MACMILLAN NETWORK ARCHITECTURE
AND DEVELOPMENT SERIES

Understanding and Deploying LDAP Directory Services

Timothy A. Howes, Ph.D.
Mark C. Smith
Gordon S. Good

MACMILLAN
TECHNICAL
PUBLISHING
U·S·A

Feedback Information

At Macmillan Technical Publishing, our goal is to create in-depth technical books of the highest quality and value. Each book is crafted with care and precision, undergoing rigorous development that involves the unique expertise of members from the professional technical community.

Readers' feedback is a natural continuation of this process. If you have any comments regarding how we could improve the quality of this book, or otherwise alter it to better suit your needs, you can contact us at ciscopress@mcp.com. Please make sure to include the book title and ISBN in your message.

We greatly appreciate your assistance.

Publisher
Jim LeValley

Executive Editor
Alicia Buckley

Managing Editor
Caroline Roop

Acquisitions Editor
Brett Bartow

Development Editor
Kitty Wilson Jarrett

Project Editor
Laura N. Williams

Copy Editor
Greg Pearson

Indexer
Chris Wilcox

Proofreader
Mary Ellen Stephenson

Acquisitions Coordinator
Amy Lewis

Manufacturing Coordinator
Brook Farling

Book Designer
Gary Adair

Cover Designer
Sandra Schroeder

Production Team Supervisor
Daniela Raderstorf

Production
Benjamin Hart
Louis Porter, Jr.

About the Authors

Timothy A. Howes is vice president and chief technology officer of Netscape Communications Corporation's Server Product Division. He was one of the original authors of the Internet LDAP directory protocol and remains a driving force behind its continued evolution. He is cochair of the IETF LDAP Extensions working group and a member of the Internet Architecture Board. In addition to being a coauthor of *LDAP: Programming Directory-Enabled Applications with Lightweight Directory Access Protocol*, he has written numerous Internet RFCs, papers, and articles. He received his Ph.D. in computer science and engineering from the University of Michigan.

Mark C. Smith is a principal engineer and directory architect at Netscape Communications Corporation, where he is responsible for the technical evolution of Netscape Directory Server and related products. He was previously a driving force behind the University of Michigan's LDAP implementation, and a key designer of the university's directory service. Mark is coauthor of *LDAP: Programming Directory-Enabled Applications with Lightweight Directory Access Protocol*, and has written many RFCs and Internet drafts.

Gordon S. Good is a senior member of the technical staff at Netscape Communications Corporation, where he leads the directory server replication development team. Previously, he was instrumental in the development of the University of Michigan's LDAP implementation and in designing and running the university's Web and email services. Gordon has also written several Internet drafts on directories.

About the Technical Reviewers

These reviewers, Leif Hedstrom, Chuck Lever, and Mike SoRelle, contributed their considerable practical, hands-on expertise to the development process for *Understanding and Deploying LDAP Directory Services*. As the book was being written, these folks reviewed all the material for technical content, organization, and flow. Their feedback was critical to ensuring that *Understanding and Deploying LDAP Directory Services* fits our readers' need for the highest quality technical information.

Leif Hedstrom is a principal UNIX architect for Netscape Communications Corporation, where he is responsible for internal infrastructure and deployment of UNIX servers and clients, as well as email, directory, and calendar services. He was the primary architect for Netscape's internal LDAP directory server environment. He has several years' experience resolving complex email- and LDAP-related issues, and he developed a large software system to convert Netscape's information infrastructure to LDAP by integrating with legacy directory services and traditional databases. Before joining Netscape in 1996, Leif developed and helped to manage Infoseek Corporation's first HTTP front-end server for its popular search engine.

Charles Lever is a computer science researcher working on LDAP server performance on Linux for Netscape Communications Corporation. Previously, Chuck was the technical lead for teams providing production-quality UNIX and LDAP directory services to the University of Michigan main campus in Ann Arbor. In this capacity, he provided technical leadership and strategic architectural direction for teams supporting LDAP servers and clients, UNIX systems, electronic mail, and high-performance statistical computation. Before coming to LDAP and UNIX production work, he helped port Transarc Corporation's AFS and DFS to IBM mainframe systems and developed operating system software for MTS, U-M's proprietary mainframe operating system.

Michael SoRelle is a systems operations group leader for MCI Telecommunications, where he manages a team of engineers in the day-to-day operation of server and workstation support for the U.S. Postal Service Network Management Center. He provides support to servers, workstations, and LAN equipment, and he tests and deploys new applications and equipment throughout the network. He is responsible for several Microsoft Exchange servers as part of the MCI InnerMail team—with more than 55,000 employees in the directory. He is the local contact for the Enterprise Security Task Force, encompassing all aspects of data security from Web server security to firewalls. Previous to joining MCI, Michael was a network analyst responsible for enterprise network planning, design, implementation, and support at Texas Children's Hospital.

Contents at a Glance

Contents

Dedication

For Nancy, whose love and support make it all worthwhile.

—Tim Howes

For my wife, Kathy, who supports me wonderfully in everything I do.

—Mark Smith

For my mother and father, and my brothers, Brian and Kevin.

—Gordon Good

Acknowledgments

We'd like to thank our management and the publishing relations department at Netscape, whose support enabled us to write this book. Specifically, our thanks go out to Claire Hough, John Paul, Ben Horowitz, David Weiden, Neel Phadnis, Susan Walton, and Suzanne Anthony.

In addition, we'd like to thank the Netscape IS department for their help in writing the Netscape case study. Bob Ferguson, Gene Irvine, and especially the incredible Leif Hedstrom deserve special thanks.

We'd like to thank the people who reviewed parts of this book, including Leif Hedstrom, Mike SoRelle, Chuck Lever, Kathleen Brade, and Nancy Cartwright.

We'd also like to thank the team at Macmillan Publishing. Kitty Jarrett deserves special thanks for her professionalism in making the process go so smoothly. Thanks to Brett Bartow for his guidance and gentle prodding, which kept us almost on schedule, and to the rest of the Macmillan team.

Preface

In the past three years, LDAP directories have risen from a relatively obscure off-shoot of an equally obscure field to become one of the linchpins of modern computing on the Internet. Increasingly, LDAP directories are becoming the nerve center of an organization's computing infrastructure, providing naming, location, management, security, and other services that have traditionally been provided by network operating systems. Design and deployment of a successful LDAP directory service can be complex and challenging, yet until now little information was available explaining the ins and outs of this important task.

When two of us (Mark and Tim) finished writing a previous book, *LDAP: Programming Directory-Enabled Applications with Lightweight Directory Access Protocol* in early 1997, we soon realized there was another, much bigger piece of the directory puzzle still to be addressed. The previous book was aimed at directory application programmers, but nothing similar was available to address the needs of directory decision makers, designers, and administrators. This book is aimed at that audience.

Recognizing the size of the task ahead of us and remembering the joys of giving up evenings and weekends for months at a time to meet deadlines for our first book, we quickly decided to expand our team. Just as quickly, we decided there was no one we'd rather share the fun with than our longtime friend and colleague, Gordon Good. Aside from being the third leg of the LDAP development team at the University of Michigan (U-M) and now a senior directory developer at Netscape, Gordon brought a wealth of system administration experience from his past life as a directory and email administrator and Web master for U-M. With Gordon on board, the three of us set about writing a book that we only half-jokingly referred to as the "LDAP Bible."

The Book's Organization

This book includes 26 chapters in 6 parts. Part I introduces directories and LDAP. Parts II through IV each address a different part of the directory life cycle. Part V discusses how to leverage your directory service once it's up and running. Finally, Part VI presents four directory services deployment case studies.

Part I provides a fairly comprehensive introduction to directories and LDAP. For readers unfamiliar with the topic, this section should bring them up to speed and provide the background necessary to understand the rest of the book. It also includes a section on the history of directories for readers interested in how all this technology came about.

Part II begins to delve into the directory life cycle by covering the first and in many ways most important phase: design. We cover all aspects of directory design, from determining your needs, to designing your data sources, schema, namespace, topology, replication, and finally privacy and security.

Part III covers the next phase in the directory life cycle: deployment. We cover everything from choosing the right directory products to piloting your service to going production. We've also included a section about analyzing the cost of your service and how to help reduce those costs.

Part IV concludes our coverage of the directory life cycle with a look at the maintenance phase. We cover such topics as backup and disaster recovery, maintaining data, monitoring your directory system, and troubleshooting problems when they occur.

Part V talks about how to take advantage of the service you have designed and deployed. We discuss the benefits and pitfalls of directory-enabling existing applications, creating new applications that use the directory, and how your directory can coexist with other data sources.

Part VI closes the book by presenting a number of directory case studies. Some of the case studies presented are real and some are fictitious, but all are designed to illustrate the concepts of directory design, deployment, and maintenance in action.

The Book's Audience

This book is primarily intended for three kinds of readers: decision makers, designers, and administrators. In addition, anyone who wants to know more about LDAP or directories in general will find the book useful, as will directory developers.

Directory decision makers will find this book useful in understanding directories and the kinds of business problems they help solve. Decision makers will find Part I useful for explaining the basics of directories. Part VI should also prove useful by providing some real, or at least realistic, examples of how directories are used and the benefits they can bring.

Directory designers will find this book useful in defining the design problem and providing a methodology for producing a comprehensive directory design. The design methodology is focused on a practical approach to design based on real-world requirements. We highly recommend that designers read the whole book, with special emphasis on Parts II, III, and IV. A good directory design results in large part from a clear understanding of the other aspects of the directory life cycle and how the directory will be used.

Directory administrators will find Part IV especially useful. It focuses on the maintenance phase of the directory life cycle, where administrators spend much of their lives. We also highly recommend that administrators read the rest of the book to get an idea of the directory big picture, as well as to understand some of the directory design decisions that are bound to make their lives either miserable or enjoyable.

Other interested readers can pick and choose from the sections of the book that interest them. We encourage all readers to at least skim Part I, to ensure that they have the background required to benefit from the rest of the book. We've tried to structure the book so that each chapter stands by itself as much as possible. Readers should be able to read the chapters covering topics that interest them, without wading through chapters of less interest. Finally, we think all readers will find the case studies presented in Part VI interesting. They give different perspectives on directories designed to illustrate the trade-offs that different directory needs imply.

Contacting Us

Finally, if you have comments or suggestions about this book or if you'd like to tell us about an interesting directory deployment or application you've developed, we'd like to hear from you. Feel free to drop us a line at the following addresses:

Tim Howes   howes@netscape.com

Mark Smith   mcs@netscape.com

Gordon Good   ggood@netscape.com

We'll try our best to get back to you, but keep in mind that we all have day jobs!

PART I

An Introduction to Directory Services and LDAP

CHAPTER 1

Directory Services Overview

The fact that you have picked up this book and started to read it suggests that you have some idea what a directory service is and what it can do for you. This chapter assumes you have an everyday understanding of directories and expands on that notion to answer three simple but important questions:

- *What is a directory?* In brief, a directory is a specialized database. In this chapter you'll learn what makes a directory specialized, what separates it from a traditional database, the defining characteristics of a directory, and why they are important.

- *What can a directory do for you?* Directories can do many things, and you probably chose this book with some particular set of problems in mind that you'd like a directory to help you solve. We'll take you through the basic uses of a directory, many of which may have already occurred to you, as well as covering some more-advanced uses that may be new to you.

- *What* isn't *a directory?* The answer to this question is sometimes even more important when defining a successful directory environment than learning what a directory is. In this chapter you'll learn what separates a directory from a file system, a Web server, and other things you have deployed on your network. The distinctions drawn here are crucial to narrowing the task of designing your directory service.

This chapter aims to answer each of these questions in detail, formalizing the answers to give you a common understanding of the task before you:

designing a directory service. You'll learn why directories are important, the scope of a directory solution, and what they can do for you. Armed with this knowledge, you'll be ready to read the rest of the book, which deals with the details of understanding, designing, deploying, maintaining, and finally making use of your very own directory service.

Directory Service Defined

We will use many terms throughout this book that may be new to you. A *directory service* is the collection of software, hardware, processes, policies, and administrative procedures involved in making the information in your directory available to the users of your directory. Your directory service includes at least the following components:

- Information contained in the directory

- Software servers holding this information

- Software clients acting on behalf of users or other entities accessing this information

- The hardware on which these clients and servers run

- The supporting software, such as operating systems and device drivers

- The network infrastructure connecting clients to servers and servers to each other

- The policies governing who can access and update the directory, what can be stored in it, and so on

- The procedures by which the directory service is maintained and monitored

- The software used to maintain and monitor the directory service

As you can see, it's quite a list! Some of these components are depicted in Figure 1.1. Generally, we will use the term *directory* as a synonym for *directory service*. It's important to keep in mind that your directory is a sophisticated system of components that work together to provide a service. Concentrating exclusively on one set of components without thinking about the others is sure to lead to trouble.

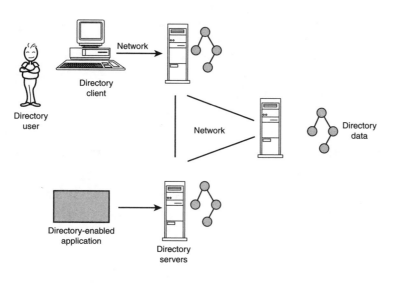

FIGURE 1.1 *Directory system components.*

What Is a Directory?

Most people are familiar with various kinds of directories, whether they realize it or not. Directories are part of our everyday lives. Everyday examples of directories we encounter include the phone book and yellow pages, *TV Guide*, shopping catalogs, the library card catalog, and others. We refer to these directories as *everyday directories*, or sometimes *offline directories*.

Using these examples as a guide, it's clear that directories help people find things by describing and organizing the items to be found. Information in such directories ranges from phone numbers to television shows, from consumer goods to reference material, and more.

Directories in the computer and networking world are similar in many ways, but with some important differences. We call these directories *online directories*. Online directories differ from offline directories in the following ways:

- Online directories are *dynamic*.

- Online directories are *flexible*.

- Online directories can be made *secure*.

- Online directories can be *personalized*.

These differences are explored in the sections that follow. It's also important to understand that there are different kinds of directories. We expand on this notion more in Chapter 2, "A Brief History of Directories." We'll give a brief categorization here in order to frame the rest of our discussion. We divide directories into the following categories:

- *NOS-based directories.* Directories such as Novell's NDS, Microsoft's Active Directory, and Banyan's StreetTalk Directory are based on a network operating system (NOS). NOS-based directories such as these are developed specifically to serve the needs of a network operating system.

- *Application-specific directories.* These directories come bundled with or embedded into an application. Examples are the Lotus Notes name and address book, the Microsoft Exchange directory, and Novell's GroupWise directory.

- *Purpose-specific directories.* These directories are not tied to an application, but are designed for a narrowly defined purpose and are not extensible. An example is the Internet's Domain Name System (DNS).

- *General-purpose, standards-based directories.* These directories are developed to serve the needs of a wide variety of applications. Examples include the LDAP directories we focus on in this book and X.500-based directories.

In this chapter we will make reference to all four types of directories. Our focus is squarely on the general-purpose type of directory, however.

Directories Are Dynamic

The everyday directories you are familiar with are relatively static; that is, they do not change very often. For example, the phone book comes once a year; you have to call information to get more up-to-date information. A new *TV Guide* is produced every week, but still your favorite show is pre-empted without notice more often than you'd like. The shopping catalogs you receive in the mail are updated only several times a year, at most; also, they do not contain such useful information as which items are in stock in which colors and sizes. Why? Because that information changes so often that by the time the catalog got to you, it would be out-of-date.

By contrast, online directories have the capacity to be kept much more up-to-date. This feature is not always used, of course. Directories are usually only as up-to-date as their administrators choose to keep them. Sometimes administrative procedures are put in place to update the directory automatically. Often, online directories are much better if they are their own ultimate authority for the information they hold. As soon as information changes, it can be updated in the directory and made available to users.

It's easy to see how this online update capability can be used to make directories more accurate, resulting in a more useful directory. This kind of improvement is incremental. But online updates have the potential to produce more revolutionary improvements, too. These improvements open the door to brand new directory applications that have no offline analogy.

For example, consider a directory that contains up-to-date information on who's employed at your organization. Such a directory could be consulted by an automated card reader to authorize access to buildings and rooms at your company. In this case, access could be revoked easily and instantly, simply by making a change to the directory.

As another example, consider a directory containing location information that is updated as you move from office to office, from hotel room to hotel room, and to other locations. This directory could be consulted to route your phone calls, faxes, and messages to you wherever you are. Traditional paper directories could never be used for such a purpose. However, the very nature of this application requires very frequent updates of the information.

This superior update capacity of online directories not only tends to keep information more up-to-date, it also can be used to distribute the update responsibility. The closer information is to its source, the more accurate and timely the information is likely to be. There are at least three reasons for this:

- The source of the information is, by definition, the most accurate.

- Extra delay and opportunity for error between the source and the directory are eliminated if the source makes the update itself.

- Depending on the information and the application, the source is likely to be the party most motivated to maintain the information correctly.

To illustrate, consider the location directory example described previously. The source is the user (you) and the information is your current location. Who knows better than you where you are? (One would hope you know that best!) Which is the more accurate path for an update to be received on: directly from you or from your administrative assistant (your typing skills not withstanding)? Suppose the update came from a directory administrator typing in information reported by your assistant relayed from you? At each step, opportunity for error is introduced, and the accuracy is further decreased. Finally, who is most motivated to have accurate information about you in the directory? Again, it is likely to be you, the source, because you do not get your phone calls, faxes, and mail unless the information is accurate. Of course, this example assumes that you are responsible enough to want the information to be accurate and that you have the tools and expertise to make it happen.

Directories Are Flexible

Another important difference between static, everyday directories and online directories is that online directories offer far greater flexibility. This flexibility has two aspects:

- Online directories are flexible in the types of information they can store.

- Online directories are flexible in the ways that information can be organized and searched.

Flexible Content

Offline directories are static in terms of their content. By that we mean that offline directories contain a very restricted and seldom extended set of information. For example, if you wanted to know something beyond the phone number, address, and name information provided by your phone book, you are probably out of luck. But there is a whole host of other useful information you might like to have. Fax number, mobile phone number, pager number, email address, even a picture or short biographical sketch, to name a few, are all items in the same category as the traditional phone information. But these items are seldom, if ever, included.

By contrast, online directories can easily be extended with new types of information. The cost of additions like these are huge with printed directories but relatively small with online directories. A printed directory would need to be redesigned, reprinted, and redistributed. The cost of this is enormous. The cost of printing the previous directory cannot be leveraged much at all.

Online directories, however, are typically designed to be extended without a redesign. There is no need for reprinting because changes are reflected automatically and immediately. Nor is there a need to redistribute the directory because clients access the directory online and do not keep their own copy. Some clients may cache or replicate portions of the data, but these copies can be updated automatically.

Extending a printed directory in this way is usually done only if a large majority of the users of the directory is clamoring for the information. This is the case because of simple economic and practical reasons. First, as a producer of a printed directory, you could not afford to double or triple the size of your directory to include more information without a compelling reason; doing so would double or triple your cost in producing the directory. Also, from a practical standpoint, the directory itself could become unwieldy and inconvenient for the very customers you are trying to serve.

An online directory, on the other hand, can be extended without incurring such costs. Adding a new data item used by only a small proportion of your users suddenly becomes cost-effective. The cost is incremental to the cost of providing the basic service. It may only involve adding some more disk space to your system and marginally increasing backup time, management, and support costs. No inconvenience is experienced by users of your service, however, because they need not even see the additional information. Those customers who want the new information can easily get it. An economic incentive exists as well: You could charge extra for these premium directory services.

Flexible Organization

The second way online directories provide more flexibility is in how they let you organize your data. Let's continue with our phone book example. The phone book contains name, phone number, and address information, organized to facilitate searching by name. If you wanted to search by phone number or by address, you would find it difficult, to say the least.

Other specialized directories that are organized to facilitate these kinds of searches may exist, but there is no guarantee of consistency with differently organized directories. Your phone book organized by name might be more or less up-to-date than your special phone book organized by phone number. Such directories contain duplicate information, which often leads to inconsistencies and out-of-date information. Also, such directories are usually not readily available, and they are usually expensive. The types of data organization that can be supported are limited. They are also limited by the nature of the medium on which the directories are distributed (e.g., paper) and by the capabilities of their end users (people without specialized training, perhaps).

By contrast, online directories can support several kinds of data organization simultaneously. The online analogy to your printed phone book can easily let you search by name, phone number, address, or other information. Furthermore, online directories can provide more-advanced types of searches that would be difficult or impossible to provide in printed form.

For example, if you are not sure of the spelling of a name, an online directory can let you search for names that sound like the one you provide. It can also provide searches based on common misspellings, substrings of names, and other variations. These different kinds of searches can be performed simultaneously or in some defined order (for example, an exact search first, then a sounds-like search, then a substring search, and so on) until a match is found. This kind of power in searching is key to providing users with the kind of "do what I mean" behavior they often desire.

Directories Can Be Secure

Offline directories offer little, if any, security. The phone book, for example, is public. Your company's printed internal phone book may have "do not distribute outside the company" stamped on it in big red letters, but this kind of security is advisory at best. This lack of security reduces the number of applications that can be served by an offline directory. It also forces users to make difficult choices, if any choice is available to them at all. Most people are familiar with unlisted phone numbers, a service most phone companies offer for a premium fee. Opting out of the directory makes your number unavailable to telemarketers and other annoying callers. However, it also makes your number unavailable to people you probably want to have it.

The root of this problem is the lack of any security in an offline directory. Its information is accessible to anybody with access to the directory, or information can be left out of the directory and accessible to nobody. This is a natural consequence of the methods used to distribute and access offline directories. Distribution is often very wide, and everybody gets his or her own copy. The access method consists of flipping through pages or calling a public number, such as 411. None of these methods provide any way of determining who is accessing the directory and, therefore, what information they should have access to.

Online directories can solve these problems. Online directories centralize information, allowing access to that information to be controlled. Clients accessing the directory can be identified through a process called *authentication*. The directory can use the identity established in conjunction with access control lists (ACLs) and other information to make decisions about which clients have access to what information in the directory.

Returning to our phone book analogy, consider how security features such as ACLs would change the situation. You could be listed in the directory, but your information would be accessible only to a subset of directory clients. You might be able to specify this subset as a list of friends. You might be able to specify it via some criteria, such as "anyone who lives on my block." You could allow your information to be available to everyone *except* a list of people you specify. The possibilities go on, and the results are quite powerful.

It's important to realize that even this level of powerful and flexible security is not a panacea. For example, ACLs can be effectively, if somewhat awkwardly, defeated by a trusted user copying confidential information off of his or her screen and distributing it outside the company. Still, online directories have security capabilities that are far more advanced than those of offline directories.

Directories Can Be Personalized

Another difference between printed directories and online directories is the degree to which each can be personalized. There are two aspects to this personalization:

- Personalized delivery of service to users of the directory

- Personalized treatment of information contained in the directory

TV Guide and the phone book are personalized on a regional basis. But everyone gets the same LL Bean catalog and accesses the same card catalog at the library. Furthermore, everyone within the same region gets the same phone book or *TV Guide*. It would be nice to get catalogs tailored to your specific interests, a phone book organized to do searches in the way you prefer, or a card catalog that remembers the kinds of books you like. This is the first aspect of personalization: the ability to deliver information tailored to your needs as an information consumer.

The second aspect of personalization concerns your ability to determine who has access to information about you and other things. This is your ability to tailor the directory to your needs as an information provider. In offline directories, as we saw previously, you have only two broad choices about the accessibility of directory information about yourself: You can either be included in the directory or not—with no in-between. Furthermore, many directories do not even provide you with this choice. Trying to get yourself unlisted can be a frustrating and time-consuming experience.

Online directories offer both of these features. The mechanism for doing so is rooted in the directory security capabilities described previously. By identifying users who access the directory and storing profile information about them, an online directory can easily provide personalized views of the directory to different users. For example, an online catalog can show you the types of products you are most likely to be interested in. This personalized service could be based on interests explicitly declared by you. It could also be based on your previous interactions with the service.

From a user's perspective, personalization of this kind is great because it gives the user a more desirable service. The user does not need to wade through information that is of less interest just to get to the information the user does consider interesting. From a service provider's perspective, personalization of this kind is great because it provides a more desirable service to the service provider's users. It also allows the service provider to better target all kinds of special services. For example, the service provider can provide information about promotions and sales, new product offerings, and advertisements, all tailored to a user's preferences.

Directory Described

So far we've been relying primarily on a common-sense understanding of the word *directory* in our discussion. We've used everyday printed directories that you are probably familiar with to explain what online directories are and how they differ from those offline. Now it's time to glean from our previous discussion the defining characteristics of online directories. The definition we will give is not a formal or mathematical one. Instead, we will expound on a list of characteristics that online directories share.

Design Center Defined

We use the term *design center* to refer to the defining set of assumptions, constraints, or criteria driving the design or implementation of a system. When designing or implementing a system, you have to make all kinds of decisions about what's important, what's not, what the system must do well, and what it can afford to do less well. A system's design center is an expression of the focus the designer or implementer had when making these decisions. Design center is a concept that applies to software and other systems and products as well.

For example, suppose you were going to design and implement a vehicle for yourself. Aside from needing a few common characteristics that essentially boil down to a wheeled, motorized conveyance, you have a lot of flexibility. A designer who has a large family

might design a station wagon or van. His design center might be focused on large passenger capacity. Another designer with a lot of stuff to haul around might design a truck. Her design center might be focused on cargo capacity. Another driving enthusiast designer might focus on performance.

Software and service design centers work in similar ways with the following questions. Does the software system or service need to serve a large community or a small one? Is the community technically sophisticated or inexperienced? Is performance a critical feature of the system? Is security? The answers to these questions and others drive the focus of the design and implementation efforts and ultimately determine the character of the system.

A directory can be thought of as a specialized database. It is interesting to compare databases and directories, because the differences have more to do with environment and design center than with anything fundamental. The comparison is also interesting because most people generally have a better understanding of what a database is and does than they do a directory. The differences between a database and a directory fall into the following broad categories:

- *Read-to-write ratio.* Directories typically have a higher read-to-write ratio than databases.

- *Extensibility.* Directories are typically more easily extended than databases.

- *Distribution scale.* Directories are usually more widely distributed than databases.

- *Replication scale.* Directories are often replicated on a higher scale than databases.

- *Performance.* Directories usually have very different performance characteristics than databases.

- *Standards.* Support for standards is important in directories, less so in databases.

Each of these points is explained in the remainder of this section.

Read-to-Write Ratio

One defining characteristic of a directory is that it is typically read or searched far more often than it is written or updated. This is quite often not the case with a database. A database might be used to record transaction information or other auditing data that is read only under exceptional, or at least infrequent, conditions. For example, such data might be read only once a month to produce a summary report, or once a year when an internal audit is conducted.

Information in a directory, on the other hand, is usually read many more times than it is written. In fact, it is not unusual for a piece of directory information to be read 1,000 to 10,000 times more often than it is written. If you think about the types of information usually stored in a directory, this makes sense. Information about people, for example, changes relatively infrequently, especially compared to the number of times the information needs to be accessed. How often do you change phone numbers compared with the number of times somebody calls you? How often do you change addresses compared with the number of times you receive mail?

Data with this "often read, seldom written" characteristic is not restricted to information about people. Catalog data, most location information, configuration information, network routing information, reference information, and many other types of information are all read far more often than they are written. The domain of applications that can be served by a directory is quite large. For some applications, the information is never updated online; instead, it is updated only periodically via some batch process initiated by an administrator.

Why is this characteristic important? It sets a design center for directory implementations. Implementers can make important, simplifying design decisions based on this characteristic. Directory implementations can be highly optimized for the types of operations that will be performed most often. If one operation is performed 10,000 times more often than another, it's a good idea to spend more time making that operation perform quickly. Contrast this with databases, which must be optimized for write and read operations. This kind of optimization has implications on other directory features—such as replication—which we will discuss later.

Information Extensibility

Another important, defining characteristic of a directory is that it supports information extensibility. The term *directory schema* refers to the types of information that can be stored, the rules that information must obey, and the way that information behaves.

Directories are not limited to a fixed set of schema that can be stored and retrieved. This information can be extended in response to new needs and new applications. A directory usually comes with a useful set of predefined types of information that can be stored, but many installations have special requirements that dictate the extension of this predefined set. Your organization may have special attributes you want to store, including, for example, employee status for people or the building location code for a printer. Sometimes these new attributes may even define new kinds of behavior from an existing attribute.

Although databases are used to store many kinds of information organized in all kinds of ways, they are usually constrained in the types of information that can be stored. It is rare to find a database that allows you to introduce a new, primitive data type with new semantics.

Data Distribution

Distribution of data is another area in which directories differ from databases. Data distribution refers to the placement of information in servers throughout your network. Data can be centralized in a single server, as shown in Figure 1.2, or data can be distributed among several servers, as shown in Figure 1.3.

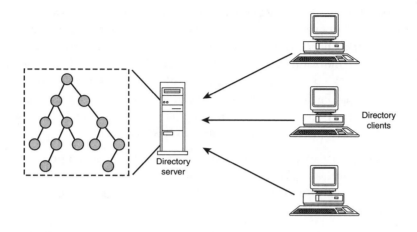

FIGURE 1.2   *Centralized directory data held in a single server.*

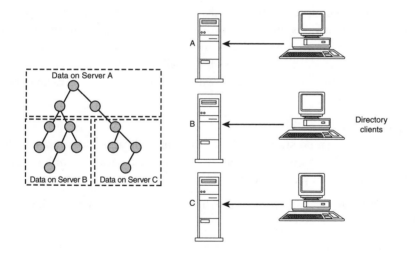

FIGURE 1.3   *Distributed directory data held in three servers.*

Although you can find databases that allow limited distribution of data, the scale of the distribution is quite different. The typical relational database allows you to store one table over here and another table over there. This distribution is usually limited to a few sites. The ability to make queries that involve both of these sites exists, but performance is often a problem. This causes the distribution features to be rarely used.

Data distribution is a fundamental factor in the design of directories. Part of the directory's purpose is to allow data to be distributed across different parts of your network. This capability is aimed at addressing environments where authority and administration must be distributed. An example of an organization needing this kind of distribution is one with offices in several countries around the world. Each office wants to have authority over its own directory; thus, the country-specific directories must appear to the outside world as a single, logical directory for the organization as a whole.

Another example in which data distribution is important is in support of large-scale directories. As your directory gets bigger, at some point the tactic of buying a bigger server with more disk and memory and CPU horsepower produces diminishing returns.

A better approach may be to construct your directory from a set of smaller machines that work together to provide the overall service. This solution is cheaper in many cases. It has the advantage of harnessing the parallel processing power of all the machines holding the directory. It also has certain attractive practical implications on the performance of some system administration functions, such as performing backups, recovering from disasters, and so on. Consider a directory distributed across ten small machines: Backing up or recovering one of the small machines is easier than backing up or recovering a single large machine.

Data Replication

Closely related to data distribution is the topic of replication. *Replication* is the process of maintaining multiple copies of directory data at different locations. There are a number of reasons to do this:

- *Reliability.* In case one copy of the directory is down, others can be accessed.

- *Availability.* Clients are more likely to find an available replica, even if part of the network has failed.

- *Locality.* Clients get better and more reliable performance from a directory the closer they are to it.

- *Performance.* More queries can be handled as additional replicas are added.

More-detailed information on replication can be found in Chapter 10, "Replication Design."

Databases sometimes support replication, but typically they do so only for a very small number of replicas. Historically, performance has been a big problem with database replication implementations. This is partly because database replication is almost always strongly consistent; that is, all copies of the data must be in sync at all times.

Directory replication, on the other hand, is almost always loosely consistent. This means that temporary inconsistencies in the data contained in different replicas are acceptable. This characteristic has important implications for the number of replicas that directories can support and the physical distribution of those replicas across the network.

As we shall see later, performance is an important directory characteristic. One good way of helping to ensure great performance is to make sure that each user of the directory has a copy of it close by. There are two reasons for this:

- Moving directory data close to the clients accessing it cuts down on the network latency of directory requests.

- The total number of directory queries processed by the system as a whole can be increased. As the number of replicas increases, so does the number of queries that can be handled. If one directory server can handle a million queries per day, adding another server could increase the capacity of the system to two million queries per day.

Availability of the directory is also a key factor. Directories tend to be used by many different applications for such fundamental purposes as authentication, access control, and configuration management. The directory must always be available to these applications if they are to function at all.

It is important to note that availability is not the same thing as reliability. A reliable directory may have redundant hardware and an uninterruptible power source. Such a directory may almost never go down, but that does not mean that it is always available to the clients that need to access it. For example, entire networks between clients and servers might go down. From the client's perspective, this causes the same problem as the directory going down.

You could try to solve this problem by building into your network the same kind of hardware reliability that is available for servers. Redundancy, uninterruptible power, and other techniques are all valuable, although not always practical. The other approach is to replicate your directory data to bring the data closer to the clients needing access to it. This helps to mitigate network problems that might otherwise prevent clients from accessing the directory. A sample unreplicated scenario is shown in Figure 1.4, and a sample replicated scenario is shown in Figure 1.5.

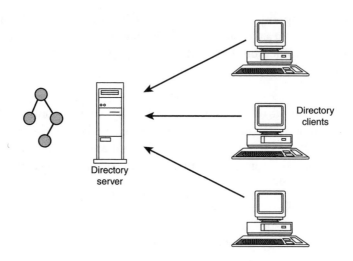

FIGURE 1.4 *An unreplicated directory service with data held by only one server.*

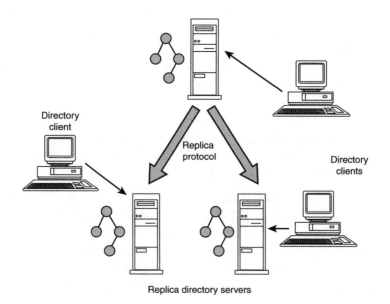

FIGURE 1.5 *A replicated directory service with data held by three servers.*

There are several implications of these facts on directory replication. Directories are replicated on a far greater scale than databases. It is not unusual for a directory replica to be maintained on each subnet in your network to minimize latency and increase availability. In some cases, a replica might be maintained on each machine, which can lead to literally hundreds or thousands of replicas. These replicas may be many network hops away from the central directory. They may even be connected over links that are only up intermittently. These kinds of replication requirements set directories apart from databases.

Performance

As mentioned previously, high performance is another characteristic that differentiates directories from databases. Database performance is typically measured in terms of the number of transactions that can be handled per second. This is also an important measure of directory performance, but the requirements on a directory are far more stringent than on most database systems.

A typical large database system might handle hundreds of transactions every second. The aggregate directory performance required by a typical large directory system may be thousands or tens of thousands of queries per second. These queries are usually simpler than the complex transactions handled by databases. As described earlier, the read-to-write ratio is typically much higher on a directory than on a database. Therefore, update performance is not as critical for directories as for databases. As we shall see later, though, it is important nonetheless.

Some of the directory's increased performance requirements are caused by the wide variety of applications that use the directory. Whereas a database may be designed and deployed with a single or a small set of driving applications in mind, directories are often deployed as an infrastructure component that will be used by an unknown but continually increasing number of applications developed across your company, and even across the Internet at large. Access to the directory is distributed, as is the development of the applications causing this access. This means that you, as the directory administrator, often do not have control over the kinds of queries your directory must answer. Therefore, it is important that your directory be flexible and capable of good performance regardless of the types of queries it must respond to.

Another root of directory performance requirements is the types of applications that typically access the directory. Applications access the directory for many different purposes. If your directory is used by your email software to route email, for example, one or more directory lookups are required for each piece of mail. Depending on the volume of mail your site processes, this can be a significant load on the directory.

There are many more examples that require high performance. If your directory is used by Web application software as an authentication database, it is accessed each time a user launches a new application. If your directory is used by these applications to store user preference and other information needed to provide location independence, even more directory accesses are called for. If your directory is used to store configuration and access control information for your Web, mail, and other servers, there is a potential directory access each time those services are accessed by clients. If you have a large user population, this quickly adds up to a lot of traffic. In these environments, using directory locality to minimize network latency is critical to providing adequate performance.

As you can see, directories are at the center of a lot of things that cause performance requirements to increase quickly. Of course, client-side caching can and should be used to minimize the number of times the directory itself is accessed, but even these techniques can only slow the flow of directory queries. High performance is still one of the most important characteristics of a directory.

Earlier we stated that the read-to-write ratio for directories is very high. The natural conclusion you could draw from this is that write performance is not nearly as important as read and search performance. Although this is true in a way, the scale of data handled by many directories makes write performance an important factor as well. And, as we described earlier, the capacity for online updating is one of the key enablers of some exciting new online directory applications. Clearly, the ability to update is important, and it must function at a certain level of performance.

For example, consider a directory with a million entries. This may seem like a lot, but this is not unreasonable for a very large corporation (after you're finished adding entries for all users, groups, network devices, external partners, customers, and other things). If each entry changes only once a month on average, that is a million updates per month, 250,000 updates per week, almost 36,000 updates per day, or around 1,500 updates per hour. That's quite a few updates! And the peak number of updates that must be handled is much higher because user-initiated changes are usually made during business hours. Administrator-initiated changes may need to be saved up and applied in a batch during limited off-peak hours, further increasing performance requirements.

Standards and Interoperability

The last important factor sets directories apart from databases is standards. The database world has various pseudo-standards, from the relational model itself to SQL. These pseudo-standards make it easier to migrate from one database system to another. They also make it so that when you've learned the concepts behind one vendor's system, you can easily apply that knowledge to come up to speed on another's quickly. These standards do not provide real interoperability, however. In the directory world, because applications from any vendor must be able to use the directory, real interoperable standards are critical.

This is where LDAP comes in. LDAP provides the standard models and protocols used in today's modern directories. LDAP makes it possible for a client developed by Microsoft to work with a server developed by Netscape, and vice versa. LDAP also makes it possible for you to develop applications that can be used with any directory. In the database world, an Oracle application cannot be used with an Informix database. An Informix application cannot be used with a Sybase database. This kind of interoperability, lacking in databases, is important to directories for two reasons:

- It allows the decoupling of directory clients from directory servers.

- It allows the decoupling of the development process from a decision about a particular directory vendor.

Before LDAP came along, each application that needed a directory usually came with its own directory built right in. This may seem a convenient solution at first glance, but consider what things are like when you've installed your 24th application and, therefore, your 24th directory. Each user in your organization who requires access to these applications needs an entry in each directory—a lot of duplicate information to maintain. This is one of the primary sources of headaches for system administrators and increased costs for IT organizations. This situation is illustrated in Figure 1.6.

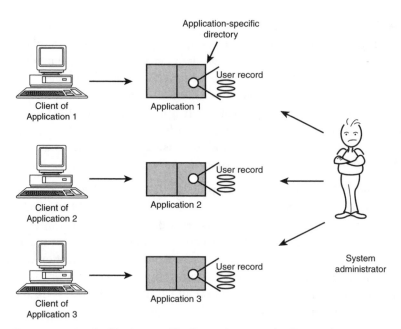

FIGURE 1.6 *Application-specific directories cause duplicate information and system administration headaches.*

Application developers everywhere can write applications using the standard directory tools of their choice. These applications will run with any LDAP-compliant directory, which essentially turns the directory into a piece of network infrastructure. This dramatically increases the number of applications that can and will be written to take advantage of the directory. It also frees you from having to rely on a single vendor for your directory solution. These same advantages are what drove the success of other Internet protocols, such as HTTP (for the Web), IMAP (for accessing email), and even TCP/IP itself. A standards-based directory infrastructure is illustrated in Figure 1.7.

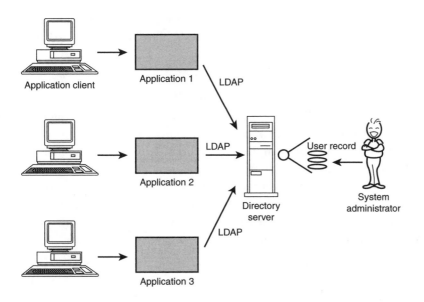

F I G U R E   1 . 7   *A standards-based, general-purpose application directory eliminates information duplication.*

Directory Description Summary

Here is a reasonably concise description to summarize a directory: It is a specialized database that is read or searched far more often than it is written to. A directory usually supports storing a wide variety of information and provides a mechanism to extend the types of information that can be stored. Directories can be centralized or distributed. They are often distributed in large scale, both in how and where information is distributed. Directories are usually replicated so that they are highly available to the clients accessing them. The scale of directory replication often involves hundreds, if not thousands, of replicas. Replication also helps increase directory performance, which is important to providing applications with a fast, reliable infrastructure component that can be used with confidence. Finally, with LDAP, directories have become standardized. This allows applications and servers from different vendors to be developed, sold, and deployed independently.

What Can a Directory Do for You?

We've already talked about some applications of offline directory services that you deal with every day. Also, we've talked about how these same applications can be improved, and sometimes revolutionized, by the timely update capabilities, extensible nature, and personalization possibilities of online directories.

Now it's time to turn our attention fully to this exciting aspect of online directories: the types of new applications that can be developed to take advantage of all the capabilities of the online directory.

Finding Things

As mentioned at the beginning of this chapter, most everyday directories are aimed at the problem of finding things. Finding the right book in the library or the telephone number of your friend or a business you want to contact; the right style, size, and color of shirt you want to order from a catalog; or the time and channel of the television show you want to watch tonight—directories organize information in this way so that it is easy to find what you are looking for. Finding things is also an important application for online directories. And as we will see, online directories have capabilities that allow far more advanced ways of finding things.

Perhaps the most basic and best understood application of an online directory is the online analogy to a phone book. Directories in this category start on one end with the large Internetwide or countrywide directories provided by Internet directory service providers, such as Four11 (www.four11.com), BigFoot (www.bigfoot.com), WhoWhere? (www.whowhere.com), and AnyWho (www.anywho.com). On the other end of the spectrum, you can apply directory technology to create a local phone book for your organization. The service provided by these directories is remarkably similar to the analogous paper directories, with some important differences.

First, online directories let you greatly increase the scale and coverage of the directory. The BigFoot directory, for example, contains essentially every phone book in North America. Try keeping that many phone books in your house for quick and easy reference! More importantly, online directories allow you to organize information, even in an application as simple as a phone book, in new and exciting ways. For example, you can use your directory to search by name, phone number, address, and other information not even contained in a traditional phone book. You can also perform new kinds of searches in case you are unable to correctly spell the name you are looking for—if you think the phone number you have might be off by a digit, or if you have only part of a name. You can also browse the contents of the directory in different ways.

Searching Versus Browsing

Directories usually support both searching and browsing, but you must take into account their differences.

Thinking about the offline analogies again, it becomes clear that both searching and browsing are needed. When you are looking for the phone number of Pete's Pizza delivery service, you know what you want and you want to go right to the answer. Phone books keep alphabetized listings to make this easy. This is *directory searching*.

On the other hand, when you are in the mood to buy some new clothes, it is seldom the case that you know exactly what you want. You probably have some general characteristics in mind (you know what you like and are in the mood for). It is unlikely that you know the make and model of the shirt you want to buy. You want to flip through the pages of a catalog, looking at pictures of clothes until you come to what you want. This is *browsing*.

Browsing and searching are not mutually exclusive. Often, you perform some kind of search to narrow down the choices, which you then browse. Sometimes the reverse is true: You browse some possibilities to find the place where you want to search. The important point to remember is that browsing and searching are complementary. Some applications require one, some the other. And some applications require both, either used together or at different times.

This flexibility of searching and browsing methods is a direct result of the directory's ability to organize information in different ways simultaneously. This kind of flexibility is important in a wide variety of applications. Consider, for example, a network printing application. This application allows users to choose the desired attributes of a printer. These attributes might be location, color or black-and-white, print quality, size or type of paper, single- versus double-sided capability, and others. Typical interaction with the user might involve the user selecting the most important attributes (for example, color and print quality). The user can then choose from a list of printers, perhaps choosing one based on location.

As a final example of finding things, consider a client in search of a network application service. This service might be a database service, an employee benefit enrollment service, a stock reporting or trading service, an online dating service, a discipline-specific research service, or just about anything. As long as these services register themselves with the directory, users or other application programs can later query the directory to locate the services. The directory's online update capability allows users to find the services they need even when those services change locations. The service simply updates the directory with its new location.

Managing Things

One application topic that sets online directories apart from their offline counterparts is information management. Online directories provide a big piece of the management puzzle in a distributed environment, providing a central repository for objects that need to be managed. The example cited most often in this category is the expensive task of user and group management—one of the most important management services a directory can provide. A centralized directory can help reduce costs of this service substantially.

The N+1 Directory Problem

Until recently, just about every application you deployed came with its own incompatible directory. Mail applications such as cc:Mail, groupware applications such as Lotus Notes and Microsoft Exchange, and even earlier versions of Netscape's Commerce Web server all came with their own directory. UNIX, too, was not immune, with applications such as `sendmail` using the `/etc/aliases` database. Although this situation is convenient if you are installing only one application, it quickly becomes unmanageable as the number of directories in your environment increases.

Imagine that you have a user needing access to all the applications you have installed on your network. The user must be added to all the application-specific directories. If any information about the user changes, it must be changed in all these directories. This is known as the *N+1 directory problem*; that is, each new application adds one more directory to manage. This is quite a troublesome and costly problem for administrators everywhere (refer to Figure 1.6).

Consider how this situation changes when you install a centralized directory. In this case, you need to enter or change user information in only one place. As new applications are added to the network, they use the centralized directory instead of their own. Of course, the flaw in this beautiful plan is clear: All applications must be rewritten to use a centralized directory, at least as an option, rather than their own proprietary directories. These changes are taking place, although the pace at which they are occurring may not be as fast as you'd like. The improved situation was depicted in Figure 1.7.

Another advantage of storing user and group information in a centralized directory is enjoyed by application developers. Instead of having to develop a proprietary directory service integrated with each application, application developers can use what's already provided and focus their activities on making a better application.

Another important application of directories to the management problem relates to the task of configuration management. Historically, the configuration for an application has been kept in a set of files or an OS-specific repository such as the Microsoft Windows Registry. This solution is simple to implement and works just fine for many applications. But network applications often have different needs, especially when deployed in large numbers.

Consider, for example, a network of Web servers. There may be hundreds of them within a large corporation. If they share one or more configuration items, imagine the onerous task of changing the configuration in all of them. With the configuration file approach, you would need to visit each Web server and edit its configuration file. With hundreds of servers, this task would indeed be tedious. You could develop an ad hoc configuration management system based on tools, such as `rdist` and `rsync`, but this system itself needs to be managed.

Now consider the implications of these servers storing their configuration information in the centralized directory. First, remote management of the server becomes possible; the server's configuration can be accessed from anywhere on the network. Second, the configuration can be shared among servers, making cluster management of servers possible. In our earlier example, the hundreds of Web servers could have their configuration changed quickly and easily from a central location. An example of this application is shown in Figure 1.8.

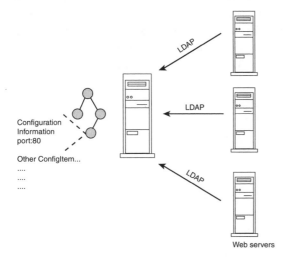

FIGURE 1.8 *Using a directory for centralized configuration management.*

A similar and potentially more powerful application of directory-based management is in the area of user configuration and preferences. Like application configuration, user preferences have historically been maintained in configuration files or local databases, such as the Microsoft Windows Registry, dot files in home directories on UNIX, and Macintosh preferences files. In an environment where centralized user configuration management is important (and there are many such environments), this proves to be a rather inconvenient solution. However, by having applications store and read this information from the directory, thousands of user configurations can be changed at one time. Imagine being able to change a piece of configuration one night, and the next day when your users arrive and start their applications, the configuration is seamlessly changed.

When this approach is combined with the storage of per-user state information in the directory, location independence can be achieved. This is an important feature in many environments. Consider a user who accesses applications from a machine at home and one at work. The user probably has her preferences set up just the way she prefers. Perhaps she has a personal email address book she needs to access from each location, or personal bookmarks in her Web browser. Storing these things in a directory and retrieving them from the network allows the user to have the same environment both at home and at work.

Similar requirements exist in shop floor situations or on university campuses, where kiosk access is provided to users without a dedicated machine of their own. (We use the terms "nomadic" or "roaming" to describe these types of users.) IS professionals and others who find themselves in front of many different machines in the course of a normal day can also benefit from location independence enabled by a directory. This application is illustrated in Figure 1.9.

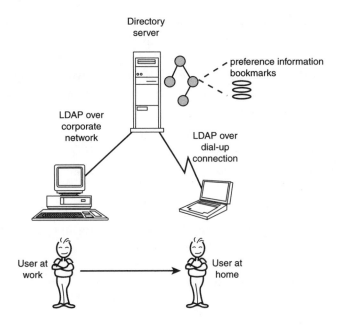

FIGURE 1.9 *Using the directory to provide location independence.*

Lightweight Database Applications

In the first section of this chapter we described a directory by comparing it to a database. In the next section we will go into more detail about the differences between the two.

Directories are good at storing and retrieving relatively small pieces of information. The fact that LDAP directories provide a standard protocol and API access to this information is also attractive. Prior to LDAP's arrival, application developers with a need to maintain a simple database for their application had just a couple choices:

- *Build a proprietary special-purpose database.* This approach means extra work for the application developer and the application administrator who must install and maintain the database. It also means a lot of wasted time solving problems that have already been solved.

- *Embed a commercial database package.* This approach is more attractive because it generally involves less work for the application developer and avoids duplicating existing efforts. However, it can still be inconvenient for users and administrators who have to install and maintain the database. Embedding a full-fledged database such as Oracle is overkill and comes with a high price tag. Other simpler, embedded databases exist, but they are usually proprietary and hard to integrate.

Embedding a simple directory server can often solve the same problems with some distinct advantages. Directories are generally smaller, less complex applications than full-fledged databases. LDAP directories provide a standard access protocol, meaning that your application can work with other directories, and other applications can work with your directory. This helps to avoid the N+1 directory problem we described earlier.

LDAP directories also provide de facto (soon-to-be-official) standard APIs you can use to access the directory, making your application more portable. This reduces the amount of work required for application programmers to embed directory services in an application.

One example of an embedded database like this can be found in Netscape's Communicator Web and mail client. The client maintains several local databases containing user bookmarks, local address book information, security information, and other things. These all used to be stored in separate proprietary databases, meaning that the information could not be shared and could not be accessed from anywhere but the local machine. Introducing a directory server to store the information solves both of these problems.

Another example of an embedded database is found in the Netscape Certificate Server. This server maintains a database of certificates it has issued to users. Version 1.0 of the product stored these certificates in an Informix database. This proved to be unwieldy, hard to manage and install, and generally a poor choice. The next version of the Certificate Server used an embedded directory server to manage this database of information. This directory-based solution is much easier to install and manage, easier to develop with, and it is much more flexible.

Security Applications

Another interesting directory application is security. Of particular interest are public key–based security systems. We cover these systems in more detail in Chapter 11, "Privacy and Security Design." For now, it's enough to know that the public key infrastructure (PKI) required to provide security like this is hard to manage. PKI requires a way to distribute security objects such as certificates to clients and servers, to keep those security objects up-to-date, to revoke them when they are compromised, and to handle other functions. Without a directory, this task is difficult to manage.

Directories help solve two problems that certificates and PKI in general introduce:

- *The PKI life cycle management problem.* This refers to how certificates are created, maintained, and destroyed. Without a directory, this process is up to you to manage. If you are lucky, you might have some proprietary software acting on your behalf that manages the process for you.

- *The certificate location problem.* This refers to how you find the certificates of the people with whom you want to communicate securely, and how people who wish to communicate with you find your certificate. Without a directory, you and your friends might have to resort to calling each other on the phone and reading off strings of hexadecimal (base 16) digits to each other.

Introducing a directory helps solve these two problems. The directory acts as a central point of administration throughout the PKI life cycle. Your various security objects can even live in the directory, where you or an administrator you trust can maintain them. When you need a new certificate, one can easily be issued to you through the directory. When your certificate needs to be revoked, again the directory provides the means to do so quickly and efficiently—and the means by which other parties can be notified of the change.

The directory also helps locate the certificates of others. In this application, the certificate or other security information is just another attribute of a user's directory entry. A certificate can be retrieved from the directory as conveniently and efficiently as a name, phone number, or email address. A more detailed and formal description of these problems and processes is presented in Chapter 11.

What a Directory Is Not

In our experience, people sometimes have one of two extreme reactions upon learning about the wonders of directories. One reaction is negative: "What good is this directory really going to do? Why can't I just use X to fill that same need? I don't see how this directory is going to be as reliable and perform as well as you say, and I am hesitant to make my application depend on it!" This reaction can usually be overcome by additional education, helping the skeptic see a directory in action, and better explaining all the great things a directory can do for the person.

The other reaction is equally misguided, but can be harder to overcome: "This directory is great! I bet there's nothing it can't do. I can now use the directory instead of my file system, Web server, FTP server, and a host of other things. Finally, a handy, all-in-one tool that chops, slices, dices, makes homemade desserts, but best of all, it cleans itself!" The enthusiasm of this reaction is to be admired, but there is danger here, too. There is an old saying that states that if the only tool you have is a hammer, every problem begins to look like a nail. Needless to say, not all problems are nails, and trying to treat them as such tends to lead to poor carpentry.

A directory is no different—like any other technology, it is best suited to solving one set of problems. A directory can be usefully applied to many other problems as well, though with somewhat less satisfaction. A directory can be abused by trying to make it solve problems that it was not intended to solve.

In this section we examine this area more closely, explaining some of the many applications for which directories are *not* well suited. We will explain why directories are different from the following network services that may look similar on the surface:

- Databases

- File systems

- Web servers

- FTP servers

- DNS servers

We will explain how your directory can complement all these services and why each one fills a valuable niche in your computing infrastructure. We will conclude this section with a summary of when to use a directory to store information and when to use something else.

Database Comparison

In the previous section we described what a directory is, and we spent quite a bit of time comparing directories to databases. We will not repeat that comparison here, but we will highlight a few important points. First, recall that directories are typically read-focused rather than write-focused. So if your application is writing large volumes of data, say for recording logs or merchandise transactions, you should choose a database over a directory.

Second, directories support a relatively simple transaction model. Directory transactions involve only a single operation and a single directory entry. Databases, on the other hand, are designed to handle large and diverse transactions, spanning multiple data items and many operations. If your application requires this kind of heavy-duty transaction support, again a database is a better answer than a directory. On the other hand, if you have an application that does not have these requirements but instead wants to read and occasionally write information to a network-accessible database in simple transactions, a directory server may well be a good, cost-effective, much simpler choice than using something like an Oracle database.

File System Comparison

A directory makes a poor file system. Files have characteristics that are different from directory information. Files are often very large, containing many megabytes or even gigabytes of information, whereas directories are optimized for storing and retrieving relatively small pieces of information.

Although there is often no restriction on the size of a directory entry or attribute, the question is one of design center. Some files are written far more often than they are read, such as log files and files used to hold a database. Directories, as you'll recall, are optimized for read over write. Some files, of course, are read far more often than they are written. Application binaries are a good example of files in this category, but the size of these files is often larger than should be stored in a directory.

Applications often access files in chunks, especially if the file is large. File systems support calls—such as seek(), and read() and write()— can be used to write only a portion of a larger file for this very purpose. Directories do not provide support for this kind of random access. Instead, a directory entry is split up into attributes. You can retrieve attributes separately, but you usually have to retrieve all of any attribute you ask for. There is no way to retrieve only part of a value, starting at some byte offset. File systems, on the other hand, are not good at storing attribute-based information. They do not typically support any kind of searching capability like directories do.

Web Comparison

Since the World Wide Web burst onto the computing scene a few years ago, Web servers have become ubiquitous. Chances are good that your organization, depending on its size, runs anywhere from one to several hundred. Web servers have certain similarities to file systems. They are made to serve clients accessing documents or files that can vary greatly in size. Although Web server documents usually share the typical read-many-write-few characteristic of directory information, directories are not well suited to the task of delivering to clients multimegabyte JPEG images or Java applications.

Web servers also often serve as a springboard to a development platform for Web applications. These platforms range from simple CGI (common gateway interface) to more-complex platforms, such as the one found in the Netscape Application Server. Directories typically do not provide this kind of flexibility in application development, even when they do provide directory application development platform services, such as those provided by the Netscape Directory Server.

Directories are optimized for providing sophisticated searching capabilities of the data they hold. Web servers can be used to develop similar search applications, but such applications are not standards based. Web servers are tuned to providing GUI-style interfaces on applications; they are not tuned to providing generic application access to directory data. If you have a specific database of information you want to make available to users, a Web server might be a good choice. If you have information you want to make available to a wide variety of applications, a directory server is a better choice.

FTP Comparison

An argument similar to the previous one for Web servers applies to File Transfer Protocol (FTP) servers. One could argue that the days of FTP servers are numbered now that Web servers have arrived, but they are hardly threatened by the arrival of directory services. Again, the main differentiating factor is the size of the data and the type of client that needs access to it. Another important point is that FTP is a very simple protocol, tuned to do one thing and do it well. If all you want to do is create a means to transfer files from one place to another, the extra directory infrastructure needed to perform replication, searching, updating, and so on is overkill.

On the other hand, if your application involves more than simple retrieval and storage of information, a directory is a more appropriate choice. Unlike directories, FTP provides no capability for search, no attribute-based information model, and no incremental update capability.

DNS Comparison

DNS, the Internet's Domain Name System, translates host names, such as `home.netscape.com`, into IP addresses. Host names are good for users wanting to remember how to connect to their favorite Internet service. IP addresses are required by the networking infrastructure underlying the Internet that is responsible for actually making the user's connection happen. The DNS and a typical directory like LDAP have certain similarities, such as providing access to a hierarchical distributed database. But there are some important differences that set the two apart.

DNS is highly optimized for its main purpose; most directories are meant to be more general purpose. The DNS has a specialized, fixed set of schemas; directories allow schemas to be extended. DNS does not allow updates of its information; directories do. DNS can be accessed over the UDP connectionless transport; directories are usually connection-based.

Note

Some recent work on dynamic DNS by the Internet Engineering Task Force (IETF) is aimed at providing update capabilities. Proposed IETF work on connectionless LDAP is aimed at providing LDAP access over UDP. These efforts and others may bring DNS and LDAP closer together. But for now, the best argument for not trying to replace the DNS with LDAP is that the DNS seems to be working just fine. If it's not broken, don't fix it!

The Complementary Directory

There are certain similarities between directories and many of the services just listed. Directories tend to complement most of these services. We will now take a moment to explore this notion of a complementary directory, what it means, and how it can create synergy among all the services in your enterprise.

A good example of the complementary directory is how it relates to a Web server. Here the directory has a number of important supporting roles to play.

First, the directory can serve as an authentication database. When clients authenticate to the Web server, their credentials are checked against the directory. When the Web server needs to make an access control decision, the directory can again be consulted to determine group membership and other information pertinent to the decision. The value of the directory in this role is especially apparent when you consider an environment that is running many Web servers, all of which need access to the same authentication database. By sharing a directory, the Web servers reduce the user management problem to a manageable level. Other services can benefit from this type of use as well.

Second, the directory can serve as a network-accessible storage device for information about configuration, access control, user preferences and profiles, and other things. The value of the directory in this role is twofold:

- If any of this information is to be shared across servers, the directory can act as a central repository, eliminating redundant administration much as it does for user and group information. Imagine the convenience of being able to change a shared configuration item on a hundred Web servers with a single change to the directory, as opposed to visiting each Web server and making the change redundantly or maintaining a separate, ad hoc system to manage configuration.

- The directory can provide a standard, network-accessible way to administer all this information. This opens up a whole new set of possibilities for standardized management tools and common administration frameworks.

As a third example of its complementary nature, the directory can be used to help organize and access information contained in the Web server itself. Today, Web search engines exist to catalog and organize Web-based content. But as anyone who has spent much time using these services can attest, you often spend more time wading through irrelevant matches to your query than reading the actual information desired. The problem is simply that Web content lacks structure and, therefore, is hard to organize and search in an automated way. With the advent of XML (Extensible Markup Language), this lack of structure is beginning to change. This is where directories come in.

Directories are great at organizing and providing subsequent access to information. Imagine today's Web search engines driven by directories: Using the directory query language and typed information structure to more accurately specify the information you are looking for, the directory could return a much more focused set of results. Keep in mind that in this scenario the content itself is still stored in a Web server and that free-text searches would still be conducted as they are today. The directory's value is to provide some structure on top of this arrangement and also provide a precise, yet flexible, query mechanism.

Another good example of a directory complementing existing services is found in examining file systems and FTP servers. In this case a directory can be used not to hold the contents of files, but rather to hold meta-information about those files, their locations, who owns them, and other things that might be useful in locating them. Most importantly, the directory can hold the information that a file system or FTP client needs to access files contained in that service. An FTP server could also use a directory server for authentication purposes.

This idea of using directories to organize and search for information that you really want to access is a common theme. Directories often don't hold the content for which you are searching, but they can hold the location of that information along with other attributes that can help you find what you are looking for.

The dividing line between what should be held in a directory and what should be held elsewhere is not always clear. In fact, sometimes it can be quite difficult to tell. General guidelines are that the more information there is, the less likely it should be put in a directory. The more frequently the information changes, the less likely it should be maintained in a directory. The less structured a piece of information is, the less benefit you will likely derive from placing it in a directory. However, the more often a piece of information is shared, the more benefit you will likely derive from placing it in a directory.

Directory Services Overview Checklist

Here's a brief summary of things to think about when deciding whether to use a directory or some other piece of technology for storing information:

- ☐ *Size of the information.* Directories are best at storing relatively small pieces of information, not multimegabyte files. Directories are good at storing pointers to large things, but not the large things themselves.

- ☐ *Character of the information.* Directories typically have an attribute-based information model. If you can express your information naturally in this form, a directory might be a good choice. If you can't, consider using a database, file system, or other approach.

- ☐ *Read-to-write ratio.* Directories are best for information that is read far more often than it is written. If the information is to be written more frequently, a database or file system might be a more appropriate choice.

- ☐ *Search capability.* Directories are made to search the information they contain. If your application requires this, a directory might be a good choice.

- ☐ *Standards-based access.* If you need standards-based access to your information, a directory is a good choice.

Keeping these principles in mind when you are deciding what to use for your application will keep you out of trouble. By this time, you should have a good understanding of what a directory is, what a directory is not, and how a directory relates to other services in your network. Hopefully, this will help you avoid the "hammer syndrome," where every problem looks like a nail you can use your directory hammer to solve.

Further Reading

A Survey of Advanced Usages of X.500 (RFC 1491). C. Weider, R. Wright, 1993. Available on the World Wide Web at http://info.internet.isi.edu:80/innotes/rfc/files/rfc1491.txt.

Introduction to White Pages Services Based on X.500 (RFC 1684). P. Jurg, 1994. Available on the World Wide Web at http://info.internet.isi.edu:80/innotes/rfc/files/rfc1684.txt.

Programming Directory-Enabled Applications with Lightweight Directory Access Protocol. T. Howes, M. Smith, Macmillan Technical Publishing, 1997.

Understanding X.500: The Directory. D. Chadwick, International Thomson Computer Press, 1996. Now out of print; selected portions available on the World Wide Web at `http://www.salford.ac.uk/its024/X500.htm`.

X.500 Directory Services: Technology and Deployment, S. Radicati, S. Van Nostrand Reinhold, 1994.

Looking Ahead

This chapter gives you an overview of directories and directory services. Starting from a layman's understanding of everyday, offline directories, we've explained analogous online directories and the features that enable them to be used for new types of applications. By now, you should have a good idea what a directory is and what it can do for you. Equally important, you should have a good idea of what a directory is not, and what you should not try to use it for.

In Chapter 2 we will look at directories from a historical perspective. Then in Chapter 3 we will introduce LDAP more formally in preparation for in-depth coverage of directory design.

CHAPTER 2

A Brief History of Directories

Directory services have recently emerged as an essential part of the network infrastructure. In the past few years, LDAP-based directory services in particular have captured the hearts and minds of many information systems professionals, application software developers, and end users. However, LDAP owes a great debt to all the other directory services and related developments that led up to its creation.

In this chapter we present a brief and necessarily incomplete history of directory services. The emphasis is on developments that are interesting and note-worthy and on the ideas that led directly to the birth and subsequent dominance of LDAP. Our goal in this chapter is to complement the technical information provided in the rest of this book by providing some historical context in which to view LDAP. Note that we do not present events in strict chronological order, so please refer to the time line located near the end of this chapter to see an ordered view of the major directory-related events.

Our look at the history of directories is divided into five major sections:

- Prehistory and early electronic directories
- Application-specific and special-purpose directories
- Network operating system (NOS) directories
- General-purpose, standards-based directories
- The future of directory services

Each of the first four sections describes a different type of directory service, differentiated both by the needs each service was designed to meet and when it was developed. For each directory type, we describe important related historical developments and also examine the current status of such directories. LDAP itself falls within the fourth section (general-purpose, standards-based directories), so that section is much larger than the others. In the fifth section, we take a brief look at the future of directory services.

Prehistory and Early Electronic Directories

Even before the birth of the computer, people had access to a variety of directories. Examples include the following:

- Catalogs used to present merchandise, course guides, and the like

- Schedules of events, as presented in publications such as *TV Guide*

- Public telephone directories of people and businesses (white pages and yellow pages)

- Internal (corporate) telephone directories and organizational charts

Typically, these directories are printed on paper and updated relatively infrequently. Many of these directories are still in use today.

Early Electronic Directories

Electronic directories were born shortly after the digital computer itself was created. One of the first widespread uses of electronic directories was to store information about accounts within multiuser timesharing systems. Many of these directories have their roots in the 1960s and early 1970s, and some of them are still in use today. Examples include the following:

- MVS PROFS (IBM)

- Michigan Terminal System (MTS)

- *UserDirectory (University of Michigan)

- UNIX /etc/passwd (Bell Labs)

These directories were used to authenticate users, control access to resources, and account for the resources consumed by individual users. As people began to use computer systems to collaborate and communicate with others, the role of these directories was expanded to include basic contact information about the users of the systems.

Distributed Computing Research and the Grapevine System

Some of the most important developments that led to the general-purpose, highly distributed directories that are increasingly popular today took place in the late 1970s and early 1980s within the research laboratories of commercial companies and universities. Distributed systems emerged as a popular research topic, growing out of the interest created by the availability of open operating systems such as UNIX and by the availability of inexpensive, relatively high-speed networking technology. The early distributed systems research covered a lot of territory, ranging from the design of simple email systems to the creation of large distributed computers based on Remote Procedure Calls (RPC).

One of the most significant early distributed systems, Grapevine, was developed and deployed at Xerox Palo Alto Research Center (PARC) by the early 1980s. Grapevine was implemented using the Mesa programming language on Xerox Alto computers. The computers were connected by Ethernet local area networks (LAN) and 56Kbps wide area network (WAN) links. All communication within the Grapevine system was via a replicated, store-and-forward message-passing system. Figure 2.1 shows the major components of Grapevine.

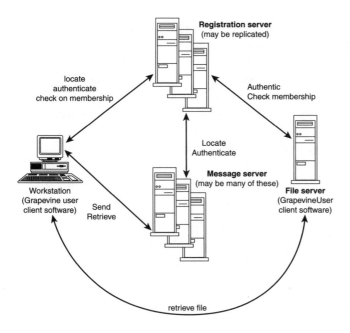

FIGURE 2.1   *The Grapevine distributed system.*

Grapevine included a Registration Database that served many of the same purposes as the directory systems of today. The Registration Database contained information about people, groups of people, and sites on the network (servers). It was highly replicated and designed for fault tolerance. Administration was decentralized and the entire system was designed to be very scalable. Xerox eventually produced a commercial directory service called Clearinghouse that was based in part on the Grapevine work.

The Arrival of the Internet

In the mid-1980s, computer networks in the form of both LANs and WANs became increasingly popular. WANs typically connect independent organizations over long distances; the best-known WAN is the Internet itself, which has its roots in Arpanet. Arpanet was a distributed research project funded by the U.S. Defense Advanced Research Projects Agency (DARPA) in the 1970s and early 1980s. Large WANs such as the Internet are actually networks of networks that join together thousands of WANs, each of which is made up of many LANs. The Internet has spawned many interesting directory services developments, including the development of LDAP itself.

The Domain Name System

In 1984, the Domain Name System (DNS) came online on the Internet to provide a mapping between textual names (e.g., `whitehouse.gov`) and the IP addresses (e.g., `198.137.241.30`) that the Internet uses behind the scenes. DNS is a widely distributed service that replaced an unwieldy scheme in which each computer on the network had a copy of a file that contained the names and IP addresses of all hosts on the Internet. DNS has evolved some since 1984, but it is still used today when a user of the Internet accesses a service using a textual name. Figure 2.2 shows the DNS hierarchical namespace.

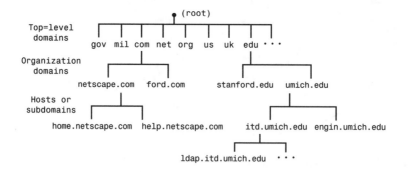

FIGURE 2.2   *The Domain Name System's hierarchical namespace.*

DNS was designed to serve a specific, limited function—not to be a general-purpose directory service. It also was not designed to be as extensive as to meet the directory needs of applications; it was designed to hold a limited set of data about Internet hosts and networks and to respond to a few types of queries.

Nevertheless, DNS was novel for its day. It was designed from the start to be a widely distributed system with distributed administration and control. It was also designed to allow the data to be replicated among multiple servers on the network. Finally, DNS has proven itself to be extremely scalable, growing with amazing aptitude from servicing a few hundred thousand hosts in 1990 to an estimated 37 million by mid-1998. Part of the reason for DNS's success is that it provides a simple, limited set of services.

The Internet WHOIS Database

Another early Internet directory was the WHOIS database, which still serves as a network-accessible registry of contact information for hosts, networks, and individual IP addresses. WHOIS accepts a limited number of text-based queries and returns text-based results to clients on the Internet. Listing 2.1 shows an example of a WHOIS query in bold, along with the results returned by the service.

LISTING 2.1 AN EXAMPLE OF A WHOIS QUERY

```
% whois excite.com
Registrant:
Excite, Inc (EXCITE-DOM)
   555 Broadway
   Redwood City, CA 94063
   USA

   Domain Name: EXCITE.COM

   Administrative Contact, Technical Contact, Zone Contact:
      DNS admin   (DA1596-ORG)   dnsadmin@EXCITE.COM
      (415)943-1200
Fax- (415)943-1299
   Billing Contact:
      Accounts Payable   (AP707-ORG)   ap@EXCITE.COM
      (415)943-1200
Fax- (415)943-1299

   Record last updated on 09-Jun-97.
   Record created on 19-Sep-95.
   Database last updated on 24-Aug-98 04:10:05 EDT.

   Domain servers in listed order:
```

continues

LISTING 2.1   CONTINUED

```
NS00.EXCITE.COM                198.3.98.250
NS01.EXCITE.COM                198.3.98.251
NSE00.EXCITE.COM               198.3.102.250
NSE01.EXCITE.COM               198.3.102.251
```

As previously mentioned, the Internet spawned a variety of other directory services developments, the most important of which are covered in other sections of this chapter.

Application-Specific and Special-Purpose Directories

In this section we discuss directories that are tied to a specific application (or to a tightly integrated suite of applications). These directories are distinguished from other, more general-purpose directories (such as LDAP directories) by their tight integration with specific applications and their use of proprietary interfaces and protocols. Typically, it is difficult or impossible to use these directories with directory-enabled applications they were not designed to support.

Application-Specific Directories

In the early 1990s, application-specific directories entered the mainstream (although they existed in various forms for many years before then). Application-specific directories are typically embedded in electronic mail and groupware products and are intended to serve the needs of only one application or a small suite of applications. The design of these directories is often driven by the user interface requirements of email or groupware applications. Examples of these directories include the following:

- The IBM/Lotus cc:Mail Directory

- The IBM/Lotus Notes Address Book

- The Novell GroupWise Directory

- The Microsoft Exchange Directory

- The UNIX `sendmail` `/etc/aliases` file

Most of these application-specific directories are still sold and used today. Over time, they have become somewhat less proprietary in that most of them now provide LDAP client access. Typically, the LDAP support is second-rate and accomplished through gateways that are retrofitted to the existing service. By their very nature, application-specific directories tend to be hard to extend for use by other directory-enabled applications.

Centralized Internet Directories

A second category of special-purpose directories has recently emerged since the explosion of Internet content services: large, centralized directories that hold information about Internet users. Some of the best known directories are

- AT&T Labs' AnyWho Directory (http://www.anywho.com)

- Bigfoot Directory (http://www.bigfoot.com)

- Yahoo!'s Four11 Directory (http://www.four11.com)

- Switchboard Directory (http://www.switchboard.com)

- WhoWhere? Directory (http://www.whowhere.com)

These directories often acquire this information about users from a combination of Usenet News postings and voluntary registration. Typically, the centralized Internet directory services also provide a directory based on public telephone directory information and are quite popular with users who are looking for lost loves or their old high school buddies.

Now that Internet email clients and Web browsers can act as LDAP clients, many of these directories support access over LDAP in addition to their primary HTML form-based interfaces. Like most Internet content providers today, they fund their services through the sale of advertisements that appear at the service access points or within search results.

Network Operating System Directories

The term *network operating system* (NOS) describes a category of products that provide a variety of services to clients and servers on LANs. LANs take many forms, but they typically operate at relatively high speeds and are used within organizations to connect a set of related computer systems. LANs, and later NOSs, originally became popular as a way to share expensive resources such as printers and file servers.

Arguably, the success of LANs can be traced to the invention of Ethernet in 1973 by some clever engineers at Xerox PARC. Today the majority of LANs are connected to the global Internet, although they also continue in their original role as providers of high-speed local connectivity within organizations. A typical configuration is shown in Figure 2.3.

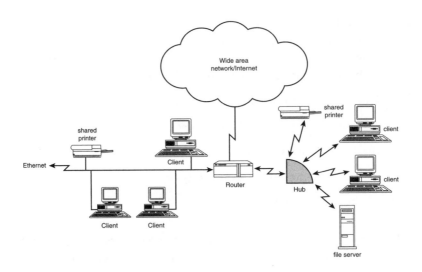

FIGURE 2.3   *A local area network (LAN).*

The best-known example of a NOS is Novell NetWare, which made its debut in the mid-1980s. Other popular NOSs include Microsoft Windows NT (a relatively late arrival), Banyan VINES (which has a sophisticated directory service called StreetTalk), and Apple Computer's Appleshare service. NOS directories grew out of the need for network operating systems to authenticate users, track network resources, and provide efficient, centralized management capabilities.

Novell Directory Services

Early versions of Novell NetWare relied on a simple directory of user- and network-related information called the Bindery. With the debut of NetWare 4.0 in 1993, NetWare gained a full-fledged distributed directory service called NetWare Directory Services, which was eventually renamed Novell Directory Services (NDS).

NDS is a mature product whose underlying models and design are closely modeled after the X.500 standards, except that it uses a proprietary suite of directory protocols. NDS can support a highly distributed network environment and offers excellent management utilities. It includes directories that can be highly replicated (even across slow WAN links), along with other sophisticated capabilities, such as a network login that allows users to type their password just once to access all network services.

NDS, which has historically focused on serving the needs of NetWare, is still weak in the areas of performance and scalability. Currently, NDS supports

LDAP only through a gateway. One telling fact is that Novell's own GroupWise messaging and collaboration suite does not use NDS—it uses its own application-specific directory. Nevertheless, NDS is one of the most widely deployed directory services.

Microsoft's Active Directory

Microsoft's LAN Manager and Windows NT Server products prior to version 5.0 include a simple directory service called the NT Domain Directory. This directory has a number of shortcomings. Although machines are grouped into related groups called domains, the NT Domain Directory does not provide a hierarchical view of the directory contents. It is not a general-purpose directory and can't be extended for use by third-party applications. An NT Domain directory is also difficult to manage when it gets large, and it does not scale up easily to accommodate tens of thousands of directory entries. Finally, LDAP is not supported by the NT Domain Directory; all access is through proprietary protocols and APIs.

To improve on the weaknesses inherent in its previous offering, Microsoft will include a new, native LDAPv3 directory called Active Directory with Windows NT Server version 5.0. Although Active Directory is primarily aimed at meeting the needs of the Windows NT 5.0 operating system, it is much closer to a general-purpose directory service than the NT Domain Directory is.

Unlike most NOS directories, Active Directory uses LDAP as its core protocol, and it actually supports a variety of Internet protocols, including LDAPv3, HTTP, and DNS. Following the lead of Netscape, Microsoft has placed Active Directory at the center of its intranet application and security strategy. Active Directory boasts advanced features such as multimaster replication, a global directory catalog to ease lookups in large-scale deployments, and support for dynamic directory applications such as chat clients and servers. At the time of this writing, Active Directory is scheduled to ship in late 1999.

Status of NOS Directories

As evidenced by Active Directory, NOS directories are embracing open standards such as LDAP and opening themselves to a wider variety of directory-enabled applications. NOS directories such as NDS boast the largest installed base of any kind of distributed directory services.

General-Purpose, Standards-Based Directories

In addition to application-specific, special-purpose, and NOS directories there is another category of directories, which we refer to as general-purpose directories. These directories are not limited to a specific purpose, a particular application, or a single operating system. Instead, they are designed to meet the needs of a very wide range of directory-enabled applications. Typically, these directories are designed around open, standard protocols; thus, implementations from multiple vendors can interoperate. These directories are the focus of this book.

The Dawn of Standards Directories: X.500

In the mid-1980s, two separate standards bodies independently started work on directory services that could work across system, corporate, and international boundaries. The first body was the International Telegraph and Telephone Consultative Committee (CCITT), which later changed its name to the International Telecommunications Union (ITU). CCITT member organizations (mainly telephone companies) wanted to create a white pages directory that could be used to look up telephone numbers and electronic mail addresses.

The other standards body was the International Organization for Standardization (ISO) , which wanted a directory to serve as a name service for Open Systems Interconnect (OSI) networks and applications. (A name service provides information about network objects; DNS is a familiar example.)

Eventually, the two independent international directory specification efforts merged into one effort, and X.500 was born. The first X.500 standard was approved in late 1988 and published in early 1990 by CCITT; it was subsequently updated in 1993 and 1997, and work continues today. The specification itself references other ISO standards and consists of a series of recommendations, including all of the following:

- *X.501: The Models*—Describes the concepts and models that underlie an X.500 directory service

- *X.509: Authentication Framework*—Describes in detail how the authentication of directory clients and servers is handled in X.500

- *X.511: Abstract Service Definition*—Describes in detail the functional services provided by X.500 directories (for example, search operations, modify operations, and so on)

- *X.518: Procedures for Distributed Operation*—Describes how directory operations that span multiple servers are handled, among other details

- *X.519: Protocol Specifications*—Describes all the X.500 protocols, including Directory Access Protocol (DAP), Directory System Protocol (DSP), Directory Operational Binding Protocol (DOP), and Directory Information Shadowing Protocol (DISP)

- *X.520: Selected Attribute Types*—Defines attribute types used by X.500 itself, and some that are generally useful as well (such as the `telephoneNumber` attribute)

- *X.521: Selected Object Classes*—Defines object classes used by X.500 itself, and some that are generally useful as well (such as the `person` object class)

- *X.525: Replication*—Describes how directory content is replicated among X.500 servers

As you can see, X.500 developers must absorb quite a few documents before they can begin to develop X.500 directory services software! The X.500 documents are published both online and in paper form by the ITU, which currently charges money to access them.

X.500 Innovations

At the time it was originally defined, X.500 had many novel qualities. First, it was one of the first truly general-purpose directory systems, and it was designed from the beginning to be extensible in order to serve the needs of a great variety of applications. Second, X.500 provided a very rich search operation that can support many different kinds of queries. Third, like Grapevine (but on a much broader scale), X.500 was designed to be a highly distributed system in which the servers, data, and administrators could span the globe. Finally, X.500 was an open standard that was not controlled by any one vendor or tied to any specific operating system, networking technology, or application. The dream of the X.500 designers was that there would eventually be one fully interconnected global directory service—THE Directory.

The major components of an X.500 directory service are shown in Figure 2.4.

X.500 directories rely on a large suite of protocols, including DAP, DSP, DOP, and DISP. Some of X.500's strengths are its information model (which is very flexible and complete), its versatility, and its openness. As we will see, the LDAP designers adopted many of the best ideas from X.500 while removing unneeded complexity.

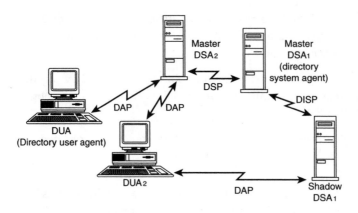

FIGURE 2.4   *Components of an X.500 directory service.*

X.500 Flaws

In practice, X.500 directories suffered from some significant flaws, especially in their first decade of existence. The early implementations were buggy and did not perform or scale very well. Those who tried to deploy distributed X.500 directories discovered some significant barriers to adoption, many of which were not specific to X.500 (such as difficulty obtaining and maintaining good data in a directory service). Also, because of the complexity of the standards themselves and the associated difficulty of implementation, it has taken a very long time for interoperability between different X.500 implementations to become possible.

In addition, X.500 was based on the OSI network protocols. The dream of the OSI designers was that OSI would eventually replace TCP/IP as the networking protocol suite of the future. Unfortunately for them, this never happened. The simplicity, speed, and low cost of TCP/IP proved to be an unbeatable combination.

Finally, the origins of X.500 itself have to some extent prevented it from succeeding. The Internet grew rapidly in a bottom-up fashion as independent organizations deployed hosts and services at their own pace and without a lot of reliance on others. In contrast, X.500 was designed with the large public service providers in mind, which implies a top-down deployment. This has proved to be impossible to achieve—and it is certainly at odds with the prevailing Internet culture.

Early X.500 Implementations and Pilots

One of the best-known early X.500 implementations, called Quipu, was developed at University College, London. Its name refers to the complicated system of knot-tying the Incan culture used for communication. Part of the reason for Quipu's early popularity was that it was freely available in source code form. Quipu is built on top of an OSI networking package called the ISO Development Environment (ISODE), which allows OSI protocols to run on top of TCP/IP and, thus, the Internet.

The availability of Quipu encouraged many organizations to experiment with X.500 directories. The Quipu implementation served as the basis for a number of X.500 white pages pilot projects centered mainly in Europe and the United States. Unfortunately, these worldwide X.500 directory pilots didn't grow as fast as their sponsors hoped, and interest has waned.

X.500 found its greatest success in large organizations that could afford the time and effort needed to deploy a large, complex directory service. Some early deployers of X.500 included the United Kingdom academic community, Boeing Corporation, The National Aeronautics and Space Administration (NASA), the University of Texas, and the University of Michigan.

The Status of X.500 Directories Today

The X.500 standards themselves have grown from basic user access and distribution to encompass single-master replication (or *shadowing*, as X.500 calls it), along with a choice of standard access control schemes and many other features. The future of X.500 standardization activities is somewhat unclear at this time because development within ISO has slowed.

A number of available products implement the recent X.500 standards. Without exception, the X.500 products all support LDAP access to their directory services. Some of the prominent X.500 products include

- ISOCOR's Global Directory Server

- Datacraft's OpenDirectory Dxserver

- Control Data's Rialto Global Directory Server

X.500 directories are generally aimed at meeting the needs of organizations performing synchronization of email systems. Typically, the deployment of an X.500 directory service is done in partnership with the X.500 software vendor.

Most vendors provide extensive consulting services to help organizations deploy and integrate an X.500 directory into their existing environment.

The Creation and Rise of LDAP

The early adopters of X.500 found that DAP (X.500's directory client access protocol) was fairly complex and not well suited for or available on the desktop computers of the day (PCs and Macintoshes). DAP is large, complex, and difficult to implement, and most implementations perform poorly. Because the majority of potential directory services users had ordinary machines on their desks, the people deploying X.500 began to look for an approach that avoided the heavyweight DAP.

Forerunners of LDAP: DIXIE and DAS

Around 1990, two independent groups devised similar protocols that were simpler and easier for desktop computers to implement than DAP. The desktop clients spoke one of these new protocols directly over TCP/IP to an intermediate server, which in turn implemented X.500 DAP. These two groups both brought their work to the Internet Engineering Task Force (IETF).

The IETF

The IETF is a large, open, international group of network researchers, designers, and operators who work on evolving Internet architecture and enhancing its capabilities. The IETF was formally chartered in 1986, although it existed informally for some time before that. The IETF is primarily focused on the task of protocol development and engineering for the Internet. The group is open to any interested individual; there are no membership requirements and only a small fee to cover the cost of meetings. The IETF holds face-to-face meetings three times each year.

The technical work is primarily done within IETF working groups (although individual or vendor contributions are

also accepted). The working groups have one or more chairpersons, and the group members meet three times each year at the regularly scheduled IETF meetings. However, most of the work happens outside the meetings on electronic mailing lists that each working group maintains. The working groups are organized into several large areas (routing, security, transport, applications, and so on).

Specifications produced by IETF members are first published in draft documents called, logically enough, *Internet Drafts*. When consensus is reached in a working group and a series of technical and administrative requirements are adequately met, documents may be published as requests for

continues

continued

comments (RFCs). All IETF documents are freely available at no cost on the Internet. It is worth noting that there are several categories of RFCs, ranging from Informational to Experimental to Standards Track, and that very few RFCs are intended to become official Internet Standards. As of mid-1998, almost 2,500 RFCs had been published, but only 58 had reached full Internet Standard status.

The first IETF meeting, held in San Diego in January 1986, was attended by 21 network engineers. A recent IETF meeting held in August 1998 in Chicago was attended by more than 2,000 people. As of late 1998, there were more than 100 active working groups organized into 8 areas within IETF. More information about IETF can be found on its World Wide Web site at http://www.ietf.org.

The two lightweight protocols for desktop computers were called Directory Assistance Service (DAS), defined in RFC 1202; and Directory Interface to X.500 Implemented Efficiently (DIXIE), defined in RFC 1249. The architecture of a directory system that uses a DIXIE client/client/server architecture is shown in Figure 2.5.

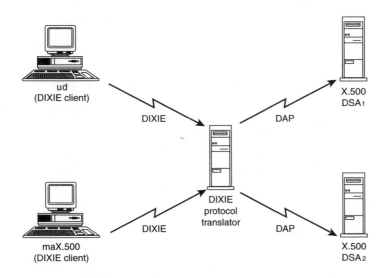

FIGURE 2.5   *DIXIE provides a front end to an X.500 directory.*

Both protocols were very successful; DIXIE, though, was quickly adopted as the preferred method to access X.500 directory systems. However, one shortcoming of the DAS and DIXIE protocols is that both were tied closely to a single X.500 implementation (Quipu).

The Creation of LDAP

After DIXIE and DAS showed the utility of a lighter-weight access protocol for X.500, the members of the Open System Interconnection–Directory Services (OSI–DS) working group within the IETF decided to join forces and produce a full-featured, lightweight directory access protocol for X.500 directories. Thus, LDAP was born.

The developers of the first LDAP specification were Wengyik Yeong, Steve Kille, Colin Robbins, and Tim Howes, who is one of the authors of this book. It is important to also note that contributions were made by many people from the Internet and X.500 communities. The first LDAP specification was published as RFC 1487 in July 1993. The first version of LDAP to see widespread use was version 2 (LDAPv2); the final specification for LDAPv2 was published as RFC 1777.

LDAP Innovations

The LDAP developers simplified the heavyweight X.500 DAP protocol in four important areas:

- *Functionality*—LDAP provides most of DAP's functionality at a much lower cost. Redundant operations and rarely used features of DAP were eliminated, simplifying the implementation of LDAP clients and servers.

- *Data representation*—Most data elements are carried as simple text strings in LDAP, although messages are still wrapped in binary encodings for efficiency. This simplifies implementations and increases performance.

- *Encoding*—The LDAP protocol data elements are encoded using a subset of the encoding rules used by X.500, thus simplifying implementation.

- *Transport*—LDAP runs directly over TCP instead of requiring the unwieldy, multilayer OSI networking stack. Implementation is simplified, performance is increased, and the need for OSI is eliminated, which eases the deployment of LDAP directories.

Early LDAP Implementations

At first, LDAP was used exclusively to provide a front end for X.500-based directory services. The first and best-known LDAP implementation was produced by the authors while at the University of Michigan. The U-M LDAP implementation, as it came to be known, was small and fast, and it ran on a wide variety of popular computing platforms. Most important of all, it included a simple, well-specified C language API that implemented all of the client side of LDAP and could be used to develop any kind of LDAP client application. The LDAPv2 client API eventually became a de facto standard and was published in RFC 1823. The components of the early U-M LDAP software releases are depicted in Figure 2.6.

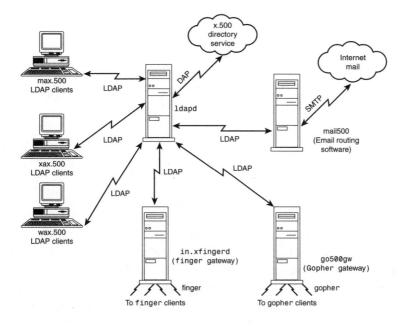

FIGURE 2.6   *Major components of the early U-M LDAP releases.*

The first version of the U-M LDAP implementation was released publicly on the Internet in 1992 with a copyright notice that allowed unrestricted use of the software. A wide range of freely available and commercial LDAP client software soon followed, much of which was based on the University of Michigan implementation.

LDAP as a Standalone Directory Service

In early 1995, the LDAP group at U-M found itself on the brink of another revelation. When examining the directory access statistics for the U-M service, the group noticed that well over 99% of the X.500 directory access came through LDAP. This was true of most X.500 directories. The architecture prevalent at the time is shown in Figure 2.7.

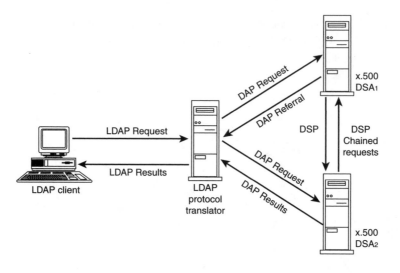

FIGURE 2.7   *LDAP directory system architecture, circa 1995.*

Although LDAP had solved the directory client access problem, the server implementations were still large, complex, and difficult to deploy. The U-M LDAP group realized that by eliminating the intermediate ldapd server, the overall complexity of the system could be greatly reduced and the performance greatly increased. After all, ldapd spent all its time translating LDAP requests into DAP requests and recasting the DAP results returned from the X.500 servers as LDAP results.

In addition, the promise of a global, interconnected X.500 directory didn't seem to be achievable, and so the need for an X.500 directory server at all was questioned. The concept of a standalone, or native, LDAP server was born. The new server was dubbed SLAPD (for standalone LDAP daemon), and with the aid of a grant from the National Science Foundation, it was quickly implemented. The revised LDAP system architecture is shown in Figure 2.8.

While keeping the best pieces of the X.500 models (see Chapter 3, "An Introduction to LDAP," for more information), LDAP had now broken free of the last bit of X.500 and could proudly stand on its own. At the same time, referrals were added to the LDAPv2 protocol as an experimental extension to support an interconnected mesh of SLAPD directory servers. These changes moved LDAP out of its role as a simple, useful protocol for accessing X.500 directories to a much broader role as the foundation for a complete directory service. The first release of the U-M LDAP software to include SLAPD was the U-M LDAP 3.2 release in December 1995.

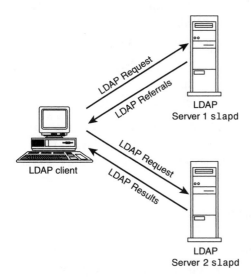

FIGURE 2.8 *LDAP system architecture after the introduction of SLAPD.*

LDAP Momentum

LDAP's commercial success was assured in April 1996 when Netscape headed a coalition of more than 40 prominent software companies that endorsed LDAP as the Internet directory service protocol of choice. Today, Netscape produces a complete set of enterprise software that is centered around an LDAP-based directory service, and all major network application software vendors support LDAP in their client and server products.

LDAP Version 3 Developed

Recently, LDAP entered an even more mature phase in its evolution with the release of version 3 of the protocol (LDAPv3). Mark Wahl of Innosoft International, Inc., along with some of the original LDAP authors and a cast of hundreds from across the Internet, contributed to the LDAPv3 specification. LDAPv3 improves on LDAPv2 in the following important areas:

- *Internationalization*—The UTF-8 character set is used everywhere it is appropriate. Because UTF-8 is an encoding of the universal Unicode character set, all the characters used in every language in the world can be stored and manipulated by LDAPv3 directory servers and clients.

- *Referrals*—A standard mechanism for returning referrals to other servers was added, which allows LDAP servers to be deployed in a bottom-up fashion, just as World Wide Web servers are.

- *Security*—Support for Simple Authentication and Security Layer (SASL) and Transport Layer Security (TLS) were added to increase LDAP's security and allow a richer set of applications to be supported.

- *Extensibility*—LDAPv3 can be extended to support new operations, and existing operations can be extended through the use of controls, allowing LDAP to be incrementally enhanced to meet future needs.

- *Feature and schema discovery*—All LDAPv3 servers publish the versions of the LDAP protocol they support along with other useful information in a special directory entry called the *root DSE* (DSA or Directory Server-Specific Entry). In addition, LDAPv3 servers publish their supported directory schemas as a set of LDAP attributes. These features help LDAP clients and servers work together more intelligently.

In late 1997, LDAPv3 was the winner of the *PC Magazine* Award for Technical Excellence in the Networking category. Some vendors are shipping LDAPv3-compliant products today, and you can expect many more to follow. In late 1997, LDAPv3 was approved as a proposed Internet Standard (the first step on its way to becoming a full Internet Standard). The LDAPv3 specification is available as the following series of RFCs:

- *RFC 2251: LDAPv3 Protocol*—Describes the LDAP protocol itself

- *RFC 2252: LDAPv3 Attribute Syntax Definitions*—Defines attribute syntaxes used by LDAP and its applications, including how these values are represented as simple strings

- *RFC 2253: LDAPv3 UTF-8 String Representation of Distinguished Names*—Describes how distinguished names are represented as simple strings using the UTF-8 character set

- *RFC 2254: The String Representation of LDAP Search Filters*—Defines a scheme for representing LDAP search filters (which may be complex Boolean expressions involving multiple terms) as simple strings for use in LDAP URLs and APIs

- *RFC 2255: The LDAP URL Format*—Defines a uniform resource locator (URL) scheme to represent LDAP search requests

- *RFC 2256: A Summary of the X.500(96) User Schema for Use with LDAPv3*—Provides a list of useful directory schemas (attributes and object classes) that are pulled from the X.500 specifications

Like their X.500 counterparts, developers of LDAP directories must absorb quite a few documents before they can successfully develop LDAP software. Fortunately, all RFCs are freely available on the Internet, and most related to LDAP are fairly short and easy to read. Unfortunately, some of the LDAP documents assume that the reader has knowledge that can only be obtained by consulting the X.500 standards.

Status of LDAP Directories Today

LDAP is now shepherded by the LDAP Extensions (LDAPEXT) working group within the IETF. People from a variety of companies, universities, and research organizations are contributing to the evolution of LDAP. Current areas of work include access control, replication, and a variety of small but useful extensions to the LDAPv3 protocol. Thanks to the simple but flexible extension mechanisms that are included in LDAPv3, no one expects an LDAP version 4 to be needed any time soon.

Most of the available LDAP directory services products are modeled after the original University of Michigan SLAPD concept. Typically, they are built around a standalone LDAP server that includes a high-performance embedded database. In some cases, the implementation is actually based on the U-M code; in other cases, vendors of X.500 or other directory services embraced LDAP strongly and have made it their directory access and operational protocol of choice. Some examples of general-purpose LDAP directory services available at the time of this writing include

- Netscape's Directory Server

- Innosoft Distributed Directory Server

- Lucent Technologies's Internet Directory Server

- Sun Microsystems's Directory Services

- IBM's DSSeries LDAP Directory

- University of Michigan's SLAPD server

These directory products are designed to support a variety of Internet, intranet, and extranet applications. They usually provide good integration with other services that are based on Internet protocols, such as SMTP-based messaging servers, HTTP-based Web servers, and the like. They provide good administrative tools, are relatively inexpensive, and aim to be easy to deploy

IETF Directory Services Working Groups

Over the years, a number of different IETF working groups have dealt with LDAP. All these groups have been chartered within the Applications or Operations areas of the IETF.

The first group to deal with LDAP was OSI–DS. Some work that was focused on adapting X.500 for the Internet along with all the early DAS, DIXIE, and LDAP work was done within the confines of OSI–DS.

In 1993, the directory services efforts in the IETF were split into several groups. These groups included Access, Searching, and Indexing of Directories (ASID) and Integrated Directory Services (IDS). The core LDAPv3 work was done within the ASID group; IDS focused mainly on directory service issues that were not specific to LDAP, such as security and privacy.

Recently, the ASID and IDS groups were disbanded, and a series of new working groups was chartered to continue LDAP's evolution. The LDAPEXT working group is focused on standardizing important extensions to LDAPv3 itself, such as a common access control scheme. The LDAP Duplication/ Replication/Update Protocol group (LDUP) is working on a multimaster replication standard for LDAP directory services. The SCHEMA group is designing a schema registration service for LDAP. Finally, the LDAP Service Deployment (LSD) group concerns itself with work that makes it easier for LDAP deployments to succeed.

More information about these IETF working groups can be found on the IETF's World Wide Web site at `http://www.ietf.org./html. charters/wg-dir.html`.

and maintain. Netscape has gone farther than most of the other vendors, as it has articulated and pursued a comprehensive strategy to move all of its intranet applications, administration, and security services to LDAP.

Other Standards-Based, General-Purpose Directories

A variety of other directory services were developed in parallel with or shortly after the X.500 and LDAP directories. Many of these directories came out of the Internet community and were either niche services or competitors to X.500 and LDAP themselves. Although none of these services were ever widely endorsed like LDAP was, a number of organizations experimented with these services and may in some cases still be running directory services based on them.

CSO Nameserver

One of the best-known and widely used early Internet directories was the CSO Nameserver, which was developed at the University of Illinois. Sometimes known as ph (referring to the name of one of the programs used to access it), this service is typically used to store information about electronic mail users. CSO Nameserver, used by many Internet sites (mostly universities), became popular because of the availability of free software and client support from one of the earliest and best Internet email clients, Eudora. QUALCOMM, Inc. now develops and markets Eudora as a commercial product.

Competitors to LDAP

When it became clear that X.500 directories were not going to take the world by storm, several other efforts to produce lighter-weight services sprung up. Among these are WHOIS++ (RFC 1834), RWHOIS (RFC 1714), and SOLO. As you can guess by the names, the first two of these were designed as extensions (albeit, extensive in and of themselves) to the original WHOIS Internet protocol. SOLO, designed to fill some of the same needs as LDAP, borrowed ideas from both WHOIS++ and LDAP.

Directory Services Future

It is clear that directory services—especially the open, general-purpose directories based on LDAP—have a very bright future. We see a number of trends in the directory services marketplace:

- Metadirectories are emerging as an important directory product category.

- Directory services are being more tightly integrated with operating systems.

- Open standards–based directories are making operating systems less important.

- LDAP is branching out to become a lightweight database access protocol.

- LDAP directories continue to dominate.

- Directories are becoming truly ubiquitous.

Each of these important directory trends is discussed in greater detail in the following sections.

Metadirectories as an Important Product Directory Category

Although nearly all new directory service deployments are based on LDAP, most organizations are not starting from scratch with their directory deployment. There are at least a handful and sometimes dozens of proprietary, outdated, or application-specific directories that the new directory service must coexist with. Because these legacy directories are difficult and expensive to replace, organizations are increasingly looking for ways to lower the costs associated with managing these redundant systems. One solution to this management problem is a *metadirectory*—a directory service designed to aggregate and help manage a multitude of other systems. This topic is covered in greater detail in Chapter 22, "Directory Coexistence."

Tighter Operating System Integration

Some directory vendors are tying the directory service and operating system tightly together. The most prominent example is the Microsoft Active Directory, which ships with Windows NT 5.0. Many of the operating system functions depend on the directory service, and in turn the directory service depends on the operating system. This kind of integration may make the system as a whole work better, but it has a disadvantage: For Microsoft's customers, the choice of directory service is tied to the choice of operating system. Thus, for different directory vendors, the level of operating system integration pursued and provided varies because of differences in customer base and target applications.

Directories Are Making Operating Systems Less Important

Competing with the previous trend is the fact that, much as the Internet Web browser has diminished the importance of the desktop operating system, open standards–based directories are making network operating systems less important. Many services that were traditionally provided by an operating system, such as service location and naming, are now provided by LDAP directories. Applications can avoid tying themselves to a platform-specific set of APIs, and software vendors can provide a more portable set of tools for customers. More and more, applications—instead of operating systems—are driving the deployment of new directory services. When coupled with the emergence of platform-independent operating environments, such as those based on Java, this trend has the potential to significantly change how software applications are written and deployed.

LDAP as a Database Access Protocol

Many applications that have relatively simple database needs are currently written to use a full-blown relational database. Database independence is surprisingly difficult to achieve; although there are several database-independent

APIs to choose from, there is no standard protocol for database access. Some independent software vendors and developers within enterprises have discovered that LDAP can provide most of the database functionality needed by their applications. This discovery will broaden LDAP's influence.

LDAP's Continued Dominance

LDAP directories continue to gain momentum and dominate the directory services space. In the standards area, LDAP is also flourishing, and a great deal of energy is being put into LDAPv3 and its extensions. Software vendors, customers, analysts, and users all see the benefits of open standards–based directories. Just as no one buys a Web browser who doesn't understand HTTP and HTML, no one purchases a directory service who does not understand LDAP.

Directories Are Becoming Truly Ubiquitous

Finally, directories are everywhere. They are "moving down the network stack" as vendors of networking switches, routers, and other devices enable LDAP on our network infrastructure. Directories are also "moving up the network stack" and into desktop applications such as Web browsers and word processors.

Millions of people access directories every day from their email clients and Web browsers. Corporate phone directories are among the most popular intranet applications; and, increasingly, server software can't function without a directory service. The powerful forces shaping the directory services landscape come from many sources. Whether you are deploying an LDAP directory service, writing directory services software, directory-enabling a network application or device, or just using directories, you, too, are contributing to the future of directories.

Conclusion

For many years, a number of different directory services competed for the interest of information service professionals, application software developers, and users. Today it is clear that LDAP has moved to the front and center of the directory services space, and there is much excitement and energy being put into developing and deploying LDAP directories. LDAP emerged from the rest of the pack to dominate the directory services space because of the following factors:

- *LDAP is simple, yet versatile*—LDAP supports a wide variety of directory-enabled applications that have widely varying needs.

- *LDAP is ubiquitous*—A good implementation of LDAP was developed and distributed freely on the Internet by researchers at the University of Michigan. This provided much of LDAP's early momentum. Today, LDAP implementations are available for every major and most minor computing platforms that are in use.

- *LDAP directories are inexpensive and easy to understand*—Organizations that choose LDAP directories find them to be relatively inexpensive to deploy and maintain. LDAP directory systems are simple enough that an army of consultants is not needed to understand and deploy them.

- *LDAP directory services simply work better*—The high reliability, performance, and scalability of LDAP directory products, combined with their general-purpose design, allows them to meet the most important directory services needs.

- *LDAP has a lot of "mindshare"*—Shortly after Netscape and 40 other software companies put their support behind LDAP in early 1996, interest in LDAP exploded. The hunger for a single directory standard is being filled by LDAP, and momentum continues to grow.

In short, LDAP is making the dream of a universal, general-purpose directory service a reality on the Internet and within organizations.

Directory Services Time Line

1953	First issue of *TV Guide* published.
1969	First Arpanet node comes online; first RFC published.
1973	Ethernet invented by Xerox PARC researchers.
1982	TCP/IP replaces older Arpanet protocols on the Internet.
	First distributed computing research paper on Grapevine published by Xerox PARC researchers.
1984	Internet DNS comes online.
1986	IETF formally chartered.
1989	Quipu (X.500 software package) released.
1990	Estimated number of Internet hosts exceeds 250,000.
1990	First version of the X.500 standard published.

1991	A team at CERN headed by Tim Berners-Lee releases the first World Wide Web software.
1992	University of Michigan developers release the first LDAP software.
1993	NDS debuts in Netware 4.0.
July 1993	LDAP specification first published as RFC 1487.
December 1995	First standalone LDAP server (SLAPD) ships as part of U-M LDAP 3.2 release.
April 1996	Consortium of more than 40 leading software vendors endorses LDAP as the Internet directory service protocol of choice.
November 1997	LDAPv3 named the winner of the *PC Magazine* Award for Technical Excellence.
December 1997	LDAPv3 approved as a proposed Internet Standard.
January 1998	Netscape ships the first commercial LDAPv3 directory server.
July 1998	Estimated number of Internet hosts exceeds 36 million.

Further Reading

Development of the Domain Name System. P. Mockapetris, K. J. Dunlap, ACM SIGCOMM Symposium, August 1988.

"Grapevine: An Exercise in Distributed Computing." A. D. Birrell, R. Levin, R. M. Needham, M. D. Schroeder, *Communications of the ACM*, 25, April 1982, pp. 260–273.

History of the Net. S. Feizabadi, Virginia Tech University. Available on the World Wide Web at `http://ei.cs.vt.edu/book/chap1/net_hist.html`.

The ISO Development Environment Version 7.0 Users' Manual Volume 5—Quipu. S. Kille, C. Robbins, July 1991.

LDAPv3 Specifications. M. Wahl, Critical Angle, Inc. Available on the World Wide Web at `http://www.critical-angle.com/ldapworld/ldapv3.html`.

The Lightweight Directory Access Protocol: X.500 Lite. T. Howes, CITI Technical Report 95-8, July 1995. Available on the World Wide Web at `http://www-leland.stanford.edu/group/networking/directory/doc/ldap/ldap.html`.

NameFLOW-Paradise International Directory Service. Available on the World Wide Web at `http://www.dante.net/nameflow.html`.

Overview of the IETF. Available on the World Wide Web at `http://www.ietf.org/overview.html`.

A Scalable, Deployable, Directory Service Framework for the Internet. T. Howes, M. Smith, INET '95. Available on the World Wide Web at `http://info.isoc.org:80/HMP/PAPER/173/abst.html`.

Understanding X.500: The Directory. D. Chadwick, International Thomson Computer Press, 1996. Now out of print; selected portions available on the World Wide Web at `http://www.salford.ac.uk/its024/X500.htm`.

University of Michigan LDAP Page. Available on the World Wide Web at `http://www.umich.edu/~dirsvcs/ldap/index.html`.

X.500 and Internet Directories. C. Robbins, NEXOR. Available on the World Wide Web at `http://www.nexor.com/public/directory.html`.

Looking Ahead

In this chapter we presented the most significant directory services developments of the past and very briefly looked at some future trends. Moving forward, we will probe much deeper into the ins and outs of LDAP-based directories. Chapter 3 describes LDAP in detail, covering all the components that help make LDAP directory services the best choice.

CHAPTER **3**

An Introduction to LDAP

In Chapter 2, "A Brief History of Directories," we talked about the history of directories and how LDAP was born. In this chapter, we take a much closer look at LDAP, both in its role as a network protocol and as a set of models that guide you in constructing and accessing your directory. We'll also examine two other important aspects of LDAP: the LDAP application programming interfaces (APIs), which you can use to develop LDAP applications; and the LDAP Data Interchange Format (LDIF), which is a common, text-based format for exchanging directory data between systems.

What Is LDAP?

At its core, LDAP is a standard, extensible directory access protocol—a common language that LDAP clients and servers use to communicate with each other. Standardization of the protocol has the benefit that client and server software from different vendors can interoperate. When you buy an LDAP-enabled program, you can expect that it will work with any standards-compatible LDAP server. This has many advantages, but we'll discuss those later in this chapter.

LDAP is a "lightweight" protocol, which means that it is efficient, straight-forward, and easy to implement, while still being highly functional. Contrast this with a "heavyweight" protocol, such as the X.500 Directory Access Protocol (DAP). X.500 DAP uses complex encoding methods and requires use of the OSI network protocol stack—a networking system that has failed to gain wide acceptance.

LDAP, on the other hand, uses a simplified set of encoding methods and runs directly on top of TCP/IP. Every major desktop and server computing platform currently available (Microsoft Windows, DOS, UNIX, and the Apple Macintosh) either ships with a TCP/IP implementation or can be easily equipped with one. OSI networking, on the other hand, is not universally available, and it is almost always an extra-cost option. LDAP, by virtue of its light weight, removes significant barriers to implementation and deployment.

As mentioned in Chapter 2, there have been two major revisions of the LDAP protocol. The first widely available version was LDAP version 2, defined in RFCs 1777 and 1778. As of this writing, LDAP version 3 is a Proposed Internet Standard, defined in RFCs 2251 through 2256. Because it is so new, not all vendors completely support LDAPv3 yet. As we discuss LDAP in this chapter, we will focus our discussion on LDAPv3. However, we will point out new features found only in LDAPv3 so that you can understand the limitations you will encounter if you are using LDAPv2.

In addition to its role as a network protocol, the LDAP standards also define four models that guide you in your use of the directory. These models promote interoperability between directory installations while still allowing you the flexibility to tailor the directory to your specific needs. The models borrow concepts from X.500, but they generally lack many of the restrictions that the X.500 models include. The four LDAP models are as follows:

- The LDAP information model, which defines the kind of data you can put into the directory.

- The LDAP naming model, which defines how you organize and refer to your directory data.

- The LDAP functional model, which defines how you access and update the information in your directory.

- The LDAP security model, which defines how information in the directory can be protected from unauthorized access.

In addition to guiding you in the use of your directory, the LDAP models guide directory developers when designing and implementing LDAP server and client software. The LDAP models are discussed in detail later in the chapter.

There are several LDAP APIs, the oldest of which is for the C programming language. The C API is supported by several freely available software development kits (SDKs), including one available in binary and source code format from Netscape Communications Corporation. In addition to the C API, Netscape's freely available Java SDK (also available in binary and source code formats) supports all LDAPv3 features. Netscape also provides PerLDAP, a toolkit for the Perl language that allows you to access LDAP directories.

SunSoft's JNDI is a proprietary, unified directory access API that supports access to multiple types of directory services (NIS+, LDAP, and others). Microsoft offers its own proprietary unified directory access API, known as Active Directory Services Interface (ADSI). These APIs and their various strengths are covered later in this chapter and in Chapter 20, "Developing New Applications."

LDAP also defines the LDAP Data Interchange Format (LDIF), a common, text-based format for describing directory information. LDIF can describe a set of directory entries or a set of updates to be applied to a directory. Directory data can also be exported from one directory and into another using LDIF. Most of the commonly available command-line utilities also read and write LDIF. The LDIF format is discussed in more detail later in this chapter.

What Can LDAP Do for You?

If you are a system administrator, then LDAP

- Makes it possible for you to centrally manage users, groups, devices, and other data.

- Helps you do away with the headache of managing separate application-specific directories (such as LAN-based electronic mail software).

If you are a IT decision maker, then LDAP

- Allows you to avoid tying yourself exclusively to a single vendor and/or operating system platform.

- Helps you decrease the total cost of ownership by reducing the number of distinct directories your staff needs to manage.

If you are a software developer, then LDAP

- Allows you to avoid tying your software exclusively to a single vendor and/or operating system platform.

- Helps you save development time by avoiding the need to construct your own user and group management database.

For example, before the advent of LDAP, each of your applications probably had its own directory of user information. If you had a LAN-based email package, there was probably an interface you used to create and manage users and groups. If you had a LAN-based collaboration package from a different vendor, it most likely had its own directory and method of accessing that directory. And, often, if you used LAN-based file server software, it probably had its own distinct user directory.

Some vendors offered packaged solutions, which made it possible to manage users and groups in one place—as long as you used only their software suite. However, if you needed to mix and match software from multiple vendors, you probably ended up developing an elaborate procedure for ensuring that new employees were added to each package's proprietary directory.

With LDAP comes the promise of eliminating this management nightmare. Instead of creating an account for each user in each system he or she needs to access, you will be able to simply create a single directory entry for the user— and all directory-enabled applications will simply refer to the user's entry in the LDAP directory. When an employee is terminated, access to all systems can be revoked by removing the user's directory entry instead of hunting down all accounts granted to the person and disabling each one. Users benefit as well because they need to remember and manage only a single password instead of one for each system.

In addition to consolidating the management of your users' access privileges, LDAP directories allow easier sharing of directory information with trading partners in an extranet environment. If you have established business relationships with other companies, you can use the directory to share common user information between your two organizations. This allows you to set up workflow processes that cross company boundaries, making both organizations more efficient.

LDAP directories also can be used to build entirely new applications. An Internet service provider, for example, might create an LDAP directory that contains information about all its subscribers and the special add-on services it may have purchased. The directory can be consulted each time the user wants to access a given service. If the user has appropriate permissions, as registered in the directory, the application grants the user access; otherwise, access is denied. Management of all the value-added services is handled by updating the directory.

Not all software vendors have made the transition to LDAP-based management, but LDAP has tremendous momentum in the software industry.

Over time, more and more applications will be directory-enabled with the net benefit of reducing the total cost of ownership of your applications.

How Does LDAP Work?

In this section, we'll delve into the LDAP protocol in detail. We'll start with an overview of LDAP as a client/server protocol. We'll then discuss the individual LDAP protocol operations and show how clients can use them to perform useful tasks such as sending secure email. We'll also discuss LDAP extensibility, and we'll conclude by showing you how LDAP works "on the wire" by discussing the actual wire protocol.

A *client/server protocol* is a protocol model in which a client program running on one computer constructs a request and sends it over the network to a computer (possibly the same computer) running a server program. The server program receives the request, takes some action, and returns a result to the client program. Examples of other client/server protocols are Hypertext Transfer Protocol (HTTP), which is typically used to serve Web pages; and Internet Message Access Protocol (IMAP), a protocol used to access electronic mail messages.

The basic idea behind a client/server protocol is that it allows work to be assigned to computers that are optimized for the task at hand. For example, a typical LDAP server computer will probably have a lot of RAM that it uses for caching the directory contents for fast performance. It will also probably have very fast disks and a fast processor, but it probably doesn't need a large-screen monitor and expensive graphics support. A client computer, on the other hand, might be on an employee's desk, probably optimized for the type of work that the employee does. Rather than putting a copy of the corporate directory on every employee's workstation, it's a better idea to maintain the directory centrally on a server (or replicated set of servers).

The LDAP protocol is a message-oriented protocol. The client constructs an LDAP message containing a request and sends it to the server. The server processes the request and sends the result or results back to the client as a series of LDAP messages.

For example, when an LDAP client searches the directory for a specific entry, it constructs an LDAP search request message and sends it to the server. The server retrieves the entry from its database and sends it to the client in an LDAP message. It also returns a result code to the client in a separate LDAP message. This interaction is shown in Figure 3.1.

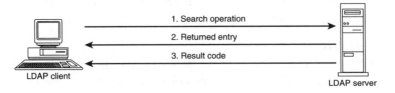

F IGURE 3.1 *A client retrieves a single entry from the directory.*

If the client searches the directory and multiple matching entries are found, the entries are sent to the client in a series of LDAP messages, one for each entry. The results are terminated with a result message, which contains an overall result for the search operation, as shown in Figure 3.2.

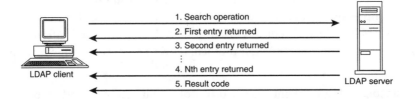

F IGURE 3.2 *A client searches the directory, and multiple entries are returned.*

Because the LDAP protocol is message-based, it also allows the client to issue multiple requests at once. Suppose, for example, a client might issue two search requests simultaneously. In LDAP, the client would generate a unique message ID for each request; returned results for specific request would be tagged with its message ID, allowing the client to sort out multiple responses to different requests arriving out of order or at the same time. In Figure 3.3, the client has issued two search requests simultaneously. The server processes both operations and returns the results to the client.

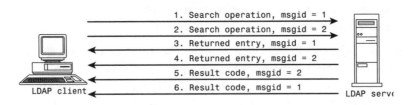

F IGURE 3.3 *A client issues multiple LDAP search requests simultaneously.*

Notice that in Figure 3.3 the server sends the final result code of message ID 2 to the client before it sends the final result code from message ID 1. This is perfectly acceptable and happens quite frequently. These details are typically hidden from the programmer by an LDAP SDK. Programmers writing an LDAP application don't need to be concerned with sorting out these results; the SDKs take care of this automatically.

Allowing multiple concurrent requests "in flight" allows LDAP to be more flexible and efficient than protocols that operate in a "lock-step" fashion (for example, HTTP). With a lock-step protocol, each client request must be answered by the server before another may be sent. For example, an HTTP client program—such as a Web browser that wants to download multiple files concurrently—must open one connection for each file. LDAP, on the other hand, can manage multiple operations on a single connection, reducing the maximum number of concurrent connections a server must be prepared to handle.

The LDAP Protocol Operations
LDAP has nine basic protocol operations, which can be divided into three categories:

- *Interrogation operations: search, compare.* These two operations allow you to ask questions of the directory.

- *Update operations: add, delete, modify, modify DN (rename).* These operations allow you to update information in the directory.

- *Authentication and control operations: bind, unbind, abandon.* The bind operation allows a client to identify itself to the directory by providing an identity and authentication credentials; the unbind operation allows the client to terminate a session; and the abandon operation allows a client to indicate that it is no longer interested in the results of an operation it had previously submitted.

We will discuss each of the individual protocol operations when we describe the LDAP functional model later in this chapter.

A typical complete LDAP client/server exchange might proceed as depicted in Figure 3.4.

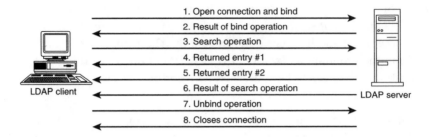

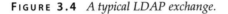

FIGURE 3.4 *A typical LDAP exchange.*

In Figure 3.4, an LDAP client and server perform the following steps:

Step 1: The client opens a TCP connection to an LDAP server and submits a bind operation. This bind operation includes the name of the directory entry the client wants to authenticate as, along with the credentials to be used when authenticating. Credentials are often simple passwords, but they might also be digital certificates used to authenticate the client.

Step 2: After the directory has verified the bind credentials, it returns a success result to the client.

Step 3: The client issues a search request.

Steps 4 and 5: The server processes this request, which results in two matching entries.

Step 6: The server sends a result message.

Step 7: The client then issues an unbind request, which indicates to the server that the client wants to disconnect.

Step 8: The server obliges by closing the connection.

By combining a number of these simple LDAP operations, directory-enabled clients can perform complex tasks that are useful to their users. For example, as shown in Figure 3.5, an electronic mail client such as Netscape Communicator can look up mail recipients in a directory, helping a user address an email message. It can also use a digital certificate stored in the directory to digitally sign and encrypt an outgoing message. Behind the scenes, the user's email program performs a number of directory operations that allow the mail to be addressed, signed, and encrypted. But from the user's point of view, it is all taken care of automatically.

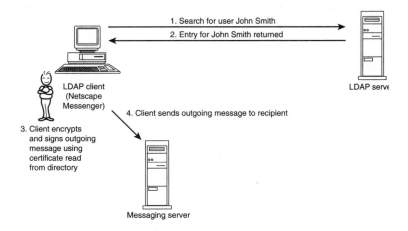

F I G U R E   3 . 5   *A directory-enabled application performing a complex task.*

Although end-user applications can certainly be directory enabled, they are not
the only kind of directory enabled applications. Server-based applications often
benefit from being directory enabled, too. For example, the Netscape
Messaging Server can use an LDAP directory when routing incoming electronic
mail, as shown in Figure 3.6.

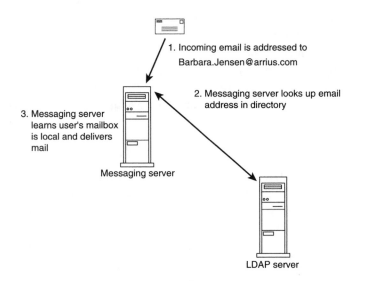

F I G U R E   3 . 6   *A directory-enabled server application.*

These are just two examples of how directory-enabled applications can leverage the power of the directory to add functionality and ease of management. We will see more and more of this in the future.

In addition to providing the nine basic protocol operations, LDAP version 3 is designed to be extensible via three methods:

- *LDAP extended operations*—A new protocol operation, like the nine basic LDAP operations discussed earlier. If in the future there is a need for a new operation, it can be defined and made standard without requiring changes to the core LDAP protocol. An example of an extended operation is StartTLS, which indicates to the server that the client wants to begin using transport layer security (TLS) to encrypt and optionally authenticate the connection.

- *LDAP controls*—Extra pieces of information carried along with existing LDAP operations, altering the behavior of the operation. For example, the manageDSAIT control is sent along with a modify operation when the client wants to manipulate certain types of meta-information stored in the directory (this meta-information is normally hidden from users of the directory). In the future, additional controls may be defined that alter the behavior of existing LDAP operations in useful ways.

- *Simple Authentication and Security Layer (SASL)*—A framework for supporting multiple authentication methods. By using the SASL framework to implement authentication, LDAP can easily be adapted to support new, stronger authentication methods. SASL also supports a framework for clients and servers to negotiate lower-layer security mechanisms, such as encryption of all client/server traffic. SASL is not specific to LDAP, though; its general framework can be adapted to a wide range of Internet protocols.

How does an LDAP client know whether a particular LDAP extended operation, LDAP control, or SASL mechanism is supported by the server it is in contact with? LDAP version 3 servers are required to advertise the extended operations, controls, and SASL mechanisms they support in a special directory entry called the root DSE. The root DSE contains a number of attributes that describe the capabilities and configuration of the particular LDAP server.

Standardization of LDAP Extensions

How does an enhancement such as a new extended operation, LDAP control, or SASL authentication method become a standard? It goes through a standardization process in the Internet Engineering Task Force (IETF).

First, the enhancement is described in a document called an Internet Draft. The draft is reviewed by participants in the IETF, changes and improvements are made, and revised drafts are submitted by the authors. Once there is consensus in the IETF that the enhancement is a good idea, and is soundly designed, the document becomes a Proposed Internet Standard. It then goes through more peer review, becomes a Draft Standard,

and finally becomes a full Internet Standard. However, multiple interoperable implementations are required before a document makes it all the way through the standards process to prove that implementation is feasible.

At all times during this process, the document is freely available on the Internet for anyone to download, read, comment on, and implement. The whole process is designed to encourage open development of standards and thorough peer review, without bogging it down with a complex standardization process. This approach has worked quite well historically; it's how the Internet was designed and built!

The LDAP Protocol on the Wire

What information is actually transmitted back and forth between LDAP clients and servers? We won't go into a great deal of detail here because this book isn't about protocol design, but we do feel that there are a few things you might want to know about the LDAP wire protocol.

LDAP uses a simplified version of the Basic Encoding Rules (BER). BER is a set of rules for encoding various data types, such as integers and strings, in a system-independent fashion. It also defines ways of combining these primitive data types into useful structures such as sets and sequences. The simplified BER that LDAP uses is often referred to as lightweight BER (LBER). LBER does away with many of the more esoteric data types that BER can represent, and instead it represents most items as simple strings.

Because LDAP is not a simple string-based protocol like HTTP, you can't simply telnet to the LDAP port on your server and start typing commands. The LDAP protocol primitives are not simple strings, so it's difficult, if not impossible, to converse with an LDAP server by typing at it. If you are familiar with text-based Internet protocols such as POP, IMAP, and SMTP, this may seem like an unfortunate limitation. On the other hand, DNS, a very successful distributed system, uses a protocol that has nontextual protocol primitives. The presence of universal implementations of client libraries for both DNS and LDAP makes this limitation less problematic.

The LDAP Models

LDAP defines four basic models that fully describe its operation, what data can be stored in LDAP directories, and what can be done with that data. These models are described in the following sections.

The LDAP Information Model

The LDAP information model defines the types of data and basic units of information you can store in your directory. In other words, the LDAP information model describes the building blocks you can use to create your directory.

The basic unit of information in the directory is the *entry*, a collection of information about an object. Often, the information in an entry describes some real-world object such as a person, but this is not required by the model. If you look at a typical directory, you'll find thousands of entries that correspond to people, departments, servers, printers, and other real-world objects in the organization served by the directory. Figure 3.7 shows a portion of a typical directory, with objects corresponding to some of the real-world objects in the organization.

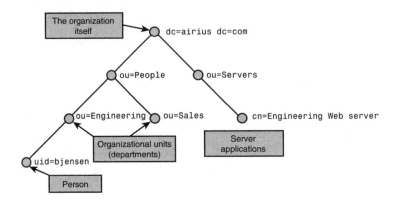

FIGURE 3.7 *Part of a typical directory.*

An entry is composed of a set of *attributes*, each of which describes one particular trait of the object. Each attribute has a *type* and one or more *values*. The type describes the kind of information contained in the attribute, and the value contains the actual data. For example, Figure 3.8 zooms in on an entry describing a person, with attributes for the person's full name, surname (last name), telephone number, and email address.

Attribute type	Attribute type
cn:	Barbara Jensen
	Babs Jensen
sn:	Jensen
telephonenumber:	+1 408 555 1212
mail:	babs@airius.com

FIGURE 3.8   *A directory entry showing attribute types and values.*

LDIF

Throughout this book you'll see directory entries shown in the LDIF text format. This is a standard way of representing directory data in a textual format that is used when exporting data from and importing data into a directory server. LDIF files consist solely of ASCII text, making it possible to pass them through email systems that are not 8-bit clean. Because it's a legible and text-based format, LDIF is used in this book when we want to represent a directory entry.

Let's look at a typical directory entry represented in LDIF:

```
dn: uid=bjensen, dc=airius, dc=com
objectClass: top
objectClass: person
objectClass: organizationalPerson
objectClass: inetOrgPerson
cn: Barbara Jensen
cn: Babs Jensen
sn: Jensen
mail: bjensen@airius.com
telephoneNumber: +1 408 555 1212
description: A big sailing fan.
```

An LDIF entry consists of a series of lines. It begins with dn:, followed by the distinguished name of the entry, all on one line. After this come the attributes of the entry, with one attribute value per line.

continues

continued

Each attribute value is preceded by the attribute type and a colon (:). The order of the attribute values is not important; however, it makes the entry more readable if you place all the objectclass *values first and keep all the attribute values of a given attribute type together.*

There are other, more-sophisticated things you can do with LDIF, including representing modifications to be applied to directory entries. We'll cover these more-sophisticated uses of LDIF later in this chapter.

Attribute types also have an associated *syntax*, which describes the types of data that may be placed in attribute values of that type. It also defines how the directory compares values when searching. For example, the caseIgnoreString syntax specifies that strings are ordered lexicographically and that case is not significant when searching or comparing values. Hence, the values Smith and smith are considered equivalent if the syntax is caseIgnoreString. The caseExactString syntax, by contrast, specifies that case *is* significant when comparing values. Thus, Smith and smith are not equivalent values if the syntax is caseExactString.

With both caseIgnoreString and caseExactString syntaxes, trailing and leading spaces are not significant, and multiple spaces are treated as a single space when searching or comparing. The rules for how attribute values of a particular syntax are compared are referred to as *matching rules*.

X.500 servers typically support a number of different syntaxes that are either some primitive type (such as a string, integer, or Boolean value) or some complex data type built from sets or sequences of the primitive types. LDAP servers typically avoid this complicated abstraction layer and support only the primitive types. The Netscape Directory Server, for example, supports the case-ignore and case-exact string, distinguished name, integer, and binary syntaxes. However, a plug-in interface allows new syntaxes to be defined.

Attributes are also classified broadly in two categories: user and operational. *User attributes*, the "normal" attributes of an entry, may be modified by the users of the directory (with appropriate permissions). *Operational attributes* are special attributes that either modify the operation of the directory server or reflect the operational status of the directory. An example of an operational attribute is the modifytimestamp attribute, which is automatically maintained by the directory and reflects the time that the entry was last modified. When an entry is sent to a client, operational attributes are not included unless the client requests them by name.

Attribute values can also have additional constraints placed on them. Some server software allows the administrator to declare whether a given attribute type may hold multiple values or if only a single attribute value may be stored.

For example, the `givenName` attribute is typically multivalued, for when a person may want to include more than one given name (e.g., Jim and James). On the other hand, an attribute holding an employee ID number is likely to be single-valued.

The other type of attribute constraint is the size of the attribute. Some server software allows the administrator to set the maximum size value that a given attribute may hold. This can be used to prevent users of the directory from using unreasonable amounts of storage.

Maintaining Order: Directory Schemas

Any entry in the directory has a set of attribute types that are required and a set of attribute types that are allowed. For example, an entry describing a person is required to have a `cn` (common name) attribute and an `sn` (surname) attribute. A number of other attributes are allowed, but not required, for person entries. Any other attribute type not explicitly required or allowed is prohibited.

The collections of all information about required and allowed attributes are called the *directory schemas*. Directory schemas, which are discussed in detail in Chapter 7, "Schema Design," allow you to retain control and maintain order over the types of information stored in your directory.

In summary, the LDAP information model describes *entries*, which are the basic building blocks of your directory. Entries are composed of attributes, which are composed of an attribute type and one or more values. Attributes may have constraints that limit the type and length of data placed in attribute values. The directory schemas place restrictions on the attribute types that must be or are allowed to be contained in an entry.

However, building blocks aren't very interesting unless you can actually use them to build something. The rules that govern how you arrange entries in a directory information tree are what comprise the LDAP naming model.

The LDAP Naming Model

The LDAP naming model defines how you organize and refer to your data. In other words, it describes the types of structures you can build out of your individual building blocks, which are the directory entries. After you've arranged your entries into a logical structure, the naming model also tells you how you can refer to any particular directory entry within that structure.

The flexibility afforded by the LDAP naming model allows you to place your data in the directory in a way that is easy for you to manage. For example, you might choose to create one container that holds all the entries describing people in your organization, and another container that holds all your groups. Or, you might choose to arrange your directory in a way that reflects the hierarchy of your organizational structure. Chapter 8, "Namespace Design," guides you in making good choices when you design your directory hierarchy or namespace.

The LDAP naming model specifies that entries are arranged in an inverted tree structure, as shown in Figure 3.9.

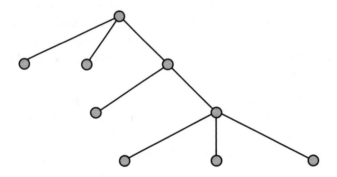

FIGURE 3.9   *A directory tree.*

Readers familiar with the hierarchical file system used by UNIX systems will note its similarities to this directory structure. Such a file system consists of a set of directories and files; each directory may have zero or more files or directories beneath it. Part of a typical UNIX file system is shown in Figure 3.10.

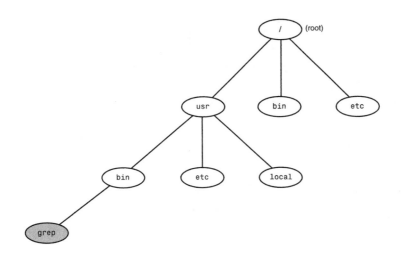

FIGURE 3.10 *Part of a typical UNIX file system.*

There are three significant differences between the UNIX file system hierarchy and the LDAP directory hierarchy, however.

The first major difference between the two models is that there isn't really a root entry in the LDAP model. A file system, of course, has a root directory, which is the common ancestor of all files or directories in the file system hierarchy. In an LDAP directory hierarchy, on the other hand, the root entry is conceptual—it doesn't exist as an entry you can place data into. There is a special entry called the root DSE that contains server-specific information, but it is not a normal directory entry.

The second major difference is that in an LDAP directory every node contains data, and any node can be a container. This means that any LDAP entry may have child nodes underneath it. Contrast this with a file system, in which a given node is either a file or a directory, but not both. In the file system, only directories may have children, and only files may contain data.

Another way of thinking of this is that an entry in a directory may be both a file and a directory simultaneously. The directory tree shown in Figure 3.11 illustrates this concept. Notice how the entries dc=airius, dc=com, ou=People, and ou=Devices all contain data (attributes) but are also containers with child nodes beneath them.

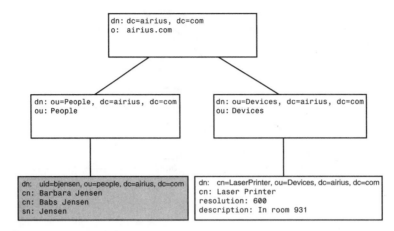

FIGURE 3.11 *Part of a typical LDAP directory.*

The third and final difference between the file system hierarchy and LDAP hierarchy is how individual nodes in the tree are named. LDAP names are backward relative to file system names. To illustrate this, let's consider the names of the shaded nodes in Figures 3.10 and 3.11. In Figure 3.10, the shaded node is a file with a complete filename of /usr/bin/grep. Notice that if you read the filename from left to right, you move from the top of the tree (/) down to the specific file being named.

Contrast this with the name of the shaded directory entry in Figure 3.11. Its name is uid=bjensen, ou=people, dc=airius, dc=com. Notice that, if you read from left to right, you move from the specific entry being named back up toward the top of the tree.

As you've seen, LDAP supports a hierarchical arrangement of directory entries. It does not, however, mandate any particular type of hierarchy. Just as you're free to arrange your file system in a way that makes sense to you and is easy for you to manage, you're free to construct any type of directory hierarchy you desire. Of course, some directory structures are better than others, depending on your particular situation; we'll cover the topic of designing your directory namespace in Chapter 8.

The one exception to this freedom is if your LDAP directory service is actually a front end to an X.500 service. The X.500 naming model is much more restrictive than the LDAP naming model. In the X.500 1993 standard, directory structure rules limit the types of hierarchies you can create. The standard accomplishes this by specifying what types of "objectclasses" may be direct children of an entry. For example, in the X.500 model, only entries representing countries, localities, or organizations may be placed at the root of the directory tree. The LDAP naming model, on the other hand, does not limit the tree structure in any way; any type of entry may be placed anywhere in the tree.

In addition to specifying how you arrange your directory entries into hierarchical structures, the LDAP naming model describes how you refer to individual entries in the directory. We mentioned this briefly when we were discussing the similarities and differences between file system hierarchy and LDAP directory hierarchy. Now let's go into more detail about naming.

Why Is Naming Important?

A naming model is needed so that you can give a unique name to any entry in the directory, allowing you to refer to any entry unambiguously. In LDAP, distinguished names (DNs) are how you refer to entries.

Like file system pathnames, the name of an LDAP entry is formed by connecting in a series all the individual names of the parent entries back to the root. For example, look back at the directory tree shown in Figure 3.11. The shaded entry's name is uid=bjensen, ou=People, dc=airius, dc=com. Reading this name from left to right, you can trace the path from the entry itself back to the root of the directory tree. The individual components of the name are separated by commas. Spaces after the commas are optional, so the following two distinguished names are equivalent:

```
uid=bjensen, ou=People, dc=airius, dc=com
uid=bjensen,ou=People,dc=airius,dc=com
```

In any entry's DN, the leftmost component is called the relative distinguished name (RDN). Among a set of peer entries (those which share a common immediate parent), each RDN must be unique. This rule, when recursively applied to the entire directory tree, ensures that no two entries may have the same DN. If you attempt to add two entries with the same name, the directory server will reject the attempt to add the second entry; this is similar to a UNIX host, which will reject an attempt to create a file with the same name as an existing file within a directory.

Note that RDNs have to be unique only if they share a common immediate parent. Look at the tree in Figure 3.12. Even though there are two entries with the RDN cn=John Smith in the directory, they are in different subtrees—making the tree completely legal. Whether this is a good way to construct your directory is another matter, one we will address in Chapter 8.

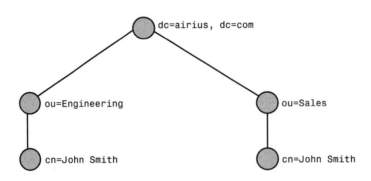

FIGURE 3.12 *Entries with the same RDNs are permitted if they are in different parts of the tree.*

Messy RDN Topics: Multivalued RDNs and Quoting

You've probably noticed that each RDN we've shown is composed of two parts: an attribute name and a value, separated by an equal sign (=). It's also possible for an RDN to contain more than one such name/value pair. Such a construction, called a *multivalued RDN*, looks like the following:

```
cn=John Smith + mail=jsmith@airius.com
```

The RDN for this entry consists of two *attribute=value* pairs: `cn=John Smith` and `mail=jsmith@airius.com`.

Multivalued RDNs can be used to distinguish RDNs that would otherwise be the same. For example, if there is more than one John Smith in the same container, a multivalued RDN would allow you to assign unique RDNs to each entry. However, you should generally avoid using multivalued RDNs in your directory. They tend to clutter your namespace, and there are better ways to arrive at unique names for your entries. (Approaches for uniquely naming your entries are discussed in Chapter 8.)

Recall that the individual RDNs in a DN are separated by commas. You may be curious how to proceed if an RDN contains a comma. How do you tell which commas are contained in RDNs, and which commas separate the individual RDN components? For example, what if you have an entry named `o=United Widgets,Ltd.` in your directory?

If you have DNs like this in your directory, you must escape all literal commas (those within an RDN) with a backslash. In our example, then, the DN would be

```
o=United Widgets\, Ltd., c=GB
```

Certain other characters must also be quoted when they appear within a component of a DN. Table 3.1 shows all the characters that must be quoted, according to the LDAPv3 specification.

TABLE 3.1 CHARACTERS REQUIRING QUOTING WHEN CONTAINED IN DISTINGUISHED NAMES

Character	Decimal Value	Escaped as
Space at the beginning or end of a DN or RDN	32	\<space>
Octothorpe (#) character at the beginning of a DN or RDN	35	\#
Comma (,)	44	\,
Plus sign (+)	43	\+
Double-quote (")	34	\"
Backslash (\)	92	\\
Less-than symbol (<)	60	\<
Greater-than symbol (>)	62	\>
Semicolon (;)	59	\;

Aliases

Alias entries in the LDAP directory allow one entry to point to another one, which means you can devise structures that are not strictly hierarchical. Alias entries perform a function like symbolic links in the UNIX file system or shortcuts in the Windows 95/NT file system. In Figure 3.13, the dotted entry is an alias entry pointing to the "real" entry.

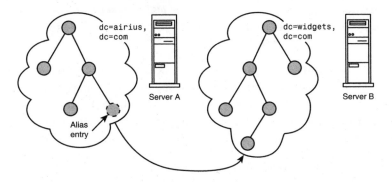

FIGURE 3.13 *An alias entry points to another directory entry.*

To create an alias entry in the directory, you must first create an entry with the object class `alias` and an attribute named `aliasedObjectName`. The value of the `aliasedObjectName` attribute must be the DN of the entry you want this alias to point to.

Not all LDAP directory servers support aliases. Because aliases can point to any directory entry, even one that is on a different server, aliases may exact a severe performance penalty. Consider the directory trees shown in Figure 3.13. Alias entries in one of the trees point to entries in the other tree, which is housed in another server. To support searching across the entire `ou=Marketing, dc=airius,dc=com` tree, Server A must contact Server B each time an alias entry is encountered while servicing the search operation. This can significantly slow down searches, which is the main reason certain software does not support aliases.

Often, the goals you are trying to achieve by using aliases can be met by using referrals, or by placing LDAP URLs in entries that clients can use to chase down the referred-to information. More information on using referrals can be found in Chapter 9, "Topology Design."

The LDAP Functional Model

Now that you understand the LDAP information and naming models, you need some way to actually access the data stored in the directory tree. The LDAP functional model describes the operations that you can perform on the directory using the LDAP protocol.

The LDAP functional model consists of a set of operations divided into three groups. The *interrogation operations* allow you to search the directory and retrieve directory data. The *update operations* allow you to add, delete, rename, and change directory entries. The *authentication and control operations* allow clients to identify themselves to the directory and control certain aspects of a session.

In addition to these three main groups of operations, version 3 of the LDAP protocol defines a framework for adding new operations to the protocol via LDAP *extended operations*. Extended operations allow the protocol to be extended in an orderly fashion to meet new marketplace needs as they emerge. Extended operations were described earlier in this chapter.

The LDAP Interrogation Operations

The two LDAP interrogation operations allow LDAP clients to search the directory and retrieve directory data.

The LDAP search operation is used to search the directory for entries and retrieve individual directory entries. There is no LDAP read operation. When you want to read a particular entry, you must use a form of the search operation in which you restrict your search to just the entry you want to retrieve. Later in the chapter we'll discuss how to search the directory and retrieve specific entries, as well as how to list all the entries at a particular location in the tree.

The LDAP search operation requires eight parameters. The first parameter is the base object for the search. This parameter, expressed as a DN, indicates the top of the tree you want to search.

The second parameter is the scope. There are three types of scope. A scope of subtree indicates that you want to search the entire subtree from the base object all the way down to the leaves of the tree. A scope of onelevel indicates that you want to search only the immediate children of the entry at the top of the search base. A scope of base indicates that you want to limit your search to just the base object; this is used to retrieve one particular entry from the directory. Figure 3.14 depicts the three types of search scope.

The third search parameter, derefAliases, tells the server whether aliases should be dereferenced when performing the search. There are four possible values for this parameter's value:

- neverDerefAliases—Do not dereference aliases in searching or in locating the base object of the search.

- derefInSearching—Dereference aliases in subordinates of the base object in searching, but not in locating the base object of the search.

- derefFindingBaseObject—Dereference aliases in locating the base object of the search, but not when searching subordinates of the base object.

- derefAlways—Dereference aliases both in searching and in locating the base object of the search.

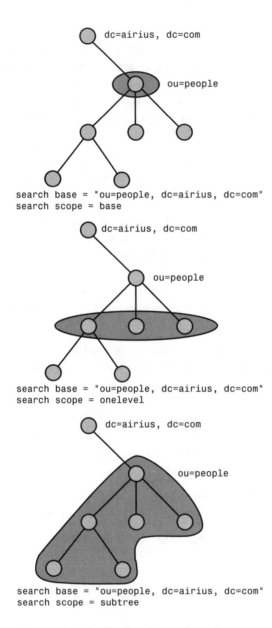

search base = "ou=people, dc=airius, dc=com"
search scope = base

search base = "ou=people, dc=airius, dc=com"
search scope = onelevel

search base = "ou=people, dc=airius, dc=com"
search scope = subtree

FIGURE 3.14 *The three types of search scope.*

The fourth search parameter is the size limit. This parameter tells the server that the client is interested in receiving only a certain number of entries. For example, if the client passes a size limit of 100, but the server locates 500 matching entries, only the first 100 will be returned to the client, along with a result code of LDAP_SIZELIMIT_EXCEEDED. A size limit of 0 means that the client wants to receive all matching entries. (Note that servers may impose a maximum size limit that cannot be overridden by unprivileged clients.)

The fifth search parameter is the time limit. This parameter tells the server the maximum time in seconds that it should spend trying to honor a search request. If the time limit is exceeded, the server will stop processing the request and send a result code of LDAP_TIMELIMIT_EXCEEDED to the client. A time limit of 0 indicates that no limit should be in effect. (Note that servers may impose a maximum time limit that cannot be overridden by unprivileged clients.)

The sixth search parameter, the attrsOnly parameter, is a Boolean parameter. If it is set to true, the server will send only the attribute types to the client; attribute values will not be sent. This can be used if the client is interested in finding out which attributes are contained in an entry but not in receiving the actual values. If this parameter is set to false, attribute types and values are returned.

The seventh search parameter is the search filter, an expression that describes the types of entries to be returned. The filter expressions used in LDAP search operations are very flexible, and are discussed in detail in the next section.

The eighth and final search parameter is a list of attributes to be returned for each matching entry. You can specify that all attributes should be returned, or you can request that only specific attributes of an entry be returned. We'll focus on how to request specific attributes later in this chapter. First, though, let's look at the different types of LDAP filters you can use when searching the directory.

An LDAP filter is a Boolean combination of attribute-value assertions. An attribute value assertion consists of two parts: an attribute name and a value assertion, which you can think of as a value with wildcards allowed. The following sections look at the various types of search filters.

Equality Filters

An equality filter allows you to look for entries that exactly match some value. Here's an example:

```
(sn=smith)
```

This filter matches entries in which the sn (surname) attribute contains a value that is exactly smith. Because the syntax of the sn attribute is a case-ignore string, the case of the attribute and the filter is not important when locating matching entries.

Substring Filters

When you use wildcards in filters, they are called substring filters. Here's an example:

```
(sn=smith*)
```

This filter matches any entry that has an sn attribute value that begins with smith. Entries with a surname of Smith, Smithers, Smithsonian, and so on will be returned.

Wildcards may appear anywhere in the filter expression, so the filter

```
(sn=*smith)
```

matches entries in which the surname ends with smith (e.g., Blacksmith). The filter

```
(sn=smi*th)
```

matches entries in which the surname begins with smi and ends with th, and the filter

```
(sn=*smith*)
```

matches entries that contain the string smith in the surname attribute. Note that the wildcard character matches zero or more instances of any character, so the filter (sn=*smith*) would match the entry with the surname Smith as well as any surnames in which the string smith is embedded.

Approximate Filters

In addition to the equality and substring filters, servers support an approximate filter. For example, on most directory servers, the filter

```
(sn~=jensen)
```

returns entries in which the surname attribute has a value that sounds like jensen (for example, jenson). Exactly how the server implements this is particular to each vendor and the languages supported by the server. The Netscape Directory Server, for example, uses the metaphone algorithm to locate entries when an approximate filter is used. Internationalization also throws an interesting wrinkle into the concept of approximate matching; each language may need its own particular sounds-like algorithm.

"Greater Than or Equal To" and "Less Than or Equal To" Filters

LDAP servers also support "greater than or equal to" and "less than or equal to" filters on attributes that have some inherent ordering. For example, the filter

```
(sn<=Smith)
```

returns all entries in which the surname is less than or equal to `Smith` lexicographically. The ordering used depends on the ordering rules for the syntax of any particular attribute. The `sn` attribute, which has the case-ignore string syntax, is ordered lexicographically without respect to case. An attribute that has integer syntax would be ordered numerically. Attributes that have no inherent ordering, such as JPEG photos, cannot be searched for with this type of filter.

If you find that you need a greater than or less than filter (without the equals part), note that "greater than" is the complement of "less than or equal to" and "less than" is the complement of "greater than or equal to." In other words,

```
(age>21)
```

which is equivalent to

```
(!(age<=21))
```

Similarly, the filter

```
(age<21)
```

which is also not a valid LDAP filter, is equivalent to

```
(!(age>=21))
```

In these cases, `!` is the negation operator, which we will discuss in more detail shortly.

Presence Filters

Another type of search filter is the presence filter. It matches any entry that has at least one value for the attribute. For example, the filter

```
(telephoneNumber=*)
```

matches all entries that have a telephone number.

Extensible Matching

The last type of search filter is the extensible match filter. It is only supported by LDAPv3 servers.

The purpose of an extensible match filter is to allow new matching rules to be implemented in servers and used by clients. Recall our earlier example involving the `caseIgnoreString` and `caseExactString` syntaxes. Each syntax has an associated method for comparing values, depending on whether case is to be considered significant when comparing values. When new attribute syntaxes are developed, it may also be necessary to define a new way of comparing values for equality. Extensible matching also allows language-specific matching rules to be defined so that values in languages other than English can be meaningfully compared.

As an added benefit, extensible matching allows you to specify that the attributes that make up the DN of the entry should be searched. So, for example, using extensible matching you can locate all the entries in the directory that contain the attribute value assertion `ou=Engineering` anywhere in their DN.

To see the usefulness of this feature, consider an entry named `cn=Babs Jensen, ou=Engineering, dc=bigco, dc=com`. Suppose you're interested in finding all the Babs Jensens in the engineering department, and you search from the top of your subtree using a search filter like `(&(cn=Babs Jensen)(ou=engineering))`. Normally, this filter would not find Babs's entry unless it explicitly contained an `ou` attribute with a value of `engineering`. Using extensible matching feature, you can treat the attribute values contained in a DN as attribute values of the entry that can match the search.

The syntax of an extensible matching filter is a bit complicated. It consists of five parts, three of which are optional. These parts are

- An attribute name. If omitted, any attribute type that supports the given matching rule is compared against the value.

- The optional string `:dn`, which indicates that the attributes forming the entry's DN are to be treated as attributes of the entry during the search.

- An optional colon and matching rule identifier that identifies the particular matching rule to be used. If no matching rule is provided, the default matching rule for the attribute being searched should be used. If the attribute name is omitted, the colon and matching rule must be present.

- The string `":="`.

- An attribute value to be compared against.

Formally, the grammar for the extensible search filter is

```
attr [":dn"] [":" matchingrule] ":=" value
```

The elements of this syntax are as follows:

`attr` is an attribute name.

`matchingrule` is usually given by an Object Identifier (OID), although if a descriptive name has been assigned to the matching rule, that may be used as well. The OIDs of the matching rules supported by your directory server will be given in its documentation.

`value` is an attribute value to be used for comparison.

Object Identifiers

Object Identifiers, commonly referred to as OIDs, are unique identifiers assigned to objects. They are used to uniquely identify many different types of things, such as X.500 directory object and attribute types. In fact, just about everything in the X.500 directory system is identified by an OID. OIDs are also used to uniquely identify objects in other protocols, such as the Simple Network Management Protocol (SNMP).

OIDs are written as strings of dotted decimal numbers. Each part of an OID represents a node in a hierarchical OID tree. This hierarchy allows an arbitrarily large number of objects to be named, and it supports delegation of the namespace. For example, all the user attribute types defined by the X.500 standards begin with 2.5.4. The cn attribute is assigned the OID 2.5.4.3, and the sn attribute is assigned the OID 2.5.4.4.

An individual subtree of the OID tree is called an *arc*. Individual arcs may be assigned to organizations, which can then further divide the arc into *subarcs*, if so desired. For example, Netscape Communications has been assigned an arc of the OID namespace for its own use. Internally, it has divided that arc into a number of subarcs for use by the various product teams. By delegating the management of the OID namespace in this fashion, conflicts can be avoided.

The X.500 protocol makes extensive use of OIDs to uniquely identify various protocol elements. LDAP, on the other hand, favors short, textual names for things: cn to describe the common name attribute and person to identify the person object class, for example. To maintain compatibility with X.500, LDAP allows a string representation of an OID to be used interchangeably with the short name for the item. For example, the search filters (cn=Barbara Jensen) and (2.5.4.3=Barbara Jensen) are equivalent. Unless you are working with an LDAP-based gateway into an X.500 system, you should generally avoid using OIDs in your directory-enabled applications.

Although LDAP largely does away with the mandatory use of OIDs, you will see them from time to time, especially if you use extensible matching rules or if you design your own schema extensions. The topic of extending your directory schema is discussed in Chapter 7.

Let's look at some examples of extensible matching filters.

The following filter specifies that the all entries in which the cn attribute matches the value Barbara Jensen should be returned:

```
(cn:1.2.3.4.5.6:=Barbara Jensen)
```

When comparing values, the matching rule given by the OID 1.2.3.4.5.6 should be used.

The following filter specifies that all entries that contain the string jensen in the surname should be returned:

```
(sn:dn:1.2.3.4.5.7:=jensen)
```

The sn attributes within the DN are also searched. When comparing values, the matching rule given by the OID 1.2.3.4.5.7 should be used.

The following filter returns any entries in which the o (organization) attribute exactly matches Airius and any entries in which o=Airius is one of the components of the DN:

```
(o:dn:=Airius)
```

The following filter returns any entries in which a DN component with a syntax appropriate to the given matching rule matches Airius:

```
(:dn:1.2.3.4.5.8:=Airius)
```

The matching rule given by the OID 1.2.3.4.5.8 should be used.

Negation

Any search element can be negated by preceding the filter with an exclamation point (!). For example, the filter

```
(!(sn=Smith))
```

matches all entries in which the sn attribute does not contain the value smith, including entries with no sn attribute at all.

Combining Filter Terms

Filters can also be combined using AND and OR operators. The AND operator is signified by an ampersand (&) symbol, and the OR operator is signified by the vertical bar (¦) symbol. When combining search filters, you use *prefix notation*, in which the operator precedes its arguments. Those familiar with the "reverse polish notation" common on Hewlett-Packard calculators will be familiar with this concept (although reverse polish is a postfix notation, not a prefix notation like that used in LDAP search filters).

Let's look at some examples of combinations of LDAP search filters. The filter

```
(&(sn=Smith)(l=Mountain View))
```

matches all entries with a surname of `smith` that also have an `l` (locality) attribute of `Mountain View`. In other words, this filter will find everyone named Smith in the Mountain View location.

The filter

```
(¦(sn=Smith)(sn=Jones))
```

matches everyone with a surname of `Smith` or `Jones`.

You use parentheses to group more-complex filters to make the meaning of the filter unambiguous. For example, if you want to search the directory for all entries that have an email address but do not have a telephone number, you would use the filter

```
(&(mail=*)(!(telephoneNumber=*)))
```

Note that the parentheses bind the negation operator to the presence filter for telephone number.

Technically speaking, parentheses are always required, even if the filter consists of only a single term. Some LDAP software allows you to omit the enclosing parentheses and inserts them for you before sending the search request to the server. However, if you are developing your own software using one of the available SDKs, you need to include the enclosing parentheses.

Table 3.2 summarizes the six types of search filters and the three Boolean operators.

TABLE 3.2 TYPES OF LDAP SEARCH FILTERS

Filter Type	Format	Example	Matches
Equality	(attr=value)	(sn=jensen)	Surnames exactly equal to jensen
Substring	(attr=[leading] *[any]*[trailing]	(sn=*jensen*)	Surnames containing the string jensen
		(sn=jensen*)	Surnames starting with the string jensen
		(sn=*jensen)	Surnames ending with the string jensen
		(sn=jen*s*en)	Surnames starting with jen, containing an s, and ending with en
Approximate	(attr~=value)	(sn~=jensin)	Surnames approximately equal to Jensin (for example, surnames that sound like Jensin—note the misspelling)
Greater than or equal to	(attr>=value)	(sn>=Jensen)	Surnames lexicographically greater than or equal to Jensen
Less than or equal to	(attr<=value)	(sn<=Jensen)	Surnames lexicographically less than or equal to Jensen
Presence	(attr=*)	(sn=*)	All surnames
AND	(&(filter1) (filter2)...))	(&(sn=Jensen) (objectclass=person))	Entries with an object class of person and surname exactly equal to Jensen
OR	(¦(filter1) (filter2)...))	(¦(sn~=Jensin) (sn=*jensin))	Entries with a surname approximately equal to Jensin or common name ending in jensin
NOT	(!(filter)	(!(mail=*))	All entities without a mail attribute

Quoting in Search Filters

If you need to search for an attribute value that contains one of five specific characters, you need to substitute the character with an escape sequence consisting of a backslash and a two-digit hexadecimal sequence representing the character's value. Table 3.3 shows the characters that must be escaped, along with the escape sequence you should use for each.

TABLE 3.3 CHARACTERS THAT MUST BE ESCAPED IF USED IN A SEARCH FILTER

Character	Value (Decimal)	Value (Hex)	Escape Sequence
* (asterisk)	42	0x2A	\2A
((left parenthesis)	40	0x28	\28
) (right parenthesis)	41	0x29	\29
\ (backslash)	92	0x5C	\5C
NUL (the null byte)	0	0x00	\00

For example, if you want to search for all entries in which the cn attribute exactly matches the value A*Star, you would use the filter (cn=A\2AStar).

Readers should note that the rules for quoting search filters and the rules for quoting distinguished names are different and not interchangeable.

Specifying Which Attributes Are to Be Returned

As previously mentioned, the last search parameter is a list of attributes to be returned for each matching entry. If this list is empty, all user attributes are returned. The special value * also means that all user attributes are to be returned, but it allows you to specify additional nonuser (operational) attributes that should be returned. (Without this special value, there would be no way to request all user attributes plus some operational attributes.)

If you want to retrieve no attributes at all, you should specify the attribute name 1.1 (there is no such attribute OID, so no attributes can be returned). Table 3.4 provides some examples of attribute lists and the attributes that are returned by the server.

TABLE 3.4 EXAMPLES OF ATTRIBUTE LISTS AND CORRESPONDING ATTRIBUTES RETURNED BY THE SERVER

Attribute List	Attributes Returned
cn, sn, givenname	cn, sn, and givenname only
*	All user attributes
1.1	No attributes
modifiersname	modifiersname only (an operational attribute)
*, modifiersname	All user attributes plus modifiersname

Common Types of Searches

Although the LDAP search operation is extremely flexible, there are some types of searches that you'll probably use more frequently than others:

- *Retrieving a single entry*—To retrieve a particular directory entry, you use a scope of base, a search base equal to the DN of the entry you want to retrieve, and a filter of (objectclass=*). The filter, which is a presence filter on the objectclass attribute, will match any entry that contains at least one value in its objectclass attribute. Because every entry in the directory must have an objectclass attribute, this filter is guaranteed to match any directory entry. And because you've specified a scope of base, only one entry will be returned by the search (if the entry exists at all). This is how you use the search operation to read a particular entry.

- *Listing all entries directly below an entry*—To list all the directory entries at a particular level in the tree, you use the same filter (objectclass=*) as when retrieving a particular entry; but you use a scope of onelevel and a search base equal to the DN just above the level you want to list. All the entries immediately below the searchbase entry are returned. The search base entry itself is not returned in a onelevel search. (The search base entry *is* returned in a base or subtree search if it matches the search filter.)

- *Searching for matching entries within a subtree*—Another common search operation occurs within a subtree of the directory for all entries that match some search criteria. To perform this type of search, use a filter that selects the entries you are interested in retrieving—or (objectclass=*) if you want all entries—along with a scope of subtree and a search base equal to the DN of the entry at the top of the tree you want to search.

Hiding LDAP Filters from Users

You might justifiably be thinking that your users will never be able to understand LDAP filter syntax. The prefix notation it uses is hardly intuitive, after all! Bear in mind, though, that any good directory access GUI will hide the details of filter construction from end users.

Instead of requiring users to type raw LDAP filters, a set of pop-up menus and text boxes is typically used to allow the user to specify the search criteria, and the GUI client constructs the filter for the user. For example, in Figure 3.15, Netscape Communicator's Search window uses the provided information to construct the filter (&(cn=*smith*)(l=*Dearborn*)).

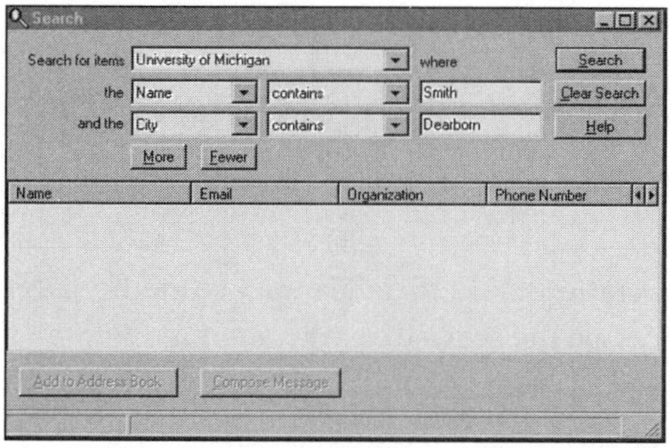

FIGURE 3.15 *A GUI interface for searching the directory.*

If you are a directory administrator, it's a good idea to become familiar with LDAP filter syntax. You can use this knowledge to provide complex "canned" queries for your end users, for example. Filter syntax also crops up in LDAP URLs and configuration files. Spending a little time understanding filter syntax is well worth the effort.

The Compare Operation

The second of the two interrogation operations, the LDAP compare operation, is used to check whether a particular entry contains a particular attribute value. The client submits a compare request to the server, supplying a DN, an attribute name, and a value. The server returns an affirmative response to the client if the entry named by the DN contains the given value in the given attribute type. If not, a negative response is returned.

It may seem odd that the compare operation even exists. After all, if you want to determine whether a particular entry contains a particular attribute value, you can just perform a search with a search base equal to the DN of the entry, a scope of base, and a filter expressing the test you want to make. If the entry is returned, the test was successful; if no entry is returned, the test was not successful.

The reasons that the compare operation exists are historical and related to LDAP's roots in X.500. There is only one case in which the compare and search operations behave differently. If a comparison is attempted on an attribute, but the attribute is not present in the entry, the compare operation will return a special indication to the client that the attribute does not exist. The search operation, on the other hand, would simply not return the entry. This ability to distinguish between "the entry has the attribute but contains no matching value" and "the entry does not have the attribute at all" may be convenient in some situations. The other advantage of the compare operation is that it is more compact in terms of the number of protocol bytes exchanged between the client and the server.

The LDAP Update Operations

There are four LDAP update operations: add, delete, rename (modify DN), and modify. These four operations define the ways that you can manipulate the data in your directory.

The add operation allows you to create new directory entries. It has two parameters: the distinguished name of the entry to be created and a set of attributes and attribute values that will comprise the new entry. In order for the add operation to complete successfully, four conditions must be met:

- The parent of the new entry must already exist in the directory.

- There must not be an entry of the same name.

- The new entry must conform to the schema in effect.

- Access control must permit the operation.

If all these conditions are met, the new entry is added to the directory.

The delete operation removes an entry from the directory. It has a single parameter: the DN of the entry to be deleted. In order for the delete operation to complete successfully, three conditions must be met:

- The entry to be deleted must exist.

- It must have no children.

- Access control must permit the entry to be deleted.

If these conditions are all met, the entry is removed from the directory.

The rename, or modify DN operation, is used to rename and/or move entries in the directory. It has four parameters: the DN of the entry to be renamed, the new RDN for the entry, an optional argument giving the new parent of the entry, and the delete-old-RDN flag. In order for the modify DN operation to succeed, the following conditions must be met:

- The entry being renamed must exist.

- The new name for the entry must not already be in use by another entry.

- Access control must permit the operation.

If all these conditions are met, the entry is renamed and/or moved.

If the entry is to be renamed but will still have the same parent entry, the new parent argument is left blank. Otherwise, the new parent argument gives the DN of the container where the entry is to be moved. The delete-old-RDN flag is a Boolean flag that specifies whether the old RDN of the entry is to be retained as an attribute of the entry or removed. Figures 3.16 through 3.20 show the various combinations of renaming and moving entries that can be performed with the modify DN operation.

FIGURE 3.16   *Renaming an entry without moving it.*

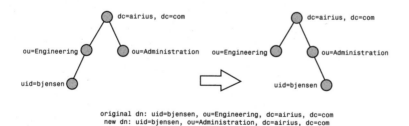

FIGURE 3.17   *Moving an entry without changing its RDN.*

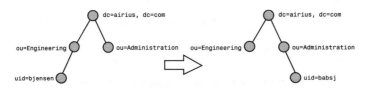

original dn: uid=bjensen, ou=Engineering, dc=airius,dc=com
new dn: uid=babsj, ou=Administration, dc=airius,dc=com

FIGURE 3.18 *Moving an entry and changing its RDN simultaneously.*

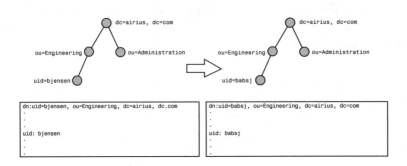

FIGURE 3.19 *Renaming an entry,* `deleteoldrdn=true`.

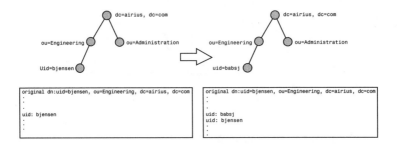

FIGURE 3.20 *Renaming an entry,* `deleteoldrdn=false`.

LDAPv2 did not have a modify DN operation—it had only a modify RDN operation. As the name implies, modify RDN allows only the RDN of an entry to be changed. This means that an LDAPv2 server may rename an entry but may not move it to a new location in the tree. To accomplish a move with LDAPv2, you must copy the entry, along with any child entries underneath it, to the new location in the tree and delete the original entry or entries.

The modify operation allows you to update an existing directory entry. It takes two parameters: the DN of the entry to be modified and a set of modifications to be applied. These modifications can specify that new attribute values are to be added to the entry, that specific attribute values are to be deleted from the entry, or that all attribute values for a given attribute are to be replaced with a new set of attribute values. The modify request can include as many attribute modifications as needed.

In order for the modify operation to succeed, the following conditions must be met:

- The entry to be modified must exist.

- All of the attribute modifications must succeed.

- The resulting entry must obey the schema in effect.

- Access control must allow the update.

If all these conditions are met, the entry is modified. Note that all the modifications must succeed, or else the entire operation fails and the entry is not modified. This prevents inconsistencies that might arise from half-completed modify operations.

This last point raises one additional but very important topic about the LDAP update operations: Each operation is *atomic*, meaning that the whole operation is processed as a single unit of work. This unit either completely succeeds or no modifications are performed. For example, a modify request that affects multiple attributes within an entry cannot half-succeed, with certain attributes updated and others not updated. If the client receives a success result from the server, then all the modifications were applied to the entry. If the server returns an error to the client, then none of the modifications were applied.

The LDAP Authentication and Control Operations
There are two LDAP authentication operations, bind and unbind, and one control operation, abandon.

The bind operation is how a client authenticates itself to the directory. It does so by providing a distinguished name and a set of credentials. The server checks whether the credentials are correct for the given DN and, if they are, notes that the client is authenticated as long as the connection remains open or until the client re-authenticates. The server can grant privileges to the client based on its identity.

There are several different types of bind methods. In a simple bind, the client presents a DN and a password in cleartext to the LDAP server. The server verifies that the password matches the password value stored in the userpassword attribute of the entry and, if so, returns a success code to the client.

The simple bind does send the password over the network to the server in the clear. However, you can protect against eavesdroppers intercepting passwords by encrypting the connections using secure sockets layer (SSL) or TLS, which are discussed in the next section. In the future, LDAPv3 will include a digest-based authentication method that does not require that a cleartext password be sent to the server.

LDAPv3 also includes a new type of bind operation, the SASL bind. SASL is an extensible, protocol-independent framework for performing authentication and negotiation of security parameters. With SASL, the client specifies the type of authentication protocol it wants to use. If the server supports the authentication protocol, the client and server perform the agreed-upon authentication protocol.

For example, the client could specify that it wants to authenticate using the Kerberos protocol. If the server knows how to speak the Kerberos protocol, it indicates this to the client that sends a service ticket for the LDAP service. The server verifies the service ticket and returns a mutual authentication token to the client. Whenever the Kerberos authentication completes, the SASL bind is complete and the server returns a success code to the client. SASL can also support multistep authentication protocols such as S/KEY.

Incorporation of SASL into LDAPv3 means that new authentication methods, such as smart cards or biometric authentication, can be easily implemented for LDAP without requiring a revision of the protocol.

The second authentication operation is the unbind operation. The unbind operation has no parameters. When a client issues an unbind operation, the server discards any authentication information it has associated with the client's connection, terminates any outstanding LDAP operations, and disconnects from the client, thus closing the TCP connection.

The abandon operation has a single parameter: the message ID of the LDAP operation to abandon. The client issues an abandon operation when it is no longer interested in obtaining the results of a previously initiated operation. Upon receiving an abandon request, the server terminates processing of the operation that corresponds to the message ID. The abandon request, typically used by GUI clients, is sent when the user cancels a long-running search request.

Note that it's possible for the abandon request (coming from the client) and the results of the abandoned operation (going to the client) to pass each other in flight. The client needs to be prepared to receive (and discard) results from operations it has abandoned but the server sent anyway. If you are using an LDAP SDK, however, you don't need to worry about this; the SDK takes care of this for you.

The LDAP Security Model

We've discussed three of the four LDAP models so far. We have a set of directory entries, which are arranged into a hierarchy, and a set of protocol operations that allow us to authenticate to, search, and update the directory. All that remains is to provide a framework for protecting the information in the directory from unauthorized access. This is the purpose of the LDAP security model.

The security model relies on the fact that LDAP is a connection-oriented protocol. In other words, an LDAP client opens a connection to an LDAP server and performs a number of protocol operations on the same connection. The LDAP client may authenticate to the directory server at some point during the lifetime of the connection, at which point it may be granted additional (or fewer) privileges. For example, a client might authenticate as a particular identity that has been granted read-write access to all the entries in the directory. Before this authentication, it has some limited set of privileges (usually a default set of privileges extended to all users of the directory). After it authenticates, however, it is granted expanded privileges as long as the connection remains open.

What exactly is authentication? From the client's perspective, it is the process of proving to the server that the client is some entity. In other words, the client asserts that it has some identity and provides some credentials to prove this assertion. From the server's perspective, the process of authentication involves accepting the identity and credentials provided by the client and checking whether they prove that the client is who it claims to be.

To illustrate this abstract concept with a concrete example, let's examine how LDAP simple authentication works. In simple authentication, an LDAP client provides to an LDAP server a distinguished name and a password, which are sent to the server in the clear (not hashed or encrypted in any way). The server locates the entry in the directory corresponding to the DN provided by the client and checks whether the password presented by the client matches the value stored in the userpassword attribute of the entry. If it does, the client is authenticated; if it does not, the authentication operation fails and an error code is returned to the client.

The process of authenticating to the directory is called *binding*. An identity is bound to the connection when a successful authentication occurs via the bind operation we introduced in the previous section. If a client does not authenticate, or if it authenticates without providing any credentials, the client is bound anonymously. In other words, the server has no idea who the client is, so it grants some default set of privileges to the client. Usually, this default set of privileges is very minimal. In some instances, the default set of privileges is completely restrictive—no part of the directory may be read or searched. How you treat anonymously bound clients is up to you and depends on the security policy appropriate to your organization. You can find more information on security and privacy in Chapter 11, "Privacy and Security Design."

There are many different types of authentication systems available that are independent of LDAP. LDAP version 2 supported only simple authentication, in which a DN and password are transmitted in the clear from the client to the server.

Note

The previous statement is not completely correct because LDAPv2 also supported Kerberos version 4 authentication, which does not require that passwords be sent in the clear. However, KerberosV4 was not commercially successful and has been superseded by Kerberos version 5. Kerberos support was therefore dropped from the core LDAPv3 protocol, although it's entirely feasible to support it via an SASL mechanism.

Acknowledging the need to support many different authentication methods, LDAPv3 has adopted the SASL framework. SASL provides a standard way for multiple authentication protocols to be supported by LDAPv3. Each type of authentication system corresponds to a particular SASL mechanism. An SASL mechanism is an identifier that describes the type of authentication protocol being supported.

Note

The IETF's Internet Engineering Steering Group (IESG) has requested that the LDAPv3 specification be altered to mandate that all clients and servers implement some authentication method more secure than sending cleartext passwords over the wire. The intent is to raise the bar for interoperability so that people using LDAPv3 clients and servers can be assured that their authentication credentials are not susceptible to network eavesdropping. As of September 1998, the details about the new mandatory-to-implement authentication methods were still to be worked out within the IETF. If you are considering purchase of LDAP software, you should ask your vendor about support for the final version of the LDAPv3 standard.

After the server has verified the identity of the client, it can choose to grant additional privileges based on some site-specific policy. For example, you might have a policy that, when authenticated, users may search the directory, but that they may not modify their own directory entries. Or, you might have a more permissive policy that allows some authenticated users to modify certain attributes of their own entries whereas other users (your administrative staff) may modify any attribute of any entry. The way you describe the access rights, the entities to which those rights are granted, and the directory entries to which those rights apply is called *access control*.

Access Control Models

It may come as somewhat of a disappointment to learn that LDAP does not currently define a standard access control model. However, this does not mean that individual LDAP server implementations have no access control model. In fact, any commercially successful server software must have such a model.

The Netscape Directory Server, for example, has a rich access control model. The model works by describing what a given identity can do to some set of entries, with granularity down to the attribute level. For example, with the Netscape Server it is possible to specify an access control item (ACI) that allows a person to modify only the `description` attribute of his or her own entry. Or, the model can allow you to grant complete rights to the directory to all persons who are in a particular group. This allows easy creation of a set of directory administrators; a given person's rights can be easily revoked by removing them from the group. The model is fully documented in the *Netscape Directory Server Administrator's Guide*.

Work has begun in the IETF on defining a standard access control model and a standard syntax for representing access control rights. The promise for the future is that you, as a directory deployer, will be able to deploy directory servers from several vendors and implement a consistent security policy across those servers—whether they cooperate to serve a distributed directory or they are replicas of each other. Unfortunately, that is not the case today. You would be wise to document your access control policy in plain language so that you can adapt it to whatever model and syntax emerge from the standards bodies in the future.

SSL and TLS

SSL and TLS are new security technologies that encrypt all the data flowing between a client and a server. SSL, the older of the two technologies, has been a successful technology for the World Wide Web, securing electronic commerce and other transactions that depend on transmission of data being hidden from eavesdroppers. TLS, the follow-up to SSL, is an emerging Internet standard. LDAP offers a standard way for clients to begin encrypting all data flowing to and from LDAP on the connection using TLS.

Just as SSL enabled a new class of applications on the Web, TLS will enable new uses of directory technology. For example, two companies in a trading partner relationship can allow directory queries from their trading partners to travel over the Internet. Because TLS encrypts these queries and the results, each company can rest assured that the directory data is protected while in transit over the Internet. Figure 3.21 depicts this scenario.

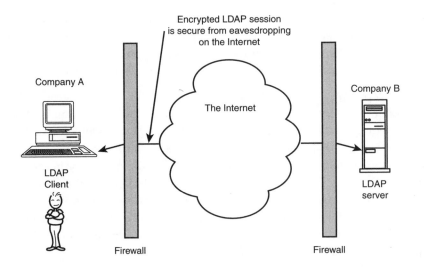

FIGURE 3.21 *TLS allows secure transmission of directory data over the Internet.*

In addition to allowing bulk encryption of all data flowing between clients and servers, SSL and TLS both allow mutual authentication using strong cryptography. Using X.509-based certificates, clients may prove their identity to servers while in turn verifying the identity of the server to which they are connected.

This technology is already widely deployed on the World Wide Web. The Hypertext Transfer Protocol over SSL (HTTPS) is used to provide secure Web access and client authentication. In a similar fashion, LDAP over SSL (LDAPS) allows secure LDAP client access and client authentication facilities today. In the future, LDAPv3 clients can use the startTLS extended operation to begin encrypting an LDAP connection, and TLS to prove their identity to the server, as well as verify the server's identity.

LDAP APIs

Early on, the developers of LDAP realized that the creation of directory-enabled applications would happen much more quickly if there existed a standard API for accessing and updating the directory. The original LDAP distribution from the University of Michigan (often referred to as the U-M LDAP release; refer to Chapter 2) included a C programming library and several sample client programs built on this library. For quite a while, the C API included in the U-M distribution was the only API/SDK available. With the current industry momentum behind LDAP, however, the number of SDKs is increasing, and additional SDKs are becoming available. (We will discuss these additional SDKs later in this section and in Chapter 20.) Figure 3.22 shows how the LDAP SDK fits into a directory-enabled client application.

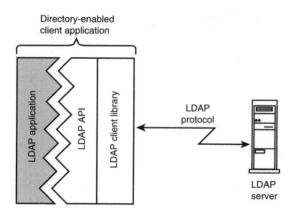

FIGURE 3.22   *The LDAP API provides a common interface to an LDAP client library SDK.*

The LDAP C API for LDAP version 2 is documented in RFC 1823, and a proposed C API for LDAP version 3 is in draft form at this time (available from the IETF Web site at http://www.ietf.org). The C API document simply defines the API calls and their semantics.

To obtain an actual SDK, you need to download one from one of a number of sources:

- The original University of Michigan SDK, which supports LDAPv2, is available in source code form from http://www.umich.edu/~dirsvcs/ldap/.

- An updated C SDK that supports LDAPv2 and LDAPv3 is available free of charge in binary form from Netscape at http://developer.netscape.com.

- Source code for the Netscape SDK is publicly available from mozilla.org at `http://www.mozilla.org`.

- Another LDAPv2/LDAPv3 SDK is available from Innosoft at `http://www.innosoft.com`.

All of the C SDKs can, of course, be used from a C++ program.

An Overview of the C LDAP API

The LDAP C API defines a set of core functions that map almost one-to-one onto the LDAP protocol operations. Those core functions are shown in Table 3.5.

TABLE 3.5 THE MAIN LDAP C API FUNCTIONS

Function	Description
ldap_search()	Searches for directory entries
ldap_compare()	Sees whether an entry contains a given attribute value
ldap_bind()	Authenticates (proves your identity) to a directory server
ldap_unbind()	Terminates an LDAP session
ldap_modify()	Makes changes to an existing directory entry
ldap_add()	Adds a new directory entry
ldap_delete()	Deletes an existing directory entry
ldap_rename()	Renames an existing directory entry (this call is named ldap_modrdn() in LDAPv2-only SDKs)
ldap_result()	Retrieves the results of one of the previous operations

The APIs listed in Table 3.5 provide an asynchronous interface to the directory; that is, the calls are used to initiate a protocol operation to the server, and the ldap_result() call is used later to collect results from the previously initiated operations. This allows your client to issue multiple protocol requests or perform other work, such as updating window contents, while the operation is in progress on the server.

The API also provides a synchronous interface, in which the API calls are blocked until all results are returned from the server. The synchronous calls are generally simpler to use and are appropriate for simple command-line clients and multithreaded applications.

In addition to the API calls listed in Table 3.5 and their synchronous counterparts, the LDAP API defines a set of utility routines that can be used to parse returned results from the server; iterates over sets of entries, attributes, and attribute values; and performs other useful operations. For a complete description of the various API calls available in the SDK you are using, consult the documentation.

A useful reference book that covers the C API in detail and offers general advice on building directory-enabled applications was written by two of the authors of this book. It is called *LDAP: Programming Directory-Enabled Applications with Lightweight Directory Access Protocol*, by Tim Howes and Mark Smith, published by Macmillan Technical Publishing.

Other LDAP APIs

In addition the various implementations of the C API, four other APIs are available:

- Netscape has developed an LDAPv2 and LDAPv3 Java API that, like the C API, has a close mapping onto the LDAP protocol. The Java API specification, currently in draft form, is available from the IETF Web site at `http://www.ietf.org`. An SDK that implements the draft API is available from `http://developer.netscape.com/` and, like the C SDK, is available in source code form at `http://www.mozilla.org`. Online documentation is also available. The Java classes that implement the Netscape SDK are also included with versions of Netscape Communicator currently being shipped.

- Perl fans can use PerLDAP, available from `http://www.mozilla.org`.

- JavaSoft has developed the proprietary Java Naming and Directory Interface (JNDI). This API/SDK defines a common interface for accessing a number of different directory systems from a Java application or applet. Additional types of directory systems and protocols can be supported by developing additional service provider interfaces (SPIs) for JNDI. This allows a JNDI client to access a number of distinct directory services, such as NIS, DNS, LDAP, NDS, or X.500. JNDI is available from JavaSoft at `http://www.javasoft.com/`.

- Microsoft also has a proprietary, object-oriented SDK, called ADSI, for accessing multiple directory systems. ADSI APIs are available for Visual Basic, C, and C++. For more information on ADSI, see `http://www.microsoft.com`.

These "directory-agnostic" access APIs (APIs that can access a number of different directory systems) can be useful if you are writing client software that must simultaneously access multiple directory services running incompatible protocols. However, because they present a single API across all the different directory protocols they support, these tools may not have sufficient fidelity for your needs. In other words, some features supported by the underlying protocol may not be available in the unified API.

In order to support these new features, the unified API must be revised to expose the new features. If the new feature exposes functionality in some protocol you aren't using, this is unnecessary clutter and overhead. LDAP-only APIs don't suffer from this problem.

LDIF

LDIF is a standard text-based format for describing directory entries. LDIF allows you to export your directory data and import it into another directory server, even if the two servers use different internal database formats. In the database/spreadsheet world, the tab-delimited format performs a similar function: It provides a simple format that virtually all spreadsheets and databases can import and export.

There are two different types of LDIF files. The first form describes a set of directory entries, such as your entire corporate directory, or perhaps a subset of it. The other type of LDIF file is a series of LDIF update statements that describes changes to be applied to directory entries. In the following sections we'll look at both formats in detail.

LDIF Representation of Directory Entries

Listing 3.1 represents two directory entries in LDIF format.

LISTING 3.1 A TYPICAL LDIF FILE

```
dn: uid=bjensen, ou=people, dc=airius, dc=com
objectclass: top
objectclass: person
objectclass: organizationalPerson
objectclass: inetOrgPerson
cn: Barbara Jensen
cn: Babs Jensen
givenname: Barbara
sn: Jensen
uid: bjensen
mail: bjensen@airius.com
telephoneNumber: +1 408 555 1212
description: Manager, switching products division

dn: uid=ssmith, ou=people, dc=airius, dc=com
```

```
objectclass: top
objectclass: person
objectclass: organizationalPerson
objectclass: inetOrgPerson
cn: Steve Smith
cn: Stephen Smith
givenname: Stephen
sn: Smith
uid:ssmith
mail: ssmith@airius.com
telephoneNumber: +1 650 555 1212
description: Member of Technical Staff.
```

An individual entry expressed in LDIF format consists of two parts: a distinguished name and a list of attribute values. The DN, which must be the first line of the entry, is composed of the string dn followed by a colon (:) and the distinguished name of the entry. After the DN comes the attributes of the entry. Each attribute value is composed of an attribute type, a colon (:), and the attribute value. Attribute values may appear in any order; for readability, however, we suggest that you list the objectclass values for the entry first and group multiple values for the same attribute type together, as in Listing 3.1.

Any line in an LDIF file may be folded into multiple lines, which is typically done when an individual line is extremely long. To fold a line, insert a newline character and a space character into the value. Folding is not required, but some editors do not handle extremely long lines. Listing 3.2 shows an entry with a folded line; note how the description attribute is folded into four lines.

LISTING 3.2 AN LDIF FILE WITH A FOLDED ATTRIBUTE VALUE

```
dn: uid=bjensen, ou=people, dc=airius, dc=com
objectclass: top
objectclass: person
objectclass: organizationalPerson
objectclass: inetOrgPerson
cn: Barbara Jensen
cn: Babs Jensen
givenname: Barbara
sn: Jensen
uid: bjensen
mail: bjensen@airius.com
telephoneNumber: +1 408 555 1212
description: I will be out of the
 office from August 12, 1998, to September 10, 1998. If you need
 assistance with the Ostrich project, please contact Steve Smith
 at extension 7226.
```

If an LDIF file contains an attribute value or a distinguished name that is not ASCII, that value or DN must be encoded in a special format called *base 64*. This encoding method can represent any arbitrary data as a series of printable characters. When an attribute is base 64–encoded, the attribute type and value are separated by two colons, instead of a single colon. Listing 3.3 shows an entry in LDIF format that contains a base 64–encoded binary attribute (jpegPhoto). Notice how, in addition to being base 64–encoded, the attribute is folded.

LISTING 3.3 AN ENTRY IN LDIF FORMAT CONTAINING A BASE 64–ENCODED ATTRIBUTE VALUE

```
dn: uid=bjensen, ou=people, dc=airius, dc=com
objectclass: top
objectclass: person
objectclass: organizationalPerson
objectclass: inetOrgPerson
cn: Barbara Jensen
cn: Babs Jensen
givenname: Barbara
sn: Jensen
uid: bjensen
mail: bjensen@airius.com
telephoneNumber: +1 408 555 1212
jpegPhoto:: /9j/4AAQSkZJRgABAAAAAQABAAD/2wBDABALDA4MChAODQ4
 SERATGCgaGBYWGDEjJR0oOjM9PDkzODdASFxOQERXRTc4UG1RV19iZ2hnP
 k1xeXBkeFxlZ2P/2wBDARESEhgVGC8aGi9jQjhCY2NjY2NjY2NjY2N
 jY2NjY2NjY2NjY2NjY2NjY2NjY2NjY2NjY2NjY2NjY2P/wAARCACcA
 LgDASIAAhEBAxEB/8QAHwAAAQUBAQEBAQEAAAAAAAAAAAAECAwQFBgcICQo
 L/8QAtRAAAgEDAwIEAwUFBAQAAAF9AQIDAAQRBRIhMUEGE1FhByJxFDKBk
 aEII0KxwRVS0fAkM2JyggkKFhcYGRolJicoKSo0NTY3ODk6Q0RFRkdISUp
 TVFVWV1hZWmNkZWZnaGlqc3R1dnd4eXqDhIWGh4iJipKTlJWVl5iZmqKjp
 KWmp6ipqrKztLW2t7i5usLDxMXGx8jJytLT1NXW19jZ2uHi4+Tl5ufo6er
 x8vP09fb3+
```

More formally, the syntax of an entry represented in LDIF format is

```
("dn:" <DN of entry> ¦ "dn::" <base 64-encoded DN of entry>)
<attribute type> (":" <attribute value> ¦"::" <base 64 attribute value>)
...
```

A complete formal definition of the LDIF syntax is available from the IETF Web site at http://www.ietf.org.

LDIF Update Statements

The second type of LDIF file describes a set of changes to be applied to one or more directory entries. An individual LDIF update statement consists of a DN, a change type, and possibly a set of modifications. Typically, you will use this type of LDIF file as input to a command-line utility such as the ldapmodify program, which is included with the Netscape Directory Server and Netscape LDAP SDK. The ldapmodify program reads the update statements, converts those statements to LDAP protocol operations, and sends them to a server for processing.

There are four types of changes that can be described by an LDIF update state-ment. These change types correspond exactly to the types of update operations that can be performed over the LDAP protocol: add a new entry, delete an existing entry, modify an existing entry, and rename an existing entry. Although the examples in the following sections do not show either folding or base 64-encoding, both are permitted in LDIF update statements.

Adding a New Entry

The add changetype statement indicates that an entry is to be added to the direc-tory. The syntax of this update statement is

```
dn: <dn of entry to be added>
changetype: add
<attribute type>: value
...
```

For example, you would use the following to add a new entry to the directory:

```
dn: uid=bjensen, ou=people, dc=airius, dc=com
changetype: add
objectclass: top
objectclass: person
objectclass: organizationalPerson
objectclass: inetOrgPerson
cn: Barbara Jensen
cn: Babs Jensen
givenname: Barbara
sn: Jensen
uid: bjensen
mail: bjensen@airius.com
telephoneNumber: +1 408 555 1212
```

Deleting an Entry

The delete changetype statement indicates that an entry is to be removed from the directory. The syntax of this type of update statement is

```
dn: <dn of entry to be deleted>
changetype: delete
```

For example, you would use the following to delete an entry from the directory:

```
dn: uid=bjensen, ou=people, dc=airius, dc=com
changetype: delete
```

Modifying an Entry

The modify changetype statement indicates that an existing entry is to be modi-fied. It also allows you to add new attribute values, remove specific attribute values, remove an attribute entirely, or replace all attribute values with a new set of values. The syntax of the modify update statement is

```
dn: <dn of entry to be modified>
changetype: modify
<modifytype> <attribute type>
[<attribute type>: <attribute value>]
-
...
```

Note that there is an additional operator: modifytype. This is either add, delete, or replace, and is interpreted as follows.

To add one or more new attribute values, use a modifytype of add and include the attribute values you want to add. The following example adds two new values to the telephoneNumber attribute; if there are already existing values for this attribute, they are unaffected:

```
dn: uid=bjensen, ou=people, dc=airius, dc=com
changetype: modify
add: telephoneNumber
telephoneNumber: +1 216 555 1212
telephoneNumber: +1 408 555 1212
```

To delete one or more specific attribute values, use a modifytype of delete and include the values you want to delete. The following example removes the value +1 216 555 1212 from the telephoneNumber attribute; any other telephoneNumber attribute values are unaffected:

```
dn: uid=bjensen, ou=people, dc=airius, dc=com
changetype: modify
delete: telephoneNumber
telephoneNumber: +1 216 555 1212
```

To completely remove an attribute, use a modifytype of delete, but do not include any specific attribute value to be deleted. The following example completely removes the telephoneNumber attribute from the entry:

```
dn: uid=bjensen, ou=people, dc=airius, dc=com
changetype: modify
delete: telephoneNumber
```

To replace an attribute with a new set of values, use a modifytype of replace and include the values that should replace any existing attribute values. The following example replaces any existing values of the telephoneNumber attribute with the two given values:

```
dn: uid=bjensen, ou=people, dc=airius, dc=com
changetype: modify
replace: telephoneNumber
telephoneNumber: +1 216 555 1212
telephoneNumber: +1 405 555 1212
```

Multiple modifytypes can be combined into a single update statement. Each set of lines comprising one modifytype must be separated by a line that contains only a single dash. For example, the following update statement adds a new value to the mail attribute, removes a specific value from the telephoneNumber attribute, completely removes the description attribute, and replaces the givenname attribute with a new set of values:

```
dn: uid=bjensen, ou=people, dc=airius, dc=com
changetype: modify
add: mail
mail: bjensen@airius.com
-
delete: telephoneNumber
telephoneNumber: +1 216 555 1212
-
delete: description
-
replace: givenname
givenname: Barbara
givenname: Babs
-
```

When multiple modifications are included in a single LDIF update statement and the ldapmodify program sends the corresponding LDAP operations to an LDAP server, the server performs the update only if all the individual attribute modifications succeed. In the last example, if the entry did not contain the telephone number attribute value +1 216 555 1212, it would not be possible to delete that specific value. The server treats each update statement as a single unit, so none of the attribute modifications would be made, and an error would be returned to the client.

Renaming and/or Moving an Entry

The moddn changetype statement indicates that an existing entry is to be renamed and optionally moved to a new location in the directory tree. The syntax of the moddn update statement is

```
dn: <dn of entry to be modified>
changetype: moddn
[newsuperior: <dn of new parent>]
[deleteoldrdn: ( 0 ¦ 1 )]
[newrdn: <new relative distinguished name for the entry>]
```

If an entry's RDN is to be changed, the newrdn and deleteoldrdn parameters must be provided. If an entry is to be moved to a new location in the tree, the newsuperior parameter must be provided. Both operations can be performed at once; that is, an entry can have its RDN changed at the same time it is moved to a new location in the tree.

For example, to change an entry's name without moving it to a new location in the tree, you'd use the following:

```
dn: uid=bjensen, ou=People, dc=airius, dc=com
changetype: moddn
newrdn: uid=babsj
deleteoldrdn: 0
```

After this update is performed on the server, the entry would look like this:

```
dn: uid=babsj, ou=People, dc=airius, dc=com
[other attributes omitted for brevity]
uid: babsj
uid: bjensen
```

Notice how the old RDN, uid: bjensen, is still present in the entry. When 0 is provided for the deleteoldrdn flag, the old RDN is retained as an attribute of the entry. If you want the old RDN to be removed from the entry, include deleteoldrdn: 1 in your moddn update statement. If this were done, the entry would look like this after being renamed:

```
dn: uid=babsj, ou=People, dc=airius, dc=com
[other attributes omitted for brevity]
uid: babsj
```

If you want to move an entry to a new location in the tree, you can use the newsuperior parameter to specify the DN of the entry you would like the entry to be moved to. For example, if you want to move Babs's entry under the Terminated Employees organizational unit, you would use the following LDIF update statement:

```
dn: uid=bjensen, ou=People, dc=airius, dc=com
changetype: moddn
newsuperior: ou=Terminated Employees, dc=airius, dc=com
```

The moddn changetype statement may behave differently depending on whether the server supports LDAPv3. If the server supports only LDAPv2, the newsuperior parameter may not be used; LDAPv2 does not support moving an entry to a new location in the tree.

LDAP and Internationalization

Directory services, by their very nature, span language boundaries. Multinational companies might have offices in dozens of countries, each with a distinct language. To address this growing need, LDAPv3 has been designed so that it can easily support multiple languages.

LDAPv3 uses the UTF-8 (Unicode Transformation Format-8) character set for all textual attribute values and distinguished names. UTF-8 is a standard character coding system that can represent text in virtually all written languages in use today. It is defined and developed by the Unicode Consortium, an industry group.

There are two important points to understand about UTF-8. First, because of the way UTF-8 is designed, ASCII data is also valid UTF-8 data. This has the benefit of being highly compatible with existing English-language directory data; no work needs to be done to transform the data into valid UTF-8.

The second point is that when you use UTF-8, it becomes unnecessary to declare an attribute value to be in a particular character set. In other systems, values must be tagged with their character set (e.g., Latin-1, Shift-JIS) so that the data may be correctly interpreted. However, because the UTF-8 character set contains codes for the glyphs of virtually all languages, this is unnecessary. It's even possible to use multiple languages within a single attribute value.

Because LDAPv3 servers can store text in multiple languages, it is useful to have some way to store and access attributes by language type. For example, in an international corporation with offices in the United States and Japan, it may be desirable to store several representations of a Japanese employee's name in the directory, including a version in Japanese and a version in English. The LDAP Extensions Working Group in the IETF has proposed a method for accomplishing this through the use of language codes.

A language code is an option on an LDAP attribute name. Separated from the base attribute name with a semicolon, it gives the particular language for the attribute in a standard format. For example, the attribute type `cn;lang-fr` refers to a common name in the French language, and the attribute type `sn;lang-ja` refers to a surname in the Japanese language. All language names are represented by a two-character code defined in ISO Standard 639, "Code for the representation of names of languages."

The LDAP language code standard also allows for names to be represented in a particular regional dialect or usage of a particular language. For example, there are some minor differences in how the English language is written in the United States and the United Kingdom. The language code `lang-en-US` identifies an attribute in the U.S. dialect, whereas the language code `lang-en-GB` indicates the British dialect. The country codes used to specify the region are defined in ISO Standard 3166, "Codes for the representation of names of countries."

An LDAP client may use language codes in search filters and attribute lists. In other words, an LDAP client may limit its search to only those attributes in the specific language it is interested in, and it may request that only specific languages be returned by specifying language codes in the list of attributes to be returned. For example, a client could search the French common name attribute with the filter (cn;lang-fr=Jules) and specify that the French common name and description attributes be returned by including only cn;lang-fr and description;lang-fr in the list of attributes to be returned.

Note that there is no way to retrieve all dialects of a particular language code. For example, the attribute type cn;lang-en is not the same as the attribute type cn;lang-en-US. Each dialect must be specifically requested. In general, avoid the use of dialects unless necessary. However, attributes with language codes are treated as subtypes of attributes without language codes. So, for example, the attribute cn;lang-en is a subtype of the attribute cn. Requesting the cn attribute will retrieve all language code variations of the cn attribute.

Language codes are a relatively new development, and not all servers support them at this time. Check with your software vendor to see if language codes are supported.

LDAP Overview Checklist

The term *LDAP* has come to mean four things:

☐ A set of models that guides you in your use of the directory; a data model that describes what you can put in the directory; a naming model that describes how you arrange and refer to directory data; a functional model that describes what you can do with directory data; and a security model that describes how directory data can be protected from unauthorized access.

☐ The LDAP protocol itself.

☐ An API for developing directory-enabled applications.

☐ LDIF, a standard interchange format for directory data.

Further Reading

A Summary of the X.500(96) User Schema for use with LDAPv3 (RFC 2256). M. Wahl, 1997. Available on the World Wide Web at http://info.internet. isi.edu:80/in-notes/rfc/files/rfc2256.txt.

Active Directory Services Interface (ADSI). Available on Microsoft's SDK World Wide Web site at `http://www.microsoft.com/msdn/sdk/`.

Code for the representation of names of languages, ISO Standard 639. The International Organization for Standardization, 1st edition, 1988.

Codes for the representation of names of countries, ISO Standard 3166. The International Organization for Standardization, 3rd edition, 1988.

Java Naming and Directory Interface (JNDI). Available on JavaSoft's JNDI Web site at `http://java.sun.com/products/jndi/`.

LDAP Data Interchange Format: Technical Specification, Internet Draft. G. Good, 1998. Available on the World Wide Web at `http://www.ietf.org`.

Lightweight Directory Access Protocol (v3) (RFC 2251). M. Wahl, T. Howes, S. Kille, 1998. Available on the World Wide Web at `http://info.internet.isi.edu:80/in-notes/rfc/files/rfc2251.txt`.

Lightweight Directory Access Protocol (v3): Attribute Syntax Definitions (RFC 2252). M. Wahl, A. Coulbeck, T. Howes, S. Kille, 1998. Available on the World Wide Web at `http://info.internet.isi.edu:80/in-notes/rfc/files/rfc2252.txt`.

Lightweight Directory Access Protocol (v3): The String Representation of LDAP Search Filters (RFC 2254). M. Wahl, T. Howes, S. Kille, 1998. Available on the World Wide Web at `http://info.internet.isi.edu:80/in-notes/rfc/files/rfc2254.txt`.

Lightweight Directory Access Protocol (v3): UTF-8 String Representation of Distinguished Names (RFC 2253). M. Wahl, T. Howes, S. Kille, 1998. Available on the World Wide Web at `http://info.internet.isi.edu:80/in-notes/rfc/files/rfc2253.txt`.

PerLDAP: an Object-Oriented LDAP Perl Module for Perl5. Available on Netscape's Directory Developer Central Web site at `http://developer.netscape.com/tech/directory/`.

Programming Directory-Enabled Applications with Lightweight Directory Access Protocol. T. Howes, M. Smith, Macmillan Technical Publishing, 1997.

The C LDAP Application Program Interface, Internet Draft. M. Smith, T. Howes, A. Herron, C. Weider, M. Wahl, A. Anantha, 1998. Available on the World Wide Web at `http://www.ietf.org`.

The Java LDAP Application Program Interface, Internet Draft. R. Weltman, T. Howes, M. Smith, 1998. Available on the World Wide Web at `http://www.ietf.org`.

The Unicode Standard, Version 2.0. The Unicode Consortium, Addison-Wesley, 1996.

Understanding X.500: The Directory. D. Chadwick, International Thomson Computer Press, 1996. Now out of print; selected portions available on the World Wide Web at `http://www.salford.ac.uk/its024/X500.htm`.

Looking Ahead

In Part I of this book, "An Introduction to Directory Services and LDAP," we've laid the groundwork for the rest of the book by giving you an overview and history of directory services and an introduction to the LDAP protocol and models. In Part II, "Designing Your Directory Service," we'll focus on designing your directory service from the ground up. We'll discuss the life cycle of a directory system and how you should assess your directory needs. Then we'll cover each major directory design topic in detail.

PART II

Designing Your Directory Service

CHAPTER 4

Directory Road Map

It's important to spend time designing your directory service. The more time you spend up front getting your design right, the less likely you are to run into trouble later. Naturally, there is a middle ground between spending forever trying to design a perfect service and diving into deployment of a service that is not thought out very well. You should strive to find this middle ground.

Keep in mind that no design, regardless of how thorough it may be, can anticipate all the problems that can occur in a real deployment. This is why piloting is such an important phase of your directory deployment. Remember also that design mistakes can be costly, and often the later the mistake is recognized, the more costly it is to correct. This too argues for early piloting and prototyping.

This chapter introduces three phases in the directory life cycle, briefly describing the role of each. The chapters in the remainder of Part II, "Designing Your Directory Service," focus on the first phase of the life cycle—design—and provide a road map to each aspect of this task. Subsequent parts focus on other aspects of the life cycle.

The Directory Life Cycle

The life cycle of your directory can be broken down into three general phases: the *design phase*, the *deployment phase*, and the *maintenance phase*. It will come as no surprise to many of you that the life cycle is not actually this simple, nor is it so easily segmented. In practice, you may design for a while (until you think you've got it right), then discover during the deployment phase that there are problems with your design that send you back to the design phase.

New features introduced at any phase can cause a new, miniature design-deploy-maintain cycle. Requirements can also change, even in the maintenance phase, causing a redesign of parts of the service.

You should view the life cycle of your directory, then, as a series of design, deployment, and maintenance tasks for the original service itself, for new applications that use the directory, and for new features of your directory service. The tasks may appear distinct, or they may blend together. The important thing is that all the phases are covered.

Nevertheless, it is still helpful to think of the three phases as being separate, especially for discussion purposes. Each phase has distinct tasks:

- During the design phase you will do a lot of data gathering about your environment and data sources, your users, applications that will use your directory, and other things. Using this data, you will design a service that fits your needs.

- During the deployment phase, you will pick a directory vendor; pilot your service in a test configuration; and do stress, scale, and performance testing. You will also test the reliability, redundancy, and fault tolerance capabilities of the system. This phase is also where you first expose the system to a relatively small group of users to get its feedback. After the pilot is complete, you will put your directory service into production.

- During the maintenance phase, you will continually update the data in your directory, keep the service running smoothly, and continue to improve the service.

As your service grows and matures, you may often find yourself in all three of these phases at once. For example, you may be designing a new aspect of the service, deploying the latest addition to the service, and maintaining the current service all at the same time.

The following sections delve into each phase of the life cycle in more detail. Design is first, followed by deployment and maintenance. Our goal in this chapter is to give an overview, or road map, of each topic, but not a complete treatment. Subsequent chapters cover each topic in more detail.

Design

During the design phase of your directory service, your most important task is to understand the requirements that will be placed on your directory. Armed with a clear understanding of these requirements, the rest of your design task will be much easier. The directory will not exactly design itself, of course, but your decisions are relatively uncomplicated if you fully understand your requirements. The result of the design phase is most likely a document or set of documents describing your directory service, the applications it will serve, the major design decisions made during the design process, and the tradeoffs those decisions represent.

There are many ways to segment your design process. We've chosen to break things up in the manner described in this chapter. In our experience, this approach is a good one because it helps you organize and divide your design decisions. Breaking down the task in this manner also helps us provide a framework for discussion. Keep in mind, however, that other methodologies may be equally valid. Feel free to explore different approaches, but make sure that you cover all the bases mentioned here. You will find in practice that design decisions you make in one area affect the design of other areas as well.

The design phase is aimed at designing a directory to suit your environment in the following areas:

- *Directory needs.* Your directory service will need to meet the needs of the directory-enabled applications you plan to deploy and the needs of the people who will use those applications. Understanding your applications' needs is covered in Chapter 5, "Defining Your Directory Needs."

- *Data.* Whatever type of directory service you want to create, you can be assured that it involves some kind of data. Chances are good that you have in your organization many existing sources of data that may prove useful in creating your service. Cataloging these data sources and understanding their relationship to your directory is important. Designing specifically for your organization's data is covered in Chapter 6, "Data Design."

- *Schema.* Your directory exists to support one or more directory-enabled applications. These applications have certain requirements concerning the data contained in the directory, its format, and how the data is interpreted. These characteristics are determined by the directory schemas, as discussed in Chapter 7, "Schema Design."

- *Namespace.* After you determine what data you want to put in your directory, you need a way to organize and reference that data. This is the purpose of a directory namespace. As we shall see in Chapter 8, "Namespace Design," the choices you make here can have wide-ranging implications for other aspects of the service.

- *Topology.* Topology design involves determining the number of servers you will need, how your directory data will be split among those servers, and where those servers need to be located. The directory topology that determines these factors is discussed in Chapter 9, "Topology Design."

- *Replication.* Directory-enabled applications often place severe performance and reliability requirements on the directory. Replication is the means by which the same directory data is maintained in multiple directory servers, leading to a more reliable service and more servers that can answer application queries—thus increasing performance. Replication design is covered in Chapter 10, "Replication Design."

- *Security.* The security aspect of your design cuts across all other design areas. You must plan to protect the data in the directory itself as well as design the other aspects of the service to meet the security and privacy requirements of your users and their applications. Many directory design decisions have these security implications. This topic is covered in Chapter 11, "Privacy and Security Design."

After you've answered the questions posed by these design areas, you will have the beginnings of a fairly complete directory service. The next phase in the development of your directory service is to deploy the service you've designed.

Deployment

The directory deployment phase is where things start to get real. Until now, you've been collecting data and creating paper designs. In this phase of the project you actually try things out. You'll work all the kinks out of your design, select appropriate directory software, and perform tests to ensure that your design can handle the anticipated load. Finally, you'll roll the directory service into production.

Although the deployment phase varies somewhat depending on your design and your user community, there are certain things you should be sure to do. The following list describes some tips for picking the right directory software, the importance of piloting your directory, doing performance and scale testing, and getting user feedback during the deployment phase:

- *Choosing directory software.* Choosing the proper directory software is important. If you choose software that cannot satisfy your design requirements or cannot scale or perform up to your requirements, it's back to the design drawing board—or time to choose some new directory software. Either way, you are in for a costly, miserable experience that will delay final deployment of your service.

Evaluating and choosing directory products can be complicated. You may have requirements not reflected in your ideal design, such as an organizational preference for a particular vendor. Directory products that are acceptable technically might be disqualified for other, non-technical reasons. For example, you might have concerns about the long-term viability of the product's vendor, the support provided by the vendor might be inadequate, or the product might just be too expensive.

Try to consider all factors that affect your choice of vendor, be they technical or practical. Don't choose a vendor without some real hands-on experience with its software. This topic is discussed in more detail in Chapter 12, "Choosing Directory Products."

- *Piloting.* The purpose of the deployment phase is to validate your design decisions (or prove them invalid, which calls for a redesign) and determine whether your directory service is functioning properly. The best way to do this is by piloting your directory service.

  A directory pilot requires you to set up, usually on a smaller scale, the directory you have designed and expose it to a limited user community to get feedback. Piloting your directory service can tell you whether the software you have chosen is appropriate (for example, whether it supports the access control capabilities your design calls for or if it supports your replication design). Piloting can also tell you whether the schema you've designed fulfills the needs of the applications that will be using it and whether the data gathering techniques you've designed are feasible. Most aspects of your design can be validated by piloting. More information on piloting your directory service can be found in Chapter 13, "Piloting Your Directory Service."

- *Performance and scale testing.* After you've verified that your design is functionally correct, your next task is to ensure that both your directory design and the directory software you have chosen are capable of handling a production environment. Can the directory scale up to the size required? Can it handle the load a production environment will place on it? What about future plans for expansion? These questions and others can be answered by doing performance and scale testing of your directory service.

  It's important to know what your goals are during this phase. How high must the system scale? How do you know when you are reaching the capacity limits of the current system? Answering these questions will help you avoid unpleasant surprises in your deployment.

- *Tuning the service.* Tuning the service goes hand-in-hand with performance and scale testing. Your goal is to make sure your directory is tuned to be as efficient as possible. Doing so can increase performance and the scale your directory can support. In this task, you should observe your directory in action, looking for bottlenecks or other inefficiencies. Make sure that your directory vendor has documentation describing how to tune the service for optimal performance in various configurations.

  It's equally important to examine the nonsoftware aspects of your service. For example, are your data gathering and maintenance procedures as efficient as possible? How does your service interact with other services on your network? Are the network links between your servers and clients optimal? Asking these questions before getting into full production is a good way to head off problems.

  It is also crucial to look at the costs of your directory service from all angles; you need to analyze not only implementation costs, but maintenance and other costs as well. This is discussed in Chapter 14, "Analyzing and Reducing Costs."

- *User feedback.* Whatever type of service you are deploying, it's important to expose it to some users. They are, after all, the reason you're doing all this work in the first place. The service may look great to you but still not meet the needs of your users. Getting user feedback is one of the most important steps in validating your design. It is imperative to get feedback from a cross-section of users representing a wide variety of requirements. Without it, you won't know whether you've done a good job meeting your objectives with the service.

- *Going to production.* Finally, during the deployment phase you need to develop and execute a plan for taking the directory service from a pilot to production. Think about how you can do this smoothly and incrementally, if possible. Moving into production is discussed in Chapter 15, "Going Production."

A more complete treatment of directory deployment is covered in Part III, "Deploying Your Directory Service."

Maintenance

The maintenance of your directory service is the longest-lasting phase, but this important aspect of the service often receives the least amount of attention during the design phase. Designing up front for an easy-to-maintain directory can really pay off in lower maintenance costs and happier users and administrators. Not thinking about maintenance until your directory is deployed can result in a fragile system strung together with various kludges. This kind of system leads to higher administrative overhead, higher costs, and, ultimately, unhappy users.

For example, consider a directory service design that does not take into account data maintenance. Other aspects of the service may be designed well, and users may be quite happy with the service initially. But what happens in the weeks and months that follow when the data contained in the directory becomes out-of-date? The service becomes less useful, user satisfaction plummets, calls to the help desk skyrocket, and the service designer goes from hero to zero quickly.

When designing for a maintainable directory service, think about the everyday or other periodic tasks you will need to perform. How will users be added to the directory? How will data obtained from other sources be kept up-to-date? How often will entries change names, and how painful a process will this be? It's okay to recognize some tasks as exceptions that don't happen very often and therefore don't need to be made all that convenient. But keep in mind that your definition of exceptions may change as the number of users in your directory changes. For example, an annoying administrative task that needs to be done once per month on average for every 1,000 users may be perfectly acceptable for a 1,000-user directory. But if your directory grows to 100,000 users, you'll be doing this task more than three times per day!

You should consider the following aspects of directory maintenance:

- *Data maintenance.* This is quite often the most important and time-consuming task involved in maintaining your directory. If you do not keep the data in your directory up-to-date, the whole service is much less useful. Make sure you have in place maintainable and scalable procedures for keeping your directory data updated. The topic of data maintenance is addressed in Chapter 17, "Maintaining Data."

- *Data backups.* Another important aspect of maintaining a reliable service is performing regular backups of your directory data. Make sure you design for this from the beginning, taking into account any limitations of your directory software. For example, does the software allow online backups, or does the system need to be taken down? You may be able to use the directory's inherent replication capabilities to provide backups. We discuss data backups in Chapter 16, "Backups and Disaster Recovery."

- *Schema additions.* As you deploy new directory-enabled applications, you will often need to extend your directory's schema. Make sure your directory software allows this and that you have in place a procedure for administrators or users deploying new applications to request their schema additions. Also bear in mind that applications may require other changes as well, such as a new indexing configuration.

- *Monitoring.* Naturally, you'll want to monitor your directory service. You need to know when it goes down so that you can bring it back up quickly. You also need to ensure that it's performing well for your users and then tune it if it is not. You may have an existing monitoring infrastructure in your organization that you want to plug into. The topic of monitoring your directory service is covered in Chapter 18, "Monitoring."

- *Expansion.* A natural part of maintaining your directory is managing the process by which it expands. In most environments, use of your directory will increase, as will the number of entries in the directory. Sometimes the change will be gradual; sometimes it will happen all at once. Make sure you have planned for this kind of expansion from the outset.

  It's a good idea to have some rules of thumb for when to upgrade. For example, you might want to begin upgrading relevant parts of the system when CPU utilization reaches 75% or when network bandwidth utilization reaches 50%. Knowing in advance what actions to take and when helps protect against unnecessary outages and makes the upgrade process a seamless part of service operation instead of a panicked fire drill.

- *Changing requirements.* Finally, part of your maintenance plan should include contingency plans for handling changing requirements beyond the normal expansion already described. Think about what you would do if any of your fundamental design assumptions were to change.

Directory Design Checklist

- ☐ Determine your directory needs and what applications will use the directory.

- ☐ Determine your data needs.

- ☐ Design your namespace.

- ☐ Design your schema.

- ☐ Design the topology of your directory.

- ☐ Design your directory replication scheme.

- ☐ Design for security and privacy.

Further Reading

Building an X.500 Directory Service in the US (RFC 1943). B. Jennings, May 1996.

Directory Deployment and Installation. Netscape Communications Corporation, February 1998. Available on the World Wide Web at
`http://home.netscape.com/eng/server/directory/3.0/deploy/contents.html`.

Introduction to White Pages Services based on X.500 (RFC 1684). P. Jurg, August 1994.

Check with your directory vendor for any product-specific documentation available about directory design, deployment, and maintenance.

Looking Ahead

Now that you've studied the road map presented in this chapter and mapped out your route, it's time to get out there on the road! The following chapters, comprising the rest of Part II, take you through a detailed design process for each of the design areas mentioned in this chapter. How to identify your directory needs is tackled first. Subsequent sections cover the topics of directory deployment and maintenance.

CHAPTER 5

Defining Your Directory Needs

Directory needs encompass all the reasons for designing and deploying a directory service. Before beginning work on any task, it is a good idea to understand why you are working on it and what you hope to accomplish. Ask yourself why you decided to deploy a directory service. These are some possible answers:

- To support a few important directory-enabled applications

- To save money by consolidating a multitude of proprietary directories into one standards-based service

- To help system administrators manage information with less effort and greater automation

- To make it easier for end users to locate resources within your organization

No matter what the initial impetus, your directory service ultimately must serve the needs of applications and people, and it should be designed with those needs in mind. Your design will likely be evaluated based on how well it serves these needs; therefore, it is very important to understand the needs up front.

It is also important to choose a directory design and deployment approach that fits your situation well. A variety of organizational and environmental constraints, along with the preferences of the design and deployment team itself, determines what approach works best. A successful approach also balances short-term needs with the need to lay a good foundation for future use of the directory service.

This chapter will help you gather and organize information on all the different needs and constraints that affect the design of your directory service. After working through the material in this chapter, you should be able to produce a good first draft of a directory requirements document. You will also be able to begin to form a project plan for your directory design and deployment effort.

This chapter begins with an overview of the needs definition process and then helps you analyze the environment in which you will deploy the directory ser-vice. Then we discuss needs and constraints that come from a variety of sources: the directory applications, the users, the deployment process and team, and the environment within your organization. Next, we talk about how to choose an overall approach that fits your needs and situation, and we finish up with a discussion of how to set good goals and milestones for your directory design and deployment project.

An Overview of the Directory Needs Definition Process

Your boss, co–workers, and customers (users) will measure the success of your directory service based on how well it meets their needs and the needs of the entire organization. Whether this evaluation is formal (for example, part of a yearly performance review) or informal (for example, casual conversation that takes place near the cappuccino machine), it will take place. The best way to meet everyone's directory-related needs is to gather and understand as many of them as possible up front, and keep them in mind throughout the stages of directory design and deployment.

In this section, we present an overview of the directory needs definition process. In subsequent sections, we cover each part of the process in detail.

Analyzing Your Environment

The first step in gathering your directory-related needs is to understand the environment in which your directory service will be deployed. *Environment* is a broad term that covers a wide range of topics, including organizational struc-ture and geography, computer systems, networks, application software, users, the directory deployment team, other system administrators, and any other people the directory serves.

Determining and Prioritizing Needs

When you have a good understanding of the overall environment, the needs and constraints that come from each area should be gathered and prioritized.

It does not matter in what order this is done as long as no stone is left unturned. We recommend that you look at each of these areas:

- *Application needs.* Application needs include all the things the directory service must do to help directory-enabled applications perform their own tasks correctly and efficiently. Applications are usually the primary force behind deployment of a directory service. For example, a modern messaging system typically relies on a directory service for its knowledge of email users and groups of users. It may be impossible to deploy the messaging system without first deploying a directory service that holds the required information. Gathering information about the needs of applications can be complex and time-consuming, but it is probably the most important task and, therefore, the one you should spend the most time on.

- *User needs and expectations.* User needs and expectations include all the things that people who use your directory service expect or desire from it. For example, end users may expect to always find accurate and up-to-date telephone numbers in the directory. Or, they may have privacy concerns about the personal data held in the directory service. Your directory service design should take all the users' needs into account, although you should realize that it is often difficult to know what your end users want (especially if the concept of a directory service is new to them).

- *Deployment constraints.* Deployment constraints arise from the organizational situation or the characteristics of the people charged with designing and deploying the directory service itself. Resource constraints, personal and organizational philosophies, the needs of those who will administer the directory service, and other realities affect your directory design and largely determine your overall approach. Because you are probably a member of the deployment team yourself, you should not have to go far to gather these deployment constraints, but you need to be careful to examine your situation objectively.

- *Other environmental constraints.* Other constraints may arise from the environment in which the directory service is deployed. These include everything from system- and network-related constraints to any constraints imposed by the other data sources and directories with which your directory must coexist. For example, the computers and operating systems already being used in your organization may limit your choice of directory service software. Also, security needs vary depending on the overall audience for your service; if your directory service lives inside a firewall, it probably needs less protection than if it is accessible to everyone on the Internet.

For each of these areas, you must gather information, produce a list of needs, and assign priorities to each item on the list.

Choosing an Overall Directory Design and Deployment Approach

After you have gathered and prioritized all the different directory-related needs and constraints, it is important to choose an overall approach to directory design and deployment that fits your needs and situation. In this book, we guide you through a design and deployment process that has served us well, but your personal philosophy and organizational realities may lead you to adopt a different approach. The amounts of time spent in the design stage, the piloting stage, and in deployment of the initial directory service all vary widely from organization to organization. The most important thing is to choose an approach that will help you succeed with your directory service deployment.

Setting Goals and Milestones

The final step in the needs definition process is to set some goals and milestones that will measure the progress of your directory deployment. This seemingly simple task is often overlooked, but defining goals and milestones is well worth spending time on up front. Most projects go more smoothly when people working on them have good targets to aim for. Good goals and milestones are easily understood, realistic, and significant enough to be worth celebrating.

The results of this process feed into the rest of the directory design process that is discussed in subsequent chapters. The remainder of this chapter is devoted to exploring each of these tasks in more detail.

Analyzing Your Environment

To accurately determine your directory needs, it is essential to understand the environment in which your directory service will operate. Unless you are new to your organization, you probably already know quite a bit about the overall environment. Spending some time during the early stages of design to record what you do know, and additional time on research to fill in any missing details, will pay off later in the directory design process. Explore the eight areas described in this section to help you produce a complete portrait of the environment in which your directory service will be deployed.

Organizational Structure and Geography

Create a list of the major units within your organization and all the physical locations your   directory service must serve. Note significant differences about the environment at each location and refer to them as you proceed with the remaining environment topics. For example, some locations will have more users than others, different kinds of computer systems, better network connectivity, and so on.

Organizational structure and geography will influence everything from how many physical servers you need to deploy to how you maintain the data stored in your directory service. The needs of a small organization located in a single building are generally simpler than those of a multinational organization with offices located in many different time zones. In the latter case, seemingly simple decisions, such as choosing a time of day to perform system maintenance, are difficult because of the multitude of time zones in which the users of the system live and work.

The amount of   independence that individual departments within an organization have varies widely from organization to organization as well. In a decentralized organization, it may be appropriate or perhaps even required that you delegate responsibility for directory content to each department or location. In a centralized organization, management of the directory may be centralized for better efficiency.

Computer Systems

Create an   inventory that characterizes the different types of computers that exist in your organization. Also record approximately how many of each different type are in use and the role of each system. A sample computer system inventory is shown in Table 5.1.

TABLE 5.1 A SAMPLE COMPUTER SYSTEM INVENTORY

Role	OS	Processor	Speed	RAM	Quantity
Low-end desktop	Windows 3.11	Pentium	133 MHz	16MB	75
Typical desktop—Mac	MacOS 8.0	PowerPC 604	150 MHz	32MB	25
Typical desktop—PC	Windows 95	Pentium II	166 MHz	32MB	100
CAD workstation	Windows NT 4.0	Pentium II	333 MHz	128MB	50
Intranet server	Sun Solaris 2.6	2 x UltraSPARC	200 MHz	256MB	18

You should also consider the following system-related topics:

- Whether machine upgrades are likely to occur soon

- Whether you will be able to purchase new systems for the directory servers themselves to run on

- Which machines will need to reach the directory servers

- How you will distribute directory service software to machines that need it

- How much control you have over the machines

If you are a system designer, administrator, or other information services (IS) professional, you already know how important it is to understand what computer systems are used in your organization. The variety of systems that must be supported by your directory service constrains your choices for directory server and client software. In some cases, the systems in use provide a hint of your users' expectations. For example, if most of the computers installed on their desks are high-end PCs or workstations, they will expect your directory to be fast and responsive too.

The Network

Obtain or create a map of your organization's network (or the portion of it on which your directory service will be deployed). This map should show all the backbone and branch networks that exist in the part of your organization your directory service will serve. Each network link should be labeled with information about its bandwidth, latency, and reliability, along with any usage-based costs. In large organizations, there is usually a central group that oversees the network; hopefully, this kind of information can be easily obtained from them. If necessary, you can measure the characteristics of the link or simply estimate based on the technology employed.

A sample network map is shown in Figure 5.1.

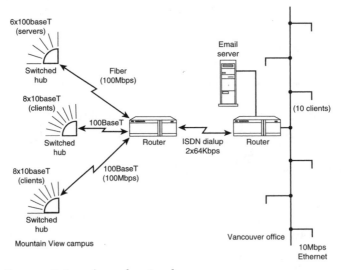

FIGURE 5.1   *A sample network map.*

The network shown in Figure 5.1 is generally very good except for the intermittent ISDN line that links the Vancouver office to the main campus in Mountain View. When designing your directory service topology, special consideration should be given to any part of the network that is particularly weak. For example, it may be necessary to place a directory replica in the Vancouver office to provide good service there.

All directory services depend on a computer network to exchange data with applications and for communication between the directory servers themselves. The composition, speed, and reliability of your network will heavily influence how many servers you need and where best to locate them. The network may partially determine how many users and applications your directory can serve. Finally, in some cases the characteristics of the network may limit the types of directory applications   you can support.

For example, because most messaging systems employ store-and-forward designs, a messaging server can usually tolerate some delay in receiving responses from a directory service. In contrast, people who use an online phonebook application are unlikely to tolerate delays that exceed a second or two. To the messaging server high throughput is very important, but to end users low latency (response time) is very important. The network between the directory server and the applications or end users is one factor that influences the overall throughput and latency of a directory service.

Application Software

In most   organizations there are typically a large number of different application software packages in widespread use. For planning purposes, concern yourself with only the most popular, the most critical, and the most directory-enabled applications. Much of the design of your directory service will in fact be driven by the needs of the directory-enabled applications you plan to deploy. These needs are discussed in more detail in the next section of this chapter and in Chapter 6, "Data Design."

Users

It has been said that there are only two businesses that refer to customers as *users*: the illegal drug trade and the computer industry. Regardless of what that says   about the computer industry, the term is widely used and is generally well understood. In the context of directory services, it refers to all the people who use a directory service or an application that depends on a directory service.

It is essential to know how many users you are serving, who they are, where they are located, what different categories they occupy, and what their expectations are. Successful computer professionals know that their primary mission is to meet and exceed users' expectations. Users' needs are discussed later in this chapter.

System Designers and Administrators

We use the term *system designer* to refer to a person who designs and plans for the deployment of information systems. A *system administrator* is someone who is responsible for the care and maintenance of a production service. When planning your directory service, the most important system designers whose needs must be   considered are those who design and plan the deployment of the directory service itself. Similarly, the most important system administrators whose needs must be considered are those charged with running the directory service. The characteristics of the system designers and administrators lead to a set of deployment constraints that may affect your approach. Deployment constraints are examined in more detail later in this chapter.

The Political Climate

Geographical boundaries and organizational structure often lead to differences in thinking among   groups. Political climate is an important but often misunderstood aspect of an organization's environment. Because political differences often occur due to lack of communication between groups, they tend to be more pronounced in large, mature, or hierarchically managed organizations.

Tip

You will probably find it difficult to paint an accurate picture of the political climate within your own organization. The best approach is to ask some experienced employees from a variety of organizational units for their own views and look for common themes and complaints. You will still need to sort out fact from fiction, of course.

Political disagreements are usually centered on how to use resources (people, money, time), the direction of the organization as a whole, or philosophical differences between managers. These disagreements may hurt your directory service deployment efforts if you get caught in the middle. We examine politics again later in this chapter when we discuss deployment constraints.

Resources

Resources include all the scarce commodities that limit the amount of work that can be accomplished. The most important resources are people, time, and money.   Resource-rich organizations tend to do things on a larger scale; of course, expectations of those working in such an environment are high as well. In contrast, if you work in a resource-poor organization, you typically are held accountable for all expenditures, and you may have to do more work up front to show that your directory service project will pay for itself.

No matter what kind of organization you are associated with, your directory deployment project will be expected to show a good return on investment, so it is important to use resources wisely. We discuss resources again later in this chapter when we discuss deployment constraints.

Determining and Prioritizing Application Needs

It is important to focus first on LDAP-enabled applications when pondering your directory needs. This is because in most organizations one or possibly two important applications are the driving force behind the initial deployment of the directory service. If this is true in your organization, you can focus most of your energy on meeting the needs of these high-profile applications. If you succeed in deploying a directory service that makes these important applications look good, your co-workers, employees, and users will label the directory service a success as well.

Note that you should avoid creating a directory service that is so focused on the needs of a small number of applications that it must be heavily redesigned later to accommodate other applications that come online. As you work through the various stages of designing your directory, remember to consider the broader, long-term picture. For example, you should favor general object classes over extremely specialized ones, assuming that the more general object classes meet the needs of your initial set of important directory applications.

Applications' directory-related needs generally fall into one of these categories: data, performance, availability, level of service, security, and priorities. These are described in the following sections.

Data

All directory-enabled applications access data that is stored in a directory service. For each application you plan to support, consider in general terms how it will use the directory and what data it requires to accomplish its mission.

Does the application need to store a lot of data? A directory service may have limited capacity for data or may simply slow down as the number of entries and attributes stored in the service increases. It is important to understand the data-capacity needs of each application so you can plan appropriately.

For example, a network printer location service may impose modest data scalability requirements; each printer entry will probably be small and most organizations do not own millions of printers. In contrast, a calendar or scheduling application that creates an entry for every meeting and task that appears on users' calendars may need to store a dozen or more attributes with each entry—creating literally millions of entries in the directory. Meeting the needs of a scheduling application may require partitioning entries among several servers to achieve the required level of performance.

How flexible is the application in terms of the schemas used in the directory? For example, a directory-enabled workflow system may require access to a lot of information about people and their organizational roles and relationships. Such an application may also use the directory for its security needs, so the directory may also be required to store passwords, public key-based certificates, and access-control information. Depending on how the workflow system is designed, it may be flexible or rigid about what schemas are used in the directory.

Does the application have any special data needs such as storing unusual data that might require new syntaxes to be defined in the directory service? Is the information so dynamic that it does not necessarily need to be written to persistent storage? Special data needs may severely limit the choices of directory service software.

Performance

Most applications expect the directory service to meet certain standards for performance. Two aspects of directory performance are of special interest: latency and throughput. *Latency* refers to the elapsed time between when an application makes an LDAP request and when it receives the expected response. Typically, low latency is most important for applications that use the directory service as part of a larger task, or when an end user is waiting for a response. For example, telephone operators require very fast response time from a directory because they cannot move on to another call until they receive a response and pass it on to the current caller.

Throughput refers to the total sustainable operation load that the directory can handle. It is possible for a directory service to have high latency (for example, each search takes two seconds to complete) and still have high throughput (for example, the server can process 1,500 searches every second). For applications that make heavy use of the directory, such as an email delivery system, throughput is the most important performance metric. You will need to think about how much work each application expects to be able to accomplish in a given time period. Be sure to distinguish read throughput requirements from write throughput requirements.

An example of the throughput needs of a hypothetical email delivery system is shown in Figure 5.2.

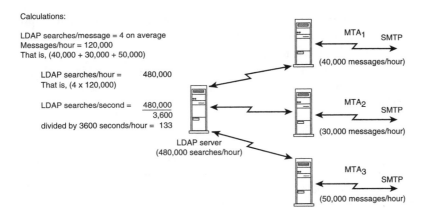

Calculations:

LDAP searches/message = 4 on average
Messages/hour = 120,000
That is, (40,000 + 30,000 + 50,000)

LDAP searches/hour =   480,000
That is, (4 x 120,000)

LDAP searches/second = $\dfrac{480,000}{3,600}$

divided by 3600 seconds/hour = 133

LDAP server
(480,000 searches/hour)

MTA₁ SMTP
(40,000 messages/hour)

MTA₂ SMTP
(30,000 messages/hour)

MTA₃ SMTP
(50,000 messages/hour)

FIGURE 5.2   *Throughput needs of a busy email service.*

Getting a handle on how well your directory service must perform will help produce a good design and ultimately result in a production directory service that enables the applications to perform well. It is always good to avoid a situation in which your directory service becomes a bottleneck for an important application.

Availability

Availability refers to the percentage of time the directory service is available for use by applications. This is another area in which different applications have different needs. If your mission is to support a telephone directory assistance service that is unavailable between midnight and five o'clock in the morning or on weekends, there is no need to design a directory service that is available 24 hours a day, 7 days a week (24x7). You could schedule backups and system maintenance during nights and weekends, taking the entire system down during that time, if necessary.

On the other hand, if the directory service is consulted by an application that controls access to a set of card-key activated doors within a hospital, 24x7 availability may be crucial. Features such as the ability to perform backups and system maintenance while the directory service is running are essential to meet the need for 24x7 availability.

Level of Service

Related to availability is the level of service needed by an application. Level of service typically encompasses availability, robustness (that is, whether the directory data store is transactional and self-repairing), service monitoring, and disaster recovery procedures. If the application itself provides an experimental service that is not expected to always be available, it is acceptable to build the application on top of an experimental directory service. Much of the characterization of service level has to do with the expectations of the people who rely on a directory-enabled application. It is important to know what level of service each application expects so that you can design a service that meets this expectation.

TIp

Over time, your directory service will probably need to support a wide range of service levels, from experimental to production to mission-critical. You should keep this in mind as you define your needs, set requirements, and design your directory service. Sometimes it is difficult to raise the service level after a directory is deployed, so you need to make sure the software and hardware you select can meet your future needs.

Security

You should consider the security requirements of your directory-enabled applications. Some application security requirements impose security requirements on your directory service as well. Consider these topics:

- *Privacy requirements.* How secret is the data that is to be transferred between the application and the directory servers? Should encryption be used to protect the information? For information that needs protection, what strength of encryption is required?

- *Authentication requirements.* Are simple passwords sufficient? Should one-time passwords be used instead? Must public key-based certificates be used to authenticate applications and users? Or smart cards?

- *Access control requirements.* Does the application need to be able to restrict access to directory information? What special needs does the application have?

- *Auditing requirements.* Must a log of all directory activity be maintained so that a security audit can be performed? For how long must the activity log be kept?

These topics are covered in greater detail in Chapter 11, "Privacy and Security Design."

Prioritizing Application Needs

The final step when examining any set of needs is to assign a set of priorities to each one. In principle this is a simple task, but if the applications your directory service is expected to support have a wide range of conflicting needs, setting priorities can be a challenge. A good technique is to make several passes through all the needs.

In the first pass, just assign each application need to one of these three categories:

- Must have for the application to function
- Would help the application do its job better
- Nice to have, but not critical

For example, the ability to customize the directory may be absolutely required in order to support an inflexible application. In contrast, extremely high directory throughput may help a heavily directory-dependent application work well, but there is probably some room for negotiation on the performance requirements.

In the second pass, think about how important each application is and sort the needs within each category you assigned in the first pass. Because it is unlikely that you will be able to satisfy all the application requirements from the start, ordering the list of requirements is an important step that shows you where to focus your attention.

Finally, make one more pass to check your work. This time, just look at the needs in the bottom half of your ordered priorities list and make sure none of them seem particularly important. If they do, move them up and reorder your list.

Determining and Prioritizing Users' Needs and Expectations

A great way to measure the overall success of any service is to ask its users whether it meets their needs and expectations. Even if you don't measure your success based on user satisfaction, someone else (such as your boss!) will. Thus, you should ask users about their needs and expectations in advance of the directory service deployment.

Because most end users are probably not familiar with the concept of an open, general-purpose directory service, you may need to educate them before you can extract useful information about their directory needs and expectations. If you already have some application-specific directories or an existing general-purpose directory in your organization, the task of determining user needs will be easier.

This section discusses some ways you can determine and prioritize your users' needs and expectations.

Asking Your Users

One of the best ways to determine users' needs is to ask them. If it is unrealistic at this point in your directory-planning process to conduct a general survey of your users, begin with an unscientific sample that includes your co-workers and friends and expand your survey later. Some good questions to ask users to help deduce their directory-related needs are these:

- How would you make use of a directory if you had access to one?

- What kind of data about other people would you like to have access to?

- What kinds of information do you expect to find in a directory?

- What data about yourself would you like to see published in a directory for others to use?

- What applications could benefit from being directory-enabled? How do you expect such applications to behave?

- How could a directory help you get your own work done more efficiently?

- How often will you search for or read information from the directory?

- How often will you make changes to directory information?

- How would you like to access directory information?

Keep in mind that you will need to provide more context and some additional explanations for users who are unfamiliar with the concept of a directory service. It is also useful to ask yourself these same questions (putting yourself in the users' shoes) and think about how you expect users to take advantage of the directory service in the future. As someone in the process of becoming a directory expert (or who is one already), you almost certainly have ideas that your users do not.

In addition to or instead of directly asking users about their needs, you should ask administrators of existing systems about the needs of the users they support. Managers and directors of specific departments are also a good source of information about the people who work for them. Talking to people who support or manage users is an especially valuable approach if your directory deployment will replace one or more existing proprietary directories. For example, the people who administer an electronic mail system should have some insight into how the users they support would use the new directory service.

Accuracy and Completeness of Data

One area that users often have great expectations for (even if it is not mentioned explicitly) is the completeness and accuracy of the data stored in the directory service. Many people expect the data to be very complete and up-to-date, and they may become disillusioned with your service if they discover otherwise. For example, one of the most common reasons users access a directory service is to look up contact information about other people, including voice and fax telephone numbers, email addresses, and postal mailing addresses. If the information in your directory is incomplete or stale, people will quickly learn to not trust your directory service.

Because users may not volunteer these data-related expectations, be sure to ask them in a way that makes sense to them. For example, a question like "What is the maximum tolerable propagation delay when replicating directory data?" is much more intimidating than one like "If you change your telephone number, how soon do you expect the change to appear in all the online systems?" Even better is to provide choices for the user, such as "Within five minutes," "Within one hour," and "The same day."

Privacy

Another interesting and sometimes contentious set of user needs and expectations is centered on personal privacy. Because your directory service will probably store some data about each person in your organization, it is important to ask your users about their privacy expectations. Some users will be relatively unconcerned about who has access to personal information, whereas others will be very concerned.

When asking people about their privacy concerns, be sure to explain what data you plan to store and to whom you plan to grant access. A lack of understanding of the needs and expectations surrounding personal privacy can lead to some unpleasant political problems as you begin to deploy your directory, so be sure to put some thought into it during the design process. The topic of privacy is discussed in greater detail in Chapter 11.

Audience

Next, consider how broad the audience for your directory service might become. For example, will the service be accessible only to people inside your organization, or do you plan to replicate some information to a server outside your firewall? If your site does not have a firewall, the audience for the directory service potentially includes everyone on the Internet, although access control could be used to restrict the audience. It is up to you to decide who the important members of your user base are and design an appropriate service. Access control rules may be used, for example, to limit access to anonymous users of the directory.

Also consider any special needs of your users. For example, in a multinational corporation, the directory service must serve people who come from a variety of cultural backgrounds; thus, differences in language, privacy expectations, laws, and other areas may be important.

The Relationship of User Needs to Application Needs

User needs and application needs are often tied together. Most directory-enabled applications ultimately serve a set of users, so some of your user needs come to your service indirectly via the needs of applications. You should work with those responsible for deploying the applications to understand how the needs of the users of each application impact the design of your directory service.

It is also important to consider the needs of the system administrators of your directory-enabled applications and all the other administrators within your organization. The directory service itself and the tools provided for maintenance of it must ultimately meet the needs of both end users and all the different kinds of administrators within your organization. For example, you may need to develop a special tool that Help Desk personnel can use to easily reset an end user's directory password. The needs of system administrators often lead to some deployment constraints, as discussed in the next major section of this chapter.

Prioritizing Your Users' Needs

As for all directory needs, you should try to order the list of users' needs by importance. The process of setting priorities is based partly on fairness (for example, "Many people mentioned this need.") and partly on politics (for example, "The director of my department thinks this is very important."). Try to be realistic about what you can accomplish, but also be careful not to place a lower priority on a user's need just because you don't agree that it is important.

Determining and Prioritizing Deployment Constraints

Both the organizational situation and the characteristics of the system designers and administrators involved in the directory design and deployment impose some constraints that affect the deployment strategy and possibly the design of the directory service itself. If you are one of the system designers or administrators, some of these constraints arise from your personal views. There is often little you can do to alter the organizational situation or people's personal characteristics, but by understanding the constraints imposed by them you can choose the directory design and deployment approach that is most likely to succeed. This section discusses some of the areas to consider when determining and prioritizing deployment constraints.

Resources

One important set of constraints involves the quantity of resources—money, time, and people—available for the directory deployment effort. When creating any new service, it is important to know how much money is available to spend, how much time you have for planning and deployment, and how much effort can be applied to the project. In turn, the leader of the directory deployment effort should provide detailed information to the project sponsors about what resources will be needed.

Be sure to set realistic goals. For example, it may be okay to spend three months planning before beginning a directory service pilot, but not if a workflow application the directory must serve is expected to be fully deployed within that same time period.

Openness of the Process

Another set of deployment constraints relates to the openness of the directory design and deployment process. If the directory project is officially blessed and well funded by a centralized information services organization, it probably makes sense to have a fairly open process in which you publish and solicit comments on your preliminary directory design.

It is especially helpful to get feedback from administrators of applications, people who manage other databases within your organization, and end users themselves. However, if the directory project is being conducted in secret on time borrowed from other projects, the design process should be closed. Although in some organizations a secret "skunk works" project of this sort may not be tolerated, in others it is an acceptable approach that can be used to make progress in the face of organizational opposition or indifference.

Skills of the Directory Project Team

Also consider the skills of the people working on the directory design and deployment. Information systems professionals with many years of experience assigned full-time to a directory project are more likely to succeed with a "from scratch" approach than people who are asked to work on a directory project in their spare time. Also, some organizations and individuals have a tendency to look for turnkey solutions that require less design and experimentation. Alternately, some people are inclined to learn everything there is to know about the problem and design a solution from start to finish. Understanding the skills and experience of your team will help you set realistic goals.

The Skills and Needs of System Administrators

Consider the skills and needs of the people who will maintain your directory service and associated applications after they are deployed. Most system administrators prefer to eliminate or at least automate boring, repetitive tasks. In large organizations, system administrators typically spend a lot of their time and effort managing organizational data—an area in which your directory service might be able to help make their job easier. By talking to a group of system administrators, you can generate a lot of good ideas for directory management tools, application management aids, and process improvements.

The Political Climate

Finally, consider the political climate within your organization. If you have been asked to succeed in designing and deploying a fully functional directory service, even though several other groups have failed in the past, a short time to market may be an important requirement. Showing some early, useful results will help gain support for continuing work on the directory service. You may also find that you need to spend considerable time and resources to defuse political conflicts with other parts of your organization. As a directory expert, part of your job is to sell everyone on the benefits of a general-purpose, standards-based directory service. Remember that good communication is the best weapon you have to help reduce the impact of political conflicts.

For example, if you find at some point during your directory design and deployment effort that you are blocked due to a lack of cooperation from another group, you may be able to defuse the situation by gaining the support of the other group's management. An effective method for achieving this is to prepare a presentation on the benefits the directory deployment will bring, and then sell management on the idea. It is important not to let your project lose too much momentum or collapse due to political conflicts.

Prioritizing Your Deployment Constraints

As with the application and user needs discussed earlier, list all the deployment constraints you can think of and then try to assign priorities to each one. Because many of the deployment constraints come out of organizational or personal characteristics, it is important to be as objective as possible and make sure the most important constraints overall are near the top of your list. Keep in mind that no matter what you do, you probably will not satisfy everyone, and that it may be more important, for example, to make the director of the personnel department happy than to make yourself happy.

Determining and Prioritizing Other Environmental Constraints

The final set of constraints to consider is of those related to the environment in which the directory service is to be deployed. There are many of these potential constraints, and the list will vary depending on your situation, but we do touch on a few of the most important areas in this section.

Computing Hardware and Software

A lot of information about existing systems was discussed earlier in this chapter in the section "Analyzing Your Environment." When thinking about your directory service, consider the computer hardware and operating systems it must support. The use of a standard protocol for directory access such as LDAP largely insulates you from the characteristics of any specific computer platform; however, as a practical consideration your directory service may need to accommodate a variety of existing systems.

Some directory or directory-enabled application software is available for only one or two platforms. Ask yourself the following questions to ensure that you take into account these system-related constraints:

- Can you purchase new hardware and software to deploy the directory servers, or do they need to run on hardware you already own?

- What kind of computer hardware and operating systems do your users have?

- What kind of computer hardware and operating systems will your directory-enabled applications need to run on?

- What up-and-coming computing platforms do you need to worry about?

There may be a trend away from certain existing systems and toward others, so be sure to note them. For example, suppose the use of the Linux operating system is on the rise and Microsoft Windows 3.1 is on its way out. By the time your directory service is fully deployed, support for Linux may be much more important than support for Windows 3.1.

The Network

Another set of environmental constraints relates to your organization's network. As discussed earlier, the physical deployment of directory servers may be largely governed by the cost, reliability, and performance characteristics of the network your directory service relies on. Even worse, if the network within your organization is managed by a completely separate group, you may be powerless to effect much change in the network (in which case, you will need to design your directory service to fit the existing network constraints). If you can have changes made to the network to accommodate your directory needs, so much the better. The physical deployment of directory servers throughout your network is covered in depth in Chapters 9, "Topology Design," and 10, "Replication Design."

Criticality of Service

Next, think about whether your organization provides mission-critical services or whether things are a bit more relaxed. For example, if you are deploying a directory service that will be used within a hospital emergency room, the standards that your directory service will be held to may be very high indeed. In contrast, within a software company it may be acceptable for a directory service to fail sometimes because the users are familiar with and may be more tolerant of such failures.

Security

Some security and privacy constraints come from the directory users (as previously discussed), but some arise from the environment in which the service operates. For example, if a directory service operates in an open network environment such as the Internet, it is more likely to be attacked by malicious intruders. Similarly, if your organization is secretive by nature or deals with sensitive data, the value of breaking the directory service's security may be higher—and the security-related expectations of users may be higher as well. Because privacy and security are so important, we devote all of Chapter 11 to those topics.

Coexistence with Other Databases and Directories

Finally, a directory service typically must co-exist with a wide variety of directories and database systems. These external systems may be completely independent of your directory service or tightly integrated with it. In the latter case, these systems will impose additional constraints on your directory service, covering a very wide range of areas. You can find more information about integrating with other directories and databases in Chapters 6, "Data Design," and 22, "Directory Coexistence," where we cover the topic of integration with other data sources.

Prioritizing Your Environmental Constraints

As you did for all the needs and constraints discussed earlier, list the remaining environmental constraints and assign priorities to each of them. Try to distinguish between absolute constraints that you cannot overcome and those that you may be able to work around or avoid. For example, it may be difficult and expensive to upgrade all the computer hardware and operating systems that users have, but you may be able to successfully lobby to purchase new systems on which to run the directory servers themselves.

Choosing an Overall Directory Design and Deployment Approach

In this book, we present a comprehensive approach to directory design and deployment. Our main goal is to share our experience and expose you to all the directory design and deployment issues you should consider. We purposefully break the design and deployment process down into smaller pieces from which you can pick and choose because no one approach works best in all situations. Each chapter covers one aspect of the design, deployment, and maintenance tasks that you may need to do. It is up to you to assemble the pieces in a way that fits your situation and choose an approach that will help you succeed with your own directory deployment.

Matching the Prevailing Philosophy

It is important to choose an approach that fits your philosophy as well as that of your team and your organization. Some people prefer to spend a lot of time in the design and piloting phases before moving a directory service into production. Others prefer to jump in with both feet and deploy a pilot service with the knowledge that iteration and redesign will take place in the future.

The organization in which you are deploying the directory service may also have expectations that are important to meet. For example, if most of the deployed computing services are 24x7 services that are heavily financed and staffed, it may make little sense to deploy a directory service that is not of similar quality.

Taking Constraints into Account

Another factor in choosing an approach that works for you is to consider the constraints under which the deployment must operate. Earlier in this chapter we listed some of these deployment and environmental constraints. Resource constraints (time, money, and people) usually impact your approach the most because they tend to limit in a very real way what you can do and how fast you can do it.

For example, one of the lessons from the large university directory case study (presented in Chapter 24, "Case Study: A Large University") is that initially there was no official support for the directory services project, and so it took a while for a production service to emerge. It was not until the service became widely used that resources were allocated explicitly to the project.

Political constraints are also worth considering, especially if they imply a specific schedule or a specific way of doing things. For example, if there is strong political opposition to or just strong skepticism about the directory project, it may make sense to deliver a basic, useful service as soon as possible rather than trying to design a be-all, end-all directory service.

Favoring Simple Solutions over Complex Ones

Another important point is that simple solutions generally work better than complex ones. Combined with a deep knowledge of the subject matter and an incremental approach to design, a "keep it simple" approach is probably your best bet. This book provides in-depth coverage of directory services, but we encourage you to adopt an incremental approach to design and deployment to go with good knowledge of all of the issues.

In an incremental approach to design, you begin by choosing simple solutions that address your most important needs and then revisit design decisions later as necessary. In this way, you can feed real deployment experience gained during pilot or production phases of the directory service back into the design process. Finding and deploying a simple solution is not necessarily quicker than finding and deploying a complex one, but simple solutions do tend to be easier to debug, easier to understand, and more flexible.

Focusing on Your Most Important Needs

Finally, it is best to focus initially on the most important directory-related needs, perhaps the top five. If, instead, you try to meet all the needs you are aware of, you may end up not meeting any of them well. Using the process outlined in this chapter to locate and prioritize application and user needs should help you find the most important areas to focus your efforts. Having focus will also make it much easier to measure your progress, as discussed in the next section.

The Bottom Line

In summary, we recommend that you choose an approach to directory design and deployment that is founded on these principles:

- Make sure the approach fits the philosophy of those doing the work.

- Operate within existing constraints.

- Be aware of political constraints and pressures.

- When in doubt, keep it simple.

- Favor flexible, incremental approaches over "design it once and forever" approaches.

- Focus initially on your most important directory-related needs.

Most important of all, choose an approach that fits your way of doing things and your specific situation. That will help you to succeed—and in the end, that is what matters the most.

Setting Goals and Milestones

Although not directly specific to the topic of directories, it is important to set some good goals and milestones for your directory design and deployment efforts. This task is often overlooked, even though everyone knows that goals and milestones are part of any good project plan. In this section, we discuss the purpose of goals and milestones and explain how to choose them.

Goals

Good goals help to motivate people by providing a target to aim for. They help to set and communicate expectations both inside and outside the directory deployment team. Goals are used to measure accomplishments and recognize success. For your directory service effort, you should try to choose some goals early so you have something to shoot for throughout the project.

A good goal tells both *what* is expected and *when*, and it is easily understood by everyone involved in a project. Goals should be realistic, and the people who are asked to meet them should believe they are achievable. Goals should also be measurable; that is, it should be clear to everyone when a goal has (or has not) been reached.

Some examples of good directory-service design and deployment goals might include

- Requirements document completed and published for other groups to comment on.

- Initial directory design completed and published.

- Directory service up and running in a pilot environment.

- Revised directory design completed and published.

- Production-quality directory service deployed with one directory-enabled application relying on the service.

- Achieve during every week 8 out of 10 employees directly or indirectly use the directory service.

- Achieve an X percent reduction in the time it takes to create all the necessary accounts and prepare the computing environment for a new hire.

- Achieve an X percent reduction in the time and effort required by system administrators to manage data within your organization.

Of course, you should choose target dates for these goals. Assigning accurate dates is usually difficult unless you have worked on a similar directory design and deployment project in the past. For some of the more distant goals, you should avoid trying to set a target date initially and just plan to set it as the project progresses. In some situations a schedule may be imposed on you and you won't have that luxury!

Milestones

Use a set of milestones to measure progress toward your goals. Milestones are especially important when the time frame in which you might achieve a particular goal is well into the future (more than a few months away); this way, you can use the milestones to check if you are on track to meet the goal. Milestones also help you know when to adjust your overall schedule. If you achieve a milestone early, it might be possible to pull your entire schedule in and shorten the project plan. If you are late in reaching a milestone, the overall schedule probably needs to be lengthened. Finally, showing advancement against a set of milestones demonstrates real progress, which can help you when you need additional funding or buy-in from other groups.

Like good goals, good milestones help motivate people by providing intermediate targets they can aim for. As someone once said, "If not for deadlines, nothing would ever get done." If you are managing a directory design and deployment project, be sure you set achievable milestones and encourage individuals and the team to celebrate when they are reached.

Choosing milestones is often easy after you have picked your goals. The milestones should simply fall out of the goal as a series of tasks that must be accomplished to achieve the goal. For example, some reasonable intermediate milestones for the second sample goal we mentioned earlier (initial directory design completed and published) might include the following:

- Data and schema design completed.

- Namespace design completed.

- Server topology and replication design completed.

- Privacy and security design completed.

- Initial draft of complete design shared with your immediate colleagues to solicit feedback.

Keep in mind that the purpose of milestones is to help motivate you and your team and to mark progress. If creating and tracking a lot of detailed milestones do not fit with your work habits and you feel you can succeed without them, feel free to ignore our advice here. For most people, though, milestones are a useful tool for marking progress as they move through a large project. It is usually rewarding to complete small projects at intervals rather than waiting for the entire, long project to be completed.

Recommendations for Setting Goals and Milestones

We recommend that you select two or three short-term goals (achievable within the next three to six months) and two or three long-term goals for your directory design and deployment effort. Then, for each goal set some intermediate milestones. The milestones can be as frequent as you like, but a good rule of thumb is to create milestones that you will hit every couple weeks.

If you have a team of people working on the directory service, be sure to involve them in the goal- and milestone-setting process and make sure they know what is expected of them individually. People who are involved in setting the goals and milestones will have a better understanding of them—and they'll be more motivated to achieve them.

> **Tip**
>
> Share status information about goals and milestones with all who are involved or interested in your directory service efforts. Actively use the milestones to track progress toward your goals. By advertising exactly what you hope to accomplish and when, you implicitly enlist the aid of others and set reasonable expectations for the directory service deployment process.

Defining Your Directory Needs Checklist

☐ Analyze your environment.

☐ Determine application needs and prioritize them.

☐ Determine user needs and prioritize them.

☐ Determine deployment constraints and prioritize them.

☐ Determine other environmental constraints and prioritize them.

☐ Choose an appropriate directory design and deployment approach.

☐ Set some achievable short- and long-term goals and milestones.

Further Reading

Building an X.500 Directory Service in the US (RFC 1943). B. Jennings, May 1996. Available on the Web at `ftp://ftp.isi.edu/in-notes/rfc1943.txt`.

Netscape Directory Server Deployment Guide. Available from Netscape's Web site at `http://home.netscape.com/eng/server/directory/3.0/deployrtm/contents.html`.

Looking Ahead

In Chapter 6, we will discuss data design for your directory service. We will use the list of directory-enabled applications you made in this chapter to seed the process of determining what data must be stored in your directory service. We will also examine the characteristics of data, relationships between different pieces of data, and sources for data.

CHAPTER 6

Data Design

Because a directory service is (among other things) a specialized database, it should not come as any surprise that some of the most important directory design considerations involve data. It is critical that you put some effort up front into thinking about what kind of information you will store in your directory service and how you will obtain and manage that information. Planning for and maintaining data will probably be the most complex and challenging aspect of deploying your directory service.

In this chapter we first examine the major issues surrounding directory data and describe some common data-related problems that are well worth avoiding. We also explain what a data policy statement is and how to define one that is appropriate for your deployment. Next, we explore some techniques for identifying what data should be stored in your directory service. Then we take a step back and look at some general characteristics of data. Finally, we discuss some potential sources for data and tips for maintaining good relationships with the other data sources that exist within your organization.

Data Design Overview

The term *data* refers to the entire collection of information stored in your directory service. We also use *data* as a general term to refer to information of any kind regardless of where it is stored. Data is what makes a directory service interesting—after all, your directory service is only as useful as the data it holds. Furthermore, the issues surrounding data sometimes evoke strong emotional and political responses because people care about their personal information, their department's information, and the organization's information. In addition, those who write or deploy directory-enabled applications have their own data-related needs. Some of the different needs will inevitably conflict, and so data design is an important and potentially complex area.

A number of other data-related topics are explored in upcoming chapters. For example, when designing a schema (see Chapter 7, "Schema Design"), we use the results obtained in this chapter to choose LDAP object classes and attributes to hold your data. The design of your directory's namespace (see Chapter 8, "Namespace Design") also builds on the material in this chapter as you strive to organize your directory data in a logical structure to optimize administration and operation of the directory service.

In Chapter 5, "Defining Your Directory Needs," we examined directory needs in detail, with a focus on the applications that will use your directory. As already noted, the applications deployed against your directory greatly influence the design and deployment of the entire directory service. Applications are the strongest driving factor in identifying which pieces of data should be stored in your directory and how you should manage them.

We use the term *data element* to refer to the pieces of data and the term *data source* to refer to any system that stores a collection of data elements. Data sources are sometimes called *repositories*. In LDAP terms, data elements correspond closely to *attribute types*. Examples include a person's full name, a printer's paper capacity, or a computer's processor type. Specific instances of data elements are called *data element values,* or just *data values* (for example, the full name "Babs Jensen"). In LDAP terms, data values are called *attribute values.*

Note

In this chapter we use less-specific, non-LDAP terms such as data element so we can direct all of our attention to the issues surrounding the data itself. When we tackle schema design in Chapter 7, we return to using the LDAP terms as we focus on how data elements are mapped specifically onto the LDAP information model.

Within your organization, there are probably many places where data is stored. For example, the personnel or human resources department may manage a data source that includes information about all people at the company who receive a paycheck. The information may be stored on paper in filing cabinets, but it is much more likely to be managed by an accounting system that is a front end to a relational database management system (RDBMS).

Of course, the directory service you are designing is also a data source. Figure 6.1 shows the relationship between data sources, data elements, and data values.

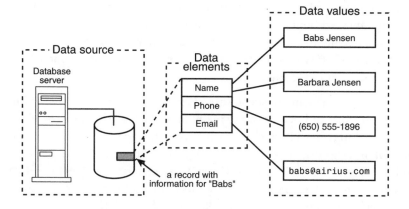

FIGURE 6.1   *Data sources, data elements, and data values.*

One of the important questions you will need to answer is "How does the data stored in the LDAP directory service relate to the data held in the other important data sources within my organization?" To answer that, you will want to learn as much as you can about the other data sources that exist within your organization.

Common Data-Related Problems

Although we live in the information age, it is rare to have the right information available to us at the right time. As individuals we typically are affected by one or more of the following problems:

- *Too much information* (it is hard to find exactly what we are looking for)

- *Not enough information* (the information we need is not available)

- *Poor quality or just plain wrong information* (we may be misled)

- *Out-of-date information* (we may be acting on yesterday's news)

Applications that use your directory service will also suffer from these same problems unless you give careful consideration to which data elements you include in your directory service, where to obtain the data, and how to manage it. For example, applications that rely on the directory as a source of contact information such as phone numbers or email addresses will succeed in their users' eyes only if the information is accurate and up-to-date. The key to understanding and avoiding these data-related problems is to develop a good understanding of how both end users and applications use your directory service.

Another potential problem is especially common within large organizations: data redundancy without coordination. *Data redundancy* refers to multiple copies of data elements and values kept in more than one data source. Problems arise when two or more systems store the same data element but do not coordinate changes to the element.

For example, if your home postal address is stored both in a centralized human resources database and in a database maintained by the corporate travel office, you may need to contact both offices when you change your address. It is not uncommon in large organizations for such personal information to be stored in several uncoordinated data sources. Often, these different sources are difficult and expensive to manage because they all use different computer systems and software packages to manage the same kind of information.

Don't be surprised to find data redundancy problems that do not involve people-related data. For example, within an organization's Information Services division the Networking group and Help Desk group may maintain separate data sources that include information about the computers and other devices connected to the network. The best solution to this problem is to eliminate redundant data sources and synchronize the remaining ones. This challenging task requires good communication and cooperation among all the data owners. This topic is discussed in greater detail later in this chapter in the section "Maintaining Good Relationships with Other Data Sources," and in Chapter 22, "Directory Coexistence."

Creating a Data Policy Statement

Before you begin the somewhat arduous task of identifying and characterizing each of the data elements you plan to store in your directory service, it is important to develop some general guidelines about directory data. These guidelines should be collected in a written data policy statement. The purpose of such a statement is to help everyone who is affected by your directory service to understand in general terms how data will be handled. Because this group includes you, your directory deployment team, data source owners, application authors, and end users, you should widely publish your data policy statement throughout your organization.

Your data policy statement should cover the following topics:

- *Guidelines for determining what data will and will not be stored in your directory service.* For example, your general guideline could be that any data element that is likely to be shared by more than one application will be stored in your directory. You might decide that large values (greater than 10KB) would never be stored in your directory.

- *Guidelines for access to directory data.* This is especially important if you plan to store any sensitive information in your directory service. You should also include general guidelines on the kind of authentication and encryption required when accessing directory data.

- *Guidelines for modification of directory data.* This might include information about whether you expect end users to be allowed to update their own entries, the ability of applications to modify entries, and other "data ownership" issues. You should also include general guidelines on the kind of authentication and encryption required when making changes to directory data.

- *Legal considerations.* There may be certain kinds of information that you simply cannot store in your directory service or give people access to because of privacy laws, employment contracts, or other legal considerations. It is best to involve your organization's legal staff when formulating this aspect of your policy.

- *Guidelines for maintaining data that is stored in more than one location.* Typically, you will have some data elements that are stored in your directory service as well as in one or more data sources that are not part of your main service. A general policy should cover topics such as how to handle data flow between the sources and which source will be authoritative.

- *Guidelines for handling exceptions to your general policies.* Because no policy can cover all possible situations, you should define a simple process for handling exceptions.

Your data policy statement should be a fairly stable document. However, you will inevitably need to evolve your policy as your organization changes, as you learn more about managing your directory service, and when external factors such as privacy laws change.

Because your data policy statement will cover a lot of ground, it is essential that you involve other groups within your organization in the process of creating and reviewing the policy. In many cases the actual data policy will in fact be defined mainly by people outside your directory team. For example, the owners of important data sources and your legal department will undoubtedly have a lot to say about how you should handle data.

Here are some specific groups to enlist when defining your directory data policy:

- Your directory design and deployment team

- People who maintain other important data sources within your organization, (namely, the human resources department)

- Authors and deployers of important directory-enabled applications

- Your legal department

- Upper management, including your chief information officer (CIO) or even the office of your chief executive officer (CEO)

Now that you have a good start on creating a data policy statement, it is time to examine the specific data elements you will store in your directory. Looking at specific examples of data elements will also help you firm up your data policy.

Identifying Which Data Elements You Need

As we saw in Chapter 5, much of the design of your directory service will be driven by the applications that use it. Therefore, the first step in determining which data elements you should include in your directory service is to start with a list of directory-enabled applications that you plan to deploy. We talked about forming just such a list in Chapter 5.

Now you should examine each application to determine what data it has access to in the directory service. In the first pass through the list, just look at each application and list all the data elements each will use. To obtain this information you will either need to become an expert on the application itself or enlist the help of others. For commercial software that supports LDAP, a list of data elements in the form of attributes should be provided somewhere in the documentation. If not, contact the company that produced the software and request the information. For custom applications that are created in-house, a design document should be available that includes the information. As the directory expert you may want to help adjust the design so that the application uses the directory wisely.

Table 6.1 shows some examples of applications and the data elements they might require.

TABLE 6.1 APPLICATIONS AND DATA ELEMENTS

Application	Vendor	Class of Information	Data Elements
Authenticated Web server	Netscape	People	User ID, password
		Groups	Group name, description, list of members, owner
Electronic mail system	Netscape	People	User ID, password,email address, mail host, vacation message, delivery options, forwarding address
		Groups	Group name, description, list of members, owner
Company phone book	Developed in-house	People	Name, email address, phone numbers, user ID, password, mailing address, department, manager, home page URL, license plate number
Organizational chart generation utility	Oblix	People	Manager, employee type, job title
Asset management application	Developed in-house	Computers	Owner, make, model, processor, speed storage capacity, IP address, host name

After you have compiled a list of the data elements used by each application, locate any identical (or nearly identical) data elements used by more than one application. It is almost always better to simplify and use as few data elements as possible. Failure to do this can create data redundancy problems within your directory service itself! For the applications shown in Table 6.1, you can see that several data elements can be shared between the applications. For example, the first three applications require access to a person's user ID and password.

The compilation of all the data elements used by each application can be a large undertaking, but you may be able to use an incremental approach. Try to divert some of the work from this initial directory design stage to future design iterations that will occur after the initial deployment of the service.

Often, one or two applications drive the initial directory service deployment, and it is appropriate to focus only on the needs of those applications. Keep in mind that you will probably need to revisit decisions made now when other directory-enabled applications come online, especially if they use some of the same data elements as the first round of applications. Unlike traditional database management systems, directory services are designed so that it is relatively easy to incrementally add new data elements. However, be careful not to combine data elements that may need to be separated later; it may be hard to determine how to split up any existing data values (for example, reliably extracting a person's surname from their full name).

Try not to let your thinking become too specialized during the data design phase of directory planning. Always consider what will happen if your directory is asked to support new applications. It makes sense to do a significant amount of up-front data planning if one or more of the following apply:

- You are replacing a directory service that is already deployed and in use.

- You plan to serve a wide variety of applications with your directory service (as opposed to a specialized service that is focused on just one or two applications).

- Your organization has a lot of data sources for your service to interact with.

- You need to involve people outside your team in the data design process for political or practical reasons.

In large organizations, it is likely that you will need to involve people from a variety of groups in any directory service design work concerned with data. This is because some of the data elements you want to include in your directory service may already exist in other data sources (e.g., a human resources database). Eventually, you will need to overcome political hurdles and work with the people who manage the other data sources to ensure that your directory service is not viewed as creating more data-related problems than it solves. On a more practical note, if you are not well-versed in data matters yourself, you can probably learn a lot by talking to the experts.

Tip

If you choose your directory data elements without consulting the experts who already manage similar information, you will probably ruffle some feathers. For example, you should consult your personnel or human resources department when choosing data elements for people-related information. Similarly, it may make sense to consult the networking group within your IS department if you plan to store information on switches and routers.

If you do not consult your colleagues, be aware of the potential consequences. In our experience, such decisions can and do come back to haunt you later. If you are having trouble getting cooperation from other groups, make sure you have buy-in from your management, and let everyone know that your directory project is important. If you have support from the top, political barriers should fall more easily!

When you need to get a handle on the data elements already in use, it helps to create a *data sources inventory*. Simply put, this is a list of all the data sources (databases and directories) in use within an organization. It should include a fair amount of detail about the actual database tables in use, including information on each of the fields that appear in each table. Similarly, it should show all the attributes and object classes in use in the directory services. The data sources inventory should also include pointers to supporting documentation, when available, and may also include contact information for those responsible for each database.

Performing a data sources inventory can be costly and time-consuming for large organizations, but it can also be valuable when you are pondering the relationship between the data elements you plan to store in your directory service and those held in other data sources. Table 6.2 shows a sample data sources inventory.

TABLE 6.2 A SAMPLE DATA SOURCES INVENTORY

Data Source	Software/Contact	Class of Information	Data Elements
Human resources database	Peoplesoft `jeffw@hr.airius.com`	People	Name, address, phone, employee number, and so on
Email system	Microsoft Exchange `leif@is.airius.com`	People	Name, user ID, email address, email preferences
		Groups	Group name, list of members
Product development phone list	Excel spreadsheet `johnb@pd.airius.com`	People	Name, email address, phone extension, home phone

In smaller organizations there is invariably less need to involve people from other groups in your directory design. There may not even be any other groups!

After you have completed your data sources inventory, you may find that you have a very long list of data elements. This is not something to be too concerned about—directories are designed to handle many data elements without a lot of overhead. The next step is to look at the characteristics of each data element in more detail.

General Characteristics of Data Elements

All data elements can be described by several general characteristics:

- Format

- Size of data values

- Number of occurrences

- Data ownership

- Consumers

- Dynamic versus static

- Shared versus application-specific

- Relationship with other data elements

You should examine each data element you plan to include in your directory service during this data design phase to determine what characteristics it shares with other data elements. By doing this you will save time during the schema and namespace design stages and avoid deployment problems.

For example, suppose a certain dynamic data element will be rewritten many times, but a second is used by only one application. It may not make sense to include the dynamic data element in the directory service at all because most directory implementations are optimized for read access, and writes are relatively expensive.

Each of the characteristics mentioned in the preceding list is discussed in more detail in the following sections.

Tip

Before you design your directory schema (a topic we will tackle in the next chapter), you should character-ize each element using the guidelines included in the following sections. You should add this information to the list of data elements you created when you examined your applications' needs.

Format

Data elements can be grouped based on the natural format of the information. For example, people's names are always textual data, but telephone numbers consist primarily of digits. Table 6.3 shows some of the more common data formats and provides sample data elements for each.

TABLE 6.3 DATA FORMATS

General Format Elements	Common Variations	Example Data
Text string	Case sensitive, case insensitive	Person's name, printer's name, URL
Multiline text string	Case sensitive, case insensitive	Postal address, description
Phone number	Local, international	Work phone number, fax number
Numeric	Integer, floating point	Employee number, cost
Multimedia	Image, sound, movie	Photograph, musical sample
Binary	(Many variations)	Digital certificate, preferences data

If your textual data is written in more than one character set or language, be sure to note that as well. As we will see in Chapter 7, each LDAP attribute must be mapped to a *syntax* that precisely defines the rules for interpreting the stored values. For example, the cn (common name) attribute is of the syntax caseIgnoreString, which means that the case of letters that make up a name are not significant when comparing one cn value with another.

Size of Data Values

Size refers to the number of characters or bytes that a data element value consumes. Knowing the approximate size of each value will help with the more directory-specific design work that we will tackle in subsequent chapters. Although it is sometimes hard to assign hard limits for the size of a data element, it is usually relatively easy to come up with a range that encompasses the typical data values that will be used. For example, Figure 6.2 shows how the elements of a North American telephone number combine to require approximately 14 characters of storage.

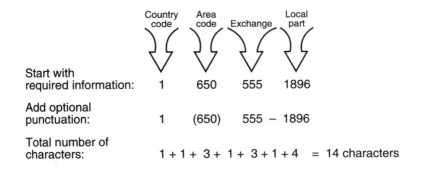

	Country code	Area code	Exchange	Local part
Start with required information:	1	650	555	1896
Add optional punctuation:	1	(650)	555 −	1896
Total number of characters:		1 + 1 + 3 + 1 + 3 + 1 + 4	= 14 characters	

FIGURE 6.2   *Size of a telephone number value.*

At the other end of the scale, if you choose to store images in your directory service, the size of each value will be much larger (perhaps in the 25KB–1MB range). Be sure to check your directory server software to see if it places any arbitrary restrictions on the size of the data values that can be stored.

When considering how large text data values will be, do not forget to take into account the character set if you have any data that is not plain ASCII. In LDAP directories, international data is typically represented using the UTF-8 encoding of the Unicode character set (as explained in Chapter 3, "An Introduction to LDAP"). UTF-8 is a variable-length encoding, and each character in a UTF-8 string requires between 1 and 4 bytes.

Tip

In some cases it makes more sense to store a pointer to a data value in the directory service instead of storing the data value itself. This pointer-based approach is especially useful when the data value is large but related to another data element that you plan to store in your directory.

For example, if you are storing in the directory information about all your department's current projects, you may want to include HTTP URLs that point to the detailed project plans. The project plans themselves should remain on Web servers as they are probably large, complex documents; but users and applications will still be able to locate these documents by consulting the directory service.

Number of Occurrences

For each data element you should answer the question "How many data values will there typically be for this element?" For example, a person will usually have only one user ID but may have several phone numbers. This information will help in directory capacity planning. It may also be useful if you replicate or synchronize with other data stores which may have different characteristics, since it will be important to know if, for example, a data store can only hold one value for a person's name when your directory allows many values.

Data Ownership

Dealing with data ownership issues is one of the more challenging aspects of directory design. When thinking about access control, privacy, and security it is important to know exactly which people and applications should be allowed to view or modify a data element. Data ownership also affects whether you will allow a data element to be changed by directory clients and whether and how a data element is kept in sync with other data sources.

Related questions include "Who should be notified when this data element is modified?" and "If this data element is stored in more than one data source, which system has final authority over the data element?" Unfortunately, the answers to these questions may be muddy and will likely change over time but just make a note of the muddiest areas and move on.

Consumers

The consumers of a data element are those directory-enabled applications that use it. When planning directory replication and topology, and when managing the relationships between your directory service and other data sources, it is helpful to know about the consumers of each data element.

For example, a mail transfer agent (MTA) is a piece of application software whose job is to route electronic mail messages to their correct destinations. When processing email, MTAs may look at an attribute in a user's entry called mailHost, which gives the hostname of the server that holds the user's email. This is depicted in Figure 6.3.

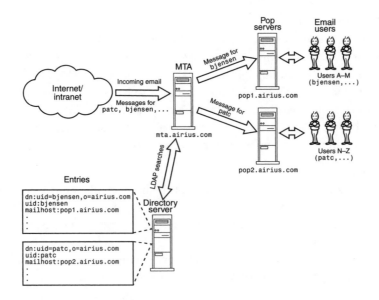

FIGURE 6.3   *An MTA and the* mailHost *attribute.*

The MTA is thus an important consumer of the mailHost attribute, so it may be important that the MTA always gets the most up-to-date copy of the mailHost attribute that is available. Email client software might also use the same mailHost attribute to determine where a user's mail drop is, in which case this becomes a shared attribute.

Similarly, users may be allowed to change their home telephone numbers in the directory service, changes that may be propagated to a personnel system that stores its data in an Oracle database. This scenario is shown in Figure 6.4.

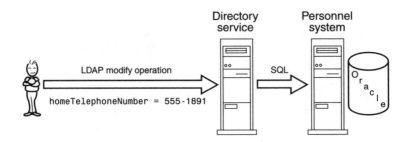

FIGURE 6.4   *Home phone number propagated to personnel database.*

In this scenario the personnel system is a consumer of the home telephone number, but it is also a source for other non-LDAP applications that may access the phone number directly from the personnel system. If the home phone number is not a piece of data critical to the personnel system, it may be okay for information between it and the directory service to be updated fairly infrequently. If the phone number is critical to both the personnel system and the directory service, however, a process that accomplishes frequent synchronization may need to be developed.

If you compile detailed information about all the consumers of a data element, you can aggregate all the information into an estimate of how often a given data element will be accessed. Again, this information is useful when doing capacity planning for your directory service.

Dynamic Versus Static Data Elements

It is also helpful to know which data elements are dynamic (i.e., have values that change) and which are static (i.e., have values that do not change). You will need this information when designing your directory server topology as well as for capacity planning. For example, if you use a replicated directory service that allows writes for a given entry to occur on only one server (a single master system), and you have a lot of attributes whose values change often, you may need to partition your data to avoid overwhelming any one master server with the write traffic.

One way to characterize the dynamic or static nature of attributes is by estimating the ratio of reads-to-writes for each data element. For example, a user ID may be written once when a student joins a university but read dozens of times each day as email is delivered; this attribute is static. In contrast, if a Web browser stores a user's personal bookmarks in the directory service, they may be changed once a day or more often; these attributes are dynamic.

Shared Versus Application-Specific Data Elements

Some data elements are used by many applications; others may be used by only one application. Data elements that are shared require careful planning so that the needs of all the applications are met adequately. On the other hand, if a data element is used by only one application and the data values are large or accessed frequently, you should consider keeping the values outside your directory service to avoid performance problems when accessing the values. You may want to include some guidelines for making this kind of decision in your data policy statement (as discussed earlier in this chapter).

> **Tip**
>
> *One thing to watch out for if you conclude that a data element is application-specific is that, over time, new applications may come online that also use the data element. Because your directory service is a great place to put shared data, when in doubt assume that a data element will be shared.*

Note that even if data elements are not shared by more than one directory-enabled application, it may make sense to store them together to ease manage-ability or improve the availability of the information (through directory replication). For example, it may be desirable to delete a person's email-related data elements when the person is deleted from the corporate phonebook. The easiest approach is to store the email-related elements in the directory service along with all the person's contact and other information. That way, you won't need to delete the information in both the directory and the mail system to delete a user's record.

Relationship with Other Data Elements

When selecting schema and laying out the namespace for your directory service, it is useful to know how your data elements are related. Because directory entries typically represent real-world objects, it is important to know which data elements relate to the same kind of object.

For example, if you have an entry in your directory service for each printer attached to your network, you want to make it easy for an application to find all the printer-related data elements. You can accomplish this by choosing a schema that defines an all-inclusive printer object (see Chapter 7 for more information on schema).

Some relationships between data elements are more subtle and may be easily overlooked. For example, if you will use the directory service to determine who used a printer in the last 24 hours, there is a need to relate information about some users to the printer's entry. This need could be addressed by including in the printer entries a set of data elements that refer to user entries.

A Data Element Characteristics Example

Suppose that we work at a large university with a great variety of installed electronic mail systems. (See Chapter 24, "Case Study: A Large University," for a related example.) Electronic mail is often a major factor affecting the expenditure of information technology dollars, and we would like to show our boss the value of our new directory service.

To do this we decide to develop as our first directory-enabled application a service that reroutes all email entering the university from the Internet to the correct system. The basic setup is shown in Figure 6.5.

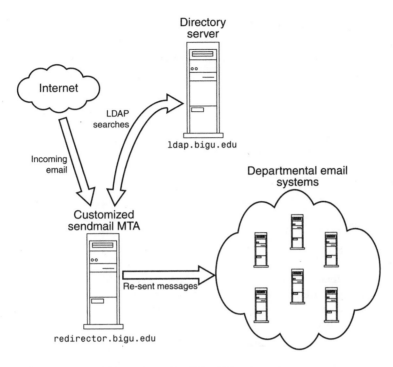

FIGURE 6.5   *The Business Card Email Service.*

By configuring our domain name system correctly, we arrange for all electronic mail messages sent to STRING@bigu.edu to arrive on the machine called redirector.bigu.edu. This machine runs a customized copy of the sendmail software that searches the directory service running on ldap.bigu.edu for a user's entry using criteria constructed from STRING. For example, if a message is addressed to babs.jensen@bigu.edu, a search with an LDAP filter of cn=babs jensen is performed. If an entry is found, the email message is re-sent to the user's mail delivery address, which is typically a mail server in the individual's department or school within the university.

We christen this service the "Business Card Email Service," or *BCES*, because now people can safely put one centrally managed email address on their business card that will not change even if they switch departments within the university.

One of the first design questions we need to answer is "What data elements do we need and what are their essential characteristics?" Table 6.4 provides one potential answer (the real answer depends on what application software we use to develop and deploy our new service).

TABLE 6.4 DATA ELEMENT CHARACTERISTICS EXAMPLE

Element (Example)	Format	Size/ # Values	Owner	Consumers	Related To
Full name (for example, John Jones)	Text	<128 chars./ one or a few values	Personnel Dept.	Users; BCES	User's entry
User ID (login; for example,, jjones)	Text	<8 chars./ one value	IS Dept.	BCES	User's entry
Email Address (jjones@ bigu.edu)	Text (Internet mail address)	Many chars./ one or a few values	IS Dept.	Users; BCES	User's entry
Delivery address (for example, jjones@math. bigu.edu)	Text (Internet mail address)	Many chars./ one value	User and system admins.	BCES	User's entry

Note that some characteristics are missing from Table 6.4. We don't include any information on how dynamic each data element is because we believe all the data elements hold data values that do not change very often. Also, because we are focused on just one application, we have not yet needed to think about which of these data elements will be shared with other directory-enabled applications.

Sources for Data

Now you should have a list of all the data elements you want to include in your directory service. It is time now to take a slightly broader view and determine where you will obtain the values for the data elements and manage the relationships with other data sources.

By now you probably have a pretty good idea what data elements exist in electronic form in the other data sources within your organization. Some data elements are unique to a new application you plan to deploy; thus, the data values themselves may not exist anywhere yet. Figure 6.6 depicts some common data sources.

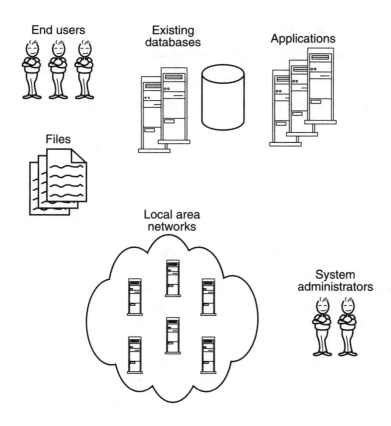

FIGURE 6.6 *Some common data sources.*

The following are common data sources:

- Other directory services

- Network operating systems

- Databases that your organization already has online

- Simple files or spreadsheets that hold data in electronic form

- Applications

- Administrators

- End users

You may need to obtain data from any or all of these sources. For each data element you plan to include in your directory, you should decide the following:

- What data source will be consulted to obtain the initial data values?

- Who will be allowed to access the data element?

- Who will be allowed to modify the data element?

- Will the data element be updated from other data sources on an ongoing basis?

- Will changes made in the directory be propagated back to any other data sources?

The information you have already gathered about each data element should help with these questions. You may not have all the answers when you initially deploy your directory service, but it is important to give some thought to these issues in advance. You do not want your directory service to hold out-of-date information, nor do you want your directory service to be accused of trying to supplant the human resources department's database (unless that is your goal). Some of the common data sources and surrounding issues are discussed in more detail in the following sections.

Tip

When surveying the data sources present in your organization, be sure to ask yourself whether each one will be important a year or two from now. If a system is being decommissioned in the near future, you may not want to invest much effort in studying it (unless of course your directory service is destined to replace it).

Other Directory Services and Network Operating Systems

Your organization may already have a large, central directory service. If not, you probably have departmental LANs that include some kind of network operating system such as Novell NetWare (with data held in the NetWare Bindery or Novell Directory Service servers), Microsoft Windows NT Server (with data held on NT domain controllers), or Sun's Network Information Service (with data held in NIS servers). You probably also have data in domain name system (DNS) servers.

Find out what data is contained in these systems and how it is being used. You should think about whether the LDAP directory service you deploy can take the place of some of these existing directories. You should also consider replicating data between the various systems; this should prevent the problem of having different values for a data element that is duplicated in several systems.

Databases

There are probably several database systems (relational, hierarchical, or other) that hold interesting data in your organization. Examples include human resources or personnel databases, student databases, and databases used to manage network resources. If you have an in-house Private Branch eXchange (PBX) telephone system, its database probably has the most up-to-date telephone number information.

In general, you will view these existing databases as gold mines when populating your directory service with an initial set of data. Do not be surprised if these systems are hard to work with though. Typically, they are expensive to run, difficult to make changes to, and hard to tie into other systems. Some databases may impose unreasonable restrictions on certain data fields, making the databases fairly useless as data sources. For example, a PBX database may be able to store only six characters for a login ID, whereas most other systems allow eight to be used. These kinds of restrictions also make it difficult to propagate information from your LDAP directory back into the database if you ever want to do so.

You will need the cooperation of whoever runs these databases to get the data you are interested in. Thus, you may need to spend time lobbying to convince them that your new directory service is valuable to them and the organization as a whole.

Files

In smaller organizations or within departments, it is common for a secretary to maintain a complete phone list in a simple file or spreadsheet. If the information is maintained at the department level, it can be a good source for the most up-to-date contact information on people. Of course, the data may not be in a form that is easily pulled into a structured data system such as an LDAP-based directory service. However, you should investigate these file-based data sources anyway in case they prove useful.

Applications

Many network or collaborative applications have a built-in database or directory that stores information about users of the application and other objects the application needs to know about. These application-specific directories tend to be proprietary, closed systems that may not even provide APIs for accessing the data. Examples include electronic mail systems that are not LDAP-aware, Web servers, and electronic calendar systems.

One of the most important reasons to invest in a directory service based on LDAP is to replace many of these application-specific directories, or at least to coexist with them. You need to develop a coexistence strategy or actively manage a transition to the replacement service (this may be a lengthy strategy). The existing directories are the best source for the application-specific data elements you plan to store in your directory service, so try to work *with* them and not around them.

Administrators

A lot of interesting data is managed by the administrators who are charged with caring for the computer systems, networks, and telephone systems within an organization. If the data these administrators manage is not available in electronic form or another manageable format, you will still want to directly enlist the aid of these administrators in setting up and maintaining the data held in your directory service.

End Users

Last, but certainly not least, end users are often the best source of data about themselves. This is especially true with personal contact information (such as home telephone numbers and addresses) and preferences.

Because you probably do not have time to ask each person for information, you should provide an easy-to-use interface to your directory service so that individuals can update their own information. Some data elements come from other databases or are maintained by administrators or applications, so be prepared to explain to end users why they can't change those data elements themselves. It is a good idea to publish information about the origin and owner of each data element held in your directory service. This is usually covered in your data policy statement (as discussed earlier in this chapter).

Maintaining Good Relationships with Other Data Sources

It is important to put some thought into how the data held in your directory service relates to that stored in other data sources within your organization. Many organizations today suffer from data redundancy problems in which data elements are stored in multiple, uncoordinated databases and directory systems.

Most people encounter this problem on a personal level when they move and want to notify their company or school of their new home address. Often, there are four or five (or more) places where you must submit the new information so it reaches all the systems that have their own copy of your home address. Your directory service could help solve this problem, and you should certainly strive to avoid making the problem worse!

In the following sections we provide an overview of some techniques you can use to make your directory service a success in an environment where there are multiple data sources that hold the same data elements. Chapter 22 includes a more extensive discussion on integrating with other data sources.

Replication

If you are working with directory products that come from the same vendor or use the same protocols for replication, you should be able to use the built-in replication features to maintain consistent values for data elements across many servers. There is also third-party software that attempts to provide replication.

Replication has many potential benefits, including the possibility of spreading your directory application load across many servers, providing for redundancy in the face of server failures, and so on. See Chapter 10, "Replication Design," for more information on replication design considerations.

Synchronization

Synchronization is a process in which changes made in one system are propagated to another. It differs from replication in that the protocols, schema, and data formats may vary widely between the data sources involved. Synchronization is typically done fairly frequently (every hour, day, or week), but consistency of the data is usually not as tight as with replication. Synchronization can be performed in one or both directions and between two or more data sources.

For example, if employee name changes are always handled by the human resources department, it may be appropriate to propagate those changes to your directory service—a one-way synchronization. If you allow telephone numbers to be changed both in the human resources database and in your directory service, you may want to set up two-way synchronization between the systems. If two-way synchronization is used, you will need to carefully consider what the outcome is if the same data element is changed in two different systems.

Synchronization tools are available from a variety of vendors, either bundled with their directory products or as standalone tools. For example, the Netscape Directory Server package includes a Windows NT Synchronization Service that provides two-way synchronization between Windows NT domain controllers and the Netscape Directory Server. As LDAP directory service products mature, you can expect more synchronization tools to become available from the major vendors because nearly all customers are asking for them.

Good synchronization tools allow you to hook into the synchronization process and cause other things to occur as a result of changes to data. For example, when a person is added to a human resources database, an entry might be created in your central directory service. This same event could also be used to trigger actions outside of your directory service, such as creating operating system accounts or granting access to network devices such as printers and file servers.

If you do set up synchronization between data sources, be prepared for some bumps along the way. Often, a lot of tuning and some in-house development are needed to smooth over the differences between the data sources. In many cases the synchronization software is produced by one vendor, the directory software by another, and database software used by other data sources comes by yet another vendor. Clearly there is some system integration work to be done, but synchronization can be a good solution whenever you overcome these issues.

Batch Updates

Batch updates are really a kind of "loosely coupled" synchronization. Typically, these are done less often (for example, once a month) and may involve the merging of data that comes from radically different sources. With very few exceptions, today the data merging process must be developed in-house. This can be an expensive prospect because it usually takes several iterations working with real data before all the bugs are worked out.

When the authors were at the University of Michigan, a complicated C language program called munge was developed to merge data from the human resources database, student database, and a central directory service (see Chapter 24 for more information). The actual "munging" was done once or twice a month and usually took about a day. During that time no modifications could be made to the data held in the directory service, and a system administrator typically had to keep a close eye on the munge process. If anything went wrong during the data merging process, the poor system administrator had to fix the data by hand or restart the entire munge process. This invariably created some very grumpy system administrators.

Political Considerations

As the new kid on the block, your directory service may be viewed by your colleagues as something that creates more work for them rather than as the liberating tool it can become. This attitude is especially common in large organizations in which the keepers of data sources have limited resources, are focused on their own problems, or are just set in their ways.

Hopefully, this is not the situation with your own organization, but if it is the best solution is to convince your peers who maintain other important data sources that your directory service will help them in some way. This is obviously more difficult than it sounds, but it is well worth spending some energy on. For example, if by working together you can eliminate four or five redundant "change of address" forms and replace the entire collection with a single electronic form, you will all be recognized as heroes.

It is also a good idea to make sure that the top people within your organization are aware of your directory project and 100% behind it. Gaining the support of your CEO or CIO will often spur other people to action, or at least break down political barriers that prevent you from making progress. The best way to get buy-in from decision makers is to put on your sales and marketing hat and produce a short document that lists the key benefits your service will provide. Share the document with the people you aim to convince and then arrange to meet with them to ensure that all their questions are answered and that they are behind the project.

If you are one of the people who manage non-LDAP directories or databases, you have our congratulations; you have already proven yourself to be a forward-thinking individual by reading this book. Please try to be helpful and friendly to the person who is trying to design and deploy the LDAP directory service (if you are not lucky enough to also own that task).

Data Design Checklist

- ☐ Develop an understanding of what applications will use your directory initially and in the future.

- ☐ Create a data policy statement.

- ☐ Create a list of the data elements needed by each directory-enabled application.

- ☐ Examine the application-specific lists to locate overlap among data elements.

- ☐ Characterize each data element by:
    - ☐ Format
    - ☐ Size of values
    - ☐ Number of occurrences
    - ☐ Data ownership

□ Consumers
□ Dynamic or static?
□ Shared or application-specific?
□ Relationship with other data elements

□ Create a data source inventory for your entire organization.

□ Create a plan for managing the relationship between data sources.

Further Reading

Netscape Directory Server Deployment Guide: Chapter 3, "Planning Your Directory Data." Available from Netscape's World Wide Web site at
`http://home.netscape.com/eng/server/directory/3.0/deployrtm/contents.html`.

Looking Ahead

The first few chapters have covered the directory design process, helping you define your directory-related needs and identifying issues surrounding the data to be stored. In the next few chapters we will begin to look at topics more specific to the design of LDAP directories. First up: directory schema design, a topic closely related to the material we covered in this chapter.

CHAPTER 7

Schema Design

If you have some background in database systems, you are already familiar with the concept of a schema. Simply put, a schema is a set of rules that determines what data can be stored in a database or directory service. Schemas are important because they help maintain the integrity and quality of the data stored in a directory service. Schemas also help reduce duplication of data and provide a well-documented, predictable way for directory-enabled applications to access and modify the collection of directory objects.

In this chapter you will learn what role schemas play, why they are important, how to locate predefined schema elements, and how to design your own custom schema. First we discuss the purpose of a schema, and then we provide a detailed description of the elements comprising LDAP schemas. Then we illustrate several formats commonly used to describe schemas, and we explain the process servers go through to check directory entries against the schema rules. In the second part of the chapter, we describe a schema design process you should follow for your directory service. We cover locating and selecting predefined schemas, designing and documenting your schema, and planning for schema maintenance and evolution.

The Purpose of a Schema

A *directory schema* is a set of rules that determines what can be stored in a directory service and how directory servers and clients should treat information during directory operations such as a search. Before a directory server stores a new or modified entry, it checks the entry's contents against the schema rules. Whenever directory clients or servers compare two attribute values, they consult the schema to determine what comparison algorithm to use.

Chapter 6, "Data Design," covers the importance of combining redundant data elements (i.e., those needed by more than one application) into as few data elements as possible. One of the main purposes for a schema is to ensure that poorly behaved applications or directory interfaces play by the rules and do not store redundant data in the directory service. Imagine the consequences if every directory-enabled application stored a person's name in a different directory attribute. This would result in wasted storage space and values that should be the same but are different—and it would ultimately lead to a lot of confusion on the part of applications and end users.

Schemas can also be used to impose constraints on the size, range, and format of data values stored in the directory. For example, according to the Internet mail standards, email address values should use a restricted set of characters and should conform to a specific format (`addr@domain`). In many cases schema rules impose simple restrictions such as "this value must be an integer." Ensuring that the data values in the directory service conform to a collection of simple rules increases the quality of the data.

Finally, directory schemas can help slow the effects of directory entropy. Although they are not a substitute for appropriate access control rules (as described in Chapter 11, "Privacy and Security Design"), schema rules do help a bit in preventing chaos within your directory service.

Suppose you allow end users to modify directory entries, but there is no schema enforcement; you should not be surprised when your directory servers become overburdened with a lot of information that does not belong there. Some users will store a lot of information that is of interest to only themselves, some will store very large values, and others may be silly or even malicious. For example, somebody might try to use an LDAP-based directory as a file system backup service for their PC, although most people would agree that this is inappropriate and should be discouraged!

Tip

If you have a lot of experience with traditional databases, you probably can't imagine a data store that does not impose schema rules. However, keep in mind that many of the users of your directory service may be novices without any directory service, database, or schema experience. Part of your job as the directory architect is to educate your users and developers and help them understand that schemas improve the directory service by increasing its reliability and the quality of the data.

Elements of LDAP Schemas

In LDAP-based directories, a schema consists of attribute types, attribute syntaxes, and object classes. These terms were introduced in Chapter 3, "An Introduction to LDAP," when we described the LDAP information model, but they are described in greater detail here.

Attributes

Recall that directory entries contain a collection of attribute types and values. *Attribute types* (or simply *attributes*) hold specific data elements such as a name, business phone number, or printer's rated speed in pages per minute. In LDAP, the definition of an attribute type includes the following:

- A name that uniquely identifies the attribute type

- An object identifier (OID) that also uniquely identifies the attribute

- An indication of whether the attribute is multivalued or single-valued

- An associated attribute syntax and set of matching rules

- A usage indicator (for applications or for operation of the directory service itself)

- Restrictions on the range or size of the values that may be stored in the attribute

Attribute names are usually fairly short and somewhat cryptic, although they do not have to be. Attribute names have the following properties:

- Attribute names are not case sensitive; that is, `cn` and `CN` both refer to the same attribute.

- Characters used within attribute names are limited to ASCII letters and the hyphen character. Attribute names must begin with a letter.

- An attribute name must be unique across your entire directory service because LDAP applications generally refer to an attribute using its name.

Examples of valid attribute names include `cn`, `telephoneNumber`, `postalAddress`, `one-way`, and `pagesPerMinute`. Some examples of invalid attribute names are `last#`, `2for2`, `my.boss`, and `favorite_drink`.

Some standard attributes have historically been known by both a longer name and a shorter name (e.g., commonName and cn), but in most cases the shorter name is the standard that LDAP clients and servers use. Confusion about which attribute name to use caused LDAP client and server interoperability problems in the past. Some implementations such as the Netscape Directory Server support longer names as aliases or synonyms for the shorter, standard names to increase compatibility with older LDAP applications.

An attribute's OID is a unique numerical identifier usually written as a sequence of integers separated by dots. For example, the OID for the postalAddress attribute is 2.5.4.16. OIDs are required by X.500 directory implementations because they are used within the X.500 family of protocols to identify attribute types. Although LDAP clients and servers can use OIDs in place of attribute names, names are almost always used in practice because they are much easier to work with than OIDs.

In an entry stored in a directory server database, attributes have one or more *attribute values* associated with them. These values correspond to the data element values discussed in Chapter 6. The attribute type provides the semantic meaning for a set of values. For example, the value 12 by itself is not very meaningful; but if you know that it is a value for the pagesPerMinute attribute, you can begin to imagine several uses for the value. The definition of the attribute type includes an indication of whether the type is allowed to hold only one value (single-valued) or several values (multivalued). Most attribute types are multivalued, which is the default.

The *attribute usage indicator* is usually omitted from the definition of an attribute type because it defaults to user applications, which means that the attribute is of general purpose and can be used by any directory application. The other type of usage is operational (note that X.500 systems actually support several subcategories of operational usage). *Operational attributes* are used by the directory service itself for administrative or system-related purposes, and they are usually maintained by the directory servers themselves. These attributes are not visible to directory clients unless specifically asked for, and they often cannot be modified by a client.

Some examples of operational attributes are shown in Table 7.1.

TABLE 7.1 EXAMPLES OF OPERATIONAL ATTRIBUTES

Attribute Name	Where Found	Description
modifyTimeStamp	Any entry	Date/time an entry was last modified
modifiersName	Any entry	Name (DN) of the entry that made the last modification
namingContexts	LDAPv3 root DSE	Partitions of the directory held in a server
supportedLDAPVersion	LDAPv3 root DSE	Versions of the LDAP protocol supported by server
aci	Any entry	Access control information (Netscape-specific)

Operational attributes are not returned when a directory client asks for all attributes, but clients can retrieve them by explicitly asking for them by name.

An Attribute Type Example

People generally like names and are pretty good at remembering them. Almost all real-world objects have a name of some kind, and we have already mentioned the cn (common name) attribute several times. Sometimes, though, it is helpful to associate longer text with an LDAP entry that describes the entry in more detail. LDAP defines a handy attribute called description for just that purpose. Its definition is shown in Listing 7.1.

LISTING 7.1 THE DEFINITION OF THE description ATTRIBUTE

```
description ATTRIBUTE ::= {
    WITH SYNTAX                 DirectoryString {1024}
    EQUALITY MATCHING RULE      caseIgnoreMatch
    SUBSTRINGS MATCHING RULE    caseIgnoreSubstringsMatch
    ID 2.5.4.13 }
```

We will explain this format in more detail later in this chapter when we talk about using ASN.1 to describe schemas. Translated to English, this definition says that the attribute named description is a string that can hold up to 1024 characters. This attribute type uses the case-ignore family of matching rules; therefore, the case of letters and leading and trailing space characters are ignored when comparing values. Its OID is 2.5.4.13, a sequence assigned by the X.500 standards committee.

Attribute Hierarchies

Some LDAP implementations, notably those closely aligned with the most recent X.500 standards, support *attribute subtypes*. Subtypes are used to define attribute hierarchies in which general attribute types can be used to construct more-specific types. For example, X.500 defines the cn attribute as a subtype of an attribute called name. Similarly, the sn (surname) attribute is also a subtype of name. The attribute called name is said to be the *supertype* of cn, and cn is said to be *derived from* name.

Attribute subtypes inherit the characteristics of their supertype. In addition, a supertype can be used to simplify searches and retrieval of attributes derived from it. For example, because both the cn and sn attributes are subtypes of the attribute name, a search request that asks for all values for the name attribute type will actually get back all values for name, cn, sn, and any other subtypes of name. Figure 7.1 shows a portion of the attribute hierarchy for the name attribute type.

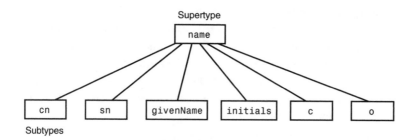

FIGURE 7.1   *The attribute hierarchy for the* name *attribute type.*

Note that several other attribute types not shown in Figure 7.1 are also subtypes of name (it is a very popular supertype!).

Attribute subtypes are an interesting but potentially confusing feature. Most LDAP implementations do not even support attribute subtypes. Even if you like the idea of subtypes, think twice before you design a schema that relies on them.

Attribute Syntaxes and Matching Rules

As mentioned earlier, each attribute type has an associated *attribute syntax* that specifies exactly how data values are represented and how comparisons between values are made. Although in LDAP most data values are carried as text strings (unlike in X.500's DAP), there may be additional structure rules for the string. For example, the pieces of information in a postal mailing address are separated by dollar sign characters in LDAP.

Another piece of the puzzle is that special rules must be used when comparing the values of different attribute types. For example, when comparing filenames on a UNIX system, the case of the letters must be taken into account; however, on a Microsoft Windows system filenames aren't case sensitive (Windows would match WINDOWS).

The rules used for making attribute value comparisons are called *matching rules*. Recent revisions of the X.500 standard separate the attribute syntax from the matching rules associated with an attribute type, but many directory service implementations still use the term *syntax* to refer to both the data representation itself and the matching rules. Also note that most directory server implementations support only a predetermined set of syntaxes and matching rules. Adding support for new attribute syntaxes and matching rules usually requires code to be written, or it may be impossible to do at all.

Object Classes

In LDAP, *object classes* are used to group related information. Typically, an object class models some real-world object such as a person, printer, or network device (although this is not required). Each directory entry belongs to one or more object classes. The names of the object classes to which an entry belongs are always listed as values for a special multivalued attribute called objectclass. The set of object classes associated with an entry serves the following needs:

- Determines which attribute types *must* be included in the entry

- Determines which attribute types *may* be included in the entry

- Provides a convenient way for directory clients to retrieve a subset of entries during search operations

For example, an object class designed to hold information about people might require that a name be present and allow a number of specific optional attributes to be included to hold personal and contact information about a person. If the object class is called person, a directory client could provide a way to search for only people entries by adding a component such as objectclass=person to the LDAP search filter it constructs.

The definition of an LDAP object class includes all the following pieces of information:

- A name that uniquely identifies the class

- An OID that also uniquely identifies the class

- A set of mandatory attribute types

- A set of allowed attribute types

- A kind (structural, auxiliary, or abstract)

The *name* of an object class is usually mnemonic and easily understood by humans, but good directory clients try to hide these names from end users. A name is the most common way for humans, clients, and servers to refer to the object class. As for attribute types, both the name and OID must be unique throughout your entire directory service. Some examples of object class names include `person`, `printer`, `groupOfNames`, and `applicationEntity`.

The set of *mandatory* (required) attribute types is usually fairly short or even empty. The set of *allowed* (optional) attribute types is often quite long. It is the job of each directory server to enforce attribute type restrictions of an object class when an entry is added to the directory or modified in any way. The one exception is that read-only directory replicas do not need to check for schema violations—they can simply rely on the writable server that supplies them to do the checking.

The *kind* of object class indicates how the class is used. *Structural classes*, for example, describe the basic aspects of an object. In some directory server implementations, structural classes can be used to place restrictions on where an entry can be stored within the directory information tree (DIT). Most object classes are structural classes, and all entries should belong to exactly one structural object class. Examples of structural object classes include `person` and `groupOfNames`.

Auxiliary classes do not place any restrictions on where an entry may be stored, and they are used to add a set of related attributes to an entry that already belongs to a structural class. As many auxiliary classes as desired can be "mixed in" to an entry; thus, auxiliary classes are sometimes called *mix-in classes*. Examples include `simpleSecurityObject`, `mailRecipient`, and `cacheObject`.

Abstract classes, the third and last kind of object class, are rare and are used only for classes needed to support LDAP's basic information model. Two examples of abstract classes are `top` (discussed later in this chapter in the section called "Object Class Inheritance") and `alias` (which is used to create entry aliases, as described in Chapter 3).

Many LDAP directory server implementations, including Netscape Directory Server, do not rigidly enforce restrictions based on the kind of object classes used in a schema (e.g., they do not prevent you from creating an entry with two structural classes). However, the distinctions implied by the different kinds of classes are useful when designing your own schema.

An Object Class Example

One of the most common uses for a directory system is to store information about people. To model this real-world object, we might define an object class called person. The information about people that is typically stored in a directory service includes name, contact information, department, job title or position, and any information needed to support software applications. For each piece of information we would define an attribute type. For naming entries and to help directory clients, we may want to require that all person entries include a name. Other attributes would be allowed in an entry but optional.

Not surprisingly, the X.500 designers had a lot of these same thoughts and defined a standard person object class that was adopted by the LDAP designers as well. It is shown in Figure 7.2.

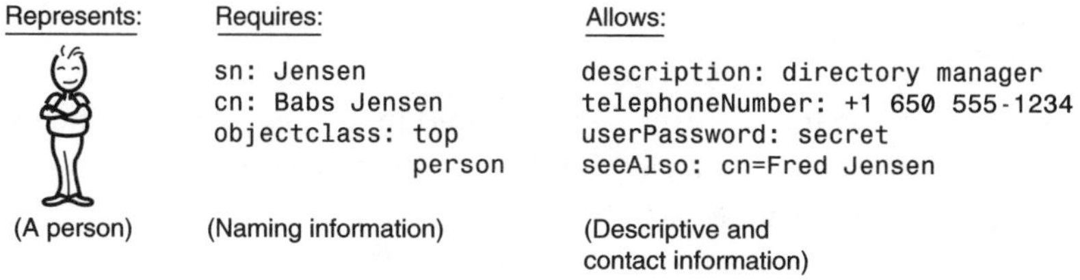

Represents: Requires: Allows:

```
                         sn: Jensen                     description: directory manager
                         cn: Babs Jensen                telephoneNumber: +1 650 555-1234
                         objectclass: top               userPassword: secret
                                      person            seeAlso: cn=Fred Jensen
```

(A person)   (Naming information)   (Descriptive and
                                                        contact information)

FIGURE 7.2   *The standard LDAP* person *object class.*

The person class is a structural object class used for entries that represent people. Some name-related attributes are mandatory, and all others are optional.

The Presence of Multiple-Object Classes

There is no limit to the number of different object classes a single entry can belong to as long as only one of the classes is a structural class. If an entry belongs to more than one object class, the set of attributes allowed in the entry is determined by simply computing the union or aggregate of the attributes listed in all the object classes. Similarly, the set of mandatory attributes is the union of all of the required attributes listed in all the object classes. This means that if an attribute is required in one of the object classes that an entry belongs to, it is required in the entry. Note that because the entire attribute namespace is flat, LDAP avoids some of the problems of multiple inheritance that plague other systems.

For example, suppose the printer and networkDevice object classes are defined as shown in Listing 7.2 (using the simple slapd.conf schema format that is described in more detail later).

LISTING 7.2 `printer` **AND** `networkdevice` **OBJECT CLASSES**

```
objectclass printer
    requires cn
    allows    description, pagesPerMinute, languages
objectclass networkDevice
    requires ipaddress
    allows    cn, connectionSpeed
```

Given these definitions, the following attributes must be present in any entry that belongs to both classes:

```
cn
ipaddress
```

The following attributes are optional:

```
connectionSpeed
description
languages
pagesPerMinute
```

Notice that because the `cn` attribute is required in the `printer` class, a `cn` value must always be present in entries that belong to both classes (even though it is merely optional in the `networkDevice` class).

Tip

Even if an attribute type is listed in more than one object class, an entry that belongs to both classes still has only one instance of that attribute type. That is, the attribute type space is flat and unrelated to the way in which attributes are assigned to object classes. In the printer example in Listing 7.2, it is impossible to distinguish between the cn attribute included in the `printer` *class and the cn attribute included in the* `networkDevice` *class. They are the same attribute, and there is only one set of cn values in an entry that belongs to both object classes.*

Object Class Inheritance

One object class can be derived from another, in which case it inherits some of the characteristics of the other class. This is sometimes called *subclassing,* or *object class inheritance.* An example of this is shown in Figure 7.3.

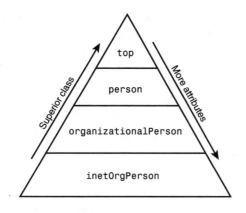

FIGURE 7.3   *Object class inheritance.*

The inetOrgPerson object class defined by the directory designers at Netscape is also supported by some other implementations. It extends the person class and includes additional attribute types to store data elements commonly used on the Internet and within organizations. It is actually derived from an intermediate class called organizationalPerson, which is derived from the person class. Therefore, inetOrgPerson entries require all the attributes required of organizationalPerson entries (and, therefore, of person entries as well). Similarly, inetOrgPerson entries are allowed to include any of the optional attributes from the superior classes.

In general, the class that another class inherits some of its characteristics from is called the *superior class,* or *superclass* (i.e., organizationalPerson is the superior class of inetOrgPerson). When one class is derived from another, it inherits the set of required attribute types, the set of optional attribute types, and the kind of object class from its superior.

There is one special abstract object class called top, from which all structural object classes are ultimately derived. The definition of the top class consists of a single mandatory attribute called objectclass, which ensures that all LDAP entries contain at least one value for objectclass.

Be careful when comparing LDAP's object class inheritance with the more sophisticated class inheritance supported by many object-oriented programming languages. For example, LDAP implementations do not support multiple inheritance, in which a single object class is derived from two or more superior classes. However, as we have seen, LDAP does support aggregation because an entry can be a member of more than one object class. Also, there is no way to "override" any of the schema rules defined by the superior class. For example, if the superior class requires that the cn attribute be present, then it must always be present in all subclasses.

The LDAPv3 extensibleObject Object Class

LDAP version 3 defines a special object class called extensibleObject that is supported by all compliant implementations. This object class allows an open-ended set of attribute types—that is, any valid attribute is allowed in extensibleObject entries.

In general, this class is rarely used for the same reasons that most administrators do not entirely disable schema checking: It may give users and applications too much freedom to store unstructured data in the directory. This class can be useful when you want to create entries that are largely free from schema constraints, especially if it is used by only a small set of applications that you control.

Schema Element Summary

In summary, LDAP schemas are made up of attribute types, each of which has a syntax and a set of matching rules. Attributes are used to hold specific kinds of data, and they are grouped into logical units through the definition of object classes. It is the job of each directory server to enforce the restrictions imposed by the schemas when entries are created or modified. Figure 7.4 shows all the elements of LDAP schemas and how they relate to one another.

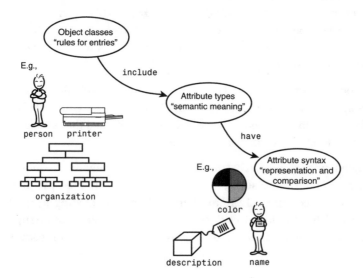

FIGURE 7.4   *Directory schema elements.*

> **Tip**
>
> *The schemas used by a directory service typically include dozens of object classes and hundreds of attribute types. Thankfully, the number of attribute syntaxes is usually small (a dozen or fewer), and the actual number of widely used object classes is also quite limited. Do not be overwhelmed by the number of available schemas. Focus on your needs and use an incremental approach as you select schema elements for your service.*

Directory Schema Formats

When reading vendor documentation or standards documents, or when working with directory service software, you will encounter several different formats that are used to describe a directory schema. It is useful to be able to read and understand all the popular schema formats. You will use this knowledge to choose a format to use when documenting the schemas for your directory service deployment. Three popular schema definition formats are described in this section.

The first schema format we describe, slapd.conf, is the one used throughout this book. The other two formats we describe (the ASN.1 and LDAPv3 formats) are included to help you read schema documentation that comes from other sources. You can safely skip over the description of the latter two formats if you want to move more quickly to the important task of designing schemas for your directory service.

The slapd.conf Schema Format

The schema format used in Netscape Directory Server's configuration files is based on the format used by the original University of Michigan Standalone LDAP server (`slapd`). We refer to this simple but widely used format as the *slapd.conf schema format* because `slapd.conf` is the traditional name for U-M's and Netscape's primary directory server configuration file. The format we describe here, the one supported by Netscape Directory Server 3.0 and 4.0, differs slightly from the format in the U-M LDAP 3.3 `slapd` release.

The slapd.conf schema format is based on two simple configuration file directives—one for defining attribute types and one for defining object classes. These are described in the following sections.

`slapd.conf` Attribute Type Definitions

Each attribute type is defined using a line in the following form (all the items enclosed in square brackets are optional):

```
attribute NAME [ALIASES] [OID] SYNTAXID [OPTIONS]
```

NAME is the attribute type name (e.g., cn); *ALIASES* is an optional space-separated list of alternative names for the attribute (e.g., commonName); *OID* is the object identifier for the attribute; and *SYNTAXID* is a short string that identifies a syntax and the associated matching rules that the directory server implementation supports.

OPTIONS is a space-separated list of one or more of these options: operational and single. The operational option indicates that the attribute is used by the directory service itself in a special way. The single option limits to one the number of attribute values that may be stored.

Note that the concept of aliases for attribute names is somewhat unique to the U-M and Netscape implementations and is included only for compatibility with directory clients that use longer names for attribute types. The six standard syntaxes supported by Netscape Directory Server 4.0 are shown in Table 7.2.

TABLE 7.2 STANDARD SYNTAXES SUPPORTED BY THE NETSCAPE DIRECTORY SERVER 4.0

slapd.conf Syntax ID	X.500 Equivalent	Description
cis	DirectoryString; caseIgnoreMatch	Text string; case of letters and leading, trailing, and multiple spaces are ignored during comparisons.
ces	DirectoryString; caseExactMatch	Text string; case of letter is significant during comparisons; leading, trailing, and multiple spaces are ignored.
tel	PrintableString; telephoneNumberMatch	Text string that represents a phone number; like cis except space and hyphen characters are also ignored during comparisons.

slapd.conf Syntax ID	X.500 Equivalent	Description
int	Integer; integerMatch	Integer numbers; comparisons follow rules for comparing integers.
dn	DistinguishedName; distinguishedNameMatch	Directory names (a pointer to another entry); comparisons follow special rules for comparing distinguished names (DNs).
bin	OctetString; octetStringMatch	Arbitrary binary data; byte-by-byte comparisons.

Note that the Netscape Directory Server software allows additional syntaxes to be defined through the use of software plug-ins.

The following are a few examples of `slapd.conf`-style attribute type definitions:

```
attribute cn commonName 2.5.4.3 cis
attribute labeledURI 1.3.6.1.4.1.250.1.57 ces
attribute seeAlso 2.5.4.34 dn
attribute supportedLDAPVersion 1.3.6.1.4.1.1466.101.120.15 int
attribute ntUserHomeDir 1.2.840.113556.1.4.44 cis single
attribute passwordExpirationTime 2.16.840.1.113730.3.1.91 cis operational
```

slapd.conf Object Class Definitions

Each object class is defined using a line in the following form (all the items enclosed in square brackets are optional):

```
objectclass NAME [oid OID] [superior SUP] [requires REQATTRS]
➡[allows ALLOWATTRS]
```

NAME is the object class name, OID is the object identifier for the class, SUP is the class's superior or parent class, REQATTRS is a comma-separated list of required attribute types, and ALLOWATTRS is a comma-separated list of attribute types that are allowed to be included in entries that belong to the class. The order in which the attributes are listed following the requires and allows keywords is not significant.

Any attribute types used in the *REQATTRS* or *ALLOWATTRS* lists must be defined using `attribute` lines that precede the `objectclass` line. Note that if the first character on a slapd.conf line is a space character, it is logically considered part of the previous line. This feature is used to write object class definitions as a series of physical lines because the list of allowed attributes tends to make it quite long.

Listing 7.3 shows an example of a fairly simple slapd.conf-style object class definition.

LISTING 7.3 THE country OBJECT CLASS IN SLAPD.CONF FORMAT

```
objectclass country
  oid 2.5.6.2
  superior top
  requires
    c
  allows
    searchGuide,
    description
```

This is the definition for the standard country object class. It is derived from top, requires the c (country) attribute be included in all entries of the country class, and allows a searchGuide and a description to optionally be included. Remember that attributes may be used in many object classes. For example, the c attribute used here could also be included in an object class that describes a person.

Although the slapd.conf schema format has the slight disadvantage that it is tied to a specific family of directory server software products (i.e., those derived from the U-M LDAP software), it is simple, easy to understand, and easy to use for writing your own schema definitions.

The ASN.1 Schema Format

Some of the LDAP and X.500 standards documents use Abstract Syntax Notation One (ASN.1) to document the schema they use, the elements of their protocols, and many other details. Although a complete discussion of ASN.1 is beyond the scope of this book, it is useful to learn to read and understand ASN.1-based schema definitions. If you are not interested in understanding ASN.1-based schema definitions, feel free to skip this entire section. You can always come back and read the material here if you run into ASN.1 when you are searching for schema elements to use for your own directory service.

At its most basic level, ASN.1 is a language that can be used to describe abstract types and values. Like most declarative programming languages, ASN.1 defines a series of simple types and allows them to be combined in various ways to build more-complex descriptions. An ASN.1 definition, described in the next section, generally consists of a number of interrelated definitions called *ASN.1 macros*.

ASN.1 Attribute Type Definitions

ASN.1 attribute type definitions are generally of the form shown in Listing 7.4 (all the items enclosed in square brackets are optional).

LISTING 7.4 THE GENERAL FORM OF AN ATTRIBUTE TYPE DEFINITION IN ASN.1

```
ATNAME ATTRIBUTE ::= {
    WITH SYNTAX SYNTAXNAME { BOUNDS }
    EQUALITY MATCHING RULE EQMATCHINGRULE
    [ ORDERING MATCHING RULE ORDMATCHINGRULE ]
    [ SUBSTRINGS MATCHING RULE SUBMATCHINGRULE ]
    [ SINGLEVALUED ]
    ID OID }
```

ATNAME is the attribute type name, *SYNTAXNAME* identifies the attribute syntax, *EQMATCHINGRULE* identifies the rules that are used when testing two attribute values for equality, *ORDMATCHINGRULE* identifies the rules that are used when performing less-than-or-equal and greater-than-or-equal comparisons between values, *SUBMATCHINGRULE* identifies the rules that are used when matching substrings to values, and *OID* is the object identifier for the attribute type.

Typically, *SYNTAXNAME* and all the matching rule identifiers refer recursively to other ASN.1 macros. In most ASN.1 macros the case of the letters used is not significant; upper- and lowercase letters may be used interchangeably. The following is a simple example:

```
name ATTRIBUTE      ::= {
    WITH SYNTAX DirectoryString { ub-name }
    EQUALITY MATCHING RULE caseIgnoreMatch
    SUBSTRINGS MATCHING RULE caseIgnoreSubstringsMatch
    ID id-at-name }
```

This is the definition of the `name` attribute, which is really a supertype from which other naming attributes are derived. It has the syntax `DirectoryString`, which is one of the standard syntaxes LDAP uses. The `ub-name` following the syntax identifier, which probably stands for "upper bound on name," is a limit on the size of the values for this attribute type. It is defined elsewhere as the integer value 64. Similarly, the OID `id-at-name` is defined as follows:

```
id-at-name OBJECT IDENTIFIER ::= { id-at 41 }
```

This expands to the complete OID `2.5.4.41` because `id-at` is defined somewhere else as `2.5.4`. The matching rules `caseIgnoreMatch` and `caseIgnoreSubstringsMatch` also have their own ASN.1 definitions, but we will not explore them in detail here.

If an attribute type is a subtype of another attribute type (i.e., if it is derived from another attribute), the ASN.1 attribute definition will generally be in the form shown in Listing 7.5.

LISTING 7.5 THE GENERAL FORM OF A SUBTYPED ATTRIBUTE TYPE IN ASN.1

```
ATNAME ATTRIBUTE ::= {
    SUBTYPE OF SUPERTYPE
    [ EQUALITY MATCHING RULE EQMATCHINGRULE ]
    [ ORDERING MATCHING RULE ORDMATCHINGRULE ]
    [ SUBSTRINGS MATCHING RULE SUBMATCHINGRULE ]
    [ SINGLEVALUED ]
    ID OID }
```

SUPERTYPE is the type that *ATNAME* is derived from. The matching rules and any other information defined in the type's supertype need not be included. Listing 7.6 shows a simple example of this kind of attribute type definition.

LISTING 7.6 THE ASN.1 DEFINITION OF THE *cn* ATTRIBUTE TYPE

```
-- upper bound for cn:
ub-common-name INTEGER ::= 64

-- OID branch for X.500 standard attribute types:
id-at OBJECT IDENTIFIER ::= { 2.5.4 }

-- OID for cn:
id-at-commonName OBJECT IDENTIFIER ::= {id-at 3}

-- the cn attribute type itself:
commonName ATTRIBUTE    ::= {
    SUBTYPE OF name
    WITH SYNTAX DirectoryString {ub-common-name}
    ID id-at-commonName }
```

Note that the definitions of `ub-common-name` and `id-at-commonName` were included because the `commonName` definition depends on these other ASN.1 elements. A complete ASN.1 schema definition must always define or import all the elements it references, except for some very basic elements defined by the ASN.1 specification itself. The lines that start with two hyphens (--) are simply comments included to aid humans who are reading the ASN.1 macros.

Some common ASN.1-based syntaxes are listed in Table 7.3.

TABLE 7.3 COMMON ASN.1-BASED SYNTAXES

Syntax	Description
DirectoryString	Text string; choice of several possible character sets. In LDAP, the character set is always UTF-8.
PrintableString	Text string; characters are from a restricted set that includes letters, digits, and a few punctuation characters (such as comma).

Syntax	Description
PostalAddress	Sequence of text strings that holds a postal (mailing) address.
BOOLEAN	Boolean values (TRUE or FALSE).
INTEGER	Numbers; comparisons follow rules for comparing integers.
DistinguishedName	Directory names (a pointer to another entry).
OctetString	Arbitrary binary data.

DirectoryString is by far the most popular syntax used for attribute types. Some common ASN.1-based matching rules are listed in Table 7.4.

TABLE 7.4 COMMON ASN.1-BASED MATCHING RULES

Matching Rule	Description
caseIgnoreMatch	Case of letters and leading, trailing, and multiple spaces are ignored during comparisons.
caseExactMatch	Case of letters is significant during comparisons; leading, trailing, and multiple spaces are ignored.
telephoneNumberMatch	Like caseIgnoreMatch, except hyphen and space characters are also ignored during comparisons.
integerMatch	Comparisons follow the rules for comparing integers.
booleanMatch	Comparisons follow the rules for comparing Boolean values; only equality match is supported.
distinguishedNameMatch	Comparisons follow special rules for comparing DNs (number of relative distinguished names (RDNs) must be the same, each RDN must have the same number of values, and each type and value must match).
octetStringMatch	A binary (byte-by-byte) comparison if performed on values.

ASN.1 Object Class Definitions

ASN.1-based object class definitions use the format shown in Listing 7.7.

LISTING 7.7 THE GENERAL FORM OF AN ASN.1 OBJECT CLASS DEFINITION

```
OCNAME OBJECT-CLASS    ::= {
SUBCLASS OF  { SUPERCLASS }
MUST CONTAIN { REQATTRS }
MAY CONTAIN  { ALLOWATTRS }
ID OID }
```

OCNAME is the name of the object class, *SUPERCLASS* is the object class it is derived from, and *REQATTRS* and *ALLOWATTRS* are the sets of required and allowed attribute types, respectively. If there are multiple attribute types in the *REQATTRS* or *ALLOWATTRS* sets, each is separated from its neighbor by a vertical bar character in this manner:

```
cn ¦ sn
```

The order in which the attributes are listed is not significant. Sometimes other ASN.1 macros are used in place of an attribute type to refer to an entire set of attributes.

Listing 7.8 shows a sample object class definition written using ASN.1.

LISTING 7.8 THE ASN.1 DEFINITION OF THE `locality` OBJECT CLASS

```
-- OID branch for X.500 standard object classes:
id-oc OBJECT IDENTIFIER ::= 2.5.6

-- OID for locality object class:
id-oc-locality OBJECT IDENTIFIER ::= {id-oc 3}

-- A set of attributes that are useful for describing locales:
LocaleAttributeSet ATTRIBUTE ::= {
    localityName ¦
    stateOrProvinceName ¦
    streetAddress }
-- An object class that represents a physical location
locality OBJECT-CLASS ::= {
    SUBCLASS OF     { top }
    MAY CONTAIN     { description ¦
                        searchGuide ¦
                        LocaleAttributeSet ¦
                        seeAlso }
    ID id-oc-locality }
```

This `locality` class, OID 2.5.6.3, is used for entries that represent physical locations of various kinds, such as "the state of California" or "222-B Baker Street." It is a subclass of the class called `top`, which means that, like all structural object classes, the `objectclass` attribute is mandatory. The following attributes may optionally be included in `locality` entries: `description`, `searchGuide`, `localityName`, `stateOrProvinceName`, `streetAddress`, and `seeAlso`. Several of these attribute types are defined in the `LocaleAttributeSet` ASN.1 macro so that the set can easily be included in other object class definitions.

As you can see, reading ASN.1 is complex and often involves peeling away several layers until you get to the information you need. This can be a tedious process because there is no way to tell in advance how many layers you will need to remove before you are done. ASN.1 is a general-purpose tool; unfortunately, general-purpose tools are usually harder to use than those designed to do one simple thing well. An advantage of ASN.1 schema descriptions is that they tend to be complete and precise.

The LDAPv3 Schema Format

Version 3 of the LDAP protocol requires that directory servers publish their supported schemas through LDAP itself. This allows directory client applications to programmatically retrieve the schema and adapt their behavior based on it. For example, a client that allows administrators to add new directory entries can query a directory server to find the complete list of structural object classes it supports and present it to the administrator.

Clients locate schema by reading the values of the subschemaSubentry operational attribute that is located in an LDAPv3 server's root DSE (directory server–specific entry) or by reading the same attribute from any directory entry. Values of the subschemaSubentry attribute are LDAP DNs that point to entries that belong to the subschema object class. Such entries are called *subschema entries*. In the Netscape Directory Server, for example, the global set of schema for the server can be found in the subschema entry named cn=schema.

The subschema object class allows these seven attribute types to be present:

- attributeTypes
- objectClasses
- matchingRules
- matchingRuleUse
- dITStructureRules
- nameForms
- ditContentRules

We discuss only the first two because they are by far the most important and widely used. For information on the rest, please refer to the LDAPv3 Attribute Syntax Definitions document (RFC 2252).

The LDAPv3 specification encourages servers to allow their schema to be modified over LDAP. If an implementation supports this, the `attributes` and `objectclasses` attributes of a subschema entry can be modified by a directory client (subject to access control restrictions, of course).

LDAPv3 Attribute Type Definitions

The `attributeTypes` attribute contains one value for each attribute supported by the server. Each value is as shown in Listing 7.9, broken up into multiple lines for clarity and with optional items in brackets.

LISTING 7.9 THE GENERAL FORM OF **LDAPv3** `attributeTypes` VALUES

```
( ATOID NAME ATNAME
➡              [ DESC ATDESC ]
➡              [ SUP SUPOID ]
➡              [ EQUALITY EQMATCHOID ]
➡              [ ORDERING ORDMATCHOID ]
➡              [ SUBSTR SUBMATCHOID ]
➡              [ SYNTAX SYNOID ]
➡              [ SINGLE-VALUE ]
➡)
```

ATOID is the object identifier for the attribute, *ATNAME* is the attribute name, *ATDESC* is a text description of the attribute, *SUPOID* is the object identifier of the type it is derived from (if any), *SYNOID* is the object identifier of the attribute's syntax, and *EQMATCHOID*, *ORDMATCHOID*, and *SUBMATCHOID* are the object identifiers for the matching rules associated with the attribute type. By default, attributes are assumed to be multivalued unless the SINGLE-VALUE phrase is present. Parameters that are strings should be enclosed in single quotes.

The following uses the LDIF notation introduced in Chapter 3 to show how the `attributeTypes` value that describes the `cn` attribute might appear in an LDAPv3 server's subschema entry:

```
attributetypes: ( 2.5.4.3 NAME 'cn' DESC 'commonName Standard
        ➡Attribute' SYNTAX 1.3.6.1.4.1.1466.115.121.1.15 )
```

LDAPv3 Object Class Definitions

The `objectClasses` attribute type contains one value for each object class supported by the server. Listing 7.10 shows the general form for each value, broken up into multiple lines for clarity and with optional items in brackets.

LISTING 7.10 THE GENERAL FORM OF **LDAPv3** *objectClasses* VALUES

```
( OCOID NAME OCNAME
➡              [ DESC OCDESC ]
➡              [ SUP SUPOID ]
➡              [ OCKIND ]
➡              [ MUST REQATSET ]
➡              [ MAY ALLOWATSET ]
➡)
```

OCOID is the object identifier for the class; *OCNAME* is the name of the object class; *OCDESC* is a text description of the class; *SUPOID* is the object identifier of the class it is derived from; *OCKIND* is ABSTRACT, STRUCTURAL, or AUXILIARY (the default is STRUCTURAL); and *REQATSET* and *ALLOWATSET* are the names or OIDs of the required and allowed attribute types, respectively. The attribute sets are enclosed in parentheses, and each attribute type name is separated from the next with a dollar sign. Parameters that are strings should be enclosed in single quotes.

Here is how the `objectClasses` value that describes the standard `person` object class might appear in an LDAPv3 server's subschema entry:

```
objectclasses: ( 2.5.6.6 NAME 'person' DESC 'Standard Person
        ➡ Object Class' SUP 'top'
        ➡ MUST ( objectclass $ sn $ cn )
        ➡ MAY ( description $ seealso $ telephonenumber $ userpassword)
        ➡ )
```

The LDAPv3 schema format is quite hard to read and is optimized for programmatic access rather than human readability.

Tip

We recommend that you use either the slapd.conf or ASN.1 schema format when designing your own directory's schema. The slapd.conf schema format is our favorite because it is the simplest and it can be used directly as server configuration information for some of the most popular LDAP server implementations.

The Schema Checking Process

When a new entry is added to the directory or an existing entry is modified, the directory server that processes the request goes through a *schema checking process* before committing the add or modify request. The schema checking process is done before the directory database itself is altered and ensures that all new or modified directory entries conform to the schema rules. If an entry violates any of the schema rules in effect, the request is rejected by the directory server and a `Constraint Violation` error is returned to the LDAP client.

The steps a server typically performs when checking schema are as follows:

1. Verify that all new or modified values conform to the syntax rules.

2. Verify that at least one value for the `objectclass` attribute is present.

3. For each object class, ensure that at least one value for each of the mandatory attributes is present.

4. Check each attribute to make sure it is allowed by one of the object classes and that the attribute only has one value if it is a single-valued attribute.

Note that the specifics and order of execution of some of the steps shown may vary in different directory service implementations. However, the basic idea is always the same: the resulting entry (whether new or modified) is checked for complete conformance with the server's schema rules, and an error is sent to the directory client if any problems are found. If there is a schema violation, the entire add or modify operation is rejected by the server.

Some implementations, such as the U-M `slapd` server and the Netscape Directory Server, provide a way to disable schema checking entirely, in which case entries that are added or modified are not checked against the schema rules at all.

Schema Design Overview

Schema design is the process of selecting and defining schemas to be used in a directory service. Before tackling schema design, you should first follow the data design process described in Chapter 6; to complete your schema design you will need detailed information on what data elements you plan to store in your directory service.

Schema design involves these steps:

1. Locate schemas provided with the applications you plan to deploy.

2. Locate standard and directory vendor-provided schemas.

3. Choose predefined schema elements to meet as many of your data element needs as possible.

4. Develop schema extensions or define new schema elements to meet your remaining needs.

5. Plan for schema maintenance and evolution.

6. Document your schema design.

Overall, it is best to use existing schema elements whenever possible, with a preference for widely published and well-documented schemas. This strategy is the easiest way to choose schema, and it should enhance compatibility with the directory-enabled applications you will deploy in the future. One of the challenges in schema design is to locate good predefined schemas to use, so we cover that topic in some depth.

If no existing schema can be located that meets your needs, you will need to create a custom schema by subclassing an existing object class definition or by defining completely new schema elements. When defining your own schema elements, it is important to use proper techniques to avoid potential problems down the road. You will also want to document your schema design (a simple but important step that many people overlook). Finally, it is a good idea to develop a strategy for maintaining your schemas and to plan for future changes.

A Few Words About Schema Configuration

In most directory server implementations, the administrator of the server determines what schema rules are in effect on a given server. Although we assume that schema customization is possible, the ease and degree to which it can be done varies widely among implementations.

An administration interface that can be used to customize schema is included with most, but not all, directory service software. In some systems schemas can be changed only by writing code that calls vendor-specific APIs. If you have already chosen your directory server software or are considering a specific implementation, check the documentation to ensure that you can and know how to perform any necessary schema customizations.

Another way implementations differ is in whether all data stored throughout the entire directory service is subject to the same set of schema rules or whether schema configuration can vary from server to server. In some implementations, different portions of the directory namespace can have their own schema rules. This allows the administrator to arrange for different subtrees within the directory to use different schemas. The term *subschema* refers to the schema that is in use for a specific subtree of the directory.

If you are deploying a centrally managed directory service, in most situations you should use the same schema everywhere. On the other hand, if you are actually deploying more than one service, or if you are an ISP that is providing directory service to more than one customer, it may be appropriate to use different schemas in different parts of the service.

Finally, you should check to see if the directory server software you plan to use supports automated replication of schema information or if you will need to take your own steps to ensure that the correct schema rules are installed on all servers you deploy. Not all implementations that support replication of user directory data can replicate schema information.

The Relationship of Schema Design to Data Design

When we tackled data design in Chapter 6, our main focus was on creating a detailed list of data elements to be included in your directory service. Most of the data design work was driven by the requirements of the applications that will use the directory service. During schema design, each data element is mapped to an LDAP attribute type, and related elements are gathered into LDAP object classes.

If some of the applications you plan to deploy come with a set of recommended schema definitions, the schema design process will probably be easier. There are also a lot of standard schemas you can choose from for common objects such as people, groups, and departments. However, you may need to design your own schemas or refine the vendor-provided and standard schemas based on your requirements. Also, if two different directory-enabled applications recommend the use of radically different schemas for the same type of object, such as a person, you will need to sort that out during the schema design process as well. Harmonizing schemas is important, so look for a high degree of configurability when selecting your directory server and application software.

Let's Call the Whole Thing Off

Some of you may wonder if you really need schema rules. Sometimes it seems like the schemas just get in the way of applications and users who want freedom when using the directory service. Based on our experience, and for all the reasons mentioned earlier in this chapter, it is important to use schemas within a directory service. However, depending on how you use your directory, it may be appropriate to de-emphasize schema rules or eliminate schema checking altogether.

Some implementations, such as Netscape Directory Server, allow you to disable schema checking entirely. Also, as discussed earlier, all LDAPv3-compliant servers support a special object class called extensibleObject that, when applied to an entry, allows any attribute type to be stored in the entry. Most directory service administrators will want to keep schema checking enabled and use the extensibleObject class only in special situations (for example, for applications that need to store their own configuration information and do not need the directory server itself to enforce schema rules).

Tip

If you do decide to downplay or disable schema rules, be careful. It is nearly impossible to impose order later on a collection of data that was created free from the constraints of schema checking! We suggest that you proceed with caution and at least begin your directory service deployment with schema checking enabled, even if you believe you will turn it off eventually.

Sources for Predefined Schemas

Predefined schemas are provided by application vendors, directory standards documents, and directory service software vendors. By choosing predefined schemas to meet as many of your needs as possible, you avoid reinventing the wheel and help ensure compatibility with as many directory-enabled applications as possible.

Directory-Enabled Applications

All directory-enabled application software should include documentation that describes its schema requirements. If you can't locate the schema information for an application that you plan to deploy, contact the vendor or author of the software and ask for the information. Often this important information is buried in an appendix or available only on a vendor's Web site.

Some applications have very specific requirements, whereas others are more liberal in the schemas they can use. It is important to find out if an application requires a specific set of object classes and attributes or whether it can be configured to work with a variety of schemas. The directory-enabled application that is the least flexible of those you plan to deploy may in practice dictate many of your schema choices.

For example, routing of electronic mail is a fairly exact process. If you plan to deploy a directory-enabled email routing system, you may find that the email software requires a specific object class to be present in all person and group entries and that specific attributes must have values for the mail-routing algorithms to function. The Netscape Messaging Server is an example of LDAP-enabled mail-routing and delivery software that has fairly strict schema requirements.

In contrast, consider a directory lookup client such as a Web-based phone book. This kind of application probably supports the standard person object class and its associated attributes out of the box. It probably also supports other schemas chosen by the vendor, such as the inetOrgPerson extended person object class. A good lookup client also provides some degree of customization so that it can be modified to accommodate organization-specific schemas.

Standard Schemas

Schemas endorsed by more than one vendor and published by some kind of standards body can be good choices for use in your directory service. Usually, a schema that has made it into a standards document has been reviewed and agreed to by a number of different implementers and users of directory services. Standard schemas also have the advantage that they are generally well-documented and widely published.

It is especially useful to choose a standard schema when you are caught between two different vendors of directory-enabled applications that are each promoting their own proprietary schemas. If the schema needs of two applications conflict, asking the application vendors to support a standard schema is a good approach. Because everyone claims to support open standards, it would be hard for them to explain why they cannot support the standard schema (unless it simply does not meet the needs of their particular application).

There are several sources of standard schemas that you should consult:

- LDAP standards documents

- X.500 standards documents

- Industry consortium standards

Most of the standard schema information is available free of cost on the World Wide Web. In some cases you may need to contact the standards body directly to purchase a copy of the standards documents. If you design your own schemas, you should consider submitting them to a standards body as well. Some URLs and other pointers to help you locate standard schemas are included in the "Further Reading" section near the end of this chapter.

Schemas Provided by Directory Vendors

Last, but certainly not least, most directory software comes with a generous collection of predefined schemas. In most cases, these schemas are a mix of standard schemas, application-specific schemas, and schemas that are being promoted by the directory vendor itself. One of the big advantages of directory vendor-provided schemas are that they are more than likely already installed in the directory service software, so it requires less work to use them.

On the other hand, just because a schema comes pre-installed does not mean it will meet your needs. As with all schema-related decisions, read through the documentation and the schema definitions carefully to evaluate a vendor-provided schema against the needs of the applications you plan to deploy.

Defining New Schema Elements

If your schema needs are not adequately met by existing, predefined schemas, you will need to define your own object classes and attributes. It is fairly easy to define your own schemas, but like with all design tasks there are pitfalls and tradeoffs to be considered. In this section we describe an approach that should produce good results. We do not discuss definitions of new attribute syntaxes because in most implementations adding new attribute syntaxes requires the directory software vendor or customer to write code to support it.

Choosing Names for New Attribute Types and Object Classes

You should choose a naming scheme for the new object classes and attributes you define. All names should be made as meaningful as possible but not too long or cumbersome. Attribute names and object classes are generally hidden from end users, but directory service administrators and applications developers will work with them extensively.

It is also important to make some effort to avoid collisions with the names chosen by other parties (standards committees, directory vendors, other software vendors, and so on). Remember, the entire attribute namespace is flat. The same is true for the object class namespace. A good strategy is to prefix the names of all the schema elements you define with something that resembles your organization's name. If you do that, collisions with other definitions are unlikely.

For example, the ACME Corporation might use the prefix acme and create attributes and object classes such as those shown in Listing 7.11.

LISTING 7.11 ACME ATTRIBUTES AND OBJECT CLASS NAMES

```
objectclass acmePerson ...
attribute acmePrinter ...
attribute acmeID ...
attribute acmeHoursAllowedAccess
```

> **Tip**
>
> If you define schema elements that you intend to publish widely and submit to a standards body such as the Internet Engineering Task Force (IETF), there is no need to prefix the names of the attributes and object classes with a string that identifies your organization. In fact, acceptance of your schema by others will likely be hindered if the names include something specific to your organization!

Obtaining and Assigning Object Identifiers

Recall that each LDAP object class or attribute type must be assigned a unique name and OID. One of the biggest stumbling blocks faced by people new to LDAP directories is how to obtain OIDs for the new attribute types and object classes they want to define. Simply put, OIDs can be obtained from anyone who has one. In fact, one OID is sufficient to meet all your schema needs; you can simply add another level of hierarchy to create new branches or *OID arcs* for your attributes and object classes. An OID arc is an OID that has been reserved for use as a container for defining additional OIDs. The process of assigning an arc of the OID space to another party is called *delegation*.

As already mentioned, an OID can be obtained from anyone who has one—they just need to delegate it to you as an arc and record this so that they do not use the OID for any other purpose. The Internet Assigned Numbers Authority (IANA) gives out OIDs to any organization that asks. IANA calls the OIDs *enterprise numbers* because it gives them out primarily for use with Simple Network Management Protocol (SNMP). The IANA OIDs work fine for LDAP as well because each OID is as good as another. A form for obtaining an OID from IANA can be accessed on the Web at `http://www.isi.edu/cgi-bin/iana/enterprise.pl`.

Other organizations known to give out OIDs are ANSI (for U.S. organizations) and BSI (for U.K. organizations). General information on OIDs maintained by a gentleman named Harald Alvestrand can be accessed using the URL `http://www.alvestrand.no/objectid/`.

As an example of obtaining and assigning OIDs, consider the University of Michigan directory services team, which contacted IANA to obtain an OID arc (`1.3.6.1.4.1.250`) for its own use. The team then created the OID arcs shown in Table 7.5 for use in defining its own directory schema.

TABLE 7.5 UNIVERSITY OF MICHIGAN OID SCHEMA ARCS

OID Arcs	Description	Owner/Contact
`1.3.6.1.4.1.250.1`	U-M defined attribute types	U-M directory services team
`1.3.6.1.4.1.250.2`	U-M defined attribute syntaxes	U-M directory services team
`1.3.6.1.4.1.250.3`	U-M defined object classes	U-M directory services team

The team assigned the OID `1.3.6.1.4.1.250.1.1` to the first attribute type it defined, `1.3.6.1.4.1.250.1.2` to the second, and so on.

Tip

After you obtain an OID, you should maintain a registry similar to Table 7.5 to ensure that no OID is ever used for more than one purpose. You should then publish the list of OIDs with your schemas (more on this topic later). Although it may seem unimportant to establish an OID registry when you are just getting started, you will want to have one because the number of attributes and object classes you or others in your organization create may be quite large in the end.

Modifying Existing Schema Elements

It may be tempting just to alter some predefined schema elements to meet your needs, perhaps by adding a new attribute to a predefined object class. At first glance, this seems like a reasonable thing to do.

> **Warning**
>
> *Do not modify existing schema elements! Changing existing schemas will break some directory servers and clients, and it will probably lead to a lot of confusion. If the person object class that everyone knows about is different within each directory service deployment, chaos will rule.*

You should also be careful when completely deleting object classes or attributes from any of your directory server software's pre-installed schemas. It may be okay to do this as long as you are sure the schema is not used internally by any of the directory service software. However, you may run into trouble when you upgrade your software because the upgrade process may require that all of the vendor's schemas be present. In general, there is no reason to remove schema elements even if you do not plan to use them; there is little or no penalty associated with leaving the schema elements installed.

Subclassing an Existing Object Class

It is fairly common to extend, or *subclass*, an existing, predefined object class in order to add new attributes to it. To do this, define a new object class that is a subclass of the existing one by indicating in the definition of the new class that the existing class is its superior. You also need to define the new attribute types and include them in the new object class as required or optional attributes.

When you subclass an existing object class in this way, the new class should generally be used to represent the same type of object as the class from which it was derived. For example, you might create a new subclass of a printer object class called hpPrinter that allows additional attributes specific to Hewlett-Packard printers. The hpPrinter class is still used to represent printers; it just holds more information.

Also, the new object class should be the same kind as the class from which it is derived. For example, if you are subclassing a structural object class, the new class should also be a structural class. Note that in some directory service implementations such Netscape's, little or no distinction is made between different kinds of object classes, so this may not be something you have to deal with in practice.

As another example of subclassing an existing object class, suppose the ACME Corporation is deploying a directory service in which one of the directory-enabled applications being developed is a "birthday notification service" (which managers will subscribe to so they remember to take each employee out to lunch on his or her birthday). The designers of the ACME directory might define a new attribute to hold the day and month a person was born. Using the slapd.conf schema format, the attribute type definition might look like this:

```
attribute acmeBirthday bday-OID cis
```

Note that *bday-OID* would need to be replaced by a real OID assigned by the ACME directory administrators. An extension of the inetOrgPerson class that allows the new acmeBirthday attribute to be included in entries could be defined as shown in Listing 7.12.

LISTING 7.12 THE DEFINITION OF THE acmePerson OBJECT CLASS

```
objectclass acmePerson
        superior inetOrgPerson
        oid acmePersonOID
        allows acmeBirthday
```

Note that *acmePersonOID* should be replaced by a real OID assigned by the directory administrators. The acmePerson class would be used whenever a user entry is created inside ACME. The following is a sample entry:

```
dn: uid=scarter, o=acme.com
objectclass: top
objectclass: person
objectclass: organizationalPerson
objectclass: inetOrgPerson
objectclass: acmePerson
cn: Sally Carter
sn: Carter
uid: scarter
userPassword: secret
acmeBirthday: 29-February
```

Now we all know why Sally claims to be so much younger than she looks—she must be counting birthdays instead of elapsed time!

Note

In the LDIF just shown, values for all the superior object classes (top, person, organizationalPerson, and inetOrgPerson) are explicitly shown in the entry's objectClass attribute. This is always how an entry will look when you retrieve it from an LDAP server. When adding or modifying entries, it should not be necessary to explicitly provide values for all the superior classes in this way, although some implementations do require it. Because there is no harm in listing all the superior object class values, it is safest always to do so.

Adding Auxiliary Information to a Directory Object

Sometimes it is preferable to create an auxiliary object class that allows attributes to be added to any type of LDAP entry regardless of what kind of real-world object it represents. A class like this is sometimes called a *mix-in class* because it allows additional attributes to be "mixed into" an existing class. A mix-in class may be added to a wide range of entry types—a much simpler approach than creating a subclass for each object class you want to allow the new attributes to appear in.

To create an auxiliary object class, simply define a new class that is not sub-classed from any existing object class (it should have the special class top as its superior). It is best to make all the attributes in the auxiliary class optional rather than mandatory. That way, the auxiliary object class itself can be associated with an entry regardless of whether any values for its attributes are present. This reduces the burden on directory clients because they do not have to worry about removing the object class value when an attribute required by the auxiliary class is removed.

An example of a useful auxiliary object class is shown in Listing 7.13 (using the ASN.1 schema description format). This class was defined by the authors while they were at the University of Michigan.

LISTING 7.13 THE `labeledURIObject` OBJECT CLASS

```
labeledURIObject OBJECT-CLASS ::= {
    SUBCLASS OF     { top }
    KIND            auxiliary
    MAY CONTAIN     { labeledURI }
    ID              1.3.6.1.4.1.250.3.15
```

This class can be added to any LDAP entry to allow uniform resource identifiers (URIs) to be included in the entry. The labeledURI attribute itself consists of a URI and an optional text label. The most common type of URIs are those that are now so much a part of the computing infrastructure: User entries might contain a URL that points to a person's home page; group entries might contain a URL that points to a Web site that contains information about the group's activities; and printer entries might contain a URL that provides access to a printer administration utility or the printer itself.

The following is an example of a group entry that also contains a URL:

```
dn: cn=UNIX Wizards, ou=Groups, dc=airius, dc=com
cn: UNIX Wizards
objectclass: top
objectclass: groupOfNames
objectclass: labeledURIObject
member: uid=bjensen, ou=people, dc=airius,dc=com
member: uid=bjornj, ou=people, dc=airius,dc=com
labeleduri: http://www.airius.com/unixwizards/ UNIX Wizards Home Page
```

As another example of an auxiliary object class, suppose you develop a directory-enabled application that keeps track of your organization's network-related inventory by storing information in the following custom attributes (shown here using the slapd.conf schema format):

```
attribute inventoryID OID int
attribute inventoryDatePlacedInService OID cis
attribute inventoryContactPerson OID dn
attribute inventoryComments OID cis
```

Note that all the *OID*s would, of course, need to be replaced with real object identifiers you assign. Because you want to mix these attributes into several different types of entries (printers, hosts, and so on), you could handle your schema needs by defining an auxiliary object class such as the `inventoryItem` class shown in Listing 7.14.

Listing 7.14 The `inventoryItem` Auxiliary Object Class

```
objectclass inventoryItem
    superior top
    oid OID
    requires
        inventoryID
    allows
        inventoryDatePlacedInService,
        inventoryContactPerson,
        inventoryComments
```

Here is a sample printer entry that has inventory information attached to it:

```
dn: cn=2nd floor HP 5Si MX, ou=printers, dc=airius, dc=com
objectclass: top
objectclass: printer
objectclass: inventoryItem
cn: 2nd floor HP 5Si MX
pagesPerMinute: 24
inventoryID: 1290-555-81
inventoryDatePlacedInService: 19970501000000Z
inventoryContactPerson: uid=bjensen,ou=people,dc=airius,dc=com
inventoryComments: on loan to the art department
```

Accommodating New Types of Objects

If you cannot find a predefined object class that is similar to the type of object you need to represent in your directory service, simply define a new structural class to hold whatever attributes are appropriate. This is similar to creating a new auxiliary class except that the structural class can stand on its own as the primary object class for an entry.

For example, if our friends at the ACME Corporation plan to use their directory to track company-owned and -operated telephone sets, they might reuse some predefined attributes but create a new object class such as the one shown in Listing 7.15.

Listing 7.15 The `acmeTelephone` Object Class

```
objectclass acmeTelephone
    superior top
    oid OID
    allowed
        cn,
        telephoneNumber,
        owner,
        l
```

Here is a sample entry:

```
dn: cn=Mark Smith's phone, ou=phones, o=acme.com
objectclass: top
objectclass: acmeTelephone
cn: Mark Smith's phone
telephoneNumber: 3477
owner: uid=bkady, ou=people, o=acme.com
l: security office
```

Note that when you create an object class for an entirely new kind of object, you will need to put some thought into which attribute will most likely be used to form the RDN of entries that belong to the class. For most object classes, the cn (common name) attribute is a good, generic choice.

In the acmeTelephone object class we just looked at, the telephoneNumber itself might actually be a better choice for naming phone entries simply because it is more likely to be unique. The sample entry we just used might instead be defined as shown here:

```
dn: telephoneNumber=3477, ou=phones, o=acme.com
objectclass: top
objectclass: acmeTelephone
cn: Mark Smith's phone
telephoneNumber: 3477
owner: uid=bkady, ou=people, o=acme.com
l: security office
```

The only difference is in the RDN (the first part of the DN), which uses the telephoneNumber attribute instead of cn to name the entry. See Chapter 8, "Namespace Design," for more information on entry naming.

Tips for Defining New Schemas

Defining a good schema is as much art as science, and the more of it you do, the easier the process becomes. The following are some tips that will help you produce better results:

- *Reuse existing elements as much as possible.* Even if you need to define a new object class, you may find that many of the attributes you need already exist. When you reuse existing elements, make sure the meaning and expected use is the same; otherwise, directory applications and users may be confused. For example, there is an attribute called drink that stores the name of a person's favorite beverage. Do not try to reuse the drink attribute with intended values of "yes" or "no" to indicate whether a person consumes alcohol or not. If you need to store a data value for that purpose, define a new attribute such as drinksAlcohol.

- *Define several smaller auxiliary object classes to mix needed attributes into existing objects.* The alternative is to subclass a lot of object classes, which in many cases requires the definition of a lot more new classes. By providing a general solution in an auxiliary class, your schema will be simpler and easier to understand.

- *Minimize the number of mandatory attribute types within your object classes.* If you are thinking of making an attribute required, proceed with caution. In our experience, required attributes inevitably get in the way at some point in the future. Even the cn and sn attributes that are required by the standard person class can be a burden if, for example, a user needs to appear in the directory to get access to various systems but wants his or her name to remain private.

- *Do not define more than one object class or attribute type to hold the same kind of information.* To maintain consistency in your schema and, thus, in your directory service, strive to use a single schema element for a given purpose. For example, the following three attributes should all be consolidated into one:

```
attribute dateOfBirth ...
attribute birthDate ...
attribute birthDay ...
```

- *When in doubt, keep it simple.* Remember that the goal of a collection of schemas is to provide a framework for your data elements that is easily understandable and usable by directory applications, administrators, and users. The more complicated the schemas you define, the less approachable your directory service.

Documenting and Publishing Your Schemas

There are several reasons why it is important to document all the schemas you use within your directory service. First, you may need the schema information when you add additional servers to your service. You can also share your schema documentation with software vendors and authors of custom applications to aid in design, development, and troubleshooting. Finally, if you create a new, useful schema, you can easily share your design with others and consider promoting it as a standard.

When documenting schemas, you can use any of the three formats described earlier or choose your own format. The best approach is to match as closely as possible the format used by your directory service implementation. If you haven't made that decision yet, just pick a format you are comfortable with. You should also identify the attribute types and object classes to which they belong and add them to the data elements list you created during the data design process (see Chapter 6).

We recommend that you publish your directory schema definitions at least within your own organization. Schema information is useful to users of the directory and developers of directory-enabled applications. If you want other organizations and independent software vendors to adopt your schemas, you should publish them on an external Web site or in another appropriate place where everyone will have access to them.

Finally, if you plan to promote some schema elements that you designed for consideration as a standard, you should publish them using the process defined by the standards body. For the IETF, which handles most Internet standards (including LDAP), this means writing an Internet Draft and submitting it to the IETF secretariat for publication. Connect to the IETF World Wide Web site at `http://www.ietf.org` for more information on how to contribute.

Schema Maintenance and Evolution

Your schema needs will change over time as you bring up new applications and find new and interesting ways to use your directory service. So far in this chapter we have generally assumed that one person or a small group of people will look after the schema for the directory service as a whole. This is a good model to follow initially, but when your directory service becomes popular and new applications are rapidly being proposed, it may be difficult to keep up with the demand for new schemas. A more decentralized approach to schema design would then be needed.

After you gain some deployment experience, you may also find yourself wishing you could change some of the schema rules that you defined when you initially deployed your directory service. This is tricky, but it is possible in certain situations described later in this section. There are also some schema-related issues to be aware of when upgrading directory service software, which we discuss as well.

Establishing a Schema Review Board

One option is to allow people to define and submit schemas to a centralized review committee to approve it before it is installed in the directory service. The main job of the review board (which can be just one or two people) is to check for inconsistencies in the schema, ensure that redundancy is not being introduced, and make sure the schema is well-defined and well-documented. This same group can also perform clerical tasks such as assigning OIDs, and it can serve as a central point for schema advice and consent.

Granting Permission to Change the Schema Configuration

If your directory server software supports it, you may want to allow people installing new applications to perform online schema updates over LDAP. Be careful to limit the number of people who have the access rights necessary to do this; you do not want frivolous, inappropriate, or inconsistent schemas to be installed. Check with your directory server software vendor to see if online schema updates are allowed and how to control access.

Changing Existing Schemas

As with all aspects of design, it is difficult to produce a perfect, complete schema design the first time. Because the use of your directory service will change over time, so will your schema needs. It may be tempting to change your defined schemas to accommodate your changing service, but proceed with caution. It is probably okay to add optional attribute types to an object class you previously defined, but it is risky to try to remove any attribute types or add required attribute types. In practice, there is usually no reason to remove attributes or add mandatory ones.

If you defined an attribute type that has the wrong syntax or name, you need to define a new type but keep the old one around and transition away from it. The most important consideration when contemplating changes to an existing schema is to make sure you have thought carefully about how it affects users, directory-enabled applications, and the directory itself.

Upgrading Directory Service Software

When the time comes to upgrade your directory service software, you should make sure all your schema additions are preserved during the upgrade process. Well-designed software takes care of this for you, but otherwise you need to reconfigure the new version of the software to make it aware of your schema rules. Also, the potential trouble with software upgrades is the most compelling reason not to remove any of the schemas that come preconfigured with your directory service software.

Schema Design Checklist

☐ Locate schemas provided with applications.

☐ Locate standard and directory vendor-provided schemas.

☐ Choose predefined schema elements to meet as many needs as possible.

☐ Define new schemas to meet your remaining needs.

☐ Document your schema design.

☐ Plan for schema maintenance and evolution.

Further Reading

A Layman's Guide to a Subset of ASN.1, BER, and DER: An RSA Laboratories Technical Note. B. Kaliski, 1993.

A Summary of the X.500(96) User Schema for Use with LDAPv3 (RFC 2256). M. Wahl, 1997; available on the World Wide Web at `http://info.internet.isi.edu/in-notes/rfc/files/rfc2256.txt`.

ITU-T Recommendation X.501, "The Directory: Models," 1996; available for purchase from the ITU World Wide Web site at `http://www.itu.ch/`.

ITU-T Recommendation X.520, "The Directory: Selected Attribute Types," 1996; available for purchase from the ITU World Wide Web site at `http://www.itu.ch/`.

ITU-T Recommendation X.521, "The Directory: Selected Object Classes," 1996; available for purchase from the ITU World Wide Web site at `http://www.itu.ch/`.

ITU-T Recommendation X.680, "Abstract Syntax Notation One (ASN.1)— Specification of Basic Notation," 1994; available for purchase on the ITU World Wide Web site at `http://www.itu.ch/`.

Lightweight Directory Access Protocol (v3): Attribute Syntax Definitions (RFC 2252). M. Wahl, A. Coulbeck, T. Howes, and S. Kille, 1998; available on the World Wide Web at `http://info.internet.isi.edu/in-notes/rfc/files/rfc2252.txt`.

Netscape Directory Server Administration Guide, Appendix A, "Object Classes." Available from Netscape's World Wide Web site at `http://home.netscape.com/eng/server/directory/3.0/agrtm/objclass.htm`.

Netscape Directory Server Administration Guide, Appendix B, "Attributes." Available from Netscape's World Wide Web site at `http://home.netscape.com/eng/server/directory/3.0/agrtm/attribut.htm`.

Netscape Directory Server Deployment Guide, Chapter 4, "Planning Directory Schema." Available from Netscape's World Wide Web site at `http://home.netscape.com/eng/server/directory/3.0/deployrtm/contents.html`.

Novell Directory Services Schema Specification. Available from Novell's World Wide Web site at `http://developer.novell.com/nds/schema.htm`.

Understanding X.500: The Directory. D. Chadwick, International Thomson Computer Press, 1996. Now out of print; selected portions available on the World Wide Web at `http://www.salford.ac.uk/its024/X500.htm`.

Windows NT 5.0 Directory Schema. Available from Microsoft's World Wide Web site at `http://www.microsoft.com/msdn/sdk/techinfo/schema/schema.htm`.

Looking Ahead

You should now have a plan that lists all the data elements you will place in your directory service along with the complete collection of schemas you will use to represent the data elements as LDAP entries. Data and schema design is very important, but it can be somewhat tedious. The next chapter covers an area in which you will have a chance to be much more creative: directory namespace design.

CHAPTER **8**

Namespace Design

Designing a directory namespace is one of the most important tasks you will undertake when designing your directory service. Your directory namespace provides the basic means by which you reference information in your directory, but it has many other implications as well. A properly designed namespace can lead to

- Easier data maintenance

- More flexibility in setting access control and replication policies

- The ability to satisfy a wider variety of directory-enabled applications

- More natural navigation through the directory

- Happy directory users and administrators

On the other hand, a poorly designed namespace can lead to administrative hassles when directory entries change names, replication or access-control requirements change, or users try to find information. In the worst case, a redesign is necessary to support some vital new directory application. The result of this poor design is generally unhappy directory users and certainly frustrated, overworked administrators.

The namespace you design for your directory has far-reaching implications that are often not at all obvious when you set out. The design of your namespace can affect replication, whether and how you are able to partition your data among servers or distribute administration of the directory, and other aspects of the service. Furthermore, changing your namespace after you've designed and deployed your directory service is a difficult task, unpleasant for administrators and often inconvenient for users.

This is what makes namespace design one of the most critical tasks you will face during your directory design process. Don't be surprised if your initial namespace design proves inadequate when you move on to designing your replication or access control framework, or even when you begin to pilot your directory service. Don't be afraid to redesign during these early stages; a later redesign is much more costly.

This chapter introduces the fundamentals of namespace design, starting with a brief review of the syntactic structure of an LDAP namespace, followed by the purposes of a namespace. Next, we describe how to analyze your namespace needs and design the best namespace for you. Several different namespace designs addressing a variety of needs and environments are presented near the end of the chapter, followed by a checklist of things to consider when designing your namespace. As always, we also list sources for further reading on the subject.

The Structure of a Namespace

The LDAP model defines a flexible namespace framework, which means that you can almost certainly design a namespace to satisfy your requirements no matter what they may be. However, it also means that you have more choices to make than you might like.

The LDAP namespace model is inherited from the X.500 directory standard, which is intended to be used in a fairly rigid, worldwide, hierarchical directory service. A typical X.500 namespace starts with countries at the top of the namespace, perhaps followed by states in the United States, and then organizations below that, with further hierarchy in each organization (see Figure 8.1). While such a hierarchical namespace may suit your needs and has a certain aesthetic appeal, it has some serious drawbacks, which are discussed later in this chapter. Fortunately, the LDAP model is flexible enough to allow other, more practical designs such as those discussed in the next section.

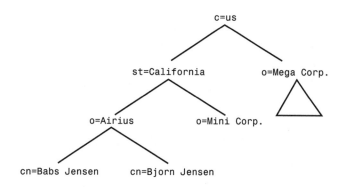

FIGURE 8.1   *A typical X.500 namespace.*

The basic LDAP model is hierarchical, or tree-structured. Of course, the
simplest hierarchical case of a one-level, flat namespace is also allowed. LDAP
does not directly support an arbitrarily connected namespace, or graph structure, in which an entry might be both child and parent of the same entry.
LDAP does, however, support the concept of aliases, which can be used to construct such structures (see Chapter 3, "An Introduction to LDAP," for more
information on aliases).

Also, keep in mind that through the use of seeAlso and other directory name-
valued attributes, you can construct arbitrary relationships among entries. This
approach is similar to the way relations work in a relational database. We prefer the use of this latter approach to the use of aliases, which tend to cause performance and consistency maintenance problems. Some examples of supported
and unsupported namespace structures are shown in Figure 8.2.

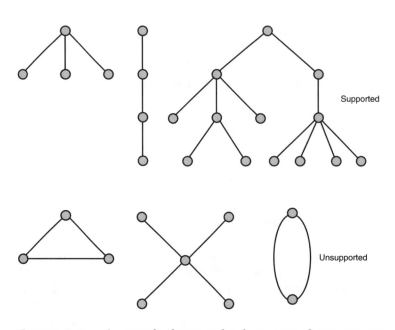

FIGURE 8.2   *An example of supported and unsupported namespace structures.*

After determining the hierarchical relationship among entries (a subject we tackle later in this chapter), the next question is how each entry in the hierarchy is named. First, recall from Chapter 3 that an LDAP directory entry is a collection of attribute values. The name of an entry is created by choosing one or more of these attribute values to form a relative distinguished name (RDN). Multiple attribute values may be chosen, but only one from each attribute.

For example, for the entry depicted in Figure 8.3, you could choose any of the RDNs shown, provided none of the entry's sibling entries have the same name. An entry's RDN must be unique among all entries sharing the same parent entry.

```
cn: Barbara Jensen          cn= Barbara Jensen
cn: Babs Jensen             uid= babs
sn: Jensen                  uid= babs+sn=Jensen
title: Director             mail= babs@airius.com
uid: babs
mail: babs@airius.com
```

            Entry   Examples.of RDNS

FIGURE 8.3   *Examples of relative distinguished names (RDNs).*

We recommend not using multivalued RDNs for reasons discussed in more detail in the next section. In short, multivalued RDNs introduce needless complexity, can adversely affect performance, and often don't solve the problems they are intended to solve.

When the RDN of an entry is chosen and its position relative to other entries in the hierarchy is determined, forming the entry's full name is simple: Just combine the RDNs of the entry and all of its ancestor entries. The resulting name is called a distinguished name, or DN.

In LDAP, DNs are written in little-endian order, like an email address, rather than big-endian order, like a file system name. *Little-endian* means that the least significant component is written first, with increasingly more significant components written subsequently. Each component of the name is separated by a comma, and multiple components of an RDN are separated by a plus sign. If these or other troublesome characters actually occur in one of the values used to form the name, they are escaped using a backslash quoting mechanism. Some examples of distinguished names are shown in Figure 8.4.

```
cn= Barbara Jensen, o=Netscape, c=us
cn= Barbara Jensen, o=Netscape.com
c=us
o=Netscape, c=us
dc=airius, dc=com
o="Mega Corp., Inc.", c=us
```

FIGURE 8.4 *Examples of distinguished names.*

More information on the LDAP namespace model, along with a formal grammar for generating and recognizing distinguished names, is described in Chapter 3.

The Purposes of a Namespace

A namespace provides the means by which directory data is named and referenced. In this respect, directory entries need names for the same reason that you or I need a name— so that we can be referred to by a more meaningful and precise term than "Hey, you!"

In some environments few, if any, additional requirements are placed on the namespace. In others, requirements for access control, replication, data partitioning, application access, and perhaps other aspects of the service impose additional requirements. This section summarizes the more common purposes of a namespace, some of which may not have occurred to you:

- *Data reference.* A namespace provides the means by which directory data is referenced, which is important for two reasons. First, of course, is that there must be a way for directory clients to refer unambiguously to a directory entry when retrieving or modifying the information associated with it. Second, the directory name provides a compact and efficient way to support groups of directory entries and directory entries that refer to one another (for example, through the use of a seeAlso, owner, or manager attribute). An example of this application is shown in Figure 8.5.

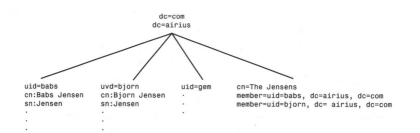

FIGURE 8.5   *A data reference example.*

- *Data organization.* A namespace provides a way to organize data. For example, you might place all entries corresponding to people in one portion of the namespace, entries corresponding to devices (such as printers) in another, and groups in yet another part of the namespace. Further subdivisions of organization are also possible, perhaps based on geographical or organizational information. Such organization can help facilitate browsing of the directory. For example, a printing application that enables a user to choose a nearby printer based on characteristics such as speed, color, and duplex ability can more easily present only printers in a user's vicinity if that portion of the directory is organized by locality. A namespace designed for this purpose is shown in Figure 8.6.

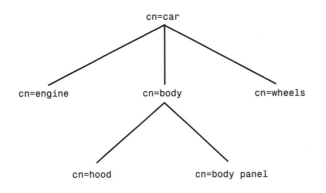

FIGURE 8.6   *A namespace example for data organization.*

- *Data partitioning.* A namespace enables directory data to be partitioned, or divided among multiple servers. Typically, partitioning can be performed only at certain well-defined namespace points (for example, on a subtree basis). If your namespace does not contain such partitioning points, you cannot partition your data. An example partitioning scheme in which the namespace enables a company's three main offices each to own and manage its own part of the data is shown in Figure 8.7. Partitioning is discussed in more detail in Chapter 9, "Topology Design."

- *Data replication.* Although not directly related to replication, your choice of namespace can constrain the replication scenarios your directory can support. This is a logical consequence of the partitioning restrictions described previously. Most replication solutions require partitioning on well-defined namespace boundaries. For example, if you choose a completely flat namespace, it is more difficult to replicate only a portion of your data. Some directory implementations may allow directory partitioning based on criteria other than the namespace. For example, imagine a directory server with a filtered replication feature that allows data to be partitioned based on an arbitrary LDAP filter. An example of a replication scheme, in which the more traditional namespace partitioning example just described is replicated to multiple servers, is shown in Figure 8.7. More on this topic can be found in Chapter 10, "Replication Design."

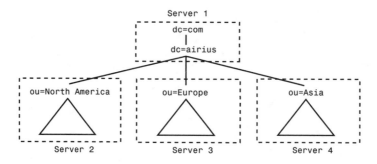

FIGURE 8.7   *A namespace example for partitioning, replication, and delegation through access control.*

- *Access control.* Like replication, access control can be affected by your choice of namespace. Some products allow the setting of access control only at namespace branch points. This is especially true when delegating authority to some of your data. This may be possible only if the data is divided on a subtree basis. Some better products have a more flexible access control scheme, allowing control to be delegated on a basis other than namespace. For example, the Netscape Directory Server allows you to specify access control rules that apply to any entry in your directory that satisfies a given directory search filter. This ability to delegate authority over portions of data is one of the most important features of a directory service. Access control is discussed extensively in Chapter 11, "Privacy and Security Design."

- *Application support.* The foregoing purposes of a namespace have all been related to the operation of the directory itself. The final purpose we will mention is that your namespace should support the applications that you are designing your directory for in the first place. This may seem almost too obvious to mention, but in our experience it is easy to get caught up in the excitement of directory design and lose track of the big picture. Make sure the namespace you design satisfies the requirements of your applications, both present and future.

You may be tempted to ascribe another purpose to your namespace, perhaps requiring that it should hold some aesthetic value of its own. After all, if people are going to have to look at the names, you might as well make them meaningful, even pleasing to look at. Perhaps your users might even be able to guess the names of entries given a standard, intuitively constructed namespace. Perhaps this is a nice idea in theory, but such dreams seldom work out in practice. Do not be fooled into considering such ideas.

A namespace should have functional value primarily, and the structure of your namespace should be hidden from users as much as possible. The primary purpose of a name is to provide a unique way of referencing the entry, and the driver behind its design is ease of administration. The other purposes described, including the effect your namespace may have on replication and access control, may also affect your choice of namespace. But these goals are administrative, and they should not be inflicted upon your users.

A directory client should hide the directory namespace from users of the client (or at the very least it should provide this option), which most modern clients do successfully. Failure to hide directory names often results in users being confused or upset by the name given to their entry, and users are unlikely to be sympathetic to the administrative concerns that caused you to name entries as you did. Furthermore, if you ever need to redesign your namespace, you will be glad you hid the original namespace from your users.

Tip

Choose names for administrative convenience, not aesthetic value. Try to hide names from users of the directory as much as possible. When developing applications, avoid making any assumptions about namespace design. Be sure to make your application flexible enough to adapt to different namespaces.

In summary, a namespace is required to reference entries and provide features such as groups, and it should support the applications using the directory. Your choice of namespace interacts with other important design decisions, often constraining the choices available when distributing, replicating, or controlling access to your data. These considerations are primary; other considerations, such as the aesthetics of your namespace, should be given less weight.

Analyzing Your Namespace Needs

Now that you have some idea what you're going to do with your namespace after you define it, it's time to turn our attention to the design process itself. The first step in designing a namespace is to understand what your needs are. Do you need a flat namespace or a hierarchical one? What attributes should you use to name entries? Do you have replication or data partitioning needs that may affect the design of your namespace? What about access control? What applications will the directory be supporting? Are your needs constant, or might they change over time? These questions and others need to be answered before you can have confidence in your namespace design.

This section takes you through the major decisions you'll need to make when designing your namespace. Keep in mind that like many other design problems, namespace design involves a series of tradeoffs, such as administrative convenience for future flexibility. As we examine each of these trade-offs, we'll try to point out what you gain and what you sacrifice at each step. At the end of this chapter we provide a checklist summary of the issues you should consider during the design process.

Choosing a Suffix

Your directory may have only a local scope, or it may be part of a larger, even a global, directory system. In either case, one of the first choices you have to make when designing your namespace is the suffix below which your namespace will live. Picture your namespace as a tree: A suffix (known as a context prefix in X.500 parlance or a domain in Active Directory) is the name of the entry at the top of the subtree you are designing.

If you are designing a strictly local namespace, your suffix may be the null string. All this means is that your namespace begins at the top of the tree (not all servers support this ability). If you are designing a namespace for your department, which is only one part of a larger tree designed for the company, your suffix would name the entry at the top of your department's tree. Examples of suffixes are shown in Figure 8.8.

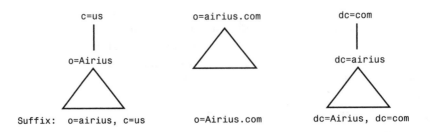

FIGURE 8.8   *Examples of directory suffixes.*

Often, a directory server may hold more than one suffix. Some directory implementations do this automatically: One suffix holds your data and the other holds data needed for the internal operation of the directory itself. You may want to design a service with multiple suffixes if you have two or more directory trees of information that do not have a natural common root.

How Suffixes Work

It may help to understand how a suffix is used by a directory server when answering a typical directory query. For example, suppose a client wants to modify the entry named uid=bjensen, dc=babs, dc=com. A Netscape Directory Server receiving the modification request compares the DN in the request to the directory suffixes it holds to determine if the entry to be modified is beneath one of the suffixes held by the server. If the server holds the suffix dc=babs, dc=com or the suffix dc=com, the modification proceeds. If the server holds the suffix dc=abc, dc=com or another suffix not matching the query, the server might refer the client to a different directory server that does hold the requested data. Or, the directory server might simply return an error, assuming that the requested entry does not exist. This depends on the directory's configuration.

Flat and Hierarchical Schemes

One of the earliest and most basic choices you have to make in designing a namespace is whether to go with a flat or hierarchical scheme. Of course, this is not a binary decision; your real decision is how much hierarchy and what type to introduce. As a guiding design principle, you should strive to make your namespace as flat as possible.

Name changes are typically one of the more burdensome administrative tasks of running a directory, inconvenient both for administrators and users. However, the flatter a namespace is, the less likely names are to change. All other things being equal, one would expect the likelihood of a name change to be proportional to the number of components in the name with the potential for change. The more hierarchical a namespace, the more components and the longer the names. The longer a name, the more likely it is to change. Thus, shorter, flatter names will change less frequently.

Tip

Make your namespace as flat as possible. Flatter names change less and are easier to administer. Long names introduce needless complexity and administrative burden.

Other considerations favor a flat namespace as well. For example, shorter names take up less space. Extra space can be used up if your directory implementation stores full names with entries or if it stores entry names as group members, in `seeAlso` and other attributes, or in directory configuration parameters.

For example, increasing the average name by only 20 bytes (the approximate result of adding just one extra component), represents an increase of 2MB in a directory containing 100,000 entries. Add to this the cost of storing and manipulating the extra directory entries used to create the hierarchy. Not overwhelming, perhaps, in today's world of cheaply available multigigabyte disk drives, but it does add up. And not all environments have the disk space to spare.

Further constraints may be imposed if an application is performing in-memory caching. Other important, related implications include the extra time it takes to do backups, the extra network bandwidth required to replicate the directory, and so on.

The shorter a name, the easier it is to remember—a clear benefit to users and administrators. Of course, we just got through telling you that names should never be inflicted upon users, and therefore the aesthetics of a name should not be an important consideration. The same argument could be made regarding the benefit of mnemonic names. But other things being equal, easy-to-remember names are better than hard-to-remember names. Figure 8.9 shows an example of a flat namespace that requires only short names.

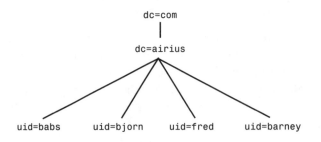

FIGURE 8.9 *An example of a flat namespace.*

Of course, there are some reasons to introduce a certain amount of hierarchy into a namespace. As described in the previous section, hierarchy can be used to enable data partitioning among multiple servers, replication, and certain kinds of access control. In addition, hierarchy can be useful to applications that want to browse the directory, although these applications are often better served by constructing virtual directory browsing views using attributes such as seeAlso, which can refer to other directory entries.

If you anticipate a centralized directory small enough to exist on a single machine, there is no need to introduce hierarchy to enable data distribution. Such a directory is not as constraining as it may sound. An average-sized

Pentium II–class machine can handle a directory on the order of millions of entries (depending on your directory implementation, of course), and it could be replicated to several other machines to handle additional read query load.

Write load is more problematic. Write load cannot be distributed with replication (assuming all copies of the data are to be kept in sync) because modifications must be made on all replicas. However, a directory that supports multimaster replication may be able to help handle peak write loads. More on these topics is discussed in Chapter 10.

Another reason to introduce hierarchy is to enable the distribution of administrative authority via access control. For example, suppose you want to allow an administrator from the marketing department to have control over marketing entries, the engineering administrator to have control over engineering entries, and so on. Many directory products, however, allow this kind of administrative distribution of control only at hierarchical namespace points. With such a system, different access control rules cannot easily be applied to the same subtree.

Some modern systems allow the setting of access control based on directory content rather than the directory namespace. With Netscape Directory Server, for example, you could define a single access control rule stating that the engineering administrator has access to all entries with an attribute value indicating they belong to the engineering department (for example ou=engineering). Carefully examine your chosen directory implementation's access control capabilities to ensure that you understand how they will restrict your namespace design, or look for software that supports your preferred design.

If you do need to introduce hierarchy in your namespace, try to do so sparingly and in a way that avoids problematic name changes as much as possible. Much of your flexibility may be removed because of the reason for needing hierarchy in the first place. For example, if you need hierarchy in order to distribute authority to different departments, there is not much hope in avoiding a name change when a user changes departments.

However, name changes can be avoided if you are able to design your hierarchy based on information that is not connected to directory information that is likely to change. For example, you could base your hierarchy on the type of objects in each tree, with one area of the tree for people, another for groups, and so on. It is unlikely, to say the least, that an entry would need to move from one area of the hierarchy to another with a scheme like this. This kind of partitioning can make replication easier in some cases as well. Figure 8.10 shows an example of this kind of hierarchical namespace.

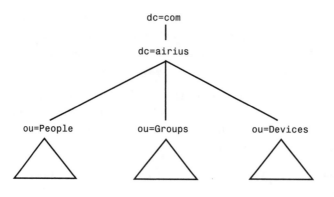

FIGURE 8.10   *A hierarchical namespace example.*

Naming Attributes

Once you've decided on the basic structure of your namespace and the level of hierarchy you need, you need to decide on attributes to use when naming entries. The attribute you should use depends on the type of entry you are naming and other requirements at your site. In this section, we present some general principles that you can apply to naming all kinds of entries.

The LDAP model requires taking an attribute from the entry and using it to form the entry's RDN. This might lead you to believe that only attributes naturally occurring in an entry should be used for naming (for example, the cn, or common name, attribute for a person's entry). Actually, there is often little reason for a name to serve any other purpose than to be unique. It is perfectly reasonable, for example, to use an otherwise meaningless attribute that has this uniqueness property. This approach fits well with our earlier admonition about trying to avoid name changes. If the attribute you choose to name an entry serves only that purpose and has no other meaning, the chance of it changing is small.

Creating a new attribute may be in conflict with other goals, such as supporting existing (bad) applications that make assumptions about the namespace. If this is the case, you can still use the unique value you created but place it in a compatible, more general-purpose standard attribute such as cn or uid. Although this may offend the sensibilities of some designers, it is a practical alternative that has many advantages.

When naming entries, take care to ensure that no two sibling entries (entries with the same immediate parent entry) have the same RDN. This requirement of the LDAP naming model is necessary to ensure that a DN can refer to at most one entry in your LDAP server. One strategy for ensuring uniqueness among RDNs is to choose the kind of naming attribute just described: one that is unique across your entire space of entries. You might accomplish this by assigning entries a sequentially increasing number as they are created (either a time stamp or a number you maintain), or by using some existing unique attribute (for example, an employee number or login ID for person entries).

Another approach to guaranteeing uniqueness is to artificially make the attribute you have chosen unique, perhaps by appending a number. For example, suppose you choose the cn attribute to name entries and have two entries with the same parent that would otherwise both be named cn=Barbara Jensen. You could append a number to one or both of the names, making cn=Barbara Jensen 1 and cn=Barbara Jensen 2 the names of the two entries.

Although this approach may have some aesthetic value, it also is harder to maintain. In our experience, users generally dislike having their names changed in any way, even for such a clear administrative reason. It may well be better to use something more arbitrary with no value to the user. This scheme may be more difficult to maintain because it requires some external mechanism to manage the process of making names unique. Be sure to pilot any user naming decisions with your user community; it's often hard to predict what they will like and dislike (see Figure 8.11 for examples). This is another good reason to hide DNs from your users.

```
   uid=babs        cn=Barbara Jensen 1   mail=babs@babs.com

     uid or            uniquified            email
     login               name               address

cn=123456789              employeeNumber=246810
                             employee
     hashed                    number
      SSN
```

FIGURE 8.11   *Examples of entry names.*

Some naturally occurring naming attributes may be sensitive in nature, and you may not want to use them for fear of unintentionally revealing information that should not be revealed. A U.S. Social Security number is a good example of such an attribute. If you use it to name your people entries, you guarantee uniqueness—but at the expense of publishing everybody's Social Security number, a practice guaranteed to make you highly unpopular.

In a case such as this, consider using some one-way hash of the value in question rather than the value itself. As long as you choose a good hashing function, the uniqueness property is maintained, and you need not fear anyone being able to deduce easily the sensitive information from the naming attribute. Two popular and good hashing functions are provided by the MD5 and SHA algorithms.

The LDAP model also allows the use of multiple attributes from an entry to form a *multivalued RDN*. The idea behind this capability is to use the additional attributes to distinguish entries that otherwise would have the same name. For example, suppose you have two users named Barbara Jensen, one in the California office and the other in the Michigan office. Using multivalued RDNs, you could distinguish between these two entries by naming one cn=Barbara Jensen + l=California and the other cn=Barbara Jensen + l=Michigan.

This practice tends to lead to long, complicated names that change frequently (what if either Barbara moves?). Also, some directory implementations, such as the Netscape Directory Server, do not fully support multivalued RDNs. For these reasons, we strongly discourage their use and encourage you instead to use one of the other naming conflict-resolution strategies discussed.

Tip

When choosing a naming attribute, use something that is unlikely to change and is unique across your directory. Try to use a standard attribute name and avoid unintentionally exposing sensitive information. Sensitive attributes can sometimes be used by employing a hash of the sensitive value rather than the value itself. Avoid using multivalued RDNs for naming. Pilot your naming scheme to make sure users do not hate it.

Application Considerations

Most people do not design and run a directory service for its own sake. Typically, the directory is required to support one or more directory-enabled applications. The requirements these applications place on the namespace and other aspects of your design are important design considerations. After all, if your directory does not satisfy the requirements of the applications driving its deployment, your chances of postdeployment employment are small.

The requirements an application can place on your directory are as varied as the applications themselves. Lest you become dismayed and think that anticipating the needs of an endless parade of different applications is a lost cause, consider the following.

First, focusing on the needs of directory applications existing or being deployed in your organization today will probably provide you with a fairly representative cross-section of requirements. Make sure you understand these needs as well as possible before you consider yourself finished with your directory design (see Chapter 5, "Defining Your Directory Needs"). Piloting your directory on a smaller, test-scale deployment is also a good idea.

Second, some general principles you can follow will help prepare you for that future parade of directory-enabled applications. These principles are important to keep in mind both when designing your directory and when writing a directory-enabled application. For more information, see Chapter 20, "Developing New Applications."

A well-written, directory-enabled application makes a concerted effort to assume as little as possible about the directory service it will access. An application should be configurable and able to adapt to new namespaces, new types of acceptable queries, schema differences, nonstandard port numbers, new host names, and more. Of course, not all applications are able to provide this kind of flexibility. How can you design your namespace to anticipate as many of these problems as possible?

If your existing needs allow it, one good approach is to use a standard namespace design. Although no real standard exists today, there is ongoing work in this area. For example, there is a current Internet Draft that describes an Internet domain component namespace model. This model solves several namespace design problems, such as choosing the suffix under which the rest of your namespace lives.

In the domain component namespace, your suffix is constructed by taking your domain name (for example, netscape.com) and algorithmically turning it into a DN (for example, dc=netscape, dc=com). Beneath this suffix, namespace design is up to you. This namespace allows you to automatically go from a domain name (as found in an email address, for example) to a DN. An example of this approach to naming is shown in Figure 8.12.

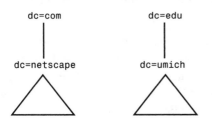

FIGURE 8.12   *Examples of standard namespaces.*

Earlier, we advised that when it comes down to picking the attribute used to name entries, try to use a standard attribute such as cn or uid. If you are considering creating a new attribute to hold the naming value—for example, `employeeID`—consider placing the value of the `employeeID` attribute in the `cn` or another standard attribute, and then use that attribute for naming instead of `employeeID`. Although this might seem aesthetically unpleasant, applications that assume standard attributes for the namespace will not become confused.

Namespace and other directory design choices like this are common. When starting from scratch, you can often afford to make things aesthetically pleasing as well as functional. It is rare, unfortunately, that you will be able to start completely from scratch without worrying about any existing applications.

Administrative Considerations

When designing your namespace, consider the effect the namespace will have on common administrative tasks. For example, when adding an entry, can the naming attributes be generated automatically, or is it a manual process? When entries are deleted, can their naming attributes be reused, or should they forever be reserved for the deleted entry? What effect will a name change have? How often are name changes likely to take place? What other dependencies are there on the namespace? The answers to these questions are seldom independent of the design decisions discussed in the previous sections. In this section, we discuss the administrative implications of those decisions.

If your organization already has some unique identifier assigned to users (for example, an employee number, login name, or user ID), it may make sense to use it as the value of the naming attribute. This saves you the administrative burden of devising and maintaining another unique identifier and is a good solution for naming user entries.

Other entries, perhaps for printers, groups, or other entities, are another matter. In either case, using an existing attribute type can eliminate another small administrative task: defining a new attribute type to use when naming entries. It also reduces the likelihood that a less-than-intelligent client could be confused by an unknown attribute.

The maintenance of the naming attribute is also a consideration. Whether or not the directory is the ultimate source of authority, the problem of reusability must be addressed. Depending on your policies, namespace identifiers might be assigned only once and never reassigned, reassigned after a suitable interval, or reassigned immediately. Whatever policy you choose, there must be some way to enforce the policy.

Most directory software does not support an out-of-the-box namespace reuse policy. Instead, you have to enforce such a policy either through some external administrative agent or through an extension to the directory software itself.

An example of the former might be a tool for adding entries to the directory that consults an external database managing the reuse policy. An example of the latter might be a plug-in to the Netscape Directory Server that performs that same process.

Almost inevitably, name changes will occur for various reasons. If you choose a naming attribute that has any significance other than its uniqueness, it can change. If you choose a naming attribute that has a relation to some real-world attribute of the entity being named, or if you choose a hierarchical namespace whose upper components could change, names will also change. The consequences of a name change should be carefully considered. How much trouble will it cause and what is the likelihood of its occurrence?

Tip

Beware of thinking that a name change will be the exceptional case, so rare that you would not mind handling such occurrences through even a tedious manual process. Our experience shows that such trouble has a habit of occurring more frequently than you might imagine. You also need to consider what will happen as your directory grows (a prediction likely to come true). What may seem uncommon in a small directory can become a downright nuisance in a large one.

A final consideration is whether there are other dependencies on the namespace you choose. For example, there might be an application someone has written that assumes a particular structure to the namespace. Without question, this is an example of an evil application. Yet, if the application is servicing your users, you must be concerned about breaking it.

Privacy Considerations

Directory names are usually public information available to anyone who can access the directory. Trying to control access to names via your directory's access control mechanism can often lead to difficulties. For this reason, you must carefully consider the privacy implications of your namespace design. Your goal should be not to divulge any information through the namespace that you do not intend to divulge.

For example, if you design a namespace for your people entries based on organizational hierarchy, you reveal the part of your organization an entry (and presumably the corresponding person) resides in. The same problem holds true for many other hierarchical namespace designs.

As described earlier, the attribute you choose to name your entries after may be considered sensitive. We saw an example earlier involving the use of Social Security numbers for naming attributes. Clearly, this would be a bad idea, so we suggested using a hashed-value form of the sensitive information.

There are other, more subtle privacy concerns as well. For example, using the cn attribute containing a person's name to name entries has a host of implications. A person's gender can often be inferred from his or her name, as can other information such as nationality or ethnicity. Not to mention the fact that a name is often enough to gain other information—such as an address, phone number, and so on—from other publicly available sources.

Care should be taken to protect privacy and to ensure that unwanted disclosure of information is minimized. Keep in mind that things that are obviously acceptable to you may be completely unacceptable to some of your users. For example, you might not mind disclosing your name or even your address to everyone in your company or the world. However, one of your users who might be concerned about potential harassment or stalking—or even worse—might feel quite differently.

Try to design a namespace that is free of such considerations, and be prepared to make exceptions for people who have legitimate concerns with any design you come up with. It may be a good idea to involve your legal department to help interpret legal issues associated with directory information privacy. Directory privacy is covered in more detail in Chapter 11.

Anticipating the Future

Finally, as difficult as it may be, you must try to anticipate the future when designing your namespace. The reason is simple: A namespace redesign is a costly and inconvenient process that you want to avoid. Because none of us has a crystal ball, the best we can do is try to avoid common situations in which namespace changes are required.

The question naturally arises, therefore, about the kinds of situations that precipitate a namespace redesign. Some of the more common situations are described in the following list:

- Choosing the wrong naming attribute can easily lead to a namespace redesign. For example, if you choose to name entries with the cn attribute using a value of first name followed by last name, what do you do when two people turn out to have the same name? Either a namespace redesign is required or you must be prepared to artificially make one of the names unique, as described previously.

- If your directory starts out under central administrative control, but you later decide to delegate control of some portion of the data, a namespace redesign may be required. As we mentioned earlier, some access control implementations do not allow delegation except at subtree boundaries. The same is true for replication and partitioning of the data.

- If you choose a hierarchical namespace with a hierarchy based on a geo-graphical, organizational, or other scheme that is likely to change, constant namespace redesigns, both big and small, may haunt you. It is best to avoid this situation altogether from the start. If you choose to reflect your organizational hierarchy, for example, a namespace redesign is required each time your company reorganizes. For some reorganization-happy companies, this can be quite a problem!

Although no one can accurately predict the future, there are some defensive namespace design tactics you can use to minimize your risk. Choosing a flat namespace is one such tactic. Subdividing your namespace based on unchanging information—perhaps into areas for people, groups, devices—permits redesigns in one space that do not affect the others.

Examples of Namespaces

Now that we've described the purposes of a namespace and the major decisions that must be made when designing one, we turn our attention to some examples that should help illustrate the points we've been discussing. Here we consider both flat and hierarchical namespaces. (More design examples can be found in Part VI, "Case Studies.")

Flat Namespace Examples

We advised you to design your namespace to be as flat as possible within the constraints created by your replication, access control, and other needs. This section describes two examples of flat namespaces for the mythical Airius company.

In the first example, a completely flat space is created. The naming attribute chosen is cn for simplicity. Each entry is named using a sequentially generated number that has no other significance. The resulting namespace is shown in Figure 8.13.

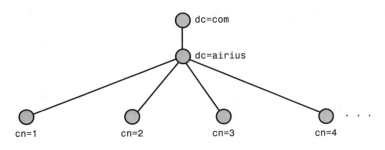

FIGURE 8.13   *An example of a flat namespace.*

Our second flat namespace example introduces a bit of hierarchy, with a flat namespace beneath each hierarchical component. The small amount of hierarchy in this namespace is used only to group different types of objects under a common portion of the tree. This has the effect of insulating namespace changes in one space from the others. It also makes it possible to partition and therefore replicate information on these same boundaries. Administrative control can also be distributed on these boundaries. The resulting namespace is shown in Figure 8.14.

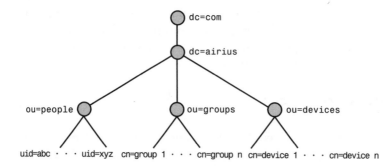

F IGURE 8.14   *An example of a flat hierarchical namespace.*

In our experience, a namespace like the one shown in Figure 8.14 is nearly optimal in many environments. It has enough hierarchy not to hinder you when your needs change (for example, in replication or access control); however, the hierarchy it does have is not based on information likely to change (for example, geographical or organizational information).

Hierarchical Namespace Examples

There are reasons you may need a hierarchical namespace, perhaps because of limitations in the directory software you've chosen or because of constraints imposed upon your directory by applications. This section illustrates two examples of hierarchical namespaces based on different hierarchical schemes. Again, we use the mythical Airius company as our guinea pig.

For the first hierarchical example, consider that Airius is a global company distributed across three continents. Airius has an office in each continent that must have control over its own data, yet the sum total of the data must appear to the outside world as a single, coordinated information tree.

Taking a lesson from the flat namespace example, Airius decides to use a similar namespace in each of its divisions. Because divisions need autonomy in their ability to manage, access, and change their own data, the top-level namespace hierarchy is divided using a geographical scheme. The resulting namespace is shown in Figure 8.15.

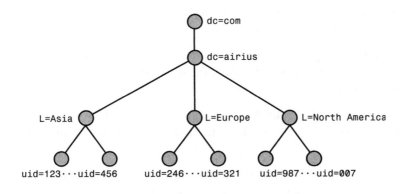

FIGURE 8.15   *An example of a hierarchical namespace.*

Our second example of a hierarchical namespace is based on Airius's internal organizational structure. Although you might be able to rationalize building such a namespace, we don't recommend it. But, in this example, the misguided Airius directory designer has decided to forge ahead. To reflect the organizational hierarchy, he's chosen to use the ou attribute with values corresponding to department names. To name leaf-level entries, the cn attribute has been chosen with a value of first name, middle initial, and last name. Name collisions are handled by appending a number to entries that collide. The resulting namespace is depicted in Figure 8.16.

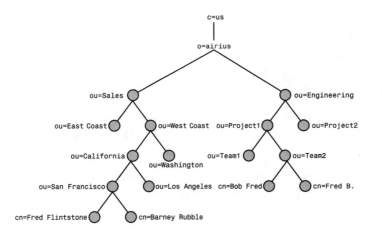

FIGURE 8.16   *Another example of a hierarchical namespace.*

Namespace Design Checklist

This section summarizes a list of issues you should consider when designing your namespace.

- ☐ Consider the number of entries your directory will need to support, and try to predict the rate at which that number will increase.

- ☐ Consider the types of entries your directory will store. Decide whether the entries are all the same or of different types and whether new types will likely be added in the future.

- ☐ Determine whether your directory data needs to be centralized or distributed. When choosing a directory product, make sure it supports your choice.

- ☐ Consider the requirements for delegating authority to different parts of your directory and how they affect the design of your namespace.

- ☐ Consider the effects of replication requirements on your namespace design.

- ☐ Keep firmly in mind the applications that will access your directory and any special requirements they may have.

- ☐ Think carefully about the attribute you will use to name entries and how best to maintain it.

- ☐ Design a system for ensuring and maintaining uniqueness of names in your directory.

- ☐ Formulate a name reuse policy that determines if, when, and how names may be reused.

Further Reading

Lightweight Directory Access Protocol (v3) (RFC 2251). M. Wahl, S. Kille, and T. Howes, December 1997.

Lightweight Directory Access Protocol (v3): UTF-8 String Representation of Distinguished Names (RFC 2253). M. Wahl, S. Kille, and T. Howes, December 1997.

Naming and Structuring Guidelines for X.500 Directory Pilots (RFC 1617). P. Barker, S. Kille, and T. Lenggenhager, May 1994.

Naming Guidelines for the AARNet X.500 Directory Service (RFC 1562). G. Michaelson and M. Prior, December 1993.

NIST, FIPS PUB 180-1: Secure Hash Standard. April 1995. This document is available online at `http://nvl.nist.gov/`.

The MD5 Message-Digest Algorithm (RFC 1321). R. Rivest, April 1992.

Using Domains in LDAP/X.500 Distinguished Names (RFC 2247). S. Kille, M. Wahl, A. Grimstad, R. Huber, and S. Sataluri, January 1998.

Looking Ahead

Now that we've covered the topic of namespace design, it's time to turn our attention to an even more exciting aspect of directory service design: server topology. This topic is covered in Chapter 9, "Topology Design."

Topology Design

LDAP directory services are designed to support a *distributed directory*, in which the complete directory tree is spread across multiple physical directory servers. Your directory service's *topology* describes the way you divide your directory tree among physical servers and how you allocate those servers among your organization's physical locations. Making good choices about your directory topology will help you:

- Achieve the best possible performance for your directory-enabled applications

- Increase directory availability

- Better manage your directory

In this chapter we first examine how a distributed directory works. We discuss several important background concepts, including the definition of a directory partition, name resolution in a distributed directory, and how separate partitions are hooked together into a single directory through the use of referrals or chaining. Finally, we discuss why you might or might not want to partition your directory, and we work through two sample scenarios.

This chapter is closely related to Chapters 8, "Namespace Design," and 10, "Replication Design." In fact, we suggest that you read all three chapters as a unit because decisions concerning namespace design have direct consequences for your directory topology, which in turn has a direct bearing on your replication strategy. After you read this chapter, you'll know how to partition your directory service for maximum performance and manageability and how to allocate servers across your LAN or WAN. This knowledge, along with the information presented in Chapter 10, will help you design a highly robust, high-performance directory service.

Directory Topology Overview

A directory service can be asked to store a potentially large number of entries—far more entries, in some cases, than one server can be reasonably expected to hold. To enable a directory to hold such large numbers of entries, it may be necessary for it to reside on more than one server.

A directory that resides on more than one server is a *distributed directory*. When you carve a single directory into manageable chunks and assign them to separate servers, you are *partitioning* the directory. For example, a large corporation might choose to partition its directory as shown in Figure 9.1.

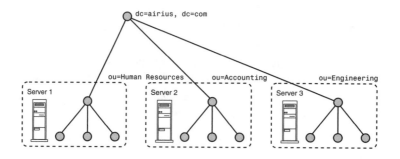

FIGURE 9.1   *A distributed directory.*

The dotted lines surrounding each server computer in Figure 9.1 indicate that the partition resides on that particular server. This is a convention we will use throughout this chapter.

When the directory tree is divided among a number of servers, each server is responsible for only a portion of the tree, which reduces the amount of work it needs to do. Using this principle of dividing a directory namespace into a number of partitions and assigning those partitions to separate servers, the directory can be made to scale to a much larger number of entries than would be possible with a single server. The Domain Name Service (DNS) operates in a similar fashion, with each portion of the DNS namespace (for example, airius.com) assigned to a particular DNS server that may be replicated to improve availability.

The unit of division is known by several different names depending on the directory server software you are using or the standards documentation you may be reading. Novell Directory Services (NDS) uses the term *directory partition*, whereas the X.500 standards documents use the term *naming context*. Both terms mean essentially the same thing, but we'll use the term *partition* throughout this chapter.

An important point to remember is that the directory itself is responsible for hiding all these partitioning details from the user. As far as users and applications are concerned, there is simply a single directory that answers their directory queries. The actual mechanics of how these details are hidden from users are discussed in detail later in the chapter. For now, simply remember that the various partitions are glued together into a single, logical directory tree from the client's or application's point of view.

A directory partition is a complete subtree of the directory information tree (DIT), minus any subtrees that are held within other partitions. A given directory entry resides in only one directory partition, and all entries within a partition must share a common ancestor known as the *partition root*. Figure 9.2 shows a very basic directory partition with a partition root of dc=airius, dc=com. The partition, denoted by the dotted line, extends downward from the partition root (dc=airius, dcom) and does not exclude any entries. In other words, it is a complete subtree.

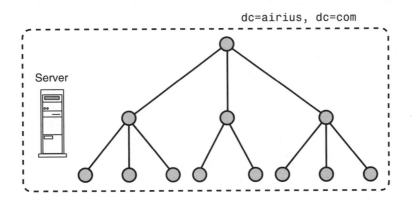

dc=airius, dc=com

Server

FIGURE 9.2   *A DIT contained in a single partition.*

It is also possible to selectively exclude subtrees from a partition. In Figure 9.3, there are two partitions. One is rooted at dc=airius, dc=com and includes all entries beneath dc=airius, dc=com except for those in the other partition. This second partition contains the entry ou=External Customers, dc=airius, dc=com and all entries beneath it.

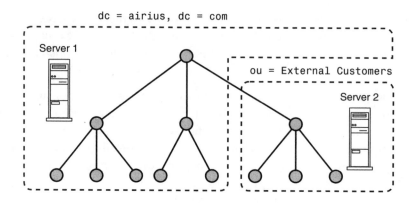

FIGURE 9.3   *A DIT split into two partitions.*

This partitioning arrangement would allow the subtree ou=External Customers, dc=airius, dc=com to reside on a different server than the rest of the directory tree.

Using this principle, you can divide a single large directory tree into a number of smaller partitions. Each partition can be assigned to a separate server, if required, either to handle the client load or because of limits on the number of entries that can be held by a server. For example, Airius's directory could be divided into partitions and assigned to four servers, as shown in Figure 9.4.

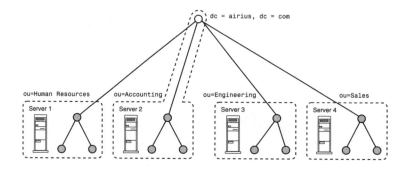

FIGURE 9.4   *A DIT partitioned across four servers.*

To further clarify the concept of a directory partition, let's also look at some illegal directory partitions. In Figure 9.5, partition 1 is invalid because it contains a "hole": Entry b is missing from the partition. Partition 2 is invalid because it is not a proper subtree: Not all the entries in the partition share a common ancestor. Partitions 3 and 4 are invalid for a similar reason as Partition 2: Although all entries do share a common ancestor, the ancestor is not contained within the partition.

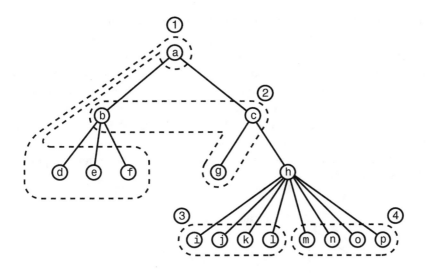

F I G U R E 9.5 *Examples of illegal partitions.*

Although we've only shown examples in which a given server holds a single partition, this need not be the case. A server can actually hold many directory partitions. For example, a directory server might hold a read-only copy of the top-level partition along with the master copy of a particular organizational unit's partition. Or, an Internet service provider might choose to offer directory services to corporate clients and deploy a number of "virtual" directories on a single server—with sufficient RAM, CPU, and disk resources, of course.

Gluing the Directory Together: Knowledge References

So far, we've described the directory partition in terms of the entries it contains. However, we still need some way to describe the relationships between directory partitions. The LDAP and X.500 standards define these relationships in terms of *knowledge references*—pointers to directory information held in another partition. There are two types of knowledge references:

- *Immediate superior knowledge references*. This type of knowledge reference points upward in the DIT toward the root and ties the naming context to its ancestor. In effect, it provides the "hook" at the top of the directory partition that you use to hang a partition from its ancestor.

- *Subordinate references.* These knowledge references point downward in the DIT to other partitions. They are the hooks onto which you hang other naming contexts.

Figure 9.6 illustrates how directory partitions fit together into a larger DIT. In this example, the partition root `ou=London, dc=airius, dc=com` denotes the top of the partition. The partition contains the partition root and all the entries underneath it, except for those entries held in partitions pointed to by the two subordinate references, `ou=Accounting, ou=London, dc=airius, dc=com` and `ou=Engineering, ou=London, dc=airius, dc=com`. An immediate superior knowledge reference also points upward in the DIT, connecting this partition to its parent partition. Knowledge references always come in pairs; although not shown, the parent partition would thus have a subordinate reference pointing to the partition in the figure.

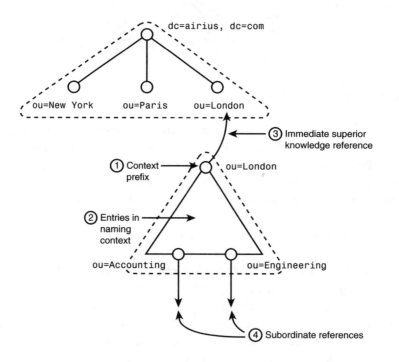

FIGURE 9.6   *A naming context in a DIT.*

> **Note**
>
> Directory servers based on the LDAPv3 standard advertise the partitions they hold in a special entry called the root DSE (DSA-specific entry; DSA stands for Directory System Agent and is the X.500 term for a directory server). The root DSE is a special entry that contains information about the directory server, including its capabilities and configuration. To discover the partitions held by a given server, you can perform a search for the entry with a zero-length name, with a scope of base and a search filter of (objectclass=*). The attribute namingContexts contained in the returned entry gives the partition roots of all partitions held by the server.

Your directory server software may use these same terms, or it may have some alternative way of talking about how partitions are named and related. But in virtually all cases, this model is a good basis for understanding how your server software can be used to construct real-world directories.

Dividing a directory in this fashion isn't useful all by itself. If we were to just leave the partitions as a series of isolated islands, locating an entry or searching across a series of partitions would be tedious. The user of the directory would need to know which servers to contact to perform an operation that spans multiple partitions. Clearly, directory partitions need to know about each other to work together as a single, cohesive unit.

Name Resolution in the Distributed Directory

Now that we understand partitions and knowledge references, the basic building blocks of a distributed directory, let's examine an important concept: *name resolution*. This is the process by which a directory maps a distinguished name (DN) provided by a client to an actual object in the directory. This process is used in the following circumstances:

- When locating the base object of an LDAP search or compare operation

- When locating an entry to modify, delete, rename, or bind as

- When locating the parent of an entry to be added to the directory

A DN presented in this fashion is called a *purported name*. The client purports that it exists, and it is up to the directory system to check whether this is true.

In the simplest case—a client contacts a directory server and presents the DN of an entry contained in that server—the name resolution process is quite simple: The server simply checks whether the entry exists and takes the appropriate action. For example, if a directory client attempts to read an entry via LDAP, the server checks whether the DN of the entry is within one of the naming contexts it holds; if it is, it checks its database for the entry. If the entry exists, any requested attributes are returned. Otherwise, a "no such object" error is returned to the client.

If the client presents a purported name whose DN is not within any of the naming contexts held by a server, the server must use any available knowledge references either to resolve the name itself or aid the client in locating the server that can resolve the name. Conceptually, the name is resolved by "walking up" or "walking down" the directory tree until the appropriate server is located. The knowledge references fully describe how a given naming context fits into the DIT, so a server always knows whether the next step in the name resolution process involves walking up or walking down the DIT.

For example, suppose that the directory client depicted in Figure 9.7 contacts Server 1 and presents the purported name cn=Barbara Jensen, ou=PCB Design, ou=Engineering, dc=airius, dc=com. Name resolution would proceed as follows:

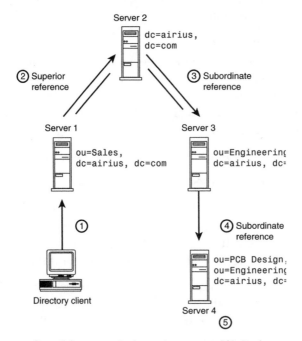

FIGURE 9.7   *Name resolution in a distributed directory.*

1. The directory client presents the purported name.

2. Because Server 1 does not hold a naming context that could contain the entry, the immediate superior knowledge reference allows the name resolution process to walk up the tree to Server 2.

3. Server 2 contains a subordinate reference for the naming context `ou=Engineering, dc=airius, dc=com`, so the name resolution process walks down the tree to Server 3.

4. Server 3 holds a subordinate reference for the naming context `ou=PCB Design, ou=Engineering, dc=airius, dc=com`, so the process walks down the tree again.

5. Finally, Server 4 is consulted to check whether the entry actually exists.

Up to this point, we've been discussing knowledge references and name resolution in an abstract sense, and you may be curious about the software in the directory system that actually performs this tree walking operation. To answer that, we'll discuss the specifics of how this knowledge reference "glue" works as we discuss the two methods directory servers use to carry out distributed operations: referrals and chaining.

Gluing Together a Directory with Referrals

A *referral* is a piece of information returned by an LDAP server that indicates to the client that other servers need to be contacted to fulfill the request. The client then typically contacts the other servers, resubmits the original request, and presents the results to the user.

Let's illustrate this with an example (see Figure 9.8). Suppose that an LDAP client issues a search operation to Server 1 with a search base of `ou=Engineering, dc=airius, dc=com`, a scope of `subtree`, and a filter of `(¦(objectclass=person)(sn=smith))`. In other words, the client wishes to find all persons within `dc=airius, dc=com` whose surname is `smith`.

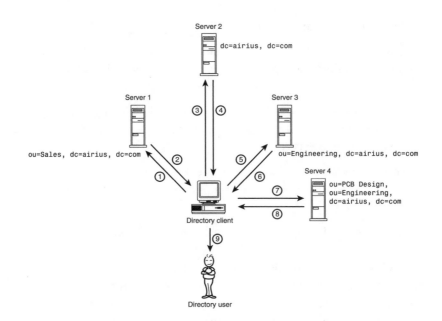

FIGURE 9.8 *Distributed searching with referrals.*

To service this search request, the distributed directory first uses name resolution to find the base object of the search. It then uses any knowledge references to refer the client to all the servers it needs to contact to obtain the entire set of matching entries.

The following sequence describes this search procedure in greater detail:

- Part 1: Resolve the name of the base object of the search.

    Step 1. The client submits the search request to Server 1.

    Step 2. Server 1 does not hold an appropriate naming context, so it examines the superior reference and returns to the client a referral to Server 2.

    Step 3. The client submits the search operation to Server 2.

    Step 4. Server 2 contains a subordinate reference to Server 3 for an appropriate naming context, so it returns to the client a referral to Server 3.

    Step 5. The client submits the search operation to Server 3.

- Part 2: Service the search operation.

    Step 6. Server 3 searches its database and returns any matching entries to the client. Because it also contains a subordinate reference to server 4, it returns to the client a referral to Server 4.

    Step 7. The client submits the search operation to Server 4.

    Step 8. Server 4 returns any matching entries to the client.

    Step 9. The client combines the lists of entries returned from Server 3 and Server 4, and presents them to the user.

This example shows how the directory, through the use of knowledge references, can direct a client to the correct servers—even if the client happens to ask the wrong server.

The Structure of an LDAP Referral

The information in an LDAP referral is in the format of an LDAP uniform resource locator (URL), as defined in RFC 2255. A referral gives the following information:

- The host name of the server to contact.

- The port number of the server.

- The base DN (if processing a search operation) or target DN (if processing an add, delete, compare, or moddn operation). This part is optional; if absent, the client should use the same base DN it used when performing the operation that resulted in the referral.

This information is all that is required for the client to chase the referral. For example, if a client searches the subtree dc=airius, dc=com for all entries with a surname smith (as in the preceding example), the referral would be returned as the following LDAP URL:

```
ldap://server1.airius.com:389/ou=Engineering, dc=airius, dc=com
```

This LDAP URL indicates that the client should contact the host server1.airius.com on port 389 and submit a search rooted at ou=Engineering, dc=airius, dc=com to collect the rest of the search results. Notice that the base DN in the referral is different from the one originally supplied by the client. When a server issues a referral in this manner, it is indicating to the client that, in addition to contacting a different server, it must also search another part of the DIT to complete the search processing. By contrast, referrals issued in response to update operations normally contain either the same target DN specified in the original operation or no target DN at all, which have the same effect.

The method for configuring referrals depends on your particular directory server software. For Netscape Directory Server, there are two places you configure referrals. The *default referral* is returned when an operation submitted by a client is based at a DN that is not contained within any of the server's naming contexts. For example, if a server holds only the naming context dc=airius, dc=com, and a client performs a search rooted at the DN dc=acme, dc=com, the server will return the default referral. Generally you configure the default referral to point to a directory server that has more knowledge about the directory partitioning arrangement at your site. The default referral functions like an immediate superior knowledge reference.

The other type of referral supported by the Netscape Directory Server, a *smart referral*, is essentially a subordinate reference. The smart referral is stored in the ref attribute of a directory entry and gives the LDAP URLs of other directory servers that have knowledge of the subtree whose DN is the same as the DN of the entry containing the smart referral. Note that the entry must have an auxiliary objectclass of referral in order to permit storage of the ref attribute. Smart referrals are being standardized as part of the LDAPv3 extensions process.

In Figure 9.9, a client that performs a search rooted at dc=airius, dc=com is returned any matching entries held within Server 1, along with a referral to Server 2. The client then automatically follows this referral and presents the complete list of matching entries to its user. In this way, smart referrals can be used to glue together a set of cooperating servers into a single, logical directory tree.

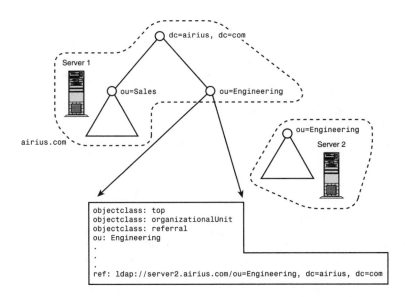

FIGURE 9.9   *Placement of a smart referral in a directory entry.*

Tip

Support for LDAP referrals is standardized as part of the LDAPv3 specification. Servers and clients based on the older U-M LDAPv2 source code distribution support an experimental implementation of referrals that is incompatible with the LDAPv3 standard. The Netscape Directory Server operates with both v2 or v3 clients by sending LDAPv3-format referrals to LDAPv3 clients and LDAPv2-format referrals to LDAPv2 clients.

Note

If you are developing an application using either the Netscape C LDAP software development kit (SDK) or the Netscape Java LDAP SDK, you can either instruct SDK to automatically follow, or "chase," referrals (the default), or you can tell it to pass referral information back to your program for action.

One reason you might not want to automatically chase referrals is if you want to provide feedback to the user indicating that a referral is being followed. Or, you might want to warn the user if a referral outside your corporate firewall is returned.

As a developer, you have total control over how your application handles referrals. Good directory client software even allows the end user to configure whether referrals should be automatically followed and how to handle authentication when following referrals.

Because these smart referrals are stored as attributes in directory entries, you might ask how it's possible to manage these attributes. Won't the directory just return a referral when you attempt to manipulate them? To manage the `ref` attribute, your client needs to include the `manageDSAIT` LDAP control along with the operation. This control is an extra piece of information sent by the client to the server informing it that the operation intends to manipulate these types of attributes. With the Netscape command-line LDAP tools, include the `-M` command-line flag to cause the `manageDSAIT` control to be included with the request. You must, of course, have sufficient access to perform this operation.

Note

Where does the term `manageDSAIT` *come from? In X.500 terminology, the DSA information tree, or DSAIT, is the set of entries held by a particular X.500 server. This set of entries includes the actual directory entries that users can retrieve, but it also includes additional entries needed to attach the server's tree to the global directory namespace and additional attributes within entries that control the behavior of the directory. These entries and attributes are not normally visible to users. When an administrator manipulates these entries and attributes, he is managing the DSA Information Tree— hence, the name* `manageDSAIT`.

Gluing Together a Directory with Chaining

Another way to glue together directory partitions is through the use of *chaining*. When this approach is used, the client starts by submitting an operation to a server in the usual way. If the server is unable to completely process the request because it does not hold all the required data, it contacts other servers on behalf of the client. It then returns the combined results to the client when the other servers have completed the operation. Figure 9.10 shows how a directory distributed using chaining would respond to the same query shown in Figure 9.8.

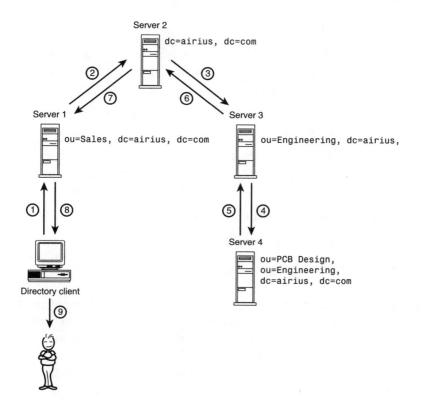

FIGURE 9.10   *Distributed searching with chaining.*

When using chaining, servers perform the following steps to service a search operation:

- Part 1: Resolve the name of the base object of the search.

   Step 1. The client submits the search request to Server 1.

   Step 2. Server 1 does not hold an appropriate naming context, so it consults its immediate superior reference and chains the operation to Server 2.

   Step 3. Server 2 contains a subordinate reference to Server 3 for an appropriate naming context, so it chains the operation to Server 3.

   Step 4a. Server 3 verifies that the base object exists.

- Part 2: Service the search operation.

    Step 4b. Server 3 searches its database for any matching entries. It also discovers that it holds a subordinate reference to Server 4, so it chains the operation to Server 4.

    Step 5. Server 4 searches its database and returns any matching entries to Server 3.

    Step 6. Server 3 combines the entries retrieved from its own database with those returned by Server 4 and sends the resulting set to Server 2.

    Step 7. Server 2 returns the set of entries to Server 1.

    Step 8. Server 1 returns the set of entries to the client.

    Step 9. The client presents the set of entries to the user.

As you can see, the same number of steps is involved when chaining and referrals are used. In both cases, the knowledge information is stored in the directory itself. The major difference is the location of the intelligence that knows how to locate the distributed information. In a chained system, this intelligence is implemented in the servers; in a system that uses referrals, this intelligence is implemented in the clients.

Deciding Between Referrals and Chaining

Each method of linking distributed directory servers has advantages and disadvantages. Chaining generally reduces client complexity, but at the cost of increased server complexity. Servers that support chaining must be able to collect search results from remote servers and send the resulting set to directory clients. Referrals, on the other hand, require more client complexity to handle the chasing of referrals and collation of search results. Referrals do, however, offer more flexibility for client applications writers and allow a developer to provide the user of the application more feedback about the progress of a distributed directory operation.

You may not have a choice about which method you use if your directory server supports only one method. Typically, standalone directory servers, such as the Netscape Directory Server, support only referrals. In fact, servers based on the LDAPv3 protocol specification must support referrals. However, there is nothing in the LDAP protocol specification that precludes chaining.

Servers based on X.500 standards usually support chaining and may also support referrals. The X.500 specification does not actually mandate that servers support chaining, so the type of distribution method (chaining or referrals) again depends on the software in use. Consult your server software documentation to determine which methods are supported and recommended.

Putting Knowledge Information into Your Directory

The procedure by which you get this knowledge information into your directory depends on the type of directory server software you are using. The following are the three most common types of directory service software:

- *X.500.* X.500 servers based on the 1993 standard define a protocol for setting up and tearing down these relationships between servers. The actual protocol is known as the Hierarchical Operational Binding Protocol. As the name implies, it is used to establish a hierarchical relationship between two X.500 naming contexts and sets up the superior/subordinate references. Your software may not use this rather frightening terminology (in fact, one would hope not!); instead it may provide a more user-friendly interface for specifying partitions and how they relate to one another. Consult your server's documentation for specific procedures.

- *Novell Directory Services.* NDS, which is based on the X.500 standards, has a similar model, but it uses proprietary methods to establish new partitions and set up the hierarchical relationships between them. Novell's Partition Manager utility allows a manager to create new partitions and assign them to NDS servers.

- *Netscape Directory Server.* Netscape Directory Server requires that you manually configure the relationship of each server to other directory servers in your organization. As discussed previously, there are two types of knowledge information you can specify in the Netscape server. The *default referral* is given by the slapd.conf configuration file parameter named referral. You can configure the default referral through the Netscape Administration Server (in Netscape Directory Server 3.0) or the Netscape Console (in Netscape Directory Server 4.0). *Smart referrals*, also in the format of an LDAP URL, are stored within the directory itself. You manage smart referrals by using the ldapmodify command-line tool with the -M option (for manageDSAIT) to add the auxiliary objectclass referral and ref attribute to a directory entry. This procedure is documented in the *Netscape Directory Server Administration Guide*.

Authentication in a Distributed Directory

Handling authentication of directory clients in a distributed directory presents some challenges. The server or servers that ultimately handle a client request must verify the identity of the client so that they can enforce access control restrictions. This is true even if the server handling the request is not the server to which the client originally authenticated. For example, consider what happens when a directory client connects and authenticates to a server and then submits a search operation chained to another server (see Figure 9.11).

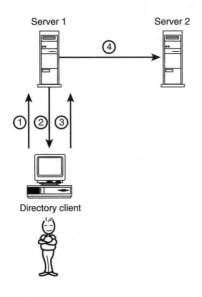

FIGURE 9.11   *Authentication in a chained topology.*

The following steps describe how authentication is performed in a chained environment:

1. The directory client connects to Server 1 and authenticates.

2. If the client's authentication credentials are successfully verified, Server 1 returns a success code to the client.

3. The client submits a search operation to Server 1.

4. Server 1 determines that it does not hold the appropriate partition, so it chains the operation to Server 2.

For Server 2 to enforce access control while performing the search operation, it needs to know the identity of the client. There are two ways it might learn this information:

- Server 1 might tell Server 2 who the client is, and Server 2 might simply choose to believe Server 1. This requires that Server 2 trusts Server 1 to correctly verify authentication credentials.

- Server 1 might pass on to Server 2 the client's identity and authentication credentials. Server 2 could then independently verify the credentials. This requires that Server 1 trust Server 2 not to misuse the authentication credentials (for example, if the credentials are a plaintext password, Server 2 must not reveal them to a third party).

In a chained environment, the chaining server (Server 1) can pass along the identity of the client when it chains the operation. If the server it chains to (Server 2) trusts the other server (presumably because the chaining server authenticated to Server 2, and the server is on a list of trusted servers), the operation can proceed. This is, in fact, how X.500 servers handle authentication in a distributed environment if the client uses simple authentication.

If, on the other hand, the client has authenticated to Server 1 using certificate-based client authentication, Server 1 can just pass along the digitally signed request and allow Server 2 to verify the client's identity directly because the digital signature contains the identity of the client. This is how X.500 servers operate when certificate-based client authentication is used. This is also how NDS servers operate (all NDS authentication is handled with digital signatures).

In a directory distributed via referrals, the client resubmits its request to each server it is referred to during the course of processing an operation. Therefore, each server it refers to authenticates the client directly. This means that no pre-arranged trust relationships need to be established between servers. If simple authentication is used, the server referred to will likely need to verify the client's password by contacting another server because it's unlikely to contain the actual entry corresponding to the client identity.

For example, if a client submits a bind operation to the Netscape Directory Server, and the bind DN is not held in any of the server's naming contexts, the server attempts to locate and contact the server that does hold the entry. If it can locate the server, it verifies the credentials by binding to that server using the credentials supplied by the client.

> **Note**
>
> *In order for certificate-based client authentication to work in a distributed directory, all servers must trust some common set of certification authorities. If this is not the case, it's possible for one server to successfully authenticate a client while another server rejects the client's credentials during chaining or following referrals. This can lead to end-user confusion.*

Security Implications

Both methods of combining directory partitions—chaining and referral—require some careful thought about security. When you construct a distributed directory using referrals, you should take precautions to ensure that you have absolute control over the referrals contained in your directory. Additionally, you should allow referrals only to directories you trust.

This is important because some directory clients may choose to automatically resubmit any referred operations and authenticate to the referred-to server using the same credentials that were used when authenticating to the original server. This means that if a rogue referral were placed in a directory, the directory clients might be tricked into resubmitting their authentication credentials to the rogue server. If the authentication method in use does not preclude a replay attack (for example, if the authentication credentials are in the clear), the rogue server can record the credentials and use them to masquerade as the client.

To prevent this possibility, you should ensure that the ability to place a `ref` attribute in the directory is limited to a set of people you trust so that rogue referrals cannot end up in the directory. In addition, consider using an authentication method impervious to replay attack, such as public-key cryptography or Kerberos. With these authentication systems, even if a rogue server happens to capture a client's authentication credentials, those credentials cannot be used indefinitely to masquerade as the client.

When you construct a distributed directory using chaining, you must use caution when establishing any trust relationships between servers. You should trust only remote servers under your direct control or run by organizations you trust.

In both types of environments, if you are using certificate-based client authentication, you should trust only digital signatures signed by a trusted certification authority. This requires that you trust that certification authority to issue certificates only to persons who have adequately proven their identity. Usually, this means that you trust only those certificates granted by your in-house certification authority. But in an extranet environment, you might choose to relax this restriction and accept certificates from your trading partners' certification authorities, assuming you trust them or an independent certification authority such as VeriSign.

As with all complex distributed systems, designing a secure directory requires careful thought and planning. It's always useful to think like a "bad guy" and imagine ways you might compromise the security of the system you're designing. More information on directory security may be found in Chapter 11, "Privacy and Security Design."

Advantages and Disadvantages of Partitioning

For many smaller directory deployments, it is perfectly reasonable to keep all your directory data in one partition. This generally results in better search performance because a single server can provide the data requested by the client without requiring that other servers be contacted.

If you have only a few thousand entries in your directory, there is probably no benefit to partitioning regardless of the type of server software you are using. Even larger partitions (sometimes as big as millions of entries) are supported by certain server software. Consult your server documentation to determine the largest number of entries that is reasonable to place in a single partition. If the number of entries stored in your directory significantly exceeds the number that can be practically stored in a single partition, you should split your directory into multiple partitions. Otherwise, try to limit your directory to one or just a few partitions.

Another reason to maintain a single large partition has to do with the types of directory-enabled applications you are using. Some applications tend to search the entire directory namespace repeatedly; these types of applications perform best if they have to search only one server to obtain the data they need.

For example, the Netscape Messaging Server, when delivering electronic mail, must look up the recipient's email address in the directory to determine routing information. It's quite likely that the entire directory namespace of your enterprise must be searched to perform this function. If your directory is split into a very large number of partitions, this can have a significant negative impact on the performance of such a directory-enabled application. If your directory services these types of applications, try to limit the number of directory partitions or point these applications to a server that aggregates all the partitions into a single location. We describe this configuration in more detail in the design example later in this chapter.

Another factor to consider is the amount of replication traffic required to service your replicated servers. If your directory services a large number of write operations and sends updates to many replica servers (a replica server holds a copy of a partition), the amount of replication traffic may be a significant burden on each server. By partitioning your directory, you reduce the number of entries contained within each server and therefore reduce the amount of update traffic that any given server must generate. Of course, the total amount of update traffic on your network is still the same; each server simply needs to handle less of it.

You may also want to partition your directory if your physical network topology includes many slower WAN links and partitioning the directory enables you to place partitions close to the applications and users that use the data in that partition. For example, if you are running Novell's IntranetWare and NDS, it often makes sense to construct a namespace that reflects the physical WAN structure of the company and assign partitions to servers located in each location. When users log in to NDS, their login preferences and scripts are retrieved from the directory. If the partition is assigned to a server located with its users and traffic does not need to span a WAN link, performance is improved. If, on the other hand, your organization's network is well-connected—perhaps if all links are T1 or faster—there isn't much to be gained from this type of approach. These are only general guidelines, and you need to examine your network layout and application needs carefully.

Finally, if you know that your directory will expand significantly in the future and exceed one of the limitations, it may be best to partition the directory sufficiently to accommodate the growth without having to redesign your partitioning scheme. Although it is certainly possible to split and combine partitions, this is generally a time-consuming task. Avoid it if you can.

Following is a summary of the factors to examine when deciding whether to partition your directory.

You should consider partitioning your directory if the following are true:

- The number of entries is too great for a single partition or server.

- Your directory-enabled applications tend only to read and modify entries from the local workgroup.

- The amount of replication traffic from a single partition is too great.

- Partitioning allows data and update traffic to remain local and avoid spanning WAN links.

- Directory use will expand significantly in the future, beyond the point where a single partition is feasible.

You should maintain your directory data in a single partition if the following are true:

- All your directory entries fit easily within a single partition and server.

- Your directory-enabled applications tend to read and modify entries across the whole enterprise.

- Not much replication traffic is generated.

- The entire organization is centrally located on a single high-speed network.

- Directory size will remain fairly static, or you know that it will not exceed the capabilities of your software.

We will discuss these partitioning issues in more detail when we look at a sample design later in this chapter.

Designing Your Directory Server Topology

The optimal directory server topology for your organization depends on these four factors:

- The directory-enabled applications you use or plan to use, and the expectations of the users of those applications

- Your directory server software and its capabilities

- Your physical network topology

- Your directory namespace

As you begin work on your directory topology, you may find that you want to revisit your namespace design. Recall that each partition needs a partition root, which is the DN of the entry at the top of the naming context. This means that you may create a partition only at a branching point in your directory. Also, if you've decided on a completely flat namespace design, but you later decide that you need to partition your directory, you'll need to go back and think about your namespace again.

Also, don't worry too much about getting every last detail exactly correct. Requirements will change. New directory-enabled applications will be developed. Your company will reorganize. Upgraded server software will become available. Your company will reorganize again. Change is a fact of life. Directory services are flexible, and you can tweak your solution as your needs evolve.

With those things in mind, here are the four steps toward designing your topology.

Step 1: Inventory Your Directory-Enabled Applications

To decide how your directory should be partitioned, you need to understand where the directory network traffic will be coming from. To get this information, you should start by taking an inventory of your directory-enabled applications. You probably already have such an inventory if you followed the steps outlined in Chapter 5, "Defining Your Directory Needs." We'll augment that inventory somewhat, focusing on the specific aspects of the applications that will affect your partitioning design.

While you're taking this inventory of your directory-enabled applications, you need to understand the demands those applications make on the directory. For each application, you should be interested in understanding the scope of directory operations performed by that application. In other words, what part of your organization's DIT does the application need to work with? Does it need to manipulate only a particular entry? Does it need to work only within a particular organizational unit? Or, does it need to search the entire directory?

Knowing something about the scope of requests an application makes allows you to decide if that application can tolerate the overhead associated with a partitioned directory. If an application needs to consistently search across the entire namespace, it may be detrimental to performance if a large number of servers must be contacted. In this case, the application will perform better if it needs to contact only a single server.

Additionally, you should know the performance requirements of the application. For some applications, performance requirements are stringent enough that you need to configure your directory so that only one server needs to be contacted to meet that application's needs. On the other hand, for applications with relaxed performance requirements, it may be perfectly acceptable for the client application to experience delays introduced by a highly partitioned directory.

You can inventory your applications in whatever manner you feel comfortable with. We have provided a form in Table 9.1 as a starting point; feel free to modify it as you see fit.

TABLE 9.1 TAKING INVENTORY OF YOUR APPLICATIONS

Application	Scope	Performance Requirements
Mail transfer agent: Netscape Messaging Server	Entire Directory	Intermittent delays acceptable. However, overall throughput must be at least 10 messages per second.
Netscape Communicator Address Book	Entire Directory	Searches based on cn or uid should require no more than one second.
Network login (for example, Novell Netware login program)	User's org unit	Delay of a few seconds acceptable.

If you're just in the planning stage, you may not be able to produce such an inventory because you don't have any directory-enabled applications. Use the following list as a starting point to think about the types of applications you might obtain and install. Although this list is not exhaustive, it does describe some of the more common types of directory-enabled applications:

- *Authentication and login applications.* These types of applications typically verify the user's login ID and password via a two-step process. First, the directory is searched to find the entry that corresponds to the login ID presented by the user. Then, the application attempts to bind to the directory using the entry's DN and the password supplied by the user. If the bind operation succeeds, the user is granted access to the application. Such applications typically make light use of the directory, and a response time of a second or so is acceptable.

- *Authorization applications.* These applications perform some sort of authorization check for the purpose of granting or denying access to some resource. For example, a Netscape Enterprise Server can be configured to use an LDAP-based directory server for access control. The access control information for a particular Web page or set of Web pages is stored in the directory so that it can be shared by a number of servers. This type of application makes heavy use of the directory because a directory lookup may be required for each HTTP request made to the Web server. Although caching of the resulting access control information can reduce the load on the directory server, these types of applications generally place a heavy load on the directory server, and users of these applications expect high performance. A response time of less than one second is necessary, and faster response is desirable.

The scope of these operations, however, is also quite important, and it is quite dependent on the way the application is configured. NDS, for example, requires that the user or administrator configure a default context, which specifies the subtree under which searches are performed and therefore limits the scope of the search operation that maps the user login ID to a directory entry. If users log in primarily from a single physical location, this works quite well because the server that can provide the requested information can be located on the same network as the client. On the other hand, if you have a large population of "nomadic" users, such as the student population described in Chapter 24, "Case Study: A Large University," little benefit is gained from a highly partitioned directory.

- *Address book applications.* These applications, typically embedded inside electronic mail applications such as Netscape Communicator, are usually used by people to look up information about other people or groups. The searches generated by these applications usually span the organization's entire namespace. Response times of a second or two are usually tolerable. The Netscape Communicator address book and Qualcomm's Eudora 4.0 address book are both examples of this type of application.

- *Messaging applications.* These applications use the directory to route electronic mail messages to their destinations. They can generate a heavy load on a directory server, especially when delivering mail to groups of users. The searches generated usually span the entire organizational directory namespace. The performance of an individual search request is generally not important, but the overall throughput of the directory can be a limiting factor in the number of messages delivered. Examples of this type of application include Netscape's Messaging Server and most other LDAP-aware electronic mail servers.

After you inventory the directory applications that will use the directory and understand their scope and the expected response times, you can begin to understand the performance implications of a highly partitioned directory versus a nonpartitioned directory.

Tip

It is our experience that directories increasingly are becoming the nerve center of IT organizations. In the past, it was possible to lay out your directory in such a way that clients could get almost all the information they needed from a local server, which held information only about the local workgroup. But now that LDAP has provided a standard way for client applications to retrieve directory information, a much richer, more functional set of directory-enabled software is becoming available. These applications leverage the enterprisewide knowledge contained in your directory and tend to search across your entire organizational directory space.

For example, an electronic mail client might support sending signed, encrypted mail by using the directory to look up the public keys of mail recipients. This type of application has a wide scope—it typically needs to look up an email address in your directory and retrieve the public key associated with the entry. You should not be surprised to learn that a majority of your directory-enabled applications require fast access to your entire directory tree. If you are in this situation, a highly partitioned directory will perform poorly. You should strive to reduce the number of partitions if at all possible.

Step 2: Understand Your Directory Server Software and Its Capabilities

Your directory server will no doubt have some practical limitations on the following:

- Number of entries that can reasonably be stored in a partition

- Number of partitions that can be held on a server

- Number of entries that can be held on a server

- Number of subordinate references that can be maintained at a given level of the DIT

- Number of replicas of a partition that can be maintained

- Number of indexed searches that can be serviced per second

- Number of concurrent client connections that can be supported

As you design your topology, you may find that some previous decisions you made are at odds with the limitations of your directory server software. For example, if you've decided on a flat namespace design for your 100,000-entry directory but need to implement it with server software that has a practical limitation of 5,000 entries per server, you need to revisit your namespace design to accommodate the server software.

If you have not yet decided on a particular vendor's directory server software, you can use the preceding list as a checklist as you go through the decision-making process described in Chapter 12, "Choosing Directory Products."

Step 3: Create a Map of Your Physical Network

Start with the map of your organization's physical network that we discussed in Chapter 5, "Defining Your Directory Needs." The components you should now focus on are your LANs and the connections between them. Label each LAN segment with its physical location, and then label the connections between LANs with the bandwidth, latency, and reliability of the connection. The bandwidth of a network connection is the maximum speed at which data can be transferred, and the latency of a connection is the time it takes for data to travel across the connection. A low-latency connection is ideal for LDAP traffic. High-latency links such as satellite links result in slow round-trip times for interactive traffic such as LDAP authentication, which can result in poor performance for applications. Such links, however, are often adequate for protocols such as FTP, which transfers data in bulk.

If you know that the connection is not 100% reliable or is active only during certain times of the day, note that on the map as well. Consider the hypothetical organization shown in Figure 9.12. The main office, located in Boulder, Colorado, consists of several Ethernet segments connected via a high-speed backbone network. A branch office in London is connected via a 56Kbps leased line that is quite reliable but exhibits a relatively high latency of 200 milliseconds (1/5 of a second).

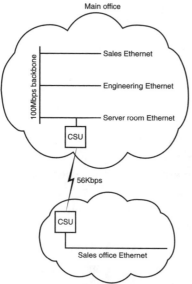

FIGURE 9.12   *A basic network map.*

Next, label on your map the locations of any directory-enabled applications you currently have. For example, if you have deployed (or plan to deploy) LDAP-enabled electronic mail client software to users on each LAN, note this on your map. If you know the scope and performance requirements of the directory operations these clients execute, note those as well. As an example, note in Figure 9.13 that there are two types of directory-enabled applications on the Engineering LAN segment: NDS login clients and Netscape Communicator clients.

You should also, if possible, include server-based directory-enabled applications such as electronic mail servers, LDAP-enabled Web applications servers, and so on. You may not have installed these servers yet; that's fine, because you can experiment with their placement to optimize availability. Note on the map any other details such as applications that perform a large number of updates. You may need to enlist the help of other system and network administrators to accomplish this task.

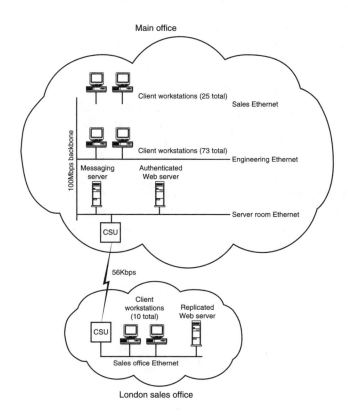

FIGURE 9.13   *An expanded network map showing locations of directory-enabled applications.*

After you have your directory clients and servers on your map, you can start to see traffic patterns emerge. Look for the locations of your high-volume directory clients, especially mail servers. Strive to limit traffic across slower WAN links; make sure that clients on remote networks have the information they need on the local LAN so that client requests need not traverse the WAN links.

Step 4: Review Your Directory Namespace Design

Now that you have a good idea of how your client and server applications are laid out, you can revisit your namespace design. Does it fit well with your WAN infrastructure and partition design? A properly designed namespace allows you to place partitions close to the users and applications that use the data they contain. If you find that your namespace makes this difficult, try other ways of arranging the namespace. For example, if you are designing a directory for a multinational company and you've chosen a namespace that reflects the company's organizational structure, you may have problems defining partitions that minimize traffic across WAN links. In this case, consider an alternative namespace design. Rather than having the top-level branch points correspond to organizational structure, try making them correspond to network layout.

Directory Partition Design Examples

This section describes two examples of directory partition design: a single-partition example and a multiple-partition example. Your directory partition design will almost certainly not be exactly like one of the two scenarios described here. However, you may find some elements in common between your situation and these examples, and we hope you can draw useful conclusions from those common themes. You should also become familiar with the case studies in Part VI of this book. The case studies represent real-world directory deployments and do even more to illustrate the issues you will face as you set out to design the best directory topology for your environment.

A Single-Partition Directory Design Example

Background: Airius Electronics is a small manufacturer of electronics modules for the airline industry. It employs 1,000 people, most of them at its large Boulder, Colorado, office. It has two branch offices, one in London and one in Paris. The branch offices are connected to the main campus by 56Kbps leased lines. The Boulder campus consists of 30 Ethernet segments connected via a 100Mbps backbone network.

Inventory of directory-enabled applications: Airius is deploying its directory to initially support two major applications. The first is a directory-enabled messaging application; the second is an intranet Web application in which the directory will be used to store access control information. Additionally, each user's workstation will run an address book application used to address and digitally sign internal electronic mail. The inventory of planned directory-enabled applications is shown in Table 9.2.

TABLE 9.2 AN APPLICATION PERFORMANCE REQUIREMENTS TABLE

Application	Scope	Performance Requirements
Messaging server	Entire directory	Intermittent delays acceptable. However, overall throughput must be at least 10 messages per second. Each message delivery requires one search per recipient. Estimated peak directory load is 50 searches per second.
Intranet Web server	Entire directory	Approximately 100 authenticated page-views per second. Assuming that each page contains four inline images, this corresponds to approximately 500 hits per second. Web server caching of ACL information will reduce the load on the directory server to about 10 directory searches per second. Maximum acceptable delay time to send the entire Web page is one second.
Address book application	Entire directory	Total directory load will be approximately 5 searches per second. Searches should require no more than 3 seconds for indexed attributes.

Capabilities of directory software: Airius has not yet chosen a particular directory server package. Part of the planning phase of the directory deployment will be the development of a set of requirements for the directory server.

Physical network topology: Whereas all users on the Boulder campus enjoy high-speed connectivity to other hosts on the Boulder campus, the two European offices are connected via slower leased lines (see Figure 9.14). Frequently, these connections see heavy use from other applications. Actual throughput on the leased lines is likely much less than 56Kbps. Directory clients are present on each Ethernet segment and at both remote office locations. These remote clients require access to the entire directory tree to address and sign electronic mail. Additionally, a number of local intranet web servers are planned so that each department or remote sales office can publish information to the intranet with access control. To guarantee fast response at the remote offices, it was decided that a replica of the entire directory needs to be available at each remote office.

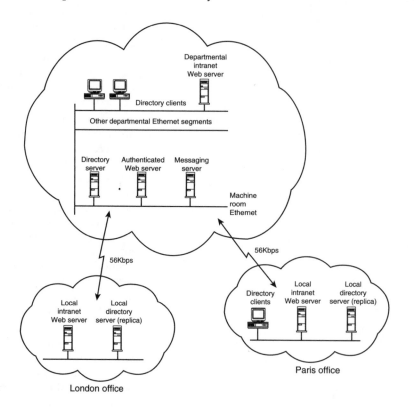

FIGURE 9.14   *A network topology map showing the location of Airius's directory-enabled applications.*

Namespace design: Airius is organized by projects, and individual employees move among projects fairly frequently. For this reason, Airius has decided on a flat namespace (see Figure 9.15) with all employee directory entries contained directly below ou=People, dc=airius, dc=com. Individual attributes within a person's entry denote the projects the person is working on, so it is not necessary to rename an entry if the employee changes projects.

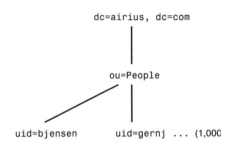

FIGURE 9.15   *Airius's namespace design.*

Conclusions: After reviewing all this information, Airius's information systems organization has decided to retain the flat namespace and put all directory entries within a single partition. Two additional replicas of the directory will be placed at the main office for load-balancing and fault tolerance. Replicated directory servers will be placed at both of the European offices, and clients at those offices will be configured to use the local replica, falling back on using the server at the Boulder campus only if the local server fails. A diagram of the final design is shown in Figure 9.16.

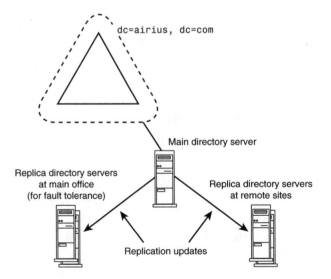

FIGURE 9.16   *Airius's final topology design.*

A Multiple-Partition Directory Design Example

Background: Our hypothetical company in this example, Airius Software, is a company with about 10,000 employees in three separate offices: New York, the corporate headquarters; San Francisco, which houses the software developers and support staff; and a London office, which houses European sales and support staff. The company organizational chart is shown in Table 9.3.

TABLE 9.3 ORGANIZATIONAL CHART OF AIRIUS SOFTWARE

New York Office	London Office	San Francisco Office
Finance Department	European Sales	Software Development
Legal Department	European Support	Western Region Support
Eastern Region Support	Human Resources	Human Resources
Human Resources		U.S. Sales

The company has chosen to deploy NDS as it upgrades its existing NetWare 3 network to Novell IntranetWare. It also plans to deploy a third-party email hub that leverages information stored in NDS to route inbound Internet mail to internal destinations, including a number of shared mailboxes used by the support staff to handle support requests that come via email.

Inventory of directory-enabled applications: As previously mentioned, Airius is planning to deploy two applications that use the NDS directory: NetWare login and electronic mail delivery. The scope of the NetWare login application is generally limited to the local workgroup, whereas the mail hub software needs to search across the entire organizational namespace and has a high throughput requirement (see Table 9.4).

TABLE 9.4 AN APPLICATION PERFORMANCE REQUIREMENTS TABLE

Application	Scope	Performance Requirements
Netware Login	Local to workgroup	Retrieval time of a few seconds for user login scripts acceptable
Electronic mail hub	Entire directory	Must sustain throughput of 10 messages per second

Capabilities of directory software: In general, NDS guidelines recommend limiting the number of directory entries within a single partition to a few thousand, so it is probably not prudent to place all 10,000 entries within a single partition.

Physical Network Topology: The three offices are connected via a frame relay network. This is very reliable, but the speed (1.544Mbps peak) is modest compared to the intracampus backbone networks. Furthermore, the intercampus links have only a 64Kbps committed information rate, which means that the actual throughput is often much less than the peak. For this reason, it is a good idea to limit traffic across the WAN links to the greatest extent possible. These intercampus links are shown in Figure 9.17.

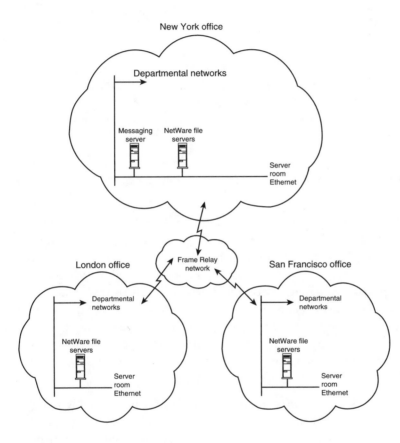

FIGURE 9.17 *Airius Software's network map.*

Traffic across the WAN links can be limited by placing the data needed by clients at each campus on an on-campus server.

Namespace design: Airius originally decided on a namespace that reflected its organizational structure. This initial namespace layout is shown in Figure 9.18.

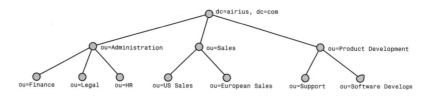

FIGURE 9.18   *Airius Software's original namespace design.*

Recall that directory partitions can be defined only at branch points in the directory. This means that any possible partition must have a partition root corresponding to one of the organizational units in the design. This means that the partitioning choices are as follows:

- A single partition rooted at dc=airius, dc=com. This is a poor choice because it would exceed the practical limits for the number of entries in a single partition.

- Three partitions, rooted at ou=Administration, dc=airius, dc=com; ou=Sales, dc=airius, dc=com; and ou=Product Development, dc=airius, dc=com. This arrangement probably allows for adequate distribution of entries among three partitions, assuming that roughly an equal number of people work in each division. However, such an arrangement makes it difficult to avoid sending directory traffic across WAN links. Note in Table 9.3 that the human resources staff is divided among the three campuses. No matter where the ou=Administration partition is located, human resources staffs at the other two locations would need to traverse WAN links to retrieve their directory data.

- Eleven partitions corresponding to each of the individual workgroups. Although this would allow partitions to be placed locally to each workgroup, management of all these partitions would be more time-consuming, especially if replication were used to provide additional copies of the partitions.

When you find yourself facing this kind of dilemma, it's often beneficial to step back and re-examine your choice of namespace layout. In this case, doing away with the existing namespace based on organizational structure and replacing it with one based on geographical layout makes the topology fit much better with the WAN infrastructure. Figure 9.19 shows a revised namespace design.

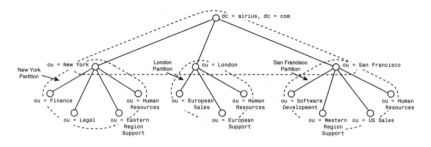

FIGURE 9.19   *Airius Software's revised namespace design.*

Notice how the three organizational units based on geography fit well with the WAN infrastructure. If we make these organizational units the roots of three partitions and locate those partitions at their respective campus, we succeed in localizing user traffic to the individual campuses. Note that there are actually four partitions, as denoted by the dashed lines in Figure 9.19. There must be a partition rooted at dc=airius, dc=com to tie the three subordinate partitions together and allow name resolution. This partition, which is very small, can be replicated to each of the three locations via NDS replication.

One problem remains, however. The mail hub application needs to search across the entire organizational namespace frequently—perhaps several times per second. Without taking some special action, the mail hub's directory traffic would span two of the WAN links.

We can solve this problem by creating a dedicated server that holds replicas of all the partitions (replication will be covered in more detail in the next chapter). Because the mail hub has high-performance requirements, it's probably a good idea to provide it a dedicated server anyway. We call this an aggregating server because it aggregates the directory data into a central location for the mail hub's use. The one drawback to using an aggregating server is that placing all the entries on a single host may tax the system hosting the aggregating server.

Another more expensive but higher-performance alternative would be to place each replica on a separate server and locate all the replicas on the same network as the mail hub application. If that approach still does not provide adequate performance, another alternative would be to make a copy of the NDS data in a single Netscape Directory Server that would service the mail hub. The Netscape server, designed specifically with search performance in mind, is a better choice for this particular application than NDS, which is designed primarily to support Netware.

Conclusions: The final allocation of partitions to servers is shown in Figure 9.20. The three campus directory servers each hold a copy of the top-level partition, rooted at dc=airius, dc=com, and each campus directory server holds a partition comprising the data local clients need. Additionally, the aggregating server, which resides on the same network segment as the mail hub, holds read-only copies of all directory partitions and receives replication updates from the read-write partitions located at each campus site.

dc=airius, dc = com (read
ou=New York (read-write)

New York server

dc=airius, dc=com (read-or
ou=London (read-write)

London server

dc=airius, dc=com (read-or
ou=San Francisco (read-writ

San Francisco server

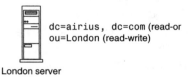

dc=airius, dc=com (read-or
ou=New York (read-only)
ou=London (read-only)
ou=San Francisco (read-onl\

Aggregating server
(on same Ethernet as mail hub)

FIGURE 9.20   *Allocation of partitions to servers at Airius Software.*

This example shows that it's beneficial to spend some time thinking about namespace design and topology as a unit.

Topology Design Checklist

☐ Take a survey of your directory-enabled applications. Understand the scope of the directory data they need to interact with. Understand the performance requirements.

☐ If you have already decided on a particular vendor's directory server software, understand its practical limitations, especially the number of entries that can be stored in a partition and how easily partitions can be managed. If you are still in the decision-making process and selecting server software, you should take these factors into consideration when making your purchase decision.

☐ Review your physical network topology. Are there WAN links that might be saturated by excessive directory traffic? If so, strive to limit the amount of traffic that needs to span those links.

☐ Review your directory namespace requirements and design. Does your namespace fit naturally with a partitioning arrangement that minimizes WAN traffic? Is there some other namespace arrangement that is a better fit?

Further Reading

Netscape Directory Server Deployment Guide. Available online at http://home.netscape.com/eng/server/directory/3.0/deployrtm/contents.html.

Novell's Guide to IntranetWare Networks. J. Hughes and B. Thomas, Novell Press, 1996.

Novell's Four Principles of NDS Design. J. Hughes and B. Thomas, Novell Press, 1996.

Microsoft Active Directory documents. Available from Microsoft's Web site at http://www.microsoft.com.

Understanding X.500: The Directory. D. Chadwick, International Thomson Computer Press, 1996. Now out of print; selected sections available on the Web at http://www.salford.ac.uk/its024/Version.Web/Contents.htm.

Looking Ahead

In this chapter, we examined how the distributed directory works and the issues you should consider when deciding how to partition your directory among servers. In Chapter 10, "Replication Design," we will examine how to improve the reliability and performance of your directory through the use of replication.

CHAPTER **10**

Replication Design

Directories play a pivotal role in your organization's computing infrastructure. The services they provide are so crucial that downtime of your directory due to equipment failure probably cannot be tolerated. If your directory data is available from only a single server, and that server fails or becomes unreachable, your users will have trouble getting their work done.

Directory replication protects you from this unfortunate situation by making your directory data available on multiple servers. It also improves performance by allowing you to make more copies of directory data available and place them close to the users and applications that use them.

In this chapter, we first discuss a number of important replication concepts. Next, we examine some related issues such as replication scheduling and how schema and access control interact with replication. Finally, we spend some time explaining how you should design a replication solution for your directory environment.

Replication, topology, and namespace design are all closely related. If you have not read Chapter 8, "Namespace Design," and Chapter 9, "Topology Design," we suggest that you do so before attempting to design your replication. Having a good understanding of all these topics will enhance your ability to build a reliable, scalable directory.

Why Replicate?

When you replicate directory content, you increase the reliability and performance of your directory service. Let's examine these two benefits and how they are achieved.

By making the directory data available in more than one location, you improve the reliability of your directory service. In the event that a single server fails, your directory clients and directory-enabled application programs could contact a different server for their directory service. Figure 10.1 illustrates how a client can use this redundancy to obtain service from a replica in the event of a server failure.

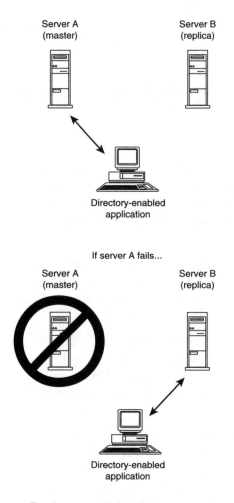

Server A
(master)

Server B
(replica)

Directory-enabled
application

If server A fails...

Server A
(master)

Server B
(replica)

Directory-enabled
application

The directory-enabled application can obtain its
directory service from server B.

FIGURE 10.1 *Increasing reliability through redundancy.*

When you replicate directory content, you also make your directory more impervious to outages as a result of network failures. In Figure 10.2, the directory-enabled application running on the LAN at the branch office can continue to function even if the network link between the branch office and company headquarters is down. Of course, the directory content on the replicated server may not be entirely up-to-date, but for the vast majority of applications this is entirely acceptable. When the network connection between the offices is restored, Server B will once again be synchronized with Server A, eliminating any temporary differences.

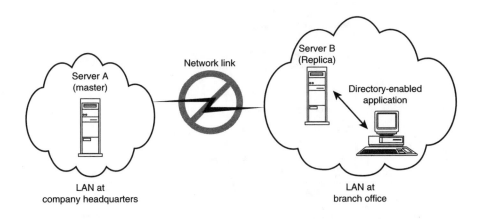

FIGURE 10.2 *Replicating to minimize the impact of a network failure.*

The situation in Figure 10.2 also has the benefit that replicas can be located close to the users and applications that need them. This improves performance because there are fewer network nodes between the LDAP clients and the directory data.

Thus, when you replicate directory content, you can also improve the performance of your directory. Your directory can be made to handle more directory client requests by distributing the load across more servers. Figure 10.3 illustrates distribution of client load across multiple replicas.

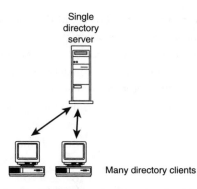

Single
directory
server

Many directory clients

A single directory server may not be able to handle all the
directory client applications in your environment.

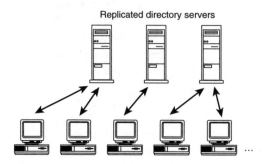

Replicated directory servers

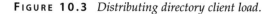

With replication, you can have the client load distributed across as
many servers as is required. Additional servers can be installed
as the need arises.

FIGURE 10.3   *Distributing directory client load.*

Replication Concepts

Before we dive into designing our replication system, we should spend some
time understanding the basic issues concerning directory replication. These
issues are as follows:

- Suppliers, consumers, and replication agreements

- The unit of replication

- Consistency and convergence

- Incremental and total updates

- Initial population of a replica

- Replication strategies: single-master, floating-master, and multi-master

- Conflict resolution in multi-master replication

Each issue is discussed in the following sections.

Suppliers, Consumers, and Replication Agreements

In replication systems, we use the terms *supplier* and *consumer* to identify the source and destination of replication updates, respectively. A supplier server sends updates to another server; a consumer server accepts those changes. These roles are not mutually exclusive: A server that is a consumer may also be a supplier.

The configuration information that tells a supplier server about a consumer server (and vice versa) is termed a *replication agreement*. This configuration information typically includes the unit of replication (discussed next), the hostname and port of the remote server, and other information about the replication to be performed, such as scheduling information. In other words, the replication agreement describes *what* is to be replicated, *where* it is to be sent, and *how* it will be done.

The Unit of Replication

When we talk about replication, we need some common language to describe what is to be replicated. In an abstract sense, we are interested in specifying

- Which entries are to be replicated

- Which attributes from those entries are to be replicated

A natural way to describe a set of entries to be replicated is to specify the distinguished name (DN) at the top of a subtree and replicate all entries subordinate to (below) it (see Figure 10.4).

In Figure 10.4, the complete subtree rooted at ou=Accounting, dc=airius, dc=com is being replicated. Virtually all directory server implementations support this ability to specify that a complete subtree is to be replicated. This subtree usually corresponds to a directory partition, as described in Chapter 9.

We might be interested in selecting only certain entries from a subtree. A reasonable thing to do would be to select entries based on their object class. For example, we might want to replicate only those entries that represent people or organizational units (see Figure 10.5).

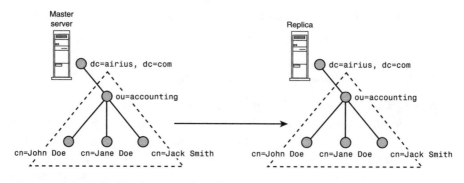

FIGURE 10.4 *Replicating an entire subtree.*

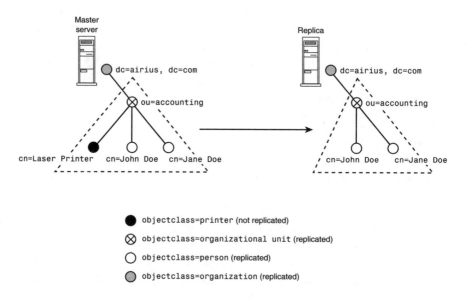

FIGURE 10.5 *Replication of selected entries.*

In Figure 10.5, the root of the replicated subtree is once again ou=Accounting, dc=airius, dc=com, but only organizationalUnit and person entries are being replicated. The X.500 standards define this ability as the *specification filter* component of the unit of replication.

One complication that can arise from selecting only certain entries is that the replicated directory may contain "holes." In the example depicted in Figure 10.5, if entries of objectclass organizationalUnit had not been selected, the replicated tree would look like the one shown in Figure 10.6. To be a valid directory tree, every entry except the root entry must have a parent; however, the consumer's directory tree violates that rule. To remedy this situation, the supplier could create on the consumer a placeholder in place of the entry that was not replicated. The X.500 model describes a specific type of placeholder, termed a glue entry, used for just this purpose.

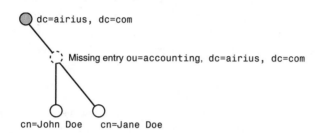

FIGURE 10.6 *A hole in the directory information tree (DIT) arising from filtered replication.*

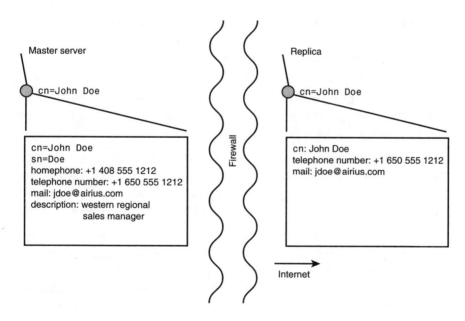

FIGURE 10.7 *Replicating only selected attributes from an entry.*

In addition to selecting only certain types of entries for replication, we might want to replicate only certain attributes. For example, when providing a publicly searchable directory of employee information outside a corporate firewall, an organization might elect to replicate only full names, email addresses, and office telephone numbers and omit all other personal information. Notice in Figure 10.7 how the copy of John Doe's entry accessible outside the firewall contains fewer attributes than the master entry inside the firewall. The X.500 standards define this as the *attribute selection* component of the unit of replication.

Consistency and Convergence

Consistency describes how closely the contents of replicated servers match each other at a given point in time. A *strongly consistent* replica is one that provides the same information as its supplier at all times; that is, a change made on one server is not visible to any other client until it has been propagated and acknowledged by all replicas. On the other hand, a *weakly consistent* replica is permitted to diverge from its supplier for some period of time. For example, Figure 10.8 shows that there is a period of time after a supplier has been updated but before the update has been propagated to a replica; during that time the supplier and the replica contain different data.

We say that a supplier and a replica have *converged* when they contain the same data. It is important that replication systems eventually converge over time so that all clients see the same view of the directory.

In a directory system that uses weakly consistent replication, directory clients should not expect their updates to be immediately reflected in the directory. For example, a directory application should not expect that it can update an entry and then immediately be able to read it to obtain the updated values.

It may come as a surprise that all practical directory systems use weakly consistent replicas. Why? The answer has to do with performance. Imagine that a single supplier feeds three replicas, and that each of the replicas handles a large client load of search requests. If the supplier maintains strong consistency with its replicas, it must send a change to each replica and receive a positive acknowledgment before returning a result to the client that sent the change. Because each replica is heavily loaded, it may be slow in sending the result to the supplier. The supplier can therefore return a result to the client no faster than the slowest replica acknowledges the update. This can reduce performance unacceptably.

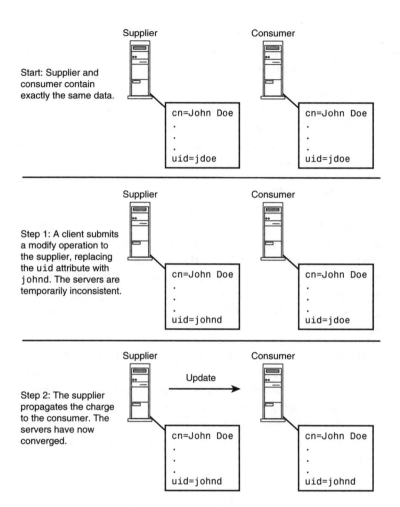

Figure 10.8 *Weakly consistent replicas.*

Additionally, implementing strong consistency among replicas requires that replicas support a two-phase commit protocol. This is necessary so that the supplier server can back out an update if any of the consumers should fail to acknowledge the change. The supplier would then return an error code to the client, and the client would presumably retry the operation later. This means that all consumer servers must be functional for a supplier server to accept a change, which is undesirable.

In addition to its lower performance, strong consistency is incompatible with scheduled replication, an advanced feature we'll discuss later in this chapter. Briefly, scheduled replication permits updates to be deferred to some particular window in time, perhaps to the middle of the night. Because a strongly consistent system requires that updates be propagated immediately, it is essentially at odds with scheduled replication.

Given all these challenges, weakly consistent replication systems are much easier to implement and provide better performance at the expense of temporary inconsistencies between supplier and replica servers. For virtually all directory applications, this is perfectly acceptable and represents a well-informed compromise on the part of directory designers.

Incremental and Total Updates

To bring two servers into synchronization, we might choose to either completely replace the contents of the consumer server or transmit only the minimum information necessary to bring the servers into synchronization. The former approach, termed a *total update* in X.500 parlance, is useful when initially creating a replica (you'll learn more about this creation operation later in this chapter). It is very inefficient, however, to always use a total update strategy when updating consumer servers because all entries are transmitted even if they have not been modified.

In an *incremental update*, only the changes made to the supplier's directory are sent to the consumer server. For example, if a directory client modifies an entry by replacing its description attribute, it's necessary to perform only that same change on all replicas to bring them into synchronization. It's not necessary to send the entire entry, and it's certainly not necessary to transmit the entire contents of the database to all replicas. Incremental updates are much more efficient, and all widely used LDAP directory server software supports them.

Note

If a replica's directory tree is in some unknown state (perhaps it has been damaged or reloaded from an extremely out-of-date backup), it may then be desirable to wipe out any existing contents and perform a total update. This is also what is done when a replica is initially populated with data.

To better understand how the incremental update process works, let's look at the process from a general view, and then we'll examine how real-world directory services perform incremental updates. Following is an outline of the incremental update process:

1. The supplier server connects to the consumer server and authenticates.

2. The suppler determines which updates need to be applied.

3. The supplier sends the updates to the consumer.

4. The consumer applies those updates to its copy of the directory data.

5. The supplier and/or the consumer save state information that records the last update applied. This information is used in step 2 of subsequent synchronization runs.

In this way, a supplier transmits only the minimum number of updates necessary to bring the consumer server into synchronization. To provide some more concrete examples, let's examine how two popular directory services—Netscape Directory Server and Novell Directory Services (NDS)—incrementally update a consumer.

The Netscape Directory Server Update Process

The Netscape Directory Server updates consumers by replaying changes it receives. For example, if a client connects to a Netscape Directory Server and adds a new entry, the supplier connects to all of its consumers and adds the same entry. Each change, when received by the supplier, is assigned a unique *changenumber*; this is then logged to a *changelog*, a database that records all changes made to the server. The supplier keeps track of the changes it has replayed to consumer by storing in the consumer's directory tree the number of the last change applied. Figure 10.9 illustrates the Netscape Directory Server update process.

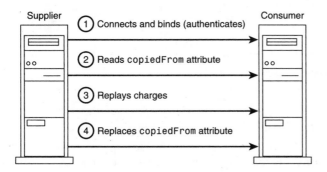

FIGURE 10.9 *The Netscape Directory Server update process.*

The Netscape Directory Server performs the following steps when incrementally updating a replica:

1. The supplier server connects to the consumer server and authenticates.

2. The supplier reads the copiedFrom attribute in the entry at the top of the replicated subtree. The copiedFrom attribute contains, along with other information, the number of the last change replayed to the consumer.

3. The supplier server replays any changes with a changenumber larger than the number read from the consumer in step 1 until it runs out of changes to replay.

4. The supplier server stores in the copiedFrom attribute the number of the last change it replayed. The consumer is now in sync with the supplier.

The Novell Directory Services Update Process

NDS servers track updates by storing along with each attribute a timestamp that indicates when that attribute was last updated. To determine which updates need to be applied to a consumer server, an NDS supplier locates all attribute values in which the timestamp is greater than the last update timestamp for the consumer. An NDS server updates a consumer server's copy of a directory partition by sending any attributes that have changed since the last replication session. The timestamp of the last update is stored in the Synchronize Up To vector (or SynchUpTo vector) on the consumer server, and it is retrieved by the supplier server at the beginning of each replication session. The NDS update process is shown in Figure 10.10.

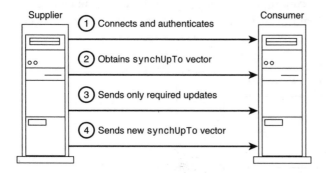

FIGURE 10.10   *The NDS update process.*

An NDS server performs the following steps when sending changes to another NDS server:

1. The supplier server connects to the consumer server and authenticates.

2. The supplier requests the SynchUpTo vector from the consumer. The consumer returns this information to the supplier.

3. The supplier sends any needed updates (those in which the timestamps are larger that the timestamp in the SynchUpTo vector).

4. After all updates have been transmitted, the supplier sends an updated SynchUpTo vector to the consumer. The consumer stores this for use during the next synchronization run.

As you can see, the update processes for Netscape Directory Server and NDS are quite similar. The main difference is in how the updates themselves are stored on the supplier. Netscape Directory Server stores a record of each change in the changelog as it is received and processed, and it replays these changes to consumer servers. NDS (and Microsoft Active Directory as well) places a unique, ever-increasing number on each changed attribute value and sends updates as a series of attribute values to be updated on the consumer servers.

The changelog approach has the advantage that no special action needs to be taken when an entry is deleted, renamed, or moved—the changelog simply records the operation that the client performed. On the other hand, NDS and Active Directory must create a placeholder entry (called a *tombstone* or *obituary*) that records the previous location of the entry and any associated timestamp or sequence number values.

The main disadvantage of the changelog approach is that it records all changes, even when the same attribute of the same entry is modified multiple times. If the supplier simply replays all changes in order, as is typically done, more changes might be transmitted than necessary. The approach used by Active Directory and NDS simply requires one update that reflects the final state of the attribute.

Initial Population of a Replica

When a consumer server is initially configured, it contains no data. The replica must somehow be populated with a consistent snapshot of the supplier's data so that it can subsequently be kept in synchronization. Or, in the event that a consumer server has become damaged, the consumer must be brought back into synchronization, usually by removing the damaged data and creating a fresh copy of the directory data from the supplier.

Tip

Be sure that the replica does not attempt to service requests until it has been completely initialized. Were it to begin servicing requests before being completely populated, it might give erroneous results. For example, it might claim that a given entry does not exist when in fact it has not yet received the entry from the supplier. Virtually all directory server software automatically takes care of arranging for a replica to be offline during replica initialization. The replica typically issues a referral to the master server or chains the operation to the master.

How is a replica initialization performed? Directory vendors accomplish this task by using various methods, although all are similar. X.500's Directory Information Shadowing Protocol (DISP) supports a total update strategy while synchronizing, which allows a supplier server to completely repopulate a unit of replication on the consumer. (An X.500-compliant server from one vendor should, in theory, be able to re-initialize a consumer server from another vendor.) NDS uses a proprietary protocol for all replication operations, including creation of a replica. Netscape Directory Server 3.0 uses LDAP itself to initialize a replica, sending a series of delete operations to remove undesired entries and a series of add operations to populate the directory.

Replication Strategies

The term *replication strategy* refers to the way updates flow from server to server and the way servers interact when propagating updates. But after a client has successfully modified, deleted, added, or renamed an entry, how does the server that received the change make it visible on all the other replicated servers? There are three main approaches toward solving this problem: single-master replication, floating-master replication, and multi-master replication.

In *single-master* replication, there is one (and only one) server that contains a writable copy of a given directory entry. All other replicas contain read-only copies of the entry. Note that this does not imply that you can have only a single master server for all of your directory content. If you have divided your directory into several directory partitions, each one of them should have a supplier server feeding consumer servers. The master server is the only one that can perform write operations, whereas any server may perform a search, compare, or bind operation (see Figure 10.11).

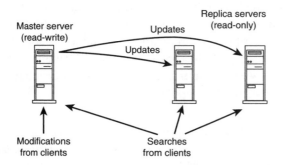

FIGURE 10.11 *Single-master replication.*

Because a typical directory-enabled application performs many more search operations than modify operations, it's beneficial to use read-only replicas. The read-only replica server can handle search operations just as well the writable master server.

If the client attempts to perform a write operation on the read-only server (e.g., adding, deleting, modifying, or renaming an entry), we need some way to arrange for the operation to be submitted to the read-write server. There are two ways this can be made to happen. The first way is via a referral, which is simply a way for a server to say to a client: "I cannot handle this request, but here is the location of a server that should be able to." Figure 10.12 shows the steps involved when a directory client submits a change to a read-only replica.

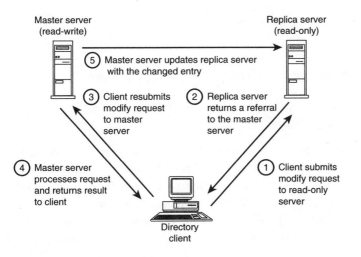

FIGURE 10.12 *Directing an update to a master server by using referrals.*

The other way to get a write operation to go to the read-write copy is by chaining the request. That is, the server resubmits the request, on behalf of the client, to the read-write copy; it then obtains the result and forwards it to the client (see Figure 10.13).

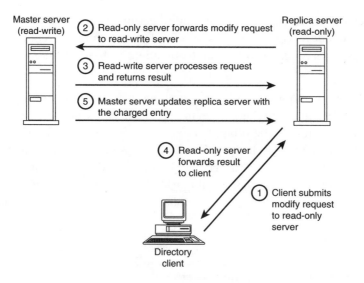

FIGURE 10.13 *Directing an update to a master server by chaining.*

A more thorough discussion of referrals and chaining may be found in Chapter 9, "Topology Design."

Typically, all these multistep interactions between clients and servers are handled automatically by the application software. Directory client users are unlikely to witness all of this—instead, they simply see the modify operation complete, and the change is eventually available on the replica. (Note that there is a period of time when the read-write copy of the server contains newer data than the read-only copy, as mentioned in the discussion on consistency and convergence.)

The astute reader will notice that in a single-master replication system there is a single point of failure: the read-write server. There is only one server that can process write operations for a given entry; if it goes down, no client can modify that portion of the directory (although search and read operations can continue at read-only replicas). Depending on the type of directory client software and directory-enabled application in use, this may or may not be acceptable. However, single-master replication is simpler to implement than the other types of replication, so it can be found in most directory server software products on the market.

One replication strategy that avoids a single point of failure is *floating-master replication*. This strategy still has only one writable copy at any given time. However, if the read-write server should become unavailable for some reason, a new read-write master server is selected by some algorithm—typically a voting algorithm in which the remaining servers collectively agree on a server to become the new master (see Figure 10.14). The actual mechanism of selecting a new master server is typically complicated and beyond the scope of this book.

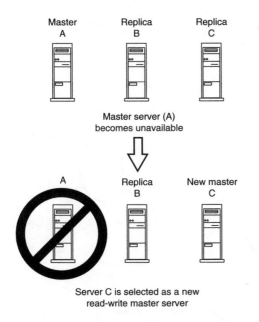

FIGURE 10.14 *Floating-master replication: selecting a new master.*

Additional complications arise when a network becomes partitioned and a new master is elected on each side of the network partition (see Figure 10.15). The procedures for reconciling what happens to the two masters when the network is rejoined can be rather complicated. Although no traditional directory products use a floating-master scheme, Microsoft Windows NT 4.0 uses this approach when designating a given domain controller as either a primary domain controller (PDC), which can be modified; or a backup domain controller (BDC), which holds a read-only copy of the NT domain controller database.

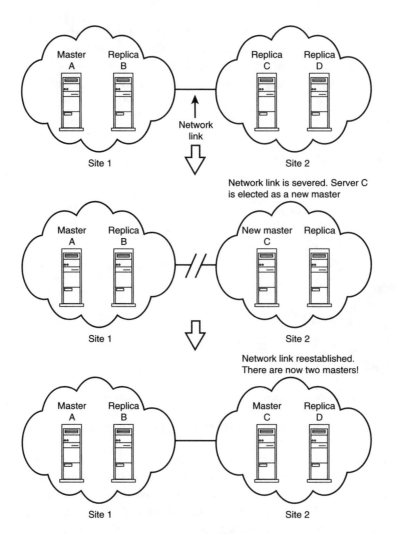

FIGURE 10.15   *Multiple masters selected in a partitioned network.*

In a *multi-master* replication system, there may be (and almost always is) more than one read-write copy available. Clients may submit a write operation to any of the read-write replicas. It then becomes the responsibility of the set of cooperating servers to ensure that changes are eventually propagated to all servers in a consistent manner. Figure 10.16 shows two replicated servers that are capable of handling client write requests.

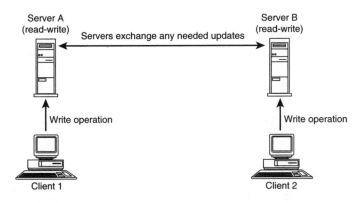

FIGURE 10.16 *Multi-master replication.*

Like floating-master replication, multi-master replication eliminates the single point of failure and thus offers greater reliability for directory clients. However, allowing more than one server to accept write operations brings additional complexity, most notably the need for an *update conflict resolution policy*. This is used to resolve an update conflict, which can occur when an attribute of an entry is modified at the same approximate time on two different master servers. We will discuss this topic later in the next section.

One obvious question might be: "If multi-master replication offers better reliability, why do most implementations use single-master replication?" In the case of X.500, the designers felt that the added complexity of conflict resolution made a multi-master approach unworkable in the globally distributed directory they were designing. As of this writing, however, this decision is being revisited, and there may emerge a multi-master version of X.500 DISP. Work has also begun to define a standard replication protocol for LDAP servers, which is likely to involve multi-master and/or floating-master replication (in addition to single-master replication).

Conflict Resolution in Multi-master Replication

In multi-master replication systems, more than one directory server may accept modifications for a given entry. Sometimes this creates a situation in which two directory clients modify the same entry on two different servers at the same time. But what happens when the clients use a different value for the same entry (see Figure 10.17)?

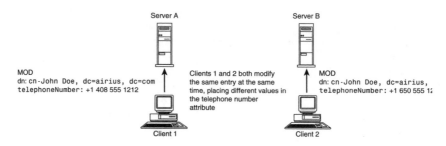

FIGURE 10.17 *Setting the stage for an update conflict.*

In Figure 10.17, Client 1 modifies the entry cn=John Doe, dc=airius, dc=com and replaces the telephoneNumber attribute with the single value +1 408 555 1212, submitting the change to Server A. At the same time, Client 2 modifies the entry cn=John Doe, dc=airius, dc=com and replaces the telephoneNumber attribute with a *different* value, +1 650 555 1212, submitting the change to Server B. After these operations complete on each server, the entries are in conflict: It's impossible for both changes to be retained, so one must be discarded.

Because we require that the set of cooperating servers eventually converge, we need to invent some way of resolving this conflict. Note that there isn't really any correct way to resolve the conflict; each client's change is as good as the other's. Of course, each user thinks that his or her change will be made on all replicas—and they may be somewhat surprised to discover otherwise.

All currently available multi-master directory replication systems use a "last writer wins" policy to resolve such conflicts. Every attribute is marked with a timestamp that indicates the most recent time it was modified. If, while synchronizing with another server, the synchronization algorithm detects a conflict, the attribute value with the later timestamp value is selected—and the other value is discarded. It follows, then, that in order to implement such a policy, the system clocks on each cooperating server must be kept in close synchronization so that timestamps from different servers can be meaningfully compared. NDS has an extensive time synchronization system that keeps the NDS server clocks in synchronization.

Resolving Identical Timestamps

Astute readers might ask what happens if two NDS servers assign the *same* timestamp to the same updated entry. Which server wins? In fact, NDS timestamps are structured such that it is impossible for this to happen. An NDS timestamp, which is 64 bits in length, consists of three parts: a 32-bit quantity that represents the number of seconds since the epoch (0000 UTC on January 1, 1970); a 16-bit quantity that represents the replica number that received the update; and a 16-bit event ID field sequentially assigned by the server that allows up to 65,536 updates within a single second. Because the replica number is guaranteed to be unique (unique replica numbers are assigned by the partition master during replica creation), there can never be a timestamp collision.

You might imagine other, more sophisticated conflict resolution policies that reflect some set of business rules. For example, it may make sense to have a rule stating that changes made by a person in the human resources group always take precedence over changes made by other users. Whatever the conflict resolution policy, it is critical that all cooperating servers use exactly the same policy; if different policies are in use, it cannot be guaranteed that the directory contents will eventually converge. This fact will become increasingly important as vendors standardize a vendor-independent multi-master replication protocol.

Advanced Features

The advanced replication features described in the following sections are found in some, but not all, directory implementations. They offer finely tuned control when scheduling the replication process.

Scheduling Replication

There are some cases in which a directory administrator might not want changes to be sent to all replicas immediately. For example, a remote office connected via a dialup link might be better served if updates can be transmitted in one batch to save connect time charges. Or a remote office connected via a slow network link might be configured to have updates propagated to a consumer server during off-hours to improve network response for other applications during working hours.

Unfortunately, scheduling replication in this fashion means that users connecting to the consumer will see old data for potentially long periods of time. For many applications, this is perfectly acceptable; but think carefully about any requirements you might have down the road. For example, if an employee is terminated, it may be necessary to reset his password immediately so he cannot log in. However, if the directory is not scheduled to be updated for another eight hours, the password revocation will not make it to the consumer immediately, as required.

Scheduling Update Latency by Attribute Type

One solution to this latency problem is to incorporate a scheduling policy that propagates changes to certain attributes immediately and others less rapidly. With NDS—the only system we know of that currently offers this capability—certain attributes such as login passwords are propagated on a fast synchronization schedule (10 seconds after the attribute value is modified), whereas other attributes, such as last login timestamps in user entries, are scheduled for update on a slow synchronization schedule (30 minutes after the attribute value is modified). This feature seeks to improve update time for critical values and defers other updates to conserve network bandwidth and server processing time. The NDS synchronization schedule is fixed and may not be altered.

Schema and Replication

The purpose of replication is to provide copies of directory data in multiple physical locations. It makes sense, therefore, that supplier and consumer servers should have the same schema. Serious problems would arise if, for example, a supplier server attempted to add an entry of some object class not allowed by the consumer's schema (the operation would be rejected, and the consumer could never be brought into synchronization).

Hence, suppliers and consumers must agree on schema before replication can take place. Some directory services, such as NDS, handle this automatically; others, such as Netscape Directory Server 4.0, rely on the supplier server to enforce schema. Consumer servers assume that updates coming from the supplier comply with its schema, so they do not check the schema when applying updates.

Access Control and Replication

Virtually all directory products offer some way of controlling access to the data contained in the directory tree, usually via an access control list (ACL) mechanism. When the contents of the tree are replicated, it is desirable to also replicate any associated ACL information so that the same protections apply to both the replicated data and the original data. More information about access control can be found in Chapter 11, "Privacy and Security Design."

Most, if not all, directory software stores ACLs as attributes of entries. In most cases, this means that the ACLs merely need to be replicated along with other directory content. As long as the supplier and consumer server use the same ACL syntax, and as long as those ACLs mean the same thing on both, their directory entries will have the same access control.

Again, in most cases, it's sufficient to replicate ACLs along with directory content. The one time this gets a bit tricky is when ACLs have a scope that extends down the directory tree and crosses a unit of replication (see Figure 10.18).

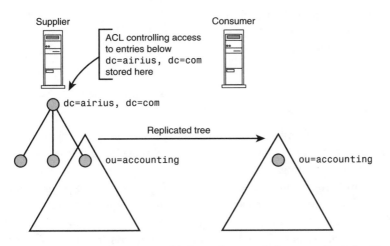

FIGURE 10.18 *Access control information stored above a replicated subtree.*

In Figure 10.18, the entry dc=airius, dc=com on the supplier server contains an access control directive that applies to all entries below it. However, this entry is not contained within the replicated subtree, so the consumer server lacks the access control information it needs to properly control access to its replicated subtree.

Netscape Directory Server allows you to configure replication in this manner, so be sure when designing your replication strategy that you include ACLs at the top of all replicated subtrees. (The default in Netscape Directory Server is to completely deny access in the absence of ACL information, so a problem like the one in Figure 10.18 would not expose any directory information to unauthorized access.) NDS, on the other hand, always maintains links between partitions that allow it to automatically find and enforce ACLs stored in superior entries—at the cost of additional network traffic, however. The X.500 model, meanwhile, specifies that any access control information contained in subentries must be provided to the consumer by the supplier, even if that information is contained in subentries above the replicated subtree.

To summarize, lightweight directory servers such as Netscape's place the responsibility for managing ACL information across replicas on the administrator, but they offer fast performance because all needed ACL information is local to the replicated server. More-heavyweight systems such as X.500 and NDS attempt to manage this information for the administrator.

Designing Your Directory Replication System

To maximize the reliability and performance of your directory service through replication, you should spend some time planning for both your current requirements and future expansion. To begin your planning, gather the following information:

- A network map of your organization, showing all locations and the types of network connectivity between them.

- An inventory of any directory-enabled applications you are running or intend to run. For example, LDAP-enabled messaging products such as Netscape Messaging Server and Enterprise Web Server utilize the directory for authentication and access control. If you know the physical locations of these applications and clients, note them on your network map. If you don't yet have a plan for deploying these servers and clients, that's okay; estimate as best you can and revisit your assumptions as you gain experience through the piloting phase of your deployment.

As we work through the design process, realize that it's very easy to over-engineer a replication solution. Think about airplanes: Very few have ten engines—most commercial jets these days have two because that's been found to be an optimal number given fuel costs, plane sizes, and engine reliability. Now think about your directory: Although it's certainly possible to put three redundant directory servers on every Ethernet segment in an office building—which would definitely increase your directory's reliability—don't forget that someone has to set up and manage all those replicas!

In an office in which all workstations and servers have 10Mbps connectivity, connectivity is probably so reliable that it's unnecessary to worry about the network being partitioned. Even if that's not a valid assumption, it's probably still cheaper to fix the network problem than it is to set up and manage a lot of directory replicas! On the other hand, if your organization is spread over a wide geographical area and your sites are linked by slower, less-reliable network links, you should definitely pay very close attention to how you allocate replicas across your network.

Finally, view this design process as an iterative one. Make a pass through it, thinking about maximizing reliability and performance. As your solution evolves, you may find that you want to revisit a design decision. Also, as you think about replication, you may find that you want to revisit some of your design decisions about directory topology and even your namespace design. Don't be afraid to do this; it will be time well spent.

Designing for Maximum Reliability

When you design for maximum reliability, you make your directory impervious to the failure of a single directory server. Then, if one of your servers fails, directory clients can use another replica to obtain their directory services.

How exactly do directory clients deal with the failure of a particular server? LDAP client applications are responsible for detecting the failure of their primary server and reconnecting to an alternate server. At present, there is no standard method for locating an alternate server that can provide service, so it's useful to ask the supplier of an LDAP-based application how this is handled.

For example, client applications that use the Netscape C language Software Development Kit (SDK) can provide multiple server names when establishing a connection; if a given server is unavailable, the SDK tries another. Another option is to use a hardware failover device such as Cisco Systems' LocalDirector, which can balance client load across a number of servers. It can also detect when a server has failed and avoids directing clients to it until it is returned to service.

To maximize reliability, locate within each major zone of your network at least one replica that is connected via a network link of less than 10Mbps. (If you have a single well-connected network, you have only one zone to worry about.) For example, if your network comprises a single set of buildings connected by high-speed fiber-optic links, you might choose to deploy two replicated servers. If either server fails, client requests would be handled by the remaining server (see Figure 10.19).

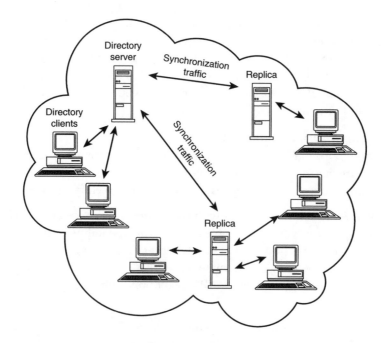

FIGURE 10.19 *Multiple replicas located at a site.*

Suppose now that your organization consists of a central office with a series of remote offices connected by slower, 56Kbps network connections. In this case, you might choose to place a replica at each remote site (see Figure 10.20). This allows you to avoid wasting your scarce network bandwidth on LDAP client traffic.

Under normal circumstances, the directory clients shown in Figure 10.20 in the remote office would contact the onsite replica for directory operations. In the event that the server fails, the remote clients could contact one of the servers in the central office. You could even place more than one replica in each remote office so that even if one of the onsite servers fail, the clients can obtain directory service without sending requests across the slower interoffice network link. If you use such a configuration, you may want to schedule replication updates to occur only during off-peak hours, if your directory server software supports it.

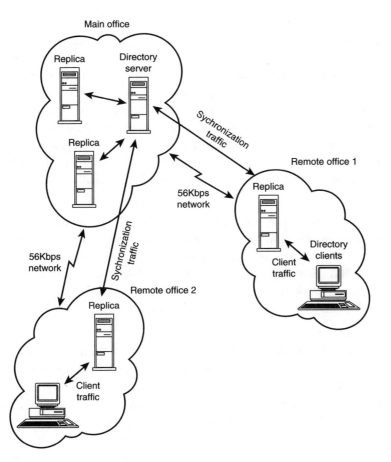

FIGURE 10.20 *Replicas placed to limit client traffic on WAN links.*

Designing for Maximum Performance

When you design replication to enhance performance, you strive to design a system that can handle your existing client load today but can be expanded easily to handle a larger load in the future.

You should strive to provide a sufficient number of replica servers to handle your client load. Estimating your client load involves a bit of guesswork, but you should be able to get a pretty good idea by understanding how often a given client makes a request and how a typical request from that client would impact the server. Then multiply this by the number of clients you expect to make use of the directory.

For example, suppose 1,000 users will use a Web-based address book application to look up other employees in the directory. Begin by making some assumptions about how often people will use the service. (These assumptions can be verified, and adjusted if necessary, during the pilot phase of your deployment; see Chapter 13, "Piloting Your Directory Service"). Let's assume that each person will perform 10 lookups during the 8 a.m.–5 p.m. workday; that means you should expect to see 10,000 queries in 8 hours. This translates to 1,250 queries per hour—approximately 1 query every 3 seconds. If you have some additional knowledge that leads you to believe that usage will not be uniform, but instead it will have spikes during the day, take that into account as well.

Next, understand the impact the load will place on the directory server. Are the queries typically made on indexed attributes—which perform well and place a lighter load on the server—or might some of the queries be on unindexed attributes? Will the searches typically return a single entry or many entries? Will the retrieved entries contain large attributes, or will the amount of transmitted data be small (perhaps up to a kilobyte or two)?

Finally, determine how many replicated servers you will need to handle the load. You may be fortunate enough to have some data from the software vendor that tells you how many typical queries the software can service while running on some standard hardware in a given time period. For example, the Netscape Directory Server can perform several hundred searches per second on a typical 200Mhz Pentium II computer, so a single server would be entirely capable of handling the client load in the previous example. If, however, you don't really know how many operations the server can perform per second, you should measure it when evaluating server software or piloting your directory.

Tip

When doing capacity planning, always take vendor-supplied performance figures with a grain of salt. Performance figures that appear in vendor data sheets reflect the performance measured by the vendor on one system with one particular set of assumptions. Performance may be affected by many other factors, including the operating system platform, amount of available memory, speed of disk drives, namespace design, complexity of access control rules, characteristics of LDAP clients, and much more. If possible, measure your systems under the types of loads you expect them to handle to get a better idea of individual server performance capabilities before planning your total number of replicas.

You should consider write performance of your directory separately from search performance. In a replicated environment, each change made by a client needs to be made at each replica as well. For this reason, write performance in a replicated environment does not scale as well as search performance. If you find that your application modifies the directory frequently, you may find it advantageous to partition your directory so that each server needs to handle fewer modifications. Remember that directories are typically optimized for searching, so don't be surprised to discover that your software can perform only a few write operations per second—even if it can perform hundreds or even thousands of indexed searches per second.

Another way to improve your directory's performance is to provide and tune dedicated servers for particular applications. For example, Netscape Messaging Server 3.5 imposes a heavy load on a server as it goes about its business of delivering mail. However, it uses only LDAP equality search filters (as opposed to substring or approximate filters). You could create a Netscape Directory Server replica that is dedicated to servicing the Messaging Server's queries. Because you know that substring and approximate indexes are not required on the server, you could remove them from the server's configuration, therefore improving its write performance and reducing the memory requirements.

One other consideration is how your directory clients will know that multiple servers are able to handle their requests. Some directory services handle this automatically via their proprietary protocols, but LDAP does not currently provide a way for a server to inform clients about other replicas of itself. One way to achieve load-balancing in the absence of this capability is to use the Domain Name System (DNS) round-robin capability to map a given hostname to all the IP addresses of hosts containing a copy of the replicated data. With DNS round-robin, the DNS server reorders the list of IP addresses each time it responds to a query for the hostname. This way, client load can be divided among any number of servers. As previously mentioned, it is also possible to use a hardware load-balancing and failover device such as Cisco Systems' LocalDirector to distribute load across a number of servers.

Other Considerations

In the discussion of reliability and performance, we've focused primarily on where to put replicas. But we haven't considered some other factors that may be important when designing your replication system.

First, you need to consider the maximum number of replicas your software can gracefully handle. This is highly dependent on the software in use and the number of updates that your system receives. In general, it's a good idea to try to limit the number of replicas supplied by a single server to somewhere between 5 and 10. If you try to manage a larger number of replicas, you may find that the servers spend so much time propagating updates that they are unable to answer client requests in a timely fashion. If your directory sees very few modifications, you can probably use more replicas; if your directory handles many modifications, you may need to use fewer replicas.

What if you find that your directory service is bogged down with synchronization traffic? One option is to partition your directory tree among a larger number of servers. When you do this, each server needs to handle fewer update requests and therefore needs to send fewer updates to replicas. Of course, the total amount of network traffic would still be the same (in fact, it may actually increase somewhat because of the partition management overhead of some directory systems), so if you find that your network is the bottleneck, a network upgrade may be in order. But in practice, the network is rarely the bottleneck. More often the limiting factors are server CPU, disk I/O, and memory usage.

Another option for reducing the replication burden on a master server is to use a cascading replication configuration. In a cascaded configuration, a change propagates from a supplier to a small number of consumers, and then from each of those consumers to a larger number of consumers, and so on until all replicas have been updated (see Figure 10.21). This approach lengthens the time it takes for a given change to propagate to all replicas, but it does make it possible to feed a larger number of replicas. Your directory server software may or may not allow this type of configuration, so consult your documentation.

The second factor to consider is the overhead associated with managing a very complex replication system. What if a replica goes down? How hard is it to bring it back up? How do you monitor the system to be sure it's working properly? How hard is it to find out whether a user's complaint results from a replication problem? In general, use of the KISS principle (keep it simple, stupid) is a wonderful idea: The simpler you can make the replication configuration, the better off you'll be. It'll be easier to troubleshoot, simpler to fix, and probably more reliable overall. If your boss is unimpressed because the system looks too simple, you can describe it as "elegant." That usually works.

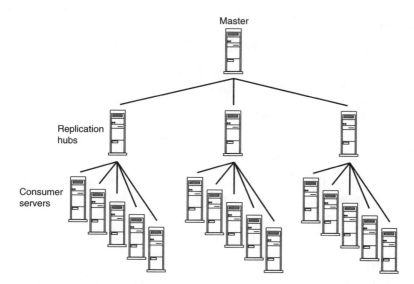

FIGURE 10.21 *Cascaded replication.*

Choosing Replication Solutions

If you need to provide a reliable, high-performance directory service, you should evaluate the software you are considering in terms of its replication capabilities. The following are some general questions to ask when performing this evaluation:

- Does the software support incremental updates, in which only the minimum set of changes needed to bring a replica into synchronization are sent?

- Does the software support single-master, floating-master, and/or multi-master replication?

- How do client applications behave when a replica becomes unavailable? Do they automatically select a new server?

- How easy is it to replace a master server that has failed?

- How easy is it to manage replication? Does the software provide tools for determining the state of replication and whether replicas are up-to-date?

- Does the software support the features you need? Does it, for example, allow replication to be scheduled at a particular time of day?

- Can the software send updates securely (for example, in encrypted form) to prevent network eavesdropping?

More information about selecting appropriate directory server software can be found in Chapter 12, "Choosing Directory Products."

Replication Checklist

☐ Create a map of your organization's physical network.

☐ Inventory your existing and planned directory-enabled applications, and understand the load they will generate.

☐ Note on the map the locations of your directory-enabled applications.

☐ Locate at least one replica within each network location connected via a slower and/or unreliable network link.

☐ Add additional replicas to handle the client load. Optionally, create dedicated replicas for directory-enabled applications that make extensive use of the directory.

Further Reading

Microsoft Active Directory documents, available from Microsoft's World Wide Web site at http://www.microsoft.com.

Netscape Directory Server Administration Guide. Available online at http://home.netscape.com/eng/server/directory/3.0/agrtm/contents.html.

Netscape Directory Server Deployment Guide. Available online at http://home.netscape.com/eng/server/directory/3.0/deployrtm/contents.html.

Novell's Four Principles of NDS Design. J. Hughes and B. Thomas, Novell Press, 1996.

Novell's Guide to IntranetWare Networks. J. Hughes and B. Thomas, Novell Press, 1996.

Understanding X.500: The Directory. D. Chadwick, International Thomson Computer Press, 1996. Now out of print; selected sections available on the World Wide Web at http://www.salford.ac.uk/its024/Version.Web/Contents.htm.

Looking Ahead

Now that you've used directory replication to provide your users with a reliable and high-performance directory, it's time to think about how to protect the data in your directory service and ensure that persons can only view and modify the data they are authorized to work with. Chapter 11, "Privacy and Security Design," describes directory privacy, security, and access control in detail.

Privacy and Security Design

No discussion of directory design would be complete without at least one chapter explaining how to secure the information in your directory and protect the privacy of your users. Without such safeguards, the types of directory applications that can be supported by your directory are severely limited.

If the information in your directory is not secured and you cannot be sure whether it has been tampered with, the applications that use the data are limited to those unconcerned with the accuracy or completeness of the information. If access to the information in your directory is not secured and the information itself cannot be kept private to those authorized to view it, only public information may be stored in the directory. Needless to say, these concerns are paramount to providing an industrial-strength directory service that can be trusted by applications and users.

This chapter describes the purposes of security and outlines the threats posed to it in a typical directory environment. We describe how to analyze your environment to determine your security and privacy needs, and we provide a section explaining how to design your directory service to meet these needs. A separate section on user privacy explains the importance of keeping data about your users private, and a section on the trade-offs between security and deployability analyzes some common decisions you will have to make.

Security Guidelines

One of the most important points to understand before you begin to design your directory's security infrastructure is that there is no such thing as "secure" or "private" in an absolute sense. Instead, there are degrees of security and privacy that come with various tradeoffs and apply only in well-defined contexts.

A good analogy can be made to the security of your own house. It probably has one or more doors and windows, each with some kind of lock on it. The security-minded among us lock the doors and windows to our house in an effort to make it secure from unauthorized entry. Clearly we can achieve only a modest level of security. A window can easily be broken. A lock can be picked. A door can be broken down. Adding bars on the windows and doors increases your level of security, but at the expense of your own convenience. Such tradeoffs are typical in the security world and may well be worthwhile if you live in a neighborhood where threats are common. The lengths to which you should go to protect yourself generally should be proportional to the security threats you face—a principle you should consider when designing your directory.

Another important security lesson is that a system is only as secure as its weakest link, so it is important to think of the whole product and protect against every avenue of likely attack. Continuing our analogy to your house, consider the futility of installing a steel reinforced door with triple dead bolt locks if you are going to leave your windows wide open. Similarly, making your directory system secure in one dimension while leaving other areas wide open can often lead to trouble. Be sure to consider every aspect of security you can think of that might be related to your service.

On the other hand, this can be taken too far. Why have windows on your house at all? If they can be broken so easily, they provide no real security. Better board them up. Why bother locking your door when anyone who really wants to get in could easily break it down? Better go live in a bank vault. But what good does that do? Even bank vaults get robbed.

The answer is that every little bit helps. Although no security system is guaranteed against a determined and capable attacker, every additional security measure you employ raises the difficulty of attack. Every time you add a level of security, you filter out more attackers. The harder it is to break your security, the more likely it is for an attacker to give up or to move on to someone else's house—or directory service.

So how far should you go to protect the security of your directory? The answer to this question depends on the kinds of threats you face—and the consequences you would suffer in case of a security failure. For example, if your directory contains name and email address information, unauthorized access to the directory might result in a lot of junk email sent to your users—which can be miserably annoying. But the most serious consequences it usually results in are lost time and a waste of system resources.

On the other hand, consider a directory that contains names, Social Security numbers, credit card numbers, and other personal information. Unauthorized access to this directory might result in far more serious consequences, including improper access to bank accounts, unauthorized use of credit cards, damaged credit reports, and worse. Clearly this information needs to be protected more strongly.

All of these principles are fundamental to security design. Keeping them firmly in mind during your design process will go a long way toward keeping you on track and help make your service secure and successful. Here is a quick summary of these security and privacy design principles:

- Recognize that there are different levels of security and privacy. Your job is to choose the level that is appropriate for your needs and the threats your directory faces.

- Remember that your system is only as secure as its weakest link. Remember also that the strength of a link in the security chain should be evaluated with respect to the likelihood of an attack.

- Keep in mind that different types of information require different security precautions; similarly, different types of users require different levels of privacy. Don't try to devise a "one-size-fits-all" solution.

The Purpose of Security

At its most basic level, the purpose of security is to protect the information in your directory so that you can access it with confidence. The obvious next question is: *Protect it from what?* We give an overview of the kind of threats you should guard against in the following section. For now, it's enough to think of these threats as being unauthorized access to or tampering with directory information, or causing users of the directory to be denied service.

If there is a security breach, often it is important to know exactly what was breached and how. Auditing provides this capability. Auditing also can be useful in determining why the system is not performing as it should, what the directory is being used for, and other interesting and useful bits of information.

Auditing information is invaluable in determining how to secure your system after a break-in. If you don't know what went wrong, it's very difficult to know how to fix it. Maintaining an adequate audit trail provides information such as who accessed the server, what operations were performed, when those operations were performed, how long they took, and other information about errors and unusual conditions. Analyzing these logs can give you insight into many problems, including the following:

- *Break-in attempts.* For example, many repeated authentication failures in the logs might alert you to a break-in attempt. This information could help you track down the attacker or take preventive measures.

- *Trawling attempts.* Trawling is any technique used to perform unauthorized bulk downloads of directory data. Look for repeated searches that download successive portions of the database in an attempt to defeat the administrative limits you have imposed. This auditing information could help you track down the trawler or take preventive measures.

- *Misconfigured applications.* For example, you might notice an application performing searches that make no sense or aren't optimal, placing unnecessary load on the directory. In extreme cases, a misconfigured application can cause others to be denied service because it consumes all available directory resources. Auditing information can help you identify and fix the misbehaving application or configure your directory to handle the searches better.

There are also nontechnical reasons for securing your directory. It's important for the users of your directory to be confident that the information they feel is private is being safeguarded in an adequate manner. Users often have concerns that go well beyond what you may consider to be a security or privacy threat. For example, you may consider a user's name or gender to be public information, but the user may have legitimate reasons for wanting this information kept private (for example, fear of stalking or being a member of a witness protection program). Such perceived threats are as real as any others as far as your users are concerned, and they should be dealt with accordingly.

Another nontechnical reason to secure your directory is for the sake of public relations. In some situations this can be the most important reason. A break-in reported in the newspaper or on TV can be devastating to your company's business. The popular press seldom digs deep enough to discover the real consequences of a break-in. If your business is banking or securities trading, or a similar business in which trust plays a vital role, a security breach can be fatal. Your customers (not to mention your competitors) usually won't distinguish between a break-in of your publicly available corporate phone book directory and the bank vault itself. The damage from this kind of a security problem can take a long time to repair.

Security Threats

There are many potential threats to security, and an entire science and industry have grownup around this important area. Several good books on the subject provide excellent coverage of security in general and treat the subject in a more complete and formal manner than we will here. Because the subject of this book is directories, not security, we will take a more pragmatic and focused approach toward describing the range of security threats. This section provides an example-driven overview of the most typical threats to directory security. We've broken up the threats into three categories: unauthorized access, tampering with information, and denial-of-service.

It's important to understand that an attacker does not necessarily have to be particularly clever to use one of these attacks. With the popularity of the Internet and the growth of the bad guy community along with it, the advantages of shrink-wrapped software have come to computer security attacks. For most of the threats we describe in this chapter, you can find ready-made software that will exploit it. People trying to compromise your security are often just running shell scripts and programs they downloaded off the Internet. They may have less of an idea how the programs operate than you do! Of course, there are exceptions, too: Wily hackers who discover security holes and write the programs that exploit them are still in abundance.

A commonly held security myth is that most attacks are made by hackers operating out of their basement computing lairs. In reality, most attacks, especially successful ones, are made by your own employees, administrators, and users. In practice, the "inside job" poses by far the greatest threat to your directory's security in most environments. When designing your security solution, be sure to consider threats both inside and outside your organization.

Unauthorized Access

The unauthorized access threat may seem simple to protect against. You should authenticate clients accessing your directory and provide access control restricting the information that these clients can access. Problem solved, right? Unfortunately, it's not quite that easy.

Think about the way directory information is delivered to authorized clients. There are several opportunities along this path for an unauthorized client to gain access to the data. Here are several breaches that can occur:

- *Credential forging.* If a client's credentials can be forged, an unauthorized client can fool the directory into thinking it is authorized. For example, suppose your directory's authentication scheme is based on plain text passwords, and no other steps are taken to protect the password as it is transmitted to the server. An attacker who is able to watch a legitimate client in an authentication exchange may be able to replay the exchange later, successfully masquerading as the legitimate client. One-time password schemes can help guard against this, as can authentication methods that do not allow replay of credentials. Connection protection mechanisms can also help reduce this risk.

- *Credential stealing.* This threat is closely related to credential forging but more low tech in nature. If your users write down their passwords on notes stuck to their computers, anyone who walks by can steal them. If you use token-based security that requires the user to present some physical token to access the directory, this token can be stolen. The same is true for schemes based on public key cryptography. If a user's private key is stolen, the thief can impersonate the user. There are a variety of ways that credentials can be stolen—many of them not technology-based.

- *Connection hijacking.* Is it possible for an unauthorized client to hijack an authorized client's connection when the authorized client has authenticated itself? Yes, barring any connection-level protection that prevents it. For this to happen, the hijacker usually has to have access to the same physical network that the victim is on. Methods of attack vary somewhat, but they all involve the hijacker responding to requests meant for the authorized client and preventing it from responding. General connection protection mechanisms, such as secure sockets layer (SSL) or its successor, transport layer security (TLS), can prevent this, as can other methods that require directory operations to be digitally signed. Digital signatures are discussed in more detail in the next section.

- *Network sniffing.* If it is possible for an attacker to eavesdrop on the information exchanged between a legitimate client and the server, the attacker can learn things he or she is not authorized to know. To guard against this, steps must be taken either to physically protect the network between clients and servers so that no one can listen in, or to protect the information exchanged so that an eavesdropper who does listen in cannot get useful information. SSL provides these benefits by encrypting the information transferred. Other schemes have this property, but SSL is by far the most widely used.

- *Trojan horses.* Remember that there can be a lot of software between an authorized directory user (or other agent) and the network that conveys that information. A "trojan horse" is software that masquerades as a legitimate program but, when run, performs some illicit functions compromising security. A popular kind of trojan horse program is a keystroke sniffer, which disguises itself as a legitimate login program. This nasty piece of software hooks into the low-level routines taking input from your keyboard, recording all keystrokes you make. These keystrokes can be analyzed later to determine, for example, what your password is. This threat is very difficult to protect against. The best approach is probably to employ administrative methods and antivirus software and to regularly back up and reinstall your machines.

- *Backdoor access.* Is it possible that there are other ways to access the data you want to protect, ways not subject to your directory's authentication and access control safeguards? The answer to this question is almost certainly yes. Directory data lives on one or more server machines, probably residing in some kind of database or file system. If an intruder gains unauthorized access to the directory server machine, he or she has a wide variety of opportunities to access the data. If your directory data comes to your server in a feed from the human resources relational database, the information in your directory is only as secure as the source database. Many other avenues of access to your data are possible, in addition to the directory access methods you are designing. Some systems are even designed for this from the ground up. The Microsoft Windows NT Active Directory, for example, is designed to make your directory data accessible over LDAP, HTTP, the file system, and other network protocols.

- *Physical access.* Obvious, perhaps, but worth mentioning is that if an attacker has physical access to the directory server machine, a whole host of problems can occur. These range from gaining increased privileges by logging in via a console or other trusted terminal, to just being able to unplug the disk drive containing the directory data and walk out the door with it! Keeping your server machines in locked rooms with limited access is a good guard against this. Encrypting directory data as it lives on the server is another good approach, although this can be expensive. Performance suffers because of the time it takes to encrypt and decrypt data. Extra hardware may be required to make performance acceptable.

- *Software bugs.* This category is a bit of a catch-all, representing one of today's most commonly exploited security problems. Bugs in the directory server software, the operating system, shared libraries, and even unrelated systems can often be exploited by an attacker to gain unauthorized privileges. There is probably not much you can do to minimize the number of bugs in your vendor's software, but you can take preventive measures. For example, avoid running any noncritical services on your directory machines to reduce the possible avenues of attack. Stay current with operating system and other software patches that may fix security bugs.

Unauthorized Tampering

Access to directory data is one thing, but if an attacker can actually change directory data—either as it resides in the service itself or en route between client and server—a new set of problems arises. If that were to happen, clients could no longer trust the information they receive from the directory, servers could no longer trust the modifications and queries they receive from clients— and the directory service would soon become useless.

Many of the attacks described in the previous section could result in data tampering, as could other new attacks. Following are the attack methods you need to be concerned about:

- *Man in the middle.* A common attack of this kind occurs when an attacker is able to insert him or herself between the directory client and server. Without any means to detect tampering, the man in the middle could change the client's requests to the server (or not forward them at all) and change the server's responses to the client (see Figure 11.1). SSL and similar technologies can solve this problem by signing information at either end of the connection. If the signature is invalid when the data arrives, the data has been tampered with.

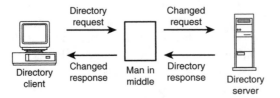

FIGURE 11.1 *The "man in the middle" security attack.*

- *Trojan horse.* As with unauthorized access to data, a trojan horse attack on a directory client (or server) can easily facilitate unauthorized tampering. The same countermeasures apply, as do the same difficulties in applying them.

- *Masquerading.* In the section on unauthorized access, we described several ways a client can fool a server into thinking the client is someone else. The same problems apply here, both for client and server. A client that can masquerade as somebody else can insert false information into the directory. An evil server that can masquerade as a legitimate server can send back incorrect information to clients and prevent legitimate client modifications from being made.

Denial-of-service Attacks

Another kind of security threat to your directory does not involve stealing or changing data at all. Instead, the attacker's goal is to prevent the directory from providing service to its clients. Such an attack is called a *denial-of-service attack.* Denial-of-service can be one of the hardest security problems to guard against and detect. There are two main types of denial-of-service attacks:

- *Direct resource consumption.* This is a general kind of attack in which the attacker simply uses the system's resources to prevent them from being used by someone else. For example, someone could write a directory client that continuously performs expensive directory operations, tying up the resources and making them unavailable to other users. Someone could also write a directory client that stores large amounts of information in the directory in an attempt to exhaust available disk space. There are many other forms of this attack.

  Placing limits on the number of directory resources any single client or user can use is a good way to guard against this. Keeping good audit records for the directory is also a good idea. Although an audit record does not prevent the attack, it does allow you to determine when it is happening, and perhaps who is perpetrating the attack and how to stop it. Monitoring can also help fight this problem. If you know the normal level of resource consumption by your directory, monitoring can alert you to any unusual events. Hopefully, you will be able to take action before the problem gets out of hand. Monitoring is discussed in more detail in Chapter 18, "Monitoring."

- *Indirect resource consumption.* This attack is similar to the direct attacks just described, but it is often more difficult to detect and guard against. This attack involves using resources that the directory server or directory clients need, thus denying those resources to the legitimate users. The difference from the direct attack is that the directory service itself is not involved, so directory auditing capabilities often don't help in detection and prevention.

For example, an attacker could write a program that uses inordinate amounts of bandwidth. Another attacker with access to the directory machine could write a program to consume CPU, disk bandwidth, memory, or other resources. Much more clever and insidious attacks are possible, too, such as initiating many half-opened connections to the directory machine until the machine runs out of system resources. The list of possibilities goes on—and can get quite nasty.

This kind of attack is very difficult to defend against, but there are some precautions you can take. Isolating your directory machines as much as possible is a good start. Reducing the number of nondirectory processes and users on the directory server machines (or, ideally, eliminating them) is another good idea. Employing firewall filters and other network-level safeguards is also possible. No amount of prevention can eliminate the threat, but it can be reduced.

There are several reasons someone might conduct a denial-of-service attack on your directory. The first and probably most likely is simply by mistake. Bugs in directory client software, misconfigured software, or simply a lack of aware-ness of the consequences of certain actions can all lead to denial-of-service. Your best guards against this kind of attacker are education, monitoring, and auditing.

The second reason someone might conduct a denial-of-service attack on your directory is simple maliciousness. The attacker might be out to ruin your day or the days of your users. The attacker might have a specific problem with you or your service, or your service might simply provide a convenient target for wreaking general havoc. Either way, you would do well to guard against this kind of attacker.

The final and most insidious reason someone might conduct a denial-of-service attack on your directory is to help them compromise another system that depends on the directory. For example, if your Web server depends on the directory to authenticate users, attacking the directory can effectively disable the Web service. This kind of attack can be difficult to defend against because the real motivation behind the attack may never be known.

Security Tools

Now that we've described some of the security threats your directory service may face, it's time to turn our attention to the tools available to help combat them. We make no attempt to provide complete coverage of all the tools out there, but we do give an overview both of the general protection mechanisms and their embodiment in specific technologies.

First, these are the general security methods at your disposal:

- *Authentication* is the means by which one party verifies another's identity. Authentication can be one-way, or it can be two-way (sometimes called *mutual authentication*). Examples of one-way authentication are when a directory client presents a password to a directory server in an LDAP bind operation, or when a directory server presents its certificate to a directory client during an SSL connection negotiation so that the connection can be encrypted. An example of two-way authentication is when both the directory client and server exchange certificates during SSL connection negotiation.

- *Signing* is the means by which the authenticity and integrity of information is ensured. If information is signed, the recipient can determine that it was in fact sent by the indicated party and that it was not tampered with in transit. An example of signing occurs when an LDAP connection is made over SSL: The SSL layer divides the stream of data being sent into a series of blocks, and each block is accompanied by a cryptographic checksum that allows the receiver of the packet to determine if it's been tampered with. In another example of signing, an application stores a signed value within an attribute in a directory entry; the authenticity of the value can then be verified regardless of the security of the server itself.

- *Encryption* is the means by which the privacy of information is protected. If information is encrypted, it is scrambled in a way that only the recipient (and possibly the sender) knows how to undo. Encrypted information intercepted by anyone else is not useful. An example of encryption occurs during an SSL LDAP session. All packets transmitted are encrypted using the method negotiated during connection setup.

- *Auditing* is the means by which you track what happens to your directory. Auditing is an element key to the overall security solution because it is often the only way to determine if your security has been compromised and in what manner. Auditing of data handling and other procedures is also important to make sure there are end-to-end security protections for your data. An example of auditing is the log files maintained by most directory server products.

These four concepts form the basis of most practical security procedures in modern directory systems. There are other, more esoteric security concepts, such as nonrepudiation, that we will not bother to cover in this book.

Now we turn our attention to some specific technologies that provide one or more of the abstract services we just described:

- *SSL* is the secure sockets layer protocol. Originally developed by Kipp Hickman of Netscape, SSL is a generic transport-layer security mechanism designed to make application protocols such as LDAP secure. SSL is based on public key cryptography and can provide very high security. It includes strong authentication, signing, and encryption services. SSL lets communicating parties negotiate a level of security that is appropriate and acceptable to both parties. A variety of different security algorithms and strengths, or security levels, can be negotiated.

- *TLS* is the transport layer security protocol. When the Internet Engineering Task Force (IETF) formed a working group to standardize an SSL-like protocol, they started with SSL version 3.0 and changed the name to TLS. There is very little difference between SSL 3.0 and TLS 1.0; in this book, we use these terms interchangeably. At the time of this writing, TLS 1.0 is on the verge of being published as RFCs with Proposed Internet Standard status.

- *Kerberos* is a security technology originally developed at the Massachusetts Institute of Technology as part of Project Athena. Unlike SSL, which is based on a public key system, Kerberos is based on a private key, or shared secret, system. Kerberos provides an authentication service but can be used to provide encryption services as well. Kerberos version 4 was the first widely used version of Kerberos. Later attempts to standardize Kerberos (although not in the IETF) with version 5 have achieved limited success. Various groups have splintered off from the core standard, producing different, incompatible versions.

- *SASL*, the simple authentication and security layer, was developed by John Myers of Netscape. SASL (pronounced "sazzle") is a generic framework for negotiating authentication and security layer semantics in application-layer protocols. SASL enables support for authentication, encryption, and signing services. Although it provides no security itself, SASL allows application protocols such as LDAP to negotiate security parameters. LDAP version 3 includes native support for SASL. At the time of this writing, SASL is a Proposed Internet Standard, documented in RFC 2222.

- *IPSec* stands for Internet Protocol security. A relatively new proposed standard at the time of this writing, IPSec is a generic network-layer security mechanism designed to make secure transport-layer connections between machines (such as with TCP, over which LDAP runs). Like SSL, IPSec is based on public key technology, but its focus is on securing connection endpoints, not users or applications.

- *SSH*, the secure shell protocol, is a generic, end-to-end security package for protecting login sessions, file transfers, and other connections between machines. SSH provides strong security and is pretty easy to use. It is a good general purpose tool you can use to secure many of the daily administrative tasks that must be performed on your directory and other systems. SSH version 2 was just released at the time of this writing.

- *Satan* is a generic host security checking package. When you point Satan at a host or network, it probes for various well-known security holes that it has been programmed to look for. When Satan is finished, it produces a report about all the problems it found and how to fix them. Tools like Satan are invaluable to system administrators (including directory administrators) who need to ensure the security of a host on the network. However, tools like Satan are also invaluable to attackers who are trying to break into those systems. You should beat the attackers to the punch and use tools like Satan before they do.

The list could go on and on, but we don't have room to mention all the possibilities here. This list should give you a basic idea of the kinds of tools available to you. Check the references at the end of this section for more reading on this subject.

Analyzing Your Security and Privacy Needs

Now that you have an idea of the kinds of threats your directory may face and the tools at your disposal to protect against them, it's time to turn our attention to analyzing your environment to determine your specific needs. It's important to tailor your security design to your environment and the needs of your users. Failure to address security needs can compromise your entire service and make an otherwise successful deployment fail. On the other hand, if you design a system that imposes needless and cumbersome security constraints on your users, the service can easily become unpopular, go unused, and fail.

The key to finding the right balance is to understand your other directory design requirements and how they affect your security design, and the security needs of your environment and your users.

Directory Requirements

Many aspects of the directory design we've discussed to this point have an impact on security, and vice versa. Some of the more important design decisions that have an impact on security are covered in the following sections.

Read or Write

If your directory is write-only, it may require more security than if you do not allow users or applications to update the directory. Directory write operations are often held to a higher standard of authentication than directory read operations. For example, you might decide that simple password-based authentication is sufficient to read information from the directory, but to update that same information, a client must authenticate using a public key certificate over a protectedSSL connection. With this setup, you can be confident about the integrity of the data in your directory and changes to that data received from clients. You can be less confident that only authorized users are accessing the directory, but you can still maintain some level of assurance.

Sensitivity of Data

Understanding the type and sensitivity of data in your directory is one of the most critical aspects affecting security. The data in your directory is what your security design is there to protect. If your directory contains publicly readable information, there may be no need for access control. You still may need to be concerned about the integrity of the information, however.

If there are different sensitivity classes of data in your directory, you need to consider how best to protect each one. For example, you may consider name data to be public data and therefore require minimal protection. On the other hand, if your directory contains Social Security numbers or salary information, a much greater level of protection is called for.

A useful design exercise is to list all the attributes that will be held in your directory and to try to categorize them based on their sensitivity and the type of access and protection required for each one. Table 11.1 shows an example of this kind of categorization.

TABLE 11.1 EXAMPLES OF ATTRIBUTES AND SENSITIVITY CLASSES

Attribute	Sensitivity	Accessed by	Updated by
cn	Low	Everyone	Administrator
mail	Medium	Everyone	User, administrator
salary	High	User, administrator	Manager
uid	Medium	Everyone	Administrator

After you choose your directory software, you can use this table to help design your directory access control.

Replication

If your directory is replicated, you need to be concerned about the security of the data as it is replicated. It's not much good to protect the data if you pass it among servers without similar protection. Also, if your replication architecture calls for copying data outside your own domain of control (e.g., onto every LAN), a lot of replicas will exist, not all of which will necessarily be held to the same stringent security requirements you place on your own machines. In other words, it's not much good to use directory access control to protect entries if they are going to be replicated to machines controlled by some of the very people you are protecting the entries against!

Think about the network links between replicas. If they are secure, or at least free from access by users, it may be acceptable to pass directory replication updates in the clear. On the other hand, if replication updates must traverse networks accessible to users who may be potential security threats, you'll probably want to protect replication exchanges from eavesdropping, tampering, and other security threats. Replicating over connections secured by SSL might be a good choice in this situation.

Make a graph representing the replicas you plan to create and indicate the security level of each network link involved. Then label each replica with its physical and administrative security levels. An example of such a graph is shown in Figure 11.2.

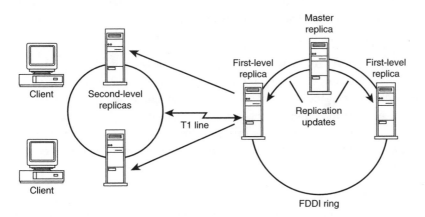

FIGURE 11.2 *Replication and network topology.*

Think about the physical and administrative environments in which the replicas of your directory will live. Are these environments under your control? Are they up to the same security standards to which you hold the replicas you operate? If not, you should reconsider your replication policy.

In Figure 11.2, replication updates between the master and first-level replicas may not need protection from eavesdropping because they occur over a network inaccessible to users. The network is also hard to tap because of the optical technology it uses. However, replication updates between the first- and second-level replicas probably do need protection because they occur over user-accessible networks.

Administration

If your directory administrative model calls for delegation, you must be concerned with the privilege level granted to subordinate administrators and their ability to increase their own privilege level.

You also need to be concerned with other aspects of the administrative environment of your directory. Recognize that you will likely need administrators of the service itself who are different than the administrators of the content held by the service. Service administrators start and stop the service and make sure it runs smoothly, is configured correctly, and is replicated properly. Typically, this function is performed by an experienced system administrator. Content administrators are responsible for day-to-day administration of directory content, adding and deleting users, resetting passwords, and similar tasks. Typically, this function is performed by data processing staff, administrative assistants, and sometimes users themselves. The two types of administration require different kinds of security considerations.

Understanding Your Environment

Analyzing your environment is another important prerequisite to understanding your security requirements. If you understand your environment, you will have a good idea of the kinds of threats your directory will face. Based on these threats and the other information you collected previously, you'll be able to choose appropriate safeguards for your directory. At a minimum, you should consider the user community, directory accessibility, network environment, and physical security.

The User Community

Think about the community of users that will be using your directory. Are they company employees who have employment contracts and other incentives not to misbehave and create directory mischief? Or are they students with far too much time and cleverness on their hands? Obviously, different user communities require different security measures.

The employee community may require relatively little security on the directory, other than that required to prevent accidental misuse of the service. It's hard to foolproof your directory from this kind of unintended abuse. Using access control and minimal authentication is a good way to guard against this kind of problem. Beware of trusting your employee community too much, however. As we mentioned previously, security problems often turn out to be inside jobs.

The student community may well require more robust protection mechanisms. Auser communities;security>determined and clever attacker is difficult to stop. Access control and strong authentication mechanisms provide a good start, but you may want to require SSL access to the directory, do extensive auditing, and institute physical security procedures around your directory servers as well.

Directory Accessibility

Think about how widely accessible your directory is. Is it behind a firewall, or is it available over the Internet? In the firewall case, the community of users that can access your directory is probably restricted to people in which you have some level of trust, however small. You can probably get by with more limited protections in this situation. Perhaps a good auditing system is enough—on the theory that anyone inside the firewall has an employment contract or case, the other incentive to be good, and all you need to know is who has been bad.

In the Internet case, your directory is available for the world to access. Even if no information in your directory is accessible to users who have not authenticated, there is still a significantly increased risk of exposure to security problems. Attackers have free reign to probe your directory for weaknesses, your directory is more vulnerable to denial-of-service attacks, and any security holes in your directory can be more easily exploited.

In this situation, your decision about how much security is required depends more on the consequences of a security breach and the attractiveness of your data and organization as a point of attack. If your organization is prominent (especially among the computer-literate), you can count on being a more likely candidate for attack by the mischievous or malicious. Typically, attacks of this kind are motivated by a desire for notoriety (or sometimes revenge, in the case of a disgruntled ex-employee, for example). There is little chance that a security breach will go unnoticed; one of the goals of the attacker is to make his or her breach of your security known.

If the data held in your directory is especially valuable, you can count on being a prime candidate for attack. This kind of attack motive can be more problematic because it is often in the attacker's best interest to conceal the fact that any security breach has taken place. Indeed, an attacker in search of credit card numbers, competitive analysis information, or other time-sensitive information may find the information they steal worthless if the fact it has been stolen is revealed.

The Network Environment

One of the most vulnerable points in your directory service can be the network over which clients access the directory and directory servers communicate with each other to pass replication updates or perform other server-to-server communication. You need to understand these vulnerabilities and the security implications they generate.

Create or obtain a map of your network's topology, such as the one shown in Figure 11.2. Make sure you understand all the paths between your servers and between servers and clients. If these paths are susceptible to eavesdropping by unauthorized entities, you must find another way to protect directory data as it travels on the network. Such a vulnerable configuration that needs protection is a network in which your server and client machines all share a broadband, nonswitched Ethernet. Any client on this network can easily listen in on traffic not intended for it. A good option might be to require SSL for client/server and server/server communication. This way, eavesdropping does an attacker no good because the traffic is encrypted.

If these paths are not susceptible or at least not wide open to access, SSL may not be required. An example of this situation might be a configuration where your server network is physically secure. Perhaps a fiber optic link (difficult to tap) connects your server network with your user networks, and your user networks consist of switched Ethernet hubs connecting user machines. In this environment it is much more difficult to eavesdrop on traffic not intended for you. You must generally compromise a router or other machine on the network to accomplish this, but it is not impossible to do. Taking these precautions raises the bar for your attackers.

Physical Security

The physical security of your servers is important. As we pointed out previously, securing your network and administrative procedures does not necessarily do you a lot of good if the physical security of your directory server machines is not protected. There are a number of steps you can take to ensure a high level of security.

Make sure your server is kept in a room accessible only to authorized users. In high-security environments, you may want to employ cryptographic smart cards or biometric security procedures to permit entry to the room and use of the server. A retinal scanner is an example of a biometric security device.

Understanding Your Users

A factor often overlooked in security design is the needs of your user community. Understanding how your users will use the directory and view the data it contains, and what their security expectations are, will go a long way toward helping you design a security infrastructure that will make them happy. This, in turn, will go a long way toward making your directory service successful and yourself happy.

How your directory will be used, both by users and applications, can have a significant effect on the security needed by your directory. For example, a directory used for phone book searches and other noncritical tasks certainly has lower security requirements than a directory used to route mission-critical email or perform other important functions.

How your users view the data in your directory is also a relevant factor. A directory that contains personal, but not secret, information about users may not need high security from your point of view, but your users may feel differently. You should be sensitive to these needs. Your users may have a sense of ownership about the data in the directory and strong feelings about how it should be protected from unauthorized access and certainly from unauthorized tampering. They may also feel differently about specific attributes such as home addresses and phone numbers. Be prepared to defend your security policy for each attribute in your directory, or be prepared to have a flexible policy that can be changed by request on a per-user basis.

Designing a flexible access control policy can be helpful. For example, suppose your directory is accessible both inside and outside your organization and contains both home and work address and phone information. The possible access combinations for these sets of information, for clients inside and outside your organization, is given in Table 11.2. If you were to poll your user community, you would likely find out that there are plenty of users who want each combination.

TABLE 11.2 POSSIBLE ACCESS COMBINATIONS FOR HOME AND WORK INFORMATION INSIDE AND OUTSIDE AN ORGANIZATION

	Accessible Inside?	Accessible Outside?
Home information	Yes	Yes
Home information	Yes	No
Home information	No	Yes
Home information	No	No
Work information	Yes	Yes
Work information	Yes	No
Work information	No	Yes
Work information	No	No

Some of these combinations may appear strange to you, but chances are that each one is desired by one or more of your users. It may seem unusual to want home information accessible to outsiders but not to your fellow employees. But one reason for this might be that publishing a home telephone number to colleagues could encourage them to call you at home—which you might want to discourage; however, you might want friends across the world to have access to your home phone number.

How do you provide a flexible access control system that allows your users to choose the model most appropriate for their needs, yet without undue administrative burden for either them or you? Although there is no one answer to this question, it is important to understand the capabilities of your software's access control features and how they deal with situations like this.

Designing for Security

To this point we've covered the basics of security threats, the tools you have in the directory world to combat them, and the effects that your environment and other directory design decisions have on your security design. By now you should have a pretty good idea of your overall security needs. For example, you should know the level of authentication required, whether you need access control, and whether you need to protect the privacy of client/server or server/server connections. You also should have thought about the relative consequences of various kinds of security breaches.

In short, you've got a good idea what your security policy should be. Now it's time to turn our attention to some more concrete steps you can take to implement your policy.

Authentication

LDAP provides several choices for authentication that are explained in the following list. Your task is not only to choose the method or methods best suited for your directory, but also to make sure that other unsuitable authentication methods are not used. Recall that authentication is really useful only in the context of access control. First, you authenticate a client, and then, based on the identity established, you interpret access control information to grant or deny access to certain resources.

Here are the choices for authentication in an LDAP environment:

- *Anonymous authentication.* This term may seem like a bit of an oxymoron. After all, authentication is all about establishing identity, and anonymous means no identity. There are circumstances, however, in which you may want to make data available to any user of the directory whether they have authenticated or not. Users who do not authenticate, or users who authenticate without providing any credentials, are called anonymous users. Such a user is treated by the LDAP server as if he did not authenticate at all and is given corresponding privileges. You can set access control on information in your directory, permitting it to be read by anonymous users.

- *Simple passwords.* With this option a client authenticates to an LDAP server by sending the server a simple, reusable password. No effort is made to protect the password. This choice might be appropriate for low-security environments in which the set of users is restricted and relatively trusted (e.g., behind a firewall). It may also be appropriate for certain secure networking environments in which eavesdropping is not a concern or in which the information being protected is of little value.

  The advantage of passwords is their simplicity, of course. Most people know and understand passwords, how to use them, and the administrative costs associated with them. Password security is also simple to implement, so there are few, if any, performance implications of choosing a password-based solution.

- *Simple passwords over SSL.* This option involves using SSL (or TLS) to protect the connection over which a simple password is transmitted. The simplicity and ease of use of passwords can be preserved, but the added security of SSL means that this option can be used in relatively high-security environments in which networks are open to eavesdropping attacks and the information protected is of relatively high value.

There are several downsides to this choice. SSL is much more complex than a password-based solution. You have to obtain certificates for your servers (but not for your clients) and renew them when necessary. Both clients and servers have to include SSL implementations, which involves a fairly substantial amount of code, increasing the cost and size of software. Not all clients and servers support SSL, which means that choosing this solution restricts your choice of software. SSL may not be much of a problem on the server side; after all, you are in charge of this choice, and if you can live with it there should be no problem. The corresponding client choice may be more problematic because users may want to use a variety of clients that do not support SSL to access your service. Think about whether supporting such clients is important for your directory. Also think about the kinds of operations for which you want to require SSL.

One more important consideration when choosing passwords over SSL is the implication it will have on the performance of your system. Using SSL to authenticate a directory session takes a substantial amount of extra computing power; encryption also requires extra cycles. Whereas the client side of this burden is distributed across the many client machines on your network, the server side is more centralized and, therefore, more of a concern. At the time of this writing, an LDAPv3 extension is nearing completion that will allow SSL protections to be turned on and off during a session. This feature will allow your password to be protected during authentication before an update operation without degrading the performance of the rest of the system. It is likely that not all servers and clients will support this extension, however, so you should check with your vendor.

Be sure to perform benchmarks during the piloting phase of your service to ensure that performance is not degraded too much. If it is, consider adding hardware acceleration to the server. A cryptographic hardware accelerator is usually a special board or other device you can add to your computer. It has processing hardware that performs cryptographic operations much faster than your computer's general-purpose processor can. Keep in mind that not all LDAP servers support hardware acceleration (Netscape Directory Server is the only one we are aware of that does).

Government Restrictions on Encryption Technology

A separate but important consideration is the effect, if any, that United States or other national laws may place on the strength of your security solution. The U.S. government considers encryption technology to be like a weapon potentially useful to foreign countries, international terrorists, and other nasty people intent on wreaking havoc on the world and the United States in particular. France actually has laws banning virtually all encryption technology. That is an extreme case, but other countries may have applicable laws you should be aware of. The remainder of this sidebar focuses on U.S. encryption policy.

The United States restricts the export of strong encryption technology (you can interpret "strong" in the sense of "hard to crack"). In encryption-speak, this means that the United States restricts the size of the keys that can be used to encrypt data. The longer the key, the more secure the encryption; the shorter the key, the easier it is for an attacker to break the encryption.

Today the U.S. government allows free export of 40-bit encryption technology. Occasionally, technology with keys as long as 56 bits have been approved for export. These key lengths are enough to stop the casual or even moderately determined attacker, but not enough to stop anybody really knowledgeable and serious about getting to your data. In today's world, the preferred key length for very secure encryption is 128 bits. However, with processors getting faster all the time and, more importantly, with people getting more clever in their methods of attack, the bar is continually being raised. For example, recent well-publicized cracking "challenges" (in which Internet users are challenged to decrypt a secret message as a test of security) have been met with lots of clever people harnessing the power of thousands of computers on the network to work in parallel on cracking the code.

What does this mean to you? Well, if your organization is outside the United States, it may mean that you cannot get very secure encryption technology from a U.S. vendor. Your choices are to live with less-secure technology, pursue a more-secure solution with a non-U.S. vendor (not bound by U.S. export laws), or wait for the U.S. government to adopt a more liberal (and reasonable!) encryption export policy.

- *Certificate authentication over SSL.* With this option, you are using the full power of SSL. This power allows you to do three things:

> Protect the privacy of data
>
> Ensure the integrity of data
>
> Authenticate clients

You end up with a much stronger level of assurance as to the identity of the client based on public key cryptographic algorithms. The components of an SSL-based system supporting certificate-based client authentication are shown in Figure 11.3. The downside is that instead of distributing the plain old passwords that we all know and understand, your clients must generate private/public key pairs and be issued certificates. Those certificates and keys must be protected and managed throughout their life cycle. You must deploy and maintain a public key infrastructure (PKI) to provide this life cycle management. Sufficient ease of use of certificates and their management has not been achieved historically.

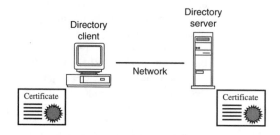

FIGURE 11.3 *Components of a PKI-based SSL system.*

Another disadvantage of this approach is the generally higher processing cost of public key security. As discussed earlier, more cycles are required than with other approaches. You may need hardware acceleration to make a public key solution feasible for a system with any kind of scale. The upside, of course, is that you get a high level of security.

If you decide you need this level of security, be sure the software you choose supports it and that the support is flexible enough to serve your other needs. For example, what kind of solution does the software provide for certificate life cycle management? When authenticating, how is the association between a subject in a certificate and an entry in the directory made? You probably want this mapping to be as flexible as possible to prevent too tight a link between your certificate authority and your directory service.

- *Another scheme via SASL.* This is really a whole set of options because SASL is a generic mechanism for hooking in just about any authentication and security mechanism you can think of. You might want to use this mechanism if, for example, you have an existing Kerberos authentication database that you want to leverage. By obtaining or writing SASL modules for Kerberos on your server and all clients that will be accessing the directory, you can continue to use your current authentication database, administration procedures, and so on.

Realize that by choosing this option you are likely putting your fate in your own hands, unless the vendor you choose supports a SASL module for your particular authentication scheme. At the time of this writing, only Netscape Directory Server supports a SASL interface that allows you to write your own plug-in modules, but Netscape does not provide any prewritten modules. The Netscape server also does not yet support security-layer plug-ins, only authentication plug-ins.

Another concern with writing your own SASL plug-in is that each client that accesses the directory must have a similar plug-in that understands the security mechanism you've chosen. Also, you should check with your server vendor to see how well a new SASL mechanism you define can be integrated with the directory's access control scheme. As with the Netscape Directory Server, you can often explicitly reference the type of authentication used when creating an access control list, but only for pre-defined authentication mechanisms. The pieces fit together as shown in Figure 11.4.

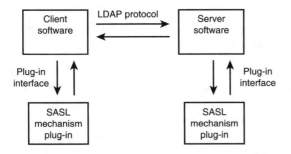

FIGURE 11.4 *Components of a SASL-based security scheme.*

Access Control

When you've decided on one or more authentication schemes to establish the identity of clients, you need to decide how to use them to protect information contained in your directory. This protection is usually provided in the form of access control, allowing you to specify that certain identities have access to certain information, whereas certain other identities or groups of identities do not.

Access control is usually specified as one or more access control lists (ACLs). Each ACL specifies three things:

- *One or more resources in the directory.* Resources, also called *objects*, are the things you control access to. They are typically entries, attributes, or values. An example might be the cn attribute in all the people entries in your directory.

- *One or more clients (users or applications) accessing the resources.* Clients, also called *subjects*, you grant or deny are the entities you grant or deny access to. A client may be specified as the name of a directory entry or other descriptive information. For example, a client might be specified as any authenticated directory user with a connection originating from within your organization's DNS domain.

- *One or more access rights.* Access rights determine what the subject can do to or with the object. For example, an access right might be "read and search," meaning that the given clients can search for and read attributes from the entry.

As we discussed in Chapter 3, "An Introduction to LDAP," there is no standard LDAP access control model today. The IETF is working on defining one, but it will likely take a while for the design to be finished, and even longer for the standard to be implemented in products and become available for you to use. In the meantime, you have to examine each directory server vendor's access control capabilities independently in the context of your needs.

As we advised earlier in the chapter, the first step in determining your access control needs is to understand your data and the users that will access it. Make a table that shows who can access each data element or attribute, the level of access that should be given, and any other relevant restrictions, such as the authentication level required, time of day the access is to be allowed, and whether the attribute can be retrieved only over an SSL connection. Try to group attributes that have related access characteristics. Table 11.3 shows an example of such a table, with attributes and access control information for a directory intended to contain some white pages data.

TABLE 11.3 SAMPLE DATA ACCESS SHOWING GROUPS OF ATTRIBUTES AND ASSOCIATED ACCESS AND AUTHENTICATION REQUIRED

Attribute(s)	User(s) or Application(s)	Access Level	Authentication and/or Connection Protection Required
cn, sn, givenName, middleInitial, name	All	Read	None
cn, sn, givenName, middleInitial, name	Administrator	Read/write	Password- or certificate-based over SSL
mail	All authenticated	Read	Password
mail	Administrator	Read/write	Password- or certificate-based over SSL
mail	Self	Read/write	Password- or certificate-based over SSL
homeAddress, homePhone	All	Read or none, depending on user's choice	Password
homeAddress, homePhone	Self	Read/write	Password
postalAddress, telephoneNumber	All	Read	Password
postalAddress, telephone- Number	Admin.	Read/write	Password- or certificate- based over SSL
salary	Self	Read	Password
salary	User's manager	Read/write	Password- or certificate-based over SSL

This table shows some examples of attributes that apply to people entries. Keep in mind that you should make similar tables for each kind of entry in your directory. If your directory stores entries for people, groups, printers, and projects, you should construct four tables.

We will not go through the design of actual ACLs for the entire table, but we will do so for three interesting parts of it using the ACL syntax understood by the Netscape Directory Server. ACLs are usually, but not always, expressed as directory attributes. The Netscape approach to representing ACLs is typical, although with some interesting capabilities not found in other approaches. An ACL is represented by an attribute called aci, which stands for access control item (ACI). An ACI can be placed anywhere in the directory tree. Depending on the ACI, it can apply to the entry in which it is placed and any of that entry's descendants.

The first access control rule we will codify is the one for the various name attributes (cn, sn, and so on). The intention of this generic rule is to make the naming attributes readable by anyone, authenticated or not. The attributes are to be updated only by the administrator. Using LDAP Data Interchange Format (LDIF) to represent the Netscape syntax for ACLs, the following aci attribute does the job:

```
aci: (target ="ldap:///dc=airius, dc=com")
  (targetattr="cn||sn||givenname||middleinitial||name")
  (version 3.0;acl "Anonymous read-search access";
  allow (read, search, compare)
  (userdn = "ldap:///anyone");)
aci: (target ="ldap:///dc=airius, dc=com")
  (targetattr="cn||sn||givenname||middleinitial||name")
  (version 3.0;acl "Admin write access";
  allow (write)
  (userdn = "ldap:///cn=directory manager");)
```

We are assuming that this ACI is placed in a directory subtree rooted at the entry dc=airius, dc=com. It applies to that entry and every entry below it in the tree, and only those attributes listed in the targetattr line of the ACI. The first value of aci grants read, search, and compare access rights to anyone accessing the directory, whether they are authenticated or not. The second value of the aci attribute grants write privileges to the directory manager. If you were going to use this ACI in your directory, you would change the dc=airius, dc=com part to point to the base of your tree. You would also change the cn=directory manager part to reference your directory manager's entry.

The next access control rule we will examine is for home address and phone information. The interesting thing about this rule is that users have a choice of which access applies to their information. You might want to do this because some of your users won't want their home address and phone information published. One way to accomplish this would be to allow users to write their own access control lists. This approach is fraught with peril, from users accidentally denying themselves access to things they should be able to access, to accidentally granting access to things they should not, to various kinds of malicious behavior. Allowing users to modify their own ACLs is almost never acceptable.

A way around this is to make ACL changes go through some mediator. The mediator might be a Web application that you develop specifically for the purpose of allowing users to make changes to the access control information in their entry. The mediator has access to make changes but also has the knowledge of what should and should not be allowed. This approach may be acceptable to you, and it is supported by most ACL schemes. The downside is that users have to go to a special application (that you must maintain) to make ACL changes.

Another approach, supported by the Netscape Directory Server, solves this problem in a more elegant way. The Netscape server allows you to predefine access rules that apply only to entries satisfying some arbitrary criteria expressed as an LDAP search filter. These entries can live anywhere in the directory. This allows you to specify the possible access control rules once in a single location, and then allow your users to update a different attribute in their entries, causing a new set of access control rules to apply. For example, consider the following pair of ACIs, shown in LDIF format:

```
aci: (target="ldap:///dc=airius, dc=com")
  (targetfilter="(homeaccess=private)")
  (targetattr = "homeAddress¦¦homePhone")
  (version 3.0; acl "keeps users' home information private";
  allow (none)
  userdn = "ldap:///anyone";)
aci: (target="ldap:///dc=airius, dc=com")
  (targetfilter="(homeaccess=public)")
  (targetattr = "homeAddress¦¦homePhone")
  (version 3.0; acl "publishes users' home information";
  allow (read)
  userdn = "ldap:///anyone";)
```

Notice the additional `targetfilter` construct in the second line of each ACI. This is a search filter used to select the entries the ACI should apply to. In the case of the first ACI, we've chosen a filter that selects entries with the hypothetical `homeaccess` attribute set to the value `private`. Entries that satisfy this filter will have their home address and phone information attributes protected by this ACL.

The second ACL contains a similar filter, but this one tests for entries with the homeaccess attribute set to the value public. In this case, the attributes can be read by anyone. Strictly speaking, the first aci value is not needed. By default, no access is granted unless specifically granted in an aci. In this case, we assumed there could be other, more general ACIs granting access to attributes by default.

With this access control scheme, a user has only to change the content of an attribute in her entry from public to private to enable a new access control policy. This kind of ACL manipulation—essentially flipping a switch in an entry—makes maintaining multiple access control policies convenient. This capability is very powerful; it allows a compact specification of complex access control policies to be made independently of directory tree structure. Use of this feature inevitably results in access control rules that are easier to understand. You can use this feature for many other policies, some examples of which are outlined here:

- Apply different access control to various types of entries by using a filter to test for different values of the objectclass attribute. For example, you could have one set of ACIs that applies only to entries satisfying an (objectclass=person) filter. Another set of rules could apply to (objectclass=group) entries.

- Apply policies based on attribute values entered by your users. For example, you could apply an access control to all entries with mail addresses not ending in the domain name of your organization by using a filter such as (!(mail=*@your.domain.com)). Thus, you could automatically prevent the routing of mail to entries that leave your domain.

- Apply policies based on reporting structures. For example, you could have an ACI that applies only to entries with (manager=<supervisor's DN>).

- Apply policies that quickly and easily grant and revoke access to users based on the content of their entries. For example, you could effectively rotate a particular role among users simply by changing a value in their entry. Any entry satisfying (role=boss-for-a-day) could be given special privileges.

As you can see, the applications of the target filter access control feature are many, and the power and flexibility are great.

The final ACL example we will investigate in detail is represented by the salary rows in Table 11.3. Our goal is to allow only an employee's manager the right to update the employee's salary. The employee should have only read access to the salary, and no one else should have any access. The latter two conditions are not much different from the simple naming attribute examples we discussed earlier. The first goal, only allowing the manager to update something, is more interesting, and we will focus our attention on that.

You could easily come up with an ACI to satisfy this goal, assuming that you know the DN of the manager in question. The problem is one of management. Taking this approach, you would need to create a separate ACI for each manager in the company, and you would need a way to apply that ACI to only those entries managed by that manager. The target filter feature mentioned previously is helpful here, but it does not help solve a basic management problem: If a user changes managers, or if a manager changes roles, you need to update the corresponding ACIs. You could use ACIs that refer to group entries for this, but then you would have to update these groups all the time.

It is also a problem that the number of ACIs required by this approach is proportional to the number of managers in your company—potentially a large list! More ACIs means more maintenance, more chance for error, and more things to change in the event of reconfiguration or reorganization. Many ACIs can also adversely affect the performance of your directory. Because all these ACIs are essentially identical, except for the value listed in one field, there must be a better way.

Fortunately, there is. The Netscape Directory Server implements a powerful feature specifically aimed at reducing this management overhead and the number of ACIs you need to store in your directory. Consider the following ACI:

```
aci: (target="ldap:///dc=airius, dc=com ")
 (targetattr = "salary")
 (version 3.0; acl "allow manager access to salary";
 allow (read, write)
 userdnattr = "manager";)
```

The interesting part of this ACI is the userdnattr construct in the last line. This means that the access is granted to the entry or entries listed in the manager attribute of the entry to which the ACI applies. So, for example, if the ACI applies to the entry shown in Figure 11.5, the salary attribute in the entry is readable and writable by the entry mentioned in the manager field, namely cn=manager babs, dc=airius, dc=com:

```
dn: cn=worker babs, dc=airius, dc=com
cn: worker babs
sn: babs
manager: cn=manager babs, dc=airius, dc=com
objectclass: top
objectclass: person
... other attributes ...
```

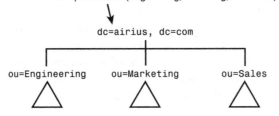

FIGURE 11.5 *ACL placement in a directory, allowing separation of ACLs and name-space.*

The power of this capability should be getting clear to you. It has the ability to reduce the number of ACIs you need to maintain in your directory and reduce management costs by avoiding the requirement to maintain duplicate information. Furthermore, it has the ability to transfer ACL decisions to directory users in a safe, efficient, and error-free way, freeing up directory administrators for more important tasks. Consider these additional applications of the userdnattr ACL construct:

- Maintain an owner attribute for groups. A single ACI can be used to allow the users listed in the owner attribute the ability to update the group. This avoids the need for a separate ACI for each group that must be changed each time the owner of a group changes.

- Maintain a proxy attribute for entries. A single ACI can be used to allow the users listed in the proxy attribute the ability to update the entry. Such a capability might be used, for example, to give an administrative assistant temporary access to an entry that the assistant will update on behalf of his boss. Again, this functionality is provided while minimizing the number of ACLs involved and the administrative effort required.

No doubt you can think of other interesting applications for this feature as well.

As with any powerful scheme, this one comes with some risks. Just as you can easily change lots of access control information in your directory for the better, you can also change it for the worse. For example, if you are not careful, you could remove access to public attributes with a simple change. More seriously, you could grant access to information that should remain private. Always be careful and triple check your work when modifying access control information.

ACL Placement

Finally, you must consider where in the directory to place the ACLs you have designed. This depends on the design approach you take and the capabilities of your software. These two things are related. If your design takes advantage of some of the features we've been discussing, and one of your goals is to limit the number of ACLs in your directory, you need directory software that supports this. If, on the other hand, your design approach is to put an ACL in each entry, your choice of software is probably expanded. You should be sure to determine the scale and performance implications of this approach. For example, some directory server implementations do not handle large numbers of ACLs well.

Tree placement of your ACLs also depends on the organization of your namespace and the capability of your directory software to separate ACL placement from the namespace. If you use software such as the Netscape Directory Server, you can separate ACL placement from namespace; your ACL placement might look something like what was shown in Figure 11.5. If you use software that does not allow such placement, you might end up with an arrangement like that shown in Figure 11.6.

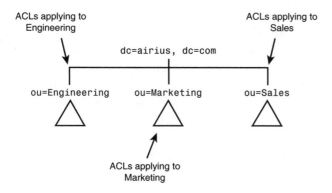

FIGURE 11.6 *ACL placement in a directory that does not allow separation of ACLs and namespace.*

If you choose to place an ACL in each entry, your tree might look something like the one depicted in Figure 11.7. We discourage you from taking this approach. In our experience, the number of ACLs in your tree is directly proportional to the administrative burden to maintain them. When things go wrong, it's much more difficult to find the offending ACL. All in all, fewer ACLs are better, and anything you can do to reduce the number of ACLs in your tree will make your life easier.

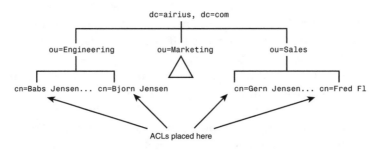

FIGURE 11.7 *ACLs placed in each entry.*

A final consideration is the relationship between ACL placement and replication. If you place ACLs at some point in the tree but replicate only a subtree below the entry containing the ACLs, some directory server software, such as Netscape Directory Server, will not replicate the ACLs (because they are not within the subtree selected for replication). If this is the case, you can either place the ACL within the replicated subtree so that it is replicated along with the data, or you can create an ACL on the consumer server in the same entry that contains the ACL on the supplier server.

Information Privacy and Integrity

You've now designed your authentication scheme for identifying users and your accesscontrol scheme for protecting information in your directory. Now it's time to design a way to protect the privacy and integrity of the information as it is passed among servers and between clients and servers. Recall that earlier in the chapter we discussed the various threats to data privacy and integrity and how the threats you face and other aspects of your environment affect your design choices. In this section, we detail these effects and lay out your design options in this area.

If your environment is such that you need to ensure the privacy and integrity of connections at a directory software level, your only real choice is SSL.

Not every vendor supports SSL, and not every vendor that supports SSL for client/server connections supports it for server/server replication connections. Be sure to check the capabilities of your software and make SSL support part of your evaluation criteria if this kind of protection is important to you.

When deciding whether you need this kind of protection, think about the different kinds of information you'll be keeping in your directory. Think about the consequences of each piece of information having its privacy or integrity compromised. You will find different answers for different attributes, of course. Consider making a table, like the one shown in Table 11.4, listing categories of attributes in your directory and how their privacy and integrity need to be protected. In practice, you might want to combine this table with the one shown in Table 11.3. We've separated them here for clarity of discussion.

TABLE 11.4 AN EXAMPLE OF AN ATTRIBUTE PRIVACY AND INTEGRITY TABLE

Attribute	Privacy	Integrity
cn, sn, givenname, name	No need for protection	No need for protection
mail	No need for protection—email addresses are public information	Must be guaranteed to avoid misrouting email
salary	Must be protected —salary information is private to an employee and the employee's manager	No need for protection —attribute is read-only in the directory

After you create a table like this, you also need to decide whether to protect privacy and integrity for client/server access, for server/server access such as replication, or for both. Protecting client/server access is usually a higher priority than protecting server/server access.

When making the decision whether to protect server/server connections, consider the topology of your replication solution. If you use replication in a tightly controlled manner, all within your authority to protect, you may not need to protect the privacy of replication connections. For example, this kind of environment might be found in a centrally administered IS department with good network connectivity throughout the organization. The directory might be replicated among three servers, all located within close proximity and on networks that no users have access to (see Figure 11.8). In this environment, there is little risk that anyone will eavesdrop on a replication exchange, so SSL may not be required. On the other hand, you might want to take a more secure approach and use SSL everywhere by default, unless there is some compelling reason not to.

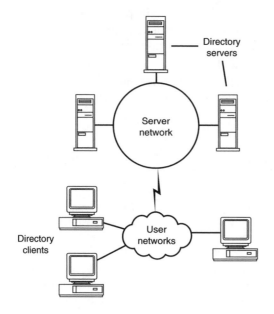

Directory servers

Server network

Directory clients

User networks

FIGURE 11.8 *A replication configuration that does not require privacy protection.*

In environments without this kind of control, or with networks that are not protected from eavesdropping, SSL may be an important component of the replication solution. For example, consider an organization without very reliable network connectivity. This could require wide directory replication onto each LAN so that the directory is always available even if the WAN link goes down. Consider also an application that has very high performance requirements. This could require that directory replicas be widely dispersed onto each LAN to reduce latency of directory queries (see Figure 11.9). In this environment, protecting replication connections may be as important as protecting client/server connections.

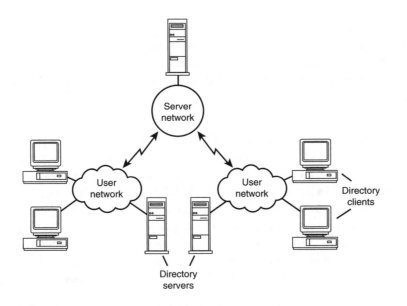

FIGURE 11.9 *A replication configuration that requires privacy protection.*

The design decisions concerning SSL include how you will address the performance issues discussed earlier and how you will handle the components of the certificate life cycle: certificate creation, distribution, renewal, and revocation. Performance is one of the most important issues to be addressed. Making your directory secure at the expense of performance is not a very good solution. Performance with security can be expensive; it takes a lot of CPU power to encrypt and decrypt data that traverses the network. Public key operations involved in initial authentication exchanges are even more expensive.

One solution is simply to buy bigger, more powerful servers. A better and often more cost-effective solution is to use hardware acceleration specifically targeted at cryptographic operations. Such solutions are readily available today, but many directory providers do not support them. If performance is important to you, be sure to make hardware cryptographic acceleration part of your selection criteria.

SSL is based on public key technology. Although it is beyond the scope of this book to explain this technology in detail (there are some excellent references listed at the end of this chapter), we do want to cover some of the administrative implications of choosing SSL or any solution based on a PKI. The important thing to know is that maintaining the PKI is different from maintaining other kinds of shared-secret or private key infrastructures. With the latter, an administrator maintains a centralized database of passwords (or the equivalent). This database exports an authentication service used by both clients and servers. The idea is that both clients and servers trust the authentication database and, therefore, can use it as a trusted third party during authentication exchanges.

The details can get significantly more complicated than this, but the principle remains the same: A centrally trusted administrator is in charge of all parts of the process of issuing identities and credentials, verifying trust, revoking credentials, imposing password and other policies related to authentication, and so on. When a user shows up for work the first day, the administrator creates an entry for the user in the authentication database. If a user forgets her password, the administrator simply resets it for her. When a user leaves the company, the administrator removes him from the database. Credentials can be temporarily suspended, usable only during certain hours of the day, or placed under other restrictions—all under the control of the administrator.

With a PKI, things are a little trickier. The basic difference is that clients and servers do not need to consult a trusted third party to perform authentication. Instead, the credentials used to authenticate are what you might call self-verifying. A user is in charge of generating his own credentials. A trusted third party is used just once, after the credentials are generated, to verify that they do indeed belong to the user in question. Subsequent authentication exchanges need not involve the third party.

PKI is helpful in terms of scale and performance because otherwise the trusted third party can often become a bottleneck in a shared secret system. However, it is often not so great in terms of deployability and manageability issues. For example, how does a user create his credentials? What happens when a user leaves the company and his credentials should be revoked? What happens when the user's credentials expire? What happens when the credentials are lost? How are new ones issued? These questions about the key and certificate management life cycle have made PKI much more difficult to administer than private key schemes.

A Look at PKI

Full coverage of public key technology is beyond the scope of this book. The purpose of this sidebar is to give you a 50,000-foot view of this important and complex technology.

The basic principle about public key technology is a mathematical concept that can be used to relate certain pairs of large numbers (called *keys*) in a special way. If one of the keys is used to encrypt a message, the other key can be used to decrypt the message, and vice versa. Fundamental to this scheme is another property: Only these two keys (called a *key pair*) are related in this way. So in other words, if a message is encrypted with one key, it can be decrypted only by the matching key in the pair (or at least, it would be very hard to do so without the matching key). One key is called the *private key* and the other is called the *public key*, for reasons that will be clear later. The idea is that you are the only one who knows your private key, and you publish your public key only as widely as you want.

Given this background, you can see how I might send a private message to you: I use your public key to encrypt the message, which I then send to you, and you use your private key to decrypt it. I know that only you can read the message because to decrypt it requires your private key, which nobody else has. As you probably see by now, there is only one flaw in this scheme: How do I know that it's really your public key I'm using to encrypt this message? This is the purpose of a certificate.

A certificate binds a public key to an identity (and possibly other information about that identity). The idea is simple: You and I share a trusted third party (e.g., a mutual friend, an organizational administrator, a government agency). If you go to that trusted third party and prove your identity and present your public key, that third party wraps up and signs your public key along with your identity and any other appropriate information. This neat little package of information is called a *certificate*, and the process of getting one is called *certificate issuance*.

A certificate has two interesting properties. First, it is signed by the trusted third party (called a *certificate authority*, or CA). This means that if it is tampered with, I'll be able to tell. Second, it is possible for me to look at the certificate and verify that it was in fact signed by the party we both trust. This is the mechanism by which I can be assured that your public key really belongs to you, at least to the level that I trust the certificate authority.

Just as in real life, you can imagine building chains of trust between certificate authorities. For example, you and I might not share a trusted third party, but the entity I trust and the entity you trust might share a trusted third party. Depending on the level of trust we both have in our trusted entities, this might be enough for us to trust each other. The area of trust management is an important and often complicated aspect of PKI.

continues

continued

Another important concept in PKI is revocation. What happens if I lose my private key or if it falls into the hands of evildoers? If your credit card is stolen, the thief can rack up charges on your account. Similarly, but with potentially more serious consequences, if your private key is stolen, the thief can read messages intended only for you and—perhaps even worse—send messages that look like they came from you. What makes this situation more serious than losing your credit card is that you might not be able to tell that your key has been compromised—you don't get a monthly statement detailing its use. Nor do you typically have any protection from the malicious things someone might do with it, whereas your liability for a stolen credit card is limited.

In this situation the solution is to revoke your certificate. This means that the CA that signed your public key wants essentially to "unsign" it. Because that's not possible, the CA might resort to publishing a list of revoked certificates—a *certificate revocation list*—that should be consulted by security-conscious applications. Another approach is to have applications ask the CA (or its agent) each time the certificate is used whether it is still good. This solution, although attractive in many ways, introduces the central bottleneck that we thought we got rid of by moving to PKI!

Figure 11.10 depicts the major components of a typical PKI solution.

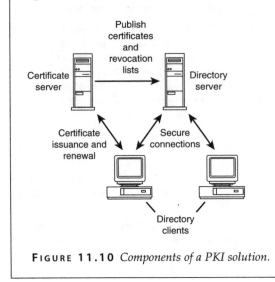

FIGURE 11.10 *Components of a PKI solution.*

Lest you be scared away from PKI by this bleak presentation of the management challenges it poses, we should quickly add that work is ongoing in this area to improve the deployability and manageability of PKI by a quantum leap. Netscape's next-generation security solution (still in development at the time of this writing) is a good example. By using the directory as a central hub for managing the PKI life cycle, you can achieve the best of both worlds. The more scalable advantages of PKI can be retained and combined with the centralized administration model of private key schemes.

The point is simply this: Although SSL comes with many benefits that often make it worth deploying, there are administrative and performance costs involved too. Administrative costs can be reduced by choosing a complete solution that includes a significant manageability component. Performance costs can be reduced by using special hardware to help speed up expensive cryptographic operations. Be sure to include PKI deployment and manageability, as well as performance requirements, in your design and evaluation criteria if you choose to deploy SSL.

Administrative Security

All the security technology in the world is not worth very much if it is improperly applied and administered. The most elaborate home security system in the world, for example, does little or no good unless it is properly installed and activated, sensible precautions are followed in its operation, and the passcode to defeat the system is not written on a note stuck to the wall near the system's keypad. Computer and directory security is similar. This section examines some of the more common administrative directory service pitfalls that can contribute to security problems.

Enforcing a password policy is important for password-based security to be effective. If you have ever run a password-cracking program on your users' passwords, you will know that people tend to choose horrible passwords that are easy to guess using either a little knowledge of the person or a brute-force attack. There are three things you can do to mitigate these problems:

- Educate your users.

- Enforce a password policy.

- Run password crackers.

First, you can educate your users on how to choose a good password, the consequences of losing a password, and the minimum precautions they should take in daily password management. Often users simply don't know what separates a good password from a bad one, or they might not realize the consequences of their password being compromised. If a user is aware of these things, she still might not think of the non–technology-oriented ways in which her password can be compromised (for example, by reading the sticky note she has stuck to her computer monitor screen). Education can go a long way toward raising awareness in your user community—and, therefore, reducing problems.

Second, you can select software that comes with some kind of password policy capability. Such software lets you specify things such as the minimum length of a password, the mix of characters it must contain, how often it must be changed, and other things. This helps enforce the policy when user education has failed either because you didn't reach users with your education campaign or because users willfully ignored all the fine advice you gave them.

Third, you can ferret out bad passwords by regularly running a password-cracking program on your directory. The reason for doing this is simple: If you can do it, you can bet that people attacking your system will do it also. Your goal is to crack and change bad passwords before an attacker does. An even more effective approach may be to crack passwords before they are entered by users and disallow the ones you can crack. Keep in mind that password cracking can be a controversial subject; it often takes careful reasoning to explain its usefulness to management. And you should be careful with the results of your cracking activities to avoid making your users upset and distrustful of you and the directory service.

Administrative data-gathering procedures are another area in which security mistakes are commonly made. Think about the path your data takes from start to finish. If you are bulk loading data from a corporate human resources relational database, consider the total path the data takes from the time it leaves the database to when it arrives in your directory. Is the data transferred via FTP? If so, how is the data protected on the way? Who has access to the data at the relational database source? Do they follow the same level of security procedures that you have instituted for your directory?

Ideally, the security of your whole system would be equal at each component. For example, if your data is protected via certificate-based authentication and encryption via SSL in your directory, you would like it to be protected in the same way in the source as it is when transferred to your directory. But be careful not to fall into the trap of viewing your solution as either "secure" or "insecure," with nothing in between. In evaluating the total security of your system, you must consider not only the possible weak links, but also how difficult and probable it is for an attacker to exploit them.

Respecting Your Users' Privacy

We've talked about privacy as it relates to the overall security design problem. In this section we talk about privacy from the perspective of the directory user. It's important to keep this perspective in mind as you design and deploy your system. Failure to do so can create irate users, headaches for you, and, ultimately, a directory service that fails to win the hearts and minds of your user community. In our experience, you will come across different kinds of users with different kinds of privacy expectations and requirements.

On one extreme is the user who does not want any information about himself published in the directory at all. This user is often very angry when information about him is published—angry not just with you, but with the maintainers of other information sources on the network, including Web-based phone books, credit reporting services, telemarketing databases, and others. This user feels these information sources are an invasion of his privacy, and he may not settle for anything less than removal from the service.

Think carefully about how important it is to your service to have complete coverage within your organization. If it's not critical, perhaps the best approach is simply to remove such users from the directory. You can often head off such problems by requiring users to sign up for service in your directory rather than publishing information about them without their permission. This latter approach is clearly to be avoided if at all possible. But in many situations, this is simply not possible. Company policy usually wins over the desire of your users. Regardless of which approach you choose, be aware of the consequences and have an answer ready for complaints like this.

Another type of user might have a specific concern about having information about her published in the directory. For example, she might have been the victim of a stalking incident and might be trying to keep as low a profile as possible. This was a real example we encountered while running the directory service at the University of Michigan. We felt we had two choices to address the situation: We could remove the user entirely, cutting off her access to computing services she wanted to use, such as email; or we could convert her entry into an anonymous entry in which all identifying information had been removed but email and other nonidentifying information remained. We chose the latter approach, and the result was a happy user.

Pay particular attention to cases like this. Users in this category have legitimate concerns about their privacy, and you should respond swiftly to remedy the situation. Do not be surprised if you receive requests that you consider to be bizarre at first. After talking to the user you can usually understand his or her perspective, and the request no longer seems quite so kooky.

Security Versus Deployability

We end this chapter by discussing the important topic of security versus deployability. Many security schemes have failed because they were not deployable. You would do well to keep in mind that the most secure service in the world is the one that is never deployed and used. Unfortunately, this is also not a very useful service. Similarly, a solution that is deployed but provides no real security will soon become useless because the information it provides cannot be trusted.

Your job when designing your directory's security infrastructure is to find the balance between these two extremes. Where that balance lies depends on the needs of your users, the security threats your system is likely to face, and the consequences that will result from a security breach. A related factor is the amount of time and money you are willing to spend to deploy and maintain your system.

It's easy to get caught in one of the two extremes of the security spectrum. At one extreme, your only interest is in deploying your directory service; security seems only to be a roadblock in the way of achieving that goal. This leads to a directory that will probably not be useful or trusted for long. Worse consequences are possible if the directory contains sensitive information that gets compromised.

At the other extreme, you can become wrapped up in security for its own sake; you forget that security is only a means to an end. This extreme can lead one of two places. One possibility is that you get bogged down trying to make the perfect security system, and meanwhile your project gets canceled or taken away from you. Another possibility is that you actually design and deploy such a system, but none of your users show up to get their fingerprints taken so they're able to use the system, and the system fails. Either way, you end up without a directory service.

You would do well to keep the security versus deployability trade-offs firmly in mind throughout your design process. This advice may seem obvious, but we have seen many directory projects go astray in this area.

Further Reading

Building an X.500 Directory Service in the US (RFC 1943). B. Jennings, May 1996.

Computer Emergency Response Team (CERT) Coordination Center, `http://www.cert.org`.

Internet Cryptography. R. Smith, Reading, Mass.: Addison-Wesley, 1997.

Privacy on the Line: The Politics of Wiretapping and Encryption. W. Diffie and S. Landau, Cambridge, Mass.: MIT Press, 1998.

Simple Authentication and Security Layer (SASL) (RFC 2222). John Myers, October 1997.

Understanding Digital Signatures: Establishing Trust over the Internet and Other Networks. G. Grant, New York: McGraw-Hill, 1997.

Looking Ahead

This chapter is the last in Part II, "Designing Your Directory Service." At this point you should have a complete directory system designed! Now it's time to move on to the deployment phase, which includes validating your design, running pilots, and going production. Part III, "Deploying Your Directory Service," takes you through these steps, showing you how to change your design as you go. First up is Chapter 12, "Choosing Directory Products."

PART **III**

Deploying Your Directory Service

CHAPTER **12**

Choosing Directory Products

In Part III, "Deploying Your Directory Service," we turn our attention to the process of turning your directory design into a concrete, functional service. In this chapter, we discuss how to select the right directory software. We will then focus on how to pilot your directory service to validate and fine-tune your design in Chapter 13, "Piloting Your Directory Service." We will pause for a moment in Chapter 14, "Analyzing and Reducing Costs," to take a look at the costs of the directory service and how they can be minimized. Finally, we will throw the switch and put the directory service online in Chapter 15, "Going Production."

It is important to choose the right software to power your directory deployment. There are a number of directory server and client products available from a variety of sources, varying widely in capabilities and cost. If you choose the wrong products, your directory service deployment may fail or at least be more painful, costly, and less effective than it should be. If you choose the right products, your deployment should succeed with maximum effectiveness and minimum pain and cost. Your challenge is to pick the products that will best meet your directory needs and work well in your environment.

In this chapter, we help you choose the right products. We mainly focus on directory server software because that is likely to be the first and most important software you choose. We also touch briefly on client software, directory-enabled application software, and software development kits (SDKs) for LDAP. Because the directory software market is evolving rapidly, we do not cover specific software products in great depth.

We begin by presenting some reasons why it is important to choose the right directory products, followed by a look at some general categories of directory services software. Next, we talk about and illustrate how to create a good set of evaluation criteria. Then, we present some advice that will help you devise a good decision-making process. In the last section of this chapter we briefly describe some of the directory services software available today.

Making the Right Product Choice

You are probably already convinced that choosing the right directory server and client software is important. Anyone who has spent any amount of time working with computer systems knows that software often makes all the difference. Let's take a brief look at why choosing the right software for your directory service is so important.

Next to developing a good directory design (which we have already discussed extensively in Part II, "Designing Your Directory Service"), choosing good software does the most to ensure the success of your directory deployment. A bad directory design can't be repaired by good directory software, but a good design can be ruined by bad software. By "bad software" we primarily mean software that does not meet your needs—although software that is buggy or poorly supported, or has some other serious defect, should also be avoided.

There is no one-size-fits-all directory solution; directory software varies widely in its capabilities. This is a good thing. Although your directory needs may overlap greatly with those of other organizations, nearly every deployment has some unique needs. The greatest challenge in choosing directory software is to find the best match between your needs and the capabilities of the available products. (Directory service needs were introduced in Chapter 5, "Defining Your Directory Needs," and were discussed throughout Part II.)

You may not notice it for a long time if you chose the wrong software. This can lead to serious and expensive problems. This situation is most likely to occur with a growing directory service in which your performance, scalability, and applications needs grow steadily over time. In the worst case, you may not notice that you have a problem until it is too late to gracefully fix it, which can lead to dissatisfaction with your service.

For example, if the use of your directory increases over time, you may notice only a gradual degradation in performance. If gradual performance loss is acceptable, there is no problem. However, if your directory server software reaches a cliff at some point and performance falls off abruptly instead of degrading gracefully, some directory-enabled applications may be unable to cope. If applications just stop working one day (which is possible), you will find yourself really scrambling to devise a quick fix.

There may be many hidden costs associated with choosing the wrong software as well. Small deficiencies in performance, scalability, ease of administration, and quality of support for applications and standards can lead to increased costs for maintaining your service and all the applications that surround it. Conversely, a directory server product that can accommodate 10% more traffic may allow you to deploy five servers instead of six, which could result in a savings of hundreds of thousands of dollars over the lifetime of your service.

Another factor that makes choosing the right software crucial is that it can be expensive and time-consuming to replace one software product with another— even though open standards such as LDAP tend to reduce such costs. Some of the costs you may still incur when replacing directory services software include the following:

- Money spent to purchase the new software. If you can't recoup the money you spent on the software you are replacing, your software costs may be double what they would have been if you had made the right choice in the first place. You may also need to purchase new hardware or upgrade existing hardware to accommodate the new software, either because of differences in supported platforms or performance characteristics of the replacement software.

- Time and money spent redesigning your directory service and directory-enabled applications to fit the new software's capabilities.

- Time and money spent to learn the ins and outs of the new software.

- Time and money spent to repilot and redeploy the new software. This can be very expensive for directory server software, especially if you have already deployed a large number of replicas or a widely distributed directory across a large number of servers.

- Lost productivity because end users and administrators have to learn how to use yet another set of software.

As you can see, this is a pretty scary list. Therefore, it is important to perform a proper evaluation of the available software products in order to make the best choice up front.

Categories of Directory Software

Because it is difficult to provide all things to all people, software vendors tend to focus their product development efforts on serving specific needs. By comparing a vendor's focus to your directory needs, you can often narrow down your list of candidate products very quickly.

Although LDAP is a general-purpose protocol, the needs of one directory deployment may be quite different than those of another. For example, an LDAP server implementation that provides strong security features might be well suited for deployment on the public Internet, whereas another product that provides minimal security may be a great product for small workgroups. These two implementations would thus require different directory software.

There are many ways to categorize the available products. One of the most useful ways to sort them is by looking at the various applications they aim to support:

- Network operating system (NOS) applications

- Intranet applications

- Extranet applications

- Internet and hosted applications

- Lightweight database applications

Each of these categories is described in the following sections.

Network Operating System Applications

From the directory software perspective, a NOS is just another application with a specific set of needs. Directories that work well with NOSs are generally focused on basic network services such as logon, access control, and management of LAN services (such as file servers and printers). In most cases, a directory that works with a specific NOS is not separable from the NOS itself, and LDAP is typically grafted onto existing products (although the current trend is toward better support for LDAP and other open standards). For products in this category, integration and ease of management are very important, and performance, scalability, and support for multiple platforms are de-emphasized.

Intranet Applications

In recent years, the term *intranet* has been adopted to describe networks inside organizations and based entirely on open Internet technology. This trend started with the adoption of Web servers and browsers inside the corporate firewall and has moved on to encompass messaging, groupware, and directory products.

Directory software that is suitable for use within intranets is typically designed to support a wide variety of end user and server applications, such as corporate phone books and high-volume messaging servers. Ease of management, performance, and scalability are all important within this category.

Extranet Applications

The term *extranet* is used to describe business-to-business communication networks that are based on open, Internet technology. Extranets are almost always *virtual* networks in the sense that they are typically formed by making secure connections over public networks such as the Internet itself rather than by pulling cable. Extranets are gaining momentum because they can be used to deploy completely new applications and replace expensive, proprietary electronic data interchange (EDI) networks.

Extranet directory-enabled applications typically serve very large numbers of people. In addition, many of the people served may not be directly employed by the organization that hosts the application. For example, extranet applications often connect manufacturing organizations to their suppliers. This leads to a need to store information about people who work for both the supplier and the consumer (the company hosting the extranet application). This kind of extranet procurement application is shown in Figure 12.1.

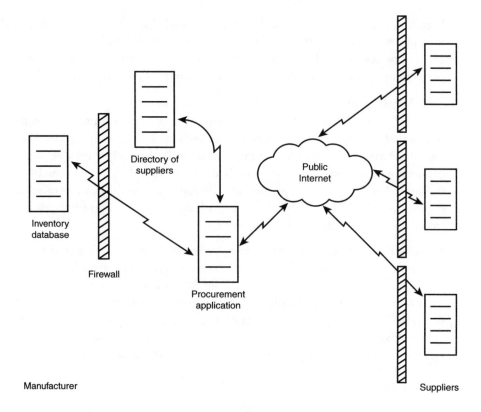

FIGURE 12.1 *An extranet procurement application.*

Security and privacy are often the most critical directory features required of extranet applications because the application and its directory service may be accessible through the public Internet. Good performance and scalability of a directory product are also critical for large-scale extranet applications.

TABLE 12.1 DIRECTORY PRODUCT CATEGORIES

Application Category	Focus	Flexibility Needs
NOS	Logon, access control, management	Low
Intranet	End user and server applications	Moderate
Extranet	Inter-organizational applications served upon the public Internet	Moderate
Internet/Hosted	End user and server applications for a variety of unrelated individuals and organizations	High
Database	Lightweight database applications in need of a standard access protocol	Very high

Internet and Hosted Applications

The business of an Internet service provider (ISP) is to provide Internet application access for end users and host applications on behalf of other organizations. ISPs typically provide services for very large numbers of users, and some ISPs provide hosting services for thousands of organizations. As Internet applications such as electronic mail increasingly depend on directory services, ISPs find themselves providing directory services too.

Recently, more large organizations that do not consider themselves ISPs are finding that the most efficient way to streamline their own business processes is to act as a service provider for their divisions, departments, external partners, and suppliers. These enterprises that have many of the same needs as traditional ISPs have been dubbed enterprise service providers (ESPs).

For ISP and ESP directory services to work well, their applications must meet a wide variety of needs and be inexpensive to manage. Flexibility, scalability, performance, and automatable management are all very important in this segment of the market.

Lightweight Database Applications

A relatively new role for LDAP directories is as a replacement for traditional database systems. The typical application being serviced is lightweight and query-intensive. Usually the data is widely distributed and actually shared by many applications. For example, a bank may need to share profile information about employees, customers, and partners among a wide variety of applications at thousands of distinct locations.

High-performance, standards-based access to any kind of data can be achieved by placing the data in an LDAP directory and replicating it widely. Directory scalability (up to tens of millions of entries!), reliability, and write performance may all be very important for these kinds of applications.

Table 12.1 provides a summary of these application categories and lists the typical needs that must be met by directory products.

Security and Privacy Needs	Performance Needs	Scalability Needs	Acceptable Cost per User
Moderate	Low	Low	High
High	High	Moderate	Moderate
Very high	High	High	Low
High	Very high	Very high	Low
High	Very high	Very high	Moderate

Just looking at the category that a specific directory product claims to address is no substitute for using the comprehensive evaluation criteria we help you create in the next section. However, it can help you quickly weed out products that are unlikely to meet your needs.

Evaluation Criteria for Directory Software

One of the first tasks in choosing directory software is to develop evaluation criteria that takes into account your current and future needs. Whether you have no idea what software you might use or you already have a specific set of products in mind, evaluation criteria are very valuable. A good set of evaluation criteria helps you decide on, justify, and feel comfortable with your product choices.

In this section, we provide some advice for developing evaluation criteria to fit your own situation. We divide the criteria into the following areas:

- Core features

- Management features

- Reliability

- Performance and scalability

- Security

- Standards conformance

- Interoperability

- Cost

- Flexibility and extensibility

- Other considerations

Each area is discussed in the following sections. As you read through these criteria, examine your own directory service needs and design to see which factors are most important to you. Your goal is to create a list of requirements and questions you have about the products. You should assign a priority or weight to each item on the list so you can make intelligent trade-offs later.

Your list of evaluation criteria will serve as a tool for evaluating products and help you ask the right questions of vendors about what they can deliver. Keep in mind that the areas we cover in the following sections are not exhaustive and that there will likely be other factors that you may want to consider as well. Use this information only as a starting point to develop your own set of evaluation criteria. And don't neglect the areas in which you have no immediate needs; be sure to take future needs into account.

Core Features

When looking at the core features of LDAP software products, your main task is to ensure that the product can meet the needs of all the directory-enabled applications you plan to deploy now and in the future. This is not a small task, of course, but the work done in Chapter 5 and throughout Part II should provide all the information you need to create a list of the features that are important to you. Some areas to consider include:

- Support for the hardware and software platforms you use or plan to use in the future.

- Support for all the core LDAP operations and extensions needed by your applications.

- Replication features, including support for all the topologies your design uses, the ability to provide uninterrupted service to client applications even if one or more replicas fail, flexible scheduling policies, and so on. Chapter 10, "Replication Design," includes detailed product criteria for replication.

- Support for distributed directories, if required by your design. This is usually accomplished with LDAP referrals or server-to-server chaining of requests.

- Directory data import, maintenance, and backup features.

- The quality, availability, and extra cost of documentation and support.

Management Features

You will need to manage both the directory service itself and its contents. When examining the management features of software, focus on your most critical needs and look for flexibility to meet future needs. Areas to consider include

- Simplicity and flexibility of installation scripts and procedures.

- Availability of good tools for configuring, monitoring, and maintaining all aspects of the service itself. Look for tools that are easy to use for complicated tasks such as security, access control, and performance tuning. Graphical and command-line tools are both often desirable, depending on your situation and preferences.

- Availability of a variety of LDAP client interfaces that users and administrators can use to find and manipulate directory content such as person entries, group entries, and any other data you plan to store in your directory. The best client interfaces can be customized to target specific needs.

- Scriptable administration and content manipulation tools that can be used to automate frequent tasks.

- The ability to manage user-specific constraints such as password policies, resource usage quotas, and other items.

- Remote administration capabilities.

Reliability

All directory services are expected to be reliable so as not to inconvenience applications and halt business processes. Specific requirements, of course, vary widely. For example, if your directory will primarily serve as an electronic phone book, but everyone has paper copies of the same data available for use if your service is unavailable, reliability is not too critical. However, extranet applications used by customers and business partners to update their contact information require great reliability.

Some reliability issues to consider when creating your evaluation criteria include

- The ability to support 24×7 (continuous) operation. Features such as the ability to back up and change the server configuration without affecting the running service can be important. Common configuration changes include extending directory schema, adding indexes to improve performance, and temporary changes needed during upgrade and maintenance activities (such as a change in the TCP port a server listens on).

- A robust, transactional server data store that is self-repairing and recovers automatically from temporary failures such as power outages.

- Support for automated failover to minimize downtime in the event of software or hardware failures. With directory server software, this can be accomplished via support for third-party or built-in high availability (HA) solutions, advanced replication features such as multimaster topologies and hot standbys, and client-side support for transparent failover to a standby server.

- Directory service monitoring tools. As discussed in Chapter 18, "Monitoring," monitoring is essential for quickly identifying and correcting problems. Support for Simple Network Management Protocol (SNMP) and the availability of proprietary monitoring tools can both be helpful. Otherwise, you need to write your own monitoring tools. (If you do this, make sure that appropriate hooks and SDKs are provided with the directory products you choose.)

Performance and Scalability

High performance and high scalability are very important in many directory deployments. The directory design process described in Part II of this book should help you expose all your performance and scalability needs. Areas to consider include:

- Latency of directory operations. For example, how fast must the directory service respond to a search or modify request?

- Throughput of directory operations. How many operations can a directory server handle in a given time period? How fast can a client application or SDK send LDAP requests and process the responses? How many search, add, and modify requests can the server process per second? Be sure to take into account the type and mix of operations you expect to have in your environment. For example, server performance for searches is typically much greater than it is for adds and modifies; thus, if your needs imply that there will be a lot of add-and-modify traffic, you should pay special attention to the write performance of the directory server software.

- The ability of the server to handle a large number of simultaneous LDAP connections while providing good performance to all the clients.

- The ability to monitor and tune the performance of the directory server to meet your needs. This is important in determining the characteristics of the hardware you should purchase as well as to optimally meet the needs of your most important directory-enabled applications.

- The ability of server and client software to maintain good performance as scale increases. Dimensions to consider include the number and size of entries, number and size of attribute values, number of access control rules, number of replicas, and number of directory partitions.

- The availability of performance information such as benchmark results and performance-focused documentation. If performance is important to you, but a directory software vendor has little to say about it, you may need to look at other products or conduct your own benchmark tests.

Directory Performance Testing

To determine how well a directory product will perform when you deploy it, you can conduct performance testing in a laboratory setting. Creating an accurate performance test that produces meaningful results is often difficult. To closely model your own directory data and directory-enabled applications, you may find that you need to develop your own custom benchmarking tools. This can be a lot of work, but it may be worth tackling up front. Understanding the performance characteristics of your directory

software will help you make informed decisions as you finalize your design and deployment plans.

DirectoryMark, jointly developed by Mindcraft and Netscape, is an off-the-shelf tool for benchmarking LDAP directory servers. This tool is highly configurable, so you may be able to use it to simulate the client load you expect to impose on your servers. Connect to Mindcraft's Web site at `http://www.mindcraft.com/benchmarks/dirmark/` for more information.

Security

As discussed in Chapter 11, "Privacy and Security Design," security needs vary widely from one directory service deployment to another. Without exception, though, security should be an important part of your product evaluation criteria. Areas to consider include:

- Access control capabilities, including adequate flexibility and granularity to meet your privacy, security, and data management needs.

- The ability to delegate administration of directory content to independent administrators and end users as needed.

- The authentication methods supported by the client and server software (e.g., LDAP basic authentication, various SASL methods, and certificate-based authentication).

- The encryption capabilities for LDAP data streams and directory data stores, including support for secure sockets layer (SSL) and transport layer security (TLS). If you need strong encryption with long key lengths, you may encounter product purchase and deployment obstacles in the form of export restrictions enforced by some governments (most notably the United States).

- The ability to use SSL or TLS to protect replication updates in transit.

- Support in server software for hardware acceleration of cryptographic algorithms. This is very important for servers that must perform a lot of encryption or routinely handle digital certificates.

Standards Conformance

To most people, standards are not interesting for their own sake; it's the products that adhere to standards that are more interesting. Standards-compliant software is important to you because it provides increased flexibility, better interoperability, more customer choice, and a proven, well-understood core feature set.

Standards documents are typically very technical and hard to understand. Although you probably do not need to read and understand all the standards documents, you should be aware of all the emerging and ratified standards so that you can ask software vendors if they comply with them. Because no available product supports all the standards, you need to determine which standards are most critical to you. You can do that by understanding what each standard specifies and how it aligns with your own directory needs.

The most important group that creates standards for LDAP is the Internet Engineering Task Force (IETF), which is the standards-setting body for the Internet. IETF standards are published as a series of documents called requests for comments (RFCs). Note that not all RFCs are destined or even intended to become standards, and that specifications are first published as Internet drafts. (See Chapter 2, "A Brief History of Directories," for more information on the IETF and how it operates.)

Other important standards are produced by industry consortiums, and some de facto standards are developed by the leading directory services vendors. Some of the directory service standards you should consider for your evaluation criteria list include:

- The core LDAP Internet protocol standards, including the complete set of LDAPv2 and LDAPv3 RFCs. The relevant documents are RFCs 1777–1779 and 2251–2256. Because these standards are the building blocks on which all LDAP-related software is built, most products claim to support these RFCs. Be sure to ask your software vendor exactly which aspects of these LDAP standards they do not support, however.

- Related Internet standards that LDAP has adopted, including Simple Authentication and Security Layer (SASL), which is defined in RFC 2222;

and the directory services Simple Network Management Protocol Management Information Base (SNMP MIB), which at the time of this writing has not yet been published as an RFC (it is available only as an Internet draft). You can use SASL to integrate with a specific authentication scheme. Support for the SNMP MIB for directory services helps you integrate your servers with off-the-shelf network management systems (NMSs).

- Emerging LDAPv3 extensions, such as those for dynamic entries, server-side sorting of search results, virtual list view, standard access control, and standard replication protocols. At the time of this writing, all these extensions are available only as Internet drafts; they have not yet been published as RFCs. In general, you should examine each extension to see if you need the feature it provides within your own directory deployment.

- The LDAP Data Interchange Format (LDIF), which defines a standard format for representing directory entries and changes to entries. At the time of this writing, LDIF is documented in an Internet draft; it has not yet been published as an RFC.

- LDAP application programming interface (API) standards within SDKs and LDAP clients. Internet standard LDAP APIs for C/C++ and Java are being developed by the IETF. Note that a number of proprietary APIs also exist, such as Microsoft's Active Directory Services Interface (ADSI) and Javasoft's Java Naming and Directory Interface (JNDI). However, support for standard APIs can be very helpful in reducing the time and cost incurred when developing LDAP applications. See Chapters 20, "Developing New Applications," and 21, "Directory-Enabling Existing Applications," for more information on available APIs and SDKs.

- Schema standards, such as those being developed as part of the Directory Enabled Networking (DEN) industry group. Good LDAP products are extensible and can accommodate a wide variety of schemas.

- Security standards, such as X.509 for certificates and the SSL and TLS protocols. Security is an area in which standards are especially important, not just to achieve basic interoperability, but also so you can more easily evaluate the security provided by the products. For example, all SSL version 3.0 implementations support a certain level of security, but for proprietary security schemes you need to trust the software vendor to provide adequate capabilities. Security is an area that is not well understood, but standards reduce the learning curve and allow you to transfer knowledge from one product to another much more easily.

- X.500 directory service standards. Because LDAP depends to some extent on the X.500 standards for its naming, information, and operations models, the X.500 standards are relevant to all LDAP directories. X.500 also specifies standards for access control and replication that have been adopted by some LDAP vendors; however, there are reportedly some interoperability problems with products that implement the more advanced X.500 features. More information on X.500 can be found in Chapter 2.

- Any other standards or certification requirements, such as Y2K compliance, certification by an operating system or hardware vendor, or support for industry-leading third-party products such as HA and backup solutions.

Interoperability

Standards conformance is an important part of any product's interoperability story. However, if you require interoperability with specific products, you should take that into account when developing your evaluation criteria. Areas to consider include:

- Availability and support for directory-enabled applications that you plan to deploy. Some vendors, such as Netscape offer a complete line of LDAP-enabled Web and messaging products designed to work with their own directory service products. When working with products from two or more vendors, you probably should verify interoperability yourself.

- Availability of synchronization tools for data sources that your directory service needs to interoperate with. For example, you may have a requirement to mirror the data held in a cc:Mail address book in your LDAP directory; therefore, you would need to buy or build a cc:Mail-to-LDAP synchronization tool. See Chapter 22, "Directory Coexistence," for more information on integrating your directory service with other data sources.

- Availability of metadirectory solutions to facilitate the joining and synchronization of disparate directories and data stores. See Chapter 22 for more information on metadirectories.

- Proof of interoperability. This can come in the form of results from vendor-to-vendor tests performed in an ad hoc fashion or at an LDAP interoperability testing forum, such as the recent DirConnect events sponsored by the Internet Mail Consortium (IMC).

Cost

The most obvious cost is that of the software itself, but you should also consider the total cost of buying, deploying, supporting, and maintaining your directory service and the applications that surround it. Chapter 14 covers cost analysis in depth, but some general areas to examine when creating your list of evaluation criteria include the following:

- *Software costs.* Be aware of the different cost structures under which the software may be sold—per server installation, per CPU, per user, per entry, yearly lease, unlimited use, and so on. Also, don't forget to take into account ongoing upgrade and support costs and the licensing costs associated with operating systems or any other software the directory software depends on. For example, Microsoft Active Directory requires that you upgrade all your servers to Windows NT 5.0 to take advantage of some features.

- *Hardware costs.* Different directory service products require different hardware, some of which may be much more expensive than others.

- *Deployment costs.* These include the cost of hardware, personnel, software deployment, and so on.

- *Maintenance costs.* These include the cost of day-to-day tasks such as performing backups, maintaining the content of the directory servers, monitoring it for failures, and any other ongoing activities. Look for products that allow management tasks to be easily automated.

- *Training costs.* These include costs to train administrators of the system, end users, and directory content administrators.

- *Support costs.* Products that are easy to learn, use, and manage cost less to support.

Keep in mind that some of your costs will be hard to quantify, especially if you have not yet deployed your directory service. Talk to people within other organizations who have already deployed a similar product to gather more concrete information about costs.

Flexibility and Extensibility

It is unlikely that an existing product can meet all your needs out of the box. For this reason, and because you can't anticipate all your future needs, it is important to choose directory products that are flexible and extensible. Areas to consider include the following

- *Configurability.* Look for the ability to selectively enable and disable features, the ability to adapt the product to work well on your available hardware and operating systems, and the ease with which you can make configuration changes. For example, if you have remote offices within your organization, you may want to run some replicated servers in those offices on inexpensive machines that have moderate amounts of memory, CPU, and disk capacity. For your main campus, you may want to run the same directory server software but tune it to take advantage of large machines that have lots of memory, CPU, and disk capacity.

- *Flexibility.* To support a variety of directory-enabled applications, you want to be able to easily extend directory schemas, add or remove indexes, and otherwise configure directory servers to provide optimal performance, for an application's queries. For example, if you bring a high-performance, directory-enabled application online in the future, it will probably come with its own schema extensions and may require the tuning of your servers to achieve optimal performance.

- *Extensibility.* Some products can be extended by writing scripts or creating software plug-ins that alter the behavior of directory clients and servers. Netscape Directory Server, for example, provides a fairly complete set of well-documented plug-in interfaces. This kind of extensibility can help when you need to support an unusual application or when you want to adapt the directory service to fit your organization's data maintenance policies.

Other Considerations

There are a few additional areas to examine as you construct your evaluation criteria. These issues are primarily related to the future of the product and the vendor that provides it. Consider each of the following topics:

- *The future of the product.* Is it evolving and moving in the direction you expect your organization to move? Is the product important enough to the organization that develops it that you can count on continued availability and support?

- *Completeness of product line.* A vendor that sells a complete line of directory-enabled applications and has made LDAP a key part of its corporate strategy may be able to meet more of your needs and serve as a good partner for all your directory services efforts. On the other hand, it is unlikely that you will buy all your directory products from only one vendor.

- *Industry and developer mindshare.* Look at how much support for the product there is outside the company or organization that develops it. A product that is widely used and supported by many third parties has a better chance of meeting the needs of most people. On the other hand, if your needs are very specialized, this isn't as important.

- *General vendor issues.* Make sure the vendor stands behind the products it sells. Determine whether the vendor has a viable business plan so you can be assured that it will be around to support you.

An Evaluation Criteria Example

In this section, we present an example evaluation criteria list for directory server software. The sample criteria were developed for a fictitious company called Airius Airlines that is deploying a directory service for the first time. The focus of the deployment is support of directory-enabled intranet applications. The first two applications that are expected to come online are an electronic phone book and an email delivery service. Airius currently has only 5,000 employees but expects to grow rapidly over the next few years.

The sample criteria are presented as a series of tables that the Airius Airlines directory services planning team created using a spreadsheet program like Microsoft Excel. Each row in the spreadsheet lists a specific characteristic used to evaluate each candidate product. A description and a weight are provided for each item. The weight is a number from 1 (not very important) to 10 (extremely important) that captures the importance of the item. Items that are extremely critical (must-have features) are marked with an asterisk (*) so that they can be spotted more easily when reviewing the results of the evaluation.

The right side of each table provides room to evaluate two products (Product A and Product B). Each product is given a rating for each characteristic. A score ranging from 0 (poor) to 100 (best) is calculated by multiplying each item's weight by a product's rating. By adding all the scores, an objective number is produced that can be consulted when making a final product choice.

Airius's evaluation criteria for core directory server features are shown in Table 12.2.

TABLE 12.2 SAMPLE EVALUATION CRITERIA FOR CORE DIRECTORY SERVER FEATURES

Feature	Weight (1–10)	Product A Rating (0–10)	Product A Score (W×R)	Product B Rating (0–10)	Product B Score (W×R)
Basic LDAP operations	7	8	56	3	21
Virtual list view LDAPv3 extension (for phone book)	5	10	50	10	50
* Runs on Windows NT 4.0	10	10	100	10	100
Runs on HP/UX 11.0	5	10	50	0	0
Multimaster replication	4	0	0	9	36
*Basic replication	10	10	100	10	100
Quality of design and deployment documentation	6	2	12	7	42
Quality of administration and configuration documentation	8	4	32	8	64
Total score (out of 550)			**400**		**413**

To illustrate how the scoring system works, consider the first row in Table 12.2: support for all basic LDAP operations. This feature was given a weight of 7 (out of a possible 10) by Airius because it is fairly important to the company (it plans to eventually make full use of its directory service, including allowing employees to update their own contact information).

Product A received a rating of 8 (out of a possible 10) because it does support all the basic LDAP operations but falls short on complete implementation of some of the added features of LDAPv3. The item score for Product A is calculated by multiplying 7 (the weight) by 8 (the product rating) to arrive at 72. Product B received a rating of 3 because it supports only search operations. Product B's score is 21 (7 times 3).

> **Tip**
>
> *For an objective numeric evaluation such as this to work, you need to ensure that the grading is done fairly. In practice, the same group of people must assign the ratings for each criterion, or you must spell out in great detail how the products are to be rated. If you can spare the resources, a good approach is to have two or more people rate each product independently and then compare the results to ensure that all parties basically agree.*

Because Airius plans to develop its own phone book application and eventually create dozens of directory-enabled applications, flexibility and extensibility of the directory software are very important. Table 12.3 shows Airius's evaluation criteria for this area.

TABLE 12.3 SAMPLE CRITERIA FOR FLEXIBILITY AND EXTENSIBILITY

Criterion	Weight (1–10)	Product A Rating (0–10)	Product A Score (W×R)	Product B Rating (0–10)	Product B Score (W×R)
Ease of configuration	4	5	20	7	28
Flexible configuration	7	9	63	5	35
Will run on low-end server machines	7	7	49	6	42
*Optimizing for new applications: tunable indexing	9	8	72	5	45
*Optimizing for new applications: extensible schemas	10	8	80	4	40
Server-side plug-in APIs	2	9	18	2	4
Total score (out of 390)			**302**		**194**

The sample evaluation criteria we have presented for Airius Airlines are, of course, far from complete. When you develop your own evaluation criteria, you should include all the areas we discussed in the previous sections, such as security, interoperability, and cost. The evaluation criteria tables shown here could be improved by adding a column to record specific comments or notes about each product feature.

Reaching a Decision

Now that you have a good set of evaluation criteria, you need to make a decision about what software products to buy. If you are new to directory services, you may want to hire a consultant to help with your directory product evaluation. Whether you hire someone or tackle this yourself, it will take some time to make a good decision.

Gathering Basic Product Information

The first step in making your decision is to gather as much information as you can about all the available products that may meet your needs. Specific examples of available LDAP software products are described briefly in the next section. Use the information you gather about each product to grade it against your evaluation criteria.

This initial fact gathering can be done using data sheets and other information that should be readily available from each vendor's marketing department. You can usually just visit a vendor's Web site to find most of what you need. You might also draw from independent reviews of directory services software, although magazines and other publications that have performed reviews to date have focused on fairly narrow portions of the directory product space, such as NOS directories.

Quizzing the Software Vendors

After gathering as much initial information as possible, you should contact people at each prospective vendor and ask to meet with them so they can tell you about their products and you can ask any remaining questions. Your main goal is to fill in your evaluation criteria for each product; however, you should also listen to what the directory vendors have to say because they may tell you something about their product that you have not considered. They may even be able to help you improve your evaluation criteria. Of course, you need to watch out for bias and hidden agendas, and you may need to steer the vendors' conversation back to your own needs if they go too far off topic.

You should also ask prospective vendors for a list of reference customers whom you can contact to learn more about how their customers are really using the product. If you know of others who have chosen a competitor's product, contact them as well and ask them why they made that choice. When obtaining references from the software vendors, ask to be referred to organizations that are similar to yours and that have undertaken similar directory service deployments.

Challenging the Vendors to Show What Their Products Can Do

If a clear winner has not yet emerged from among the prospective products, you may want to challenge each vendor to show what its software can do and how it will meet your needs. This can be done by asking the vendor to help you with a trial design and a small pilot. This will not only help you learn how well a vendor's products will work in your own environment, but it will also help you learn what it is like to work closely with the vendor.

You can also invite several vendors to come to your business or a neutral place at the same time and conduct a "bakeoff" so that you can perform a head-to-head evaluation. If you do this, make sure you are prepared with sample data, schema, and benchmarks in hand so the event is a productive one. Also, don't expect to convince any vendors to participate in this kind of event unless you plan to spend a lot of money on directory services software and support.

Conducting a Directory Services Pilot

You should always do your own in-house evaluation and piloting of whatever software you choose before deploying it. There are always surprises with software, a few of which inevitably are unpleasant and show up only in your environment. The process of creating, running, and learning from a pilot directory service is covered in Chapter 13.

Before you actually create the pilot service, you may want to do some testing in a controlled environment that is free from distractions. Lab testing is a good way to learn the basics of the software and to see how well it scales and how reliable it is under heavy load. See Chapter 13 for specific ideas on how to conduct useful laboratory tests.

Negotiating the Best Possible Deal

After you have made your final software decision, negotiate the best deal you can. Depending on your needs, you may want to buy just the software from a vendor, or you may want to negotiate a complete package that includes hardware, software, installation, support, and onsite consulting.

In some cases you also need to take political factors into account. You should fight hard to get the best software available, but if your CEO sits on the same school board as the CEO of one of the directory software suppliers, your hands may be tied. In that case, use the political relationship to your advantage by asking for a better deal, better support, additional critical features, and so on.

Directory Software Options

In the first part of this chapter we looked at product selection in an abstract way without referring specifically to any real products. In this section we briefly present information on some of the directory products available at the time of this writing. Because directory software is part of an emerging and changing portion of the software market, you should consult other sources in addition to this book when locating products to ensure that you don't overlook any newcomers or recently upgraded products.

We divide our survey of LDAP directory software into three general categories, which are discussed in the following sections:

- Directory server software

- Directory-enabled applications

- SDKs

Directory Server Software

A wide variety of directory server software that speaks LDAP is available, ranging from commercial software to freeware. Some of these products, of course, are better suited to certain kinds of directory-enabled applications than others, and we attempt to capture that information in the "Focus" item listed with each product's entry.

It is worth noting that the NOS directories (Novell Directory Services and Microsoft Active Directory) are more narrowly focused than many of the others. If you need a great directory service for your NOS, one of those two products is a good choice; if you do not, you should look elsewhere.

DSSeries LDAP Directory 1.1
Vendor: IBM

Overview: An LDAPv2 directory server for IBM's AIX operating system, with some support for LDAPv3. Also supports some strong security features (through SSL) and replication.

Focus: Extranets

For more information: Connect to IBM's DSSeries Web site at `http://www.software.ibm.com/ts/dsseries/`.

Global Directory Server (GDS)
Vendor: ISOCOR

Overview: An X.500(93)–based directory server that also supports LDAPv2. Directory synchronization capabilities that work with GDS also available from ISOCOR.

Focus: Large intranets

Significant features: X.500 standards compliance and directory synchronization tools

For more information: Connect to ISOCOR's GDS Web site at `http://www.isocor.com/products/gds.htm`.

Innosoft Distributed Directory Server (IDDS) version 4.3
Vendor: Innosoft

Overview: A native LDAPv3 directory server that supports features such as strong security (through SSL).

Focus: Intranets

Significant features: Standards compliance and security

For more information: Connect to Innosoft's IDDS Web site at `http://www3.innosoft.com/idds-descript.html`.

Internet Directory Server (IDS) 3.0
Vendor: Lucent Technologies

Overview: A native LDAPv3 directory server that supports features such as strong security (through SSL), replication, dynamic entries, and password policy management.

Focus: Large intranets, extranets, and ISPs

Significant features: Support for telephony, performance, and scalability

For more information: Connect to Lucent's IDS Web site at `http://www.lucent.com/netsys/internetservers/ids/ids.html`.

LDAP/X.500 Enterprise Directory Server
Vendor: ISODE

Overview: An X.500(93)–based directory server that also supports LDAP.

Focus: Large intranets

Significant features: X.500 standards compliance, scalability, and performance

For more information: Connect to ISODE's products Web site at `http://www.isode.com/products.html`.

Netscape Directory Server 4.0
Vendor: Netscape Communications

Overview: A native, general-purpose LDAPv3 directory server that supports advanced features such as the LDAPv3 Virtual List View extension, full international capabilities, strong security (through SSL), replication, and password policy management.

Focus: Large intranets, extranets, ISPs, and ESPs

Significant features: Open standards compliance, performance, scalability, security, multiplatform support

For more information: Connect to Netscape's Mission Control Web site at `http://home.netscape.com/missioncontrol/`.

Novell Directory Services 4.0
Vendor: Novell

Overview: A powerful directory service integrated with NetWare. Advanced features including multi-master replication and the ability to very widely distribute the directory among servers. LDAP supported via a low-performance gateway.

Focus: NetWare NOSs

Significant features: Powerful, easy-to-use administration tools, NetWare integration, and large installed base

For more information: Connect to Novell's NDS Web site at `http://www.novell.com/products/nds/`.

OpenDirectory Dxserver
Vendor: OpenDirectory

Overview: An X.500(93)–based directory server that also supports LDAPv2.

Focus: Large intranets

Significant features: X.500 standards compliance and scalability

For more information: Connect to the OpenDirectory Web site at `http://www.opendirectory.com/`.

Rialto Global Directory Server
Vendor: Control Data

Overview: An X.500(93)–based directory server that also supports LDAP.

Focus: Large intranets

Significant features: X.500 standards compliance and directory synchronization

For more information: Connect to Control Data's Rialto directories Web site at `http://www.cdc.com/products/directories.html`.

SLAPD
Vendor: University of Michigan and others

Overview: An LDAPv2 directory server that is freely available in source code form. Some groups working on adding support for LDAPv3.

Focus: Intranets

Significant features: First standalone LDAP directory server, free, multiple platforms, and source code

For more information: Connect to the University of Michigan LDAP Web site at `http://www.umich.edu/~dirsvcs/ldap/#servers`. Some SLAPD projects were recently started within the free software community as well; connect to `http://www.is.kiruna.se/~goran/ldap/` and `http://www.openldap.org` for more information.

Sun Directory Services 1.0
Vendor: Sun Microsystems

Overview: A native LDAPv2 directory server for the Solaris operating system.

Focus: Intranets

For more information: Connect to the Sun Directory Services Web site at `http://www.sun.com/solstice/telecom/LDAP.html`.

Windows NT Server 5.0 Active Directory
Vendor: Microsoft

Overview: An LDAPv3 directory service that will be integrated with the Microsoft Windows NT Server 5.0 operating system. Advanced features including multimaster replication and support for dynamic entries.

Focus: Intranets and Windows NT NOSs

Significant features: Domain Name System (DNS) integration and Windows 98 and Windows NT integration

For more information: Connect to Microsoft's Active Directory Web site at `http://www.microsoft.com/NTServer/Basics/Future/ActiveDirectory/default.asp`.

Directory-Enabled Applications

Hundreds of directory-enabled software applications are available from dozens of different sources. The different kinds of applications available include

- Web browsers that understand LDAP URLs.

- Electronic mail clients that support LDAP searches and LDAP-based address books.

- General-purpose directory browsers, many of which support adding and modifying entries as well.

- HTML-based end user and directory administration interfaces. These can often be easily customized to fit site-specific needs.

- Server applications, such as electronic mail servers, Web servers, and security servers.

To give you a taste of the different kinds of applications that are available, we list a few of the major vendors and describe some of the LDAP applications they produce.

Microsoft

Overview: Microsoft's Outlook and Outlook Express email clients can use LDAP to query remote address books and Internet directories. Microsoft's NetMeeting product uses LDAP to arrange a user-to-user rendezvous. Over time you can expect to see many of Microsoft's products become LDAP-aware.

For more information: Connect to Microsoft's products Web site at `http://www.microsoft.com/products/`.

Netscape Communications

Overview: Nearly all of Netscape's products are LDAP-aware. The email client included in Netscape's Communicator browser suite can use LDAP to query remote address books and Internet directories. Netscape's high-performance security, Web, application, electronic commerce, and messaging servers are all LDAP-enabled. Netscape Directory Server includes a customizable HTML LDAP gateway that can be used for end user and administrative tasks.

For more information: Connect to Netscape's products Web site at `http://home.netscape.com/products/`.

Oblix

Overview: Oblix specializes in directory management and publishing tools. Its Corporate Services Automation product line provides a set of Web-based interfaces for managing employee information that is stored in an LDAP server. It provides nifty features such as visual organization charts that are created based on information stored in an LDAP directory.

For more information: Connect to Oblix's Web site at `http://www.oblix.com/`.

University of Michigan

Overview: All the LDAP software developed by the University of Michigan is free, and source code is generally available as well. Available LDAP client software includes: full-featured LDAP clients for Microsoft Windows (waX.500), X-Windows (xax500), and Macintosh (maX.500); an email delivery agent called mail500; and a variety of gateways to older information delivery systems such as finger and gopher.

For more information: Connect to the University of Michigan LDAP client Web page at `http://www.umich.edu/~dirsvcs/ldap/ldclients.html`.

SDKs

A variety of libraries and tools is available for developing LDAP applications. These SDKs are generally inexpensive, and in many cases they are available free of charge. To protect your programming investment, we recommend that you code to one of the developing standard LDAP APIs for C or Java. A variety of proprietary APIs is supported by the SDK vendors. Chapters 20 and 21 discuss SDKs in greater detail.

In the following sections, we describe some of the most popular LDAP SDKs.

Active Directory Services Interface (ADSI)

Vendor: Microsoft

Overview: A collection of COM objects for Microsoft Windows that provide a unified interface for accessing a variety of directories, including LDAP directories. A DLL that conforms to the RFC 1823 and IETF draft LDAPv3 APIs also included with ADSI.

For more information: Connect to Microsoft's SDK Web site at `http://www.microsoft.com/msdn/sdk/`.

Innosoft LDAP Client SDK (ILC-SDK)

Vendor: Innosoft

Overview: C dynamic libraries that conform to RFC 1823 and IETF draft LDAPv3 C API. Supported platforms include AIX, Digital UNIX, Solaris, OpenVMS, and Windows NT.

For more information: Connect to Innosoft's ILC-SDK Web site at `http://www.innosoft.com/iii/company/ldap-sdk.html`.

Java Naming and Directory Interface (JNDI)
Vendor: JavaSoft (Sun Microsystems)

Overview: A standard Java extension that provides a unified interface for accessing a variety of directories, including LDAP directories.

For more information: Connect to JavaSoft's JNDI Web site at `http://java.sun.com/products/jndi/`.

LDAP-X
Vendor: Boldon James

Overview: A set of Microsoft Windows ActiveX controls that comprise a tool kit for constructing LDAP applications.

For more information: Connect to Boldon James's LDAP-X Web site at `http://www.bj.co.uk/ldapx.htm`.

Netscape Directory SDK for C
Vendor: Netscape Communications

Overview: C dynamic libraries that conform to RFC 1823 and IETF draft LDAPv3 C API and include support for the LDAPv3 extensions supported by Netscape Directory Server. A complete set of LDAP command-line tools also provided. Supported platforms include most major UNIX flavors; Windows 95, 98, and NT; and Macintosh PowerPC. Source code available under the terms of the Netscape Public License.

For more information: Connect to Netscape's Directory Developer Central Web site at `http://developer.netscape.com/tech/directory/`. For access to the LDAP C SDK source code, connect to the mozilla.org Web site at `http://www.mozilla.org/directory`.

Netscape Directory SDK for Java
Vendor: Netscape Communications

Overview: A set of Java classes that conform to the IETF draft LDAPv3 Java API. A complete set of LDAP command-line tools also provided with the SDK. Source code available under the terms of the Netscape Public License.

For more information: Connect to Netscape's Directory Developer Central Web site at `http://developer.netscape.com/tech/directory/`. For access to the Java LDAP SDK source code, connect to the mozilla.org Web site at `http://www.mozilla.org/directory`.

PerLDAP Modules for Perl

Vendor: Clayton Donley and Netscape Communications

Overview: A set of modules written in C and Perl that allow Perl programmers to create LDAP applications. Source code also available under the terms of the Mozilla Public License.

For more information: Connect to Netscape's Directory Developer Central Web site at `http://developer.netscape.com/tech/directory/`. For access to the PerLDAP source code, connect to the mozilla.org Web site at `http://www.mozilla.org/directory`.

University of Michigan LDAP C SDK

Vendor: University of Michigan

Overview: C libraries that conform to RFC 1823 (no support for LDAPv3). A complete set of LDAP command-line tools also provided. Supported platforms include most major UNIX flavors, Windows 95 and NT, and Macintosh. Source code is also available. (This SDK is part of the general University of Michigan LDAP 3.3 software release.)

For more information: Connect to the University of Michigan LDAP Web site at `http://www.umich.edu/~dirsvcs/ldap/`.

Choosing Directory Products Checklist

❏ Understand the categories of directory software.

❏ Develop evaluation criteria for the following:

    ❏ Core features.

    ❏ Management features.

    ❏ Reliability.

    ❏ Performance and scalability.

    ❏ Security.

    ❏ Standards conformance.

    ❏ Interoperability.

    ❏ Flexibility and extensibility.

    ❏ Cost.

    ❏ Other considerations.

❏ Conduct your evaluation and reach a decision by doing the following:

    ❏ Gather basic product information.

    ❏ Quiz the software vendors.

    ❏ Challenge vendors to show what they can do.

    ❏ Conduct a directory service pilot.

    ❏ Negotiate the best possible deal.

Further Reading

A Summary of the X.500(96) User Schema for Use with LDAPv3 (RFC 2256). M. Wahl, 1997. Available on the World Wide Web at `http://info.internet.isi.edu/in-notes/rfc/files/rfc2256.txt`.

DirConnect LDAP interoperability testing. Sponsored by the Internet Directory Consortium (part of the Open Group). Information is available on the World Wide Web at `http://www.opengroup.org/idc/`.

Directory Enabled Networks Ad Hoc Working Group. Information is available on the World Wide Web at `http://murchiso.com/den/`.

DirectoryMark, The LDAPv3 Server Benchmarking Tool. Information is available on Mindcraft's World Wide Web site at `http://www.mindcraft.com/benchmarks/dirmark/`.

Directory Server Monitoring MIB (Internet draft). Mansfield, Kille, 1998; available on the World Wide Web at `http://www.ietf.org`.

LDAP Control Extension for Server Side Sorting of Search Results (Internet draft). A. Herron, T. Howes, C. Weider, A. Anantha, 1998. Available on the World Wide Web at `http://www.ietf.org`.

LDAP Data Interchange Format: Technical Specification (Internet draft). G. Good, 1998. Available on the World Wide Web at `http://www.ietf.org`.

LDAP Extensions for Scrolling View Browsing of Search Results (Internet draft). D. Boreham, C. Weider, 1998. Available on the World Wide Web at `http://www.ietf.org`.

LDAPv3: Extensions for Dynamic Directory Services (Internet draft). Y. Yaacovi, M. Wahl, T. Genovese, 1997. Available on the World Wide Web at `http://www.ietf.org`.

LDAPv3: Extension for Transport Layer Security (Internet draft). J. Hodges, R.L. Morgan, M. Wahl, 1998. Available on the World Wide Web at `http://www.ietf.org`.

LDAPv3 Triggered Search Result Control (Internet draft). M. Wahl, 1998. Available on the World Wide Web at `http://www.ietf.org`.

Lightweight Directory Access Protocol (v3) (RFC 2251). M. Wahl, T. Howes, and S. Kille, 1998. Available on the World Wide Web at `http://info.internet.isi.edu/in-notes/rfc/files/rfc2251.txt`.

Lightweight Directory Access Protocol (v3): Attribute Syntax Definitions (RFC 2252). M. Wahl, A. Coulbeck, T. Howes, and S. Kille, 1998. Available on the World Wide Web at `http://info.internet.isi.edu/in-notes/rfc/files/rfc2252.txt`.

Lightweight Directory Access Protocol (v3): The String Representation of LDAP Search Filters (RFC 2254). M. Wahl, T. Howes, and S. Kille, 1998. Available on the World Wide Web at `http://info.internet.isi.edu/in-notes/rfc/files/rfc2254.txt`.

Lightweight Directory Access Protocol (v3): UTF-8 String Representation of Distinguished Names (RFC 2253). M. Wahl, T. Howes, and S. Kille, 1998. Available on the World Wide Web at `http://info.internet.isi.edu/in-notes/rfc/files/rfc2253.txt`.

Persistent Search: A Simple LDAP Change Notification Mechanism (Internet draft). T. Smith, G. Good, T. Howes, R. Weltman, 1998. Available on the World Wide Web at `http://www.ietf.org`.

Referrals and Knowledge References in LDAP Directories (Internet draft). T. Howes, M. Wahl, 1998. Available on the World Wide Web at `http://www.ietf.org`.

Simple Authentication and Security Layer (SASL) (RFC 2222). J. Myers, 1997. Available on the World Wide Web at `http://info.internet.isi.edu/in-notes/rfc/files/rfc2222.txt`.

The C LDAP Application Program Interface (Internet draft). M. Smith, T. Howes, A. Herron, C. Weider, M. Wahl, and A. Anantha, 1998. Available on the World Wide Web at `http://www.ietf.org`.

The Java LDAP Application Program Interface (Internet draft). R. Weltman, T. Howes, and M. Smith, 1998. Available on the World Wide Web at `http://www.ietf.org`.

The TLS Protocol Version 1.0 (Internet draft). T. Dierks, C. Allen, 1997. Available on the World Wide Web at `http://www.ietf.org`.

Use of Language Codes in LDAPv3 (Internet draft). M. Wahl, T. Howes, 1998. Available on the World Wide Web at http://www.ietf.org.

Looking Ahead

In Chapter 13 we will test the products you have selected by creating a pilot directory service. Depending on what you learn during the pilot, you may be ready to turn your directory into a production service, or you may need to revisit earlier design decisions and product choices. Either way, a pilot service is a great way to bridge the gap between the design and production phases of your directory deployment.

CHAPTER 13

Piloting Your Directory Service

One of the most important milestones in your directory's early life cycle is achieved when you pilot the service. Until this point, your design has existed only in documents, on white boards, and in your head. During the pilot stage, you move from paper to programs, from design to deployment, and from theory to practice.

During your directory pilot, you get your first look at how well the design you've labored over works in something approaching a real environment. You begin to see how well the software you've selected performs, how smoothly the data maintenance procedures that you've designed work, and how receptive the users of your directory are to the service. You will then make modifications to your design based on feedback from the pilot. You should never consider deploying a service or making a major change to your service without testing and piloting it first.

Piloting is important for the following reasons:

- No matter how complete a design you believe you have produced, there will always be things you did not think of that show up only when the service is actually running—and piloting can help find these design flaws.

- Piloting is the best way to provide users of your service—end users, administrators, and other people involved in all aspects of the eventual system—an early look at what you are planning. Getting their feedback early and responding to it is key to producing a successful directory deployment.

- Management often likes to see something tangible before committing additional resources to it. Piloting can provide an important political tool for you to gain continued funding, extra resources, or other benefits for your project.

- Piloting is the best way to determine how well your directory serves the needs of your directory-enabled applications.

There may be other benefits to piloting as well, depending on your situation.

In this chapter, we present a road map to guide you through the process of piloting your directory service. We start with pre-pilot testing, in which you ensure that the directory software you have chosen will perform well in your environment. We then focus on determining the scope and goals of your pilot, and we continue with a discussion of the piloting environment you need. Next we talk about how to collect feedback on your pilot and how to scale up your pilot to simulate the load the service will experience in production. Finally, we conclude with a discussion of how to analyze the feedback generated from your pilot experience, the implications the feedback has on your design, and how to make changes to the design.

Pre-pilot Testing

Before you go through the trouble of setting up a pilot involving users, there are some aspects of your service that you should test in a lab environment. Testing is different from piloting. Testing is done in a closed environment, usually just by you and your staff; piloting is more open, users are involved, and the scope is expanded. For example, you should do preliminary scale, performance, and functionality testing to select the software to run your pilot on. These tests are best performed in a laboratory environment, where mistakes are easily corrected and configurations are easily changed.

In Chapter 12, "Choosing Directory Products," we talked about the steps to follow when selecting software for your directory, including performing tests in a laboratory environment. However, laboratory testing should be used for more than just selecting software. In the laboratory, you can find out whether the system works for you. Perhaps you can even persuade a few of your colleagues to see whether it works for them. Such testing is a crucial step before piloting or deploying any significant change to your service. Although this doesn't necessarily mean the change will work for your users in the environment outside the lab, testing gives you some confidence that it will.

Laboratory testing is aimed at answering objective questions about the system being tested. Does it do what it's supposed to do? Does it perform within acceptable limits? Can it scale to the required size? Naturally, to answer these questions effectively, you need to have appropriate goals in mind for the features you are testing.

Make a list of objective, measurable goals for your system, similar to the one shown in Table 13.1. In this example, the component being tested is a new directory server. The objective questions to be determined are whether the new server scales and gives acceptable performance while holding a certain number of entries, serving a predefined number of client connections, and performing a predefined set of queries. The entries, connections, and queries are chosen to reflect the expected typical load the server will experience in production.

TABLE 13.1 EXAMPLES OF OBJECTIVE CRITERIA TO MEASURE IN A LABORATORY TESTING ENVIRONMENT

Description	Goal	Comments
Number of directory entries	200,000	150,000 people entries, 30,000 group entries, 10,000 organizational unit entries, 10,000 miscellaneous entries.
Number of simultaneous connections	500	Some of these connections may be idle.
Number of simultaneous active connections	50	These connections are all performing the operations listed below.
Response time	Average of 1 second. No client should experience longer than a 2-second delay.	Response time is for clients performing simple equality searches on a single indexed attribute.

Laboratory testing cannot answer subjective questions about the system being tested. Questions such as "Will users like the system?" can be answered only by asking users during a pilot. Other questions that seem to be objective at first glance also cannot be answered without piloting in a real environment. For example, the interaction between your service and other services on the network, your network topology, various hard-to-predict failure modes, and real user behavior are difficult to produce in a laboratory environment. Piloting helps produce the appropriate conditions to answer these questions.

You should enter the piloting stage only after you have answered some basic questions by testing in the laboratory. Having done so, you can be confident that your pilot will succeed.

A Piloting Road Map

The steps you will follow in establishing your pilot vary depending on your environment and the design of your service. The steps outlined in the following sections are typical and cover the most common scenarios. Don't worry if you find you need to deviate from these steps, or if you don't have the time or money to cover everything we suggest. Just make sure you cover all the bases that are important to you in your environment.

Defining Your Goals

What do you want to get out of your pilot? You will have different goals depending on the type of service you have and the environment you're in. How you define your goals leads you to focus your pilot on different aspects of the service. For example, consider the following goals:

- *To produce a directory service for direct use by many demanding users.* In this case, you might focus your pilot on the user experience. This means spending extra time designing user interfaces, involving human factors expertise, piloting with a large and diverse user community, and conducting focus groups. You should measure your success based on how much users like your service, how efficiently it answers their queries, and how completely it serves their needs.

- *To produce a directory service for use by application developers.* In this case, your emphasis should be on the interfaces by which application developers access the directory. Your pilot users in this case would be developers. You should measure your success based on how easy the system is to use, how quickly new applications can be developed, and how much functionality the system provides. More information on LDAP-enabled applications can be found in Chapter 20, "Developing New Applications," and Chapter 21, "Directory-Enabling Existing Applications."

- *To produce a directory service containing sensitive data that serves the authentication and security needs of applications.* If this is your goal, you should focus your pilot on security. This means going through a security analysis to ensure that the security measures protecting your directory are both adequate and easy to use. You should measure your success based on the security (both perceived and actual) that users of the system are afforded, the ease with which applications can use the security services provided by the directory, and the degree to which the security needs of all applications are covered. Chapter 11, "Privacy and Security Design," discusses this topic in detail.

Other potential areas of focus exist, of course. The goals in the preceding list typically have an even tighter focus. For example, an application directory might be targeted specifically at extranet applications. In practice, you probably want to focus on all of these areas to some degree, but it's important to realize that you cannot fully pilot every aspect of your service. If you could, you wouldn't have a pilot—you'd have a full-fledged directory service! The same goes for pre-pilot testing: You can't test everything, so focus your tests on the most important aspects of the service.

Defining and prioritizing the goals you have in piloting your directory service helps you focus your efforts and make your pilot more effective.

Defining Your Scope

The goals you want to achieve by piloting naturally define the scope of your pilot. This scope has several dimensions: How much will users be involved in your pilot? Will your group of users be small and focused or large and diverse? What aspects of your service will you pilot? Will you try to pilot a few aspects thoroughly, or will you cover all aspects in less depth?

Part of your scope will be determined by the time and resources you have to devote to your pilot. You may have external constraints placed on you, or you may place constraints on yourself. A successful pilot is focused and has clear goals and objectives. Try to avoid endlessly piloting with no way of knowing when you are done. Your pilot may end because of either success or failure, and it's important to be able to recognize both outcomes. In the case of a successful pilot, your next step may be full deployment of the service. In the case of a failed pilot, your next step is probably to redesign, retest, and repilot.

A good practice is to draw a timeline showing the major milestones in your pilot. This timeline serves two purposes. First, it helps you map out the stages of your pilot, which helps you decide what needs to happen when. Second, it gives you a good reality check on the pilot itself. If your timeline leaves only a week for locating, training, and getting feedback from your pilot users, you would know that you haven't budgeted enough time.

The sample time line in Table 13.2 includes some time for testing, locating pilot users, rolling out the pilot, gathering feedback, and even applying that feedback to the pilot itself. As you can see, this timeline takes just over 12 weeks—an aggressive schedule. Unless you have very dedicated and motivated pilot users, don't expect to be able to do things this quickly.

TABLE 13.2 AN EXAMPLE OF A PILOT TIMELINE

Task Description	Start Date	Duration
Laboratory testing	+0 weeks	2 weeks
Locating pilot users	+0 weeks	2 weeks
Pilot environment setup and rollout	+2 weeks	1 week
Pilot operation	+3 weeks	4 weeks
Data gathering	+4 weeks	3 weeks
Incorporating pilot feedback	+7 weeks	2 weeks
Revised pilot environment setup and rollout	+9 weeks	1 week
Revised pilot operation	+10 weeks	2 weeks
Data gathering	+10 weeks	2 weeks
Incorporating pilot feedback into design	+12 weeks	1 week

Constructing an explicit timeline also helps you work more efficiently. A timeline can help identify opportunities to perform tasks in parallel, decreasing the time necessary for the pilot. For example, you may decide that locating pilot users can be done in parallel with setting up the service, or that data gathering can completely overlap with pilot operation.

Remember that the purpose of restricting the scope of your directory pilot is to ensure that it actually happens in a reasonable amount of time with a reasonable amount of resources. Be as explicit as you can about your scope; avoid extending the pilot into areas that are beyond it.

Developing Documentation and Training Materials

Your pilot may involve users who are not familiar with the service being piloted. Therefore, you should develop documentation, training materials, and other information to prepare your pilot users to be effective participants. You might be able to revise these materials and give them to your production users, so it's important to pilot these materials along with the directory service itself.

There are at least three broad categories of users you should be sure to address:

- End users
- Administrators
- Application developers

End user documentation is often tutorial in nature. You cannot assume that your users know much about your service or directories in general to begin with. You must educate them if you expect them to use the system and be effective pilot participants.

The complexity of your end user documentation and training materials depends on the complexity of your directory service, the tasks it will be used for, and the sophistication of your users. A simple phonebook service, for example, may require only online help. A more complicated directory service may require a printed user manual. An even more complicated system may require users to attend some kind of training session. Be sure to determine the level of documentation and training required by your users.

Administrative users typically require a different kind of documentation. There are three types of administrators: directory system administrators, directory content administrators, and directory-enabled application administrators. You must document the procedures they follow, provide troubleshooting guides for when things go wrong, and perhaps train them in the use of the system. Don't scrimp on documentation for your administrative users; they are responsible in large part for making the system run smoothly.

Application developers are often the most sophisticated users of your directory. They also require the most extensive training and documentation materials. Application developers usually need to know everything users need to know, but they also have to understand how to access the directory from their application. Furthermore, they need to know about your directory's naming conventions, available schema, how to access the directory through an API, and more. You can usually count on developers to be willing to tolerate rougher edges than users, but do not underestimate the amount of information they need to do their job.

Selecting Your Users

Selecting your users is important, especially if your service is targeted at end users (as opposed to a small set of applications you control). The users of your directory service are the least predictable variable in your directory equation.

Technical problems, such as inadequate capacity, can be solved relatively easily; problems involving user perceptions and expectations can be much harder to solve. It's important to detect and correct these problems early.

It's also important to make a good first impression with your directory service. This is important in a pilot, but it's absolutely critical in a production deployment. A bad first impression, no matter what the cause, can spell disaster and sometimes demise for an otherwise worthy project. The best way to be confident that you will make good first and subsequent impressions in production is to know that you've already made a favorable impression on a similar audience. This is where your pilot users come in. A good pilot provides a smooth transition to a production service. (Chapter 15, "Going Production," describes in detail the process of moving from pilot to production.)

Tip

When making the transition from pilot to production, make sure you have a backup plan in case things go wrong. Ideally, you should be able to switch back to the old production system quickly and seamlessly in case of trouble.

If you do a good job of selecting pilot users, you will have a representative sample of your ultimate directory service user community. Making your pilot users happy translates directly into making your production users happy. No system is perfect, of course, but choosing your pilot users wisely goes a long way toward ensuring a successful directory deployment.

If you do a poor job of selecting pilot users, you will not have a representative sample of your ultimate directory service user community. Making your pilot users happy may then have no relation to the happiness of your production users. From a user perspective, you might as well have not piloted your directory service at all.

Naturally, this raises a question: How can you select a good set of pilot users? There is no foolproof method, but here are some guidelines that you should follow:

- *Know your users.* It's important to know the ultimate audience of your directory service. If you don't know this, there is little chance you will select a representative group of pilot users. Be explicit about this. Write down the types of people you expect to use your directory.

- *Pick your users—don't let your users pick you.* You may be tempted to ask for volunteers to pilot your directory service. Although this is fine in some environments, you need to realize an important point:

Volunteers are a self-selecting group that tends to be more outgoing, more comfortable with computers, and usually more experienced than the general user population. As such, they often make poor representatives of your user community.

On the other hand, if your pilot goals are focused on testing the system components of your directory more than perfecting the user experience, a self-selecting group of users might work just fine. In fact, the extra sophistication and experience these users bring to the pilot may even be an advantage in giving the system a better workout.

If your goal is accurate representation, a better approach may be to recruit users from each group in your organization. This way you can be sure to get appropriate representation from all important constituencies. Also, be sure to include users of varying degrees of sophistication. This approach may be difficult. Be prepared to offer some kind of incentive to your pilot participants, such as cash, T-shirts, a free lunch, or some other perk. If your pilot offers real advantages to users (e.g., better performance), be sure to explain that to your potential pilot users.

Another good approach is to use a combination of volunteers and hand-picked users. The volunteers are easy to get, perhaps by advertising on the Web. The hand-picked users ensure that good representation is maintained. You might accomplish this by using a staged approach: Use volunteers first to work out the early bugs, and then use representative users to make sure the system works for your community.

- *Make your expectations clear.* It's important to tell your pilot users what you expect from them and what they can expect from you. Making your expectations clear can help weed out inappropriate pilot users who are not prepared to contribute to the pilot. It also helps users prepare themselves for the pilot and budget their time.

  Explaining to your pilot users what they can expect from you also helps avoid mismatched expectations. This applies to any remuneration they will receive for participating in the pilot, the level of support you can provide to them, the quality of service they can expect, and how their feedback will be incorporated.

- *Don't forget administrators.* Piloting is not solely about end users—you also have administrative procedures to test. You should not forget this important aspect of your service, nor should you forget the important administrative users who perform these procedures. Administrative procedures you might want to pilot include data maintenance, exception handling, backups and restoring, disaster recovering, and more. Be sure to factor these procedures and the corresponding users into your plans.

After you've selected an appropriate number of pilot users, there are a number of steps you should be sure to follow before, during, and after the pilot process. The following list is a minimal set of things to accomplish:

- *Prepare your users.* Make sure the users you select have the tools and training necessary to be effective pilot users. If the goal of your pilot is to see how users with no training cope with your directory, no training is necessary. On the other hand, if your goal is to exercise the system and ensure that a wide range of experienced users are served, make sure you provide any necessary training.

- *Be responsive.* It's important to be responsive to your pilot users—after all, they are going out of their way to help you make your service better (very few of them are in it for their health). You should strive to be as responsive as you can to their needs. This includes answering questions, responding to feedback, providing support, and so on.

- *Provide feedback.* Your pilot will be more successful if your pilot users feel a sense of ownership, or at least knowledge, of your directory service. One good way to do this is to make sure you provide constant feedback to the pilot users. If the pilot encounters problems, explain what went wrong. If you make changes to the service, explain what you did. If you gather statistics on the system during the pilot, share them with your users. All these steps will make your users feel more involved in the pilot and, therefore, more likely to be motivated to provide good feedback.

  One way to respond to users is to create a mailing list or discussion group containing everyone involved in the pilot. You can send regular status reports, notification of exceptional conditions, and other information using this list, and you'll know that they will reach all pilot participants.

All of these steps can help you develop a successful and long-lasting relationship with your pilot users, which is important if you expect to conduct pilot activities in the future. It can be very handy, not to mention less expensive, to have a batch of willing pilot participants on hand.

Setting Up Your Environment

At the same time that you select your user population, you should set up the environment for your pilot. You want things ready to go as soon as your users are identified. It's important to set up the proper environment for your pilot. Remember, you are not piloting just to see whether users like the service; you are also piloting to test all the procedures you've designed for creating and maintaining the service and its content. You are also piloting to see whether the system works efficiently as a whole.

This makes your choice of pilot environment even more important. Procedures that work well in one environment may not work at all in another. For example, suppose you rely on a local disk for your directory database during the pilot, but the production service needs to run over Sun's Network File System (NFS). The product you select may not work over NFS, and even if it does, performance may not be acceptable. Similar concerns can arise with your networking, hardware, software, and so on. Try to duplicate your production environment as closely as you can. If necessary, do so on a smaller scale. For example, use fewer servers, but try to use the same type of servers found in your production environment.

The kind of environment you end up with for your pilot depends on the kind of environment you will have in production and the resources you have to duplicate it. Ideally, you would set up a pilot environment that exactly duplicates your production environment. This way, you could minimize problems resulting from environment changes from pilot to production. The same holds true for any test equipment you use during the pre-pilot testing phase: For the tests to be useful, try to make the test equipment match the production equipment as closely as possible.

Tip

When your pilot is concluded, try to maintain the pilot equipment as a testbed. As you make changes to your service, you can pilot them on your testbed hardware. The testbed provides a convenient staging service for improvements to your directory service.

More often than not, resource and financial restrictions prohibit the development of an exact duplicate of your production system. Instead, you are often forced to make do with what you have. This may run the gamut from bits and pieces of leftover equipment to less expensive versions of all your production machines. If you find yourself having to scrimp in this kind of situation, be aware that your pilots will likely not be as effective.

Whatever equipment you have at your disposal, keep the following advice in mind when designing your pilot environment:

- *Software versions.* Make sure you use the same operating system versions on your pilot machines that you will use on your production machines. This also applies to backup software, third-party software, and, of course, the directory itself (unless the purpose of your pilot is to try out a new version of the directory software).

- *Hardware configuration.* As much as possible, make sure you use similar hardware configurations in both the pilot and production environments. This includes such things as the type of processor, number of processors, type of disk drive, type of backup device, network controller, and other hardware. Some things are more likely to cause problems than others. For example, moving to a multiple-CPU machine in production might create problems not exercised on a single-CPU machine in your pilot.

- *Network configuration.* Try to ensure that the network configuration of your pilot servers and clients are similar to the production's network configuration. This includes things such as the available bandwidth, the topology of the network, the level of other traffic on the network, and the reliability of the network links. Network configuration can have an especially significant impact on the response time that users of the system perceive. Your pilot system may be pretty snappy, but the production system could seem very slow because of too much traffic on the production network or a different topology creating longer network latency.

It's a good idea to make a map of your pilot system. Identify its major components and the network links between them. Label the map with the hardware, software, and type and speed of network links at each component. Identify links between replicas and the role each replica serves. Compare this to the similar map you have made for your production system. Look for any obvious differences, especially in the trouble areas just mentioned. An example of a pilot environment map is shown in Figure 13.1.

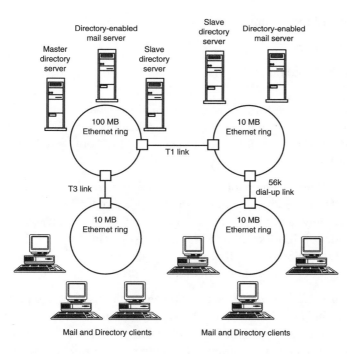

FIGURE 13.1   *An example of a pilot environment map.*

After you've designed your pilot environment, you need to build it. Make sure you do this in plenty of time to fix problems before the pilot's official start date. Like with your production system, some problems will undoubtedly crop up only in the implementation phase. Be sure to leave yourself enough time to fix any glitches that arise.

Rolling Out the Pilot

There are several steps to rolling our your pilot. The actual steps you use may vary somewhat depending on how large your pilot is and the type of users involved. The most common steps are outlined here:

1. Bring up the servers.

2. Test the servers.

3. Put system administrator feedback mechanisms in place.

4. Roll out documentation, training, and clients to system administrators.

5. Put end user feedback mechanisms in place.

6. Begin to distribute clients to users.

7. Begin to distribute documentation and perform training.

8. Get early feedback.

9. Widen the distribution of the pilot.

The basic steps are simple: Bring up the service and distribute clients and documentation, and you are off and running. We've added a couple steps to show that you should test things at each step of the way and roll out the pilot incrementally, if possible.

We recommend rolling out the pilot to system administrators before end users. This often provides a good incremental deployment. System administrators, who are relatively few in number—and with whom you should already have a good working relationship—should go first. If things go smoothly for them, begin rolling out the pilot to a small group of end users. If things go well for them, expand the scope of the pilot with other end users.

Always make sure that your feedback mechanisms are in place before rolling out each stage of the pilot. Failure to do this may result in the loss of important feedback and, more importantly, the loss in confidence of your pilot users. Also, be sure to roll out documentation and training as you roll out the pilot to users. Failure to do this can result in confused users, which leads to a bad perception of the pilot.

Collecting Feedback

With your pilot up and running, you need to begin collecting feedback. Keep in mind that this is the whole point of your pilot, so this step is important. There are several different kinds of feedback you can collect:

- *User feedback.* This is among the most important feedback to collect from your pilot. Again, you get only one chance to make that important first impression on your user population. User feedback from your pilot is your one chance to get an early look at what your users think and then modify your system accordingly.

- *System administrator feedback.* System administrator feedback comes from your pilot users administering the directory and its content. Do not underestimate the importance of collecting and incorporating this feedback. It has a direct relationship to the ease with which your directory is maintained. A well-maintained directory is a happy directory.

- *System feedback.* This type of feedback you gather yourself. During your pilot, you should monitor the performance of your servers, your network, and any other relevant system parameters. Collecting and incorporating this feedback makes your production system run more smoothly and perform better.

- *Problem reports.* Make sure you analyze all the failures and problem reports you receive during the pilot. It's a good idea to save these reports and analyze them after the pilot, looking for trends that might be missed if you were to analyze only one problem at a time.

You can use various methods to collect feedback, depending on the type. To collect user feedback, you might use any of the following methods:

- *Interviews.* Interviewing users can provide very effective feedback. An experienced interviewer can obtain much more effective feedback than practically any other method. The downside of this approach is that it is labor-intensive. For an interview be most effective, it needs to be conducted one-on-one. This can be a time-consuming process, but it's a really good idea.

- *Focus groups.* With this mechanism, a small group of users is interviewed about the pilot. This has many of the same advantages as one-on-one interviews, with less of the cost. A great deal of expertise is still needed to conduct effective interviews, but the total time is reduced by the size of the focus group. Finding a convenient time to schedule focus group sessions can be difficult.

- *Online comments.* Setting up an online service through which users can respond is another effective feedback mechanism. You need to find a balance between allowing users a completely free-form comment mechanism and providing a restricted feedback mechanism such as multiple choice. The free-form mechanism allows maximum flexibility, but users are often unclear in their comments if left to their own devices; be prepared to follow up on these unclear comments. The restricted mechanism produces results that are easy to parse and interpret, but it requires that you to ask the right questions and provide the correct choices—a difficult thing to get right.

A good approach may be to use some combination of both methods. You want good feedback, but avoid spending too much time developing fancy feedback mechanisms. Most of what you want can usually be achieved through a simple email-collection mechanism.

You can use the same techniques for collecting administrator and developer feedback that you do for user feedback. Out of all the techniques, you should probably do one-on-one interviews with administrators and developers; because there are relatively few of them, this may be more feasible. Keep in mind that you should ask administrators and developers different questions than you ask your users.

Tip

One important thing to keep in mind when asking for feedback from users and administrators is this: Do not ask for feedback unless you intend to listen. There is nothing more frustrating than to be asked for feedback but then feel that your feedback is ignored. This makes your users feel like they've wasted their time. Of course, this does not mean you need to take every suggestion made during the pilot. Sometimes you will be unable to incorporate feedback for very good reasons. In these situations, be sure to let users know why you didn't incorporate their feedback. When you do incorporate feedback, be sure to tell users about that, too. Remember that your pilot users are busy people just like you. Be proactive in soliciting feedback.

When collecting system feedback, the techniques you use are quite different. Most of the techniques involve collecting data from your automated monitoring sources. Chapter 18, "Monitoring," discusses monitoring of your directory in more detail, but some of the more common and useful techniques are listed briefly here:

- *OS monitoring.* Use whatever tools your operating system provides to measure the general performance of your servers. This includes things such as disk activity, paging activity, memory usage, system calls, and the ratio between user time and system time on the CPU.

  This kind of monitoring is aimed at identifying system bottlenecks. For example, if you notice an inordinate amount of activity on one disk, you might consider switching some files with high write traffic to a second disk on your system. This distributes the write traffic more evenly, reducing the bottleneck. As another example, if you notice a lot of paging activity, you might either buy more memory for your machine or tune parameters on your software to make it use less memory.

  Another way that system monitoring is useful is in evaluating your directory software. Look for unusual activity, especially as you scale up your service. It's better to identify bottlenecks before they degrade your production system.

- *Directory software monitoring.* This technique involves using the directory's own monitoring and audit capabilities to determine how smoothly the system is operating. These capabilities include directory error and access log files, monitoring capabilities through SNMP or via LDAP (for example, using Netscape Directory Server's cn=monitor entry), and any other information the software provides.

- *Directory performance monitoring.* This technique involves direct monitoring the performance of the directory system by using scripts or other tools. The objective of collecting this kind of data is to get a feel for the performance of the directory system itself—the performance that end users experience.

  Important things to look for here are low average response times with small standard deviation. Make sure you measure response time to typical queries so that the data you collect is meaningful.

- *Directory-enabled application monitoring.* This technique involves monitoring the performance of directory-enabled applications that depend on the directory for their own performance. Depending on the focus of your service, this can be very important feedback to collect. For example, if your directory serves the needs of a directory-enabled email delivery service, you'll want to know how well that service is functioning and whether the directory service is a bottleneck.

When collecting data, try to be as analytical as possible. Your hunches about what's good and what's bad about the pilot may well be valid, but there's no substitute for hard data. If the conclusion of your pilot is that you need to increase your budget, for example, having objective data to back up this conclusion is especially valuable.

Scaling It Up

By definition, your pilot is conducted on a smaller scale than your production service. Of course, not every aspect of your pilot is necessarily scaled down from the production version. For example, your pilot may involve only a few users, but the pilot directory servers might contain as much data as the production servers. Be careful to keep this in mind as you interpret data from your pilot.

You should also try to find ways to scale up selected portions of your pilot to increase your confidence in how the system will scale in production. There are several areas in which you can scale up your pilot:

- Number of entries

- Size of entries

- Number of connections

- Number of queries

- Number of replicas

Some of these dimensions can be tested in the laboratory. For example, you can test the number of entries and connections a single server can handle. But it's important to scale up some aspects of the service during the actual pilot while you have users using the service. Sometimes the interaction among several factors may combine to produce unexpected results. The more you can simulate these real-world interactions, the more realistic your scaling tests will be.

You can use many techniques to conduct realistic laboratory scaling tests. First, formulate a model describing the kinds of loads and conditions you want to test, and then develop test clients that simulate these loads. Each test client may make many connections to the directory, simulating many real-world clients. Develop test data that increases the size of your directory. You can increase the number of entries along with their size, the number of values in each attribute, and so on (these don't have to be real entries). Think about your future needs in each area, and focus your testing on areas you think you'll need.

Introduce other factors into the system. For example, load the network links between clients and servers with other traffic. You might accomplish this by writing a special-purpose client or by simply transferring some large files back and forth during your test runs. Most systems have good tools you can use to induce different kinds of loads. For example, `spray` is a good tool for loading the network, and `mkfile` is a good tool for loading the file system. Load the directory server machines with other processes; this will help you understand whether the machine can be shared with other services.

Simulate network and hardware failures during the test by unplugging network cables and power cords. How does the system react? Do clients fail over to directory replicas? Is the directory server able to recover its database? Does replication recover gracefully? These questions are important to answer in any kind of environment, but they become more crucial in a large-scale directory environment. For example, if your directory does not recover gracefully from a power outage, you may have to rebuild the database from scratch. This may be tolerable on a small scale, but for a big directory it can introduce unacceptable downtime.

Watch out for scaling behavior in which the directory system does not degrade gracefully. This kind of "brick wall," when met in a production environment, invariably comes as an unpleasant surprise. For example, consider a directory that can hold only a fixed number of entries or size of database: When these limits are reached, the directory ceases to function. Look for directory software that degrades gracefully as limits are reached.

Applying What You've Learned

Applying what you've learned is the most important aspect of your pilot. After all, the whole point of doing the pilot is to learn how well your design works in practice. Naturally, if you learn of flaws in your design, you should make changes to correct them.

This is especially important during your directory's pilot stage. You will get feedback from your pilot that will change your design. Be prepared to incorporate these changes into the pilot itself, providing a feedback loop to let you know when you get things right.

There are many areas in which you will receive feedback that you should incorporate. Following are some of the more important topics to listen for:

- *User experience.* The directory experience of your users is perhaps the most subjective design criterion your directory service has. Therefore, it is the most important to validate through continuous refinement and user feedback.

- *Operating system configuration.* If you find a problem with your operating system configuration, be sure to correct it and repilot. Do not assume that upgrading to a newer version of the OS will fix the problem you experienced; upgrading may work, but it could also introduce new problems. Be aware of the effect of configuration changes on your directory software.

- *Directory software configuration.* You may find that you need to change the configuration of your directory server software. For example, you may need to tune the software's database parameters to provide better performance. However, make sure that better performance in one area does not degrade performance in another. Does turning on indexing to make the database faster also make it larger? Does making the database smaller to conserve disk space also make it slower? Understand the tradeoffs you are making.

- *Directory-enabled application configuration.* You may find that one or more of the directory-enabled application clients need to be reconfigured or even recoded. For example, the application may be making inefficient use of the directory by opening a new connection each time it wants to do a query instead of reusing an open connection. Or the application may be using several searches when one would suffice. These kinds of inefficiencies can have a life-threatening impact on your directory's performance. Use any leverage you can to encourage application developers and maintainers to make their applications play nice with the directory.

- *Hardware configurations.* You may discover that you need to upgrade your hardware because of capacity or other problems. Be sure to pilot with the upgraded hardware; it may introduce other problems, or it may not solve the problem you thought it was solving. Use your laboratory and your pilot to experiment with different hardware configurations and combinations of hardware and software.

- *Network configuration.* You may discover that the network topology of your directory servers is inadequate. For example, you may find when you do scale testing that you need to move your servers to a high-speed network.

- *Server topology.* You may find that your server topology is inadequate. For example, you may decide you need a replica on each subnet because the networks between clients and the main server subnet are not reliable enough. Or you may find that the distribution topology you planned leads to poor performance. In this case, you may need to cross-replicate or collocate the distributed partitions or alter your namespace design to allow a different partitioning strategy. Be sure to pilot these changes, and make sure your clients are configured to take advantage of the new topology.

Make sure you prioritize the feedback you receive. It's important to incorporate as much feedback as possible and then repilot the service with the design changed accordingly. But you also need to be realistic. You will not be able to incorporate all the feedback you receive. Some feedback is so trivial that there is no need to repilot. Some of it will be bad advice. Some of it will not be practical. And some pieces of feedback may conflict with others. In the latter case, you have to make a choice about which feedback, if any, gets incorporated. Prioritizing feedback enables you to determine which suggestions to incorporate given your limited resources.

As mentioned earlier, be sure to return feedback to those users who have taken the time to provide you with feedback. This will make users happy and more likely to participate in future pilots. It may not be practical to personally answer each suggestion that comes in. If this is the case, publish a summary of the feedback you've received along with your planned response. This is often sufficient to make users feel they are involved in the pilot and that their feedback has been listened to—even if not implemented verbatim.

Piloting Checklist

☐ Select test criteria for scale, performance, and functionality.

☐ Perform laboratory tests for scale, performance, and functionality.

☐ Document pilot goals.

☐ Document a pilot scope.

☐ Document a pilot timeline.

☐ Develop pilot documentation and training materials.

☐ Identify pilot end users and administrative users.

☐ Set up the pilot environment.

☐ Roll out the pilot to users and administrators.

☐ Collect feedback.

☐ Incorporate feedback.

☐ Repeat the last two steps until you feel confident that you are ready to go production.

Looking Ahead

After you've completed your pilot, it's time to roll out your service in production. Before we discuss that topic in Chapter 15, "Going Production," we take a slight detour in Chapter 14, "Analyzing and Reducing Costs," to look at the costs involved with providing your production directory service.

CHAPTER **14**

Analyzing and Reducing Costs

To design, develop, and deploy a successful directory service, you need to have the proper funding. Getting funding from your organization invariably means understanding the costs of the service you plan to deploy, developing a budget, and communicating that information to those who hold the purse strings. Because budgets are often subject to negotiation, it's also wise to prioritize the items in your directory service budget so that you know which aspects of your budget are negotiable and which are not.

In this chapter, we provide an overview of the various costs associated with the phases of a directory service's life cycle. For the purposes of this chapter, we break the life cycle into two major sections: the design, pilot, and deployment phase (everything up to going production); and the maintenance and upgrade phase (everything after production service begins).

This chapter isn't meant to be a comprehensive guide to project planning and budgeting; that topic is adequately covered in other texts (see the "Further Reading" section at the end of this chapter). Instead, we focus on directory-specific costs that you need to consider when planning and budgeting. We also describe ways to reduce costs during your directory's life cycle. Your company may, of course, have a well-established planning and budgeting process in place. If that is the case, use the information in this chapter to assist you as you work with that existing process.

This chapter is necessarily incomplete. Each directory deployment is unique and targeted at meeting specific needs. Your directory may not incur some of the costs described in this chapter, and it may incur some costs we haven't thought of. Use this chapter as a guide to the general types of costs associated with providing a directory service, but be flexible as you think about your particular directory service and its budget.

The Politics of Costs

At some point in your directory service's life cycle, you may be asked to justify its costs, or you may need additional funding to accommodate growth or new applications. Communicating these needs effectively requires that you explain costs clearly and make an effective case for your needs.

When making your case, focus on the benefits that the directory can provide. Translate these benefits into cost savings for the organization, indicating how these represent a return on the company's investment in directory technology. For example, if the deployment of your directory and consolidation of LAN email packages have allowed you to reduce the time spent managing electronic mail accounts from 20 to 2 hours a week, that represents a concrete savings for your organization. There will no doubt be many of these types of cost savings. Collect them all in one document that clearly shows the total savings. In some cases, the directory will pay for itself from the beginning. In other cases, you may be too early in the directory's life cycle to have recovered all costs, but you can calculate the date when costs will be recovered.

To make your case even stronger, be sure to include revenue that is both directly and indirectly generated as a result of the directory. For example, if the directory was leveraged to develop a new application that has spawned a new revenue stream, be sure to allocate a portion of that revenue to the directory itself.

Show how your directory service is being utilized and becoming popular among your users. You might maintain some type of usage data that shows the growth of your service; present the data as evidence that the directory is providing a useful service. If these usage figures are increasing, they make an excellent case for additional funds to cover the cost of upgrading the service to provide additional capacity.

With the information we provide in this chapter, you can make a case that you've deployed your directory service in the most cost-effective manner possible.

Reducing Costs

In today's competitive business environment, efficient processes are vital to an organization's bottom line. Making your directory more efficient makes those business processes that depend on it more efficient. Understanding your directory service's costs is the first step toward making it as cost-effective as possible. In this section, we'll outline some general cost-reduction principles as they apply to directory services. We'll then provide specific suggestions for reducing the costs at each point in the directory service life cycle.

General Principles of Cost Reduction

There are three general principles you should keep in mind when striving to reduce the costs of your directory service:

- Hardware and software costs are generally lower than personnel costs. If one of your staff members feels limited by the available hardware or software, it's almost always best to make an investment to remove that bottleneck. For example, suppose you have an update process that requires manual intervention and runs on a computer with insufficient memory. Greater efficiency would be achieved by purchasing and installing a memory upgrade. The cost of the upgrade may seem high, but when you balance this against the increased productivity of your maintenance staff, you'll often find that these types of investments pay for themselves quickly. Besides, it's also easier to buy a new piece of hardware than it is to interview and hire additional staff.

- Automation of manual processes can save time and allows your deployment and maintenance staffs to concentrate on increasing the reliability and availability of the directory. It also allows new applications to be developed more rapidly. For example, moving from a manual, attended backup process to one that occurs automatically frees up a person's time to do something more useful.

- Your maintenance and deployment staffs are your best resource for identifying opportunities for improving efficiency. They work with the directory each day and routinely see where the system is less efficient than it should be. Involve them in the planning process and solicit their input for ways to reduce the costs of running the directory service.

Design, Piloting, and Deployment Costs

The first half of your directory's life cycle includes all the activity up to the point where you throw the switch and put your directory into production. The costs associated with this phase can be broken down into three major areas: design costs, piloting costs, and deployment costs. In this section we examine each of these areas, describe the specific types of costs, and offer some advice on reducing those costs.

Design Costs

As discussed in Part II, "Designing Your Directory Service," the design phase of your directory's life cycle is when you make many important decisions concerning the scope and structure of your directory service. Costs associated with this phase primarily involve staff but include all of the following:

- *Salary and benefits costs.* These include salary and benefits for you and the staff helping you during the design phase. If your design phase involves people from other groups such as your human resources department, be sure to include salary and benefits costs for them. Quantifying these costs will invariably involve some apportioning of staff time between the various phases of the directory life cycle. Also be sure to budget time for the deployers to become familiar with the software; this ensures that they fully understand its capabilities and limitations.

- *Fees paid to outside contractors.* If you retain the services of consultants to assist you in the design phase of your directory project, include the fees paid to them in your total design phase costs. As with salaries and benefits, if you employ the services of consultants beyond the design phase, you may need to assign portions of the costs to each phase of the project.

- *Cost of research materials.* As you design your directory service, you will no doubt purchase journal subscriptions, special technology reports, and, of course, books like this one to assist you in making good design choices.

- *Software costs.* During the design phase, you may need to purchase one or more copies of the software you plan to deploy. In some instances, you may be able to avoid these costs, perhaps by using evaluation copies of the software.

- *Training and conference costs.* You will probably need to develop in-house directory expertise; therefore, you may incur costs when you send staff members to training seminars and technology conferences.

Reducing Design Costs

In general, you should be careful about cutting costs in the design phase of your directory's life cycle. Studies have repeatedly shown that mistakes made during the early part of a project are significantly more expensive to correct than mistakes made later in the project. If in doubt, look for other expenses to reduce.

You should be aware of the relative efficiency of attempting your directory design process solely using in-house expertise versus involving outside consultants. Evaluate the directory-specific knowledge of your staff who will design the directory. Are they familiar with directory technology, or will there be significant training costs incurred before design can begin? If directory technology is not something your staff is familiar with, it may be better to bring in consultants who can help you with the design process.

Piloting Costs

During the piloting phase of your directory's life cycle, you obtain invaluable information about your directory design. You learn whether your design assumptions are valid and, if they're not, you have the opportunity to revisit your design and make improvements. As in the design phase, reducing costs in the piloting phase is risky; if you don't obtain useful feedback, your design may not be optimal. When reducing costs in this phase, be sure that you do not compromise your ability to obtain and respond to feedback from your pilot users.

The following are common costs associated with piloting:

- *Pilot equipment costs.* Your pilot phase, if properly done, includes an actual small-scale directory deployment. The equipment used to provide this pilot deployment might include CPUs, disks, networking hardware, and other hardware used to provide the pilot service.

- *Pilot software costs.* In some cases, you may be able to perform your pilot using trial versions of software, but in other cases you may need to purchase the software.

- *Staff costs—pilot deployment.* During your pilot phase, you will incur costs associated with installing, configuring, and maintaining the pilot hardware and software.

- *Staff costs—pilot publicity, feedback, and analysis.* During and after the pilot phase, you will incur costs associated with publicizing your pilot, gathering feedback from pilot users, analyzing that feedback, and refining the directory design and deployment plans.

- *Documentation and training costs.* Your users should have documentation available to them during the pilot, including both vendor and in-house documentation. You may also find it helpful to your pilot's success to provide training sessions for your users.

- *Incentives for pilot users.* To obtain the best possible feedback from your directory pilot, you might choose to provide incentives to reward pilot users for their participation and feedback.

Reducing Piloting Costs

The piloting phase of your directory life cycle is your opportunity to validate your directory design and anticipate potential problems before going into full production. Therefore, you should ensure that your pilot program gives you the information required for a successful deployment. If your pilot program doesn't give you this information, you need to either do another pilot or proceed without it. Neither outcome is desirable, of course.

To reduce piloting costs, try to pick your pilot participants carefully, explain very clearly what you expect from them, and tell them how they will benefit from their participation. If you don't obtain useful feedback from your pilot users, your pilot will be much less effective than it could have been. On the other hand, if your pilot participants generate useful feedback that helps you validate your basic assumptions and improves the service before it goes into production, your piloting costs represent money well spent.

Deployment Hardware Costs

During the deployment phase of your directory service, you will purchase the equipment required to provide the full directory service you've been planning. Deployment hardware costs include everything in your infrastructure that is directly used to provide the directory service, including the following:

- *Server costs.* This includes the price of server hardware used to run the directory. Be sure to include the costs of standby units you may purchase as hot or cold spares.

- *Memory upgrades.* If you purchase memory upgrades for your servers from a third-party vendor, be sure to include them in your total deployment costs. If you purchase your memory pre-installed from the same vendor who supplies your servers, memory costs will already be reflected in the price of your servers. Be aware that some server hardware vendors (in particular, those who sell high-end systems) will not honor the factory warranty if third-party options such as memory, disk drives, or network adapters have been installed. Be sure you understand the implications of adding third-party options.

- *Network hardware.* Your servers need to be connected to the network, and the hardware used to accomplish this may include network adapter cards, cabling, hubs, routers, terminal servers for remote maintenance, and other equipment. Of course, some of this equipment may already be deployed in support of other services. You may want to apportion costs

among the various services connected to the directory. For more information, see the sidebar "Apportioning Hardware and Software Costs" later
in this chapter.

- *Hardware used for monitoring functions.* A network management system
  (NMS) may already exist within your organization, in which case you
  may need to allocate a portion of your budget to maintenance and
  upgrades of the existing NMS hardware. If none exists and you plan to
  monitor your directory service, you may need to purchase a system for
  NMS functions.

- *Physical plant.* You need a place to locate the equipment that provides
  your directory service. You will almost certainly locate it with other computing infrastructure services; therefore, you may need to allocate a portion of your budget to the rental costs and upkeep of this facility.

- *Mass-storage devices.* Storage devices for your directory data might include
  disk drives or RAID (Redundant Array of Inexpensive Disks) storage
  units. As with memory, these may be purchased from your server vendor
  or from a third party.

- *Backup solutions.* Directory data must be backed up to protect against disk
  failures and disasters such as fires and floods. Backup solutions might
  include 8mm tape units (sometimes referred to as Exabyte tape drives),
  digital audio tape (DAT) units, or digital linear tape (DLT) units. You may
  also choose to back up to a mirrored disk drive or use replication to keep
  a backup server up-to-date with your directory data.

Reducing Deployment Hardware Costs

There are a number of ways to reduce the cost of hardware used to provide
your directory service. First and foremost, deploy your directory service on
reliable hardware that scales well. This means using server and network hardware that has sufficient capacity for present needs and that can be upgraded to
handle additional capacity. When evaluating hardware vendors, consider the
following questions:

- What is the maximum RAM capacity of this server? Is it sufficient for
  your current and future needs?

- Does the hardware permit the required level of reliability and redundancy? For example, are any necessary hot-swappable disks and power supplies available?

- What mass-storage options are available? Are they sufficient for the size of directory you plan to deploy?

- Do the hardware and operating system (OS) support multiple CPUs? Can additional CPUs be added easily? Does the directory server software take advantage of multiple CPUs?

- Does the operating system for this hardware limit you in some undesirable way? For example, can the operating system support very large files (greater than 2GB)? Can the operating system address a large amount of RAM? Can the operating system handle enough TCP connections to carry the load?

- Are the costs of maintaining the operating system reasonable? Do you have sufficient in-house expertise on the OS platform, and can it be managed efficiently?

- Does the network adapter have sufficient throughput to handle the I/O loads planned? Does the network have sufficient capacity to handle the traffic generated by directory clients and servers?

Purchasing a server without sufficient scaling capacity means that you'll need to replace that hardware at some point in the future. This may be unavoidable considering how quickly CPU speeds are improving and prices are dropping. Ideally, however, you should choose to replace hardware when newer, cheaper, and faster hardware is available and not because your current hardware is overburdened and cannot be upgraded.

Another way to reduce hardware costs is to choose directory server software that runs on multiple hardware and operating system platforms. Choosing this type of software allows you the flexibility to choose the best hardware for the task instead of limiting you to a single hardware and OS platform. But keep in mind that a heterogeneous computing environment is more expensive to maintain than a homogeneous one.

Being creative when negotiating pricing can also help you reduce hardware costs. This may involve purchasing hardware in larger quantities. This approach, of course, may be at odds with deploying your directory in a stepwise fashion, in which you might plan to add additional capacity only as the need arises. However, if you have some idea of how your directory needs will expand, you may be able to negotiate a better price from a vendor by committing to purchase the additional hardware over some period of time. If you can pool your purchases with other projects, you may be able to obtain even more favorable pricing.

Finally, to reduce hardware purchase costs, choose directory server software that is efficient and scales well in terms of:

- The total number of directory entries stored

- The total size of the database

- The average and maximum size of a directory entry

- The maximum number of concurrent client connections supported

- The maximum number of LDAP operations that can be performed in a given time period

Ask the software vendor to suggest reasonable hardware configurations for the directory you plan to deploy. Be sure to provide information both on the number of entries you plan to store in your directory and the type of directory client load you plan to place on the directory. You may find that the minimum hardware requirements vary widely depending on the software vendor. Obviously, a directory that can be deployed efficiently on a single server is less expensive to deploy than a directory that requires data to be partitioned among many servers. Does the server software take advantage of multiple CPUs? Or can additional replicas be easily deployed to handle additional client load? The answers to all these questions will help you understand how hardware costs will be affected by your choice of directory server software.

Deployment Software Costs

To deploy your directory service, you need several different types of software. You may also need to develop custom software for your directory service. Software costs might include the following:

- *Operating system software.* Your servers will require an operating system. Depending on the hardware platform, your OS costs may be one-time costs (possibly with upgrade costs in the future), or they may involve an up-front cost and an annual license or maintenance fee.

- *Operating system enhancements.* To enhance performance and reliability, it may be beneficial to purchase additional software that enhances the operating system. For example, you may purchase high-performance file system software, disk mirroring software, high-availability software, and clustering software.

- *Directory server software.* Directory server software may be priced on a per-server basis, a per-seat (per-user) basis, or some other method. Understand the long-term costs of your vendor's pricing model.

- *Utility software.* You may find it beneficial to purchase utility software to assist you in data maintenance tasks.

- *NMS software.* As described in Chapter 18, "Monitoring," you can use a commercially available NMS package such as Cabletron Spectrum or HP OpenView, or you can develop custom monitoring software. You may be able to leverage an existing deployed NMS system, in which case your costs will be lower.

- *Metadirectory software.* If you need to synchronize a number of dissimilar directories, you may wish to purchase a metadirectory package.

- *Directory client software for end users.* This may include commercially available client software or custom-developed software such as HTML-based interfaces that allow your users to interact with the directory.

- *Development tools for application developers.* If you plan to develop your own directory-enabled applications in-house, you may need to purchase development tools. Generally, LDAP client software development kits are available free of charge, but you may need to purchase compilers, graphical user interface (GUI) libraries, and other utility software needed to develop your applications.

- *Directory-enabled applications.* Along with the deployment of your directory, you may be able to deploy new directory-enabled applications or deploy upgrades to existing applications to make them directory-enabled. More information on directory-enabled applications can be found in Chapters 20, "Developing New Applications," and 21, "Directory-Enabling Existing Applications."

- *Backup and restore software.* Sometimes backup devices are bundled with backup and restore utility software. Even if this is the case, you may decide to purchase a more comprehensive package if you need, for example, to back up remote network nodes automatically to manage a tape carousel or jukebox.

Reducing Deployment Software Costs

As with hardware costs, software costs are often negotiable. Ask the vendor about various pricing options. Is the pricing per CPU? per server? per user? per entry? If multiple pricing options are available, one might be the best choice for your situation now, but another might benefit you down the road. Be sure to look at future growth when deciding on a pricing model.

Better pricing can often be obtained by purchasing additional software from the vendor at the same time. Take the time to find out if your organization is in (or is planning) negotiations with the vendor over other software. A vendor will often provide more favorable pricing when multiple products are being purchased.

Apportioning Hardware and Software Costs

When you consider the various hardware that comprises your directory service, some items are completely specific to the directory service itself whereas others are shared among all parts of your computing infrastructure. For example, if you have a dedicated machine that you run an LDAP server on, the CPU, memory, disks, monitor, and so on, are used solely to provide the directory service. On the other hand, the router that connects the machine room Ethernet to the rest of your network is shared among a number of services.

Similarly, some software may be shared among multiple services. For example, you might have a site license that allows you to install operating system software on a number of systems throughout your organization. A portion of the site license cost should be attributed to the directory service.

When analyzing costs, you might perform a simple calculation to apportion the costs of these shared resources among the various services. If you have a machine room that houses 50 server computers, and 5 of those servers are dedicated LDAP servers, you might allocate 10% (5 divided by 50) of the total machine room costs to the directory service. These costs cover networking (routers, hubs, cabling, monitoring software), power (AC power, uninterruptible power supplies), air conditioning, and staffing costs, if any.

Of course, this calculation can get more complicated. For example, if the attachment of your directory servers requires an upgrade to the router hardware (to handle the additional load), it might be argued that the directory service should assume the entire cost of the upgrade. On the other hand, it's quite likely that some other service will eventually be deployed or expanded, necessitating the upgrade. As with most types of budgeting, there are always opinions on both sides.

Ongoing Costs of Providing Your Directory Service

As soon as the directory service is in production, there are costs associated with maintaining the directory server hardware and software and the directory data. There are also costs associated with supporting end users and scaling the service to meet the needs of a growing company that is developing and deploying new directory-enabled applications.

Software Upgrade Costs

When your directory service is in production, you may need to invest in software upgrades from time to time. Upgrades may be needed for the following software packages:

- *Operating system software upgrades.* As new versions of operating system software become available, you may find it desirable to upgrade in order to obtain benefits such as increased performance or the ability to address larger amounts of memory or disk space. You may also need to upgrade your operating system when you upgrade your directory server software to take advantage of additional functionality.

- *Directory server software upgrades.* Upgrades of directory server software that add additional features, provide better performance, or fix bugs will become available.

- *Directory-enabled application and client software upgrades.* Directory-enabled applications (such as electronic mail server software and groupware applications) and end user client applications may need to be upgraded from time to time. New versions of these applications may require that you also upgrade your directory server software to enable new features.

- *Other software upgrades.* Other software used in support of your directory service may need to be upgraded during your directory's life cycle. Such software might include network management software and metadirectory software.

Reducing Software Upgrade Costs

To reduce software upgrade costs, you can use two techniques: negotiating the best price for the upgrade and deploying the upgrade efficiently.

When negotiating a price for the software upgrades, the same principles apply as when you make your initial software purchase. Volume discounts may be offered, so it is wise to purchase all your upgrades at once or negotiate an arrangement in which you commit to a certain number of upgrades over a set period of time. In some cases, your company may already have site licenses or support contracts in place that either cover the software you need or can be modified to include it at a nominal cost.

The second way to reduce costs is to deploy your upgrade in the most efficient manner. For example, if you need to deploy a new directory-enabled client application to all your users, there are approaches you can use to minimize the amount of staff time required. You might produce a self-extracting archive that users can install themselves (many software vendors distribute their applications in this manner anyway), or you can make use of one of the Enterprise Management packages (Tivoli, for example) to automate the distribution and installation of software packages on end user computers.

Of course, for certain types of software, such as server software, the number of places you need to install the upgrades is small, perhaps only a few servers. In that case, there isn't much efficiency to be gained by streamlining the installation process. In the case of server software, however, you can reduce overall costs to the organization by performing the upgrade in a way that provides the least disruption to end users and business processes. For example, you might schedule the upgrade during off hours when users will not be inconvenienced by unavailability of the directory. Be aware of any automated data maintenance processes that might also be scheduled during off hours, and be certain that these processes can either tolerate a temporary directory outage or be rescheduled to occur after the upgrade is complete.

Hardware Upgrade and Replacement Costs

As the demands on your directory increase, you may find it necessary to add additional capacity to existing servers or replace them entirely. The types of upgrade or replacement costs you may incur include the following:

- *Additional memory for servers.* As the number of concurrent client connections to your directory server increases, you may need to add more memory to your servers to maintain performance. When upgrading servers, keep in mind the number of available sockets for memory expansion. For example, suppose your server has four memory module sockets available. Completely populating all four slots with lower-capacity memory modules means that you will need to remove some of them later should you need to add even more memory.

- *Additional disk space for servers.* If the amount of directory data you need to store increases, you may need to purchase and install additional disk capacity for your servers. This might occur when the number of directory entries increases or if you need to maintain additional attribute indexes. Additionally, if you add more memory to your system, you may need to increase the amount of disk space used for virtual memory paging.

- *Other server upgrade costs.* You may choose to upgrade your servers by adding additional CPUs or switching to faster processors. You may also add more I/O capacity as the demands on your directory increase.

- *Replacement costs for servers.* As newer, faster hardware becomes available, you may decide to replace, rather than upgrade, your server hardware when you need additional capacity. In some cases, you may be able to reuse peripherals such as disk drives on the new servers. In other cases, you may want to replace the peripherals as well.

- *Costs for additional network capacity.* As the usage of your directory increases, you will probably find that you need to upgrade your network hardware at some point. For example, you may need to move from non-switched Ethernet hubs to switched Ethernet, or you may need to provide an additional network segment and router port to handle the increased network traffic created by your service.

- *Upgrade and replacement planning costs.* When you upgrade or replace server equipment, proper planning is required. Be sure to take the costs of this planning into account.

Reducing Hardware Upgrade and Replacement Costs

Just like negotiating a good initial price for your server hardware, you should try to negotiate the best price for your upgrades and replacements. You can also reduce costs when replacing your servers by reusing peripherals. For example, if your old servers use SCSI disk drives, purchasing new servers that also use SCSI disks will allow you to reuse the original disks on your new servers. Of course, you may want to purchase faster disks if performance is a concern. Similarly, using a new server that can accommodate the same memory expansion modules allows the reuse of memory from the old servers—as long as the memory is fast enough for the new hardware.

If you've purchased server hardware that can be upgraded, it may be significantly cheaper to add CPUs to an existing server than to add and manage a second server. Of course, this approach makes sense only if your directory service has become CPU-bound. If your server is I/O-bound, adding another CPU won't be much help.

Costs for hardware can be amortized over the lifetime of the equipment so that the entire cost of new hardware or upgrades need not all be paid for in a single fiscal year. The same principle can also be applied to software purchases and upgrades.

Monitoring Costs

Proper monitoring of your directory service involves the upkeep of your monitoring tools as well as the ongoing staff costs involved when responding to directory problems. The following are some of the monitoring costs you may incur:

- *Pager and cell phone fees.* If you have on-call staff, you probably equip them with pagers or cellular telephones so that they can be contacted in the event of a problem. There are initial purchase costs and monthly charges that must be taken into account.

- *On-call pay.* If your maintenance staff is on-call and must be available to address problems, you will incur additional salary costs.

- *Costs associated with refinement and maintenance of monitoring software.* As your directory service evolves and new servers are deployed, you will need to incorporate monitoring of those servers into your existing monitoring system.

Reducing Monitoring Costs

To reduce monitoring costs, leverage any existing network management infrastructure that might be present in your organization. For example, instead of designing your own directory monitoring system that runs in parallel with an existing monitoring system, integrate your monitoring with the existing NMS. This not only allows you to avoid reinventing the wheel, but it also provides a central focus point where your users and maintenance staff can go to learn about all system failures.

Data Maintenance Costs

Maintaining the data in your directory, which is discussed in Chapter 17, "Maintaining Data," is one of the most important ongoing activities you will perform. Good maintenance of your directory ensures the quality of the data, which in turn improves the usefulness of your service. Following are some of the data maintenance costs you may incur:

- *Personnel costs.* Your data update process may involve manual tasks. For example, you may have a process that requires a computer operator to retrieve a tape containing a dump of personnel data from an administrative mainframe computer, run the data through some sort of transformation, and load the data into the directory. Even if most routine tasks are automated, it's still necessary to periodically review the log files produced by these tasks to ensure that they are functioning properly.

- *Fees levied by data owners.* If your organization is arranged into separate cost centers, the other parts of your organization may charge you for obtaining their data. For example, a human resources division with its own IT staff may charge a fee to extract the data you need to update your directory.

- *Costs of ongoing development data maintenance tools and procedures.* When external data sources change in some way, perhaps moving from mainframe-based databases to a relational database running on a UNIX server, you may need to change your data import tools and procedures at the same time.

- *Metadirectory maintenance.* If you use a metadirectory to synchronize a number of external directories, you will need to spend time maintaining it and its relationships with the foreign directories. Metadirectories are discussed further in Chapter 22, "Directory Coexistence."

Reducing Data Maintenance Costs

To the greatest extent possible, automate your data management systems. The actual way you accomplish this will vary depending on how your data is managed. This section presents a few ideas.

If your directory is routinely updated from some central source, such as a human resources database, automate the update process as much as you can. By using automatically scheduled processes to perform the update, you free up staff to concentrate on more useful tasks. Be certain, however, that the update process provides useful diagnostics when problems are encountered and that someone periodically reviews the diagnostic output. For more information on updating directory data from external sources, see Chapter 6, "Data Design," and Chapters 17 and 22.

It's quite likely that your external data sources are themselves undergoing development and modernization; you should be prepared to deal with such changes. Whenever possible, make data transformation tools flexible. For example, suppose that you need to develop a tool that transforms a table of ASCII data into an LDIF file for import into the directory. If you can make the mapping from column locations to attribute types table-driven, you can accommodate changes in the width of the columns by simply updating a table instead of changing the program code.

Whenever possible and desirable, delegate responsibilities for updating data to departmental administrators or even end users. Of course, this is possible and desirable for only certain attributes, but it may make sense to make those groups responsible for some data updates. This distributes responsibility for data management across the organization and reduces administrative burden.

It also improves the quality of the information in the directory by improving its timeliness.

If you do allow departmental administrators or end users to modify certain attributes, be sure to deploy easy-to-use tools for this task. For example, suppose you have a Web-based application that allows users to change their own entries; such an application could perform validation of the values the users enter and reject invalid data with a helpful message that describes the appropriate format for the data.

Backup and Restore Costs

Keeping your data backed up, as discussed in Chapter 16, "Backups and Disaster Recovery," is an extremely important activity. Safeguarding your mission-critical data involves the following costs:

- *Personnel costs.* You will incur some staff costs associated with performing regular backups. Loading and unloading backup media and performing backup and restore operations are some of the tasks involved.

- *Backup media costs.* You need to have a sufficient supply of blank backup media to accommodate your backup strategy. Also be certain to plan for the retirement of older backup media to prevent failing media from endangering the integrity of your backups.

- *Transportation and offsite storage costs.* A robust backup strategy involves transporting the backup media to an offsite location to prevent its destruction in the event of a disaster. You may incur expenses for shipping the backup media to the remote location and for leasing the storage space.

Reducing Backup and Restore Costs

One obvious way to reduce backup and restore costs is to use an existing backup system if one is already in place. For example, if all your servers are backed up across the network to a central tape drive, backing up the directory servers to this system will be cheaper than deploying a new backup system. The rest of this section, however, assumes that you have decided to purchase and deploy a backup system instead of using an existing system.

When comparing expenses for various backup solutions, consider the cost of the hardware and the cost per byte of the media. In some cases, a backup device that costs more may actually be less expensive to operate over the long term because it is able to store more data on each individual piece of backup media.

Backups protect you against catastrophic data loss. They also can be used to allow end users to recover from incorrect changes made to their own directory entries. However, performing restore operations for end users can be extremely time-consuming and expensive; most backup software does not even provide access to individual entries in a backed-up directory. Usually, the entire directory must be restored to some other location and the required entries extracted. In general, you should avoid setting expectations that backups are to be used for anything other than recovery from catastrophic data loss. You might accomplish this by charging a fee to recover data from backup media.

Disaster Recovery Plan Costs

A well-designed and well-tested disaster recovery plan can protect your critical business processes from certain types of disasters, including floods, earthquakes, and fires. Development and execution of a disaster recovery plan are quite expensive; however, compared to the potential catastrophic business losses that could accompany a disaster, the development costs seem much more reasonable. For more information on disaster recovery, see Chapter 16.

Following are some of the costs you may incur for your disaster recovery plan:

- *Periodic disaster recovery (DR) service fees.* If you utilize the services of a disaster recovery vendor to provide a hot or cold backup site, you will pay that vendor on a regular basis.

- *In-house DR costs.* If DR is provided in-house, you will incur costs associated with providing the directory service portion of the entire DR solution, including space rental and backup hardware and software.

- *DR testing.* When your DR plan is deployed, it should be periodically tested. This testing may be rather elaborate because it requires simulating an actual disaster. A significant amount of planning is involved in the development of the DR test plan, and a significant amount of staff time can be spent performing the actual tests.

- *DR review and update.* Periodically, your DR plan should be reviewed and updated to accommodate new applications or changes in the underlying directory service. If new applications have been developed or your directory service has changed in some fundamental way, it may be necessary to redesign your disaster recovery solution.

Reducing Disaster Recovery Plan Costs

It's certainly possible to design a comprehensive disaster recovery plan that will protect you against most types of disasters and have your business processes back in service very quickly. However, the costs of such a plan may be prohibitive. A cost-effective DR plan takes into account the likelihood of each type of disaster.

For example, you might be deciding where to locate a cold standby location for your major servers. If you are located in an area prone to earthquakes, it probably makes sense to locate the backup site far enough away so that it's unlikely that the primary and backup sites will both be affected by a single earthquake. On the other hand, if your location is not subject to earthquakes (or other large-scale disasters such as hurricanes), you can save money by locating your backup site relatively close to your primary site. In the event that a disaster does render the primary site unusable, it will be less costly to transport your staff to the backup site.

Also consider the acceptable time for putting a backup site into service. Maintaining a hot site certainly offers the quickest turnaround, but is also significantly more costly to maintain and test. If it's acceptable to incur 48 hours of downtime with a cold site versus four hours with a hot site, you can save money by using the cold backup site.

Beyond the disaster plan itself, another way to save money is to weigh the relative costs of contracting with a DR solutions provider versus providing the backup sites yourself. If your organization has only a single location capable of supporting a backup site, it may make more sense to contract with a DR solutions provider. On the other hand, if your organization has several locations with high-speed network connectivity, sufficient power and backup generator capacity, and enough physical space, you may be able to design and deploy your own backup site at a lower cost.

Support and Training Costs

Support and training enable your end users and directory administrators to more effectively use and maintain the directory. Here is a wide range of options for providing training and support, with associated costs:

- *End user support costs.* Providing support for your end users can be accomplished by maintaining an in-house help desk or contracting with an external support provider. Tasks performed include resetting passwords, software troubleshooting, and other general end user support services.

- *Training for end users.* Training your end users may be accomplished in a number of ways depending on the application you're providing training for. For commercially available applications, you may be able to use vendor-supplied training materials or the services of a third-party training organization. You may find that online tutorials are available or that you can send your end users to training classes and seminars. For applications developed in-house, you need to develop your own training materials. These can take the form of seminars, brown-bag sessions, online tutorials, or printed training materials.

- *Training for support staff.* Your support staff will also require training on the various directory technologies used within your organization. The types and sources of training materials are generally the same as for end user training. Unlike end users, however, your support staff will require deeper knowledge and easy access to reference materials such as operations manuals and troubleshooting guides. For applications developed in-house, your application developers may be available to develop a training course for the administrators and help-desk personnel who will support the application.

- *Training for developers.* If you plan to develop directory-enabled applications in-house, you may need to provide training for your developers, especially if LDAP and directory technologies are new to your organization. Developer training resources might include seminars, conferences, and reference documentation.

Reducing Support and Training Costs

Whether your organization provides an in-house help desk or contracts with an external provider of support servers, providing your end users with better information can significantly reduce the number of support calls. Here are some suggestions for accomplishing this:

- Directory-enabled applications should provide clear and helpful error messages when a directory problem is encountered. These messages should state succinctly what the problem is and what the user should do about it. For example, it's better to provide the message "The directory is temporarily unavailable. Try again in a few minutes. If the problem persists, contact 555-HELP" instead of a cryptic message such as "LDAP_SERVER_DOWN."

- Use your intranet to deliver help documents to end users, and advertise their location. If your users know that there is a high-quality collection of help documents online that often answer their questions, you can head off a large number of support calls.

- Use your intranet and your telephone system to deliver status information about your service to your end users. For example, if your directory service is temporarily unavailable, providing this information on a central status page and via a recorded telephone message might reduce the number of calls received by your support desk.

- Providing convenient training for your users can reduce the number of support calls. Seminars and online tutorials are excellent ways to improve end user knowledge.

- Provide good reference material (such as this book) to your directory developers and deployers.

Software Support Contracts and Hardware Maintenance Contracts

Keeping your directory system running smoothly is much easier if all your hardware is functioning correctly and your software is up-to-date. The types of support and maintenance contracts you might purchase include the following:

- *Software support contracts.* Some of the software packages you use to provide your directory service may offer (or require) an annual maintenance fee, which entitles you to bug fixes and support. For example, some operating system vendors offer an online database of patches available only to customers who purchase a support contract.

- *Hardware support/maintenance contracts.* You might choose to purchase a maintenance contract for your server hardware that covers the cost of repairing any failed hardware. These maintenance contracts provide widely varying turnaround times and costs. The advantage of maintenance agreements is that their costs are fixed and can be more easily included in a budget.

- *Self-servicing costs.* An alternative to purchasing a maintenance agreement is to provide your own in-house service. This approach requires that you have adequate knowledge in-house to perform hardware failure diagnosis, and it requires that you have a supply of spare parts for all your servers. It also requires that you have an arrangement with a supplier who will exchange failed modules for new or refurbished modules (for a fee, of course). If you have a heterogeneous computing environment, consider a vendor who can stock parts for a wide range of computing systems.

Reducing Support Contracts and Maintenance Costs

Hardware maintenance contracts vary widely in terms of turnaround time. If you have sufficient extra capacity in your directory service (perhaps you've deployed a number of replicas and have spare capacity) you may be able to tolerate a longer turnaround time for repair or even use a depot service arrangement.

If your organization is very large, it may make sense to provide your own in-house service as just described. If you have sufficient knowledge in-house to consider this option, you may find that it is significantly less expensive than purchasing a service agreement.

Finally, as with the other major purchases you make to deploy your directory service, purchasing support and maintenance agreements in larger quantities may offer some benefits when negotiating prices.

Costs of Adding New Directory-Enabled Applications

If your directory service is successful, it will be widely used by your employees—and possibly by external users, if deployed in an extranet environment. Planning to accommodate new directory-enabled applications and additional load is vital to your directory's continued success. Understanding the costs of these enhancements, which are described in the following list, is therefore also necessary:

- *Additional systemwide capacity for new directory-enabled applications.* Each new directory-enabled application deployed may make additional demands on your directory. For example, if you deploy an extranet application to your distributors, you might use the directory to control access to the application. This means that your directory must be prepared to accommodate directory entries for all the users at your distributors who will use the application. Any type of new application may also place a significant load on the directory. You might choose to deploy a dedicated replica of your directory data for the exclusive use of that application.

- *Development costs for new applications.* Developing a new directory-enabled application has a set of costs associated with it.

- *Deployment costs for new applications.* Putting new applications into production involves piloting the application, developing and distributing documentation, and rolling out the application for general use.

- *Costs associated with planning for expansion.* In addition to the actual costs of capacity expansion, there are costs that revolve around planning for the expansion. These are typically staff costs that involve the process of understanding and planning for the additional capacity needed for new applications.

More information on directory-enabled applications is available in Chapters 20 and 21.

Reducing Costs of Adding New Directory-Enabled Applications

When adding additional capacity to your directory service, use the same techniques you used to obtain the best price for your original hardware. Also, be sure to purchase appropriate hardware for continued growth. For example, if you know that in the future you will need 100Mbps networking to your servers to handle your directory traffic, don't make a large investment in 10Mbps technology that will have to be replaced.

Ongoing costs of application development can be reduced by using sound software engineering techniques. Try to develop reusable components that can be shared by your developers. For example, you might be able to avoid reinventing the wheel by developing or purchasing a utility library that contains code common to all directory-enabled applications. This library can be distributed in binary form and linked with new applications. If bugs are found in the library, they can be fixed by the library maintainer, and a new library can be distributed to the application developers.

Analyzing and Reducing Costs Checklist

- ☐ Understand how your directory service impacts the overall business. How does it save money? How does it cost money? Knowing this information can help you maneuver through the politics of your organization more effectively.

- ☐ Understand the various costs associated with each portion of your directory life cycle—design, piloting, deployment, and maintenance.

- ☐ Hardware and software costs are lower than personnel costs. Reduce bottlenecks that prevent your staff from being efficient.

- ☐ Automate repetitive processes.

- ☐ Seek input from your maintenance and deployment staffs on how efficiency can be improved.

Further Reading

Best Practices in Information Technology: How Corporations Get the Most Value from Exploiting Their Digital Investments. J.W. Cortada, Prentice Hall, 1997.

Effective Measurement and Management of IT Costs and Benefits. A. Money, A. Twite (ed.), and D. Remnyi, Butterworth-Heinemann, 1996.

Information Economics: Linking Business Performance to Information Technology. M. Parker, R. Benson, and H. E. Trainor, Prentice Hall, 1988.

Strategic IS/IT Planning (Datamation Professional Series). E. Tozer, Butterworth-Heinemann, 1995.

Looking Ahead

In this chapter, we provided a sample listing of the various costs your directory service might incur during its lifetime and some suggestions for reducing those costs and making your directory service as efficient as possible. If you understand these costs, you can effectively communicate this information and negotiate the funding you need to handle additional capacity and growth. In the next chapter, "Going Production," we focus on developing a plan for throwing the switch and putting your directory into full production.

CHAPTER **15**

Going Production

Putting your directory service into production is a big step. It is what you have been working toward as you have developed an understanding of directory services and your own needs, created a detailed design, and performed a directory service pilot. Because you get only one chance to make a good first impression, it is important to execute well at this stage.

In conducting your pilot, you learned a lot about what is involved in rolling out and running a directory service. Following are the ways production directory services are different from a pilot directory service:

- *Expectations are dramatically higher.* People expect a higher level of service, including good performance, minimal downtime, and absolutely no loss of data. To meet these expectations, you need to monitor your service and have staff on call to fix problems as soon as they are detected.

- *The audience for your service is significantly larger.* You will add to the early adopters who made use of your pilot a large set of people who view computing services simply as tools to help them get their jobs done. This type of user demands an easy-to-use, well-documented, and well-supported service.

- *The scope and scale of your service may expand greatly.* In a typical pilot deployment, not all the servers and applications that you plan to use in your production service are online. Production servers are also often deployed on larger machines than pilot servers, and the larger machines may require more care and feeding for backups and other maintenance tasks.

- *Monitoring and troubleshooting responsibilities are increased.* The people deploying the directory service have a greater responsibility to keep an eye on the service and be available to fix problems that arise. This is really a consequence of the increased expectations and larger audience for the service.

Throughout this chapter, we assume that your directory service deployment is fairly large and complex. Therefore, we place a lot of emphasis on written plans and communication among the people participating in the production rollout. If your deployment is small, you can safely use less-formal methods of communication. Whether it is large or small, you can win many supporters for your service simply by providing a useful, reliable service right from the start and telling people about it.

The best way to achieve a successful production rollout is to start with a comprehensive plan. The first section of this chapter helps you create such a plan. After that, we present some advice to help you succeed with your production deployment. We finish up with a discussion on how to execute your plan successfully.

Creating a Plan for Going Production

A good production plan covers a lot of ground. Unless the scope and audience for your directory service are extremely small, you should develop a detailed, written plan before going production. Everyone who will be involved in or directly affected by the rollout should participate in the creation and review of the plan.

A good plan for going production includes five major parts:

- A list of resources needed for your rollout.

- Prerequisite tasks that must be completed before the rollout.

- A detailed service rollout plan that indicates what needs to be done, the order in which you will do it, and who will be responsible for completing each task.

- Criteria used to measure the success of your service.

- A publicity and marketing plan.

These five parts of the overall plan are discussed in greater detail in the sections that follow.

List the Resources Needed for Your Rollout

One key to a successful rollout is to make sure all the necessary pieces are in place before you bring up any services. Some of the resources you need to line up include:

- Directory service software, including appropriate licenses and any necessary documentation. Refer to Chapter 12, "Choosing Directory Products," for more information on selecting directory software.

- Hardware, operating system software, and third-party software that will be used to deploy your servers.

- Other infrastructure elements, such as network drops, physical space for servers, uninterruptible power supplies, and systems to enforce physical security of your most important servers.

- Directory management tools to meet the needs of those who manage the directory service. A combination of off-the-shelf products and custom tools developed in house are usually needed.

- Committed administrative staff to perform backups, be on call to respond to service problems, and generally be responsible for the day-to-day care and feeding of the service.

Depending on the specifics of your own environment and the goals for your deployment, you may need additional resources. Create a checklist of all the required resources, and assign a responsible person to ensure that each is obtained before you expect the rollout to begin.

Create a List of Prerequisite Tasks

There are several important things you should do before you start installing servers and rolling out your service. These prerequisite tasks include the following:

- Create a directory service testbed that you can use to simulate server load, try out new versions of directory software, try out design changes, and so on. This testbed should be completely separate from your production service if possible (i.e., locate it on a different part of the network, or use different server and client hardware).

- Obtain the data you will use to populate your directory. Obtaining this data may be difficult and time-consuming if it comes from a source outside your immediate control. If you need to merge data from more than one source, the process of obtaining the data and preparing it for use in your directory service will be even more time-consuming. Hopefully you worked out some of the procedures during your directory service pilot; if not, now is the time to do so.

- Obtain any permission needed to publish the data in your service. For example, you may need to ask your legal department to sign off on your plan for putting end user information in the directory service.

- Coordinate the deployment of any directory applications that will use your directory service. Presumably, these applications will go production at the same time or shortly after your directory service. Alternatively, they may already be in production, but they'll switch to your service from a proprietary directory service or database. Either way, you will need to coordinate with the people who run the directory-enabled applications. Your own group may be responsible for some of the applications, of course.

- Develop a complete set of well-documented, well-understood procedures for backing up and monitoring the directory service (see Chapter 18, "Monitoring," for more information).

- Develop a disaster recovery plan (see Chapter 16, "Backups and Disaster Recovery," for more information).

- Conduct appropriate training for support staff who may be asked to help users.

- Conduct appropriate training for system administrators who may be asked to resolve directory-related problems.

- Develop end user documentation and online help as needed.

- Publicize the service.

Again, depending on your environment and your directory design, there may be additional things you need to do before beginning your production rollout. Create a checklist of everything that needs to be done and include a person responsible for each item. Consider dependencies among the tasks and make sure you prioritize your efforts accordingly.

Create a Detailed Service Rollout Plan

You should create a detailed service rollout plan that indicates what needs to be done, the order in which you will do it, and who will be responsible for completing each task. This plan should include the following information:

- A list of the people who will be directly involved in the production directory service rollout, along with their primary tasks.

- A list of the people who will be indirectly involved in the rollout. This list should include people responsible for directory-enabled applications, help desk staff, and so on.

- A series of tasks for bringing up directory servers. This part of the plan should include the order in which you will bring up the servers and the person responsible for installing each one. For example, you might want to bring up a master server first, followed by three local replicas, followed later by seven remote replicas.

- A series of tasks associated with bringing directory-enabled applications online. Do not plan to bring up all applications at once. A phased approach is safer and more likely to succeed.

- A plan for increasing use of the service by applications and end users. If possible, gradually increase the service load so you can observe the system behavior and make appropriate adjustments before the service becomes overloaded.

- A plan for distributing documentation to administrators, and then to end users.

- A schedule for training end users and administrators.

- Strategies for dealing with problems that might arise, such as unanticipated software or hardware bugs. This is typically documented in the form of an escalation plan that lists whom should be notified about which kinds of problems, and what procedures will be used if critical problems are not quickly resolved.

Depending on the scope of your service, there may be either very few or a large number of people involved in the production rollout. In either case, make sure each person is involved in creating the detailed rollout plan and understands his or her role.

Develop Criteria for Success

While you are lining up all the resources you need, tackling prerequisite tasks, and developing your detailed rollout plan, you also should create a document that lists certain criteria you can use to measure the success of your directory service rollout.

If you already have goals for your directory service (as discussed in Chapter 5, "Defining Your Directory Needs"), use them to formulate criteria by which you can objectively evaluate the success of your production service. Don't be overly ambitious; it is probably sufficient to just jot down a few things you hope to accomplish. Here are some simple examples of production goals:

- To support your most important directory-enabled application without causing any unplanned service outages

- To respond to all directory-related questions from users within 24 hours of receiving them

- To handle 100,000 searches per hour on your busiest server with no unexpected errors and an average response time of one second or less

- To teach every administrative assistant in your organization how to use a new phonebook application powered by your directory service

- To get 50% of the people you trained on the phonebook application to use it to make a change to an employee's entry within the first month of your production service

It is best to keep your success criteria simple. Share the criteria with the other members of your deployment team so that everyone is aware of the big picture. Make sure all the criteria are measurable; it is important to know if you are meeting or failing to meet your targets.

Create a Publicity and Marketing Plan

Before you begin your production rollout, you should develop a publicity and marketing plan for your new directory service. Your two major goals in this area should be to make people aware of the new service and encourage them to use it.

Publicity can take many forms. A few well-crafted articles for the company newsletter or postings to appropriate discussion groups may be all you need. On the other hand, you might want to make a bigger splash by hosting a directory service party. If your organization holds brown-bag meetings or any other type of training sessions on computing topics, you should sign up to lead a session or two to promote your new service and educate people about it.

Some of the topics you may want to cover when spreading the word about your directory service include

- The basics of directory services and LDAP (for the uninitiated)

- Quick-start information on how to use the service

- How your directory service is being used now

- How you expect usage to grow in the future

- The extensive design and piloting work that was done by your team to prepare for a smooth production rollout

- All the help your directory services team had from other groups within your organization (don't forget to say thanks!)

- What a great new online service your team has created and how everyone benefits from it

It is important to tailor your publicity and marketing efforts to meet the needs of the intended audience. In practice, this means that you may need to develop separate materials for the end users, directory application developers, system administrators, executives, and so on.

If possible, enlist the marketing people who work for your organization to help draft your publicity plan and create appropriate materials. You should also consider whether you are willing to serve as a reference customer for any of your directory software suppliers. By doing so, you may be able to generate some external publicity about your organization and foster a better relationship with the supplier.

In summary, the deployment of a production-quality LDAP directory service is a major milestone for your organization. Make sure people know about it. There is nothing wrong with congratulating yourself and your team on a job well done while simultaneously raising awareness about your new service!

Advice for Going Production

There are a few more things you should consider before you begin to execute your production plan. In this section we present some advice that will help you avoid mistakes others have made and achieve a smooth rollout of your production directory service.

Don't Jump the Gun

The most important advice we can give is *Don't go production until you are ready.* The biggest mistake people often make is to skip one or more essential design steps. This usually leads to a deficient, hard-to-maintain service. You might find that you need to go back and perform the steps you left out and then redeploy your entire service. In the long run, the time you save up front by skipping some of the directory design work will be greatly outweighed by the aggravation you cause yourself and the users of your service.

The other major preproduction task that many are tempted to omit is the directory service pilot (described in Chapter 13, "Piloting Your Directory Service"). A pilot service is the best way to prove your directory design and learn what it's like to run a production service. By creating a pilot service and heeding the lessons learned, you will greatly increase the chances of success for your production service.

Don't Lose Focus

Another common mistake is to lose focus and forget what you are trying to accomplish. Always keep your production success criteria in mind as you proceed with your deployment. Remind yourself who your most important users are and think about what you need to do to meet their needs. Work diligently to ensure that your most important directory-enabled applications succeed. The success of your service is linked closely to the success of those applications.

Adopt an Incremental Approach

One of the running themes throughout this book is that an incremental approach is more likely to succeed than an all-or-nothing approach. This is especially true when rolling out a production directory service. Don't try to add too many dependent applications the first day your service is up and running. Don't create unrealistic expectations by overhyping your service. Don't try to roll out all the replicas your design includes in the first few days of service; adopt a phased approach and ensure that each new part of the service is working before increasing the complexity of the system.

Prepare Yourself Well

There is an old story about a passenger train engineer who was faced with a crisis. While traveling with a full complement of passengers at high speed, his train came upon a single empty freight car that someone had mistakenly left on the main track instead of on a nearby siding. The situation is depicted in Figure 15.1.

Without missing a beat, the engineer immediately increased his engine speed to full throttle. His passenger train struck the empty freight car at nearly full speed, knocking it off the track and out of the way and avoiding derailing his own train.

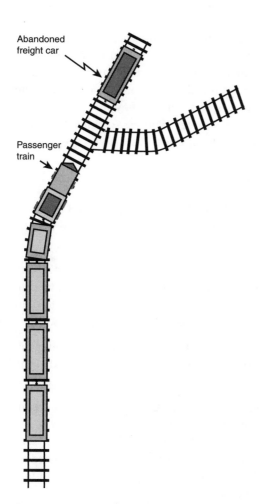

FIGURE 15.1 *A dangerous situation.*

After the incident, when the engineer was asked how he knew to increase his speed, rather than try to stop, he had a ready answer: "I knew how far I was from the empty car because many times in the past, as I passed by that same stretch of track, I imagined that same exact situation and thought about what I would do. I knew that if I was too close to stop in time, I should increase my speed because the impulse created by striking the empty car would most likely drive it off the track and safely out of the path of my own train. I didn't have to think about any of this at the time of the crisis because I already knew exactly what to do."

The moral of the story is, of course, be prepared for whatever might come your way. This is good advice, and you should apply it to your production directory service. You should think ahead and prepare yourself as much as possible for your production rollout. Consider what is likely to go right and how things might go wrong. Play "what if" games and consider how you will adapt to any situation that arises, and change your strategy if necessary. Like the train engineer, you will be able to act very quickly and decisively if you prepare yourself.

Potential problem areas to consider include the following:

- *Bugs in hardware or software.* If these crop up, you may need to adjust your design to work around the problem, or you may just need to wait for a bug fix from a vendor.

- *Flaws in your design, software, or hardware that lead to inadequate capacity for your service.* If you can afford it, pad your estimates so you have extra capacity. If necessary, be prepared to slow down your rollout to reduce the load on the system until you can install additional servers.

- *Unexpected hardware failures.* This will lead to inadequate capacity or complete disruption of your service. If you can arrange it, have extra hardware lined up that you can borrow in case an unexpected failure occurs.

- *Changes in the requirements for your service.* Any major change in requirements will require you to take a step back and consider how you need to adjust your rollout plans. For example, if you find out that your service must support a new directory-enabled application, you may need to reconfigure servers to add new schemas, configure additional indexes, or make other changes to accommodate it.

- *Staffing shortages.* These might occur because of illness, family emergency, or people being called away to address problems in other production systems they are also responsible for. You can reduce the pain caused by a staffing shortage by ensuring that each person involved in your directory service rollout has trained another person who can handle his or her tasks in an emergency.

Be realistic about the risks involved in your production plan, and think about how you will detect problems and what you will do if they occur. Make sure you inform your management and the owners of directory-dependent applications and services of the risks so they are not surprised by the problems or your actions.

As an example of the kind of thinking you should do, suppose your design calls for you to roll out five replica servers to provide service to a busy directory-enabled mail delivery service. Consider what you would do during your production rollout if you found a critical bug in your directory service software that prevents you from creating more than three replicas. Clearly this would reduce the capacity of your service. You must decide whether three replicas would be able to handle the application load long enough to get a patch from your directory server software vendor, or if instead you would need to scale back the mail service—or possibly delay your directory service rollout entirely. Depending on the situation, any of these options might be the best choice. By thinking about the options in advance, you will be able to act quickly and decisively if problems occur during your rollout.

Executing Your Plan

The final step is to roll out your production service. This involves executing each of the five pieces of your production plan:

1. Gather needed resources.

2. Perform prerequisite tasks.

3. Roll out the service.

4. Check your progress against your success criteria.

5. Publicize your new service.

You may want to have extra resources at your disposal during the early stages of your rollout. Access to spare people and machines will help you recover more quickly if someone or something fails unexpectedly. In general, be prepared to react quickly if anything goes seriously wrong.

You should also make sure you know where to turn for outside help. Create a list of contact information for hardware vendors, directory software vendors, suppliers of other software you are using, and anyone else whom you may need to ask for help if you encounter a problem or need help configuring your service. During the most critical phases of your rollout (e.g., when your first important directory-enabled application comes online and begins using your directory), we suggest that you put on alert the people you may need to turn to for help.

Hopefully your rollout will go smoothly, but it is possible that it will not. You may, for example, encounter a critical bug that did not show up during your pilot. Or you may find that some part of your design just won't work with the software you have or in the environment in which the service needs to run. If this happens, do not despair. Regroup and consider whether you need to revisit your design or conduct another pilot before proceeding with your production rollout. It is important to know what kind of problems would lead you to halt the rollout and which ones could be dealt with while the rollout proceeds.

Finally, remember to keep everyone informed about your progress. Communicate openly with your management, colleagues, developers, and end users about how the production rollout is proceeding. Try not to promise more than you can deliver. After you have met all or most of your success criteria, let everyone know that you consider the directory service to be in production. And don't forget to thank everyone for their hard work and help in reaching this major milestone!

Going Production Checklist

❏ Make sure your directory design is complete.

❏ Perform a directory service pilot.

❏ Create a plan for going production:

    ❏ List the resources needed for your rollout.

    ❏ Create a list of prerequisite tasks.

    ❏ Create a detailed service rollout plan.

    ❏ Develop criteria for success.

    ❏ Create a publicity and marketing plan.

❏ Prepare for possible problems.

❏ Execute your production plan:

    ❏ Gather needed resources.

    ❏ Perform prerequisite tasks.

    ❏ Roll out the service.

    ❏ Check your progress against your success criteria.

    ❏ Publicize your new service.

Looking Ahead

With this chapter we wrap up Part III, "Deploying Your Directory Service." Hopefully you are now well on your way to deploying a production-quality directory service. In Part IV, "Maintaining Your Directory Service," we will move our focus to the maintenance of your directory service. The topics covered in the next four chapters include backups and disaster recovery, managing your data, monitoring your service, and troubleshooting directory service problems.

PART **IV**

Maintaining Your Directory Service

## CHAPTER 16

Backups and Disaster Recovery

The data contained in your directory is (or soon will be) critical to the day-to-day operation of your organization. If that data becomes unavailable through equipment failure or data corruption, your business's bottom line could suffer. Developing sound backup and restoration procedures safeguards your important data from damage. In addition to a backup strategy, you should have a disaster recovery plan that details the procedure for your organization to put its directory systems back in service after a disaster such as a fire or flood.

Of course, comprehensive backup and disaster recovery plans involve all the various information technology (IT) services provided, including file systems, databases, and applications. We won't attempt to provide a comprehensive guide to backup and disaster recovery in this chapter. Instead, we'll focus on the specifics of backing up and restoring directories, and how these procedures differ from other backup/restore procedures you may be familiar with. We'll also discuss disaster recovery procedures as they pertain specifically to your directory. With this knowledge, you should be able to incorporate your directory into your established backup/restore and disaster recovery plans.

Backup and Restore Procedures

Like file systems and databases, a directory's data is stored on disk drives. This data can become damaged for a number of reasons, including the following:

- *Disk drive media or controller failure.* The magnetic media on which the directory data is stored can fail, resulting in corruption or total loss.

- *Software bugs.* The directory software or operating system may have a bug that corrupts the data in the database.

- *Erroneous applications.* Directory applications can go haywire, placing incorrect data in the directory or deleting directory entries that should not be deleted.

- *Operator error.* Files or directory entries and attributes can be inadvertently erased.

- *Theft.* Your directory server equipment and the data stored on it can be stolen.

- *Disasters.* These include fires, floods, and earthquakes, which can completely destroy all your equipment.

If one of these unfortunate events happens to your directory, you need some way to recover. You can accomplish this by restoring a backup of your directory data to the affected servers.

There are two ways you can back up your directory data: by using traditional backup techniques such as tape backups and disk mirroring, or by using directory replication. Each approach has advantages, and a comprehensive backup approach that aims to provide high availability benefits from using both approaches simultaneously. We'll discuss the advantages of each approach throughout this chapter.

Backing Up and Restoring Directory Data Using Traditional Techniques

Just like user files stored on a file server, your directory data should be backed up to some sort of medium such as magnetic tape. You can also back up to an alternate disk drive that is local or over the network. The backups can be used to restore the data in the event that data damage or loss occurs.

However, backing up a directory is different from backing up a file system in several important ways:

- File servers are usually much larger than directories; therefore, more data needs to be backed up. This means that it's usually feasible to back up your directory by copying it to an alternate disk, whereas file system backups generally require the use of higher-capacity backup media such as tape. However, very large directories, which may be many gigabytes in size, cannot be copied to an alternate disk.

- Unlike file systems, directories are frequently replicated, so it's important to understand the implications of restoring a replica from a backup tape. In most cases, it's better to rebuild a damaged replica from its peer replicas than to restore it from a backup tape; the data in the peer replicas should be more up-to-date.

- The tools provided to back up directories generally do not support incremental backup, in which only the data that has changed since the last backup is copied to tape. This may change in the future; but for now, directories are generally backed up as a unit.

- The directory service may be spread across a number of individual servers. To back up the entire service, you must either back up all the servers individually or back up all the directory data from a central location.

Your actual backup procedure depends on the particular directory server software you use. Backing up Novell Directory Services (NDS) server data, for example, is accomplished using an SMS-compliant backup utility in conjunction with NetWare Loadable Modules (NLMs) on each NDS server. The NDS backup utility reads the directory contents over the network and copies the data to a backup device.

Backing up Netscape's Directory Server is accomplished by running the `ns-slapd db2archive` utility, which creates copies of the database files in a backup directory. The contents of this directory can then be copied to tape, if desired.

Both NDS and Netscape Directory Server backups can be performed while servers are online and being updated. Other directory software may require that you shut down the server or place it in read-only mode to obtain a consistent backup. This is undesirable, of course, because it introduces downtime. Consult the directory server vendor's documentation for details.

It is also possible to back up a directory using mirrored disks. In a mirrored system, any writes to the disk are performed on a primary disk or disk array, as well as a *mirror*, or second copy of the data. In the event that the primary disk or disk array fails, the mirror can be used as a backup.

Note

Even if you use mirroring to back up your directory data, you should also use backup media that can be transported offsite. A backup of your critical directory data isn't much good if it goes up in flames with all of your servers!

Another way to back up your directory data is to read all the entries using the LDAP protocol and write them to disk or tape. For example, you can use the Netscape `ldapsearch` command-line utility to read all directory entries underneath `dc=airius, dc=com` in the following command:

```
ldapsearch -h directory.airius.com -p 389 -D "cn=Directory Manager"
➥ -w secret -s sub -b "dc=airius, dc=com" "(objectclass=*)"
```

> **Note**
>
> This command should all be typed on a single line; it doesn't appear on one line in this book because of page size constraints.

The example `ldapsearch` command connects to the LDAP server running on port 389 on host `directory.airius.com`, authenticates as `cn=Directory Manager` with password `secret`, and performs a subtree search rooted at `dc=airius, dc=com`. (These parameters should be tailored for your environment.) The filter, `(objectclass=*)`, matches any entry.

Assuming that `cn=Directory Manager` has read privileges on all entries within the subtree `dc=airius,dc=com`, the server will respond by sending all entries, and the client will generate LDIF output that can be redirected to a file or tape.

There are some caveats with this approach. First, the `ldapsearch` command as given would not return any operational attributes such as `modifiersname` and `modifytimestamp`. These attributes must be explicitly mentioned on the command line. This can be accomplished by adding to the command line as follows:

```
ldapsearch -h directory.airius.com -p 389 -D "cn=Directory Manager"
➥-w secret -s sub -b "dc=airius, dc=com" "(objectclass=*)" "*"
➥modifiersname modifytimestamp creatorsname createtimestamp
```

The additional arguments at the end of the command line specify that all user attributes are to be returned (as called for by the `*`), along with four operational attributes (`modifiersname`, `modifytimestamp`, `creatorsname`, `createtimestamp`).

The second caveat is that the command-line utility may return entries that do not reside on the specified server. This can happen if your directory is distributed across multiple servers using chaining or referrals (as discussed in Chapter 9, "Topology Design"). Receiving these entries may be what you want, of course, if your aim is to copy all your directory entries across your whole distributed directory. If this is not what you want, you can use the `-R` command-line flag to `ldapsearch` to instruct it not to follow referrals. If your directory uses chaining, however, there is no way to ask for entries that are local to only one server.

A third caveat is that if the directory is modified while the backup is taken, certain inconsistencies may result. For example, if a group references members, those members may not appear in the backup snapshot if they are added while the directory was being backed up.

The final caveat is that data backed up in this manner is likely to be incomplete. There may be quite a bit of additional information stored in the directory to support its operation, such as superior and subordinate knowledge. The manageDSAIT control, available on LDAPv3–compliant servers, can be used to access this type of data (this control is discussed in Chapter 3, "An Introduction to LDAP").

The bottom line is that backing up data over LDAP may not produce a backup that can be used to recover from complete data loss. However, this type of backup is quite useful in protecting against problems that arise as a result of erroneous information in the directory.

Other Things to Back Up

Although backing up your critical directory data is important, it's likely that there is additional information you should back up. For example, you should back up your configuration files for your directory server when you back up your directory data; re-creating them from scratch would be a time-consuming experience. Additionally, your directory schema configuration and access control information may reside in separate files or databases; be sure these are backed up as well. Consult your directory server documentation to learn about other configuration files and data you should back up.

Tip

When maintaining a complex set of configuration files like those in most directory server software, it's beneficial to keep a history of changes made to them. This allows you to revert to an older version of the configuration if an error is made. One way of accomplishing this is to use a revision control system such as SCCS, RCS, or CVS (all of these are available on UNIX platforms). Revision control systems allow you to retrieve any previous version of a file's contents and determine who made a particular change. Such tools can also help protect against erroneous configuration changes.

Backing Up Netscape Directory Server Configuration Data

Netscape Directory Server stores all of its configuration data within a single directory named `config` underneath the server instance directory. For example, if the directory server is installed on a UNIX host in a server root directory named `/usr/netscape`, and the server instance name is `directory`, configuration files for the server are stored in the directory `usr/netscape/slapd-directory/config`. Backing up this configuration data can be accomplished by copying all the files in that directory to a backup location such as a remote disk drive or a tape. You can use the UNIX `tar` (tape archive) utility to place all the configuration files into a single archive. For example, if you wanted to back up all the configuration files and place the `tar` archive in the directory `/n/backups`, you could use the command `tar cf/n/backups/slapd.config.backup.tar/usr/netscape/slapd-directory/config`.

Using Replication for Backup and Restore

Although traditional backup techniques can protect you against many types of problems, they have one major drawback: Restoration of data is time-consuming. Copying data from the backup media to the server may take many minutes or even hours for a large directory. However, if you use replication as your primary means of providing redundancy and fault-tolerance, you can avoid the costly downtime that would be required for the restoration phase.

Because replicas are online copies of your critical directory data, no delay is incurred while data is being restored from backup media. If a server fails, you can simply remove it from the set of replicas and repair the failure. After the server is repaired, you can bring it back online and re-establish it as a replica. Users will generally be unaware of the problem—as long as there is sufficient capacity across the remaining replicas to handle the client load.

Using replication for backup and restoration has another advantage: Directory data are usually more up-to-date on replicas than on backup tapes. Of course, most directories support loose replica consistency; that is, it's possible for changes to be held on a replica for some time before being propagated to other replicas. Thus, there is no absolute guarantee that all replicas are completely in sync at any given time.

Directory server software that supports multi-master replication makes this backup procedure simple. Because any server can accept updates in such a configuration, there is no loss of functionality when a server is missing from the replica set. The process of repairing a failed server in a multi-master environment is depicted in Figure 16.1. In the situation depicted, replica 3 experiences a failure of its disk drive. The server is removed from the set of replicas, and the disk drive is replaced. The replica is added to the set of replicas as soon as its directory data is reinitialized from one of the other replicas.

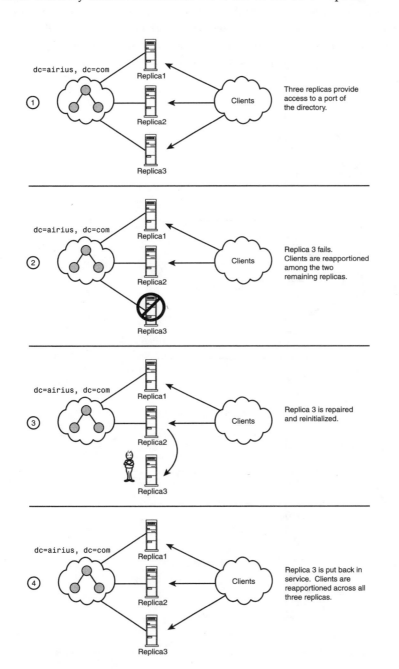

FIGURE 16.1   *Multi-master replication provides protection against server failure.*

If your directory server software supports only single-master replication, the backup process can become a bit more complicated. In single-master replication, only the master server can be updated; all other servers are read-only copies. If the master server fails, no updates can be processed by the directory until the master is repaired and brought back online (see Figure 16.2), or until a different server is designated as the master (see Figure 16.3).

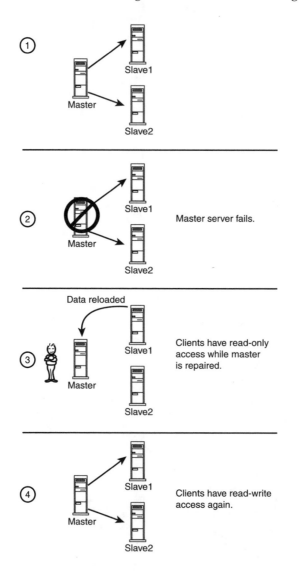

FIGURE 16.2   *Single-master replication: A master server fails, is repaired, and is brought back online.*

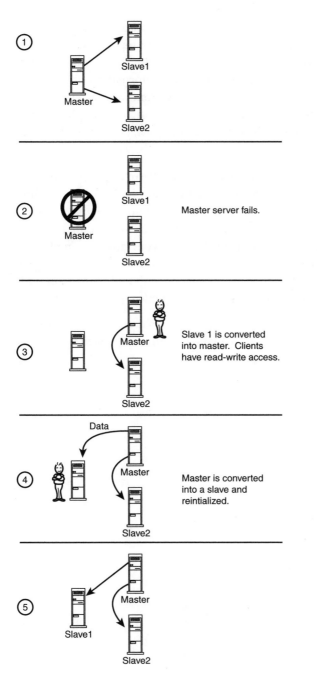

Master server fails.

Slave 1 is converted into master. Clients have read-write access.

Master is converted into a slave and reintialized.

FIGURE 16.3   *A master server fails, and a slave server is converted into a master.*

Converting a slave server to a master can be a complicated process. At the very least, it involves configuring the new master to send replication updates to all the consumer servers covered by the failed master (excluding the new master). Additionally, it may be necessary to update state information stored in each replica, such as the last update number received from the master, to reflect the update numbers on the new master. Because this can be a complicated procedure, be sure you understand the process thoroughly. For more information, consult your directory server software manual.

Using Replication and Traditional Backup Techniques Together

Although replication provides you with redundancy and high availability in the event of a single server failure, it cannot protect you from incorrect data being placed in your directory. For example, if an automatic data update process begins erroneously deleting entries from your directory, replication unfortunately ensures that these incorrect updates end up on all your replicas! To protect yourself from this type of problem, you should perform periodic backups of directory data to media such as magnetic tape.

A hybrid approach that uses both backup methods is shown in Figure 16.4. One of the replicas is equipped with a tape backup unit, which is used to back up the directory contents periodically.

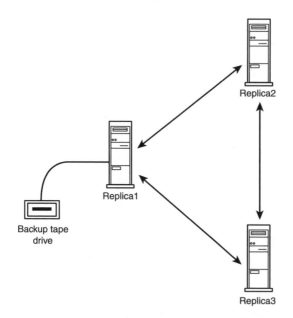

FIGURE 16.4 *A hybrid approach to backup, incorporating both replication and traditional backup techniques.*

Safeguarding Your Backups

It's important to keep your backup media in a safe place. This means protecting them from damaging environments such as extreme temperatures and magnetic fields. You should also keep copies of your backups offsite. In the event of a disaster such as a fire, the offsite backups can be used to restore data to replacement servers. You can outsource the transportation and storage of offsite backups to reduce costs. We'll discuss disasters and disaster recovery in detail later in this chapter.

Another important aspect of safeguarding your backups is the physical security of the backup media storage facility. No matter how good your privacy and security design, it is all for naught if someone can just stroll up to your cabinet holding the backup tapes and walk off with a copy of your sensitive directory data. Backups should be well-secured; this might mean placing backups in a locked, fireproof vault in an offsite facility and using a bonded courier service to transport the backups.

Finally, consider storing your offsite backups in a location that is unlikely to be affected by a natual disaster that damages or destroys your main location. For example, an offsite backup storage facility 10 miles away may be adequate in the Midwestern United States, where the primary natural disaster is severe weather. In California, where the primary concern is earthquakes, it may be prudent to store offsite backups at a location in a region that is less active seismically.

Verifying Your Backups

Backing up your critical directory data is very important. However, the act of backing up is futile if the backups can't be restored. You need to take steps to check the integrity of the backups you produce. At the very least, check that your backup media are readable and free of media errors.

How you verify your backups depends on the server software you use. One option is to actually restore the backup onto a test server, start the server, and then verify that the contents of the server are correct. This may not always be practical, however. For example, the NDS backup copies data from the entire set of distributed NDS servers onto a single backup. Restoring the directory to a test server may be impractical because of the number of partitions in the directory; it may be difficult to fit them all onto a temporary server used for verification. If you run NDS, consult your backup software documentation for instructions on verifying backups.

You should verify backups immediately after the backup completes. If the verification fails, the cause of the failure should be determined and fixed, and another backup should be performed immediately. You may also want to incorporate your backup process into your monitoring system so that you'll know if something goes wrong.

You should be especially careful to fully verify your backups when you initially develop and deploy your backup procedure or change it in some significant way. Backup software, like any other software, can contain bugs. It's always better to discover this, and other flaws in your backup procedures, before you need to restore critical directory data from a bad backup.

Disaster Planning and Recovery

Businesses are becoming more and more dependent on directories to the point where they will simply be unable to function if the directory becomes unavailable. What happens if the data processing center of your organization falls victim to a fire, a flood, or sabotage? How will you restore critical directory services?

Developing a comprehensive recovery plan is the best way to anticipate and prepare for business continuity in the face of a disaster. There are a number of books covering this subject, along with a number of disaster recovery vendors (also known as business continuity services), including SunGard Recovery Services, IBM Corporation, and Comdisco Incorporated. These vendors and others like them can help you plan and implement disaster recovery procedures.

In this section we provide a brief overview of disasters and disaster recovery planning, and we discuss how planning for directory disasters differs from other types of disaster planning. Then we discuss specific issues that can help you design and implement your directory disaster recovery plan.

Types of Disasters

A disaster is any occurrence that destroys your computing infrastructure or makes it inaccessible for an extended period of time. Examples include the following:

- Fires

- Severe weather, such as hurricanes, tornadoes, and severe storms

- Earthquakes

- Extended electrical power outages

- Hardware or software errors that cannot be fixed within a reasonable time period

- Floods

- Burst pipes

- Explosions

- Chemical spills

- Airplane crashes

- Riots

- Sabotage

- Terrorist attacks

Developing a Directory Disaster Recovery Plan

When you develop a plan for directory disaster recovery, you should follow a methodical process similar to these steps:

1. Perform a risk assessment, ranking risks from most likely to least likely.

2. Understand the business implications of each type of risk.

3. Design and implement the recovery solution.

4. Periodically review and update the plan.

Each of these steps is explained in detail in the following sections.

Step 1: Perform a Risk Assessment and Rank the Risks from Most Likely to Least Likely

When planning for disaster recovery, the first questions to ask yourself are "What risks does the computing infrastructure face?" and "How likely is each risk?" For example, if your data center is located on a hill, flooding is probably unlikely. On the other hand, if the data center is in the San Francisco Bay area, earthquakes are a risk that must be taken into account.

Ranking your risks allows you to make rational decisions about whether you should attempt to protect against that risk. Although it would be nice to provide protection against every conceivable risk, it's probably not economically possible. Understanding which risks are more important to address allows you to allocate your disaster preparedness resources wisely.

For some risks, you may decide that pre-emptive measures are appropriate. For example, if your location is subject to frequent electrical storms and power failures, you may decide to invest in a generator that can provide an alternate power source during extended power failures.

Step 2: Understand the Business Implications of Each Type of Risk

For each type of disaster, think through its implications and how it will affect your organization's business processes.

For example, assume that your directory service is completely destroyed by a fire and that it takes three business days to obtain replacement hardware and restore the directory data from backup tapes. What are the business implications of this three-day delay? What business processes are halted by the unavailability of the directory? Such impeded processes might include

- Delivery of email (inbound mail from the Internet will typically be returned to the sender if your electonic mail servers are continuously unavailable for three or more days)

- Any processes that depend on the timely delivery of email

- Login to your intranet and extranet applications

- Any intranet or extranet applications that use the directory for authentication

Next, you need to understand the implications of directory failure—and what that means for your bottom line. In other words, if the directory is unavailable, how much money will the business lose as a direct consequence of the failure? Will customers switch to an alternate vendor because you cannot provide the goods or services they require? Are there contractual obligations that you must meet even in the face of a disaster? With this information, you can determine the recovery times you need to target.

For example, you might determine that the maximum acceptable directory downtime is 24 hours before the business begins to suffer significant losses. When you know the potential costs of *not* having a disaster recovery solution, you can begin to weigh them against the costs of a recovery solution.

Step 3: Design and Implement the Recovery Solution

The next step is to design the actual recovery solution and understand its costs. You can choose to design and implement the recovery plan yourself, or you can use the services of a disaster recovery vendor to design and/or implement the plan.

Disaster recovery vendors typically offer both "hot" and "cold" recovery solutions. A *hot site* is kept up-to-date with your latest data and application software, and it can be put into service very quickly. A *cold site* contains sufficient equipment to meet your computing needs, but it is not kept up-to-date; your computing environment must instead be re-created at the cold site after the disaster recovery plan goes into effect. Additionally, disaster recovery vendors offer mobile recovery solutions, in which a portable data center can be driven to your site in the event of a disaster.

Hot sites and cold sites each have advantages and disadvantages. A hot site can be put into service much more quickly than a cold site because all the data is up-to-date and ready to go, whereas a cold site requires that data be transported to the remote site, the needed software installed, and the data restored. As you might expect, it is much more expensive to maintain a hot site, especially if you contract with a disaster recovery provider. Assuming that not too many customers experience simultaneous disasters, a disaster recovery provider can use a single cold site to support a number of businesses—lowering the cost for the customers. A hot site, on the other hand, must be dedicated to a single customer, which makes it much more expensive.

Step 4: Periodically Review and Update the Plan

Finally, after the recovery plan is implemented, it must be periodically reviewed and updated as your business requirements change and as new applications are developed and old ones retired. The plan should be reviewed at least annually, and more often if your organization deploys new applications frequently.

The disaster recovery procedures should also be tested and repaired if they are found to no longer work. Some organizations even go so far as to simulate an actual disaster to exercise the recovery procedures. Your disaster recovery tests should be in line with your disaster recovery needs; very stringent needs dictate more rigorous testing.

Directory-Specific Issues in Disaster Recovery

A cold-site disaster recovery plan for a directory is much like that for the other critical data repositories you might use. The recovery procedures are, for the most part, like recovering a database. If you use a cold site, directory server software must be installed on the replacement machines, and backup tapes containing the directory data must be restored.

With hot-site disaster recovery, however, directory replication offers unique opportunities to improve recovery time significantly. By using directory replication to maintain the hot standby servers, your directory can be made available much more quickly. For example, if you use directory replication to maintain hot standby replicas, no recovery at all is necessary; because the replicas are always updated, they are ready to take over at a moment's notice.

This does *not* mean, however, that it's impossible to lose transactions when using replication. It's certainly possible that a server at the primary site could be destroyed before it has a chance to transmit all its replication updates to its peers. This is especially true if replication is performed infrequently because directory replication is loosely consistent, as discussed in Chapter 10, "Replication Design." If this is a serious issue for your application, you should configure your directory software to always transmit replication updates immediately.

One issue that arises with replication is the reassignment of master servers. Directory server software that supports only single-master replication requires additional steps to recover from the destruction of the master server. In such a case, another server must be configured to be the updatable master and to supply updates to the backup servers at the alternate site. The recovery plan must be modified to include time for these steps if necessary.

Another issue to consider is the distributed nature of directories. Recall that a single directory tree can be spread across a number of servers, each holding a portion of the tree. To provide a backup set of servers, either at a cold or hot site, you need to either provide equivalent computing power (number of servers, speed of CPUs, and so on) or make a conscious decision that the standby site will be limited in some fashion.

For example, at your primary site your directory may be divided into three partitions, each residing on a separate server. The backup site, however, might have all three partitions on the same server. Although the backup site would have less capacity than the primary site, you might choose this approach to limit costs. Reduced capacity may be perfectly acceptable anyway, especially if you can reduce the load on the directory by shutting down less important directory-enabled applications while the backup site is in operation. However, the backup site must at least meet some minimum performance requirements for it to be useful at all.

You can, of course, install additional replicas at the backup site after disaster recovery commences. This would reduce the amount of replication update traffic that must flow from your primary site to your backup site under normal conditions. For example, if your primary site consists of three directory partitions replicated three times each (a total of nine servers), a complete hot standby site would also have nine servers. Maintaining the backup replicas might significantly increase the workload of the servers at the primary site, however. If you instead maintained a single server at the hot site that held all three partitions, replication update traffic to the remote site would be significantly reduced. Additional replicas could be rebuilt from the single server at the hot site in the event of a disaster at the primary site. This might be considered a hybrid hot/cold site approach: The online replica at the remote site is hot and the other servers are cold, put into service only if a disaster occurs (see Figure 16.5).

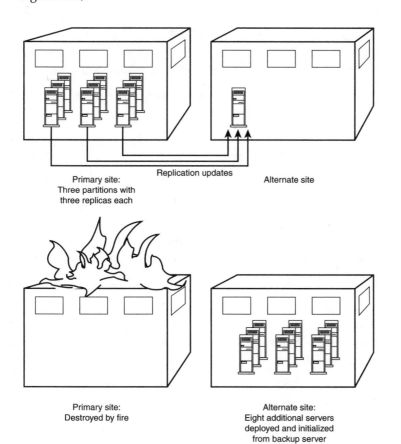

Primary site:
Three partitions with
three replicas each

Replication updates

Alternate site

Primary site:
Destroyed by fire

Alternate site:
Eight additional servers
deployed and initialized
from backup server

FIGURE 16.5 *A hybrid hot/cold strategy.*

Summary

Critical computing processes that depend on the critical data in your directory must be able to continue in the face of a directory server failure or a disaster. Backups and replication can provide you with the first line of defense against both types of problems. Directories offer unique challenges and opportunities related to backups and recovery. In this chapter we've discussed these topics and given you the information you need to incorporate directory backup and recovery into your overall data center planning.

Backups and Disaster Recovery Checklist

☐ Select a backup strategy appropriate to the criticality of the data in your directory and your directory server software.

☐ Consider using replication as your primary means of protecting against catastrophic equipment failures.

☐ Even if replication is used to provide backup, traditional procedures such as backing up directory data to magnetic tape are still needed to protect against erroneous data update procedures that destroy directory data.

☐ It is critical to safeguard your backups from damage and to ensure the security of the data they contain.

☐ Backups should be verified to ensure that the data they contain is valid and can be successfully restored.

☐ You should develop a disaster plan appropriate to your business needs and the types of disasters you may encounter.

☐ Disaster recovery services can be provided in-house or purchased from a disaster recovery vendor (sometimes also called a business continuity service). In either case, costs of a disaster recovery plan are directly related to the speed with which services can be restored.

Further Reading

Comdisco Business Continuity Services. Information available on the Web at `http://www.comdisco.com/bc/`.

Disaster Recovery Journal. P.O. Box 510110, St. Louis, MO 63151. Available on the Web at `http://www.drj.com`.

Fire in the Computer Room, What Now? Disaster Recovery: Planning for Business Survival. G. Neaga, B. Winters, P. Laufman, Prentice Hall PTR, 1997.

IBM Business Recovery Systems. Information available on the Web at `http://www.ibm.com`.

Netscape Directory Server Administration Guide. Available on the Web at `http://home.netscape.com/eng/server/directory/3.0/agrtm/`.

Novell's Guide to IntranetWare Networks. J. F. Hughes and B. W. Thomas, Novell Press, 1996.

SunGard Recovery Services, Inc. Information available on the Web at `http://www.sungard.com/drs.html`.

Windows NT Backup and Recovery Guide. J. McMains, W. Rinaldi, Osborne/McGraw-Hill, 1998.

Looking Ahead

In this chapter we describe how you can protect the data in your directory from damage resulting from equipment failure, software failure, and disaster. In Chapter 17, "Maintaining Data," we turn our attention to the topics of managing data, ensuring its timeliness and accuracy, and incorporating data from new sources.

CHAPTER **17**

Maintaining Data

Data maintenance refers to the policies and procedures used to keep the data in your directory up-to-date and accurate. Data maintenance is one of the most important tasks involved in maintaining your directory service. Your directory service is all about providing access to data; if that data is inaccurate or of poor quality, the quality of your entire service is reduced, users are disappointed, and directory-enabled applications may function incorrectly or not at all.

You will also find that without proper planning, data maintenance can become one of the most expensive tasks involved in maintaining your directory service. Failure to implement automated data maintenance procedures can cost hundreds of thousands of dollars in staff time spent updating data and resolving problems. The loss of productivity and user satisfaction caused by inaccurate data in the directory is often very expensive.

This chapter describes the process of maintaining your data. We begin with a section explaining in more detail why data maintenance is so important. Then, we describe how to formulate your data maintenance policy. Afterwards, we discuss how to manage data maintained both centrally and by your users. Next, we explain how to check the quality of your data. Finally, we explore what happens when you need to extend your directory with data from a new source.

The Importance of Data Maintenance

A directory without good data is virtually worthless. Worse yet, bad data can cause real harm. Imagine a directory providing a white pages service that users consult to find contact information of friends and colleagues. If the information they retrieve is not accurate, they will soon stop using the service.

Or, imagine a directory providing authentication and access control services to a variety of extranet applications. The directory contains information specifying which users are allowed to access the applications and their resources. If this information is not accurate, there is not much use in consulting the directory in the first place.

More serious consequences can result from inaccurate data as greater numbers of mission-critical applications use the directory. For example, consider an internal corporate directory used to control access to vital corporate resources. An employee's termination is supposed to be reflected in the directory and his access to resources instantly revoked. Failure to provide accuracy in this case can open your organization to sabotage by disgruntled ex-employees, corporate espionage, and similar situations.

User distrust and dissatisfaction with the directory service is another thing that can result from poor data maintenance. If your directory contains information about users, this dissatisfaction is especially likely. Whereas users may be disappointed to find incorrect information about others in the directory, they can get downright angry if they find incorrect information about themselves.

The potential for dire consequences that can result from inaccurate data in the directory can be used to your advantage. The very fact that the consequences are bad should result in a great deal of motivation to keep the data up-to-date. We will show later in this chapter how you can use this motivation to improve the quality of your directory data by distributing the authority to update it. Ultimately, you may want to allow users to update their own entries for some kinds of information, or you may want to empower a small group of directory content administrators to maintain directory data.

The Data Maintenance Policy

In Chapter 6, "Data Design," you learned how to identify, locate, and obtain the data needed to populate your directory. The result of that phase of your design process was a table listing all your data sources, the data you need from each, and the procedures you will use to obtain the data. This information played an important role in formulating your data maintenance policy.

Your data maintenance policy determines who is responsible for maintaining which attributes in the directory. If more than one entity is allowed to maintain an attribute, your data maintenance policy determines how conflicts are resolved. For example, suppose that users and the human resources databases are both allowed to update the telephoneNumber attribute. What do you do if both sources update the attribute with different values at the same time?

Your data maintenance policy should outline procedures to determine the answer to this question. It also should determine the frequency of updates for pieces of information in the directory and the security those updates require.

Another important procedure determined by your data maintenance policy is how exceptions are handled. Every policy has exceptions. Do not fool yourself into thinking your data maintenance policy is the exception to this rule.

There are potentially as many reasons to make exceptions to your data maintenance policy as there are users of your directory. For example, consider an operation that obtains home address information from the official payroll database. Although this might be just fine for the vast majority of your employees, consider an employee who has his checks mailed to a location different from his home. Including this address in the employee's home contact information would just be plain wrong. You may want to make an exception for this user.

How you handle data maintenance exceptions will have a great impact on the cost of maintaining your directory service. Consider the number of exceptions in relation to the projected size of your directory. Is the policy you choose applicable to 90% of your users? 99%? More? Make some educated guesses here, and realize that the larger your directory gets, the more important it is that the policy be nearly universal.

For example, consider a small directory containing entries for 100 people. If your policy correctly covers 99 out of these 100 users, it is a relatively small burden to do something special for the remaining person. On the other hand, if your directory contains entries for 100,000 people, 99% coverage is pretty close to a disaster: You would have to make special exceptions for 1,000 people, a task that can become quite arduous and expensive.

Consider automating the exception process itself. This may sound counterintuitive, but it is possible in some situations. For example, you might allow users to modify their own entries in a way that excepts them from the standard data policy. This might be accomplished by the user setting a flag in his or her entry. The flag is then read by the automated data maintenance procedure, prompting special handling of the user's entry.

For the purposes of this chapter, we'll separate the attributes in your directory into six categories:

- *Attributes maintained by directory administrators.* These kinds of attributes might include access control attributes, password policy information, or other attributes used in operating the directory.

- *Attributes maintained by directory content administrators.* These attributes might include account information maintained by system administrators of other systems or services. They may be maintained by your help desk, departmental administrative assistants, or other agents acting as a proxy for other users.

- *Attributes maintained by official data sources.* By official, we mean corporate data sources maintained by your organization's human resources, finance, or other departments. These attributes might include official name, work telephone number, employee identification number, title, salary, manager, and other attributes your organization maintains in other databases.

- *Attributes maintained by directory end users.* These attributes might include home address and telephone number, description, picture, and other attributes containing personal information about the user.

- *Attributes maintained by directory-enabled applications.* These attributes might include application-specific preference information, application or user state information, or attributes shared across multiple instances of the application.

- *Attributes maintained by the directory service itself.* This includes attributes such as modifiersName, modifyTimeStamp, and others that the directory maintains either as a convenience or to ensure its proper operation.

You probably don't need to worry about attributes the directory itself maintains. Application-maintained data is often not up to you to maintain, but it's important that you monitor and approve how applications use the directory. In the discussion that follows, we will also consider data maintained by administrators and other data sources, or centrally maintained data; and user-maintained data.

Application-Maintained Data

Data maintained by directory-enabled applications may end up being the majority of data in your directory. The health of this kind of data and the applications that maintain it can have a tremendous effect on the quality and performance of your directory service. Make sure the directory-enabled applications developed by you or others use the directory in an efficient and sensible way. Be proactive when you do this; don't wait for application developers to come to you.

There are many aspects of efficient and high-performance directory-enabled application development. It's beyond the scope of this book to give a tutorial on directory-enabled application development, but the following list highlights some of the more important things to remember. Following these tips will go a long way toward making any directory-enabled application perform better:

- *Minimize connections.* Your application and directory service will both benefit if you open a connection only once and reuse it for many operations. A search request, with a single network round-trip to the directory server, can often be processed in only a few milliseconds. Opening a connection to perform the same operation can take much longer and consume far more network and server resources.

- *Perform only efficient searches.* The capabilities of your directory software and how you configure it determine what kinds of searches your directory can handle efficiently. The difference in response time between a search your directory can respond to efficiently and one it can't is often measured in minutes. Efficient searches are important both for reducing the response time perceived by the application making the query and for increasing the overall throughput provided by your directory server. Clearly, a balance must be reached between application developers and directory administrators. Sometimes, application developers can be shown a better way to do things; at other times directory administrators may be able to reconfigure the server to better serve an application's requests.

- *Minimize the number of searches.* Application developers often don't think in terms of consolidating operations for efficiency. This can lead to performing multiple searches when only one would do. For example, if neighboring parts of the code call for an application to recover the mail and title attributes, an application developer might make two searches— one for each attribute. A more efficient approach would be to do one search asking for both attributes at the same time.

- *Retrieve only required attributes.* Another area often ripe for improvement is the number of unnecessary attributes retrieved by an application. Sometimes, developers are tempted to retrieve attributes they don't really need, perhaps even every attribute in the entry. In some directory installations, this can be quite a lot of data! For example, you might maintain a JPEG photo or audio greeting attribute that is tens of thousands of bytes long. Transmitting these needlessly wastes bandwidth and computing power and can have severe performance implications because of access control and other processing overhead. It's better to ask only for those attributes the application will use.

- *Minimize updates.* As discussed in Chapter 1, "Directory Services Overview," one of the defining characteristics of a directory is that it is better equipped to handle read operations than update operations. Typical directory implementations are able to handle several orders of magnitude more reads and searches than writes. The less writing an application does to the directory, the better performance everyone accessing the directory will experience. It's also important to make updates as efficiently as possible. Encourage application developers to change only the minimum information necessary. A common mistake is to perform a modification by deleting the old entry and adding the modified entry even if only one attribute value in the entry has changed. This kind of behavior can make updates substantially less efficient.

There are many techniques for communicating these guidelines to application developers. Among the more effective methods we've found are the following:

- *Documentation.* If you simply document and publicize good practices, developers will often follow them. You might do this in the form of printed or online documentation.

- *Training and seminars.* Most inefficiencies in the way directory-enabled applications use the directory are simply due to a lack of education. Documentation can help, but sometimes developing a formal training course is called for.

- *Sample code.* Whatever vehicle you use to distribute guidelines to developers, be sure to include plenty of sample code. Not only does this put things in a language developers can understand, but it becomes easier to incorporate into an application.

- *Consulting.* In some situations it may be worthwhile to provide one-on-one consulting to application developers. You might do this during the application's design phase, during development when you can act as a support resource, and during application testing when you can help fix any last-minute problems.

- *Laboratory testing.* One good way to root out and correct potential problems is to host application developers and their applications in your testing laboratory. This is good for developers because it gives them a chance to test their application in a controlled, easily monitored environment. It's good for you and your directory service because it gives you a chance to correct bad behavior before it is unleashed on your production service.

You may not have the resources to implement all these techniques. Think about what kind of community you are dealing with and which techniques will give you the biggest bang for your buck. Make sure you document the policy that applications must conform to. This will give you an objective tool to use in judging and correcting applications.

Centrally Maintained Data

The first thing to decide about centrally maintained data is who is the central authority responsible for the maintenance. This might be the directory administrator or some third party. In either case, you'll need to think about how the data is maintained, the frequency of updates, the effect updates will have on the operation of the directory, and other issues. These choices are summarized in the following list:

- *Online or offline update.* Do the updates come in over LDAP, or do they come in via a file or other format that is imported into the directory service by other means? Typically, such imports go directly into the underlying directory database. If possible, have the updates come in over LDAP. That way, you can use the normal LDAP security mechanisms to protect the directory and avoid taking the directory down.

- *Update security.* If the information being updated is sensitive and has to travel over insecure connections on its way to the directory, you will need to consider how to protect it. You might use SSL to protect updates that come in over LDAP. Other solutions, such as SSH, are available to protect non-LDAP data transfers.

- *Update process.* If the update process is regular, you should almost certainly automate it as much as you can. If you can't, you need to consider alternatives. Who performs the updates? What kind of training do they need? What kind of support do you need to provide for them?

- *Exception handling.* Any process, automated or not, has exceptions. Depending on the size of your database and the number of updates you process, these exceptions can be significant. Think about making exception handling as automated and low-cost as possible.

- *Update frequency.* The frequency at which data is updated depends on many factors, including the volatility of the data, the timeliness required, the consequences of out-of-date data, and other things. Scheduling updates should be done with care to avoid impacting the service and inconveniencing users.

- *Data validation.* You may be surprised at the low quality of data that creeps into some of the data sources around your organization. You should use the directory update process as an opportunity to improve the quality of this data. This will make your directory service of higher quality and serve as an incentive to the data source to increase the quality of its data.

Make sure you fully understand the implications of each of your choices. For example, opting for an offline process may involve shutting down the directory during the update. Depending on the frequency of update, this may or may not be acceptable. Opting for an online updating process, however, may degrade the performance of the directory. An online updating process may not complete as quickly as an offline one.

Update security may have implications as well. Can you arrange to give the updating entity access only to the fields it is allowed to update? Or, do you need to give it more access than it really should have? If the update is accomplished via an offline process, consider the implications for the security of your system. For example, it may mean giving physical access to the machine. If this is not acceptable, it may mean that you need to act as the update agent. You'll probably want to develop as automated a process as possible to save staff costs. How much will the development of this system cost you? If you opt to protect the security of online updates via some technology such as SSL, consider the effect this will have on your service. How much will service be degraded? Will you need hardware acceleration to get acceptable performance? These considerations are all implications of the update process.

Update frequency is another choice that can have many implications. There is a conflict between wanting the data in your directory to be as up-to-date as possible and wanting the service to always be up and performing at peak capacity. For example, an offline update process may cause you to have to take the system down while you import data. This is typically the fastest way to get data into your directory, but it means that the server being updated is totally inaccessible during the update. This limits how often you can perform such an update. Extracting update data from the data source might also be an expensive process that cannot be performed often.

For an online update process, different concerns must be addressed. Depending on the number and complexity of updates being applied, online updates can significantly degrade your directory's performance. For example, consider updates from a database with 100,000 entries, each of which changes once an hour. Keeping absolutely up-to-date with these changes requires your directory to process 100,000 updates per hour. Multiply that by the number of replicas in your system; depending on the capabilities of your directory software and the load of other queries on the system, this may be too much. A more prudent approach may be to update the directory only once a day or even once a week. Make sure you understand how up-to-date the information needs to be in order to be useful.

In general, we have found that the following principles help make centralized update processes safe and efficient:

- *Automate as much as possible.* This will reduce staff costs for updating, which can be one of the most expensive aspects of running your directory service.

- *Be prepared to handle exceptions and errors.* No process, no matter how foolproof it seems, is going to be able to handle everything. Make sure you train a group of people to field exception reports and take appropriate action.

- *Use an online update process whenever possible.* This maximizes directory availability and also allows you to make use of the directory's built-in security features to protect the update.

- *Keep logs so you can figure out what went wrong.* This is invaluable when first developing and testing the system. Keeping detailed logs of the update process will continue to be valuable as your service moves into production.

One final word of advice: You can save yourself a lot of work and potential for trouble if you avoid centralized update processes altogether. The closer you can push update responsibility to the owners of the data being updated—be they human resource administrators or end users—the better off you are.

User-Maintained Data

Some of the data contained in your directory is best maintained by the users it pertains to. This kind of data includes things such as home address and phone number, vehicle license number, user-owned mailing lists, and other information that the user has the most interest in seeing up-to-date. Having users update this information themselves can be a benefit to both administrators and users for the following reasons:

- *Accuracy of the data.* For many kinds of user information, the most accurate source is users themselves. This is true of information such as home addresses and telephone numbers, which users know better than you do.

It's also true of other information—such as title, salary, manager, and so on—that you might think would be better known by corporate sources. You rarely want to allow users to change this information, but you should make it easy for them to request that changes be made.

- *Less work for you.* There is no question that maintaining data can be a labor-intensive process—even automated systems do not relieve you of all this burden. However, these systems must be developed, maintained, and monitored, so the more you can distribute this task across your entire user population, the better.

- *Empowerment of your users.* The more empowered users feel, the happier they are likely to be. This is especially true today because users are inundated with information. Personal information is maintained in literally dozens, if not hundreds, of databases across the globe, usually with little or no opportunity for it to be corrected when it's wrong. Although your directory service cannot address the larger problem, it can provide users with the opportunity and the means to correct mistakes they notice. Make sure you ask users to update only the data for which they are the best source.

Despite these advantages, there are still problems to be overcome before you enable your users to update their own information. Although user updating of data has many long-term benefits to you, your directory service, and your users, you will have to make an investment up front to enable this process. In most cases, however, this investment is well worth this cost.

User-maintained data is not a panacea—it comes with its own set of problems. For example, users often do not have the motivation or expertise required to perform updates. They might not realize the consequences of out-of-date information, or they might not have the time to take care of it. You probably want to take control of information that you deem critically important to providing a good directory service. Another good approach is to train a small group of responsible users, such as administrative assistants or system administrators, to perform the updates.

Update-Capable Clients

The first thing a user requires to update his or her own entry is a client capable of performing the update. Depending on the type and capabilities of the service you have deployed, such clients may already be available. If not, there are three alternatives you should consider:

- *General-purpose client*. This can be one of the many generic directory clients on the market. The advantage is that such clients come ready to go, with only configuration, distribution, and training required by you. The costs involved with this can still be substantial, however. Make sure the client you select has the functionality you require but is not so general-purpose as to be overwhelming to users. Users may find it frustrating if the client has capabilities they cannot use because of access control or other restrictions. Sometimes, clients allow configuration changes to remove such extra options.

- *Special-purpose client*. This might be an application you distribute to each user's desktop or a centralized Web application accessible from any Web browser. The latter option is attractive in terms of development and distribution costs.

- *Online request system*. With this option, users don't directly make changes to their entries in real-time. Instead, they access the online request system to submit their changes. The request is then handled by administrative staff or an automated offline process. Such changes may be applied to the directory itself or to the source databases (an attractive feature). Another advantage is the human verification of update requests that can be performed when using this method. These advantages need to be weighed against the lack of instant update capability, which may confuse users.

See Chapter 20, "Developing New Applications," for tips and techniques you can use to develop some of these applications yourself.

Authentication and Security

If your users have an update-capable client in their hands, they'll need to authenticate to the directory before it allows them to make changes. This is an important step toward protecting the security and integrity of information in the directory.

Chapter 11, "Privacy and Security Design," discussed options for authentication in detail, so by this point you should already have an authentication and security plan. Part of your data maintenance plan must include provisions for distributing and maintaining authentication credentials. These provisions might involve passwords, certificates, or some other form of credentials.

As soon as users have authenticated, you need to be concerned about the security implications of the updates they make. Again, this was covered in detail in Chapter 11. We will not repeat that treatment here, except to recall that different kinds of information require different kinds of protection. For example, public information needs its integrity protected, but privacy is not generally a concern. Sensitive information needs both privacy and integrity protection.

You should also apply access controls to your directory, as described in Chapter 11. These controls ensure that users are able to update those fields you want them to update. Even more importantly, access controls ensure that users are unable to update data that you don't want them to update.

It's often important to maintain an audit trail when allowing users to update their own entries. Problems will inevitably occur, and you need to be able to distinguish between user errors, directory system errors, and security breaches. Maintaining an adequate audit trail showing who updated what and when they did it can go a long way toward resolving these problems. Most directory server software supports some kind of audit capability. Audit logs were discussed in detail in Chapter 11.

Training and Support Costs

One of the few downsides of allowing users to update their own entries is the extra training and support costs that may be required. You need to balance these costs against the savings you get by not having to spend administrative staff time performing updates.

Training costs depend on the complexity of the update process you devise and the sophistication of your user community. If your update process is embodied in a self-explanatory Web application, your training costs will be minimal. If your update process is embodied in a more complicated standalone application, there may be more extensive training required.

Support costs also can vary quite a bit depending on the update process you devise. In addition to help desk calls received from users asking how to use the update applications, you can expect to receive calls from people wanting to update fields that you don't want to allow them to update. Be prepared to explain your data maintenance policy; if possible, publish the policy as widely as possible.

One good way to lower support costs is to be proactive about giving users as much information as possible. For example, if a user's manager is responsible for updating certain fields for the human resources department before the changes are reflected in the directory, explain this in your online documentation. A user reading this may then go directly to his or her manager rather than bothering the help desk, which would not have the relevant information needed to help the user.

System Effects

Just as with centrally maintained data, you need to consider the effects of your user-maintained data policies on the directory service. The effects concern your directory's performance, its replication system, the quality of data, and other factors.

Directory performance can be affected by user updates just as it can by other updates. This type of traffic tends to slow the directory down, and many updates coming in unchecked could even result in a denial of service to other users of the directory. This might happen because of a malicious user or simply because of an error in the way someone is using the directory. For example, consider a user who tries to write a little program to update his directory entry several times a day. If this program becomes caught in some kind of loop, the load on the directory can be substantial. Use your audit trail and normal directory performance monitoring methods to guard against problems like this.

Replication performance is also affected by the number of updates your directory processes. Too many updates can cause replication to get backed up. This can cause long delays during which different copies of your directory contain different information. Although loose consistency like this is a fundamental characteristic of most directories, taken to extremes it can lead to user confusion and more calls to the help desk.

It is not always true that user-maintained data causes more updates to the directory. It may well be the case that the same or even fewer updates result. The question is one of control. With user-maintained data, you have no control over how many updates are performed, when they are performed, and by whom. You should guard against an out-of-control user update problem, even if it is unlikely to occur. You should also guard against users not updating their information in a timely manner, which leads to stale data in the directory.

Data Validation

Quality of data is another concern when allowing user updates. We stated that improving data quality is one of the main reasons for introducing user updates in the first place, so this may come as a bit of a surprise. Keep in mind that although users may be able to provide up-to-date and accurate information, they are, after all, only human. Unintentional mistakes are often made, and you should do what you can to guard against such mistakes. Also, keep in mind that user motivation to update data may be highly variable.

One good method of guarding against data quality problems is to screen the data entered by users. With data screening, some process inspects the data to be added or changed in the directory. If the data is found to be faulty, the update is not made. You can often catch syntactic errors this way, although rarely semantic ones. Examples of syntactic errors include entering an email address that contains spaces, a telephone number with nonprintable characters, a JPEG photograph that does not conform to the JPEG standard, and so on. Examples of semantic errors include entering a valid but incorrect email address, somebody else's telephone number, and more. Some semantic checks can be performed. For example, minimal verification of an email address can be performed by looking up mail exchange (MX) or address (A) records in the DNS. If a user enters the telephone number of an existing user, a simple directory search can be used to detect this and reject the change.

There are two places where you can screen users' data. First, you can modify the clients used to update their entries to do the screening. Some clients already provide support for this kind of data validation. You may be able to use this support, although if you have any special requirements you may be out of luck. An example of a special requirement might be an employee number field whose values must have a specific format. Most clients don't provide generic data validation support. This method also has the disadvantage that no checking is done if a user finds a different way to update her entry, perhaps by using a different client.

Another option is to enable data validation in the directory servers themselves. This eliminates the possibility of a user bypassing the validation because all updates come to the directory servers. As we learned in Chapter 3, "An Introduction to LDAP," attributes have a syntax associated with them that determines the kind of information its values can contain. Many directory servers provide validation at this basic syntax level. This is enough to keep nonprintable characters out of phone numbers and email addresses, but it's probably not enough to check the syntax of an email address and certainly not for something like a special employee number.

To perform more elaborate data validation checks such as these, you need the ability to change the directory's behavior. There are different ways of doing this, although few directory software products provide this capability. Netscape Directory Server provides a set of plug-in interfaces that allow you to write a little bit of code to perform a validation. This code then gets plugged into the directory server and called before an update operation is executed. Your plug-in has the option of refusing the operation (if the data is really messed up) or changing the data to an acceptable format (to remove dashes from an employee number, for example). Check to make sure your directory software supports the kind of validation you need.

Handling New Data Sources

Unless your directory is very special-purpose, there will come a time when you need to add more data to it. This involves integrating a new data source—perhaps another database within your organization, a new application that needs to store things in the directory, or your users themselves. In any case, you'll need to plan to handle the new data, as outlined in the following steps:

1. Design a schema to hold the new data.

2. Design a security policy for the new data.

3. Integrate the new data source into your data maintenance policy.

4. Design a new data update procedure for the new source (or adopt an existing one).

5. Assess the impact of integrating the new data source on your directory service as a whole.

6. Implement the new data update procedure.

7. Make sure the update procedure works correctly.

Whatever your new data source is, you'll need to design schema to hold the information in the directory. Make sure the policy governing the maintenance of the new data is integrated into and compatible with your existing data maintenance policies. Follow the same steps you did earlier in this chapter and in Chapter 6 to design the procedure by which the new information is updated. Finally, you'll need to implement the new procedure that embodies your data maintenance policy.

Following these steps should allow you to integrate new data sources with minimum disruption to the service. Make sure you have an explicit plan for handling new data sources that covers all these steps in detail. Our experience has shown that integrating new data sources is a pretty common task. If your directory service is popular and successful, many new applications will want to use it. Each application may well have some specialized data it needs to store or have available in the directory. The future success and growth of your service depend in large part on how well you respond to these needs. As with all substantial changes to your directory service, be sure to pilot the change before deploying a new data source in production.

Chapter 22, "Directory Coexistence," talks about this topic in great detail. Chapters 20 and 21, "Directory-Enabling Existing Applications," talk in great detail about creating applications that use the directory.

Handling Exceptions

As we've said repeatedly throughout this chapter, don't count on your data maintenance policies to cover 100% of the situations you encounter. Exceptions are a fact of life. You would do well to formulate policies and procedures that minimize the need for exception handling, but you should also prepare to handle the exceptions that will inevitably occur.

Exceptions take many forms. One form of exception involves simple errors. For example, you might count on data from one of your sources to be formatted in a particular way. If it is not, your data update procedure should handle this situation gracefully. Logging errors is always good, as is correcting errors when possible. Aborting the entire update process because of a single error in the data is usually a bad idea, although there are exceptions even to this advice, of course. If the error is in mission-critical data that cannot tolerate any errors, aborting the update process may indeed be the best approach. Evaluate your situation to determine which course of action is most appropriate.

Another form of exception involves the policy itself. These kinds of exceptions are usually caused by user needs. For example, your policy might state that telephone and office address information for all employees is to be published to the outside world. Some of your employees might not want this information published for reasons of privacy and security (perhaps they've been the victims of stalking, for example). You could handle this exception by placing access control on the user's entry or by simply not updating the user's phone and address information from the data source. Be prepared to respond to legitimate exceptions like this.

Checking Data Quality

The purpose of data maintenance is to ensure that the data in your directory service has the highest–possible quality. Quality of data has several aspects, but we will focus primarily on the accuracy and timeliness of data. Naturally, you will want to check the quality of your data both to monitor how well your data maintenance procedures are working and to get an idea of the kind of service you are providing to the users of your directory.

Bad data can creep into your directory service from a number of directions, including the following:

- *Bad source data.* If there is bad data in the source from which you are populating your directory, the data in your directory will also be bad. If you detect this, use the opportunity to improve the quality of the source data. If that doesn't work, you might consider filtering the data as it comes in to remove things such as nonprintable characters. If the data in the source is just plain wrong, try to find out why and correct the problem.

- *User or administrator error.* People make mistakes. Any time users or administrators are responsible for entering data, you run this risk. Increased education and training, as well as directory data validation filters, can help correct this kind of problem.

- *Systematic error.* This kind of error can be introduced by a flaw in the automated procedure used to populate the directory or by a program that has a bug in it. Fixing these kinds of problems can dramatically increase your directory's quality.

Methods of Checking Quality

There are several methods you can use to check the quality of data in your directory. The following are three common methods:

- *Source of truth.* If you have a source of truth for the data you'd like to check (typically, one or more of your source databases), you can simply compare its data with the data in your directory. This may be easier said than done, of course. You might dump the directory data and source data to files and write a script or program to compare the two files and then report any differences. Or, you might write a program that reads information directly from the directory and the source database and then does the comparison online. This is likely to be expensive however you do it. A lower-cost approach may be to incorporate this check into the regular data synchronization procedure you have developed for the source.

- *Spot check.* A second method is to perform spot checks of the directory and rely on statistical inferences to tell you about the overall quality of your directory data. You can write a program to select entries from the directory at random and compare them to the corresponding entries in the source of truth database. This method is much less expensive than doing a complete comparison. You'll need to decide for yourself how many entries to check to have confidence that you're getting an accurate and representative sample of data.

- *User survey.* A third method is to survey users to ask them about data quality or monitor user complaints about incorrect data. This method works well only for data that users care about and can judge the accuracy of. This method is also statistical in nature, so you'll need to do some educated guessing to derive the overall quality of your data.

Source of truth and spot checking can be used to check the syntactic validity of information even when no source of truth database exists or is accessible. For example, you could read all (or a sampling) of the email address attributes in the directory and determine whether they are syntactically valid.

Implications of Checking Quality

It's important to consider the implications of your data quality checking methods for the operation of your directory service. Be sure to choose a method that does not significantly reduce directory performance. Depending on the method you choose, you may have to make a trade–off between how often you check for quality and the accuracy of your checking methods. The main concerns in this area are methods that cause an excessive load on the directory or cause the directory to be unavailable.

For example, consider a method that requires reading over LDAP all the entries in your directory. Your directory might have the capacity to respond to this kind of request without degrading performance for other users, but then again it might not. If you use a method like this, you can run the check at night or another off-peak time when the directory has plenty of extra capacity to respond to the data-checking requests. This may be difficult if your directory operates in a global environment in which there is no off-peak time. Another approach then is to create a dedicated directory replica that does nothing but process these data-verification tasks.

Consider also a method that requires you to dump your directory's data to a file. Some directory server software allows you to perform this operation without taking the service down, but some does not. If you are planning to use this method, be sure the software you choose supports online production of the necessary extracts or that your service can tolerate the downtime. Remember that you have replication to help with the availability problem, so consider taking down a replica to produce the extract instead of taking down the master server. Also, consider producing your own extract over LDAP—but be careful you don't degrade performance as discussed earlier.

Correcting Bad Data

Whatever method you use to check the quality of your data, be sure to investigate the cause any time you encounter an error. This will help you correct problems with the system that produced the bad data. Although this kind of investigation can be time-consuming and expensive, it's usually well worth it. You'll often find that many errors are caused by the same underlying problem. Fixing that problem can dramatically increase the quality of your data.

Many underlying problems can cause bad data, some of which were already discussed briefly. Systematic errors in programs or procedures should be treated as bugs and corrected. Bad data introduced through human error might be the result of inadequate training or documentation for either users or administrators; increasing the quality and coverage of this training and documentation can cause corresponding quality increases in your data. Human error can also be the result of poor software design. Spend time with users and administrators responsible for updating the directory and observe the steps they take when maintaining data. This can often point out flaws in the software and procedures they use.

Finally, even if you can't eliminate poor data coming into your directory, you can mitigate the damage by installing data-validation filters. As mentioned earlier, these filters can be installed in directory clients that users and administrators use to update the directory, or they can be installed in the directory service itself.

Data Maintenance Checklist

- ☐ Identify who is allowed to update which attributes in which parts of your directory tree.

- ☐ Determine which attributes and which parts of your directory tree are centrally maintained and which are user-maintained.

- ☐ Determine the frequency of data updates from each source.

- ☐ Create a data maintenance policy.

- ☐ Design your data update procedures.

- ☐ Create a policy and procedures for adding new data sources.

- ☐ Analyze the effects of these procedures on your directory service's performance and availability.

- ☐ Develop client software needed for performing updates.

- ☐ Develop training and documentation for users and administrators who will update the directory.

- ☐ Conduct training and distribute documentation and software.

- ☐ Monitor data quality.

- ☐ Take action when you find data quality problems. This is a repetitive process that often requires you to revisit earlier steps.

Further Reading

LDAP: Programming Directory-Enabled Applications with Lightweight Directory Access Protocol. T. Howes and M. Smith, Indianapolis, IN: Macmillan Technical Publishing, 1997.

Looking Ahead

Now that you know how to ensure the accuracy of data in your directory, it's time to learn how to monitor other aspects of the service's operation in Chapter 18, "Monitoring." After that, we will close the directory maintenance part of the book with Chapter 19, "Troubleshooting."

CHAPTER **18**

Monitoring

To deploy a reliable directory service that meets your users' expectations, you need to develop and implement a monitoring strategy. Your monitoring system should help you attain two main goals:

- To quickly detect and allow you to remedy failures of your directory service

- To anticipate and resolve potential problems before they result in failure

In this chapter, we first discuss general monitoring principles and the various types of monitoring strategies you might use. Then, we cover the various types of monitoring systems available, including off-the-shelf network monitoring systems and custom monitoring tools. Next, we cover the topic of notification, in which you inform the appropriate people about any problems detected. Then, we discuss how to proceed when a failure or degradation of service is detected. We conclude with a simple monitoring tool, written in Perl, that you can use as a starting point for developing your own custom monitoring system.

An Introduction to Monitoring

It's likely that your directory service is (or will be) a vital part of your computing infrastructure. Users may depend on it for things such as login and address books, and applications may depend on it for such things as access control and email delivery. Failure or unavailability of the directory can result in downtime for users and applications, which translates into lost time and money. By monitoring your directory service, you can learn of outages as soon as they occur.

With more-sophisticated, proactive monitoring strategies, you can also anticipate problems before they result in an outage or degraded service. Information
you gather from this type of monitoring can be used to fine-tune your directory server software. For example, proactive monitoring may alert you to the
need to change directory configuration parameters to optimize performance for
common queries. Proactive monitoring can also provide data that can help you
optimize your management procedures. For example, an increase in the number of updates handled by your directory may signal the need for more-
frequent backups.

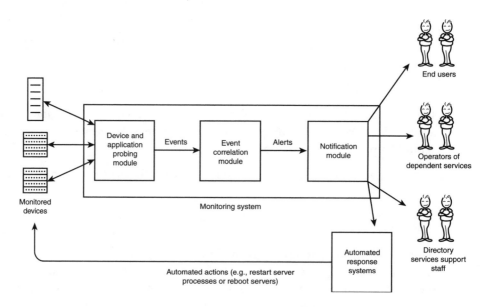

A monitoring system consists of three conceptual modules (see Figure 18.1),
described in the following list:

F IGURE 18.1 *A conceptual overview of monitoring.*

- The Device and Application Probing module is responsible for
  periodically checking the status of the monitored devices, hosts, and
  applications. When a device fails a test, an event is generated that
  describes the device and the test that was performed.

- The Event Correlation module is fed these events and correlates them to
  determine the root cause, and then it suppresses any events that might
  have occurred as a consequence of other events. For example, a network
  router might fail, temporarily making all devices, hosts, and applications

beyond it inaccessible. Any alerts for those events would be suppressed because they are probably false alarms. After suppressing any inappropriate events, the module constructs one or more alerts and sends them to the notification module.

- The Notification module receives alerts and notifies the appropriate persons who can remedy the problem. Alternatively, the Notification module might arrange for an automated system to take some remedial action such as restarting a server process or rebooting a failed server.

The monitoring system shown in Figure 18.1 is a conceptual model that we use to frame our discussion of directory monitoring. Any of the modules' functions could be performed by humans or a software program; however, if you use a commercially available network management system (NMS), you'll probably find that it implements all of these functions for you.

The most basic type of monitoring detects when the directory (or a part of it) is unavailable, perhaps because a server machine has crashed or has become unreachable as a result of a network failure. These directory failures are *hard failures*—that is, a part of the directory has failed completely.

Other types of directory problems can result in degraded performance. For example, looping electronic mail can cause the load on the directory to increase dramatically as the messaging servers attempt to deliver the looping mail. A more advanced monitoring tool could conceivably detect the increased load on the directory and alert a system administrator, who could take corrective action. A complete monitoring system should be able to detect hard failures and also detect when performance drops below an acceptable level.

In addition to detecting hard failures and unacceptable performance degradation, a well-designed monitoring solution also provides you with valuable information on performance trends. Such proactive monitoring can help you anticipate problems before they become serious enough for your users to notice.

Methods of Monitoring

There are a number of ways to monitor a directory service. Following are the various types of monitoring you should consider:

- *Monitoring with Simple Network Management Protocol (SNMP).* Although SNMP has found its widest application in the management of networking hardware such as switches, hubs, and routers, it is also possible to use SNMP to monitor and manage application processes running on server computers. SNMP allows a management application to monitor the status of an entity on the network. It's also possible for a management application to be asynchronously notified via the SNMP trap mechanism when some sort of problem occurs (if a server process terminates unexpectedly, for example).

- *Probing the directory via LDAP.* One of the most straightforward and useful ways to monitor your directory service is to probe it by connecting to it as a client and issuing LDAP requests. For example, a simple probing tool might connect to a directory server and issue a search request for a given entry. If the entry is returned within a reasonable span of time, the directory is considered functional. If not, the probing tool can report a failure.

- *Monitoring operating system performance data.* Most modern operating systems (OSs) provide tools to query their operating parameters. This type of information can help you identify when your directory server performance is suffering because of an OS problem.

- *Indirect Monitoring.* Monitoring the applications that utilize the directory provides more of an end user view of the reliability and responsiveness of your system.

- *Log File Analysis.* You can automatically scan the directory service's log files for messages that indicate an error condition, and you can watch for conditions that signal a performance problem. Log file analysis is also a good way to perform proactive monitoring, in which you identify undesirable performance trends and telltale signs of impending problems before they are noticed by your users.

Later in this chapter we discuss each of these five approaches in detail and provide specific examples of each.

General Monitoring Principles

Before we discuss specific monitoring methods, let's take a moment to introduce some general principles that apply to all methods.

Monitoring Unobtrusively

You should always understand the implications of your monitoring strategy. It's possible for a poorly designed monitoring system to adversely affect performance if it places a heavy load on the directory service. In general, you should strive to make the monitoring as unobtrusive as possible while still providing the information you need.

How do you make your monitoring unobtrusive? You should use the available method that is the most lightweight but gives you the needed information. For example, if you probe the directory, retrieving a single entry is probably sufficient; it's unnecessary to retrieve many entries. You should also perform the probe no more often than necessary to implement your desired responsiveness. For example, you can discover problems sooner if you probe the directory every five seconds, but that may be overkill; it's probably reasonable to probe every minute, or even every five minutes, depending on the level of service you are expected to provide to your users.

One Failure Causing Other Failures

It's also possible that if a failure occurs, it may trigger other alerts in your monitoring system. For example, if one of a set of replicated servers becomes unavailable, the load on the remaining servers may increase as clients reapportion themselves among the remaining replicas. If this occurs, you can try to reduce the load on the remaining servers by disabling noncritical applications or by bringing additional replicas online. In any case, such an event signals the need for additional capacity to provide some headroom should it happen again.

Keeping a Problem History

You should strive to design your monitoring system so that it provides you with a reliable history of problems. For example, if you use a commercial network management system that logs alerts in a standard format, you might periodically extract the directory-related alerts and archive them in a central location. These extracted logs can help you identify trends that you can use to plan for expansion—and demonstrate your ever-improving reliability figures to management (or hide the figures if they don't show improvement!).

Having a Plan

Finally, for every type of failure you can anticipate, you should create a written action plan to share with all operators and support personnel who might be the first to learn of a failure. It's also a good idea to have a default action plan to be followed when an unanticipated error occurs. Action plans are covered in more detail in the "Taking Action" section of this chapter.

Selecting and Developing Monitoring Tools

As you set out to design your directory monitoring system, you have two main alternatives to choose from. You can choose an NMS package, such as IBM's Tivoli TME 10, Computer Associates' CA/Unicenter TNG, Hewlett-Packard's

OpenView, IBM's NetView, or Cabletron's Spectrum; or you can choose to develop your own set of tools to monitor the directory. Which approach should you use?

NMS packages have historically been used to monitor SNMP-enabled network devices such as routers, hubs, and switches. These packages typically have excellent data archiving and reporting capabilities; allow the definition of customized alerts; and offer event-correlation capabilities, which permit the NMS to suppress spurious alerts. Additionally, many NMSs can directly perform notification via email, telephone, and pager. If your directory server software supports monitoring via SNMP, monitoring it with an NMS is a natural choice. This is especially true if you already are using an NMS to monitor the rest of your network.

If you do not already use an NMS in your organization, and if you cannot justify the cost of purchasing and deploying one, it makes sense to develop a set of tools that perform the directory monitoring function. A simple set of Perl scripts, for example, can be used to perform extensive monitoring of your directory service. We offer some general design hints for developing a set of tools and show you how you can develop notification methods later in the chapter.

If you have (or plan to deploy) an NMS, but your directory does not support monitoring via SNMP, you might use a hybrid approach in which custom-developed probing tools are integrated into your NMS. (The NMS software, of course, must support this.) The advantage of a hybrid system is that you still benefit from the event correlation, logging, and notification services provided by your NMS software. Even if your directory service supports SNMP monitoring, you may find it beneficial to use this hybrid approach because it allows you to monitor the directory in the same way your users access it.

In the following sections, we discuss the NMS and custom monitoring approaches in greater detail.

Monitoring Your Directory with SNMP and a Network Management System

If your directory server supports SNMP, you can monitor it with one of many commercially available NMS software packages. Before we discuss this topic, however, let's examine how SNMP works.

An Introduction to SNMP

SNMP is an Internet standard protocol for exchanging management information. In a typical SNMP installation, a managed device runs an SNMP agent, and the management station runs an SNMP manager application. The manager may request information from the agent with an SNMP GET request, and the agent responds with a GET response containing the requested data. Figure 18.2 shows a manager requesting a piece of information from a managed device.

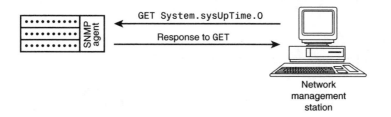

FIGURE 18.2 *An SNMP manager requests information from a managed device.*

In Figure 18.2, the NMS has issued a request to read a piece of management information from the managed device, an Ethernet hub. The device returns the requested information (systemUpTime, or elapsed time since the device was powered on) to the NMS.

SNMP also allows a manager to send a SET request to an agent. This instructs the agent to modify its operational status in some way. Figure 18.3 shows a manager issuing a SET request to a managed device. This SET request sets the system.sysContact.0 Management Information Base (MIB) variable to the string bjensen@airius.com, which represents the email address of the person responsible for the managed device.

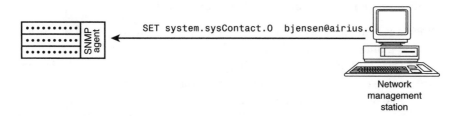

FIGURE 18.3 *An SNMP manager issues a SET request to a managed device.*

Warning

Older SNMP standards do not provide secure authentication, so SNMP SET commands are rarely enabled in managed devices.

Managed devices can also generate spontaneous messages called *traps*, which indicate some exceptional condition. In Figure 18.4, the managed device has encountered some error and has generated a trap that it has sent to the management station. As before, the NMS may choose to take some action upon receiving a trap from a managed device.

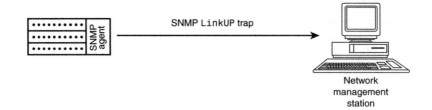

FIGURE 18.4   *A network device generates an SNMP trap.*

SNMP can be used to manage a wide range of devices on a network, including switches, routers, and hubs. But how does the manager know what types of data are made available by a particular agent? The collection of available management information for all devices in the universe is described in the MIB—a huge tree of management information. Each type of device has its own branch of the tree, and the leaves of the tree represent the actual parameters that may be managed. The actual structure of the MIB isn't particularly important to our discussion, however. Suffice it to say that the MIB assigns a unique identifier to every possible parameter on every type of device you might want to monitor. This lets managers and agents refer precisely and unambiguously to operating parameters of every device on the network.

When a vendor creates a new piece of networking hardware and wants to make it manageable via SNMP, it needs to create agent software for the device and document the MIB variables that the device supports. If the device performs some common function for which variables already exist in the MIB, no additional MIB variable needs to be defined. If, on the other hand, the device provides new functionality that is to be monitored via SNMP, the vendor needs to assign and document new MIB variables that correspond to these new functions.

In a typical enterprise, one or more NMS stations monitor large numbers of network devices. These management stations poll the devices and record the collected data in a database. Other parts of the NMS display the data graphically. For example, an NMS might offer a pictorial view of a vendor's router. If one of the interfaces on the router encounters a large number of errors in a short time, the NMS package might color the view red to indicate a problem and alert an on-call person by email or pager. NMS software makes the task of managing hundreds or thousands of network devices much easier by automating the data collection and analysis process.

SNMP and Directory Servers

Although SNMP is most often used to monitor networking hardware such as hubs, switches, and routers, it can also be used to monitor applications software such as an LDAP server. Figure 18.5 shows how Netscape Directory Server 3.0 can be monitored using SNMP.

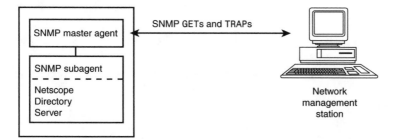

FIGURE 18.5 *Monitoring Netscape Directory Server via SNMP.*

The host that runs the Netscape Directory Server must run an SNMP master agent (on UNIX platforms, the master agent is included with the Netscape Administration Server; on Windows NT, the master agent is included with the operating system). This master agent routes all incoming communication from the NMS to the appropriate subagent (there might be more than one subagent if more than one monitored server is running on the host). The subagent processes the SNMP request and returns the result to the master agent, which routes it to the NMS. Similarly, a subagent may send a trap to the master agent, which forwards it to the NMS.

Netscape Directory Server supports a subset of the MADMAN MIB defined in Internet Draft `draft-ietf-madman-dsa-mib-1-07.txt`, which is a product of the Mail and Directory Management (MADMAN) working group in the IETF. As of this writing, this MIB is about to become a proposed standard and will be published as an Internet RFC.

The MIB variables supported by the Netscape server are divided into three sections, or tables: Operations, Entries, and Server Interaction. All the counters described in the table are reset whenever the directory server is restarted.

The MIB variables supported by Netscape Directory Server are listed in Table 18.1. (Note that any MIB variable present in the Internet Draft but absent from Table 18.1 is not supported by Netscape Directory Server.)

TABLE 18.1 SNMP MIB VARIABLES SUPPORTED BY **NETSCAPE DIRECTORY SERVER**

MIB Variable	Description
The Operations Table	
dsaAnonymousBinds	The number of anonymous bind operations processed.
dsaUnauthBinds	The number of unauthenticated bind operations processed.
dsaSimpleAuthBinds	The number of bind operations that used simple authentication.
dsaStrongAuthBinds	The number of bind operations that used SSL to authenticate the client's identity.
DsaBindSecurityErrors	The number of bind requests that failed because of invalid credentials.
dsaCompareOps	The number of compare operations processed.
dsaAddEntryOps	The number of add operations processed.
dsaRemoveEntryOps	The number of delete operations processed.
dsaModifyEntryOps	The number of modify operations processed
dsaModifyRDNOps	The number of modify RDN operations processed.
dsaSearchOps	The number of search operations (of any scope) processed.
dsaOneLevelSearchOps	The number of search operations with scope=onelevel processed.
dsaReferrals	The number of referrals returned to clients.
dsaErrors	The number of requests that could not be processed because of errors.
The Entries Table	
dsaCacheEntries	The number of entries contained in the server's entry cache.
dsaCacheHits	The number of operations that were serviced from the entry cache.
The Server Interaction Table	
dsaIntIndex	Data on the last five directory servers that this server has interacted with. The dsIntIndex variable is the index to the table.
dsaTimeOfCreation	The value of sysUpTime at the time this row was created. If this attempt was made before the NMS was initialized, the object contains the value 0.

MIB Variable	Description
dsaTimeOfLastAttempt	The amount of time since this directory server last attempted to contact the peer directory server identified by the corresponding dsIntIndex object. If this attempt was made before the NMS was initialized, the object contains the value 0.
dsaTimeOfLastSuccess	The amount of time since this directory server last successfully contacted the peer directory server identified by the corresponding dsIntIndex object. If this contact was made before the NMS was initialized, the object contains the value 0.
DsaFailuresSinceLastSuccess	The number of times this directory server has failed to contact the peer directory server identified in the corresponding dsIntIndex object since the last successful contact.
dsaFailures	The total number of times this directory server has failed to contact the peer directory server identified by the corresponding dsIntIndex object.
dsaSuccesses	The total number of times this directory server has successfully contacted the peer directory server identified by the corresponding dsIntIndex object.
dsaURL	The URL of the peer directory server identified in the corresponding dsIntIndex object.

In addition to making these MIB variables available via SNMP GET requests, the Netscape Directory Server SNMP subagent generates an enterprise-specific trap whenever the server starts up and whenever it shuts down, either normally or abnormally. You can make use of this information by configuring your NMS to generate an alert when parameters exceed some preset limits. You may also want to configure your NMS to warn you if it receives a "server down" trap, indicating that the server has shut down for some reason.

More information about using SNMP with Netscape Directory Server can be found in the Netscape Directory Server Administrator's Guide.

Monitoring Your Directory with Custom Probing Tools

If you don't have an NMS but still need to monitor your directory service, a simple set of tools can be constructed using off-the-shelf components such as command-line LDAP tools or PerLDAP. In this section, we suggest some general design principles for developing your own monitoring tools.

We suggest you probe your directory by performing the same general types of operations that your users and directory-enabled applications perform. For example, you might choose to probe your directory by periodically attempting to read an entry from the directory (see Figure 18.6).

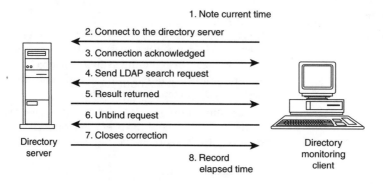

FIGURE 18.6 *Probing the directory via LDAP.*

When you probe the directory in this manner, the expected result is that a single entry will be returned. If some other result is obtained, the LDAP server is either unavailable, unreachable because of a network failure, or malfunctioning in some manner. Table 18.2 summarizes the most common failure modes for a monitoring client.

TABLE 18.2 TYPES OF MONITORING FAILURES

Result	Explanation
No route to host.	The directory server host cannot be contacted. A network failure or DNS lookup failure is the most likely cause.
Connection times out.	The directory server host is down, or the network between the monitoring tool and the directory server is down.
Connection refused.	No directory server is running on the host.
An LDAP error code other than LDAP_SUCCESS(0) is returned.	The directory server encountered an error while servicing the search request.
Server responds, but too slowly.	The directory server is experiencing some problem or misconfiguration that is degrading its performance, or the server is simply overloaded.

How do you know when to declare a failure? Think about the error conditions you consider to be critical. If the directory server is completely unresponsive, this is obviously a serious condition that must be remedied. But what if the server responds slowly? Part of your development effort involves setting thresholds. For example, you might decide that a response time of longer than three seconds for a simple search constitutes a serious degradation of performance and calls for notification of the appropriate person.

If one of the first two error conditions in Table 18.2 is encountered, the fault may lie with the network rather than the server. You can distinguish this condition by sending an ICMP echo request (a ping) to the router closest to the directory server. If the router isn't able to receive a ping, you really can't draw any conclusions about the state of the directory server. About the best you can do is declare its state "unknown." How you handle this situation is up to you. You can consider it a failure and notify the appropriate people, or you can ignore the error condition on the assumption that the server is running but unreachable.

In addition to simple searches, you might consider test probes that approximate the types of activity your users and directory-enabled applications generate. For example, if a common activity is for your users to update their personal information (such as home telephone number), you might develop a script that replaces the homeTelephoneNumber attribute of a special test entry. It's a good idea to spend some time examining any access logs your server generates; this way, you can tally the various types of operations it handles and perform similar operations in your probing tests.

Tip

The sample Perl script included at the end of this chapter implements a test like those described here: It searches for an entry and reports an error if the entry cannot be retrieved. The script is "smart"—that is, it avoids generating an alert if the directory server becomes unreachable because of a network failure.

We recommend that you use a modular approach when designing custom monitoring tools. In a modular approach, you separate the actual monitoring processes from the policy decisions about what constitutes a failure and who should be notified. One way to accomplish this is to have the probing modules simply write their test results to a log file in a standard format, then have another process read and interpret the log file and implement a notification policy. For example, you might implement a policy stating that a directory server at a remote location must exhibit slow performance twice in any five-minute period before an alert is raised (doing this requires saving state information between probes). Figure 18.7 depicts such an architecture.

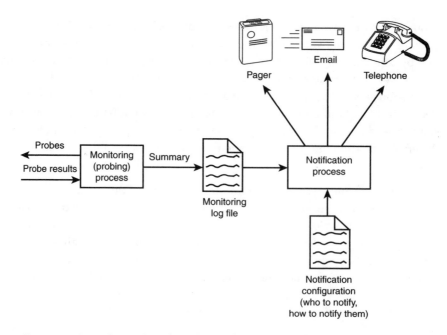

FIGURE **18.7** *Separation of monitoring functions and alert/notification functions.*

Suppose that you have an existing NMS deployed, but your directory server is not manageable via SNMP. How can you integrate monitoring of your server into your NMS? Fortunately, many NMS software packages include application management functions, which include the ability to monitor and manage application packages. Although not a trivial task, monitoring of a directory server can be performed with one of the application management–capable packages. IBM's Tivoli TME 10 and Computer Associates' CA/Unicenter TNG are two products that include these capabilities. Netscape SuiteSpot servers can be managed and monitored using the Tivoli TME 10 Module for SuiteSpot, and Lotus Notes/Domino servers can be managed and monitored with TME 10 and the TME 10 Module for Notes and Domino.

Log File Analysis

Directory server log files can provide an effective way to monitor your servers. Most server software logs warning and error messages to a well-known location. On UNIX systems, software often logs messages using the `syslog` facility. On Windows NT systems, messages are often logged to the NT Event Log and may be viewed using the Event Viewer utility. Netscape Directory Server logs error messages to a file rather than using the system-provided logging facilities.

A number of available tools can be used to monitor the directory server logs for error messages. These utilities can be configured to trigger an alert when, for example, a message matching a particular pattern appears in the log file.

Automatically analyzing log files can also be useful in identifying performance trends that indicate a problem. For example, Netscape Directory Server 4.0 writes to its access log the elapsed time each operation takes to complete. You might choose to develop a tool that keeps a running average of the elapsed times reported for the last 100 operations. If the average elapsed time exceeds some threshold, an alert can be generated.

Log file analysis is also the centerpiece of a proactive monitoring strategy, which is discussed later in this chapter.

Operating System Performance Data

OS performance data can be a valuable aid in identifying the underlying causes of performance trends. For example, you can discover the total amount of virtual memory in use on the system or the amount of free disk space on a particular disk or disk partition on virtually any OS. These types of information can help you identify when your directory server performance is suffering because of some OS problem. For example, if you note that your OS constantly writes to its virtual memory paging space, this is an indication that there is insufficient physical memory for the applications running on the machine. You can remedy this problem by reducing the number of applications running on the machine (by moving them to another machine), or by adding additional RAM to the machine.

OS performance data can be monitored by writing custom scripts that periodically check the system. Alternatively, you can install an SNMP agent that obtains this OS data and makes it available via SNMP. Then, you can monitor the server's operating system health from your central NMS, if you have one.

Indirect Monitoring

Another approach that should be part of your monitoring strategy is indirect monitoring. In this approach, you don't monitor the individual services such as your directory. Instead, you construct monitoring tools that measure availability and response times for the things that matter directly to your end users. For example, if you provide an electronic mail service that depends on the directory, you might periodically measure the time it takes to send an electronic mail message from one user to another.

Indirect monitoring is the real acid test for your servers and network because any single part of your complex, interconnected systems can be at fault. Combined with monitoring the individual devices, servers, and server processes that make up your directory-enabled application, you can quickly identify and repair problems—and ultimately improve the reliability and performance of all your directory-enabled applications.

Proactive Monitoring

Although it is certainly important to learn of directory service failures as soon as they occur, it's even better if you can identify and head off problems before they cause your service to fail or perform poorly. This technique is called proactive monitoring. The goal of proactive monitoring is to catch problems early and fix them before your users notice them.

Problems with directory services (and many other types of services) often arise when a system becomes overloaded. There are many ways that this can happen. For example, as a directory service becomes more popular and used more widely, the number of simultaneous client connections may increase dramatically. Or an upgrade to a directory-enabled application such as a messaging server may place a greater load on the directory service. A well-designed, proactive monitoring strategy can identify trends that, if left unchecked, would eventually cause a noticeable problem with the directory service.

Analyzing the log files produced by your directory server software is a good way to identify trends in the usage of the service. For example, you might write a Perl script that reads the access log generated by the Netscape Directory Server. This script might count the number of search operations performed by the server each hour and write the summary to another file. This summary data can be reviewed periodically to identify trends. Many other types of information can be obtained and analyzed using this general approach. For example, you could count the number of update operations processed by a server, or you could keep a running average of the elapsed time of each operation processed by the server.

It's also a good idea to proactively monitor the quality of your data. For example, if your directory is synchronized from some authoritative data source such as a PeopleSoft HR database, you may want to check whether the data in the directory matches the data in the HR system. Discrepancies indicate that the synchronization process is not working correctly. You can also monitor the quality of data that the directory itself is the authoritative data source for.

For example, you might check whether email addresses in the directory are in the correct format. More information on monitoring data quality via data validation techniques can be found in Chapter 17, "Maintaining Data."

Notification Techniques

The whole point of monitoring your directory is to provide the best possible service for your users by anticipating problems before they cause a failure and detecting and repairing failures quickly. If your automated monitoring tools detect a problem, they need to notify someone so that appropriate action can be taken.

This section deals with the topic of notification methods. We present some general principles you should follow when planning your notification strategy and suggest some notification methods you might use. The possibilities range from simple manual systems to sophisticated automated systems.

Basic Notification Principles

An effective notification system accomplishes four goals when a failure of the directory service is detected:

- It notifies the people responsible for fixing the directory system.

- It notifies the people who administer affected systems, such as electronic mail servers.

- It notifies the people affected by the outage.

- It notifies each person in an appropriate way.

As soon as a problem is detected, your system should notify the person who can actually fix it. This might be a rotating "firefighter" who is on call and has responsibility for taking care of any serious emergencies, or it might be the person who deployed the directory service—this depends on your organization and its policies. This type of notification is typically urgent; the person should be telephoned or paged if the directory is a critical 24x7 service.

The notification system should also send a notification to whoever administers systems that might be affected by the directory failure. For example, if the directory server provides service to several electronic mail servers, the administrators of these servers may want to know about the directory server failure, especially if they receive complaints from users. This type of notification is advisory—it might take the form of an electronic mail message to the administrator, or there might be a special Web page on your intranet that lists known outages. If you use email as a notification method, be aware that email delivery itself might be delayed by the directory outage.

Your users may also want to receive or obtain some sort of notification when the directory service is unavailable, along with an estimate of when the directory will be back in service. For this purpose you could maintain a Web page listing all known outages so that end users can learn for themselves about system failures (instead of calling the help desk). You can also publish your system maintenance messages in ways that don't depend on the network itself, perhaps via a recorded telephone message. Making this type of information available to end users improves user satisfaction and lowers help desk costs.

The type of notification should be appropriate for the intended recipient. If you have a support person on 24-hour call (and she is receiving on-call pay), it's entirely appropriate to page her at 4 a.m. and tell her about the failure of a critical directory server. On the other hand, if your organization is experimenting with directory services, and nobody is on call, be judicious with your use of intrusive notification methods such as pages and telephone calls. The last thing you want to do when piloting a directory service is to alienate the people whom you need to make the project work! For end users and system administrators responsible for dependent systems, an on-demand notification system such as a Web page or recorded telephone message is usually appropriate.

An important point to remember is that you should avoid "crying wolf." In other words, your notification system should try to get someone's attention only when there is a real problem. If it generates false alarms, the believability of future notification messages your system generates will be suspect. For example, suppose a network router fails, disconnecting your directory server from the rest of the network, including your monitoring station. You shouldn't drag the directory administrator out of bed in the middle of the night; there's nothing she can do about the problem (unless, of course, she also manages the router). Whoever or whatever looks at multiple alerts from your monitoring system needs to have the ability to correlate those alerts and determine the root cause.

When a notification message does need to be generated, the message should be tailored to the intended audience. For a directory administrator, we suggest that the notification message describe the test that failed, in what manner it failed, and when it failed. For example, if the directory is monitored via SNMP and a "server down" trap is generated, the message should state exactly that fact, as well as the time the trap was received by the NMS. The following message would be appropriate for a directory administrator:

```
Directory server ldap2.airius.com SNMP trap (server down) at 02:32:23
```

For end users, however, the message should be more descriptive of the effect the problem will have. For example:

```
Directory server ldap2.airius.com is unavailable as of 2:32 AM
```

If the person or system generating the alert message has knowledge of services that depend on the failed server, an even more informative message like the following can be generated:

```
Directory server ldap2.airius.com is unavailable as of 8:45 AM.
Electronic mail for users with accounts on mail2.airius.com and
mail4.airius.com will be inaccessible. Service should be
restored by 10:00 AM.
```

Ideally, your notification should allow a person fixing the problem to annotate any status information you provide. For example, if your notification messages are generated by an operator in a 24x7 network operations center, a directory administrator repairing a failed directory server can call the center and give the operator an estimated time for the repair. The network operations center operator can, in turn, update any status messages via the Web, automatic phone messages, or other means.

Notification Methods

There are a number of different methods you might use to notify people of problems with your directory service. If you already have a monitoring and notification infrastructure in your organization, it probably makes sense just to use that instead of developing something new. The following sections might provide some new ideas you can incorporate into an existing notification system or a custom system built from scratch.

One approach is to have an operator sit at a monitoring console and watch for alerts. If an alert is generated for a directory service, the operator can restart the directory service or call an appropriate person. With this type of manual approach, the operator needs to have clear procedures to follow, especially if he is not an expert on directory systems. The procedures should state when it is appropriate to restart the directory and when an expert should be called. Some sort of audit trail should also be generated, especially if the operator repairs the problem without expert intervention. For example, if the directory service fails at the same time each day and is simply rebooted by the operations staff, the deployment staff needs to learn about this so that it can analyze and remedy the problem.

Another approach is to use or build a software program that performs the notification function. Conceptually, the program receives an alert that names a device, server, or application, which is looked up in a table and mapped to some set of people and notification methods. Such a table might look like Figure 18.8. This excerpt from a larger notification table indicates that when a failure is detected with server ldap-hq.airius.com, one of two actions is to be taken, depending on the time of day. Between 8 a.m. and 5 p.m., a page is sent to the telephone number 1-800-555-1234 using PIN (pager identification number) 9511, and email is sent to bjensen@airius.com. Between 5 p.m. and 8 a.m., a different pager is signaled, and email is sent to oncall-directory@airius.com. A similar procedure is in effect for the LDAP server ldap-cleveland.airius.com. (Our sample Perl scripts at the end of the chapter include a simple, table-driven notification package.)

ldap-hq.airius.com	0800-1700	page 1 800 555 1234 PIN 9511 email bjensen@airius.com
	1700-0800	page 1 800 555 1234 PIN 2927 email oncall-directory@airius.com
ldap-cleveland.airius.com	0800-1700	page 1 216 555 1234 PIN 2193 email hsmith@airius.com
	1700-0800	page 1 800 555 1234 PIN 2927 email oncall-directory@airius.com

FIGURE 18.8   *A portion of a notification table.*

Testing Your Notification System

In the same way that the Emergency Broadcast System in the United States is periodically tested to ensure its functionality, you should test your notification system from time to time. There are several approaches you might use.

The notification system itself might periodically issue a special alert that causes a special test notification to be sent. Any notification generated, such as pages or email messages, should be obviously marked as a test. For example, a test of the email notification method might contain the text:

```
Testing automatic notification system. No action
is required on your part.
```

Additionally, it may be prudent to test the notification tables by injecting all possible alerts into the system and checking that the correct notifications take place. Of course, you need to schedule this well in advance and inform all the people who will receive notification during this process. You also need to take special precautions to watch for failures that actually occur during the test.

Taking Action

As soon as a failure or degradation of your directory service is detected, someone or something needs to do something about it. In this section, we describe some general principles of problem evaluation and resolution, along with some things you should be aware of when remedying problems with a directory service.

Planning Your Course of Action

When you note a failure of the directory service, take a moment to plan your course of action. Although it is certainly important to get the directory service running correctly as soon as possible, you should also be sure to proceed in a methodical fashion. Before taking any action, ask yourself the following questions:

- Exactly what part of the directory service has failed? In what way has it failed?

- Which users and directory-enabled applications depend on the failed service?

- What exactly is the effect? Is something irreparable happening as a result of this outage (e.g., is email bouncing), or has the system simply stopped performing useful work? A guiding principle here is that delayed results or degraded performance are better than downtime or incorrect results.

- Are there any log files or other evidence that might be erased or overwritten? If so, make copies of these files as soon as possible so that they don't get lost.

As soon as you know who is affected by the failure, provide some feedback to let them know the scope of the problem and that you are beginning to work on a resolution. Include an estimated time for repair, if possible. Notifying your end users is important; although it may seem like something you don't have time for, end users deal with outages much better when they aren't kept in the dark.

Minimizing the Effect

After you've achieved a basic understanding of the scope of the problem and who and what it affects, try to minimize the effects of the outage. This can buy you additional time to understand the problem. For example, if you maintain several replicas of the failed server, you may be able to reconfigure your dependent services so that they access the replicas. In some cases, failover to a replica is handled automatically by the directory software.

It may also be possible to temporarily shut down the dependent services to minimize the effects. For example, if you have a batch update process that merges changes from a foreign data source, and this process places a heavy load on the directory, you might consider waiting to run that process until the service has been repaired.

Directory-enabled electronic mail transfer agents (MTAs) that handle mail from external sites are a good example of a dependent service that can be shut down to reduce directory load. Although no inbound mail would be received if the MTA were shut down, external mail servers would queue the mail and periodically attempt to deliver it. MTAs that handle outbound mail should be kept online, if possible, so that users can send mail.

Understanding the Root Cause

After you've isolated the failing components and informed the affected parties, you need to understand the root cause of the problem as thoroughly as possible. If you don't eventually figure out why the failure occurred, it's quite likely that you'll have the same problem in the future.

Troubleshooting a complex, distributed system is tricky business, and we can't possibly hope to explain it all in this text. We do, however, outline a basic step-by-step strategy you might follow when analyzing directory service failures:

1. Gather evidence, which can include any of the following:

   - Directory usage and error logs

   - Usage and error logs of dependent applications

   - User reports of problems

   - Operating system logs

   - Alerts generated by your monitoring system

   - Core dumps from directory server software (UNIX systems) or Dr. Watson logs (Windows NT)

2. After you've collected the evidence, look for things out of the ordinary that occurred around the time of the failure. You'll often know only the time that a user complaint was received or that the monitoring system noticed a problem with the directory.

3. Starting at that time, work backward through the log files, looking for any suspicious error messages. Arrange these chronologically to get a better picture of the sequence of events leading up to the failure (but watch out for clock skew between computer systems).

These steps often lead you directly to the root cause. For example, if the directory service was unable to read database entries from a failing disk drive, you would probably find a close correlation between the time the directory failed and the time the operating system began to log failures.

If the root cause is still not obvious, you may want to involve your directory vendor's technical support staff. The log files and other evidence you collect should help the vendor understand and troubleshoot the problem. Another option you may have, depending on your software, is to enable more-verbose log output and put the directory server back into service. This would probably result in some degradation of service, but the additional log output may be very revealing, especially to your vendor's support staff. Be sure to reconfigure the server for normal logging after you've reproduced the problem with verbose logging enabled.

If the problem is intermittent and hard to reproduce, you may find that a testbed environment allows you to investigate the problem more thoroughly without affecting your production service. A testbed is also a great place to test new software versions and configuration changes before rolling them out into your production environment.

Correcting the Problem

The process of directory problem resolution is covered in detail in Chapter 19, "Troubleshooting." After you've corrected the problem, use the opportunity to improve your directory service. Ask yourself the following:

• Was there anything that could have been done to avoid the failure in the first place? Is there some workaround that can minimize the effect if the problem happens again?

• Was the correct person notified promptly? Is there some improvement that can be made to the notification system?

- Is there some specific procedure that should be followed if this problem occurs again? If the problem occurs again, and someone else needs to deal with it, any documentation you can provide will help him or her.

Documenting What Happened

Producing a detailed problem/resolution report is a great idea for several reasons. First, it serves as a learning tool for your fellow system administrators. Second, if the root cause is a bug in the directory server software, a detailed problem report can be extremely helpful to your vendor. Components of a good problem report include

- Version numbers of the directory server software.
- Version numbers of the operating system software.
- Any patches or service packs installed for the operating system.
- Any optional or third-party software installed on the system, such as the Veritas file system option on the Solaris operating system.
- Relevant portions of directory server logs, operating system logs, and dependent software logs.
- Copies of directory database files (be aware of the contents of these files—they may contain sensitive information).
- Steps to re-create the problem, if known.
- An accurate description of the observed behaviors. Try not to make any assumptions here; instead, simply report what you saw. In other words, offer "just the facts."
- Your assessment of the root cause of the problem, if any.

After a problem has been resolved, it's a good idea to conduct a postmortem and ask a number of questions of yourself. Could troubleshooting have been made easier if additional documentation were available? Did you have all the network maps for your organization? Was it clear which applications used the directory and which servers were used by those applications? Did you have all the necessary administrative passwords to gain access to the affected systems? Did you have the telephone and pager numbers of everyone you needed to contact? Always think about how to make your troubleshooting process more effective.

A Sample Directory Monitoring Utility

The following Perl scripts implement a very simple monitoring and notification system for LDAP servers. You can use the scripts as they appear here or as a starting point for a more elaborate monitoring system.

The first script, `ldap_probe.pl`, probes the directory server once per minute. It attempts to retrieve the entry whose distinguished name is given on the command line. For example, the command

```
./ldap_probe.pl dir.airius.com 389
➥"cn=Test Entry, dc=airius, dc=com"
```

would attempt to read the entry `cn=Test Entry, c=airius, dc=com` from the LDAP server. If the probe were to succeed, the script would wait 60 seconds and repeat the probe. If the probe were to fail for any reason, the script would invoke the `notify.pl` notification script. The notification script would be passed a host identifier string and an indication of whether the server has gone down or has come back up. The `notify.pl` script would then look up the host/port combination in its configuration file (`notify.conf`) and perform the appropriate notification.

This division of work illustrates a concept we introduced earlier: keeping the probing and notification functions separate. To alter the notification actions performed, all that is necessary is to edit the `notify.conf` configuration file. Notification via email is supported by the script, although it can easily be extended to support text paging.

The scripts assume that you are using a UNIX workstation, although modifying them to run under Windows NT should be simple. They also assume that the Netscape LDAP client tool `ldapsearch` is available in a directory contained in your search path.

Listing 18.1 contains the `ldap_probe.pl` script, which performs the actual probing functions. Listing 18.2 contains the `notify.pl` script, which is called by `ldap_probe.pl` when someone is to be notified about a problem. Listing 18.3 contains the `notify.conf` file. This file contains the configuration information that describes whom should be notified for each type of failure detected by the `ldap_probe.pl` script.

LISTING 18.1 THE `ldap_probe.pl` SCRIPT

```
# usage: probe.pl host port DN [router]
#
# This script periodically probes an LDAP server to check whether
# it is still responding to queries. If the server does not
# respond, the notify.pl script is called to generate a
# notification. The notify.pl script is called on each up-down
# or down-up transition.
#
# For each probe, the script connects to the LDAP server
# running on the given host and port, and attempts to read
# the entry given by "DN". If the entry cannot be read, and
# the error returned indicates that the directory server
# could not be contacted, "router" (if given) is pinged. If
# the router cannot be pinged, then the script does not
# notify, on the assumption that the directory server is
# "hidden" behind a network failure. Otherwise, notification
# is performed.

$ping_timeout = 10;      # Wait 10 seconds for a response from ping
$test_interval = 60;     # 60 seconds between probes

# Check arguments
if ($#ARGV < 2 || $#ARGV > 3) {
    print "usage: ldap_probe.pl host port DN [router]\n";
    exit;
}

# Get arguments
$host = $ARGV[0];
$port = $ARGV[1];
$dn = $ARGV[2];
if ($#ARGV == 3) {
    $router = $ARGV[3];
} else {
    $router = "";
}

$is_down = 0;

# Loop forever
while  {

    # Initialize state for this loop
    $prev_is_down = $is_down;
    $is_down = 0;
    $do_check_router = 0;
    $transition = "";

    # Attempt to read the entry named by "DN"
    $search_result = system "ldapsearch -h $host
➥-p $port -s base -b \"$dn\"
➥\"(objectclass=*)\" cn > /dev/null 2>&1;
```

```
$search_result = $search_result / 256;

# Check for errors which indicate that the server is not
# running, is unreachable, or that the domain name could
# not be looked up.
if ($search_result == 91                    # LDAP_CONNECT_ERROR
          || $search_result == 85            # LDAP_TIMEOUT
          || $search_result == 81) {         # LDAP_SERVER_DOWN
    # There errors are generated if the server is not running or
    # is unreachable, or if the domain name could not be looked
    # up.
    $do_check_router = 1;
} elsif ($search_result != 0) {
    # Some other error occurred.
    $is_down = 1;
}


# If the server is down or unreachable, check the router by
# pinging it (if a router address was provided). If the router
# is unpingable, we can't know about the state of the server.
if ($do_check_router) {
    if ($router ne "") {
        $ping_result = system "ping $router $ping
        ➥timeout > /dev/null 2>&1";
        $ping_result = $ping_result / 256;
        if ($ping_result == 0) {
            # Router was pingable, so assume that the LDAP
            # server is down.
            $is_down = 1;
        }
    } else {
        # No router address provided.
        $is_down = 1;
    }
}


# Did we just notice a transition?
if (!$prev_is_down && $is_down) {
    # Up - down transition
    $transition = "down";
} elsif ($prev_is_down && !$is_down) {
    # Down - up transition
    $transition = "up";
} else {
    $transition = "";
}

if ($transition ne "") {
    # Call the notification script
    system ("notify.pl $host:$port ldap_probe $transition");
}
```

continues

LISTING 18.1 CONTINUED

```perl
        # Wait a while until testing again
        sleep($test_interval);
    }
```

LISTING 18.2 THE notify.pl SCRIPT

```perl
# usage: notify.pl identifier test transition
#
# This script reads the file notify.conf and locates lines where the
# identifier, test, and transition match those given as input to this
# script. For each match, the notification method given by the fourth
# argument is performed. For example, if notify.conf contains the

# following
# line:
#
#directory.airius.com ldap_probe down mail bjensen@airius.com
➥"directory.airius.com LDAP down"
#
# the script will send an email message to bjensen@airius.com
# with the text "directory.airius.com LDAP down"
#
# There are three types of notification methods:
# mail:    an electronic mail message is generated and sent.
# page:    a text page is generated (you must supply your own
# command).
# "shell": if the fourth argument begins with a slash (/), the
#          argument is treated as a shell command that is
#          executed. Any additional arguments on the line
#          are quoted and passed to the shell.
#
# See notify.conf for more details.

require "shellwords.pl";
require "ctime.pl";

# Check arguments
if ($#ARGV < 2) {
    print "usage: notify.pl entity testname transition\n";
    exit;
}

$entity = @ARGV[0];
$testname = @ARGV[1];
$transition = @ARGV[2];

# Open the configuration file
if (!open(CONF, "notify.conf")) {
    print STDERR "Cannot open configuration file notify.conf.\n";
    exit;
}
```

```
# Note the current time
$now = &ctime(time);
chop $now;

$found = 0;
while (<CONF>) {
    # Skip comment lines.
    if (/^ *#/) {
        next;
    }
    # Split the line according to UNIX shell quoting conventions
    @_ = &shellwords($_);
    $nargs = @_;
    if ($entity eq @_[0] && $testname eq @_[1]
➥&& $transition eq @_[2]) {
    # Found a match. Perform the notification.
        $found = 1;
        &do_notify;
    }
}
if (!$found) {
    # There were no matching lines. Generate a warning.
    # You could also perform a default notification here; e.g.,
    # send email to the maintainer of the notify.conf file
    # to let him/her know about the error.
    print STDERR "Could not find a notification method
➥for $entity $testname $transition\n";
}

# Subroutine to actually perform the notification.
sub do_notify {
    $method = @_[3];

    if ($method eq "page") {
        # The "page" notification method is not implemented.  You
        # can activate it by adding code to dial out to your
        # paging service.
        # The pager telephone number is the 4th argument,
        # and the pager's PIN is the 5th argument. For
        # example, the following line in notify.conf might
        # be used:
        #dir.airius.com ldap_probe down 9,1-800-555-1212 3233
        ➥"dir.airius.com LDAP down"
        $pager = @_[4];
        $pager_pin = @_[5];
        $message = @_[6];
        print "Paging $pager, PIN $pager_pin, message \"$message\"\n";
        # Insert your custom paging code here.

    } elsif ($method eq "mail") {
        # Send an email notification.
```

continues

Listing 18.2 Continued

```
              $email_addr = @_[4];
              $message = @_[5];
              print "Sending email to $email_addr, message \"$message\"\n";
              open(MAIL, "¦/bin/mail $email_addr");
              print MAIL "To: $email_addr\n";
              print MAIL "Subject: $entity $testname $transition\n";
              print MAIL "\n";
              print MAIL "At $now\n";
              print MAIL "$message\n";
              close(MAIL);

      } elsif (substr($method, 0, 1) eq "/") {
              # Any method that begins with a / is treated as a shell command.
              shift(@_);
              shift(@_);
              shift(@_);
              shift(@_);
              # Quote each argument.
              for ($i = 0; $i < @_; $i++) {
                  @_[$i] = "\"@_[$i]\"";
              }
              $not_args = join(" ", @_);
              print "Sending the following command to the shell:
      ➥$method $not_args\n";
              system "$method $not_args";
      }
  }
```

Listing 18.3 The notify.conf Configuration File

```
# notify.conf
# This file contains the configuration information for notify.pl.
#
# Format:
#
# identifier test transition action [arguments...]
#
# Where:
# "identifier" is a string that identifies the service
# (typically a host name)
# "test" is a string which identifies the type of test performed
# "transition" is either "up" or "down"
# "action" describes the type of notification to perform. The
# notify.pl program  knows about the following types:
#
#    "mail email-address message"
# Electronic mail is sent to "email-address". The text
# of the message is "message".
#
#    "/shell-command [arguments...]"
# The comand "/shell-command" is executed. Any arguments
# are passed to the  shell command.
```

```
#
#
# Lines beginning with "#" are comments, and are ignored.

dir.airius.om:389 ldap_probe down mail bjensen@airius.com
➥"dir.airius.com:389 down"
dir.airius.om:389 ldap_probe up mail bjensen@airius.com
➥"dir.airius.com:389 up"
dir.airius.om:389 ldap_probe down /usr/local/bin/addnotice
➥"dir.airius.com:389 down"
dir.airius.om:389 ldap_probe up /usr/local/bin/addnotice
➥"dir.airius.com:389 up"
```

Monitoring Checklist

☐ Understand the monitoring tools at hand. Do you have, or do you plan to run, a full-fledged NMS? Or do you plan to develop your own stand-alone monitoring tools? Does your directory server software support SNMP?

☐ Ensure that any custom-built monitoring tools simulate actual directory operations.

☐ Decide what will be considered a failure of the directory. Set acceptable performance levels, taking into account any service-level agreements that may be in place.

☐ Implement log file analysis.

☐ Implement OS performance data analysis.

☐ Implement indirect monitoring.

☐ Decide on a notification strategy, implement notification methods, and develop a test plan for them.

☐ When an incident occurs, keep detailed records and use the knowledge gained while resolving the problem to improve the quality of your directory service.

Further Reading

Directory Server Monitoring MIB (Internet Draft). G. Mansfield and S. E. Kille, 1997. Available on the World Wide Web at http://www.ietf.org.

How to Manage Your Network Using SNMP: The Networking Management

Practicum. M. T. Rose and K. McCloghrie, Prentice Hall, 1995.

Netscape Directory Server Administration Guide, Chapter 13, "Managing SNMP." Available from Netscape's World Wide Web site at `http://home.netscape.com/eng/server/directory/3.0/agrtm`.

SNMP, SNMPv2, and RMON: Practical Network Management. W. Stallings, Addison-Wesley, 1996.

The Simple Book: An Introduction to Networking Management. M. T. Rose, Prentice Hall, 1996.

Total SNMP: Exploring the Simple Network Management Protocol. S. J. Harnedy, Prentice Hall, 1997.

Understanding SNMP MIBs. D. Perkins and E. McGinnis, Prentice Hall, 1996.

Looking Ahead

In this chapter, we discussed approaches you might use to monitor your directory service, as well as some general techniques for notifying people of failures. In Chapter 19, "Troubleshooting" we will focus on specific techniques for remedying problems you might encounter with your directory data, your directory server software, and the hardware on which your directory service runs.

Troubleshooting

From time to time during the course of your directory service's lifetime, things will go wrong. Sometimes these problems will result in degradation of performance. Sometimes they will cause the directory to fail completely. When something does go wrong, your objective should be to minimize the damage, return the directory to full service as quickly as possible, and understand the problem so that you can take steps to prevent its recurrence.

Directory problems can be broken down into four major groups:

- Directory outages as a result of hardware or software failure

- Performance problems

- Problems with directory data

- Security problems

In this chapter we examine each of these categories in detail and provide examples of each. We also suggest a step-by-step approach for dealing with directory problems as they arise. We conclude with troubleshooting checklists that help you resolve some typical directory problems.

Discovering Problems

How do you discover directory problems in the first place? There are a number of ways that a problem might come to the attention of the directory administrator:

- The monitoring system (if you have one) may automatically detect a failure or degradation of the directory and notify you about it.

- The maintenance or operations staff may notice problems with the directory as they go about their routine directory maintenance functions.

- Administrators of dependent services such as electronic mail servers may notice and report problems.

- End users may notice a problem and report it to your help desk. The problem might actually be described by end users as a failure in a dependent system, such as an IMAP server, or as a problem with a desktop application that relies on the directory.

A failure may be detected and reported via all the above methods nearly simultaneously. For example, if a directory server becomes unavailable, you might be notified by your NMS software at the same time your help desk receives numerous calls from your end users. Those end users may report problems with any of the dependent applications, such as address books, email servers, and authenticated Web server access. Your operations staff might also be unable to run a regular data-updating procedure.

This is typical of distributed systems in which the individual portions of the system are interdependent. Part of the problem resolution process, therefore, involves correlating the various problem reports and identifying the underlying problem. As soon as you know what the real problem is, you can then inform users of all the affected services.

Ideally, you should strive to eliminate the possibility that your users will discover problems before you do. You can accomplish this through a well-designed, proactive monitoring system. This takes careful planning, but the payoffs are significant. More information on proactive monitoring can be found in Chapter 18, "Monitoring."

When there is a problem, you should clearly communicate to your users and front-line staff the following information:

- There is a known problem.

- How long you expect it to take to fix the problem.

- Any workarounds or alternative services your users can employ in the meantime.

Plan well in advance how you will notify your users about directory problems. Common methods include publishing outage information to Web pages, posting outage information to Usenet newsgroups, and providing status information in a recorded telephone message. Whatever method you use, be certain that it does not depend on the directory itself.

Providing good information to your end users and front-line support staff serves two important purposes. First, it allows your end users to remain productive because they know which applications are affected by the failure and how long the applications will be unavailable. Second, your front-line support staff can be more effective in helping your end users understand the implications of the outage. Your end users will also have a better overall impression of your directory service and dependent applications.

Types of Problems

As mentioned earlier in this chapter, there are four main classifications of directory problems. In this section, we provide an overview of the various types of issues that can arise with each type of problem.

Directory Outages

The first type of problem we explore is the directory outage. An outage occurs when part or all of your directory service becomes unavailable. This can occur when one or more of the directory servers have become unreachable as a result of a network problem, or because the directory server software or hardware has failed in some way. When an outage occurs, users receive no service at all.

Causes

Causes of directory outages fall into two broad categories: hardware failures and software failures. Hardware that can fail includes network components such as routers, switches, network interface cards, and network cabling; and server components such as CPU boards, disk drives, memory, power supplies, and so on. An outage can also occur as a result of a power outage. Software failures can include the operating system itself or the directory server software. It's also possible that other software running on the server can malfunction and cause the directory server software to fail or become unresponsive.

Implications

When a directory outage occurs, your users and directory-enabled applications receive no directory service at all. Because LDAP is a client/server protocol, the failure would be noticed as a failure to connect to the directory service. Outages produce three different symptoms: connection timeouts, refused connections, and hung connections.

A connection timeout occurs when the client attempts to open a connection to the server but receives no response at all. In this case, the client waits some fixed period of time for a response. Eventually, the client times out and reports an error; however, this timeout period is typically on the order of minutes—longer than most users are willing to wait. Connection timeouts can occur if the directory server becomes unreachable because of a network failure, if the server itself is powered off, or if the operating system has crashed.

A refused connection occurs when the directory server's operating system is operating correctly and the server is reachable on the network, but no server process is listening for incoming LDAP connections. In this case, the operating system's TCP/IP stack returns the "connection refused" message to the client. Refused connections typically happen when the directory server process has terminated abnormally as a result of a software bug. They can also occur if the server machine has restarted, perhaps because of a power failure, but the directory server software is not configured to start automatically upon system reboot.

A hung connection occurs when the server is reachable and a directory server process is running, but the service malfunctions. In this case, the connection is still accepted, but no further data flows from the server to the client. Hung connections can result from software bugs or hardware failure, such as a hung SCSI bus on the server.

Resolution

If hardware failure is the underlying cause of an outage, the usual course of action is to replace and restart the failed hardware. For example, if the cause is determined to be a bad network cable, the obvious remedy is to plug in a new cable.

In some cases, however, outages caused by hardware failure can be more challenging to correct, either because the needed replacement parts are not available or because the directory data was damaged (which can happen if a disk drive fails). Ideally, you should maintain a stock of spare parts or purchase an onsite service agreement with a guaranteed maximum response time. Depending on the availability requirements and any service-level agreements you might have, even a short outage may be unacceptable. In this case, you need to look into providing a highly available directory service, as discussed in Chapter 16, "Backups and Disaster Recovery."

When software failure is the root of a directory outage, more vigilance is required. Simply restarting the failed software component may bring the service back online, but if the underlying condition that triggered the software failure is still present, the service may soon fail in exactly the same way. For example, suppose the directory server's cache is configured much too large and the server becomes unresponsive because of excessive paging activity. Restarting the server would probably make the service perform acceptably for a while, but as soon as the cache fills the system may again experience the problem.

When you experience any sort of software outage whose cause is unclear, try to note as much detail about the state of the service while the problem is occurring. Is the server process running? If so, how much memory is it using? Is it consuming any CPU time? Is there disk activity? Is there any useful information in the operating system or directory service log files? If the cause of the problem is still unclear, it may be appropriate to restart the service and watch carefully to see if the service degrades slowly or fails suddenly. For example, you might notice that the service fails whenever a particular query arrives at the server from a particular directory-enabled application. Information like this can be very valuable when working with your vendor's technical support organization.

Performance Problems

Another common type of directory problem occurs when your directory is performing poorly. Poor performance can manifest itself in a number of ways. The overall performance of your directory may be poor, or a specific type of directory operation such a delete operation might be slow. Performance problems can be consistent, or they can be intermittent. Troubleshooting these problems requires careful analysis and attention to detail.

Causes

Misconfigured software is the most common type of directory performance problem. A misconfigured directory server might not perform optimally, or it might not function at all. For example, most directory server software uses a RAM-based cache to improve performance. If the size of this cache is too small, performance of the directory can suffer, perhaps to the point where the server seems to be hung. To correct this problem, increase the size of the cache. On the other hand, if the cache configuration is too large, the server's virtual memory system may experience excessive paging, thereby slowing performance. Most operating systems offer a utility for observing virtual memory system paging activity (`perfmon` on Windows NT and `vmstat` on Solaris, for example).

Another common misconfiguration problem results from not maintaining appropriate indexes for the types of searches your server handles. Netscape Directory Server, for example, permits searches on any attribute. However, search performance is poor on unindexed attributes because the server might need to look through every entry in the database to locate matching entries. If your server takes a long time to respond to search requests and consumes a large amount of CPU time, you may want to check to see if clients are using unindexed attributes in search filters. The Netscape server, for example, records in its access log the search filter presented by each client, and in version 4.0 a note is logged for unindexed searches.

Your software may also encounter some specific limit within either the server software or the operating system. For example, most versions of UNIX have a hard limit on the number of file descriptors that a single UNIX process may use (one file descriptor is used for every open TCP/IP connection and every open file). This limit is usually in the thousands of connections, but it may be altered via UNIX commands.

Another type of limitation you may encounter is the size of the TCP listen queue. This parameter controls how many incoming TCP connections can simultaneously be in the process of being opened. TCP connections are usually established very quickly and removed from the listen queue as soon as they are completely established. However, if many clients attempt to connect to a server at the same time, or if some problem prevents the connection from being quickly established, the listen queue can fill up and new incoming connections may appear to hang.

Older versions of UNIX operating system had a small listen queue (often fixed at only five incoming connections) that was inadequate for high-volume network servers. Newer operating system versions are configurable, and you may need to significantly increase the size of the listen queue. HTTP servers are particularly susceptible to this problem because Web browsers tend to open many short-lived connections. It's often necessary to increase the listen queue to 64 connections or more on a heavily used Web server. LDAP clients typically use longer-lived connections, but you still may need to increase the listen queue size on an LDAP server.

If your server software runs inside a single process, it is subject to the connection limit. This means that there is a cap on the maximum simultaneous number of connections that can be handled. If there are so many clients that your server encounters this limit, you will notice that the server refuses connections (clients receive a "connection refused" error from the TCP/IP stack). The proper action in this case is to either increase the limit, add additional replicas to handle the load, or reduce the number of client connections (if the client software opens connections unnecessarily or neglects to close connections when finished).

Finally, you may encounter performance-degrading software bugs in the directory server software or the operating system. Software vendors increasingly are using the World Wide Web to distribute patches and publish knowledge bases full of information about their products. Additionally, Usenet newsgroups are a tremendous resource for learning about known bugs, workarounds, and patches.

If you find a previously unknown bug, be certain to report it to the software vendor in as clear a fashion as possible so the bug can be fixed. For information on submitting a good bug report, see Chapter 18.

Implications

The implications of performance problems can range from very slight degradation of the service to outright failure. The symptoms can affect all users equally, or they might affect only a subset of directory users. For example, a misconfigured cache can result in poor performance for all users and directory-enabled applications, whereas a missing attribute index might only result in poor search performance for users and applications who search on the unindexed attribute (unless many users do so, in which case the server's overall performance may suffer).

Resolution

When resolving performance problems, it's very important to proceed logically and deliberately. Take notes that describe the problems exactly as reported or observed, and then try to reproduce the problem yourself. For example, if your users complain that address book searches in Netscape Communicator take a long time, try the same search yourself. Ask the users how the search dialog is configured and perform the same search. If you can reproduce the problem, you're well on your way to understanding the root cause. If you can't reproduce the problem, ask yourself what's different about your environment and the user's environment. Are you connected to the same server? Are you authenticated or bound anonymously? Are you closer to the server within the network? Try to eliminate each difference, one by one, until you can duplicate the problem.

Remedying the problem may be a simple matter if a small configuration change is required, or it may be quite involved if a bug has been discovered in your software. If no fix is available, is there some workaround? Can you mitigate the effects of the problem by reconfiguring your directory in some way? For example, installing more memory, adding another CPU, or adding an additional replica may provide the additional capacity you need if you encounter a capacity limit on your software.

No matter what the remedy, take the time to document the problem, the cause, and your workaround and/or long-term fix. Software problems can be quite complex, and the more you can share troubleshooting knowledge with your peers, the more effective your organization will be at providing a high-quality service. These details can also be very useful to the operating system or directory server software vendor if a software bug is the root cause.

Tip

It's extremely helpful to understand and be able to interpret the types of information that your server software can log. For example, Netscape Directory Server writes a line to its access log under each of the following conditions:

- When a client opens a connection. *The IP address of the client is logged.*
- When a client initiates an LDAP operation. *The type of operation is logged along with additional information specific to the type of operation. For bind operations, the bind DN is recorded. For search operations, the search base, scope, and filter are recorded. For update operations, the DN of the entry being updated is recorded.*
- When a result of an LDAP operation is sent to a client. *The result code sent to the client is logged.*
- When a client disconnects.

Each of these log entries is stamped with the date and time the event occurred.

The access log can be helpful in understanding problems. For example, if a user complains of slow search performance, you can search the logs for the IP address of the user's machine. When you find the log entries corresponding to the user's session, you can see exactly the type of search base and search filters the user's client software presented to the server. This information may help you determine whether the problem is a result of a misconfiguration in the user's software or a problem with the server itself.

Problems with Directory Data

Directory data problems may be the result of missing, extra, or incorrect information. In the worst case, the database files that your directory server software uses may become corrupted because of software bugs, operating system bugs, or operator errors. In our experience with actual directory deployments, this is the most common type of problem.

Data problems are often a consequence of some other problem such as misconfigured software. In other cases, data problems can result from incorrect actions on the part of data administrators. Problems with data itself can also be a cause of many other problems. For example, if access control attributes have been erroneously changed or removed, users and applications may not be able to access needed directory entries.

Causes

When incorrect data appears in your directory, someone or some process must have put it there. For example, a confused departmental administrator might remove the entry for an active employee instead of a terminated employee. On a larger scale, an automated update process that reconciles database records from a human resources database may, as a result of a bug, place incorrect employee information in the directory.

Typical monitoring software won't detect this type of problem unless the data is so damaged that the server crashes or cannot even start up. You will usually learn of this type of problem via end user reports unless you proactively monitor data quality.

To be more proactive, you might consider developing tools to monitor the quality of data in your directory or build data validation tools into the software that you can use to synchronize your directory with external data sources. Such tools can detect problems with data before it is noticed by users or becomes a problem. More information on data quality monitoring can be found in Chapter 17, "Maintaining Data."

Implications

When incorrect data ends up in your directory, dependent applications can start behaving incorrectly. For example, if your directory is used to authenticate users accessing your internal Web servers, but some users have been incorrectly removed from the directory, they will be unable to access the protected resources. Or if a user's directory entry has been removed, electronic mail destined for that user may be returned to the sender. In general, if the directory appears to be operating correctly, but one or more of your users are having problems, check the contents of the relevant directory entries.

Even more subtle errors can occur if the directory holds information about network resources such as file servers and printers. If the directory entries corresponding to these devices are removed or damaged in some way, the services provided by those devices may become unavailable.

If database files become corrupted, symptoms may be either very obvious or very subtle. All the entries in the directory may disappear (which is easy to notice), or certain entries may simply not be returned when certain types of searches are performed. Robust server software prevents these types of inconsistencies from arising as a part of normal operation, but operator mistakes can cause any number of unanticipated problems. For example, although Netscape Directory Server uses a transactional database that ensures data consistency even in the case of operating system crashes, manually removing one of the attribute index files and restarting the server can cause unexpected and unwanted results.

If the corruption is subtle, it may go unnoticed for some time. When dealing with corrupted data, always be open to the possibility that the damage actually occurred some time ago and has only now been noticed.

Resolution

If you determine that you have a problem with the data in your directory, the first thing to do is determine the extent of the damage. To do this, of course, you need to have some idea of what should actually be in the directory. A good starting point is to take a look at the directory contents. Do you see approximately the correct number of entries in your directory? If you see too few entries, indicating that entries have been erroneously deleted, it may be prudent to shut down certain dependent services. For example, if you know that the entries for an entire department are missing from the directory, you probably should shut down the servers that handle email for those people. If the mail server cannot locate a user's email address in the directory, it may incorrectly conclude that there is no such user and return the mail to the sender.

If in doubt, the safest thing is to shut down the affected servers. Directory-enabled applications generally notice that the directory is unavailable and report a meaningful error and retry the operation at some later time. However, if the data is incorrect or missing, but the directory is not shut down, applications may behave incorrectly.

As soon as you know the extent of the damage, you need to set about repairing it. How you do this depends on the extent of the damage and the knowledge you have about the correct contents of the directory. For example, if only a single user's entry has been deleted, it's probably most appropriate to simply re-create the entry. On the other hand, if your directory's entire contents have been wiped out by a buggy automated update process, you need to restore your data from some comprehensive source such as a set of backup files or tapes. We suggest that any update scripts that you develop yourself include the capability to log their actions to a file so that you can analyze the scripts' actions later should it become necessary.

After you restore your directory, you need to understand how the damage happened. Did incorrectly configured access control allow removal of an entry? Did a data merge process go awry? You need to examine log files and other records to determine when and how the damage occurred. This step is very important for preventing similar problems. As we've learned in our own deployment experience, problems rarely resolve themselves permanently!

Security Problems

The final category of problems is related to security. The most serious type of security problem involves unauthorized access to directory data. An attacker may attempt to compromise the security of the directory with the intent of reading or damaging sensitive directory data or rendering the service useless for other users via a denial of service attack. The topic of directory access control and security is covered in detail in Chapter 11, "Privacy and Security Design." The steps outlined there should protect you against many common types of break-ins, but how do you notice and respond to security problems if they occur in spite of your best efforts?

A good way to detect compromised security is to be on the alert for telltale signs that the directory has been tampered with. Such signs, often subtle, might include access to your directory from an unexpected location on the Internet (if your directory is accessible from the Internet at all), or a report from a user that his or her directory entry has been altered in some unexpected way. This is often just a consequence of a normal automated update, but it can also signal that the user's password or other credentials have been compromised. If you suspect unauthorized access, directory server logs can help track down the date and time when the tampering occurred and the origin of the LDAP connection.

A denial-of-service attack, on the other hand, has one purpose: to render the directory unusable. The attacker seeks to consume all available resources, perhaps by issuing thousands of repeated unindexed searches against the directory, or by exploiting a known bug in the directory or operating system software and causing a crash.

Causes

If your directory is directly accessible from the Internet, it may be subject to attacks from any place in the world. If, on the other hand, your directory is accessible only from inside your corporate network, you are less susceptible to attack from the outside—but you are certainly not immune. Disgruntled employees can certainly wreak havoc on a directory server given enough time and motivation.

What motivates people to mount denial-of-service attacks or attempt to break in to your directory? In some cases, the sheer challenge of breaking in is sufficient. In other cases, a disgruntled employee may be angry enough to attempt to compromise your directory as a way of achieving revenge.

Implications

A denial-of-service attack can render a directory unresponsive by consuming excessive resources, or it can take down a directory by exploiting known bugs. A security breach is a very serious occurrence, especially if your directory is used for authentication and access control for your critical business resources. The implications of compromised security are highly dependent on the type of data stored in your directory.

Resolution

Discovering a denial-of-service attack is usually simple because the affected servers and dependent services become unresponsive or unavailable. A well-designed monitoring system will note sudden peaks in server load. When you suspect a denial-of-service attack, be sure to save any relevant log files that might help you pinpoint the origin of the attack.

If you determine that the attack originated from a location inside your company, you probably have some recourse you can use to stop the attacker. You need to be careful when tracing the attack back to the original source, however; just because a particular machine was the origin of the attack doesn't necessarily mean that the its owner was the attacker. A good hacker will cover his footprints carefully and avoid using his own desktop machine to originate an attack.

If the origin of the attack is outside your company, you might be able to use a firewall product or packet filter product to block access to your directory from the originating network.

It's also entirely possible for a user to accidentally cause a heavy load on the directory without knowing it. For example, if a user attempts to search the directory for an unindexed attribute but grows impatient and submits the search several times, the directory may become less responsive. This is not a malicious attack, and you need to be aware of this when tracing the problem to its source. In such a case, reconfiguring the directory to index the attribute or setting smaller administrative limits may be an effective way to protect the directory from such inadvertent denial-of-service attacks. Setting reasonable size limits (which control the number of entries returned in response to a search request) and time limits (which control the maximum amount of time the directory will spend responding to a search request) can help make your directory more robust. Not all directory software can be configured in this manner, so be sure to consult your documentation.

If you suspect that the security of your directory has been compromised in some way, immediate action is required. First and foremost, have a plan for who needs to be contacted. In some cases, you may have onsite computer security experts who will respond to the situation and escalate the situation as necessary. In other cases, you may be the in-house expert, and you may need to escalate the situation to your internal security department or even local, state, or federal law enforcement agencies.

In an extremely high-security environment, it may be appropriate to shut off access to the compromised services, including the directory itself and any dependent services such as authenticated intranet Web access. Shutting off services abruptly will almost certainly tip off any attacker that his actions have been detected. If it's possible to learn the network address the hacker is connecting from, it may be possible to closely observe the actions and understand the extent of the damage. Gathering more evidence like this may help you catch the intruder and prove useful if you decide to involve law enforcement agencies. Always keep a detailed log of evidence when you suspect the presence of an intruder. Compromised security is a very serious problem and is covered in more detail in Chapter 11.

Troubleshooting and Resolving Problems

When presented with a problem, you should follow a methodical, step-by-step approach to troubleshooting. The steps we suggest are covered in this section.

Step 1: Assess the Problem and Inform Affected Persons

When you first become aware of a problem, you should perform a quick initial assessment of the evidence and try to understand the scope of the problem. At this stage, the underlying cause of the problem may not be obvious. You may have only a few unrelated problem reports from your help desk that may or may not clearly point to the cause. When the underlying cause isn't clear, try to think of all the possible causes and investigate each one.

Depending on the size of your organization and how your computing support is provided, you may need to contact other people to understand the possible causes. For example, if you are in charge of running the LDAP servers, another group is responsible for the physical network, and yet another group is responsible for the network routing, you may need to get in touch with all these groups to understand if the problem is the fault of a system you administer. If you work in this type of organization, it's extremely valuable to cultivate good working relationships with the groups that provide services that you depend on and the groups that use the services you provide. Having clear escalation processes and up-to-date contact information is also crucial to this type of distributed problem solving.

For example, if you receive notification that users cannot access Web pages that require authentication, you don't really know if the problem lies in the Web server itself, the directory, or some infrastructure piece such as the network between them. Is the Web server accessible? If you access it yourself, can you observe the same problem the end users encountered? Is the directory server running? Is there some problem with the directory server data? Make a list of possible causes.

After you've completed this initial assessment, inform the affected persons. Let them know that you are aware of the problem and are working on resolving it. If you have a pretty good idea of how long it will take to solve the problem, provide an estimate (perhaps padding it a bit to give yourself time to proceed methodically). To the greatest extent possible, inform your users and help desk which services are affected by the problem and what the symptoms might be. For example, if the directory is inaccessible because of a network failure, what will users of the corporate address book application see? What will happen to incoming and outbound electronic mail? Providing information to the help desk will help them understand the problem and more effectively communicate with the end users.

Step 2: Contain the Damage

After you've thought through the possible causes, are there any causes that might result in long-term data loss or corruption? For example, if the data in the directory has been damaged and entries for some employees are missing, what will happen to electronic mail addressed to those people? Most email server software will bounce the message (return to sender) with an explanation that no such address exists. Or if a disk drive appears to be failing and an automatic update script is about to run and put a heavy update load on the directory, what will happen to the data updates? Will they be lost?

If there is any possibility of such damage, it's often best to shut down the affected parts of the directory. Remember, delayed results or service unavailability are better than incorrect results or data loss.

Step 3: Put the System Back into Service by Applying a Short-Term Fix

After you've completed your initial assessment and contained any possible damage, it's time to start putting the directory back into service with a short-term fix, if appropriate. For example, if your master directory server has a bad logic board, and it will be several days before you can obtain a replacement part, perhaps an appropriate short-term fix is to place another machine in service. Or if you've determined that an automatic directory update process has erroneously removed entries from the directory, an appropriate short-term fix might be to restore the directory from a backup tape and shut off the automatic update process until you can analyze and resolve the problem with it.

The short-term fix will often leave you with somewhat reduced capacity. For example, you might put a replacement machine into service that isn't as fast as the machine it replaces. A failed directory server might simply be taken out of service until it can be repaired, assuming that you have a sufficient number of replicas to handle the remaining client load without serious degradation. This is fine as long as the situation is eventually resolved and the full capacity of the directory is restored.

Step 4: Fully Understand the Problem and Devise a Long-Term Fix

As soon as your directory is running with your short-term fix, it's time to examine all the evidence and fully comprehend what happened. For some types of problems, you will already understand the problem fully: Perhaps a power supply failed and has to be replaced, or a bug in update software needs to be fixed. In these cases, a long-term fix isn't really necessary.

In other cases, however, you might not fully understand what happened. Perhaps the directory server machine became unresponsive and had to be rebooted, or maybe replica directory servers got out of synchronization and had to be rebuilt from the master server. If you aren't 100% certain why the problem occurred in the first place, you should spend some time analyzing the failure. The following evidence can help with this step:

- Directory server usage and error log files

- Directory audit log files showing the changes made to the directory

- Log files generated by the operating system

- Log files from dependent applications such as Web servers, messaging servers, and so on

- Output from your NMS software

- Problem reports from end users

- Problem reports from your maintenance staff

Creating a timeline of these events is often very helpful in understanding the chronology and cause-effect relationships. For example, you may note that the directory server began reporting errors writing to its files at the same time the operating system began to log errors with the SCSI bus on the host. This might lead you to suspect a problem with the cable attaching the disk drive to the server, other SCSI peripherals attached to the SCSI bus, or the disk itself.

Assuming that the underlying problem isn't something you can fix right away, you need to develop your long-term fix. This might be straightforward, such as scheduling downtime to replace a failed power supply when the replacement part arrives; or it might be quite complicated if it involves fixing a bug in an automatic update procedure, for example.

Complicated long-term fixes should ideally be tested before deployment. Maintaining a lab environment, in which you can test fixes before applying them to your production environment, is a great way to address this need. For large or mission-critical directories, it's an absolute requirement.

Step 5: Implement the Long-Term Fix and Take Steps to Prevent the Problem from Recurring

When your long-term fix has been identified and tested, it's time to deploy it. If the long-term fix requires any directory downtime, schedule it well in advance, ideally during evening or weekend hours when the directory sees low usage. For example, if you've put a replacement server in place while waiting for replacement parts for your primary server, you'll need some scheduled downtime to put the primary server in place.

Tip

One way to help ensure that changes to your directory environment are as nondisruptive as possible is to implement a change control policy. Such a policy describes the lead time required before a change can be implemented and who must be notified. An example of a change control policy might include the following:

- *At least 24 hours before any change happens, a change control notice must be submitted to all relevant persons, including administrators of dependent systems. This notice should describe the change being made, the reason for the change, and the anticipated effects on dependent services.*

- *During this 24-hour period, the change may be vetoed if one of the affected administrators believes it will conflict with a previously scheduled change. If vetoed, the change must be rescheduled for a later time.*

- *Emergency changes must, of course, be permitted.*

Such a policy will help ensure that all affected staff are prepared for the maintenance or outage and know whom to contact if the outage causes problems with dependent systems.

In some cases, you may be able to avoid the downtime entirely. For example, suppose your software supports multimaster replication and you need to exchange a server for its replacement. You could put the repaired server into place, make it a read-write replica, and then remove the temporary server from service. Making the transition in this manner is entirely transparent to end users.

When you have everything up and running, ask yourself if there is some way to either prevent the problem from happening again or mitigate the negative consequences. For example, if an outage was caused by the failure of a server, could the impact have been lessened by having more replicas of the data available? If the outage was caused by a bug in the server software or operating system, have appropriate patches been deployed to all servers? Think of each incident as providing you with valuable input for improving the quality of your directory service.

Step 6: Arrange to Monitor for the Problem

If your monitoring system did not detect the problem, is there some way to update your monitoring strategy? If you are able to update your monitoring system to catch the problem in the future, you should be able to improve the response time. If the problem is a result of a bug in OS or directory server software, but a patch is not yet available, monitoring for the condition and taking some action such as rebooting a server can improve the reliability of the directory until a patch is available and can be installed.

Step 7: Document What Happened

Finally, take the time to produce a report of the problem, the steps you followed to determine the cause, and the resolution. Also record the total time the service was interrupted. A collection of these reports can be an extremely valuable resource for new technical staff. These reports can also be useful when communicating with management, especially if you want to make the case for additional funding for things such as increased server capacity or improved monitoring support.

Troubleshooting Checklist

The following are checklists of items to note and information to gather when you have a problem with your directory.

Directory Outages

- ☐ Are directory clients timing out, or are their connections being refused by the server?

- ☐ Are all network components (routers, hubs, switches, cables) between the clients and the servers functional?

- ☐ Is the directory server machine running? If not, has the hardware failed?

- ☐ Are all hardware components on the directory server machine functioning properly? Are there any operating system logs that record hardware failures?

- ☐ Is the directory server process running? If so, is it consuming any CPU time? Is it causing any disk activity?

- ☐ If the directory server process is not running, did it fail when processing a particular client request? Does it fail each time it receives such a request? Such a request might represent a denial-of-service attack.

Performance Problems

- ☐ Are specific types of directory operations performing poorly, or is the overall performance of the server poor?

- ☐ Are appropriate attribute indexes being maintained on the directory server?

- ☐ Is the size of the directory server process too large? Does it become too large immediately upon startup or gradually over time?

- ☐ Are the cache sizes of the directory (if any) configured appropriately (neither too small nor too large)?

- ☐ Are there other processes running on the directory server machine that are causing the poor performance?

- ☐ Is the directory under a particularly heavy load? Is this load expected? If it is excessive, is there one particular client or application accounting for most of the load?

Problems with Directory Data

- ☐ Is data missing or incorrect?

- ☐ Does the data appear to be corrupted in a catastrophic manner? Such damage indicates a serious hardware or software problem.

☐ Is the data damaged in some specific way? For example, have certain entries been erroneously deleted? Can the source of the erroneous modifications be determined by examining directory server logs?

Security Problems

☐ Are there telltale signs of a break-in, such as connections from an unexpected location or unexpected modifications to directory entries?

☐ Do directory logs show unexpected client activity?

☐ Is the directory experiencing a denial of service attack? Such an attack usually overwhelms available server resources. Is the source of the attack known?

Looking Ahead

This chapter concludes Part IV, "Maintaining Your Directory Service." Now that we've discussed planning, deploying, and maintaining your directory service, we next turn our attention to the topic of leveraging your directory service and using it in new ways to lower costs and improve the effectiveness of your computing applications.

PART V

Leveraging Your Directory Service

CHAPTER **20**

Developing New Applications

In the next few chapters, we describe how to leverage your deployed directory service and get more out of your directory investment. One of the most common ways to leverage a directory is to create new applications that use it. As discussed in Chapter 5, "Defining Your Directory Needs," serving the needs of one or more directory-enabled applications is often the driving force behind the initial deployment of a directory service. The first set of applications deployed against a directory service are typically existing, commercial applications. In this chapter, we take the next step and look at creating new directory-enabled applications.

From an application developer's point of view, an LDAP directory service is a wonderful thing. LDAP provides a simple, secure, and standard way to access a shared, flexible store of information. A number of high-quality software development kits (SDKs) for writing LDAP applications are available at minimal or no cost. These SDKs free developers from worrying about low-level protocol details and allow them to focus on what they're trying to accomplish with their applications. Use of LDAP by applications is becoming the norm as organizations discover that directory services are a key component of a robust network application infrastructure.

In this chapter, we first look at some reasons why it makes sense to develop directory applications. Next, we describe the most common ways that applications use directories. We then provide an overview of the available tools for developing LDAP applications. We also include a section that contains helpful advice for anyone writing an LDAP directory-enabled application, and we conclude with two sample applications. Our goal is to expose you to some of the many different ways that applications can use LDAP, help you generate ideas for new applications that will be useful within your own organization, and show you that developing applications using LDAP is fun, easy, and rewarding. Don't be afraid to get your hands dirty—write some code!

Reasons to Develop Directory-Enabled Applications

You may already be aware from experience of many of the reasons it makes sense to integrate applications with your directory service. By creating LDAP directory-enabled applications you can do all of the following:

- *Lower your data management costs.* By avoiding application-specific data stores, your organization saves money that would otherwise be spent maintaining redundant data.

- *Adapt the directory to fit your organization.* One example of this is the creation of custom tools to streamline the directory management and application management tasks performed by various groups within your organization.

- *Save on application development, deployment, and maintenance costs.* LDAP applications are easy to develop, and, compared to a RDBMS data store, LDAP directories are cheaper to deploy and maintain.

- *Create entirely new kinds of applications.* By leveraging the directory infrastructure, applications that would normally be difficult to develop can be created with relative ease.

Each of these benefits is discussed further in the following sections. After that, we provide a few reasons why it may *not* make sense to directory-enable an application.

Lowering Your Data Management Costs

If the application being developed needs access to data already stored in your directory, or if the data it uses may be shared with other applications, using a private data store is an expensive mistake. By leveraging your deployed directory service, you avoid creating a new data store that must be designed, deployed, and maintained. By using your directory service as a rendezvous point for applications that share data elements, you avoid the need for troublesome data synchronization between data stores. (Note that we use the phrase *rendezvous point* throughout this chapter as a general term to refer to a service, such as a directory, that supports access to the same data by a set of cooperating applications.)

Suppose you plan to develop a set of Web-based applications for automating a few common employee tasks such as requesting time off, registering car license plate numbers for use by the security office, and providing feedback about manager performance. Without the use of a central directory service, each application might have its own database of information about employees, including user passwords and the names of their managers. This unhappy situation is shown in Figure 20.1.

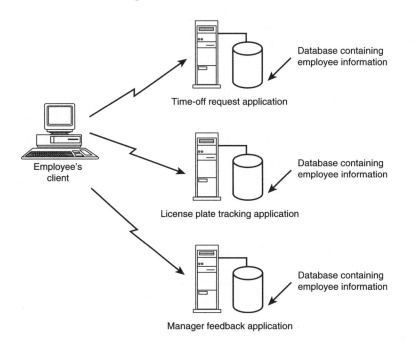

FIGURE 20.1 *Applications with redundant data stores.*

A better approach is to write each application so that it uses your directory service. The time-off request and manager feedback applications both need access to the manager's name, and all the applications need to authenticate employees with user IDs and passwords; by storing all the shared information in your directory service, redundant data elements and the extra databases are eliminated. This approach is shown in Figure 20.2.

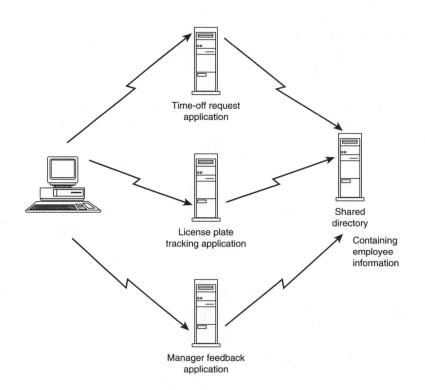

FIGURE 20.2 *Applications that share a directory service*

The picture is much simpler now. And in this case, a simpler architecture translates directly into reduced data maintenance costs.

Adapting the Directory to Fit Your Organization

It is rare to find a perfect fit between the way that different people in an organization want to work and available off-the-shelf directory tools. You'll most likely want to develop new LDAP applications yourself to help streamline maintenance and everyday use of your directory service.

For example, a common task for help desk employees is resetting user passwords. Although this simple task can be accomplished using any of the user and group management interfaces that directory vendors ship with their products, you may want to develop a more focused tool that fits your preferred way of handling password resets. Your new tool might, for example, generate a new random password to increase security (by avoiding the use of the same password over and over again by help desk employees). Such a custom password-setting tool might work as shown in Listing 20.1.

Listing 20.1 Using a custom password-resetting application

```
% setpwd bjensen
Contacting LDAP server...
Finding entry bjensen...
Modifying entry bjensen...
Password reset.  bjensen's new password is: eMpress*stinkpot8
Don't forget to remind bjensen to reset his/her password right away!
```

Applications of this type range from small, focused utilities such as setpwd to large, complex applications that perform a variety of management tasks. (Sample code for a custom setpwd command-line utility is provided later in this chapter.)

Saving on Deployment and Maintenance Costs

After you have deployed a directory service, the incremental cost incurred to support additional applications is quite low. There is no need to discard what you have already done and start over. Most of the directory design, maintenance, and support infrastructure already in place can be expanded incrementally to accommodate new applications.

For applications that require some kind of data store to function, you must often choose between using your directory service and using a traditional RDBMS such as an Oracle system. Directory servers are typically less expensive to purchase, deploy, and maintain than RDBMS servers. Through the use of replication, directories can also scale up to provide high-performance access for many applications. Directories are flexible and therefore easy to change to support the needs of new applications.

For example, adding new schema elements to an RDBMS usually requires that the existing database be shut down and rebuilt using a special utility. This is a tedious, time-consuming process that requires database services to other applications to be disabled. In contrast, new schemas can be added to LDAP directories via LDAP itself at any time; there is no need to shut down the service.

Creating Entirely New Kinds of Applications

An open, standards-based directory provides a great rendezvous point for distributed applications. It also allows organizational information previously locked inside proprietary data stores to be freed for use by innovative application developers. You may discover that some kinds of applications that were impossible or very difficult to create without the existence of a central directory service are now easy to create.

For example, in many organizations, a small army of departmental administrative assistants is responsible for creating and publishing organization charts. New charts are typically created using a manual process and then published inside the company about once a month and distributed in paper form. By leveraging a directory service that contains basic information about employee relationships, an application that creates organization charts on demand can be easily developed. Advantages of such an application include reduced costs for maintenance of the data, elimination of distribution costs, and access to more up-to-date organization charts. Figure 20.3 shows Oblix's Corporate Directory application, a commercial package that includes, among other features, an interactive, dynamic organization chart viewer that leverages LDAP directory information.

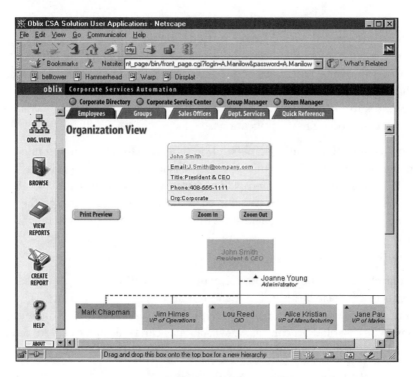

FIGURE 20.3 *Oblix's Corporate Directory application.*

The convergence of LDAP, HTTP, HTML, and other Internet standards means that it's easier than ever before to build applications that pull together essential organizational information and make it available to wide audiences at low cost.

When It Does Not Make Sense to Directory-Enable

It doesn't make sense to integrate *every* new application with your LDAP directory service. In Chapter 1, "Directory Services Overview," you learned what a directory service is and is not good for. Generally, applications that use only private data that does not need to be shared with other applications would not benefit from being directory-enabled. Or, if the data is truly application-specific and never to be shared, again, there is no reason to store it in a directory service.

Tip

One exception to this guideline: There may be some benefit to storing private data in a centralized directory service if doing so reduces the pain of managing the data or allows new end user features such as location independence (also called roaming*). In the latter case, storing application-specific data in a shared, network-accessible directory instead of a local file system or registry allows the application to retrieve the information it needs no matter where on the network it is executed.*

Another guideline is that applications whose data needs violate your directory data policy should not be directory-enabled (see Chapter 6, "Data Design", for information on creating a data policy). Unless you are willing to change your policy, it makes no sense to go through the trouble of writing the application for use with your directory service. For example, suppose your data policy stipulates that no private data such as date of birth, personal photograph, or U.S. Social Security number should be stored in your directory. In that case, you shouldn't bother directory-enabling any applications that need to store Social Security numbers. That data should instead be stored in private, application-specific databases.

Common Ways Applications Use Directories

Because directory services are so flexible, applications use them in many different ways. Although not an exhaustive list, the following are some of the most common ways applications use directories:

- Locating and sharing information

- Verifying authentication credentials

- Aiding the deployment of other services

- Making access control decisions

- Enabling location independence

These examples are discussed in the following sections.

Locating and Sharing Information

The most common use of directory services by applications is to locate information and share it with end users and other applications on the network.

Information held in directories is typically published and maintained by a small number of people or applications, but it is accessed by many. Storing information in a shared directory service has several advantages:

- Maintenance of the information can be performed over the network using LDAP, and management tasks can be easily distributed to a large number of people.

- Multiple instances of the same application and instances of unrelated applications can access the data no matter where they reside on the network.

- Access control provided by the directory service can be used to ensure that each individual and application has only the necessary and appropriate level of access to the information.

- Management of all information about people and resources can be consolidated in one logical location and managed in a consistent way using LDAP directory-enabled management interfaces (instead of residing in a number of different applications that each has its own access methods and management interfaces).

Most of the directory-enabled applications mentioned in this book store some shared information in a directory. Whether the information is shared with a single management tool or with hundreds of other applications, placing it in a directory service makes it more available and easier to manage.

Verifying Authentication Credentials

A simple but powerful way for an application to use a directory service is for authentication. The basic idea is for the application to ask the directory to verify authentication credentials presented by users or by other applications. This can usually be done through an LDAP bind operation, in which the success or failure of the bind translates directly into success or failure of the authentication attempt within the application.

Figure 20.4 shows how a Web server that is configured to serve documents only to certain people might use a directory server to authenticate users.

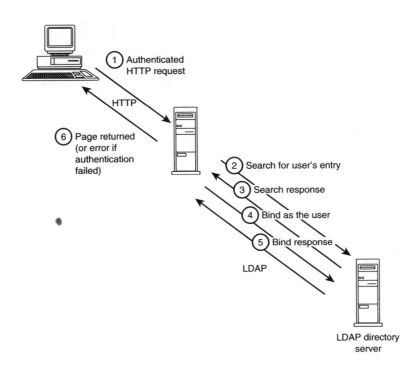

FIGURE 20.4 *A Web server that uses a directory to support authentication.*

The process illustrated in Figure 20.4 goes basically like this: The Web server obtains a user ID and password through an authenticated HTTP request. The Web server then uses LDAP to search for the user. If the search is successful, an LDAP bind operation is used to check the user's password. The Web server then uses the result of the bind operation to decide whether to return the requested Web page or an error.

Using a directory as an authentication service and sharing the directory among all applications requires end users to use only one set of authentication credentials to access all application services. This typically means that each end user needs to remember only one password or carry one certificate—which makes users happier and leads to fewer calls to the help desk.

Tip

Sometimes it is inconvenient or perhaps less secure to ask a directory server to verify a user's authentication credentials on behalf of the application. In this case, it may still make sense to store in a directory service the credentials or other information required to verify each user's identity.

Consider a public key–based authentication scheme. Usually an application can itself verify that a certificate presented by an end user is valid and not expired, but it is more difficult for each application to be aware of which certificates have been revoked. Certificates are typically revoked after a person's public key is compromised or when a person leaves an organization. In traditional public key infrastructure (PKI) designs, certificate revocation lists (CRLs) must be distributed to every application. If certificates or CRLs are stored in a directory service, revocation checking can be accomplished using online revocation checks done over LDAP itself; or a little more indirectly through a protocol designed for revocation checking, such as the online certificate status protocol (OCSP). One possible configuration is shown in Figure 20.5.

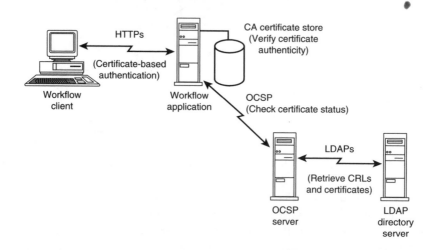

FIGURE 20.5 *Using a directory for certificate revocation checking.*

The workflow application shown in Figure 20.5 uses public key certificates for authentication, and it verifies the authenticity of the certificate using locally stored information about the certificate authority (CA) that signed the certificate. To ensure that the presented certificate has not been revoked, an OCSP server that is backended by an LDAP directory server is contacted. The OCSP server's job is to tell applications whether a certificate is still active and whether it should be honored.

Aiding the Deployment of Other Services

Because most directories provide secure access over a standard protocol (LDAP), they are good tools to use when you need to tie together a set of cooperating applications. This property of directories is especially important if you work with computing services that have historically proven to be costly to deploy and maintain. By using a directory service to facilitate self-service by end users, as a rendezvous point for a set of cooperating applications, and as a central point for service management, it is possible to reduce the cost of providing a service.

One infamous example of a technology that has proved difficult and costly to deploy is PKI, which we already discussed briefly in the last section. With PKI, increased security and greater efficiency can be achieved by putting public key certificates in the hands of end users and applications. The process of issuing, revoking, and renewing certificates for all members of an organization is commonly referred to as *certificate life cycle management*—the major headache encountered in most real world-PKI deployments.

By leveraging a directory service to assist in the certificate life cycle management process, products such as Netscape's Certificate Server are making PKI much more palatable. The main components of a complete PKI solution based on a directory are shown in Figure 20.6.

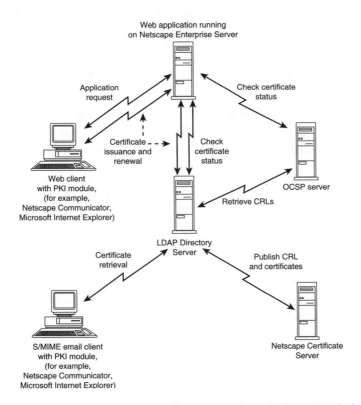

FIGURE 20.6 *Leveraging a directory service to facilitate PKI deployment.*

Certificates containing users' public keys are generated by a certificate server and published in each person's directory entry. These certificates can be accessed to support applications such as S/MIME email and to allow for online certificate revocation checking. CRLs are also published in the directory server, where they are used by one or more OCSP responders. Finally, a special attribute added to each user's entry is checked by the PKI module in each user's Web browser during application startup to see if any PKI-related actions should be taken. This feature is used to support automated renewal of certificates that are about to expire.

Making Access Control Decisions

Another way that applications can take advantage of a directory is for assistance in making decisions about who is allowed to do what. There are several advantages to using information stored in a directory service to make access control decisions:

- Administration of the access control information can be distributed among several people, and no new protocol needs to be invented for maintenance—LDAP itself does the job nicely.

- The information that access control is based on can be shared by several applications. This eliminates redundant access control information, thereby reducing management costs and lowering security risks.

- When appropriate, information maintained for access control purposes can be used for related purposes as well. For example, a group can be used both to perform access control checks and to distribute electronic mail.

- The access control information can be replicated and made available through several directory servers to meet applications' performance and reliability needs.

There are several ways that applications use directories to help with access control decisions. One approach is for the application to store a set of access control rules locally that refer to certain directory information (such as user and group entries). For example, a Web server such as Netscape Enterprise Server 3.5 stores access control rules with the documents it serves from a local file system. Enterprise Server's access control rules can also, however, refer to user and group entries that are stored in an LDAP server (see Figure 20.7).

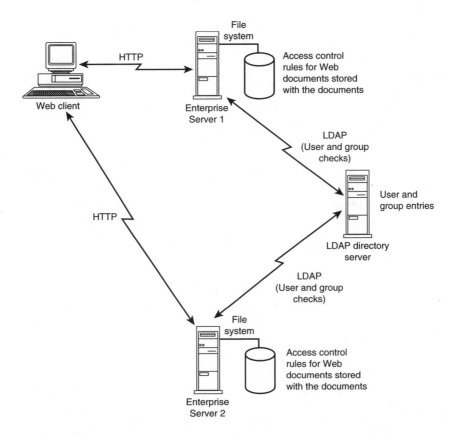

FIGURE 20.7 *How Netscape Enterprise Server 3.5 uses LDAP for access control.*

Evaluation of access control rules is performed locally by the Web server, and information about users and groups is retrieved from the directory as needed. Some advantages of this approach are that the application is free to implement an access control scheme that perfectly fits its needs, and the access control information itself can be stored close to the objects that access control is applied to.

A second method is for the application to store its own application-specific access control information in a directory. The information is read from the directory and evaluated by the application. This approach is used by Netscape's Collabra Server (see Figure 20.8) as well as Netscape Enterprise Server 4.0. The Collabra server is a high-performance, easy-to-manage news server that speaks the Network News Transfer Protocol (NNTP).

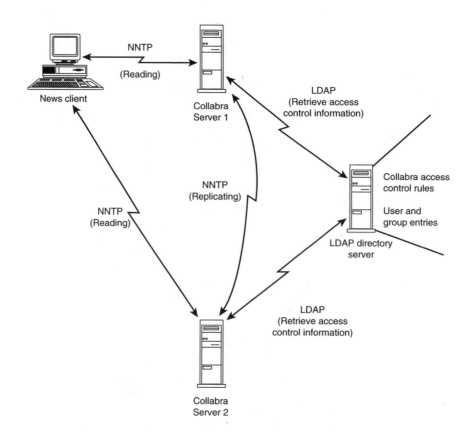

FIGURE 20.8 *How Netscape Collabra Server uses LDAP for access control.*

As it turns out, Collabra Server's access control rules can refer to user and group entries much as Enterprise Server 3.5's rules can. But, because the access control information is stored in a shared directory that can be replicated, access control information can be centrally managed and shared with other instances of the application or with related applications.

A third method is to take advantage of the access control evaluation features of the directory service itself. This is accomplished by representing in the directory service the objects or tasks for which access control needs to be enforced. By installing appropriate access control rules on the entries and authenticating as the person requesting access, the application can use the success or failure of an LDAP operation to grant or deny access to an end user. An example of this approach is shown in Figure 20.9. The computer system management application shown allows the user to perform a task if, and only if, the user is granted read access to a corresponding task entry stored in the directory service.

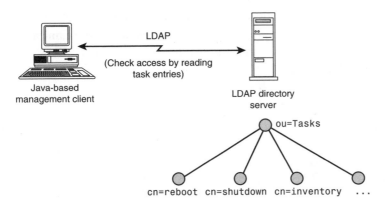

FIGURE 20.9 *Enforcing access control on a set of tasks.*

The Netscape Console, which is used for managing many of Netscape's products, uses this third approach. One advantage of leveraging the directory service's access control evaluation machinery in this way is that the application doesn't need to implement an access control evaluation engine, design a syntax for access control rules, or provide specialized tools for creating and editing the rules—directory server software typically includes all these things out of the box. As long as the access control features provided by the directory software meet the needs of your application, this approach can save a lot of work. There is one disadvantage of this approach, however: Because access control is not yet part of the LDAP standard, writing an application that leverages directory access control ties the application to a specific LDAP server implementation.

Enabling Location Independence

An increasingly popular way for software developers to use LDAP is to enable location independence features in their applications. Location independence, or *roaming*, is achieved when end users and network applications can access the information they need (such as application preferences) regardless of the machine they are using and where they are connected on the network. As long as the directory can be accessed securely from anywhere on your organization's network, your directory service is a perfect tool for implementing location independence. Then, you can simply write your applications to store all the configuration and preferences information in an LDAP directory server—instead of the typical local disk or something like the Windows Registry.

Location independence is a powerful feature that promises to unchain end users from their desktops and allow effective roaming within the network. A good example of an application that demonstrates this is Netscape

Communicator 4.5. Like traditional applications, Communicator can store end user preferences (called *user profiles*) in a local file system. Communicator can also be configured to retrieve user profile information from an LDAP server (see Figure 20.10).

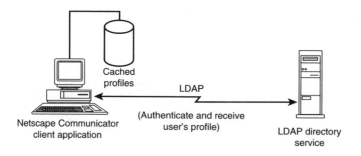

FIGURE 20.10 *Using a directory service to enable location independence.*

When configured this way, the Communicator application asks the end user for a name and password at startup. It uses this information to authenticate with a directory server, and then it downloads the user's profile information to the local disk, where it is cached. If the user makes any changes to his or her preferences while using Communicator, the changed information is written back to the directory service. For example, if the user adds or deletes a bookmark, the new bookmark data is recorded in the directory.

Tools for Developing LDAP Applications

In this section, we examine some different categories of SDKs and scripting tools that can be used to develop LDAP applications. Chapter 12, "Choosing Directory Products," and the "Further Reading" section near the end of this chapter include pointers to more-detailed information on all the kinds of tools we mention. Directory software vendors encourage developers to write LDAP directory-enabled applications, so many of these tools can even be freely downloaded from the Internet and used at no cost.

LDAP software development tools that can be used to write directory-enabled applications can be organized into four categories:

- LDAP SDKs

- LDAP scripting components for JavaScript and Perl

- LDAP command-line tools

- Directory-agnostic SDKs

Practically speaking, your choice of LDAP software development tools is constrained by the programming languages you are comfortable using. That aside, the most important criterion for choosing a tool is its quality and its documentation. You should examine several tools to see which package you like best before you choose.

LDAP SDKs

LDAP SDKs provide complete, high-performance, native access to all the features of LDAP. The application programming interfaces (APIs) they provide conform closely to the C or Java LDAP API specifications being developed by the Internet Engineering Task Force (IETF). At the time of this writing, the programming languages directly supported are limited to C, C++, and Java. However, most of the other programming languages that are widely used, such as Microsoft Visual Basic, can call C or Java APIs.

An LDAP SDK is a good choice if the application you need to LDAP-enable is written in one of the supported languages. The most widely known and used examples of these SDKs are the free Directory SDKs that Netscape produces. These and some of the other SDKs based on the original University of Michigan LDAP are even available in source code form for porting to your favorite platform or enhancing as needed.

LDAP Scripting Components for JavaScript and Perl

The ability to access LDAP directories from interpreted languages such as JavaScript and Perl is typically provided by a component that extends the language in some way. For JavaScript, this is accomplished by directly calling Java LDAP SDK classes or through a Java wrapper implemented on top of a Java LDAP SDK. For Perl, a language extension module such as PerLDAP is commonly used.

These tools are a natural choice if you prefer to use a scripting language to develop your applications. Even if that is not the case, consider invoking an interpreted language (such as Perl) outside of your compiled application code. Development and debugging time would likely be much less than if you developed your application using C, C++, or Java code. Of course, if your performance requirements are high, the overhead of invoking an external interpreter makes this option less attractive.

LDAP Command-Line Tools

Some vendors provide a set of command-line tools that provide access to LDAP directories. These tools are useful for simple LDAP integration tasks, especially those for which performance isn't critical. LDAP command-line tools are good choices for batch-oriented applications as well.

The LDAP command-line tools can be called from a variety of languages, including compiled languages such as C++, Windows NT command language, any UNIX shell scripting language, and Perl. Netscape provides command-line tools with its Directory SDKs and its Directory Server product. The University of Michigan LDAP release also includes a set of command-line tools, although they are not as full-featured as the Netscape tools.

Directory-Agnostic SDKs

Your remaining choice is to use an SDK that provides access to a variety of directory and directory-like data sources (including LDAP). We use the term *directory-agnostic* to describe these SDKs. Examples include Microsoft's Active Directory Services Interface (ADSI) and JavaSoft's Java Naming and Directory Interface (JNDI). Access to a variety of data sources is accomplished by providing a common, directory-independent API for application programmers to use. The SDK is internally designed and constructed so that a variety of directory service modules can be plugged in beneath the API. A good example of this kind of SDK architecture is JNDI, which is illustrated in Figure 20.11.

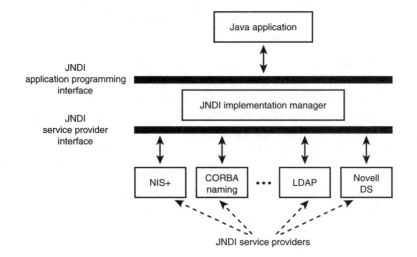

FIGURE 20.11 *JavaSoft's JNDI architecture.*

One of these directory-agnostic SDKs may be a good choice if your application needs access to directory services other than LDAP. The main disadvantages of these SDKs are that they do not provide full access to LDAP's capabilities and that they do not evolve as fast as the SDKs that are focused purely on LDAP. Other disadvantages include increased overhead and code size as a result of the extra layers and directory service modules included. In the case of ADSI, it may be difficult to call the SDK functions from existing applications that are not based on Microsoft's Common Object Model (COM).

Advice for LDAP Application Developers

As with most kinds of applications, the process of developing an LDAP directory-enabled application is filled with many choices. By planning ahead a bit and thinking about how your application will interact with the directory service and other applications, you can save yourself a lot of grief. In this section, we present some advice to help you develop good LDAP applications. (Additional information on data-related design considerations can be found in Chapter 17, "Maintaining Data.")

Striving to Fit In

A common mistake for new LDAP application developers is to treat the directory as a private application-specific store. Although in some rare cases this might be a valid practice, the focus of most LDAP directories is on sharing information among applications, end users, and administrators. Also, keep in mind that the design of the directory may be altered in the future to meet the needs of other applications or to accommodate organizational changes.

You should design and write your application so that it assumes as little as possible about the directory design and can coexist with other applications—including ones that have not yet been written. To accomplish this, follow these guidelines when designing and implementing your application:

- Use standard schema elements whenever practical to promote interoperability and easy coexistence with other applications that do the same. Using standard schemas also helps ease directory service software upgrades.

- When extending schemas, follow the procedures outlined in Chapter 7, "Schema Design." The best approach is to create auxiliary classes to hold attributes you need to add to existing objects such as persons, and to use an application- or organization-specific prefix when naming new attributes and object classes.

- Avoid including mandatory attributes in the object classes you define. If another application includes that mandatory attribute as an optional one in a different object class, it will encounter an error when it tries to include its own object class in entries without including a value for the attribute that you made mandatory.

- Assume as little as possible about the directory namespace, topology, replication, and security design. Also consider the kind of directory design changes that might affect your application; provide configuration settings or built-in intelligence to avoid problems resulting from these changes.

The challenge in developing an application that fits well with other applications and can survive directory design changes is knowing when it is okay to make assumptions. For example, it is probably unacceptable to assume much about how the people and group entries are arranged in the directory information tree (DIT). On the other hand, it is probably okay for your application to dictate the DIT structure within a portion of the directory namespace that it uses to store its own application-specific configuration information.

Tip

Make your application as configurable as possible with respect to how it uses the directory service. Do not hardwire knowledge of the DIT structure, access control rules, or other key parts of the directory design into your application. If you do not expect certain things to change, it is okay to make them somewhat difficult to reconfigure. However, it is important to ensure that there is some way to change the configuration without rewriting the application. Otherwise, you would need to modify the application and distribute new copies everywhere if a critical directory-related assumption you made ceased to hold true. Examples of techniques you can use to build a flexible application include using configuration files or templates for directory-related settings and writing your application so that it reads schema information from the directory service itself.

Communicating Your Application's Directory Needs

As part of your application design process, document how the application interacts with the directory service. Share this information with the people responsible for the design and deployment of the directory service. In many cases, deployment of a new application requires the directory design to be modified or software upgrades to be performed, both of which may be perfectly acceptable to directory administrators if known in advance.

It is important for everyone to be aware of any necessary changes as soon as possible so that the required planning and deployment tasks can be handled before your application is deployed. These are some of the things you should communicate to those responsible for running the directory:

- Schema extensions required for your application.

- Security and access control changes needed to support your application.

- Privacy issues surrounding new data your application may introduce into the directory.

- Additional directory management tasks required for your application. For example, it might make sense to extend certain existing administrative interfaces to support a new attribute used by your application.

- Data source integration requirements for the application. For example, additional synchronization procedures may need to be set up to obtain certain entries and attribute values needed by your application.

- Special LDAP protocol features you rely on. For example, you may be planning to use an LDAPv3 protocol extension that is new enough to require an upgrade of the directory server software. Sometimes your application needs such a feature to work at all; if possible, try to create a mode in which the application works, albeit less functionally, in the absence of the extension.

- An estimate of the additional load the application will impose on the service. This is typically measured in terms of the number of LDAP operations performed in a given time period. Don't forget to estimate peak loads and consider each operation separately. For example, search operations are typically much less expensive for LDAP servers to perform than modify or add operations.

- Server configuration changes required by your application, such as indexing of additional attributes.

Designing for Good Performance and Scalability

Actual performance and scalability requirements vary from application to application and site to site. It is true, however, that the use of computing services and networks is rapidly increasing in most organizations. To be safe, you should design your application to perform well and accommodate a much larger number of directory entries than are currently stored in your directory service. By considering performance and scalability of the directory-related aspects of your application up front, you may avoid a costly redesign later.

When designing and writing your application, avoid architectural choices that limit performance, require you to open a large number of connections to the directory service, or make it difficult to use performance-enhancing techniques such as caching. If your application uses LDAP heavily, you may want to implement a shared pool of connections to the directory service (see Figure 20.12).

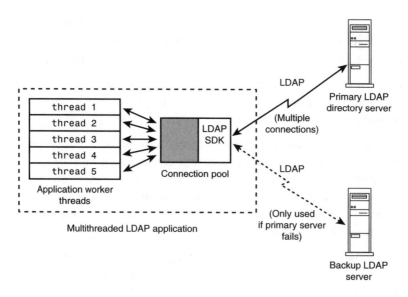

FIGURE 20.12 *LDAP connection pool architecture.*

There are several advantages to having a shared pool of connections:

- The pool provides a central place for caching of search, bind, and compare operations and for sharing results among threads within your application.

- You can easily arrange to share one connection among several application threads, thereby reducing the number of simultaneous connections your application needs to make to the directory service.

- The code to support robust features (such as automatic failover to an alternate server) can be implemented in one place in the connection pool.

Although you may not need something as complex as a shared connection pool, it is worth considering what kind of architecture will help your application use the directory service efficiently and perform well.

Tip

One danger in using any abstraction layer, including something like the LDAP connection pool just described, is that you typically sacrifice some fidelity and lose the ability to take full advantage of all the LDAP features provided by the LDAP SDK. For example, suppose you implement a connection pool that does not allow you to use arbitrary LDAPv3 controls; if you later find that your application would work better if it used an LDAPv3 extension that requires you to send a control to the server, you would need to redesign your abstraction layer. Plan ahead, and use abstraction layers only when there is a clear advantage in doing so.

All LDAP applications perform better if they avoid issuing extraneous operations and if they use simple operations as much as possible. By minimizing your application's impact on CPU, disk, memory, and other directory server resources, you improve the performance of all applications. When searching and reading entries, ask for only the attributes you need; do not retrieve all attributes from every entry. When modifying an entry, compare the new values with the ones already present in the entry and avoid sending unnecessary modify requests to the directory server. Use simple search filters whenever possible; for example, use an exact filter first, and then try a substring filter only if no entries are returned.

Avoid building into your application assumptions about the total number of entries or the shape of the directory tree (e.g., flat or deep). If you expect a lot of entries to sometimes be returned from a search operation, take advantage of the LDAPv3 virtual list view extension to build a scalable user interface and allow you to process the entries in manageable chunks. Think carefully before you create an application that relies on being able to find all the entries in the directory at once. If your application includes a user interface for selecting directory entries, make sure it supports a search-based interface instead of (or in addition to) a list-based interface. Using these techniques will help your application handle thousands of entries and scale up gracefully as the directory service itself scales up.

Developing a Prototype and Conducting a Pilot

One of the best ways to prove your design and try out alternatives is to develop a working prototype. The prototype does not have to be complete or have the prettiest interface. A prototype can be created using scripting tools or other rapid application development (RAD) techniques, even if you plan to use different development tools for building the final application. In order to learn from it, your prototype should work and interact with other systems (including the directory service) in the same way you expect the final version of your application to do so.

As soon as a working application exists, conduct a pilot test to solicit feedback and learn about any problems that should be fixed before you put the application into production service. The pilot should be done in an environment as similar as possible to the actual environment the application will be used in. Test your application's features, measure its performance, and solicit feedback from beta testers. Capture log files and other performance information and use them to conduct scaling tests to estimate the load your application will eventually place on the production directory service. Use the results of the pilot to improve your application, including how it interacts with the directory service. If you make substantial changes to your application after it is deployed, you may want to conduct another pilot.

Leveraging Existing Code

In many cases the applications you create will be similar to others for which the source code is readily available. Most SDKs come with sample code, and vendors such as Netscape and Microsoft make additional sample code available informally in newsgroups, in developer newsletters, and on developer CD-ROMs. The Internet at large is a great resource for locating complete directory-enabled applications; applications with freely available source code include LDAP-enabled mail transport agents (MTAs), several HTTP-to-LDAP gateways, and LDAP-enabled email clients.

Within your own organization you may want to create a Web site to publish LDAP-related source code so that it can be reused by anyone creating a new LDAP application. Code modules explicitly designed to be reusable should be distributed in binary form as shared libraries or Java class files. Over time, try to build up a large collection of code to serve as the starting point for new applications. You should, of course, ensure that any code promoted for reuse is of good quality and demonstrates appropriate use of the directory service.

Avoiding Common Mistakes

As when writing applications for any service that provides a lot of flexibility and functionality, the process of writing LDAP applications has some pitfalls. Many newcomers to LDAP application development make the same mistakes as those who came before them. Here are some common mistakes you should avoid:

- *Allowing abusive searches to get through to the directory service.* A search that consumes a lot of resources on a directory server is an *abusive search.* These include unindexed searches, searches that return a huge number of entries, and searches that read more information than needed for the task at hand. If your application provides an interface that end users interact with to create LDAP search filters, implement simple checks to avoid abusing the server. The kind of searches that are abusive might vary from one directory server implementation to another. For example, with Netscape Directory Server it is important to avoid substring filters that use fewer than three characters (e.g., cn=*hi*), and you should ensure that at least one "ANDed" component of all search filters references an indexed attribute type. You can detect unindexed searches processed by Netscape Directory Server 4.0 by examining the server access log for lines that include notes=U. It may also be helpful to examine the access log for searches whose elapsed time (etime) is longer than a few seconds.

- *Not taking advantage of client-side size and time limits.* To prevent searches from taking too long and monopolizing the directory service, use reasonable size and time limits in your application. Using these limits also protects your application and your users from being frustrated by slow, unresponsive service.

- *Treating multiple values stored in one attribute as an ordered list.* In LDAP, the attribute values associated with each attribute type are a set of unordered values. Although many directory servers return the values for a given attribute type in the same order they're stored in, it is dangerous for an application to rely on this behavior. If you need a way to distinguish between two or more values for the same attribute, include something in the values themselves (such as a sequence number or other identifying text) to allow your application to tell the values apart.

- *Storing extremely large entries in the directory service.* Most directory server and SDK implementations are designed with relatively small entries in mind. There is no hard and fast rule for how big is too big, but entries bigger than 100K bytes in size are unusually large.

- *Improper handling of zero-length passwords.* If your application uses LDAP simple bind operations to test passwords to see if they are valid, make sure you check for zero-length or NULL passwords before passing them on to the directory server. LDAP servers return success responses for simple bind operations that contain a zero-length password and a syntactically valid DN, but the server does not grant to the connection the privileges associated with the bind DN. In other words, LDAP simple bind operations with zero-length passwords always appear to the application to succeed when, in fact, no checking of credentials or granting of privilege was done.

- *Improperly supporting LDAP referrals.* The most common mistake developers who use the LDAP C API make with respect to referral support is forgetting to install a rebind function. The *rebind function* is a callback function that is automatically called by the SDK library to obtain credentials to use when connecting to another server. Without a rebind function in place, all referred connections are anonymous. This causes errors or confusion when modifying the directory or when accessing attributes protected by access control. Another common referral-related mistake is not providing a way to disable automatic chasing of referrals. The ability to disable referrals is useful when troubleshooting directory problems or to improve performance in the face of unreachable servers.

- *Reading an entry right after it was modified and expecting to see recent changes.* It is common for there to be a short delay before changes made on a writable directory server are visible on a read-only replica (see Chapter 10, "Replication Design," for a discussion of the loosely consistent replication strategy employed by most directory services). If your application is connected to a read-only directory replica, searches sometimes return stale data. Try to design your application so that it doesn't need to immediately read information it just changed and, if appropriate, warn users to expect a short delay before directory changes are visible. If it is essential for your application to immediately see the changes it makes, configure it to locate a writable directory server that it can use to process reads as well as writes (of course, this diminishes the value of replication somewhat). Using a client-side cache to hide replication propagation delay is also an option, but if the contents of the cache are flushed (when a user quits and reloads your application, for example), old directory data may reappear and confuse the user.

Example 1: A Password-Resetting Utility

Because end users often forget their passwords, one of the most common tasks for help desk personnel is to assign new passwords. Organizations that have deployed a directory service need to enable their help desk personnel to easily reset passwords stored in the directory. In this section, we present a command-line utility called setpwd that resets the password in a user's directory entry to a randomly chosen one.

Directory Use

The setpwd utility uses the directory service in a simple way. All interaction with the LDAP service is created using a special help desk identity that is given permission to modify the userPassword attribute in all person entries. Given a person's user ID that is supplied on its command line, the setpwd application locates the person's directory entry via an LDAP search operation. If one entry is found, a random password is generated and the existing userPassword values in the entry are replaced with the new password.

Because this is a simple directory application, there are no significant application architecture issues to consider. The setpwd application does, however, avoid reading unnecessary attributes from the user entries. In addition, setpwd uses only one LDAP connection even when it resets several users' passwords.

The Source Code

The setpwd utility is written in C, and it uses the Netscape Directory SDK for C (which provides a standard LDAPv3 C API). Nearly all the functions that are part of the LDAP C API begin with the prefix ldap_. The code was compiled and tested under the Sun Solaris 2.6 UNIX operating system, although it should be easy to port to other systems and implementations of the LDAP C API. The entire source code for setpwd consists of one file that is called, logically enough, setpwd.c. We present the code in pieces to aid understanding.

The beginning of the setpwd.c file is shown in Listing 20.2. Notice the inclusion of the standard LDAP header file on line 9.

LISTING 20.2 THE setpwd.c PRELUDE

```
1.    /*
2.     * A simple password resetting program for use by a helpdesk.
3.     */
4.    #include <stdio.h>
5.    #include <string.h>
6.    #include <stdlib.h>
7.    #include <ctype.h>
8.    #include <time.h>
9.    #include <ldap.h>

10.   #define LONGEST_WORD    100

11.   /*
12.    * Global variables:
13.    */
14.   char *base     = "dc=airius,dc=com";
15.   char *host     = "directory.airius.com";
16.   int  port      = LDAP_PORT;
17.   char *binddn   = "cn=HelpDesk, dc=airius, dc=com";
18.   char *bindpwd  = "secret#password";
19.   char *wordfile = "/usr/dict/words";
20.   int  quiet     = 0;        /* setenv QUIET to suppress chatter */

21.   /*
22.    * Function prototypes:
23.    */
24.   static int resetpwd( LDAP *ld, char *base, char *userid );
25.   static char *userid2dn( LDAP *ld, char *base, char *userid );
26.   static void print_ldap_error( LDAP *ld, int lderr, char *s );
27.   static char *randompwd( void );
28.   static char * randomword( void );
```

A series of LDAP-related global variables is defined and set on lines 14–19. The distinguished name (DN) and password used to bind to the directory service are hard-coded into this application (lines 17 and 18), which is unusual but convenient for the help desk personnel who are the audience for this application. The `wordfile` variable defined on line 19 has nothing to do with LDAP; it is used by `setpwd`'s random password generation code (described later).

The `setpwd main()` function is shown in Listing 20.3.

LISTING 20.3 THE `setpwd.c main()` FUNCTION

```
1.    int
2.    main( int argc, char **argv )
3.    {
4.        LDAP        *ld;
5.        int         i, rc;

6.        quiet = (( getenv( "QUIET" ) != NULL ));

7.        if ( argc < 2 ) {
8.            fprintf( stderr, "usage: %s userid...\n", argv[ 0 ] );
9.            return( 2 );
10.       }

11.       /*
12.        * Connect and bind to the directory server.
13.        */
14.       if ( !quiet ) puts( "Contacting LDAP server..." );
15.       if (( ld = ldap_init( host, port )) == NULL ) {
16.           perror( host );
17.           return( 1 );
18.       }

19.       if (( rc = ldap_simple_bind_s( ld, binddn, bindpwd ))
20.               != LDAP_SUCCESS ) {
21.           print_ldap_error( ld, rc, binddn );
22.           ldap_unbind( ld );
23.           return( 1 );
24.       }

25.       /*
26.        * Process userid arguments, setting random passwords
27.        * for each one.
28.        */
29.       rc = 0;
30.       srandom( time( NULL ));
31.       for ( i = 1; i < argc; ++i ) {
32.           if ( !quiet && i > 1 ) {
33.               putchar( '\n' );
34.           }
35.           rc |= resetpwd( ld, base, argv[ i ] );
36.       }

37.       /*
38.        * close LDAP server connection and exit.
```

```
39.          */
40.          ldap_unbind( ld );
41.          return( rc );
42.     }
```

After some simple argument checking and initialization, the code begins to interact with the LDAP SDK and the directory service. The code on lines 15–18 obtains an LDAP session handle for our LDAP server host and port. Note that the ldap_init() function call does not open a connection to the LDAP server. A connection to the LDAP server is opened the first time an LDAP request is made.

Such a request is made by the code on lines 19–24, which binds to the LDAP server using the help desk DN and password. The ldap_simple_bind_s() call connects to the directory server (if the session handle is not already connected, as is the case here), issues an LDAP bind request, and waits for the server response. A return code of LDAP_SUCCESS indicates that the DN and password were accepted and that the authentication was successful.

The code on lines 25–36 moves through the arguments provided on the command line and passes each one to the resetpwd() function, which is described next. The ldap_unbind() call included in the clean-up code on lines 37–42 does two things: It closes the LDAP connection and disposes of the memory and any other resources consumed by the LDAP session handle.

The code for the resetpwd() function, which is responsible for resetting one user's password, is shown in Listing 20.4.

LISTING 20.4 THE setpwd.c resetpwd() FUNCTION

```
1.      /*
2.       * resetpwd(): set an entry's password to a random string.
3.       *
4.       * Returns 0 on success and 1 on failure.
5.       */
6.      static int
7.      resetpwd( LDAP *ld, char *base, char *userid )
8.      {
9.          char         *dn, *pwd, *vals[2];
10.         int          rc;
11.         LDAPMod      mod, *mods[2];

12.         /*
13.          * Find the entry.
14.          */
15.         if ( !quiet ) printf( "Finding entry %s...\n", userid );
16.         if (( dn = userid2dn( ld, base, userid )) == NULL ) {
17.             return( 1 );
18.         }
```

continues

LISTING 20.4 CONTINUED

```
19.        if (( pwd = randompwd == NULL ) {
20.            return( 1 );
21.        }

22.        /*
23.         * Replace the userPassword attribute.
24.         */
25.        if ( !quiet ) printf( "Modifying entry %s...\n", userid );
26.        vals[0] = pwd;
27.        vals[1] = NULL;
28.        mod.mod_values = vals;
29.        mod.mod_type = "userPassword";
30.        mod.mod_op = LDAP_MOD_REPLACE;
31.        mods[0] = &mod;
32.        mods[1] = NULL;

33.        if (( rc = ldap_modify_s( ld, dn, mods )) == LDAP_SUCCESS ) {
34.            rc = 0;
35.            printf( "Password reset.  %s's new password is: %s\n",
36.                        userid, pwd );
37.            if ( !quiet ) {
38.                printf( "Don't forget to remind %s to reset "
39.                            "his/her password right away!\n", userid );
40.            }
41.        } else {
42.            rc = 1;
43.            print_ldap_error( ld, rc, "modify" );
44.        }

45.        free( pwd );
46.        ldap_memfree( dn );
47.        return( rc );
48.    }
```

The first task performed by this code is to find the user's directory entry (we need to know the DN to be able to modify the user's entry). The code on lines 12–18 calls a utility function named userid2dn() (described next) to find and return the user's DN given his or her user ID. The code on lines 19–21 calls another utility function called randompwd() (described later), which generates a new password for the user.

The remainder of the resetpwd() code (lines 22–48) accomplishes the task of replacing the userPassword attribute in the user's entry with the newly generated password. After setting up a one-element array of modifications, the ldap_modify_s() LDAP SDK function is called to direct the server to make the password change.

The source code for the `userid2dn()` utility function is shown in Listing 20.5. This function uses an LDAP subtree search operation to find a user's directory entry given his or her user ID.

LISTING 20.5 THE `setpwd.c` `userid2dn()` FUNCTION

```
1.      /*
2.       * userid2dn(): Given an entry's userid, return its DN.
3.       *
4.       * The DN returned should be freed by passing it to
5.       * ldap_memfree(). If no entry is found, NULL is returned.
6.       */
7.      static char *
8.      userid2dn( LDAP *ld, char *base, char *userid )
9.      {
10.         int         rc;
11.         char        *filter, *dn = NULL;
12.         char        *attrs[] = { LDAP_NO_ATTRS, NULL };
13.         LDAPMessage *e, *res = NULL;

14.         if (( filter = (char *)malloc( strlen( userid ) + 7 ))
15.                 == NULL ) {
16.             perror( "malloc" );
17.             return( NULL );
18.         }

19.         sprintf( filter, "(uid=%s)", userid );

20.         rc = ldap_search_s( ld, base, LDAP_SCOPE_SUBTREE,
21.                 filter, attrs, 0, &res );
22.         free( filter );

23.         if ( rc != LDAP_SUCCESS ) {
24.             print_ldap_error( ld, rc, "search" );
25.         } else if (( e = ldap_first_entry( ld, res )) == NULL ) {
26.             fprintf( stderr, "No match for %s\n", userid );
27.         } else if ( ldap_next_entry( ld, e ) != NULL ) {
28.             fprintf( stderr, "%d matches for %s\n",
29.                     ldap_count_entries( ld, res ), userid );
30.         } else {
31.             dn = ldap_get_dn( ld, e );  /* found just one! */
32.         }

33.         ldap_msgfree( res );
34.         return( dn );
35.     }
```

The code on lines 14–19 creates an LDAP search filter that looks like (uid=*ID*), where *ID* is the user ID provided on the setpwd command line. The actual search is done by the ldap_search_s() LDAP SDK call that appears on lines 20 and 21. Notice that the attrs parameter, which is an array of attribute types to

be returned with each entry found during the search, contains one type called
LDAP_NO_ATTRS (attrs is initialized on line 12). The special LDAP_NO_ATTRS macro,
defined by the LDAP API, is used to indicate that no attribute types should be
returned. This is desirable because it is wasteful to ask for attributes we do not
need, and in this instance we are interested in obtaining only the DN of the
entry. If we were to pass NULL for the attrs parameter, every attribute in the
entry would be returned. The code on lines 23–35 checks to see if exactly one
entry was found; if so, it returns the DN of the entry. If more than one entry is
found, or if no entries are found, an error is reported.

The print_ldap_error() utility function is shown in Listing 20.6. This simple
function is called from several places in setpwd.c to report LDAP-related errors
in a consistent way.

LISTING 20.6 THE setpwd.c print_ldap_error() FUNCTION

```
1.    /*
2.     * Display an LDAP error message.
3.     */
4.    void
5.    print_ldap_error( LDAP *ld, int lderr, char *s )
6.    {
7.        fprintf( stderr, "%s: %s\n", s, ldap_err2string( lderr ));
8.    }
```

The randompwd() function, which is called from the resetpwd() function we
already looked at, is shown in Listing 20.7. This code does not perform any
LDAP-related functions. It uses a file that contains a series of words (one per
line) and the standard random() number generator function to select a new
password. The actual algorithm used could easily be altered to match a specific
organization's security policy or the preferences of help desk technical staff.

LISTING 20.7 THE setpwd.c randompwd() FUNCTION

```
1.    /*
2.     * randompwd(): generate a reasonably good password using some
3.     * random words from a file.  The password should be easy to
4.     * remember and able to be passed on verbally to a user.
5.     *
6.     * The algorithm we use is this:
7.     *   a) select two random words from the words file (w1 and w2).
8.     *   b) pick a random punctuation character (c).
9.     *   c) pick a random digit 0-9 (d)
10.    *   d) construct a candidate password as:  w1 c w2 d
11.    *   e) change the case of one of the letters at random
12.    */
13.   static char *
14.   randompwd( void )
15.   {
16.       static char *punctuation = "!@#$%&*-+=,.?";
```

```
17.          char          *pwd, *w1, *w2, *p;

18.          if (( w1 = randomword == NULL ¦¦ ( w2 = randomword == NULL ) {
19.              if ( w1 != NULL ) {
20.                  free( w1 );
21.              }
22.              return( NULL );
23.          }

24.          if (( pwd = (char *)malloc( LONGEST_WORD * 2 + 3 )) != NULL ) ➡{
25.              sprintf( pwd, "%s%c%s%d", w1,
26.                      punctuation[ random() % strlen( punctuation ) ],
27.                      ➡w2,random() % 10 );
28.              p = pwd + ( random() % strlen( pwd ));
29.              if ( isalpha( *p )) {
30.                  if ( isupper( *p )) {
31.                      *p = tolower( *p );
32.                  } else {
33.                      *p = toupper( *p );
34.                  }
35.              }
36.          }

37.          free( w1 );
38.          free( w2 );
39.          return( pwd );
40.      }
```

The `randompwd()` function uses a utility function called `randomword()` to pick the two words that is uses to construct the password value. The first part of the `randomword()` function, which consists mainly of initialization tasks, is shown in Listing 20.8.

LISTING 20.8 THE `setpwd.c` `randomword()` FUNCTION (PART 1 OF 2)

```
1.      /*
2.       * randomword(): return a random, lowercase word.
3.       *
4.       * Returns a malloc'd string if successful.
5.       * Returns NULL on error, e.g., if unable to access
6.       * the words file.
7.       *
8.       * This function assumes that all words in the file are
9.       * less than LONGEST_WORD characters long.
10.      */
11.     static char *
12.     randomword( void )
13.     {
14.         static FILE *fp = NULL;
15.         static long filesize = 0L;
16.         char          *word, *p;
17.         int           len;
```

continues

LISTING 20.8 CONTINUED

```
18.        if ( fp == NULL ) {
19.            /*
20.             * initialize: open the words file and
21.             * determine its size
22.             */
23.            if (( fp = fopen( wordfile, "r" )) == NULL
24.                    ¦¦ fseek( fp, 0L, SEEK_END ) == -1
25.                    ¦¦ ( filesize = ftell( fp )) == -1 ) {
26.                perror( wordfile );
27.                if ( fp != NULL ) {
28.                    fclose( fp );
29.                }
30.                return( NULL );
31.            }

32.            filesize -= LONGEST_WORD;
33.        }
```

The remainder of the randomword() function, which randomly seeks to a location in the words file and returns a word, is shown in Listing 20.9.

LISTING 20.9 THE setpwd.c randomword() FUNCTION (PART 2 OF 2)

```
1.        /*
2.         * seek to a random location in the file.
3.         */
4.        if ( fseek( fp, random() % filesize, SEEK_SET ) == -1 ) {
5.            perror( wordfile );
6.            return( NULL );
7.        }

8.        if (( word = (char *)malloc( LONGEST_WORD )) == NULL ) {
9.            perror( "malloc" );
10.           return( NULL );
11.       }

12.       /*
13.        * read the tail (remainder) of one word and then
14.        * the entire next word, which is what we will return.
15.        */
16.       fgets( word, LONGEST_WORD - 1, fp );
17.       if ( fgets( word, LONGEST_WORD - 1, fp ) == NULL ) {
18.           perror( wordfile );
19.           free( word );
20.           return( NULL );
21.       }

22.       len = strlen( word ) - 1;
23.       if ( word[ len ] == '\n' ) {
24.           word[ len ] = '\0';
```

```
25.        }

26.        for ( p = word; *p != '\0'; ++p ) {
27.            if ( isupper( *p )) {
28.                *p = tolower( *p );
29.            }
30.        }

31.        return( word );
32.    }
```

The Help Desk Staff's Experience

Listing 20.10 shows a sample run of the setpwd application.

```
% setpwd scarter
Contacting LDAP server...
Finding entry scarter...
Modifying entry scarter...
Password reset.  scarter's new password is: Knife,attentive7
Don't forget to remind scarter to reset his/her password right away!
```

Sam Carter's password was reset to the random password Knife,attentive7.

Listing 20.11 shows another sample run of the setpwd utility.

```
% setenv QUIET
% setpwd scarter tmorris kvaughan abergin dmiller gfarmer
➥kwinters trigden cschmith jwall
ace
Password reset.  scarter's new password is: define+chaRd5
Password reset.  tmorris's new password is: cyclades@eT0
Password reset.  kvaughan's new password is: sorghum#releVant5
Password reset.  abergin's new password is: shinGle?appellant0
Password reset.  dmiller's new password is: grackLe,polish2
Password reset.  gfarmer's new password is: periClean+problematic5
Password reset.  kwinters's new password is: deforest*articulatoRy6
Password reset.  trigden's new password is: bombard+decontrolling2
Password reset.  cschmith's new password is: pessimist+lIne9
Password reset.  jwallace's new password is: paulSon,battle3
```

In this instance, 10 people's passwords were reset with a single run of the utility. The QUIET environment variable is set prior to running setpwd to reduce the amount of output.

Ideas for Improvement

The setpwd application could be improved in many ways. Here are a few ideas:

- Increase security by prompting for the help desk password, or by using a different form of authentication (such as Kerberos or public key certificates) instead of embedding the help desk password in the application.

- Increase security by taking advantage of your directory service's password policy features (if available) to force users to choose a new password the next time they bind to the directory after their password is reset using setpwd.

- Provide a way for the person who invokes setpwd to optionally specify the new password values.

- Expand the setpwd application's role by adding features to disable a user's account and change other information in user entries, such as email addresses.

- Create reusable, shared libraries that contain some of the LDAP-related code included in setpwd. Good candidates include the userid2dn() and print_ldap_error() functions.

Example 2: An Employee Time-Off Request Web Application

A common administrative task that managers must handle is a request by an employee for paid time off, usually in the form of sick days and vacation days. In a typical organization, the time off request process consists of these steps:

1. An employee fills out a paper form specifying the days she will be on vacation or the days she was out sick.

2. The employee gives the paper form to her manager.

3. The manager approves or turns down the request and informs the employee of the decision.

4. If the manager approves the request, he sends the paper form to the payroll department, where the time off is tracked and reported on the employee's paycheck.

In this section, we present a sample workflow application that uses an HTML form, an LDAP directory service, and email to automate most of these steps.

Directory Use

Our time-off request processing application uses the directory service for the following tasks:

- Finding the employee's entry given her user ID. This is done using an LDAP subtree search.

- Finding the DN of the employee's manager. This is done by checking her directory entry for a manager attribute value.

- Verifying the employee's identity by checking a password she provides against the one stored in the directory entry. This is done using an LDAP bind operation.

- Retrieving the email address of the employee's manager. This is done by reading the manager's entry using an LDAP search operation with a base object scope.

Because all the directory interaction takes place in a single Perl script, our time-off request application is able to use the directory efficiently. Because of a limitation of the PerLDAP module we use, however, two connections to the LDAP server are made instead of one. This minor problem is discussed in greater detail later.

The Source Code

The source code for our time-off request workflow application consists of two files: an HTML form called timeoff.html and a Perl common gateway interface (CGI) script called processto.pl. The HTML form provides the interface for an employee who is making the time off request. The Perl CGI script processes the form, uses email to send the request to the employee's manager, and provides feedback to the employee so she knows her request has been received and sent to her manager.

Listing 20.12 shows the contents of the timeoff.html file. The majority of the HTML code consists of a form that will be posted to the processto.pl script (as specified by line 5 of Listing 20.12).

LISTING 20.12 THE SOURCE CODE FOR THE timeoff.html FORM

```
1.      <HTML>
2.      <TITLE>Employee Time Off Request Form</TITLE>

3.      <BODY>
4.      <CENTER><H2>Employee Time Off Request Form</H2></CENTER>
5.      <FORM METHOD=post ACTION=/cgibin/processto.pl>
6.      <TABLE>
```

continues

LISTING 20.12 CONTINUED

```
7.      <TR><TD>User ID:</TD><TD>
8.      <INPUT NAME="userid" TYPE="text"</TD>
9.      <TD>Password:</TD><TD>
10.     <INPUT NAME="password" TYPE="password"></TD>
11.     </TABLE>

12.     <HR>
13.     <H3>Sick Time Requested:</H3>
14.     Start Date:
15.     <INPUT NAME="sickstart" TYPE="text" SIZE=12>
16.       End Date:
17.     <INPUT NAME="sickend" TYPE="text" SIZE=12>
18.       Total Hours:
19.     <INPUT NAME="sickhours" TYPE="text" SIZE=10>

20.     <HR>
21.     <H3>Vacation Time Requested:</H3>
22.     Start Date:
23.     <INPUT NAME="vacstart" TYPE="text" SIZE=12>
24.       End Date:
25.     <INPUT NAME="vacend" TYPE="text" SIZE=12>
26.       Total Hours:
27.     <INPUT NAME="vachours" TYPE="text" SIZE=10>

28.     <HR>
29.     <H3>Explanation:</H3>
30.     <TEXTAREA NAME="explanation" ROWS=3 COLS=60>
31.     </TEXTAREA>

32.     <HR>
33.     <INPUT TYPE="submit" VALUE="Send This Request To Your Manager">
34.         
35.     <INPUT TYPE="reset" VALUE="Clear This Form">

36.     </FORM>

37.     </BODY>
38.     </HTML>
```

This HTML file defines 11 form input fields. Two of the form fields are for employee identification (userid and password), seven are for data about the time-off request itself (sickstart, sickend, sickhours, vacstart, vacend, vachours, and explanation), and two buttons are provided to submit and clear the form.

The processto.pl Perl script is responsible for all of the directory interaction and for sending a time-off request message to an employee's manager using SMTP. It uses the PerLDAP module (which can be downloaded from the Netscape developer Web site at http://developer.netscape.com/tech/directory) and the CGI and Net::SMTP modules (which can be

downloaded from the comprehensive Perl archive network (CPAN) Web site at
http://www.cpan.org/). Because the processto.pl script is fairly long, we discuss it in several chunks. The first part of the script is shown in Listing 20.13.

LISTING 20.13 THE processto.pl PRELUDE

```
1.    #!/usr/local/bin/perl

2.    # processto.pl -- Perl 5 script to process time off requests
3.    #   submitted by timeoff.html and e-mail them to an employee's
4.    #   manager.
5.    #
6.    # Requires the PerLDAP, CGI, and Net::SMTP modules.

7.    use Mozilla::LDAP::Conn;
8.    use CGI;
9.    use Net::SMTP;

10.   # LDAP server information
11.   $ldapbase = "dc=airius,dc=com";
12.   $ldaphost = "directory.airius.com";
13.   $ldapport = "389";

14.   # SMTP server (for outgoing messages)
15.   $smtphost = "mailhost.airius.com";
16.   $smtpFrom = "timeoff-service\@airius.com";

17.   # Global variables
18.   $employeeName = "";
19.   $managerName = "";
```

The directory search base (used when locating the employee's entry), the LDAP
server information, and the information needed to send email messages using
SMTP is defined using global variables on lines 10–16. The employeeName and
managerName globals defined on lines 17–19 are used by the findManagerEmail
subroutine (discussed later) to convey additional information back to the
script's main module.

The first part of the processto.pl main module is shown in Listing 20.14. This
code makes extensive use of the object-oriented CGI processing interface provided by the CGI Perl module to transfer values from the posted form variables into local Perl variables.

LISTING 20.14 THE processto.pl MAIN MODULE (PART 1 OF 2)

```
1.    # Start of main:

2.    # Reject excessively huge posts and all file uploads
3.    $CGI::POST_MAX=1024 * 10;   # accept a maximum of 10K of data
4.    $CGI::DISABLE_UPLOADS = 1; # disallow all file uploads
```

continues

LISTING 20.14 CONTINUED

```
5.    $post = new CGI;
6.    print $post->header();

7.    # Get the values of all of the posted form variables
8.    $userid = $post->param( "userid" );
9.    $password = $post->param( "password" );
10.   $sickstart = $post->param( "sickstart" );
11.   $sickend = $post->param( "sickend" );
12.   $sickhours = $post->param( "sickhours" );
13.   $vacstart = $post->param( "vacstart" );
14.   $vacend = $post->param( "vacend" );
15.   $vachours = $post->param( "vachours" );
16.   $explanation = $post->param( "explanation" );

17.   # Validate the posted variables
18.   if ( $password eq "" ) {
19.       incompleteForm( $post,
20.               "Please go back and enter your Password" );
21.   }
22.   if ( $userid eq "" ) {
23.       incompleteForm( $post,
24.               "Please go back and enter your User ID" );
25.   }
26.   if ( $sickhours eq "" && $vachours eq "" ) {
27.       incompleteForm( $post, "Please go back and enter "
28.               . "some sick or vacation hours" );
29.   }
30.   $employeeName = $userid;          # best we have (for now)
```

Lines 17–30 perform simple validation of the form contents to ensure that the minimum required set of information was provided by the employee who submitted the form.

The remainder of the main module is shown in Listing 20.15. This code first tries to find the email address of the employee's manager. If an address is found, it constructs a time-off request email message using the information posted in the time-off request form, and it sends the message to the manager for approval.

LISTING 20.15 THE processto.pl MAIN MODULE (PART 2 OF 2)

```
1.    # find manager's e-mail address
2.    $managerEmail = findManagerEmail( $post, $userid, $password );

3.    # construct and send an e-mail message to the manager
4.    if ( $managerEmail ne "" ) {
5.        $subject = "Time off request for $userid ($employeeName).";
6.        $text = "$subject\n\n";
7.        if ( $sickhours ne "" ) {
8.            $text .= "Sick time hours:       "
```

```
9.                        . "$sickhours ($sickstart-$sickend)\n";
10.            }
11.            if ( $vachours ne "" ) {
12.                $text .= "Vacation time hours: "
13.                        . "$vachours ($vacstart-$vacend)\n";
14.            }
15.            if ( $explanation ne "" ) {
16.                $text .= "\nExplanation: $explanation\n";
17.            }
18.            $text .= "\nTo approve this request, reply and include "
19.                        . "the word APPROVE in the message text.\n";
20.            $text .= "\nTo deny this request, reply and include "
21.                        . "the word DENY in the message text.\n";

22.            $rc = sendMailMessage( $managerEmail, $smtpFrom,
23.                    $subject, $text );

24.            if ( $rc == 0 ) {
25.                print $post->h3( "Your request has been sent to "
26.                        . "your manager ($managerName). You should "
27.                        . "soon receive an e-mail message telling "
28.                        . "you if your request was approved." );
29.            } else {
30.                print $post->b( "Unable to send e-mail message. "
31.                        . "Please try again later." );
32.                displayBackButton();
33.            }
34.    }

35.    $post->end_html();
36.    # End of main.
```

All the directory interaction takes place inside the findManagerEmail subroutine (described next), which is called on line 2. The remainder of the code in the main module constructs an email message and calls on the sendMailMessage subroutine (described later) to send the message to the manager.

The first part of the findManagerEmail subroutine is shown in Listing 20.16. The job of this subroutine is to authenticate the employee, locate her manager using the manager attribute, and read an email address value from the manager's mail attribute. Because the manager attribute is a DN-valued attribute, there is no need to do a subtree search to find the manager entry—we can get to it directly using the value found in the employee's manager attribute.

LISTING 20.16 THE processto.pl findManagerEmail SUBROUTINE (PART 1 OF 2)

```
1.    # Start of findManagerEmail:
2.    #   Connect to the LDAP server and authenticate as the user.
3.    #   Locate their manager's entry via the "manager" attribute.
4.    #   Read the manager's e-mail address from his/her "mail"
5.    #      attribute and return it.
```

continues

Listing 20.16 Continued

```
6.    #  If any errors occur, a message is output in HTML and ""
7.    #    is returned.
8.    #  This function also emits some HTML to show the employee
9.    #    and manager's names, etc.
10.   sub
11.   findManagerEmail( $cgiout, $userid, $password )
12.   {
13.       local( $cgiout, $userid, $password ) = @_;
14.       local( @attrlist, $ldap, $employeeDN, $managerDN,
15.              $managerMail );

16.       @attrlist = ( "cn", "mail", "manager" );
17.       $managerMail = "";

18.   # Open an anonymous connection to the LDAP server
19.       $ldap = new Mozilla::LDAP::Conn( $ldaphost, $ldapport );
20.       if ( ! $ldap ) {
21.           print $cgiout->b( "Unable to connect to directory"
22.                       . " service. Please try again later." );
23.           displayBackButton( $cgiout );
24.           return "";
25.       }

26.   # Find the employee's entry
27.       $entry = $ldap->search( $ldapbase, "subtree",
28.                "(uid=$userid)", 0, @attrlist );
29.       if ( ! $entry ) {
30.           print $cgiout->b( "No match for User ID $userid" );
31.           displayBackButton();
32.           $ldap->close;
33.           return "";
34.       }

35.   # Extract interesting information from the employee entry
36.       $employeeDN = $entry->{"dn"};
37.       if ( $entry->{"cn"}) {
38.           $employeeName = $entry->{"cn"}[0];
39.           print $cgiout->h3( "Hello $employeeName." );
40.       }
41.       if ( $entry->{"manager"}) {
42.           $managerDN = $entry->{"manager"}[0];
43.       } else {
44.           $managerDN = "";
45.       }
```

We use the small attrlist array defined on line 16 in all the LDAP search requests we make. The code on lines 18–25 opens an anonymous, unauthenticated connection to the LDAP server using the PerLDAP modules' object-oriented interface. The code on lines 26–34 uses PerLDAP method calls to find the employee's entry by performing a subtree search with a filter based on the user ID. Lines 35–45 extract the employee's name (from the cn attribute) and the DN of the employee's manager (from the manager attribute), if they are present.

The remainder of the findManagerEmail subroutine is shown in Listing 20.17. This code checks the employee's password by binding to the LDAP server and reads the manager entry in order to return the manager's email address.

LISTING 20.17 THE processto.pl findManagerEmail SUBROUTINE (PART 2 OF 2)

```
1.     # Close existing connection and open an authenticated
2.     # connection to the LDAP server
3.         $ldap->close;
4.         $ldap = new Mozilla::LDAP::Conn( $ldaphost, $ldapport,
5.                 $employeeDN, $password );
6.         if ( ! $ldap ) {
7.             print $cgiout->b( "Unable to authenticate to "
8.                         . "the directory service.  Please check "
9.                         . "your password and try again." );
10.            displayBackButton( $cgiout );
11.            return "";
12.        }

13.    # Read manager entry to get name and e-mail address
14.        if ( $managerDN eq "" ) {
15.            print $cgiout->h3( "Your manager is not listed in your "
16.                        . "directory entry.  Please contact the "
17.                        . "IS HelpDesk for assistance." );
18.        } else {
19.            $entry = $ldap->search( $managerDN, "base",
20.                        "(objectClass=*)", 0, @attrlist ) ;
21.            if ( ! $entry ) {
22.                print $cgiout->h3( "Your manager is not listed in "
23.                            . "the directory.  Please contact the "
24.                            . "IS HelpDesk for assistance." );
25.            } else {
26.                if ( $entry->{"mail"}) {
27.                    $managerMail = $entry->{"mail"}[0];
28.                }
29.                if ( $entry->{"cn"}) {
30.                    $managerName = $entry->{"cn"}[0];
31.                } else {
32.                    $managerName = $managerMail; # best we have
33.                }
34.            }
35.        }

36.    # Clean up and return
37.        $ldap->close;
38.        $managerMail;
39.    }
40.    # End of findManagerEmail.
```

At the time of this writing, the PerLDAP module does not support binding a second time on the same connection, so the code on lines 1–12 closes the connection that was previously used to find the employee's entry and creates a new connection, binding using the employee DN and password. Short of requiring that the employee enter her DN in the time-off request form (not recommended!), there is no way to avoid using two connections like this; we need to first search by user ID to find the DN that we use in the authenticated bind.

The code on lines 13–25 reads the manager's entry by performing a base object search on the manager DN. Because just one entry needs to be examined, this kind of search is very efficient in most LDAP server implementations. Lines 26–35 extract the manager's name (from the `cn` attribute) and email address (from the `mail` attribute), if they are present. The code on lines 36–40 closes the second LDAP connection and returns the `managerMail` value.

The remainder of the code in the `processto.pl` CGI script consists of utility subroutines that do not interact with the directory service. The first two of these subroutines are the `incompleteForm` and `displayBackButton` subroutines shown in Listing 20.18.

LISTING 20.18 THE `processto.pl` `incompleteForm` AND `displayBackButton` SUBROUTINES

```
1.    # Start of incompleteForm:
2.    sub
3.    incompleteForm {
4.        local( $cgiout, $msg ) = @_;

5.        print $cgiout->b( "Incomplete form. $msg." ), "\n";
6.        displayBackButton( $cgiout );
7.        print $cgiout->end_html;
8.        exit;
9.    }
10.   # End of incompleteForm.


11.   # Start of displayBackButton:
12.   sub
13.   displayBackButton {
14.       local( $cgiout ) = @_;

15.       print $cgiout->start_form,
16.               $cgiout->button(-name=>'goback', -value=>'Go Back',
17.               -onClick=>'window.back()'), $cgiout->end_form;
18.   }
19.   # End of displayBackButton.
```

The `incompleteForm` subroutine is called by the main module to report to the employee in a consistent manner that he or she neglected to fill in one of the required form fields. The displayBackButton subroutine is called in several places to generate HTML code for a Go Back button, which provides a convenient way for the employee to return to the original form so she can make needed corrections or fill in missing information.

The last piece of the processto.pl script is the sendMailMessage subroutine shown in Listing 20.19. This >subroutine is called by the main module and uses the Net::SMTP Perl module to send an email message.

LISTING 20.19 THE processto.pl sendMailMessage SUBROUTINE

```
1.    # Start of sendMailMessage:
2.    # Returns 0 if all goes well and non-zero if not.
3.    sub
4.    sendMailMessage()
5.    {
6.        local( $to, $from, $subject, $text ) = @_;
7.        local( $smtp );

8.        $smtp = Net::SMTP->new( $smtphost );
9.        if ( ! $smtp ) {
10.           return 1;
11.       }
12.       $smtp->mail( $from );
13.       $smtp->to( $to );
14.       $smtp->data();
15.       $smtp->datasend( "To: $to\n" );
16.       $smtp->datasend( "From: $from\n" );
17.       if ( $subject ne "" ) {
18.           $smtp->datasend( "Subject: $subject\n" );
19.       }
20.       $smtp->datasend( "\n$text" );
21.       $smtp->dataend();
22.       $smtp->quit;

23.       0;  # success
24.   }
25.   # End of sendMailMessage.
```

The Employee's Experience

Now, let's take a look at the time-off workflow application in action. Employees connect to a well-advertised location (such as http://hr/timeoff.html) using their Web browser. An empty form is displayed based on the timeoff.html HTML file discussed earlier. Figure 20.13 shows a sample vacation request form completed by an employee named Babs Jensen.

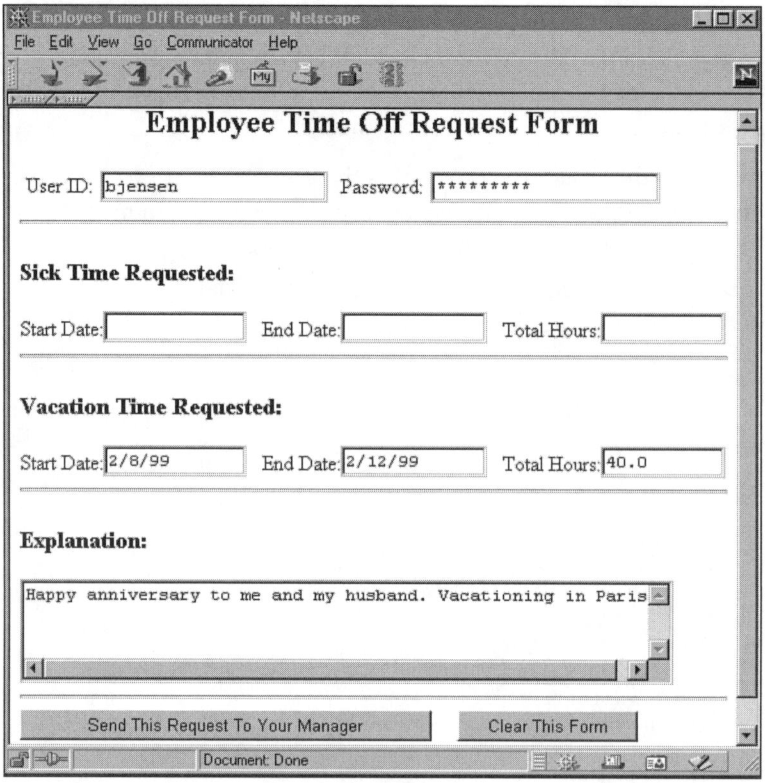

FIGURE 20.13 *A sample time-off request form.*

After the employee clicks on the Send This Request To Your Manager button, the processto.pl CGI script is invoked behind the scenes to process the form and notify the manager about the request. The script also produces confirmation output for the employee. A sample response is shown in Figure 20.14.

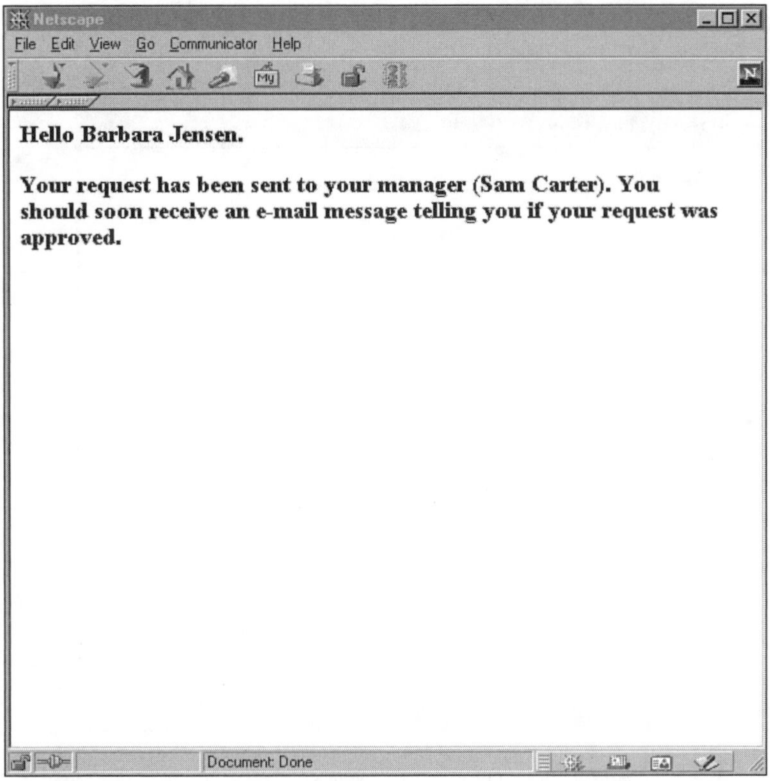

FIGURE 20.14   *A sample response to a time-off request submission.*

The Manager's Experience

Managers do not interact with the HTML form (unless they request some time off for themselves). Instead, they receive an email message that instructs them to reply and mark the request with APPROVE or DENY. The message generated by Babs' request is shown in Figure 20.15.

Replies are sent to a special address called `timeoff-service@airius.com`, which is monitored by a human or automated service within the payroll department. That person or service is responsible for recording the information as needed and notifying the employee about her request via email.

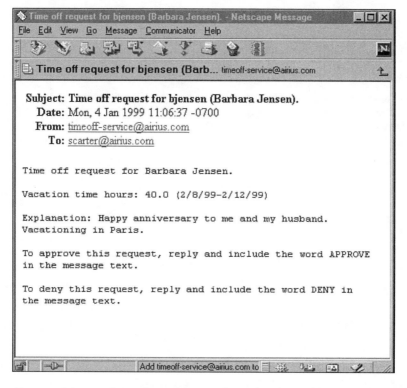

FIGURE 20.15   *A sample manager email message generated by the* processto.pl *script.*

Ideas for Improvement

Our time-off request directory-enabled workflow application could be improved in many ways. Here are a few ideas:

- Improve the timeoff.html form by having it check for empty required fields using JavaScript (instead of requiring that the employee submit the form, wait for the CGI script to validate the fields and inform her of her mistake, and then click on Go Back to fill in the required fields).

- Improve the timeoff.html form by having it calculate a value for the two Total Hours: fields using JavaScript.

- Improve the timeoff.html form by adding JavaScript code to validate the date fields.

- Write a script that can be used to process replies sent by managers to the timeoff-service email address. The script should send a message back to the employee to let her know if her request was approved or denied, and it should also submit data about time-off requests approved by managers to a payroll system.

- To further streamline the request approval process, change the processto.pl script to generate an HTML email message that contains two buttons labeled Approve and Deny that perform those respective functions.

- If you keep track of whether an employee is on vacation or not in your directory service (this is typically done to support automated vacation email responders), enhance the processto.pl script to check whether an employee's manager is currently on vacation and, if so, send the time-off request to the manager's manager instead. Be sure to inform the employee who submitted the request that this was done.

Developing New Applications Checklist

☐ Identify one or more needs that can be filled by developing a new directory-enabled application.

☐ Check that it makes sense to use an LDAP directory for the application.

☐ Choose the best LDAP development tool for the task at hand.

☐ Design your application to fit in well with other applications and the directory service itself.

☐ Document how the application will be integrated with the directory service. Share that information with the people who maintain the directory service.

☐ Consider performance and scalability during application design and implementation.

☐ Develop a prototype application and conduct pilot tests, if appropriate.

☐ Leverage existing code if possible.

☐ Avoid common LDAP application development mistakes.

Further Reading

Active Directory Services Interface (ADSI). Available on Microsoft's SDK World Wide Web site at `http://www.microsoft.com/msdn/sdk/`.

Java Naming and Directory Interface (JNDI). Available on JavaSoft's JNDI Web site at `http://java.sun.com/products/jndi/`.

mozilla.org Directory SDK Source Code. Available on the `mozilla.org` Web site at `http://www.mozilla.org/directory/`.

Netscape Directory SDK for C. Available on Netscape's Directory Developer Central Web site at `http://developer.netscape.com/tech/directory/`.

Netscape Directory SDK for Java. Available on Netscape's Directory Developer Central Web site at `http://developer.netscape.com/tech/directory/`.

Oblix Corporate Directory. More information is available on the World Wide Web at `http://www.oblix.com`.

PerLDAP, an Object-Oriented LDAP Perl Module for Perl5. Available on Netscape's Directory Developer Central Web site at `http://developer.netscape.com/tech/directory/`.

Programming Directory-Enabled Applications with Lightweight Directory Access Protocol. T. Howes and M. Smith, Macmillan Technical Publishing USA, 1997.

Programming Perl (2nd ed.). L. Wall (ed.), R. L. Schwartz, T. Christiansen, and S. Potter, O'Reilly & Associates, 1996.

The C LDAP Application Program Interface (Internet Draft). M. Smith, T. Howes, A. Herron, C. Weider, M. Wahl, and A. Anantha, 1998; available on the World Wide Web at `http://www.ietf.org`.

The Java LDAP Application Program Interface (Internet Draft). R. Weltman, T. Howes, and M. Smith, 1998; available on the World Wide Web at `http://www.ietf.org`.

The Java Programming Language (2nd ed.). Ken Arnold and James Gosling, Addison-Wesley, 1997.

X.509 Internet Public Key Infrastructure Online Certificate Status Protocol—OCSP (Internet Draft). M. Myers, R. Ankney, A. Malpani, S. Galperin, and C. Adams, 1998; available on the World Wide Web at `http://www.ietf.org`.

Looking Ahead

In Chapter 21, "Directory-Enabling Existing Applications," we will continue our discussion of how to effectively leverage your deployed directory service. By integrating LDAP support into an application, you can add exciting new features and lower the cost of maintenance.

CHAPTER 21

Directory-Enabling Existing
Applications

In Chapter 20, "Developing New Applications," we talked about developing new applications that can use your directory service. The basic idea is to leverage your deployed LDAP directory and bring its benefits to your users.

But what about existing applications? They can also benefit from being directory enabled. It is often harder to get people to use a new application than a modified one they already use. This is why it is often advantageous just to directory-enable an existing application instead of writing a new one. If the application to be modified has a split client/server, or "thin client," architecture, you may be able to LDAP-enable it by making changes only on the server side and thus avoid the need to deploy new software to end users. Most Web (HTML-based) applications can be LDAP enabled in this way.

The usual motivation for directory-enabling an existing application is to add new features that use LDAP, or to change an existing feature to use LDAP instead of an application-specific database or directory. By leveraging a deployed LDAP directory service, it is often possible to improve the end user experience and reduce system administration costs at the same time.

In the first section of this chapter, we detail why it makes sense to directory-enable an existing application. Then we discuss some techniques to help you directory-enable applications easily and successfully. In the last portion of the chapter, we present two concrete examples of directory-enabling existing applications. For information on SDKs and tools that can be used to integrate your applications with LDAP, please see Chapter 20.

Reasons to Directory-Enable Existing Applications

If you already have your own reasons for integrating existing applications with your directory service, you can safely skip this section. However, you may not be aware of many other good reasons to directory-enable an existing application. By integrating existing applications with your directory service, you can do any or all of the following:

- *Enable new features in the applications.* For example, users of an email client application can access shared address books.

- *Lower your data management costs.* This is usually accomplished by eliminating redundant copies of data and decommissioning private directories and databases.

- *Simplify life for end users by leveraging your deployed directory service.* For example, using a centralized directory for authentication reduces the number of distinct passwords end users need to remember.

- *Bring the directory service to your end users.* By enhancing an existing application instead of changing to a new one, you make it easier for end users to adopt your directory service.

Note that sometimes it does not make sense to integrate an application with a directory service. For example, the data the application uses may violate your directory data policy. Please refer to Chapter 20 for more information on when it does *not* make sense to directory-enable an application.

Each of the benefits of integrating an application with a directory service is discussed further in the following sections.

Enabling New Features in Applications

The process of LDAP integration can be used to add entirely new features to applications. The added features can increase the value of the application and expose users to your directory service in a new way. For example, suppose you have a widely used email application with only local lookup capabilities for its address book; you could add LDAP lookup capabilities so that users could access other address books shared across the organization. They would thus access your directory service more because it would be closely tied to a task they perform often: addressing and sending email.

New application features like a local-to-global address book upgrade are extensions of existing ones. However, added features can be completely new, too. For example, modifying a server application to store its configuration information in an LDAP directory service allows the configuration to be shared among a set of similarly configured servers, thereby reducing server management costs and enabling new server deployment scenarios.

Lowering Your Data Management Costs

Directory-enabling an application that has a private, application-specific data store can reduce the cost of data management: The private data store can be taken out of service, and all the resources used to run and maintain it can be eliminated. These old, application-specific directories and databases are often more expensive to maintain than a centralized, LDAP-based directory service; expertise is harder to find, management tools are weaker, and platform choices are more limited than with an LDAP directory.

Another way data management costs can be reduced is by eliminating redundant copies of data elements; the need for synchronization between a data source and your centralized directory is eliminated with them. If some of the data used by the application is personal data, your end users will appreciate that data about them is stored in one fewer place—therefore making changes to the data easier.

For example, consider an existing workflow system with its own database storing information about users of the system (see Figure 21.1). In this system, end users and administrators must update two separate information stores.

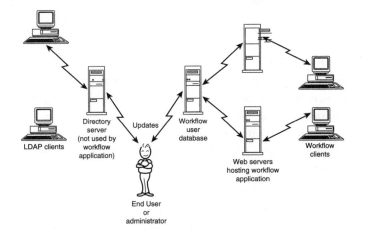

FIGURE 21.1 *A workflow application with a private database.*

By consolidating into the directory service the information held in the private database, redundant data is eliminated and the system as a whole is simplified (see Figure 21.2).

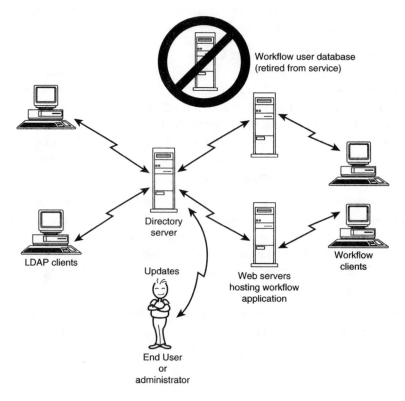

FIGURE 21.2   *The directory-enabled workflow application.*

Simplifying Life for End Users

Another important reason to leverage your deployed directory service in existing applications is to simplify life for end users. Part of this simplification is achieved by eliminating redundant, application-specific data stores. For example, if all your applications that send postal mail use a common directory service to determine a person's mailing address, employees need to change their address in only one place when they move.

Another simplification possible through use of a centralized directory is to create a consistent view of information from within a variety of applications. All applications that use the same LDAP directory service access the same information by using the same protocol. Use of a common data store and access method leads to greater consistency in the look and feel of different applications and the terminology they use. This makes it easier for end users to carry over their knowledge of one application to another.

A related motivating factor is that over time, people will expect the directory service to be used behind the scenes when they access certain kinds of information. For example, novice users who discover your Web-based directory phonebook application may assume that all contact information about them is stored in one directory service. They will be disappointed if the same information they find in the phonebook isn't returned when they execute the `finger` command on their UNIX workstation. This unfortunate situation is shown in Figure 21.3.

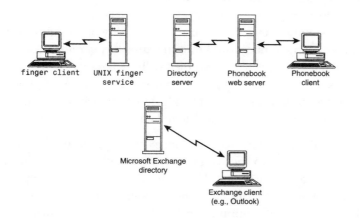

FIGURE 21.3 *Unintegrated contact information lookup applications.*

By directory-enabling the `finger` service, end user confusion and frustration can be reduced. This happier situation is depicted in Figure 21.4.

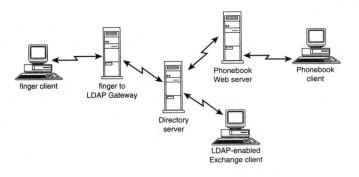

FIGURE 21.4 *Integrated, directory-enabled contact information lookup applications.*

Bringing the Directory Service to Your End Users

The benefit of directory-enabling can be somewhat self-serving, especially if one of your goals is simply to increase the use and visibility of your directory. Directory-enabling existing applications brings the directory service closer to your end users—making it more likely that they will use the service. By making your directory service an essential part of your users' everyday life, you ensure future support for it. More people using a directory service should also result in better data quality and more-consistent data across data stores.

People are more likely to try a new version of an existing software application they already use than they are to try a completely new application. For this reason, it is often better to add a little bit of LDAP support to an existing application than it is to invest in the development and deployment of a brand new, richly featured directory-enabled application. The key is to add features that are valuable to your users so they will want to use your directory service.

For example, you might have a Web-based building and conference room location service running on one of your intranet Web servers. Enhancing this application to retrieve an employee's office location from the directory so that people, buildings, and conference rooms can be located adds value for end users and increases the use of your directory service.

Advice for Directory-Enabling Existing Applications

Adding LDAP support to an existing application may be better than creating a brand new LDAP application, but it can also be much more difficult. The degree of difficulty depends on the nature of the application you are modifying, the scope of the changes you need to make, and the level of LDAP expertise you expect the application's users to have. You can use the following techniques to ease the pain of development and increase the payoff when you are done (some choices conflict with others, and they won't all apply in all situations):

- Hide the directory integration from users and systems that depend on the application.

- Make the new directory capabilities visible to the users of the application to promote new features.

- Use a protocol gateway to achieve integration.

- Avoid problematic architectural choices that adversely affect performance, involve the duplication of a lot of data, and so on.

- Consider how the directory service will be affected, and inform those who run the service of any need for increased capacity and other modifications.

- Plan for a transition from the existing application to the new directory-enabled version.

- Be creative and consider all your options.

Each idea is discussed in greater detail in this section. Again, some of these ideas conflict with one another; you should use the ideas that make the most sense in your situation.

Hiding the Directory Integration

Depending on the kind of directory-enabling you do, it may make sense to try to hide the changes from the users of the application as much as possible. This can be especially important if the application is used widely or by other systems that are difficult and expensive to modify.

For example, suppose you have an email delivery system that uses five servers, each with its own local database of information about users and mailing lists. You may want to reduce your system management costs by directory-enabling the email servers so they all share a single directory of information about users and lists. It may be possible to hide this change from users of the email service by doing all the directory integration on the back end (i.e., in the email servers themselves). This way, you can avoid deploying new email clients, and your users need not learn anything new.

Another example of hiding directory integration is to modify a client application that normally queries a proprietary directory to instead query an LDAP directory—without changing the user interface. The proprietary directory can be eliminated, and users need not learn a new interface.

The general idea behind hiding directory integration from the people or systems that use an application is to reduce the cost and pain associated with the introduction of a directory service.

Making the New Directory Capabilities Visible

An alternative to hiding directory integration is to make the new directory capabilities visible to the users of the application. If you are truly adding new features—or if you simply want to better promote your directory service—exposing the new features to the application's users is a useful technique.

For example, suppose you have a Web-based workflow application that requires users to know a person's user ID to include them in a flow. Adding a directory feature that allows lookups of people based on name, phone number, and other criteria may be a great benefit to workflow users. To ensure that people notice the new feature, you may want to alter the interface of the workflow application by adding a new button to access the new feature. As a side benefit, users who appreciate the new feature will know that it is made possible by your directory service. This in turn will help promote your service.

A more subtle technique is to modify the application in some way to simply let people know that they are using a directory service. For example, you might add a banner that reads "Directory-Enabled `finger` Service" to the output returned by an LDAP-aware UNIX finger server.

Using a Protocol Gateway to Achieve Integration

An application gateway that translates between an existing protocol and LDAP is often an effective way to directory-enable an existing, widely used application. A *gateway* is a server application that accepts a request by using one application protocol, translates it to another protocol such as LDAP, and passes it to another server. A similar translation procedure is performed—in the reverse direction—on information returned from the directory server.

Suppose you have been using the CSO Nameserver software from the University of Illinois to provide a simple directory service for your users. CSO is similar to LDAP, but simpler. A number of clients for CSO exist, including one built in to the popular email client Eudora. By replacing your CSO Nameserver with a CSO-to-LDAP gateway, end users can be given access to your LDAP directory service in a fairly transparent manner (see Figure 21.5). A freely available gateway product called CX can be used as the gateway.

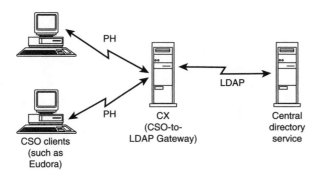

FIGURE 21.5 *Using the CX CSO-to-LDAP gateway.*

Another example is a building access system that consists of dozens of electronic card readers that communicate with a centralized building access database through a proprietary protocol (see Figure 21.6).

Let's assume that the building-access database contains redundant information about people, so you decide to replace it with your directory service. One approach would be to upgrade to card readers that speak LDAP directly. Due to high cost and lack of availability of such devices, a much cheaper and simpler approach might be to hide the directory integration from the card readers. This could be accomplished by building an intermediate server that acts as a gateway between the card readers' proprietary protocol and LDAP (see Figure 21.7).

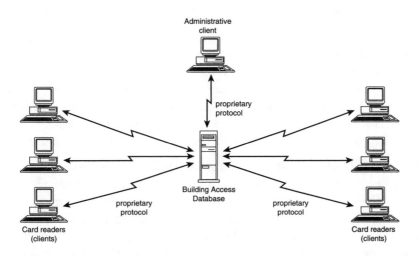

FIGURE 21.6 *A building access system before directory-enabling.*

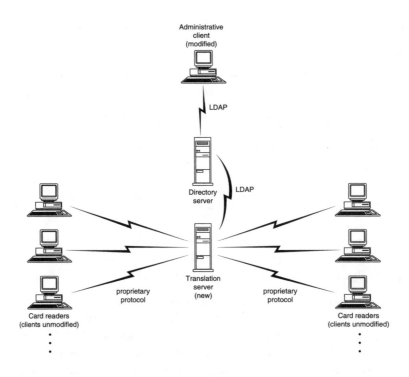

Figure 21.7 *A directory-enabled building access system.*

By using an application protocol gateway to bring directory service to your users, no changes need to be made to the client software they already use. This means that you can deploy the directory capability more quickly and with less expense.

Avoiding Problematic Architectural Choices

For all their good points, gateways have some problematic characteristics as well. Using a gateway sometimes leads to unacceptable performance, introducing delay and consuming additional system resources to translate from one protocol to another. Teaching about gateways also causes management headaches: It is one more piece of software to monitor and keep running.

In addition, gateways sometimes produce an imperfect directory experience for users of an application. A compromise must typically be made to fit any two protocols together, and if too much is lost in the translation, users may complain. For example, advanced features of LDAP aren't likely to be supported by an older protocol such as PH (which the CSO Nameserver is based on). The list view extension, for example, allows users to efficiently browse tens of thousands of directory entries; however, people who access your directory service via PH will not be able to take advantage of the feature.

Integration schemes that make copies of directory data are also troublesome. Live access to directory data (via a gateway, for example) is generally preferred over accessing data that has been duplicated and placed in another data store; such synchronization between data stores is often difficult, resource-intensive, and fragile. You need to consider the tradeoff between high-performance access to data, which might be best achieved by copying the data, and timely access to changing data. More information on integrating other data sources with your directory service can be found in Chapter 22, "Directory Coexistence."

Considering How the Directory Service Will Be Affected

When directory-enabling any application, it is important to consider how the application will use the directory service. The people who run the directory service need to know what kind of load the new directory-enabled version of the application will place on their service. Changes to the directory schema may be required to accommodate the application. Sometimes an application requires an LDAP protocol feature that is not supported by the directory server software in use. An upgrade may be necessary, or a different strategy may need to be chosen to accomplish the directory integration.

For example, the directory-enabled version of the building access system described earlier would increase the load on the directory service. The amount of the increase can easily be calculated using the number of card key accesses performed weekly using the existing, non-LDAP building access database. Suppose this number is 70,000. The new directory-enabled system might use two LDAP search operations when deciding whether to grant access: one to find the user associated with a card and one to check whether the user is in a group that has access to a given building. The total load imposed on the directory service by the new system would thus be 140,000 searches per week. Each search needs to be answered fairly quickly because people will not tolerate long delays while waiting for a door to be unlocked. You should also take into account peak load: An application may be used more often at certain times of the day or on certain days of the week. For example, it is likely that a majority of the card key accesses occur between the hours of 8:00 and 10:30 a.m. on weekdays, when most people arrive for work.

By providing detailed information about how your directory-enabled application will affect the directory service, those responsible for the service can plan to accommodate the load or new service features introduced by your application. More advice on communicating the needs of your application to those who maintain a directory service can be found in Chapter 20.

Planning for a Transition

Try to plan an orderly transition from the existing application to the new
directory-enabled version. By introducing the new directory capabilities in a
controlled way, you reduce the risk associated with the change. To transition
smoothly, you must continue to support the old application for a period of
time while users and dependent systems switch and adjust to the new version.

Try to use an incremental approach in which you pilot the new version of the
application before fully rolling it out. For most applications, this can be done
by announcing the new directory-enabled version to a small number of users,
extracting and incorporating their feedback, and then rolling it out to your
entire user base. If the application you modify is primarily used by other systems, you may be able to limit how many systems you initially switch over to
use the directory-enabled version of the application. Another approach is to
test the modified application with the dependent systems during off hours,
when any resulting problems have less of an effect on your organization.

Being Creative and Considering All Your Options

As you consider how best to directory-enable an existing application, be creative. The most obvious and straightforward approach is not always the best
one. Consider all the possible techniques we have discussed and others to
determine what makes the most sense for the application you are directory-
enabling.

When considering the alternatives, think about what you want to accomplish
by directory-enabling the application. Do you want to provide completely new
capabilities to end users? Are you trying to save system maintenance costs by
decommissioning a redundant data store? Do you want to quietly introduce
the directory-enabled application, or do you want to make a big splash and
generate publicity for your directory service? The best choice is influenced by
the answers to these and many other questions.

For example, when adding LDAP support to a widely used application such as
an email client, adopting an address book metaphor for the interface to the
new LDAP features may increase the rate of adoption and reduce the learning
curve for your users. On the other hand, introducing an entirely new user
interface paradigm, such as a "Search LDAP" screen, allows more flexibility in
exposing LDAP-specific features such as compound Boolean search filters.
With some creative thinking, you can design your application to provide access
to advanced address book capabilities for power users but preserve a familiar
address book interface for novices. A possible approach could be to allow
power users to type LDAP search filters in a search field that accepts simple
text strings.

Another example of creative thinking might arise when considering how best to integrate an LDAP directory service with a legacy application that has a proprietary data store. If performance is a key requirement, it may be appropriate to modify the application to speak LDAP natively. But suppose your primary goal of LDAP integration is to eliminate the database system used by the application and reduce your data store maintenance costs. Then the more appropriate approach to integration might involve a protocol or API-level gateway that looks to the application like its old data store but accesses data from an LDAP directory. The gateway approach may be easier to develop and deploy, thereby allowing you to achieve your primary goal of decommissioning the legacy data store more quickly.

Example 1: A Directory-Enabled `finger` Service

A `finger` service is a simple client/server account lookup mechanism supported by all UNIX operating systems. A `finger` client exists for most desktop operating systems, including all flavors of UNIX, Microsoft Windows, and Apple MacOS. A `finger` server, included with all UNIX systems, can return information about local accounts to all finger clients on the network (`finger` servers have been developed for non-UNIX systems as well). The `finger` clients and servers communicate using a simple text-based protocol.

Assuming that many end users have access to a `finger` client and know how to use it, it's sensible to make some of the people information stored in a directory service available via `finger`. In this section, we provide source code and usage examples for a directory-enabled `finger` server written in Perl. Our service searches an LDAP directory and returns information about people.

The Integration Approach

Our goal is to leverage the knowledge and client software that users already have, so we use a gateway to integrate `finger` with LDAP. On most UNIX systems, an executable called `in.fingerd` is used in response to incoming `finger` protocol requests. By replacing that executable with our own script that understands the `finger` protocol but speaks LDAP to retrieve information, we maintain compatibility with existing clients.

Our LDAP `finger` gateway is a standalone executable—it does not execute within the confines of an existing application. Therefore, nearly any programming language that provides access to LDAP could be used. We chose to write our gateway by using the Perl 5 language and the PerLDAP object-oriented LDAP access module available from Netscape's developer Web site. This choice allows rapid prototyping, provides maximum portability for our code, and performs acceptably. Our `ldapfinger.pl` script replaces the `in.xfingerd` binary program executed by UNIX's `inetd` process, which is responsible for executing a variety of Internet services.

The Source Code

The source code consists of a single script, which we present here in pieces to aid understanding. The prelude and main module are shown in Listing 21.1.

LISTING 21.1 THE `ldapfinger.pl` PRELUDE AND MAIN MODULE

```perl
1.  #!/usr/local/bin/perl
2.  #
3.  # fingerd -- Perl 5 script that implements the server side
4.  #   of the finger protocol using an LDAP server as its
5.  #   database of user information.
6.  #
7.  # Requires: PerLDAP
8.  #

9.  use Mozilla::LDAP::Conn;

10. # LDAP server information
11. $ldapbase = "dc=airius,dc=com";
12. $ldaphost = "ldap.airius.com";
13. $ldapport = "389";

14. # constants
15. $unknown = "???";
16. $separator = "\n";
17. @attrlist = ( "cn", "uid", "mail", "departmentnumber",
18.           "telephonenumber", "roomnumber", "postaladdress",
19.           "ou", "title", "displayname", "description",
20.           "labeleduri" );

21. # Start of main:

22. print "LDAP Finger Service\n\n";

23. # grab query string and chop off newline and return characters
24. $query = <STDIN>;
25. chop $query;
26. if ( $query =~ /\r$/ ) {
27.         chop $query;
28. }

29. # form filter using query string
30. $filter = "(&(objectClass=person)"
31.         . "(|(sn=$query)(cn=$query)(uid=$query)))";

32. # open an anonymous connection to the LDAP server
33. $ldap = new Mozilla::LDAP::Conn( $ldaphost, $ldapport );
34. die "Unable to connect to server at "
35.         . "ldap://$ldaphost:$ldapport\n" unless $ldap;
```

```
36. # search it
37. $entry = $ldap->search( $ldapbase, "subtree", $filter,
38.          0, @attrlist );

39. # display results
40. if ( $entry ) {
41.          $count = 0;
42.          do {
43.                    displayEntry( $entry );
44.                    $entry = $ldap->nextEntry;
45.                    ++$count;
46.          } while ( $entry );

47.          if ( $count > 1 ) {
48.                    print $count, " entries matched '$query'\n";
49.          } else {
50.                    print "One entry matched '$query'\n";
51.          }

52. } else {
53.          print "No entries matched '$query'\n";
54. }

55. # clean up
56. $ldap->close;

57. # End of main.
```

The following list summarizes the actions performed in Listing 21.1:

1. The LDAP server information is specified on lines 10–13. Constants used elsewhere in the script are defined on lines 14–20.

2. When executed, the main module displays a banner string that lets the user know that he has connected to an LDAP finger service (line 22).

3. The query string sent by the client is read and cleaned up.

4. In the finger protocol, the client sends a text query string that is terminated with a newline and a carriage return.

5. The Perl code on lines 22–28 reads the query string from standard input and removes any end-of-line characters (inetd always arranges for protocol data sent by clients to be passed to standard input).

6. The query string is used to form an LDAP search filter (lines 29–31).

7. The code on lines 32–57 uses PerLDAP calls to connect to the LDAP server, perform one search, and display any entries found.

The work to produce a nicely formatted entry display is done by the displayEntry subroutine, which is shown in Listing 21.2.

LISTING 21.2 THE ldapfinger.pl displayEntry SUBROUTINE

```
1.   # Start of displayEntry:
2.   sub
3.   displayEntry {
4.       local( $entry ) = @_;
5.       local( $value, @attrs );

6.       @attrs = ( "displayName", "cn" );
7.       printf( "Login name: %-8s             "
8.               . "              In real life: %s\n",
9.               getSimpleValue( $entry, "uid" ),
10.              getFirstValue( $entry, *attrs ));

11.      printf( "E-Mail:      %-32s Phone: %s\n",
12.              getSimpleValue( $entry, "mail" ),
13.              getSimpleValue( $entry, "telephonenumber" ));

14.      @attrs = ( "ou", "departmentnumber" );
15.      printf( "Department: %-32s Room:  %s\n",
16.              getFirstValue( $entry, *attrs ),
17.              getSimpleValue( $entry, "roomnumber" ));

18.      $value = getSimpleValue( $entry, "postaladdress" );
19.      if ( $value ne $unknown ) {
20.          print "Address:       $value\n";
21.      }

22.      $value = getSimpleValue( $entry, "title" );
23.      if ( $value ne $unknown ) {
24.          print "Title:         $value\n";
25.      }

26.      $value = getSimpleValue( $entry, "description" );
27.      if ( $value ne $unknown ) {
28.          print "Description: $value\n";
29.      }

30.      displayAllValues( $entry, "labeleduri", "URL:        " );

31.      print $separator;
32. }
33. # End of displayEntry.
```

The displayEntry subroutine is straightforward. It uses simple printf statements to produce a formatted display of an LDAP entry. The resulting text is sent to standard output, which the UNIX inetd process has arranged to be sent back to the finger client.

Three additional subroutines are used by displayEntry: displayAllValues, getSimpleValue, and getFirstValue. These three subroutines are shown in Listing 21.3.

LISTING 21.3 ADDITIONAL ldapfinger.pl **DISPLAY SUBROUTINES**

```perl
1.   # Start of displayAllValues:
2.   sub
3.   displayAllValues {
4.          local( $entry, $attr, $prefix ) = @_;
5.          local( $value );

6.          if ( $entry->{$attr} ) {
7.                  foreach $value (@{$entry->{$attr}}) {
8.                          print $prefix, $value, "\n";
9.                  }
10.         }
11.  }
12.  # End of displayAllValues.

13.  # Start of getSimpleValue:
14.  sub
15.  getSimpleValue {
16.         local( $entry, $attr ) = @_;
17.         local( $value );

18.         if ( $entry->{$attr} ) {
19.                 $value = $entry->{$attr}[0];
20.         } else {
21.                 $value = $unknown;
22.         }

23.         $value;
24.  }
25.  # End of getSimpleValue.

26.  # Start of getFirstValue:
27.  sub
28.  getFirstValue {
29.         local( $entry, *attrs ) = @_;
30.         local( $a );
31.         local( $value );

32.         $value = $unknown;

33.         foreach $a (@attrs) {
34.                 $value = getSimpleValue( $entry, $a );
35.                 last if ( $value ne $unknown );
36.         }
```

continues

LISTING 21.3 CONTINUED

```
37.          $value;
38. }
39. # End of getFirstValue.
```

All these display subroutines access values from an LDAP entry by using
PerLDAP's attribute hash array.

Finally, the system's /etc/inetd.conf configuration file has to be modified to
tell inetd to execute our script instead of the standard in.fingerd executable.
Listing 21.4 shows the altered portion of the /etc/inetd.conf file used on a Sun
Solaris 2.6 UNIX system.

LISTING 21.4 CHANGES TO /etc/inetd.conf TO ENABLE THE ldapfinger.pl SCRIPT

```
1. #finger  stream   tcp       nowait   nobody
➥  /usr/sbin/in.fingerd     in.fingerd
2. finger   stream   tcp       nowait   nobody
➥  /usr/local/etc/ldapfinger.pl ldapfinger.pl
```

Line 1, which is commented out, is the line originally used to invoke the standard in.fingerd executable. Line 2 is the line we added to invoke our new
ldapfinger.pl Perl script. It assumes that we have installed the script in the
/usr/local/etc directory.

The Resulting End User Experience

Listing 21.5 shows a finger command along with its output produced by a
standard, non–LDAP-enabled UNIX finger service.

LISTING 21.5 A NON-LDAP-ENABLED UNIX finger LOOKUP FOR dsmith

```
% finger dsmith@airius.com

Login name: dsmith                  In real life: Daniel Smith
Directory: /u/dsmith                Shell: /bin/tcsh
On since Jul 14 09:05:10 on console from :0
8 minutes 42 seconds Idle Time
No unread mail
Project: Human Resources web site
Plan:
Send me e-mail at dsmith@airius.com
```

Listing 21.6 shows a lookup using our LDAP directory-enabled finger service.
In this case, only one entry matches the query string.

LISTING 21.6 AN LDAP finger LOOKUP FOR smith

```
% finger smith@airius.com

[airius.com]
LDAP Finger Service
```

```
Login name:   dsmith                In real life: Daniel Smith
E-Mail:       dsmith@airius.com      Phone: +1 408 555 9519
Department:   Human Resources        Room:  0368

One entry matched 'smith'
```

An LDAP-enabled `finger` example that returns an entry with more attributes is shown in Listing 21.7. Babs's entry contains `postalAddress` and `labeledURI` attributes (which Daniel Smith's entry did not have in Listing 21.6).

LISTING 21.7. AN LDAP FINGER LOOKUP FOR `bjensen`

```
% finger bjensen@airius.com
[airius. com]
LDAP Finger Service

Login name:   bjensen               In real life: Barbara Jensen
E-Mail:       bjensen@airius.com     Phone: +1 408 555 1862
Department:   Product Development    Room:  0209
Address:      1234 Airius Way $ Mountain   View, CA 94043
URL:          http://www.airius.com/babs   My Home Page

One entry matched 'bjensen'
```

A final example is shown in Listing 21.8. Nine entries match the query string `jensen`; our service returns information about all of them, along with the number of entries found.

LISTING 21.8. AN LDAP FINGER LOOKUP FOR `jensen`

```
% finger jensen@airius.com

[airius.com]
LDAP Finger Service

Login name:   kjensen               In real life: Kurt Jensen
E-Mail:       kjensen@airius.com     Phone: +1 408 555 6127
Department:   Product Development    Room:  1944

Login name:   bjensen               In real life: Barbara Jensen
E-Mail:       bjensen@airius.com     Phone: +1 408 555 1862
Department:   Product Development    Room:  0209
Address:      1234 Airius Way $ Mountain View, CA 94043
URL:          http://www.airius.com/babs My   Home Page

Login name:   gjensen               In real life: Gern Jensen
E-Mail:       gjensen@airius.com     Phone: +1 408 555 3299
Department:   Human Resources        Room:  4609

Login name:   jjensen               In real life: Jody Jensen
E-Mail:       jjensen@airius.com     Phone: +1 408 555 7587
Department:   Accounting             Room:  4882
```

continues

Listing 21.8. Continued

```
Login name:  ajensen                    In real life: Allison Jensen
E-Mail:      ajensen@airius.com         Phone: +1 408 555 7892
Department:  Product Development        Room:  0784

Login name:  bjense2                    In real life: Bjorn Jensen
E-Mail:      bjense2@airius.com         Phone: +1 408 555 5655
Department:  Accounting                 Room:  4294

Login name:  tjensen                    In real life: Ted Jensen
E-Mail:      tjensen@airius.com         Phone: +1 408 555 8622
Department:  Accounting                 Room:  4717

Login name:  rjensen                    In real life: Richard Jensen
E-Mail:      rjensen@airius.com         Phone: +1 408 555 5957
Department:   Accounting                Room:  2631

Login name:  rjense2                    In real life: Randy Jensen
E-Mail:      rjense2@airius.com         Phone: +1 408 555 9045
Department:  Product Testing            Room:  1984

9 entries matched 'jensen'
```

Ideas for Improvement

Many things could be done to improve our LDAP `finger` gateway. Here are some ideas:

- Sort the entries before displaying them. This would be helpful when more than a few entries are found.

- Improve the display of special attributes. For example, `postalAddress` attributes use the dollar sign ($) character as a line separator, but the `ldapfinger.pl` script does not take this into account.

- Improve the generation of search filters. As written, the script does not examine the query string at all—it just searches for all entries whose surname, full name, or user ID exactly match the query string. A more intelligent script might examine the query string and generate different filters depending on its contents. For example, a query string that consists only of numbers might trigger a search by telephone number.

Example 2: Adding LDAP Lookup to an Email Client

Most email client software includes a private address book used to store addresses of people that users correspond with on a regular basis. A useful extension of a private address book is an LDAP directory-enabled address book that allows users to search a centralized directory service when addressing email messages.

In this example, we show how to add an LDAP lookup feature to the ICEMail client. Specifically, we provide users with the ability to look up an email address while composing an email message.

(ICEMail is a pure Java Internet email client written and maintained by Tim Endres of ICE Engineering. The source code for ICEMail is available under the terms of the GNU Public License. The changes shown here are based on the ICEMail 2.5 release. For more information, visit the ICEMail Web site at `http://www.ice.com./java/icemail/index.shtml`.)

The Integration Approach

ICEMail had no address book of any kind that we could tie into when adding our LDAP lookup feature. We decided to change the ICEMail message composition window to add a Directory Lookup menu. This menu would grab the contents of the "To:" addressing field, look it up in the directory, and replace it with a person's email address, if one was found.

To accomplish this tight integration, we modified the ICEMail client source code directly. Because ICEMail is a pure Java application, our modifications were written in Java. We chose the Netscape Java LDAP SDK as our means to access LDAP information.

The Code

ICEMail is a fairly large application with a friendly graphical user interface (GUI) written using Sun's Java Foundation Classes (JFC). We had to modify several of the classes that make up ICEMail before adding our LDAP lookup feature. In the code listings that follow, lines with an ellipses character (. . .) indicate a place in which existing ICEMail code has been omitted to save space. In each listing we include the declaration of the class that the code we add is part of; this way you can see where the code fits within the ICEMail source code. We also include context in the form of existing code that surrounds our changes; the existing code is shown without line numbers.

The first part of the code adds a character string to ICEMail's `Configuration` class. The `Configuration` class manages configuration settings for ICEMail, and its code is in the file `source/com/ice/mail/Configuration.java`. Our changes are shown in Listing 21.9; the line we added is shown in bold type.

Listing 21.9 An addition to ICEMail's Configuration class public member variables

```
1.      public class
2.      Configuration
3.                  implements ActionListener
4.          {
...
5.          public static final String        P_LDAP_DIRECTORY =
➥"ldapDirectory";
```

The new string, called P_LDAP_DIRECTORY, is the name of a property that will be stored in each user's ICEMail configuration file to specify which LDAP directory to search.

All the remaining changes are to ICEMail's ComposeFrame class, which is responsible for displaying the message composition (new letter) window and interacting with the user. This source code is in the file source/com/ice/mail/ComposeFrame.java.

The next part of the code, shown in Listing 21.10 adds imports to gain access to the Netscape LDAP classes, along with two new imports (in bold).

Listing 21.10 Changes to ICEMail's ComposeFrame class imports section

```
...
1.      import com.ice.util.UserProperties;
2.      import com.ice.util.ICETracer;

3.      import netscape.ldap.*;
4.      import java.net.MalformedURLException;

5.      public class
6.      ComposeFrame extends JFrame
...
```

When an ICEMail ComposeFrame class is created, it reads configuration information and tucks it away for use by its own methods. We need to add our LDAP directory information to the member variables so that we'll have a convenient place to access it. The code change required is shown on line 4 in Listing 21.11.

Listing 21.11 An addition to ICEMail's ComposeFrame class private member variables

```
...
1.      private JButton                    detachButton;
2.      private JComboBox                  attachCombo;
3.      private Vector                     attachFiles;
4.      private LDAPUrl                    ldapDirectoryURL;

5.      public
6.      ComposeFrame(
7.              String title, Message msg, String body,
8.              boolean forwarding, boolean edit, boolean toAll )
9.          {
...
```

Because our directory configuration can easily be represented as an LDAP URL, an ldapDirectoryURL private member variable is added to hold it. Note that the LDAPUrl class is part of the LDAP Java API.

The LDAP lookups themselves are performed by a method called ldapLookup, which is added to the ComposeFrame class. The ldapLookup code is shown in Listing 21.12.

LISTING 21.12 THE ComposeFrame ldapLookup() METHOD

```
1. public class
2. ComposeFrame extends JFrame
3.        implements ActionListener
4. {
...
5. /*
6.  * ldapLookup: grab the contents of the "to" field, look it up in
7.  * the configured LDAP directory, and replace the contents of the
8.  * "to" field with CN <MAIL> as found in the directory.
9.  */
10. private void
11. ldapLookup() {
12.     LDAPConnection ld = null;
13.     LDAPEntry      entry = null;
14.     String         ldAttrs[] = { "cn", "displayName", "mail" };

15.     String toText = this.toText.getText();
16.     if ( toText.length() <= 0 ) {
17.       return;
18.     }

19.     String ldFilter = "(&(objectClass=person)(¦(cn=" + toText
20.         + ")(uid=" + toText + ")(sn=" + toText + ")))";

21.     try {
22.       ld = new LDAPConnection();

23.       ld.connect( this.ldapDirectoryURL.getHost(),
24.           ldapDirectoryURL.getPort() );

25.       LDAPSearchResults res = ld.search(
26.           this.ldapDirectoryURL.getDN(),
27.           LDAPConnection.SCOPE_SUB, ldFilter, ldAttrs, false,
28.            null );

29.       int count = 0;

30.       while ( res.hasMoreElements {
31.         try {
32.           entry = res.next();
33.           ++count;
34.         } catch ( LDAPException e ) {
```

continues

```
35.            JOptionPane.showMessageDialog( null,
36.               "LDAP res.next error: "
37.               + e.errorCodeToString;
38.          }
39.        }

40.     if ( count <= 0 ) {
41.        JOptionPane.showMessageDialog( null,
42.           "No entries matched " + toText );
43.     } else if ( count > 1 ) {
44.        JOptionPane.showMessageDialog( null,
45.            count + " entries matched " + toText );
46.     } else {
47.        /*
48.         * exactly one match... replace contents of
49.         * "to:" field with CN <MAIL>
50.         */
51.        LDAPAttribute attr = entry.getAttribute( "cn" );
52.        Enumeration enum = attr.getStringValues();
53.        String newAddress = (String)enum.nextElement();

54.        attr = entry.getAttribute( "mail" );
55.        enum = attr.getStringValues();
56.        newAddress += " <"
57.            + (String)enum.nextElement() + ">";
58.        this.toText.setText( newAddress );
59.     }

60.  } catch ( LDAPException e ) {
61.     JOptionPane.showMessageDialog( null,
62.        "LDAP connect or search error: "
63.         + e.errorCodeToString;
64.     }

65.  if ( ld != null && ld.isConnected {
66.     try {
67.        ld.disconnect();
68.     } catch ( LDAPException e ) {
69.        /* ignore */
70.     }
71.   }
72. }
```

Although lengthy, the ldapLookup code is straightforward. After declaring some local variables, we grab the text contents of the "To:" field, and we return from the function without doing anything if there is no text (lines 15–18). We then use the "To:" field string to form a simple LDAP search filter (lines 19 and 20).

The code on lines 21–39 connects to the LDAP directory, performs one search, and counts the number of entries returned. The LDAP host, port, and search base are obtained from the ldapDirectoryURL private member variable we already defined. We retrieve only a few attributes from the LDAP server.

The code on lines 40–59 handles the three possible outcomes of a successful search. If no entries are found, the code on lines 40–42 displays a message box to inform the user. If more than one match is found, a different message box lets the user know (lines 43–45). The interesting case in which a single matching entry is found is handled by lines 46–59. If the entry has an email address, we replace the contents of the "To:" field with a string formed using the entry's common name (cn) attribute and the mail attribute. The remainder of the code in the ldapLookup method is concerned with error handling and cleanup.

A bit more code is needed to create a menu item that can be selected by the user to trigger a directory lookup. First, we need to add a top-level menu during initialization. The code is shown in Listing 21.13.

LISTING 21.13 ADDITIONS TO ICEMAIL'S establishMenuBar METHOD

```
1.          private void
2.          establishMenuBar()
3.              {
...
4.                  this.establishSignatures( this.menuBar ) ;

5.                  this.addDirectoryMenu( this.menuBar );

6.                  this.setJMenuBar( this.menuBar );
7.              }
...
```

We call a new method, addDirectoryMenu (added as line 5), to establish our own menu. The code for the addDirectoryMenu method itself is shown in Listing 21.14.

LISTING 21.14 THE ComposeFrame addDirectoryMenu METHOD

```
1. public class
2. ComposeFrame extends JFrame
3.     implements ActionListener
4. {
...
5. /*
6.  * addDirectoryMenu: if an LDAP directory is configured,
7.  * add a Directory / Lookup menu item to the compose frame
8.  */
9. private void
10. addDirectoryMenu( JMenuBar menuBar ) {
11.     String urlstr = UserProperties.getProperty(
```

continues

LISTING 21.14 CONTINUED

```
12.          Configuration.P_LDAP_DIRECTORY, null );
13.    if ( urlstr != null ) {
14.      try {
15.        this.ldapDirectoryURL = new LDAPUrl( urlstr );

16.        JMenu menu = new JMenu( "Directory" );
17.        this.menuBar.add( menu );

18.        JMenuItem item = new JMenuItem( "Lookup" );
19.        item.addActionListener( this );
20.        item.setActionCommand( "LDAP:LOOKUP" );
21.        menu.add( item );
22.      } catch ( MalformedURLException e ) {
23.        JOptionPane.showMessageDialog( null,
24.          "Malformed LDAP URL: " + urlstr );
25.      }
26.    }
27.  }
```

The code on lines 11–12 retrieves the `ldapDirectory` LDAP URL property from the configuration. If such a string property exists, we use it to create an `LDAPUrl` object, and we set the `ldapDirectoryURL` `ComposeFrame` member variable for future use (lines 13–15). Finally, we create a new top-level menu called `Directory` and add a single item called `Lookup` that posts the `LDAP:LOOKUP` action command when it is selected by the user.

A final code change is required to tie the lookup code into the `ComposeFrame` `ActionEvent` handler; this way, an LDAP lookup is performed when the Directory Lookup menu item is selected. These changes are shown in Listing 21.15.

LISTING 21.15 ADDITIONS TO ICEMAIL'S `actionPerformed()` METHOD

```
...
1. public void
2. actionPerformed( ActionEvent event )
3.   {
4.   String command = event.getActionCommand();

5.   if ( command.equals( "CLOSE" ) )
6.     {
7.     this.closeWindow();
8.     }
...
9.   else if ( command.equals( "UNDO" ) )
10.     {
11.     if ( this.messageUndo != null )
12.       this.messageUndo.undoOrRedo();
13.     }
```

```
14.     else if ( command.equals( "LDAP:LOOKUP" ) )
15.       {
16.     this.ldapLookup();
17.       }
18.     else
19.       {
20.       System.err.println
21.           ( "UNKNOWN Command '" + command + "'" );
22.       }
...
```

If an LDAP:LOOKUP event is received, we simply call our ldapLookup method (as a result of the code added on lines 14–17).

We did not implement a GUI for configuring the LDAP directory. Therefore, to enable the LDAP lookup feature, a line like the one shown in Listing 21.16 should be added to a user's icmailrc.txt file.

LISTING 21.16 A SAMPLE ADDITION TO icemailrc.txt

```
1.     ICEMail.ldapDirectory=ldap://ldap.airius.com/dc=airius, dc=com
```

The portion to the right of the equals sign (=) is an LDAP URL that specifies the LDAP server host, port, and base DN to search.

The Resulting End User Experience

The original ICEMail compose window is shown in Figure 21.8.

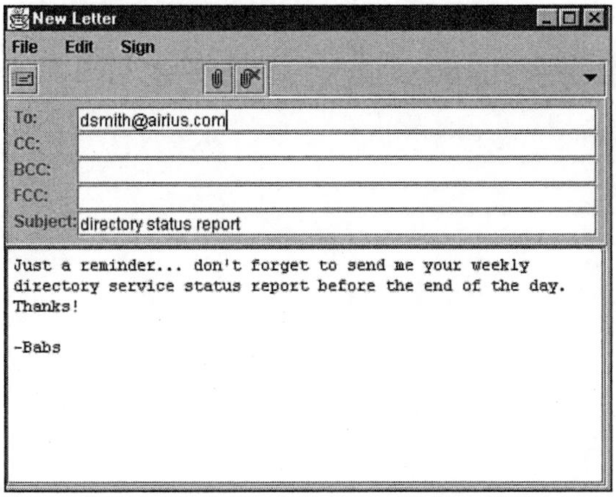

FIGURE 21.8   *The original ICEMail compose window.*

Note that a recipient's exact email address must be typed into the "To:" field when addressing a message.

Our LDAP-enabled compose window is shown in Figure 21.9. The name of the recipient (Daniel Smith) has been typed into the "To:" field, and our Directory Lookup menu command is about to be executed.

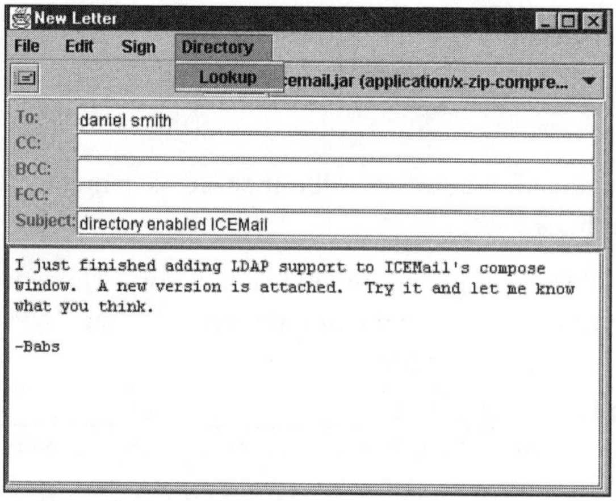

FIGURE 21.9 *The LDAP-enabled ICEMail compose window.*

After the LDAP lookup has been done, the text in the "To:" field is replaced with Daniel Smith's email address, as found in the Airius directory (see Figure 21.10).

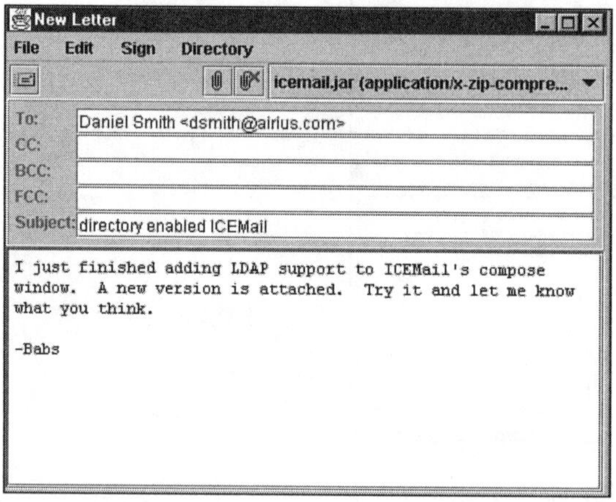

FIGURE 21.10 *The ICEMail compose window after a successful LDAP lookup.*

Ideas for Improvement

Many things could be done to improve the LDAP lookup feature in ICEMail. Here are some ideas:

- Present a list to allow the user to choose the desired entry if more than one match is found.

- Support multiple addresses in the "To:" field. As written, our code always grabs the entire contents of the field, looks it up, and replaces the entire field with the email address found. ICEMail is designed to allow a comma-separated list of addresses to be typed into the "To:" field, so we should support that paradigm, too.

- Support the LDAP lookup command within the "CC:" and "BCC:" fields, as well as in the "To:" field.

- Improve the generation of search filters. As written, the code in ldapLookup does not examine the query string (from the "To" field) at all—it just searches for entries whose surname, full name, or user ID exactly matches the query string. A more intelligent approach would be to examine the query string and generate different filters depending on its contents. For example, a string that consists only of numbers could trigger a search by telephone number.

- Provide a GUI for setting the ldapDirectory preference. This would be accomplished by making additional changes to ICEMail's Configuration class.

Directory-Enabling Existing Applications Checklist

☐ Identify one or more needs that can be filled by integrating an existing application with an LDAP directory service.

☐ Choose the best LDAP development tool for the task at hand.

☐ Choose an approach to LDAP integration that allows you to meet your goals and satisfy the users of the application.

☐ Design your LDAP integration so the resulting application coexists well with other directory-enabled applications and the directory service itself.

☐ Document how the application will be integrated with the directory service, and then share that information with the people who maintain the directory service.

☐ Consider performance and scalability during LDAP integration design and implementation.

☐ Plan for the transition from the older version of the application to the new LDAP directory-enabled one.

Further Reading

Active Directory Services Interface (ADSI). Available on Microsoft's SDK Web site at `http://www.microsoft.com/msdn/sdk/`.

CX, a PH to LDAP Superserver, UMEÅ University. Available on the Web at `ftp://ftp.umu.se/pub/wp/`.

Java Naming and Directory Interface (JNDI). Available on JavaSoft's JNDI Web site at `http://java.sun.com/products/jndi/`.

Net::LDAPapi, an LDAP Perl Module for Perl5. Available on Clayton Donley's Net::LDAPapi World Wide Web site at `http://www.wwa.com/~donley/netldap.html`.

Netscape Directory SDK for C. Available on Netscape's Directory Developer Central Web site at `http://developer.netscape.com/tech/directory/`.

Netscape Directory SDK for Java. Available on Netscape's Directory Developer Central Web site at `http://developer.netscape.com/tech/directory/`.

PerLDAP, an Object-Oriented LDAP Perl Module for Perl5. Available on Netscape's Directory Developer Central Web site at `http://developer.netscape.com/tech/directory/`.

Programming Directory-Enabled Applications with Lightweight Directory Access Protocol. T. Howes and M. Smith, Macmillan Technical Publishing, 1997.

Programming Perl (2nd ed.). L. Wall (ed.), R. L. Schwartz, T. Christiansen, and S. Potter, O'Reilly & Associates, 1996.

The C LDAP Application Program Interface (Internet Draft). M. Smith, T. Howes, A. Herron, C. Weider, M. Wahl, and A. Anantha, 1998; available on the World Wide Web at `http://www.ietf.org`.

The Java LDAP Application Program Interface (Internet Draft). R. Weltman, T. Howes, and M. Smith, 1998; available on the World Wide Web at `http://www.ietf.org`.

The Java Programming Language (2nd ed.). K. Arnold and J. Gosling, Addison-Wesley, 1997.

Looking Ahead

Another way to leverage your directory service is to integrate it with additional data stores within your organization. This complex topic is covered in Chapter 22, "Directory Coexistence."

CHAPTER **22**

Directory Coexistence

So far, the focus of this book has been on designing, deploying, and maintaining your directory service. The last two chapters talked about how to make use of the directory with existing and new applications. In this chapter we focus on integrating other data sources with your directory.

Often referred to as *directory coexistence*, integrating other data sources involves the relationship between the data in your directory and data maintained elsewhere, and the procedures and policies by which these relationships are maintained. Directory coexistence also allows your directory to coexist with and complement existing business processes within your organization. This important topic determines whether your directory is an island—isolated from the rest of your enterprise—or whether it is integrated and coexists peacefully with your existing infrastructure and business processes.

There are many reasons to integrate or link data between your directory and one or more external data sources. You might have existing data in another database that you want to make available to directory applications. You might want to provide a central management point for data, reducing the cost of maintaining it. Or you might want to use the directory as the source for new data elements used to populate other databases. There are at least as many reasons for integration as there are other data sources, and it is rare to find a directory service that does not need to coordinate with any data sources at all.

There are several different approaches toward directory coexistence. The correct approach for you depends on your requirements and the capabilities of both your directory and the other data sources and business processes you want your directory to coexist with. In some situations, a simple one-time pop-ulation of the directory from another source (or vice versa) may be all that's needed. In others, you may need an ongoing two-way relationship between your directory and a data source, in which data may be updated by either one. These two examples are extremes; requirements usually lie somewhere in between. You'll need to work with the maintainers of other data sources in your organization to determine which methods are best for you.

Whatever your needs, there are a variety of techniques for accomplishing integration and coexistence. These range from home-grown scripts and pro-grams to off-the-shelf software. After figuring out your needs, you'll need to determine whether any available software fits the bill. Chances are that even if you do find suitable software, you will have to develop certain tools to aug-ment it. Because directories, databases, and the environments in which they run are so variable, it is unlikely that any off-the-shelf software will suit your needs exactly.

This chapter takes you through the process of determining your directory coexistence needs and how to meet them. You'll learn which data sources your directory needs to coexist with, the kind of integration you need, and how to accomplish it. You'll learn the difference between directory migration, directory synchronization, and metadirectories—all of them tools that help accomplish directory coexistence. The chapter ends with a couple examples that show you how to develop directory coexistence tools for simple directories.

Why Is Coexistence Important?

In Chapter 17, "Maintaining Data," we discussed the importance of managing directory data to keep it accurate and up-to-date. The reasons are simple, and they all boil down to increasing the usefulness of the directory service. The arguments for directory coexistence are along similar lines, but they are moti-vated by the state of your enterprise. Chances are that you already have many directories, databases, and other data sources deployed in your organization. Following is a partial list of the common sources you might already have:

- *Operating system (OS) directories*. These include Novell Directory Services, Microsoft's Active Directory, Banyan's StreetTalk directory, UNIX's /etc/passwd file and NIS service, and others. These directories contain minimal information about users (such as name, login, and password), as well as information about OS-related devices and services (such as print-ers and file servers). The main job of these directories is to serve the needs of the operating system in which they are embedded. Although quite adept at that task, operating system directories make poor enterprise directories. However, they do often contain information, such as login and name, that might be useful in your enterprisewide directory.

- *Application-specific directories.* These include the Lotus Notes Name and Address Book, Microsoft's Exchange directory, Novell's GroupWise directory, the built-in authentication databases provided with most network services, and a host of other directories specific to one or a small number of applications. Each directory is designed to meet the needs of a single application. Often available only via proprietary protocols or APIs, these directories are seldom extensible, and, like operating system directories, they make poor enterprise directories. Such directories may contain information you'd like to make available in your directory, such as email address or name.

- *Corporate databases.* This broad category refers to databases such as those with information about corporate human resources, telephone operations, customer information, payroll, and so on. These databases often contain lots of interesting and useful information that should be made available through the enterprise directory service. Corporate databases are also usually integrated with existing business processes, from hiring and termination of employees to procurement and financial processes.

- *Home-grown databases.* As the name suggests, this category refers to the inevitable collection of ad hoc databases present in any organization. These might be maintained by departmental secretaries or local administrators, or they might be created for projects that have since been abandoned. Only you can determine how many of these databases exist in your organization and whether any of them contain useful information that should be included in your directory service.

- *Client data.* Do not forget your users as a source of data. If you choose to allow self-reported data, new data will flow from LDAP clients back to the servers. For example, you might allow users to update their own contact information or email address directly in the directory. It might be useful to allow this data not only to be published in the directory, but also to flow back to your human resources database.

All of these data sources serve a purpose (or did at one time). Some of them may be in the process of being phased out. Others are probably there to stay. Why should you be concerned about making your directory service coexist with these legacy data sources? Following are several reasons:

- *Jump-starting your directory.* One of the problems you face, as discussed in Chapter 6, "Data Design," is how to populate your directory with useful data. The best and easiest way to do this is to find another data source that already contains the data you want. This can save you substantial time and money in getting your directory populated with data.

- *Ease of data maintenance.* As discussed in Chapter 17, it's important to keep the data in your directory accurate and up-to-date. Continuing to feed your directory periodically from existing data sources can help achieve this goal. This arrangement can save you from having to institute complicated update procedures yourself. Instead, you can simply track data as it changes in the source database.

- *Avoiding duplicated data.* Maintaining data in multiple locations leads to inconsistencies, duplicated effort, increased costs, and a host of other problems. Using directory coexistence to maintain data in a single location helps reduce costs and problems.

- *Avoiding user confusion.* Duplicated data often leads to user confusion. Users often assume (reasonably so) that if they change some piece of information about themselves in one place, the change will be made in all other locations. Finding that a change of address made in the human resources database needs to be made again in the enterprise directory can lead to an unhappy and confused user.

Directory coexistence is often the biggest problem directory administrators face. Lack of directory coexistence can lead to user complaints, spiraling data management costs, and an ineffective and unpopular directory service. It's important to address this issue in your directory deployment, or at least to convince yourself that you don't need to.

Determining Your Requirements

The essence of directory coexistence is synchronizing data. Now that you have an idea why directory coexistence is important, we turn our attention to the task of determining your specific directory coexistence requirements. The best method to use may vary depending on your organization and the purpose of your directory service, but any requirement gathering should cover the following areas:

- *Data to be synchronized.* The first thing to do is determine which directory data needs to coexist with other data. Some data in your directory will not be needed outside of the directory. Some data in your other data sources will not be needed in your directory. But some data will need to be shared among the directory and other data sources. You need to determine which data falls into each category.

- *Type of synchronization.* Second, you need to determine how the data should coexist. Will the directory own the data and feed it periodically to an external database? Will the data source own the data and feed it to the directory? Does the data need to be co-owned? The answer to these questions determines the kind of synchronization technology you should use to maintain the coexistence. We cover this topic in greater detail later in this chapter.

- *Synchronization frequency.* Third, you need to analyze each piece of coexisting data to determine how often it needs to be synchronized among all the participating data sources. This may range from a one-time synchronization to as close to real-time synchronization as you can get. Different data elements and data sources may have different requirements. You need to strike a balance among complexity, ease of implementation and management, and system performance, which synchronization frequency can have a substantial effect on.

- *Synchronization security.* Depending on the sensitivity of the data being synchronized, security of the synchronization process may be an important consideration. Again, this varies among data elements and data sources. Seldom will you be able to choose a one-size-fits-all solution that is adequate for all your data elements and data sources. You need to strike a compromise among the complexity of maintaining multiple levels of security, the difficulty of development, and the performance and usability implications of making everything as secure as the most sensitive data element.

- *Synchronization performance.* A final, often overlooked consideration is synchronization performance. It's important to think of this in the needs assessment phase. Otherwise, you are likely to end up with unreasonable requirements, such as real-time synchronization for all data elements. Although often desirable, this kind of solution may have severe performance implications. A service that spends all of its available resources on directory coexistence and none serving directory clients is not much of a system.

You can use much of the work you began in Chapter 6 to get you started. In that chapter we showed you how to create a table of data sources and data elements within your organization. This table should show where existing data in your enterprise is located and which data elements are interesting to your directory service. Your next task is to figure out which of these data elements and sources need to coexist with the directory and which can serve as simple, one-time data sources. This process is the heart of your directory coexistence strategy.

Tip

You should always be suspicious of a decision to do a one-time data dump from a data source. This is a convenient way to jump-start your directory and load it with data, but often it can create problems down the road. Duplicate, uncoordinated data tends to increase your overall data maintenance costs and can lead to user frustration and confusion. On the other hand, if a data source is being phased out, taking a one-time dump of data may be the ideal approach. Be sure to think farther ahead than just populating your directory when you consider whether coexistence is needed.

For those data elements that must coexist, you need to determine the mode of coexistence. The key question here is *Who owns the data?* Answering this question determines where the data is updated and, therefore, who is in charge of maintaining the coexistence relationships. Most data is updated in one place, but you may also have data that you'd like to be updated in multiple places. In such a case there are multiple data sources for the same data element. Although desirable in rare circumstances, this should be avoided as much as possible. It brings with it complications that make your job of implementing and administering a coexistence solution much harder.

An example of data that might be migrated is the user name and password information contained in an old email system that is about to be decommissioned. In this case, the best approach is probably to migrate the data to the directory and then forget about the old email system. Care must be taken so that after the data is migrated, the old system does not accept updates; users might be surprised when such updates are lost.

An example of data that might need coexistence would be the user name and password information contained in an existing network operating system directory, such as Microsoft's Active Directory. If you expect this directory to continue providing service, you will probably want the common information it maintains with your enterprise directory to be synchronized on a regular basis. The source of this information could be the enterprise directory or the NOS directory, depending on your needs.

An example of data that you might want to maintain in multiple data sources is user password data. It would be nice if user passwords were synchronized across your enterprise directory, NOS directories, and various application directories. It might also be nice if a user could change his or her password in any of these systems. On the other hand, the security implications of synchronizing passwords to multiple systems might prevent you from doing so.

You'll also need to determine how frequently information should be synchronized to maintain effective coexistence. The ideal solution is usually to synchronize information in real time as soon as it is changed, but this is often unrealistic. Synchronization can be an expensive proposition, and it may consume large amounts of resources or require parts of your directory service (or other data sources) to be unavailable during the process. For these reasons, you may be forced to synchronize less frequently than you would like. Be sure to determine an acceptable range of synchronization frequency, and make sure the frequency you choose does not adversely affect the performance of your directory too much.

As discussed in Chapter 11, "Privacy and Security Design," different data elements have different security needs. Some data elements are highly sensitive in nature and should be protected from unauthorized access and tampering. Other data elements are not sensitive, and they need to be protected only from unauthorized modification. The coexistence process itself may present another way to compromise your data. Beware of designing coexistence procedures that become a security hole. Also be aware of the capabilities of the systems you coexist with. You may take great care in protecting the data in your system, but it will do you little good if your system is synchronized to another system that provides no security.

Tip

Be careful to design your directory coexistence procedures with security in mind. A badly designed directory coexistence process often presents back-door holes that can be used to compromise the security of your directory. Make sure that systems your directory receives data from and sends data to are as secure as the directory itself. Also be sure to secure the processes and links between these systems.

The result of all this design work should be summarized in a directory coexistence table that lists all your data sources, the data elements flowing to or from them, and how often the data flows. An example of a directory coexistence table is shown in Table 22.1. For this example, we've assumed that there are three sources for directory data in addition to the directory service itself: the corporate human resources database, Microsoft Windows NT domain registry, and the telephone operations database. As you can see, some information flows from the directory to these data sources, some flows from the data sources to the directory, and other information is simply maintained in the directory service and does not need to coexist with any other information.

TABLE 22.1 A SAMPLE DIRECTORY COEXISTENCE TABLE

Data Element	Data Owned By	Data Flows To	Update Frequency	Special Considerations
Name	Human resources	Directory service	Weekly	None
Title	Human resources	Directory service	Weekly	None
Manager	Human resources	Directory service	Weekly	None
Salary	Human resources	Directory service	Weekly	Sensitive
Phone	Telephone operations	Directory service, human resources	Nightly	Flows to human resources from directory service
Office location	Telephone operations	Directory service	Nightly	None
Email address	Directory service	Human resources	Weekly	New field for human resources
Description	Directory user	Directory service	User-controlled	None
Other directory attributes	Directory service	None		Directory maintains other attributes it does not share

This information can also be represented in graphical form, as shown in Figure 22.1. This can help you better picture the way data flows and how the different systems need to interact.

FIGURE 22.1   *A sample data flow graph.*

Coexistence Techniques

As mentioned in the previous section, there are multiple ways of maintaining directory coexistence. A directory implementing any of these solutions is sometimes broadly called a *metadirectory*. The idea behind the term is that the directory serves as an aggregation point for information that lives in other directories. Metadirectory is not a very well-defined term, as it covers quite a lot of ground. In this section we'll explore the various meanings of metadirectory and techniques for maintaining directory coexistence.

Migration

Data migration is the most rudimentary form of coexistence. We are hard-pressed to even describe it as coexistence because it refers to a one-time event rather than an ongoing process. Nevertheless, it is a good starting point for our discussion.

Data migration is simply a way of populating your directory from an external data source. Implicit in the migration is the fact that the source is not used after its data is entered into the directory. A good time to use data migration might be when switching from one email system to another, for example. If the old email system has its own application-specific directory containing user and group information, and the new email system uses your enterprise directory for its user and group database, migration is a good way to get the data out of the old system and installed in the new system with minimal disruption and inconvenience to your users. Data migration is illustrated in Figure 22.2.

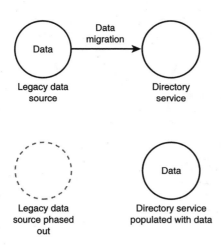

F IGURE 22.2 *Data migration.*

Most directory products come with migration tools. Some, such as Netscape's LDIF import tools, rely on you to provide a text file of information in a standard format. The system you migrate from is often able to produce a text file, either in that format or one that is easily convertible. Other tools are specific to a particular application. For example, Netscape's Messaging Server contains migration tools from a number of email packages. Other vendors provide similar tools.

One-Way Synchronization

One step up from data migration is one-way data synchronization. With this approach, the directory is periodically populated from the data source. The reverse is also possible: An external database can be populated periodically from the directory. In one-way synchronization, data is changed in the source, not in the destination. Updates are propagated either by replacing the entire contents of the directory or by applying only those changes that have occurred since the last update.

The advantage of doing a total replacement is primarily simplicity: You just delete the old data and enter the new data. Some legacy database and directory systems have no facility for tracking changes, making it difficult to generate incremental updates and easier just to perform a total replacement. The disadvantage of this method is performance: For large data sets, it can take a long time to completely re-create the entire directory each time an update occurs. The directory may even need to be down during this process.

Incremental updates typically perform much better. If only 5% of the data changes between updates, an incremental update would be cheaper than a total replacement by a factor of 20. Another advantage of incremental updating is that it can usually be done online while the directory is up and running. This tends to make the update perform better, have a smaller impact on the service, and be easier to implement. Also, because updates come in over the same mechanism as regular directory updates, there is one fewer potential security hole to worry about.

Even if the end system you synchronize with does not support incremental change reporting, consider implementing this feature yourself. For example, you could save the last full extract from the system and compare it to the next full extract, thus creating an incremental update.

One-way synchronization is often used to extract data from your directory and populate other directories. This way you retain central control over the data by making it available for use with legacy systems. One-way synchronization is also often used to extract information from corporate data sources, such as the human resources database, to populate a read-only directory. This gives directory clients access to the data they need while leveraging your corporate data management procedures already in place.

Most directory coexistence plans call for a number of different one-way synchronization relationships for various attributes. For example, a user's name and job title might be synchronized one-way from the HR database, whereas the telephone number might be one-way synchronized from the phone system database. The directory itself might one-way-synchronize its user name and email address data to a number of application-specific directories for use in email address books. A typical example of this kind of synchronization is shown in Figure 22.3.

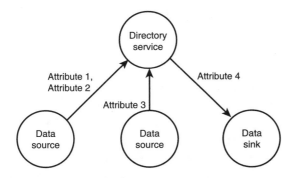

FIGURE 22.3 *Multiple one-way synchronization relationships.*

Two-Way Synchronization

Two-way synchronization involves propagating changes to a data element in two or more directions (see Figure 22.4). Changes to the data element can be made at any of two or more locations. The changes are propagated to all data repositories participating in the synchronization effort.

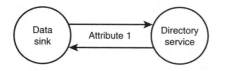

FIGURE 22.4 *Two-way synchronization.*

The advantage of this scheme is that it provides maximum flexibility. There is no need to select a single owner of the data and make other repositories read-only. Instead, every repository of the data can continue to be a read-write source for the data. The need for this kind of synchronization is illustrated by the password example previously mentioned.

The disadvantage of two-way propagation is its complexity and its occasional unpredictability. With changes occurring at any number of locations, it's relatively easy for conflicts to occur. A change made to a data element in one location may be in conflict with a change made to the same data element in another location at roughly the same time. To maintain a consistent view of the data in all locations, conflicts like this must be resolved in a predictable and efficient way.

Resolving these conflicts can be difficult. Even a simple approach, perhaps involving serializing access based on synchronized time, requires an additional service to keep the times synchronized—and ties can still occur. Other solutions, perhaps involving a policy-based conflict resolution strategy, can be simpler to implement but often result in unexpected behavior from the user's point of view. For example, if a user sees a change he made get overwritten by another change, he may not understand the conflict resolution policy that led to this behavior.

Certain circumstances may require two-way synchronization, but the added complexity and potential user confusion it causes are usually reason enough to avoid it. If you think you have a specific need for two-way synchronization, be creative about how you might avoid it. For example, you might deploy a centralized service that changes passwords in one location and uses one-way synchronization to push those changes out to all other data sources. This would probably be a minor inconvenience to users, but it would make life a lot easier for everyone in the long term. Alternatively, consider how you could intercept calls to change passwords at other data sources and reroute them to the centralized service. This approach would give the illusion of two-way synchronization without the same complexity.

N-Way Join

When synchronizing data from multiple sources, you usually want a way to match up related information in each data source. For example, if your coexistence policy calls for synchronizing names, job titles, and managers from the corporate human resources database and telephone numbers from the telephone operations database, you would like to end up with one entry in your metadirectory that contains all this information for a single person. You do not want to end up with two entries for each person—one from the HR database and one from the telephone operations database. The process of matching up entries from disparate databases is called *joining*.

To join two entries in different databases, you need to have a piece of information that is common to both databases. For example, if the databases each contain a field for Social Security number (SSN), you can use it to determine which entries correspond to the same people in both databases (see Figure 22.5). Using a uniquely identifying field such as SSN is much better than using a potentially non-unique field such as name.

Using an SSN can be less than ideal for several reasons. SSNs are sensitive information, a point explained in more detail later in this chapter. SSNs are also not immutable; they can change for a number of reasons. Such changes may be unlikely, but in large-scale directories even rare exceptions can be expensive. Finally, SSNs are not universal; not everyone has one, and you may not have access to SSNs for all the people represented in your directory. Foreign employees, customers, and others may not have an SSN or want to give theirs to you. For these reasons, it's often better to use or make up another unique identifier.

You often won't have anything better than names on which to join. This can lead to reduced efficiency in your synchronization procedure, create the need for manual synchronization, or even cause incorrect joining of information. Overcoming these problems is one of the biggest challenges in providing a metadirectory service that has reliably accurate data. A join on first and last names may typically match no better than 50% of the names in your databases. The numbers get significantly worse as the number of entries in your databases increases (e.g., the chances of having two Babs Jensens in a database of 100,000 people are significantly greater than the chances of having two Babs Jensens in a database of 100 people).

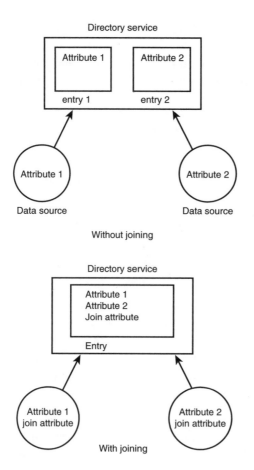

FIGURE 22.5   *A join.*

The result of this inadequate matching is usually a lot of manual work. An administrator typically goes through the unmatched entries by hand, comparing other information to try to determine a match. A worse outcome could be that the wrong match is made either automatically or by a careless administrator. In this situation, one person's information can appear in another person's entry. The consequences of this kind of error can range from annoying to serious, depending on the type of information, directory, and people involved.

The ability to join entries is an important feature that is needed for efficient synchronization. When you evaluate directory coexistence software, be sure to evaluate its ability to provide this feature. Also, investigate the software's advanced abilities, such as joining across multiple attributes and the extent to which you can tune the joining algorithm. Some environments may be willing to sacrifice accuracy for less administrative work. Other environments may be unable to tolerate inaccurate joins for any reason.

Virtual Directory

A final kind of metadirectory we will discuss is the virtual directory. A relatively new addition to the directory world, the virtual directory takes a different approach to directory coexistence. Instead of synchronizing data among directories periodically, a virtual directory provides a real-time directory view of selected data from multiple data sources.

The concept is simple: A virtual directory looks to the outside world like a regular LDAP server, but it holds no data. When it receives a request, it reformats and reroutes it to the necessary back-end data sources. The answers received are collated, reformatted, and sent back to the requestor. The virtual directory system is shown in Figure 22.6.

The advantages of this scheme are several. First, the question of who updates multiple copies of data is neatly solved. The virtual directory simply routes update requests to the appropriate data sources; no copies of the data are made. Second, the propagation delays inherent in a synchronization-based approach are also avoided. No data is copied, and each query is mapped onto the source data store in real time. Finally, the virtual directory allows you to dispense with messy and costly data management procedures designed to synchronize data.

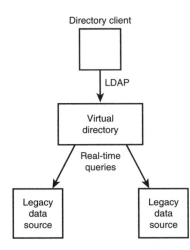

FIGURE 22.6 A virtual directory.

There are also several drawbacks to the virtual directory scheme. First, it can be pretty complex. The algorithms required to map queries here and there, collate results, deal with failures that may have occurred in one source database but not another, and so on can be difficult to determine and implement. Second, performance is likely to suffer compared to the centralized, synchronized directory approach. The source directories are not likely to be as fast as your native enterprise directory to begin with, and adding extra network round-trips, real-time query and data mapping, and result and error processing can reduce performance even further. A final disadvantage is that virtual directories are new, and they do not yet qualify as off-the-shelf software. You would probably be looking at a substantial development project to get a virtual directory up and working. Of course, you may already be looking at a substantial development project to get data synchronization working in the first place!

The pros and cons of a virtual directory add up to a few conclusions. Virtual directories are probably best in environments in which your goal is to provide access from a few well-known applications to an existing database or set of databases. Knowing the applications, and therefore the kinds of requests they generate, allows you to significantly reduce the scope of your virtual directory development project. Another important consideration is performance: The virtual directory would not be as fast as a native directory. You should be sure to benchmark the virtual directory early on to ensure that it meets the performance needs of your applications.

As far as we know, at the time of this writing Netscape is the only commercial vendor to support a virtual directory. Support is provided through a database plug-in feature, allowing you to write your own back-end database. You can develop a virtual directory by writing your own back end that maps queries and reformats results (see Figure 22.7).

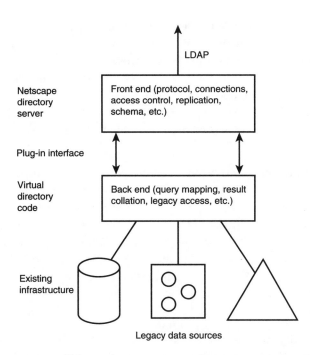

FIGURE 22.7 *Netscape virtual directory server architecture.*

Privacy and Security Considerations

In this section we explore issues related specifically to your directory coexistence strategy, including the privacy of the join attribute, the security of links in the coexistence process, and the security of foreign data sources. (General privacy and security concerns for your directory service are discussed in Chapter 11.)

Join Attribute

As described earlier in this chapter, joining data among multiple directories is much easier when you have one or more join attributes that are common among all the directories. The more likely the join attributes are to be unique, the more accurate the joining process and the less administrative burden placed on directory administrators. This feature is clearly desirable and argues for choosing a unique join attribute.

The most convenient attribute to use is often SSN or something similar. However, SSN is sensitive information that should be carefully protected. If your SSN falls into the wrong hands, all kinds of trouble can follow, such as stolen identity, ruined credit, and unauthorized access to personal information. SSNs are also considered private information by most users. These users will certainly be upset if care is not taken to protect their private information. For these reasons SSN may not be the best choice for a join attribute. But sometimes it may be the only realistic choice you have.

You must take care to protect sensitive join attributes when designing your directory coexistence processes. Consider who has access to the sensitive join attribute at all stages of the coexistence process. Do you really need to use SSN, or is there another less sensitive attribute that would work just as well? Could you use a hashed form of the SSN, providing a measure of privacy protection? Does the coexistence process expose the join attribute to other less-trusted foreign directory administrators? These questions and others all need to be answered.

Data Transport

Another common security trouble spot in the directory coexistence process is found in the procedures used to transfer information between your directory service and the foreign data sources it communicates with. If these transfers are not protected with the same care that data in the directory service itself is protected, an attacker can potentially gain unauthorized access to data or even insert fraudulent data into the directory service.

There are a variety of techniques for protecting this data transfer. If directory coexistence is maintained via LDAP, the normal security of your directory can be applied. This is probably the best approach from a security standpoint; it minimizes the possible avenues of attack and allows you to focus your security design on the directory service itself. It also minimizes directory downtime that can be caused by non-LDAP data import.

If you choose an offline technique for transferring data to and from foreign directories, consider other ways to protect the transfer. There are several techniques available, such as secure file transfer, a generic tool such as secure shell protocol, encrypting the data itself and then transferring it via unprotected means, and so on. These techniques are described in more detail in Chapter 11.

Foreign Directory Security

A final consideration in the protection of your directory coexistence solution is the security of the foreign data sources that your directory coexists with. If these data sources are not secured, there may be little point in securing the same data in your directory service. An attacker looking for the data may simply be able to access it in the foreign directory, bypassing all the security you have labored to implement for your directory service.

For example, suppose your directory obtains name and address information from the corporate human resources database. Because the address information is sensitive, you might protect it in your directory service via authentication and access controls and other techniques. A determined attacker bent on inserting invalid address data for another user cannot do it through the directory but may be able to do it through the human resources database. When that data is changed, it will find its way into your directory service via the normal directory synchronization procedures.

Be sure to consider more than just physical and technology-related security issues. Personnel and procedural security are also important. The most secure directory in the world can be compromised if an attacker is able to call up an administrator and talk him or her into making unauthorized changes. Masquerading as a legitimate user, trickery, flattery, and downright bribery are all potential weapons at an attacker's disposal. Make sure your procedures guard against such attacks and that your personnel are aware of the possibilities.

Example 1: One-Way Synchronization with Join

In this example we develop a tool that can be used to implement periodic one-way synchronization with any system whose data can be expressed as a delimited text file. Many typical data sources provide tools to make this kind of data extract easy. Some provide the ability to extract only those changes that have occurred since the previous extract, in which case the tool runs more efficiently.

Our tool is written in Perl, although it could easily have been written in another scripting language, such as JavaScript, or language, such as C, C++, or Java. We chose Perl because of its power and portability and its popularity in the system administrator community. The code for our synchronization tool is shown in Listing 22.1.

LISTING 22.1 AN LDAP PERL SYNCHRONIZATION TOOL WITH A JOIN

```
1.   #!/usr/local/bin/perl
2.   #
3.   # ldapsync -- Perl 5 script that synchronizes a comma-separated
4.   #    text file of cn values, joining on uid attribute
5.   #
6.   # Requires: LDAPP (LDAP module for Perl)
7.   #

8.   use Ldapp;

9.   # LDAP server information
10.  $ldapbase = "dc=airius, dc=com";
11.  $ldaphost = "ldap.host.com";
12.  $ldapport = "389";
13.  @attrlist = ( "uid", "cn" );

14.  # Start of main:

15.  # open an authenticated connection to the LDAP server
16.  $ldap = new Ldapp( $ldaphost, $ldapport,
         "cn=directory manager", "passwd" );
17.  die "Unable to connect to server at ldap://$ldaphost:"
18.     "$ldapport\n" unless $ldap;

19.  # for each line of input, search for the directory entry
20.  # corresponding to the first field, and see if its value
21.  # for the second field needs to be updated
22.    while (<STDIN>) {
23.  #    grab query string and chop off newline and
24.  #    return characters
25.      $line = $_;
26.      chop $line;
27.      if ($line =~ /\r$/) {
28.         chop $line;
29.      }

30.  #    parse join attribute (uid) and attribute to
31.  #    be updated (cn)
32.      @args = split(/,/, $line);
33.      $key = @args[0];
34.      $value = @args[1];

35.  #    search for entry with uid equal to the join attribute
36.      $filter = "(uid=$key)";
37.      $entry = $ldap->search($ldapbase, "subtree",
38.         $filter, 0, @attrlist);

39.  #    found a match - update if necessary
40.      if ($entry) {
41.          print "Found entry with uid $key. Checking...";
42.          if (!$entry->{@attrlist[1]} ||
```

```
43.                    $entry->{@attrlist[1]}[0] ne $value) {
44.                        print "Updating...";
45.    #                   ... update entry by replacing cn value ...
46.               }
47.            print "\n";

48.    #    no matching entry - add one
49.        } else {
50.            print "No entry found with uid $key. Creating...";
51.    #            ... add entry with appropriate cn value ...
52.            print "\n";
53.        }
54.    }

55.    # clean up
56.    $ldap->close;

57.    exit 0;
```

We've chosen to use the PerLDAP extensions to Perl 5 to give us access to LDAP in this implementation. You can get these extensions from the Netscape Web site at http://developer.netscape.com.

The LDAP server information is specified on lines 9–12. Some constants used elsewhere in our script are defined on line 13.

An LDAP connection is opened on lines 15–18, and the synchronization tool authenticates itself as the directory manager. This is necessary so that it can later update the directory.

The main body of the example is contained in the while loop spanning lines 18–50. This loop is executed as long as there is more input to be read. Each input line consists of a comma-separated pair of values. The first value is a login name used as the value of the uid attribute in the directory; we use this attribute to join entries in the directory with corresponding entries in the external data source. The second value is a name to be synchronized with the cn attribute of the directory.

Lines 23–29 trim off any trailing newline or carriage return characters. Lines 30–34 parse the resulting line to extract the uid and cn values.

The directory is searched for an entry matching the uid just read on lines 35–38. The results are processed on lines 39–53. As you will notice, the PerLDAP calls that actually update an entry or add a new entry on lines 45 and 51, respectively, have been left as an exercise for the reader.

Example 2: A Virtual Directory

In this example we give a high-level description of how to develop a simple virtual directory using the Netscape Directory Server 4.0 software development kit. Our goal is to develop a virtual LDAP directory that provides access to two other LDAP directories. A more realistic example might involve providing access to an Oracle database containing human resources information. But the LDAP example is more general, and it should adequately illustrate the basics of the virtual directory.

What we're trying to build is shown in Figure 22.8. The idea is that we have two existing LDAP directories serving different directory trees. Perhaps these directories represent two companies that have now merged. Our goal is to present what appears to be a third LDAP directory but is actually the aggregation of the original two directories. We will do this by using the Netscape Directory Server virtual directory interface.

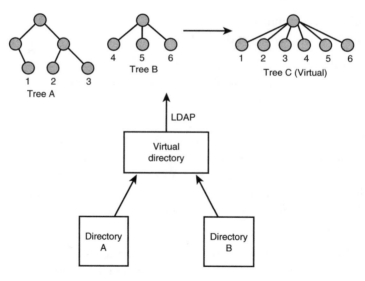

FIGURE 22.8 *A sample virtual directory project.*

The Netscape Directory Server virtual directory interface allows us to replace the directory server's existing database with one of our own. To do this fully, we need to write functions to perform the 20 tasks shown in Table 22.2.

TABLE 22.2 NETSCAPE DIRECTORY SERVER DATABASE PLUG-IN INTERFACES

Virtual Directory Function	Description
Configure	Process configuration file data
Bind	Process LDAP bind request
Unbind	Process LDAP unbind request
Search	Process LDAP search request
NextSearch	Process LDAP search request
Compare	Process LDAP compare request
Add	Process LDAP add request
Modify	Process LDAP modify request
ModifyRDN	Process LDAP modify RDN request
Abandon	Process LDAP abandon request
Close	Close down the database
Flush	Flush the database
Start	Initialize the database
Sequence	Step through database entries
Ldif2db	Convert LDIF file to a database
Db2ldif	Dump database to an LDIF file
Archive2db	Restore a database archive
Db2archive	Archive a database
Dbsize	Return the size of the database
Dbtest	Interactive database test program

Our goal in this example is fairly modest: We want only to provide unauthenticated search access to the two virtual LDAP directories. There is no need for us to develop functions that authenticate, update, or perform other tasks for the directory. Luckily, the virtual directory API makes this easy. Simply omitting a function causes the front end to return an appropriate error to the client, indicating that the function is unavailable.

For our purposes, we need to implement only four functions: Search, NextSearch, Start, and Close. In addition, we could implement the Configure function if we needed any configuration information specific to a plug-in. The implementation of these functions is left as an exercise for the reader.

Directory Coexistence Checklist

☐ Identify external data sources and elements for coexistence.

☐ Identify the desired type of synchronization.

☐ Determine the desired frequency of synchronization.

☐ Determine the sensitivity of synchronized data.

☐ Evaluate performance implications on the directory service.

☐ Formulate a directory coexistence policy.

☐ Evaluate coexistence implementation options.

☐ Design and implement a coexistence solution.

☐ Monitor coexistence and take action when you find a problem.

Further Reading

"Examining Data Quality." G. K. Tayi and D. P. Ballou, *Communications of the ACM*, February 1998, pp. 54–57.

Enterprise-Wide Software Solutions: Integration Strategies and Practices. S. Lozinsky and P. Wahl, Addison-Wesley, 1998.

Implementing Sap R/3: How to Introduce a Large System into a Large Organization (2nd ed.). N. H. Bancroft, H. Seip, and A. Sprengel, Prentice Hall, 1997.

Netscape Directory Server 3.0 Deployment Guide. Netscape Communications Corporation, 1997; available on the Web at `http://developer.netscape.com`.

Network Resource Planning For SAP R/3, BAAN IV and *PEOPLESOFT: A Guide to Planning Enterprise Applications.* A. Clewett, D. Franklin, and A. McCown, McGraw Hill, 1998.

Sap R/3 Business Blueprint: Understanding the Business Process Reference Model. T. Curran, G. Keller, and A. Ladd, Prentice Hall, 1997.

Looking Ahead

Congratulations! You now know everything you need to design, deploy, and maintain a first-class enterprise directory service. In the final section of the book we will turn our attention to several directory deployment case studies. By applying what you've learned to the case studies, our aim is to give you a more practical knowledge of directory services, as well as to show how the advice contained in Parts I–V applies to the big picture of directory design.

PART **VI**

Case Studies

CHAPTER **23**

Case Study: Netscape
Communications Corporation

Part VI, "Case Studies," shows how organizations actually plan for and deploy
directory services. Two of these case studies (this one and Chapter 24, "Case
Study: A Large University") represent real-life directory deployments with
which the authors have had direct experience. The other two (Chapter 25,
"Case Study: A Large Multinational Enterprise," and Chapter 26, "Case Study:
An Enterprise with an Extranet") are fictional, and they represent the author's
concept of how a directory could be deployed to meet the needs of such organizations.

By presenting these four case studies, we hope to show how a directory can be
applied within a number of different organizational settings. You will find that
your organization isn't exactly like any of those depicted in these case studies;
instead, you will probably find that it is a combination of several aspects from
each. Use these case studies as starting points for developing a directory strategy for your own needs.

An Overview of the Organization

Netscape Communications Corporation is a leading supplier of client and
server software that links people and information over the Internet and
intranets. In addition, Netscape's Netcenter World Wide Web portal,
located at `http://home.netscape.com`, is a leading rendezvous point for people
wanting to navigate the net, access products and services, and communicate
with others online.

Based in Mountain View, California, Netscape employs several thousand full-time employees and contractors. Most staff members are located on the Mountain View campus, which consists of a number of individual buildings connected via high-speed fiber-optic network connections. The Mountain View campus is connected to the Internet via a number of T3 connections, which are also used to support its World Wide Web presence.

In addition to the Mountain View campus, there are dozens of sales and support offices located throughout the United States and a number of European and Asian countries. Connections to each remote site vary depending on the number of employees, and they range from dial-up lines to higher-speed leased lines.

Organizationally, Netscape contains an Information Services (IS) division charged with providing computing services to the rest of the company. Netscape also contains a Human Resources (HR) division, which is responsible for personnel issues within the company. IS is responsible for developing and deploying the directory and directory-enabled applications, and HR provides the data about employees to IS for inclusion in the directory. HR uses software from PeopleSoft to manage information about its employees, contractors, and contingent workers. This information is used for business processes such as payroll and benefits enrollment.

Unlike some organizations (see Chapter 24 for a counter-example), Netscape's IS services are provided centrally rather than distributed throughout the various units within the company. This means that a high degree of control and centralization exists, so decision-making and deployment of new IS services are fast. This is a function of Netscape's size (moderate) and age (almost five years, as of this writing). Your organization may be much more "balkanized," especially if it is very large or has grown through mergers and acquisitions.

In addition to its use in Netscape's IS organization, directory technology (specifically Netscape Directory Server) is also a core component of Netscape's leading Web portal site, Netcenter. Although Netcenter would certainly make an interesting case study itself, we don't discuss it here. Instead, we focus on how directory technology is used within Netscape to support and enhance basic business processes.

This case study represents a real-world deployment of directory technology. It is a snapshot of the state of directory technology in August 1998.

Directory Drivers

There were two main factors driving Netscape to deploy an organizationwide LDAP directory:

- *Ensuring the quality of the Netscape Directory Server*—The primary motivation behind the internal deployment was to provide a testbed for the Netscape Directory Server. The internal deployment provided valuable feedback and helped the software engineers improve the quality of the product before it was made available for beta testing.

- *Supporting directory-enabled applications*—Netscape has directory-enabled nearly all its products. As these new directory-enabled products neared completion, they were deployed internally. The directory deployment directly supported those applications, which included the Netscape Messaging Server, Netscape Collabra Server, Netscape Enterprise Server, Netscape Certificate Server, Netscape Calendar Server, and Netscape Phone Book application.

Directory Service Design

In this section we describe Netscape's directory design and how it was developed.

Needs

As in many businesses, Netscape's directory needs were driven by two factors: the need to support a wide range of applications and the need to deploy them in a manageable and cost-effective manner.

As mentioned previously, Netscape's IS department is charged with providing computing support to employees at the main campus and satellite offices. With few exceptions, IS provides all the hardware, software, and network connectivity for every employee. (This is in contrast to the decentralized support methods that will be described in Chapter 25.)

Despite this centralization, minor political problems arose when the directory service was being deployed. Obtaining a synchronization file with all full-time employees, contractors, temporary employees, and contingent employees proved difficult, and the issue had to be escalated to senior management. When the synchronization file was obtained, IS staff needed to spend a significant amount of time connecting existing IS work processes to the directory. This required some modifications to existing HR database tables and associated user interfaces.

Another constraint was that the staff involved in the directory design and deployment, although extremely skilled, needed some time to become familiar with directory technology. Fortunately, the developers responsible for developing the directory server software (the Netscape Directory Server) were literally next door. This provided immense benefits for both IS and the Directory Server software engineering team; questions from IS were handled quickly and accurately, and Engineering obtained valuable information on how the product worked in an actual deployment. In essence, IS still provides an ongoing directory pilot that continually feeds back useful information to Engineering, ultimately resulting in a higher-quality, more functional product.

One of the primary drivers for the directory deployment was the support of Netscape's SuiteSpot family of directory-enabled products, including Netscape Messaging Server (electronic mail), Netscape Collabra Server (internal discussion groups), Netscape Enterprise Server (internal Web publishing), Netscape Certificate Server (for public-key certificates), and Netscape Calendar Server (for workgroup scheduling). Each of these products is directory-enabled and can utilize the directory for user and group management and access control. Additionally, employees have become very dependent on the Netscape Phone Book—an internally developed application that allows quick and easy lookup of contact information and location information for people and meeting rooms.

The directory is also used for IS-specific work processes, serving as the focal point for creation or removal of resources when a person joins or leaves Netscape. For example, when an employee is hired, a directory entry is created, triggering processes that create UNIX and Windows NT accounts, assign telephone numbers, add the employee to the security/badging database, allocate a network port, and add the employee to certain companywide, divisionwide, and workgroup-specific mailing lists.

Early in the design process, IS made the assumption that directory users needed to feel confident that the central repository of directory data was secure, stable, valuable, and accurate. These needs led to the conclusions described in the following list:

- *Security*—Users must believe that the information in the directory is protected from unauthorized use by other employees and persons outside the company. This means that each attribute type stored in the directory should be reviewed and a policy established for how that data may be used, who may use it, and how it will be protected.

- *Stability*—Users must feel that the data in the directory is stable. Data should not change unless in response to a change in the environment (for example, a new phone number). When users are allowed to change data in the directory, their changes should not arbitrarily disappear.

- *Value*—Users must find some value in the directory data. They should find useful data that allows them to perform their jobs, and they should not be forced to wade through nonessential or inappropriate data. The directory can also provide value by allowing the directory data to be put to use in new and novel applications (see the "Leveraging the Directory Service" section later in this chapter).

- *Accuracy*—Users must feel that the data in the directory is accurate. Stale data reduces the usefulness of the directory and causes users to use other, less efficient means of obtaining the information they need.

Additionally, the directory itself must be flexible enough to accommodate new applications, and it must scale well so that users always receive adequate performance.

Data

As mentioned in the previous section, the primary drivers behind the directory service revolved around the directory-enabled applications slated for deployment. Those applications had well-defined schema requirements, which made identification of the necessary data elements very straightforward.

What was less straightforward, however, was identifying the "owner," or authoritative source, of each data element. The IS organization began by developing a conceptual framework for understanding the directory, external data sources, and external users of the data. This framework is pictured in Figure 23.1.

Data owners are the databases that contain authoritative enterprise data. For example, data stored in the PeopleSoft system is considered authoritative for certain elements such as a person's name and home postal address. The Private Branch Exchange (PBX) telephone system is considered authoritative for office telephone numbers. We'll describe the process that synchronizes data between the directory and other data sources in the "Maintaining Data" section of this chapter.

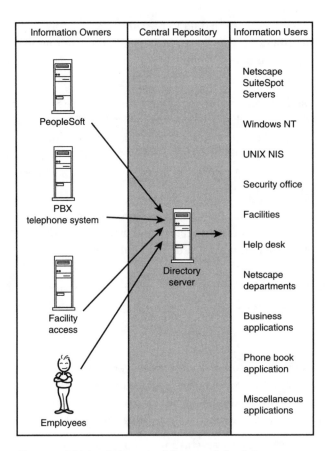

FIGURE 23.1 *A conceptual framework for data sources.*

Data is collected from the authoritative data sources and placed into the directory. In this role, the directory serves as a *central repository*—a rendezvous point where applications can meet to obtain data about people, groups, and other business-related objects. The directory serves a valuable role by publishing and grouping the data synchronized from the various distinct data sources.

In some cases, the directory itself is considered authoritative for certain data elements such as email addresses. For these data elements, the directory functions simultaneously as a data owner and the central repository.

Data users are applications, business processes, and end users that make use of the directory data stored in the central repository.

As soon as the fundamental data model had been developed, IS refined the data plan further by establishing the following basic guidelines for deciding whether a given data element should be stored in the directory:

- *If two or more applications require the data element.* If only one application needs it, the element does not need to be shared.

- *If the directory data changes in response to events that occur in the Netscape environment.* This stands in contrast to other traditional databases that change in response to minute-by-minute data processing needs, such as an order-fulfillment database. This policy is meant to discourage using the directory as a relational database.

- *If the directory data can facilitate location independence.* It is a completely valid and desirable use of the directory to store user preferences.

Next, a detailed data element inventory was completed. This inventory described each data element, the directory's attribute name for it, the authoritative source, and the consumers that use it. A portion of that inventory is shown in Table 23.1.

TABLE 23.1 A PORTION OF THE DATA ELEMENT INVENTORY

Attribute Contents	Attribute Name	Authoritative Source	Consumers
Email address	`mail`	Directory	Messaging server Phone Book application Communicator address book
Business telephone number	`telephoneNumber`	PBX	Phone Book application Communicator address book
Employee's manager	`manager`	PeopleSoft	Phone Book application
Employee Photo	`jpegPhoto`	Facility Access	Security photograph (badging)

Finally, a set of synchronization procedures were developed that propagate changes from the external authoritative data sources into the directory. These synchronization procedures were designed to capture changed data in the external authoritative data source and apply updates to the directory.

Schema

The schema used in the central directory is comprised of three distinct sets of schema definitions:

- Schemas packaged with the directory-enabled applications, such as the Netscape Calendar Server, Netscape Messaging Server, and Netscape Collabra Server.

- POSIX schemas, as defined in RFC 2307. These schema elements define the user information stored by POSIX-compliant UNIX operating systems. They allow the directory to store user information propagated to the company's UNIX systems.

- Custom schemas developed in-house. These schema elements support Netscape business processes. For example, there is an attribute that describes the termination date for an employee who is leaving the company. Automated processes revoke access to directory-enabled applications after the termination date.

The custom schema definitions were added only after carefully examining available schema elements and determining that no existing attribute types met Netscape's needs.

All schema extensions were implemented as auxiliary, or "mix-in," object classes. To illustrate, consider the definition of the nscpPerson object class shown in Listing 23.1.

LISTING 23.1. THE nscpPerson OBJECT CLASS

```
objectclass nscpPerson
    allows
        nscpBadgeImage,
        nscpPersonExpDate,
        nscpCurContactInfo,
        nscpBuildingNum,
        nscpBuildingLev,
        nscpHarold,
```

This object class contains only the Netscape-specific attributes. It is intended that entries in the directory that describe people are of object classes inetOrgPerson and nscpPerson. This allows the entry to contain any of the attributes allowed by either the inetOrgPerson or nscpPerson object classes. In this way, Netscape extended the schema with business-specific attributes without altering the standard object class definitions. The added attributes were as follows:

- nscpBadgeImage—the digitized photograph from the employee's ID badge. This attribute may be viewed only by Netscape security personnel (to protect employee privacy).

- nscpPersonExpDate—the date after which an entry is no longer valid. When an employee leaves the company, this attribute contains the date of his or her last work day.

- `nscpCurContactInfo`—a free-form text attribute that may be set by the employee to indicate how he or she may be contacted if not in the office. This allows employees to be tracked down for important customer support issues, for example.

- `nscpBuildingNum`—the number of the building where an employee works.

- `nscpBuildingLev`—the building floor an employee works on.

- `nscpHarold`—the legal name of the employee. Because the common name (cn) attribute contains the name by which people commonly know a person, there needs to be some other attribute that holds the employee's legal name. (One of the IS directory designers goes by a different name than his legal name, which happens to be Harold, in case you were wondering about the name of this attribute.)

Namespace

Netscape's directory namespace is shown in Figure 23.2.

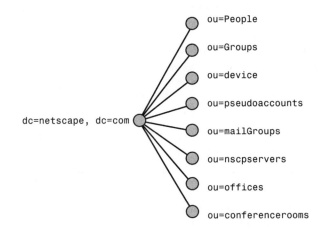

Figure 23.2 *Netscape directory namespace.*

The organizational units in Netscape's directory namespace contain the following data:

- `ou=People`—holds information on all Netscape employees and contractors. The namespace within this container is flat (that is, all people entries are located directly below the organizational unit container).

- ou=Groups—holds groups used for access control decisions. For example, the list of mailing list administrators is defined in this container. The namespace underneath this container is also flat.

- ou=device—will hold information about various network-accessible devices such as printers (not currently used). IP address, MAC address, owner, serial number, and other information will be recorded for each device.

- ou=pseudoaccounts—holds definitions of various directory identities used for special purposes. For example, when one directory server needs to authenticate to another directory server, it uses one of these identities. This namespace is flat.

- ou=mailGroups—holds group definitions used for routing electronic mail to groups of employees and external email addresses. The mail group entries are maintained in a separate directory tree because of limitations in earlier versions of internal mailing list management software. In the future, there will be a single ou=Groups container that holds any type of group, including mail groups. Like the ou=Groups container, this namespace is flat.

- ou=nscpservers—will hold contact and configuration information for all the various servers deployed within Netscape (not currently used).

- ou=offices—holds contact and location information for Netscape offices located throughout the world.

- ou=conferencerooms—holds definitions of all the conference rooms at Netscape's main campus. It is used by the Netscape Calendar Server to define the various conference rooms. This namespace is flat.

There are several important points to note about this namespace design. To some extent, the portion of the global directory namespace Netscape uses at this time is unimportant because the internal directory is not available outside Netscape's firewall. However, if Netscape should want to share this information with external business partners in the future, it would be necessary to choose a portion of the namespace that cannot conflict with namespaces in use by other businesses.

To accomplish this, Netscape chose to use a naming method that leverages the existing Domain Name System (DNS) infrastructure to provide a unique namespace. The top of Netscape's namespace is an entry named dc=netscape, dc=com. This name is derived from Netscape's assigned domain name, netscape.com. The other option would have been to use the X.500 naming method, which is based on a country-locality-organization name hierarchy. Using this scheme, Netscape's tree would have been rooted at o=Netscape Communications Inc., st=California, c=US, or possibly o=Netscape Communications Inc., c=US. Netscape chose the DNS-derived names because they are shorter and do not require registration with any standards organization (other than registered domain name).

After the directory suffix was chosen, Netscape's IS department needed to decide how the directory information would be structured. The following factors were taken into consideration in arriving at the final decision:

- IS chose to use the Netscape Directory Server to provide the service (for obvious reasons).

- The Netscape Directory Server's access control model allows for access control decisions to be based upon attribute values within entries. This means that it is not necessary to divide the directory into subtrees for the purposes of delegating administrative authority. This makes it much more feasible to use a flat namespace.

- The number of entries contained in the directory would be, at most, counted in the tens of thousands. This is perfectly within the capacity of a single Netscape Directory Server. Therefore, it was unnecessary to partition the directory across multiple servers.

- Employees within Netscape can and do move between departments. If the organizational hierarchy were part of the naming scheme, it would be necessary to change an entry's name (move it, in other words) whenever the employee changed departments. This has a number of undesirable consequences, especially when there are references in the directory to the person's entry (for example, in electronic mail groups).

- During the deployment of the Directory Server, the primary directory-enabled applications being supported were the Netscape Messaging Server, Netscape Collabra Server, and Netscape Calendar Server. All these products avoid making assumptions about directory namespace, which provides great flexibility.

A flat namespace beneath ou=People was chosen to avoid the headaches caused when people move between departments. Within the ou=People container, the uid (user ID) attribute was chosen as the naming attribute for entries. This has two desirable properties. First, the uid needs to be unique anyway because the employee's electronic mail address is *uid*@netscape.com. Second, because the namespace is flat, any attempts to create a duplicate uid would be rejected by the directory server (because the new entry would have the same distinguished name as an existing entry).

One trade-off in using a flat namespace under ou=People is that directory browsing is less interesting—all employees would appear in a single, flat list of names. Browsing is more useful when the namespace reflects some organizational hierarchy. Netscape directory deployers realized that there were multiple hierarchies present in the directory data. For example, each employee at Netscape is associated with a particular department, and this represents one type of hierarchy present in the data. Each employee also has a manager, and the reporting hierarchy represents a different type of hierarchy.

Instead of favoring one type of hierarchy, the deployers opted to make the namespace independent of any particular hierarchy. To construct multiple alternative hierarchies, such as the reporting hierarchy, DN-valued attributes are used. For example, each employee's entry contains a manager attribute that holds the DN of the employee's manager. A directory application can use this information to allow a user to jump to an employee's manager or to list all the employees who report to a given manager.

Topology

The topology chosen for the Netscape directory deployment is very simple: the entire directory is contained in a single partition. There were two considerations that led to this decision:

- The number of directory entries is small relative to the capacity of the server (the server can handle hundreds of thousands of entries or more). Therefore, it is not necessary to partition the data to achieve sufficient capacity. All the entries in the directory are contained in each replica (replicas are discussed later in the chapter).

- Netscape maintains a central IS organization; therefore, there is no need to allow separate islands of administrative control. Any required delegation of authority can be handled via the access control mechanisms supported by the server. Therefore, delegation of authority required no partitioning.

For these reasons, a single-partition design was chosen.

Replication

Netscape uses directory replication primarily as a means of providing sufficient directory capacity for its directory-enabled applications such as messaging and calendaring. This is the primary motivator behind the replication architecture. The overall replication architecture is shown in Figure 23.3.

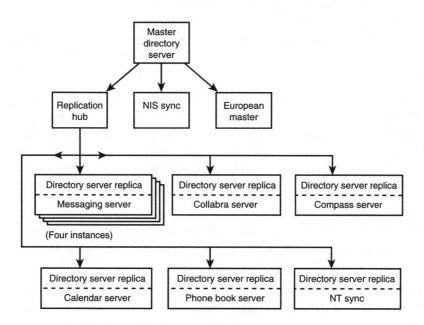

FIGURE 23.3 *The Netscape IS replication architecture.*

There are several important points about the replication architecture:

- Each of the directory-enabled applications (messaging, calendaring, and compass) are colocated with a directory server running on the same host. These applications are configured to query the local directory server first and then fall back to another server if the local server is unavailable (this situation is extremely rare). Colocation of directory and application servers improves response time and protects against network outages.

- Netscape Directory Server uses a single-master replication scheme in which one server is designated as the updatable master and all other servers are read-only. Because a relatively large number of replicas exist (there are 11 replicas providing direct end user service), it is undesirable to try to feed all the replicas from the updatable master. Instead, the updatable master server feeds a replication master, which is then responsible for distributing the changes to the remaining replicas. This has the advantage that the updatable master is freed from the task of updating a large number of replicas; it needs to update only the replication master. This results in better update performance for clients.

This particular design leverages the strengths of the Netscape Directory Server—namely, its ability to store a large number of entries while still providing excellent performance. If your directory server software limits you to a particular number of entries per partition, a more complicated replication architecture may be required.

On the other hand, the presence of the replication hub is a concession to the single-master nature of Netscape's Directory Server. Because there is a single updatable server, it is highly desirable to keep its load as light as possible—which is why a replication hub is used. If your directory server software supports multimaster replication, your architecture can do away with the concept of a replication hub.

Privacy and Security

Security design for Netscape's internal Directory Server deployment focused on two major issues: access control on directory data and protection against attack.

The data contained in Netscape's internal directory is primarily composed of public information that can be viewed by any employee. However, several attributes of person entries are potentially sensitive in nature, such as the employee home address and telephone number.

To fully understand the security issues associated with each directory attribute, Netscape's IS department developed a security matrix. For each type of object stored in the directory, the matrix describes the attributes present in that entry and the security restrictions in effect for those attributes. For example, the electronic mail address for a given employee is considered public information; it is essential for other employees to know a given employee's email address for Netscape business processes to proceed. On the other hand, the employee's home address is considered sensitive information to protect employee privacy.

During the development of this security matrix, Netscape's legal department offered advice about which attributes might be considered sensitive information. For each attribute considered sensitive, a policy was developed that describes who may view and update it. A portion of the final security matrix is shown in Table 23.2.

TABLE 23.2 AN EXCERPT FROM THE NETSCAPE SECURITY MATRIX

Attribute Type	Sensitivity	Readable By	Updatable By
cn	Low	Everyone	PeopleSoft sync process
homeTelephoneNumber	High	Everyone	Self (not automatically placed in directory by PeopleSoft synchronization process)
jpegPhoto	High	Self, Security	Badging system (security) personnel

Note that the update policy also allows an individual employee to decide whether certain information should be published in the directory at all. For example, the authoritative source for the employee's home address is the PeopleSoft database. Unlike most of the other directory attributes, the home address is not automatically synchronized from PeopleSoft to the directory. Instead, the employee may place a home address in the directory if he or she desires. This policy places complete control of certain sensitive information such as home addresses in the hands of the employee.

Another part of Netscape's directory security design involves protecting the directory from several types of assault. Because Netscape's internal directory is used only by employees and contractors, certain assumptions make it unnecessary to protect against certain types of attacks. Employees are trusted to conform to organizational policy, so disciplinary action can be levied against an employee who perpetrates a directory attack. Such attacks (of which there have been none to date) include denial-of-service attacks and impersonation attacks.

Despite this, however, certain other precautions need to be taken because Netscape uses leased lines provided by a third party. Netscape does not control the physical security of these lines; therefore, data transmitted across them cannot be guaranteed safe from eavesdropping. The following precautions are in place:

- Application and directory servers are physically secured in machine rooms that may be opened only by operations staff and security personnel. This provides a level of protection against theft or physical compromise of the physical devices (for example, breaking in by rebooting a server and starting a privileged shell).

- Login to directory and application server machines may be accomplished only via the secure shell protocol (SSH). This prevents network eavesdroppers from intercepting communication from a system administrator to a server.

- For the same reason, connections from a administrator's workstation to the Administration Server are done via the Hypertext Transfer Protocol over SSL (HTTPS) to provide encryption. This allows the administrator to be certain that the session is not susceptible to eavesdropping.

- Secure sockets layer (SSL) is used to encrypt all replication updates flowing from the master server to the replication hub, and from the replication hub to any of the consumer servers. This protects the directory data (especially sensitive user data) from eavesdropping and ensures that the data isn't tampered with in transit. This is especially important for the updates to the European directory server, which traverse a leased line owned an operated by a third-party network provider.

- All directory servers support LDAP over SSL (LDAPS) in the event that a particular employee desires that all communications with the directory take place over an encrypted connection. The servers support standard LDAP as well, of course.

In summary, Netscape's security architecture for the directory and the data it contains are tuned to the particular needs of the business.

Directory Service Deployment

The next section of this chapter describes the steps taken to put Netscape's internal directory service into production.

Product Choice

Netscape is somewhat unique in that it is a leading developer of directory technology. Netscape's products include a high-performance directory server (Netscape Directory Server) and client software development kits (SDKs). Additionally, all of Netscape's SuiteSpot server family is now directory-enabled. Because of performance and support issues, Netscape chose to deploy its own products.

Piloting

The pilot phase of the directory deployment was rather informal. The first directory pilot phase was conducted by the software engineers working on the 1.0 version of Directory Server, even before the software was officially released as a product. The developers created a directory that held information about employees (including telephone numbers, office locations, and electronic mail addresses), and they publicized the availability of the directory. The engineers also created an HTML-based interface that allowed employees to search for entries and update their own directory entries.

At roughly the same time, the Netscape Communicator development team was adding LDAP capabilities to a pre-release version of the Netscape Communicator address book. The presence of the pilot directory allowed these developers to distribute pre-release copies of Communicator to employees and obtain valuable feedback on the design and usability of the address book user interface.

20/20 Hindsight: Enabling Schema Checking

When the initial pilot phase began, not much thought had been put into analyzing schema requirements. To make it easier to add new attributes and object classes, schema checking was turned off (which allowed any attribute to be added to any entry in the directory). The developers running the pilot directory found this convenient because it allowed them to begin adding new attributes and object classes to the entries in the directory without modifying the schema configuration, assigning OIDs, and restarting the server.

Unfortunately, this also allowed a number of inconsistencies to creep into the directory data. Because developers in other groups were also using the pilot directory to become familiar with LDAP, a number of unknown and misspelled attribute types were introduced into the data.

Although these inconsistencies weren't such a serious problem in the pilot phase, they became troublesome when the pilot data was imported into the production service—in which schema checking was enabled. A rather extensive process of cleaning up the pilot data was needed before it could be imported. The pilot data could have been discarded; however, many employees had come to depend on the data stored in the pilot server, so it was decided to retain as much data as possible.

In retrospect, it would have been better to enable schema checking even during the early stages of the pilot to avoid this problem.

After initial deployment of the directory, several other pilots focused on new directory-enabled applications being developed. One such application was the Mailing List Manager (MLM), which replaced an older application that used proprietary databases to manage internal and external mailing lists. These lists were migrated into the directory, and a new, HTML-based management interface was developed, piloted, and deployed.

Going Production

The production rollout of the Directory Server coincided with the rollout of the Netscape Messaging Server. These steps were followed:

1. The server hardware was purchased and installed. The directory server and messaging server were both installed on a single host, so memory and disk space were sized appropriately.

2. Network ports (100Base-T Ethernet) were installed, and network adapters were installed in the hosts.

3. Backup procedures were developed for the messaging server. Because the directory that resides on the messaging server host is a replica, directory data wasn't backed up. Instead, only the directory configuration files were backed up.

4. An initial test was performed to ensure that the messaging server was able to support access via the POP and IMAP protocols and could receive electronic mail via the SMTP protocol. This test also verified that the messaging server was able to contact and retrieve directory data.

5. User accounts were moved over from the existing, non–directory-enabled messaging server. The service was then in full production.

Directory Service Maintenance

In this section we describe the various procedures used to maintain the Netscape internal directory.

Data Backups and Disaster Recovery

Netscape IS backs up directory data daily using the online backup capabilities of Netscape Directory Server. With this capability, data can be backed up to disk while the server is running and accepting updates; it is not necessary to shut down the server or place it in read-only mode. The backup files are then archived to tape along with directory configuration data. Tapes are then moved offsite (along with backup tapes of other critical applications) to protect against their loss in a disaster. The offsite backups are stored in a secure location to protect the security of the data.

Although tape backups are made, the primary method of restoring a directory server is to obtain recent directory data from a replica. Replicas are always kept in sync; therefore, they provide a more up-to-date copy of the directory than backup tapes. Tapes are still required, however, in the event that directory data is damaged (e.g., entries are deleted), and any changes propagate to all replicas.

The disaster recovery plan for Netscape's internal directory leverages the extensive disaster recovery plan already in place for Netscape Netcenter. In a nutshell, the plan provides for continuous operations through a combination of alternate power sources at primary sites and alternate sites that contain replicas of critical data and applications.

Maintaining Data

Netscape's directory needs to coexist with several other data repositories. For some data elements, the external repositories are the authoritative source for the data. For other data elements, the directory itself is authoritative. This section describes the procedures used to maintain the relationships between the external data repositories and the directory, and the procedures used to maintain data that the directory itself is the authoritative source for.

Three main external repositories are synchronized with the directory:

- The Windows NT domain user and group database

- Network Information Service (NIS)

- PeopleSoft

- Data, whose authoritative source is the directory itself

These repositories, and the process used to synchronize them, are discussed in this section.

The Windows NT User and Group Database

A special tool was written to run on Netscape's NT primary domain controller (PDC) and synchronize the NT user database with the directory. Specific attributes in the directory for NT users, NT accounts, NT passwords, NT directory structures, and NT access control lists (ACLs) are read from the directory, and the Windows PDC information is synchronized to match the directory. This process also ensures that the password stored in the NT authentication database matches the password stored in the directory. If it does not, the synchronization tool overwrites the NT password with the authoritative password from the directory. The NT sync process starts up every three minutes, searches the directory for any entries that have changed since the last NT sync run, and then synchronizes them.

Netscape currently places all NT users in a single NT domain to make management simpler. If Netscape ever splits its NT user and group information into multiple NT domains, a separate synchronization service will need to run on each PDC, and a policy will need to be implemented that maps newly created user entries to a particular domain.

It should be noted that the Netscape Directory Server includes a bidirectional NT Synchronization Service that can perform these same functions and could be used in place of the existing synchronization tool. However, development of the custom NT sync script currently in use predates the development of the commercially available Synchronization Service.

NIS

Netscape's UNIX workstations use NIS to distribute user and group information to all workstations throughout the company. Like the NT user database, NIS represents a repository of user information that should be kept in sync with the directory. Custom scripts were developed that read directory data and generate several NIS maps, which are then imported into the NIS master server. These maps include the `passwd` map (user and password information), the NFS automounter map files, and the aliases map, which `sendmail` uses to expand mail aliases. The NIS sync process runs every 20 minutes.

PeopleSoft

The PeopleSoft system is the authoritative source for most of the information about employees. It is vitally important that the directory data be kept in sync with PeopleSoft. For example, when a new employee is hired, he or she should immediately be able to access vital services such as UNIX login, NT login, and email. Similarly, when an employee leaves the company, access to these facilities must be immediately revoked.

This synchronization is accomplished via a set of Perl scripts that reconcile PeopleSoft data with the directory. These scripts, which are based on PerLDAP (available at `http://help.netscape.com/download/server/directory/ utilities/ldap/tar.gz`), also perform data validation and cleanup when needed, such as when data lacks attributes required by the directory. The scripts also report any exceptions they encounter, such as entries with missing `manager`, `organizationalUnit`, or `businessCategory` attributes. These exceptions are reported to the appropriate departments that can repair the problems. The PeopleSoft sync process runs once per hour.

Data Whose Authoritative Source Is the Directory Itself

The directory itself is authoritative for some of the data elements, such as email addresses. Unlike data elements that are synchronized from external sources, it's possible to delegate authority to update these directory-mastered data elements using the directory servers' ACL capabilities.

One example of this is the home mailing address for employees. These data elements are stored in the PeopleSoft database, but they are not synchronized to the directory (out of concern for employee privacy). However, employees are free to add these attributes to their directory entry if they want to. Also note that these elements are not synchronized back to the PeopleSoft database (although it's conceivable that they could be).

Monitoring

Netscape has a rather extensive SNMP-based monitoring system in place that focuses on monitoring network devices such as routers, hubs, and server network interfaces. As is the case in many organizations, the group that provides this monitoring is distinct from the group that deploys the directory. Coupled with the fact that early versions of Netscape Directory Server did not support monitoring via SNMP, this led the directory deployers to develop their own set of monitoring tools that check whether the following conditions hold:

- All directory servers are running and responding to requests.

- All replicas are in sync with the master server.

If any of these tests fail, an alert is raised and an appropriate individual is notified via electronic mail and pager.

In the future, monitoring of the directory may be integrated with the other network monitoring functions. In addition to monitoring the directory server itself, the procedures that synchronize the PeopleSoft database tables with the directory simultaneously perform extensive data validation. If a discrepancy is noted, the synchronization tools automatically route problem notifications to the appropriate person who can repair it.

Leveraging the Directory Service

When an organization has successfully deployed a directory, it becomes possible to leverage it to support new directory-enabled applications. One such example of this is Netscape's Maps application.

Netscape's Mountain View campus has many meeting rooms. Like many companies in Silicon Valley, Netscape names these conference rooms after cartoon characters, movie names, famous people, and so on. Although this naming convention is fun and part of the culture, it can make it difficult to figure out where you need to be for your next meeting unless you happen to know, for example, that the Miles Davis conference room is on the ground floor of Building 12. Similarly, employees' office numbers don't give any indication of the location of the office within the building. Some way was needed to help employees to determine the physical location of offices and conference rooms.

To address this need, the Maps application was designed. It is a Web-based, directory-enabled application that allows a person's name or conference room name to be looked up in the directory. If a match is found, a graphical map is displayed in the browser window, and the location of the cubicle or meeting room is highlighted. The location (in x,y coordinates relative to the upper-left corner of the map image) is stored in an attribute of the entry. After the map is drawn in the browser window, a small cross hair cursor moves across the screen to highlight the location. The map application is very popular, and it is used hundreds of times each day.

Directory Deployment Impact

In what ways have things changed for the better now that Netscape has deployed a directory service? The following are a few of the ways that the directory has improved life for Netscape employees:

- The employee hiring and termination processes are now automatically triggered by changes made to directory data. Before IS deployed the directory, hiring and termination were tedious processes that required departmental administrators to submit separate work orders for account activation/deactivation, computer system orders, network drop, and so on. IS treats the directory as an authoritative repository and triggers events such as account activation based on the directory data. This automation has streamlined the processes and provided significant cost savings.

- Administration of user and group information is now centralized. Instead of each application requiring its own user and group database, they obtain this information from the central directory, either directly or via a synchronization process.

- Windows NT domain user and group information is synchronized from the directory, reducing maintenance costs.

- Employees can change all their passwords (UNIX, NT, and directory) at one time using a Web-based application. The passwords are pushed from the directory into NT and UNIX NIS, ensuring that the same password is available everywhere.

- The Netscape Phone Book application allows employees to look up other employees' email addresses, telephone numbers, office locations, and so on. Employees may also update their own directory entries using the Phone Book application.

- New directory-enabled applications, such as the Maps application, are being developed and deployed.

Summary and Lessons Learned

Netscape's directory deployment has been a great success on two fronts. First, the company has benefited in the ways you've probably come to expect from a directory service having read the earlier chapters of this book. For example, business processes are streamlined, particularly the process of getting the computing environment for a new hire up and running. The deployment has also met its goal of being a useful testbed for the Netscape Directory Server and the directory-enabled applications that Netscape develops.

In any complex process such as deploying a directory, there is always some room for improvement. Here are a few words of advice based on lessons learned during the directory deployment at Netscape:

- Obtain buy-in from senior management early in the planning process. This can help ensure that you obtain the necessary cooperation from other departments that are crucial to the success of the directory deployment.

- Plan the directory namespace well in advance. It will become increasingly difficult to change the namespace as the directory gains momentum and becomes more and more essential to business processes.

- Pay particular attention to privacy needs of your directory users. It's best to obtain the opinion of your legal department when deciding which attributes will be available in the directory. Allow sufficient time for review.

- Even if your directory software allows you to disable schema checking, it's almost always a mistake to deploy the directory this way. Leaving schema checking enabled improves the quality of your directory data.

- Start early when planning for synchronization with external data sources, especially when those sources are owned by another group within your organization. Try to get the other groups to fully communicate the structure of those data sources so that you don't miss important data repositories when migrating data into the directory.

- Do not work in a vacuum. Include as many participants as possible in the initial design phase for data synchronization, work process changes, resulting information changes, and user interface development. This ensures that everything is covered and helps provide buy-in to the project.

Further Reading

An Approach for Using LDAP as a Network Information Service (RFC 2307). L. Howard, 1998; available on the World Wide Web at `http://info.internet.isi.edu:80/in-notes/rfc/files/rfc2307.txt`.

Looking Ahead

In Chapter 24 we will examine a much different organization—a large university with thousands of students, faculty, and staff.

Case Study: A Large University

An Overview of the Organization

This case study is fictional, but it is based loosely on our experience designing, deploying, and maintaining the University of Michigan's directory service. It is not meant to be an accurate chronicle of that experience; we've changed the names and several key decisions to better illustrate various points. Therefore, we'll refer to the university as Big State University.

Big State University is a leading research and educational institution with an annual budget of over $2 billion. Big State employs more than 25,000 faculty and staff and enrolls more than 50,000 students in graduate and undergraduate programs in 17 schools and colleges. Large portions of Big State's budget and staff are associated with the Big State Medical Complex, one of the largest teaching hospitals and medical research centers in the world.

The majority of Big State faculty, staff, and students are located on the main campus in Springfield. Two other campuses are located in nearby cities, and Big State has associated offices and research facilities throughout the world. In addition, Big State has an alumni base of several hundred thousand people it wants to remain in contact with for fundraising and other purposes.

Organizationally, Big State has several large, central administrative divisions, including university-wide human resources, finance, student services, and information technology (IT) departments. The remainder of Big State's organization is divided into its 17 schools and colleges responsible for administering Big State's degree programs. The schools and colleges obtain human resources, finance, and student services from the central organizations, but they otherwise operate with a great deal of autonomy. This autonomy extends to most choices about information technology, meaning that individual schools and colleges are not required to use the central IT organization's computing services.

Big State has a leading-edge physical network infrastructure that supports high-bandwidth TCP/IP, IPX, and AppleTalk protocol transport. The main campus network is based around a 100Mbps fiber optic backbone. Most of the more than 250 buildings on the main campus have Ethernet connected to the backbone via high-speed links. Some buildings that have not yet been upgraded are connected at only 128Kbps, but this is the exception rather than the rule. The two satellite campuses are connected to the main campus via 1.5Mbps T1 links. The main campus fiber ring is connected to an Internet backbone provided by a commercial Internet service provider via a 45Mbps T3 link.

In this chapter we describe how Big State's directory team addressed each of the topics covered in the previous sections of this book: design, deployment, and maintenance of a directory service. We describe how Big State's requirements affected each stage, the applications that drove the deployment, and some of the lessons learned.

Directory Drivers

Big State University had for many years been providing centralized email and directory services to the campus via the Big State mainframe computing system. The mainframe was a proprietary system, increasingly expensive to maintain, and it did not play well with the Internet. The primary driver behind Big State's directory deployment was the desire to replace the mainframe directory and email services. This meant deploying an online campus phone book, along with the more challenging task of deploying directory-based email software to provide campuswide service to the bigstate.edu domain. We discuss the needs of these applications in more detail in the following sections.

A secondary driver behind the deployment was the future need to deploy many campus-wide directory-enabled applications. The directory could serve as a central authentication and access control database that could be shared across these applications, as well as a repository of organizational and other directory information. Most of these applications could be used by university employees and students, but some could be used by prospective students, alumni, and other non-university users.

Directory Service Design

In this section we discuss Big State's directory design and how it was developed.

Needs

The main applications driving Big State's directory deployment were the online phone book and the `bigstate.edu` email service. The phone book application required that the directory be populated with up-to-date white pages information about university faculty, staff, and students. Big State wanted to provide this information to internal and external users. The end users would be able to modify some of the information about themselves; other information would come only from official university data sources. Because this application would be user-driven, response time would be important, but overall aggregate performance requirements would be minimal. For example, Big State expected the phone book application to receive on the order of a few thousand accesses per day at most.

The `bigstate.edu` email service was designed to bring some order to the chaotic post-mainframe email environment emerging at Big State. Ever since users began leaving the mainframe system, literally dozens of local email systems had been popping up all over the Big State campus. Big State had no authority or desire to dictate the email systems used on campus—it just wanted to provide the addressing consistency users enjoyed in the mainframe days while still maintaining the email diversity required by today's users. This was the purpose of the `bigstate.edu` email service, whose architecture is illustrated in Figure 24.1.

The `bigstate.edu` email service was designed to give everyone at Big State a short, consistent, easy-to-remember email address in the form *firstname*.*lastname*@bigstate.edu or *userid*@bigstate.edu. This address follows a Big State email user during his or her entire association with the university, regardless of the local system on which the user might actually receive mail. Naturally, a necessary level of indirection is needed to insulate an email address from the user's actual location; the key component of this service is the directory. To deliver mail to email addresses based on names, the system required a name collision policy. To deliver to an address based on user ID, it required a mechanism for maintaining campus-wide unique user IDs.

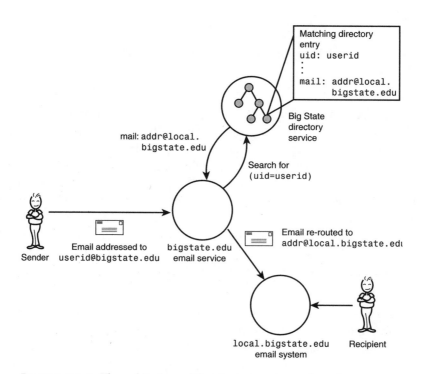

Matching directory
entry
uid: userid
:
:
mail: addr@local.
      bigstate.edu

Big State
directory
service

mail: addr@local.
      bigstate.edu

Search for
(uid=userid)

Sender

Email addressed to
userid@bigstate.edu

bigstate.edu
email service

Email re-routed to
addr@local.bigstate.edu

local.bigstate.edu
email system

Recipient

FIGURE 24.1 *The architecture of the* bigstate.edu *email service.*

Another key feature of the service is the ability for end users to create groups or mailing lists that receive mail at the bigstate.edu domain, a feature users of the mainframe system enjoyed. To implement email groups with a directory service, the directory deployment team developed specialized client software for creating and updating groups, and it imposed additional schema and performance requirements.

The overall performance requirements of the directory were driven by the most demanding directory application, which turned out to be the bigstate.edu email service. The Big State directory designers estimated that two-thirds of its 75,000 users would be active email users, receiving an average of three messages per day. If it takes three directory operations to deliver each piece of mail, you can see the load on the directory is substantial.

Throwing mailing lists into the mix increased the directory load even more. At Big State, users create more than 40,000 mailing lists, some with thousands of members (although the average group contains approximately 150 members). Delivering mail to these lists imposes a much greater load on the directory, and their creation and maintenance imposes an additional update load. This affects general directory performance as well as replication performance.

Data

The primary drivers behind the directory service revolved around the directory-enabled applications slated for deployment. These applications had well-defined schema requirements, which made for simpler identification of the necessary data elements. The broadest data requirements came from the online phone book, which aims to provide access to a wide range of the usual white pages information, such as name, title, address, phone number, organization, and so on. More-focused requirements came from the bigstate.edu email service, which needs local email addresses for users.

Data that might be useful for seeding the phone book application's white pages information was available from a number of sources within the university. In fact, Big State staff did a survey recently in which they identified 17 official university databases holding name and address information. Nevertheless, the directory designers identified two main sources of information: the university's Personnel database for faculty and staff and the Registrar's database for students. These databases were chosen for political as well as technical value.

The Personnel database had one particularly attractive quality: It was already used to publish the printed university faculty and staff directory. This made it easy to convince the keepers of this data that it should be released for the purposes of creating an online directory. The student data was also released after a similar argument was made regarding student phone information already available in the campus locator phone service.

One helpful practice was that the personnel department and the registrar both provided ways for users to request that their information be left out of any publications. This made everyone feel that enough choice had been given to users who did not want their information published.

20-20 Hindsight: Data Population

The ability for users to opt out of inclusion in the online directory was a subject of controversy for two reasons. First, the default action was to include all users, and then any user who did not want to be included had to take some action to be excluded (typically checking a box on a paper form). In the case of the student database, this box had to be checked once a year by the user, or the information would once again be published under university guidelines.

Many users believed that the default should be to omit students' information, and then anyone who wanted to be listed would have to check a box on a form. Directory service administrators did not like this scenario very well because it virtually guaranteed a decrease in the population of the directory. In fact, there was significant worry that such a scheme would cause the directory to fail to achieve a critical mass of data.

continues

continued

Second, many Big State users felt that electronic distribution of information, such as in the directory, is fundamentally different from the paper distribution of information they are used to, such as the printed university phone book. These users felt that signing up to be published in the printed directory should not automatically sign them up to have their information published in the online directory, especially for the Internet at large to see.

These kinds of tensions are typical when deploying an electronically available service using traditional printed data. Big State's answer to these problems was to allow users to opt out of the online directory independently from opting in or out of any other directories.

Another barrier against obtaining and deploying data from official university data sources was political. Big State's IT division was historically comprised of two parts: a traditional, mainframe-based corporate computing department supporting the university's business processes such as payroll, finance, and student registration; and a more progressive Internet and desktop computing department supporting the university's research and teaching missions. The directory was deployed by the latter group, but the databases holding the required information were managed by the former group. In retrospect, the Big State designers should have involved the corporate computing staff more in the design and deployment of the directory. This would undoubtedly have made the data acquisition process smoother and less troublesome. In particular, subsequent data acquisitions projects, such as adding temporary employees to the directory, would probably have been easier.

After an agreement was reached on the data to populate the directory with, procedures were developed for actually obtaining the data, reformatting it correctly, and augmenting it for inclusion in the directory. Procedures were also developed for maintaining the data through subsequent feeds from the source database. These procedures are described in more detail later in this chapter.

Another important kind of information required by the `bigstate.edu` email service was local email address information for users. This information proved to be much harder to obtain than the white pages information. The reason for this was simple: There is no centrally maintained database containing the required information. Instead, it is scattered around the campus in databases or applications maintained by local system administrators, and sometimes by users themselves.

To overcome this problem and populate the directory with useful information, the Big State designers took two courses of action. First, they worked directly with administrators of the larger systems on campus to develop tools to extract email addresses from their systems. Second, they developed a program with which campus administrators could submit lists of email addresses to the directory. Campus administrators had an incentive to do this because their users would be able to use the bigstate.edu email service. (A future email service developed by Big State and described later in this chapter automatically updated user email addresses at user registration time.)

Another category of data that Big State could store in the directory was administrative data. These data elements contain information used to manage other data elements. For example, Big State includes an expires attribute indicating when an entry scheduled for deletion will be removed. Another example is the noBatchUpdates attribute, which is used to indicate that a user does not wish his or her entry to be updated from official data sources.

As advised in Chapter 6, "Data Design," the Big State directory designers created a table showing the information to be contained in the directory, its source, and who owns the information. This information determined the Big State directory data source diagram, which is shown in Figure 24.2.

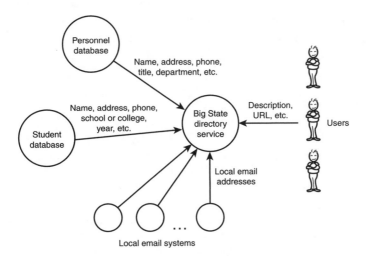

FIGURE 24.2 *The Big State directory data source diagram.*

Schema

The schema used in the central directory is comprised of two basic sets of schema definitions, one representing people and the other groups. The schema for representing people is taken from the standard person schema definition, extended with a few extra fields required by the Big State deployment. For example, Big State added a universityID attribute to hold the university-wide unique identification number. This attribute is used as a common key with external data sources, allowing entries in the directory to be matched up with the corresponding data from an external source.

Other new attributes were added to help keep track of various data handling and other procedures. For example, attributes are used for tracking data sources, noting the expiration time of entries, controlling whether entries are updated from corporate data sources, and other purposes. Attributes were also created to facilitate Big State's directory authentication scheme based on Kerberos, as described later in this chapter, as well as its proxy access control scheme.

The schema for representing groups was created from scratch in conjunction with the design of the `bigstate.edu` mail routing software. This software was written and designed by Big State staff because no commercial software found at the time satisfied the requirements. The existing standard group schema definitions also proved to be inadequate. For example, the standard group definition requires every member of a group to have a directory entry, making it difficult to create mailing lists that include non-university members. The Big State group definition, on the other hand, allows for both directory and email members. The group schema definition designed by Big State is shown in Listing 24.1 (it is somewhat abbreviated and annotated for clarity).

LISTING 24.1 BIG STATE GROUP SCHEMA DEFINITION

```
objectclass rfc822MailGroup
    requires
        objectClass,
        owner,                    # DN of the owner of the group
        cn                        # used to name the group entry
    allows
        associatedDomain,         # domain name associated with the group
        joinable,                 # flag indicating if others can join
        mail,                     # email members
        member,                   # directory members
        memberOfGroup,            # used for nested groups
        moderator,                # moderator of the group
        requestsTo,               # DN to receive list maintenance mail
        rfc822RequestsTo,         # email to receive -request mail
        rfc822ErrorsTo,           # email address for delivery reports
        errorsTo,                 # DN to receive delivery errors
        suppressNoEmailError,     # flag indicating if no members are ok
    ...                           # other attributes
```

20-20 Hindsight: Schema Design

Big State's schema definitions proved to be valuable. It would have been a good idea, however, to prefix the names of attributes specific to Big State with some kind of string that would ensure they would not collide with other attribute definitions. Some of Big State's definitions were general-purpose, suitable for use by other institutions, but others were specific to Big State. Making this distinction clear through a naming convention would have made Big State's schema easier to use by other organizations.

Namespace

Two future requirements led Big State to the namespace design it chose. First, Big State wanted the directory to be extensible so it can store other kinds of objects (not just users and groups) as future applications arose. This requirement led Big State to choose the high-level partition-by-object-type namespace recommended in Chapter 8, "Namespace Design."

Second, Big State imagined that at some later time it might want to partition and delegate portions of the directory to different units on campus. The medical campus and the College of Engineering were two likely candidates with the desire and necessary expertise to maintain portions of the directory. To facilitate this future possibility, Big State eschewed the advice to create a flat namespace; instead, it opted for a namespace in the people portion of the tree based on organizational hierarchy. To its credit, Big State let this hierarchy descend only one level. Because of difficulty in matching up the two data sources (one for faculty and staff, and one for students), Big State also decided to separate this data using the namespace (see Figure 24.3).

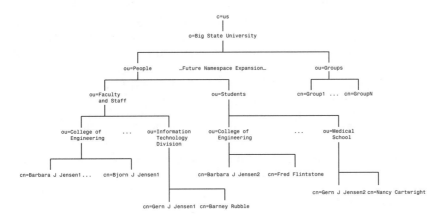

FIGURE 24.3 *The Big State directory namespace.*

To name individual people entries, Big State chose people's actual names. The names, taken from the official university staff and student databases, were constructed whenever possible to include a first name, middle initial, and last name (e.g., Barbara J Jensen). This was done in an effort to reduce the likelihood of name collisions. Recall that Big State wanted to reserve a unique email address based on name for each user.

When collisions do occur, uniqueness is guaranteed through data maintenance procedures that append a number to each name. For example, the first Barbara J. Jensen who comes to the university would be given the number 1. If another Barbara J. Jensen arrives, she would be given the number 2. The two entries would be named using the relative distinguished names `cn=Barbara J Jensen 1` and `cn=Barbara J Jensen 2`. These data maintenance procedures turned out to be rather complicated, as described in "20-20 Hindsight: Data Population" earlier in the chapter.

Although not part of the namespace, Big State also maintained a `userid` attribute that was unique across the directory. The attribute was populated and maintained from an existing database of campus-wide login names.

20-20 Hindsight: Namespace Design

Big State's decision to design an extensible namespace proved to be valuable. After the directory infrastructure was in place, many new applications were deployed and many new types of entries were added to the directory, including entries for documents and images. The extensible namespace made this possible with minimal disruption of the service.

Big State's decision to design a deeply hierarchical namespace proved to be a mistake, however. For a variety of reasons, the planned delegation of information to other units on campus never materialized. In retrospect, this possibility was not well-thought-out. With modern software, hierarchy is not necessary to delegate responsibility, and the additional hierarchy caused numerous problems in the operation of the service. For example, special tools had to be developed to handle the name changes that occur when a user moves from one department to another or from student to staff. Despite these special tools, name changes proved to be a continual plague on the directory administrators, requiring special handling.

The hierarchy also meant that users who have appointments in multiple departments are listed in only one department. The same is true for users who are both staff and student, a fairly common occurrence. This can be confusing to users. Finally, the hierarchy also led to longer names, wasting space and network bandwidth during replication. In summary, the hierarchy caused several problems and brought no perceptible benefit.

Another bad decision in hindsight was the use of names to form RDNs. Users often did not like the use of the first-middle-initial-last form of their name, and maintaining the numeric appendages for names was an administrative burden. A better choice for RDNs would have been the `userid` attribute, whose uniqueness is already maintained and which would have been less apt to encounter user resistance.

Topology

The topology design of the Big State directory service was driven by the requirements of the applications. These applications need to search the people and group portions of the namespace, so those portions of the directory need to be kept together to make these searches efficient. Big State's network is relatively fast and well-connected, indicating no need to partition the directory for performance reasons. Although as mentioned earlier Big State had thoughts of delegating portions of the directory to other units on campus, there was no immediate need to do so. Therefore, Big State decided to keep the directory together in a single server, making the topology very simple.

Replication

Two requirements drove the Big State directory replication design. The first requirement was for the service to always be up and available; the online phone book and email services depending on the directory are mission-critical and must be as available as possible. The second requirement was a certain high level of performance. The directory had to have sufficient capacity to support the directory-enabled applications using it, including the online phone book and email applications driving the directory's deployment, as well as the additional applications that would be deployed later. A replication architecture that would support this kind of incremental capacity increase was an explicit goal.

In the Big State directory replication architecture, a single-master server handles updates and feeds directory replicas serving various directory-enabled applications (see Figure 24.4). Initial deployment plans called for two small replicas to serve the online phone book application and three large replicas to serve the three directory-enabled email machines providing the `bigstate.edu` mail service. Partitioning directory usage based on the type of application makes it easier to track directory usage, bring down parts of the service for maintenance without affecting the rest of the service, and increase capacity when needed.

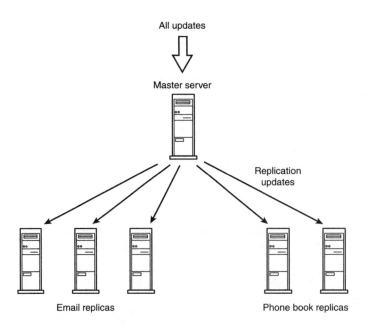

All updates

Master server

Replication
updates

Email replicas

Phone book replicas

FIGURE 24.4 *The Big State directory replication architecture.*

20-20 Hindsight: Replication

The Big State replication architecture was the right idea, but two aspects of the design needed attention soon after deployment. These problems were discovered as directory traffic increased because of the overwhelming popularity of the bigstate.edu email service.

First, the email service proved to be more of a directory hog and more popular than anticipated. This necessitated the deployment of two extra email machines with corresponding directory services to handle the load. Luckily, with the change described next, the replication architecture was able to handle this increase.

Second, the double burden of servicing all updates and feeding all replicas turned out to be too much for the single-master server to handle. The solution was to split this responsibility between the master server and a new server that now acts as replication supplier. The master server handles all updates and feeds the replication supplier, which feeds all the replicas.

When more replicas are needed than the replication supplier can feed, a second level of replication suppliers can be added. In this configuration (see Figure 24.5), the replication supplier feeds two or more second-level replication suppliers, which feed the replicas servicing directory-enabled applications. In this way, the number of directory replicas can be increased indefinitely.

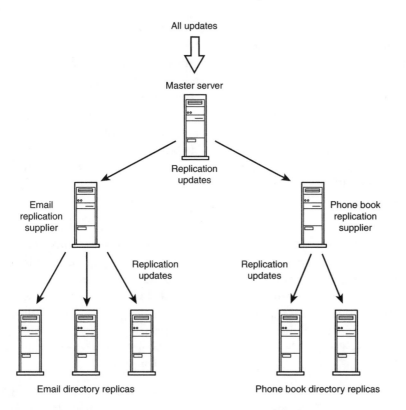

All updates

Master server

Replication
updates

Email
replication
supplier

Phone book
replication
supplier

Replication
updates

Replication
updates

Email directory replicas

Phone book directory replicas

FIGURE 24.5 *The revised Big State replication architecture.*

Privacy and Security

Privacy and security were paramount concerns for the Big State directory
designers. In a university, the general computing environment is relatively
open, and Big State has no firewall to protect services such as the directory
from the Internet at large. This means the directory service is open to access as
well as attack. Unfortunately, the university population includes a large number of students, some of whom are notorious for having too much time, cleverness, and mischievous intent on their hands. These factors combine to produce
an environment rife with an impressive array of threats to directory security
and privacy.

Because the Big State directory provides a white pages service, it contains personal information about directory users—information that must be protected.
The directory also serves various directory-enabled applications that are considered critical to the mission of the university. Making sure the applications
have secure access to accurate directory data is a requirement.

Most of the attributes held in the directory need to have their integrity protected. This means that directory clients must be assured that the information they read from the directory is authentic. A few attributes also need their privacy protected, such as the universityID attribute, which often contains a user's United States Social Security number. This attribute should be accessible only to directory administrators and select directory content administrators such as the help desk. In addition to privacy requirements, all attributes need to be protected from unauthorized tampering. The Big State directory designers constructed an access control scheme that separates the directory attributes into categories with different security requirements, meeting all these requirements. ACLs were constructed to protect each category appropriately.

Another requirement was to support delegated administration. Many faculty and staff members do not have the time or expertise necessary to update their own information in the directory, and they wanted to delegate this task to a departmental administrator or secretary. The Big State directory designers constructed a proxy access control scheme to make this possible. This scheme worked by defining an ACL allowing any distinguished name listed in the special proxy attribute of an entry to have appropriate access to the entry. This way, users can control access to their own entries simply by adding an attribute value. There is no need to modify any directory ACLs.

One important security issue was that Big State wanted to be able to leverage the existing campus Kerberos authentication service for the directory. By "kerberizing" the directory, the designers avoided designing a new authentication system and distributing and maintaining new passwords. Also, using Kerberos allowed the many thousands of Kerberos users on campus to begin their directory life with a password they already knew. This proved to be a great boon to directory use on campus. The only downside was that it required special development on both directory servers and clients. Big State found that even today no directory products support Kerberos out of the box, significantly adding to the cost and difficulty of maintaining and upgrading the existing service.

Privacy is an equally important concern in the directory. In a university environment, users are accustomed to having more control over their personal information than they might have at a big corporation. Big State is no exception, so the directory designers set out to design a system that provides maximum flexibility for directory users. This included the ability for users to opt out of the directory entirely or to hide or publish various attributes such home address information. This capability was accomplished through the use of content-based ACLs, which is similar to the targetfilter capability of Netscape Directory Server described in Chapter 11, "Privacy and Security Design."

Deployment

Deployment of the Big State directory service was a relatively simple process. Because the directory service and associated directory-enabled applications were all new, there was no existing user base to be migrated and no existing service to worry about interrupting. The deployment steps detailed in the following sections were followed.

Product Choice

Big State had several requirements driving its choice of directory product. At the time of deployment (the early 1990s), Big State was ahead of even the early adopters on the industry directory curve—meaning that no commercial products existed that served Big State's needs. So Big State embarked on a development project to build the software it needed. This software had three main components: a directory server, LDAP directory clients, and gateways linking existing services.

At the time, X.500 was the only standard directory protocol available, so Big State developed an X.500 directory server based on publicly available code. The Big State developers implemented a new, more scalable, high-performance database; a replication service; and a new, more powerful access control scheme that satisfied their needs. Big State, along with members of the Internet Engineering Task Force (IETF), also designed and implemented the LDAP protocol itself. LDAP (or something like it) was necessary to bring directory service to the rest of the Big State campus, which consists primarily of Macintosh and Windows machines. At that stage, LDAP was implemented as a front end to the X.500 directory. (See Chapter 2, "A Brief History of Directories," for more history on the development of LDAP.)

Big State developed a number of LDAP directory clients covering all the major platforms to provide users with read-and-write access to the directory. These clients include the flagship maX.500 Macintosh client, the waX.500 Windows client, and the xax500 UNIX X Window client. Also developed was a simple command-line interface client called ud. These clients know about Big State's data management procedures and are able to provide users with intelligent error messages when things go wrong. The clients also know about the special schema designed for groups and other applications, allowing users to query and update schema elements. The mailing list service and the ability to change personal information encouraged users to update the directory frequently.

Big State also developed a number of gateways linking existing services (such as finger, Gopher, and the Web) to the directory service. This strategy allowed users to access the directory immediately using their existing tools.

20-20 Hindsight: Directory Development

Big State's decision to develop rather than purchase software had mixed results. At the time the service was developed and deployed, the state of the market was very immature, so Big State would have had to make unacceptable compromises in its service by deploying off-the-shelf software. Key technology such as LDAP did not yet exist either, so it had to be invented. Big State's development efforts had a substantial and lasting effect on the industry, and many vendors have based their directory solutions on LDAP software that was developed at Big State during this time.

Unfortunately, substantial development effort was required. A lot of time and several people were committed to the effort, costing Big State real dollars. (Of course, given the payoff in terms of advancing both the directory industry and Big State's directory deployment, this price was deemed well-worth paying.) More seriously, Big State spent valuable time developing a solution from scratch. An even more serious negative consequence of Big State's decision is that Big State must continue to support the software it developed to run its service. Keeping the software bug-free and enhancing it to grow with the service it provides requires a significant ongoing investment.

Big State is contemplating moving from its home-grown environment to a more standard, vendor-based environment. Many obstacles must be overcome to duplicate the functionality of the Big State deployment using vendor-supplied products. Starting with a vendor-based solution and evolving over time with the vendor would have made this transition easier.

Given the plethora of capable directory products on the market now, Big State would have little problem finding products to support its needs if it were starting to design a service today; the idea of developing a directory server from scratch would be certainly out of the question. However, developing specialized directory-enabled applications that are aware of local schema and policies would still be a perfectly reasonable thing to do.

Piloting

The first Big State directory pilot was conducted with only the online phone book application. This allowed the service to be piloted, data-handling techniques to be tried out, and initial user reaction to the service to be tested. The phone book application was considered relatively low-risk, especially in comparison to the email application. The phone book is important, but if it is down or malfunctions, users can always resort to printed or telephone-based directory assistance. If the email application malfunctions, however, mail service can be hindered and university business can be seriously disrupted.

As part of the phone book pilot, Web, finger, and Gopher gateways to the directory were deployed to give users a variety of access methods. The pilot was conducted rather informally and without any scientific feedback-gathering techniques. Only online documentation was required for the various white pages gateways, but more elaborate documentation and training courses were developed for the various directory clients such as maX.500. These clients were rolled out in parallel with both the phone book and the email application. They became more important as more users found the need to update the contents of the directory.

When the phone book application was shown to be successful, Big State moved forward with plans to pilot the email service, which required more formal piloting procedures. The service was first tested on a very small scale in a laboratory environment using Big State's directory staff as guinea pigs. Success there led to rolling out the service in a real, although unannounced, environment. This involved securing the necessary machines, space, power, and network connectivity; configuring the machines and loading them with the required directory and other software; populating the directory with appropriate data; putting in place pilot monitoring and backup procedures; and other tasks.

The service was rolled out to select groups of individuals as well as to others who became aware of the service (there was no easy way to prevent them from using the service). Documentation was developed for both end users and support staff, and support staff were also trained. When the unannounced pilot was deemed successful, various methods were used to publicize the service for its rollout to a wider audience. These included publicizing the service in new student and new hire enrollment packages, placing articles in the campus newspapers, and other methods. The IT division's public relations department was also helpful in this endeavor.

Analyzing and Reducing Costs

One lesson the Big State directory team learned early on is that data maintenance and personnel are by far the most expensive costs associated with the service. Almost all data maintenance procedures are automated, but even the tiny fraction that are not cause lots of extra work and headaches for the Big State staff. An ongoing effort for the directory team is to automate more and more of the maintenance processes and reduce the number of exceptional cases that must be dealt with by hand.

The periodic bulk data loading procedure proved to be one of the most troublesome aspects of the service. Despite massive effort to automate this service, handle exceptional conditions, and generally make the procedure easy, problems still occurred. The goal was to get this procedure mostly automated, with a system administrator handling any reasonable exceptions. Instead, the procedure continued to cause problems, requiring attention from the service designers.

Another high-cost aspect of the service turned out to be help desk and other related support services. Users forgetting their passwords, wanting information added to or removed from their entries, and needing other exceptional conditions handled turned out to be a large burden on the support staff. Big State addressed this problem by developing more and better documentation, automating certain tasks so that users can service many requests themselves, and offering training classes to the user community.

Going Production

Moving from a pilot to a production environment was a relatively painless task. Because the service was new and deployed from scratch, the same infrastructure used for piloting could be used for the production service. By the time the pilots had been operating for a while, going production was a simple matter of making sure the production operations were in place and had sufficient capacity, and then opening the service to a wider audience. Several more robust procedures such as for monitoring were also developed as part of the production process.

Other tasks associated with going production, such as developing training classes, creating documentation, and publicizing the service, were completed after the service was up and running smoothly for some time.

Maintenance

Maintenance of the Big State directory was relatively simple, but not without its problems. Some of the more tedious and time-consuming aspects of system maintenance are covered in the following sections.

Data Backup and Disaster Recovery

Three approaches are taken to provide backup and disaster recovery for the directory service. First, each machine providing service is backed up to magnetic tape regularly. These tapes are saved for six weeks and rotated periodically. This kind of backup is used primarily to guard against any of the single systems becoming corrupted. The system's configuration can be restored from the backup tape, and its directory can be repopulated using one of the techniques described later in this section.

Second, directory replicas are also used as a backup service. If a secondary replica becomes corrupted, directory data can be restored from the master replica. If the master directory server becomes corrupted, it can be restored from the database of the most up-to-date replica server. This kind of procedure often provides more timely backups than the magnetic tape method. The tapes are typically updated with an incremental backup once per day, whereas directory replicas are constantly updated and kept in sync with the master.

Third, the directory data is dumped to a text file and transferred to a different, secure machine every night. If the master and all replica directories become corrupt, they can be restored from this saved file, losing only the intervening changes. This kind of backup is helpful in recovering from such problems as an out-of-control administrative procedure that mistakenly deletes a bunch of entries from the directory. It is also helpful in recovering data mistakenly deleted or modified by a user.

20-20 Hindsight: Backup Procedures

Maintaining three separate backup and disaster recovery procedures may seem like overkill, but Big State found that each procedure was the best choice for different situations, and sometimes the procedures can be used in combination. For example, a disk failure on a production machine is best handled by restoring the machine's file systems from the tape backup, and then restoring its directory data from one of the replica directories. This kind of creative thinking made the job of recovering from failures and catastrophes much easier. Using the right combination of procedures helps to minimize recovery time and increase system uptime.

Maintaining Data

One of the most trouble-prone and time-consuming tasks associated with the Big State directory service is data maintenance. There are several procedures related to this task:

- *Bulk data source loading.* This is the main way the directory is populated with data. Periodic data dumps are obtained from the personnel and student source databases and merged with the existing directory data to produce an updated directory. The merging procedure is accomplished by a program called "munge," which is used in conjunction with a set of step-by-step procedures that accomplish the merge. The merging procedure is quite complicated and error-prone, and it is further complicated because the directory must be restricted to read-only mode during much of the procedure.

- *Directory content administration.* These kinds of changes are primarily made by help desk and other support staff in response to user requests. This includes requests to move an entry from one department to another and to change certain attributes that users themselves are not allowed to change. For example, a `title` attribute maintained in the directory often doesn't contain exactly what a user considers his or her title to be. In this instance, the user can only request that the title be changed.

- *Other automated data source loading.* This includes various other automated links to data sources on campus. For each source, a separate data loading procedure was developed and must be maintained. One source of problems used to involve different sources fighting with each other; that is, one source would add data to the directory, only to have it overwritten by another source (this typically happened to a user with accounts on two or more local systems). The solution was to add source-tracking capabilities to the automated data source loading procedures.

The Big State directory is not unusual in the occasionally poor quality of its data. This problem leads to user complaints, which in turn lead to manual work by directory maintenance staff to correct the problems. These manual tasks can become quite burdensome and expensive.

Monitoring

Big State has an extensive monitoring system in place that focuses on network devices such as routers, hubs, and server network interfaces. As is the case in many organizations, the group that provides this monitoring is distinct from the group that deployed the directory. The Big State directory designers wanted to leverage this existing monitoring infrastructure as much as possible when monitoring the directory system.

The Big State monitoring system provides a mechanism for calling out to user-developed code to perform certain tests. The directory deployment team worked with the monitoring system maintenance staff to incorporate plug-in programs it wrote to perform a number of directory tests. These allowed directory alerts to be displayed on the monitoring system's trouble board, to be dealt with by monitoring system staff when appropriate.

The directory deployment team developed and documented procedures to help the monitoring staff know what to do in case of a directory alert. Initially, these procedures usually specified paging or emailing a directory team member, depending on the severity of the event. As both the monitoring and directory teams became more comfortable with the service, procedures were updated to allow the monitoring staff to troubleshoot certain problems. Some alerts were even automated, causing directory team members to be automatically paged in the event of a serious failure, such as the directory becoming unreachable or directory replication or email queues becoming inordinately large.

Another aspect to the Big State monitoring system is log analysis. The directory team developed log analysis software to produce daily and weekly summaries of directory-related activities. This includes the number and types of operations the directory servers themselves handle, as well as statistics on important directory-enabled applications. For example, the periodic reports detailing usage of the phone book and email applications is invaluable for predicting capacity problems, justifying funding expenditures, and general public relations.

20-20 Hindsight: Monitoring

The Big State monitoring system worked fairly well, but it tended to produce a lot of false alarms. This was partly caused by incorrect threshold parameters in the monitoring software. For example, sometimes the directory would be reported as down when it was in fact just slow. These threshold parameters were tuned to improve the situation.

More seriously, the monitoring system revealed a great deal of variance in the level of service provided to directory clients. This was partly a capacity problem, easily remedied with the introduction of bigger and faster directory server machines. But it was also an indication of problems with the directory software itself. These problems were harder to fix and required relatively expensive staff time to debug and improve the directory server software.

Troubleshooting

Big State developed a number of troubleshooting procedures for dealing with directory problems. Following are some of the more interesting problems that led to the development of these procedures:

- *Infinite email loops.* This is one of the nastier problems encountered by the directory team. Users are allowed to create mail groups that can contain addresses that point anywhere at all. Sometimes they create a condition in which email sent to a group is sent to another address that forwards it back to the group—creating an infinite loop. Most mail software has no trouble handling such loops, stopping them after some maximum hop count is achieved. Unfortunately, loops can get more complicated and hard to detect. For example, consider a group with two members, each of which points back to the group itself. This situation results in an exponentially increasing number of emails flooding the system.

- *Data feed disasters.* On a few occasions, the data feed from the staff and student source databases contains erroneous information. A typical mistake is the exclusion of a whole class of employees. Without careful safeguards, this situation can have resulted in wholesale deletion of many directory entries.

- *Replication failures*. The replication software has proved to be rather unstable. Unanticipated changes to the master server or small configuration differences between master and replica often cause changes to fail to replicate. This situation requires manual intervention by a knowledgeable directory administrator and often involves directory downtime. In the most serious situations, either the master or replica server crashes while attempting to replicate a change.

Several troubleshooting procedures developed from these problems. Perhaps the most important is related to problems with the email service. Step one in dealing with any email-related problem is to turn off email service. No harm is done by this because undeliverable mail is queued, usually for up to three days. Taking this step avoids the more serious error of bouncing email and buys the directory maintenance team valuable time to figure out and correct the problem.

The mail loop problem has never been fully resolved, but a number of steps were taken to mitigate the problem. First, the mail delivery software was modified to detect and reject the simplest forms of mail loops that it could detect. Second, an automated process was developed to trawl the directory for other situations that were likely to cause mail loops, and administrators were alerted of suspected problems. Third, the directory monitoring software was improved to more quickly and accurately detect mail loops when they occur. Finally, better tools were developed to recover from mail loop disasters. These tools make it easier to hunt down and delete the loop-generating messages clogging the mail system.

Other tools were developed to help detect data feed disasters before serious damage can occur. These include changes to the munge program to look for large, unexpected changes in the user population during the monthly data merge. Large changes are reported to administrators who can ensure they are legitimate.

Tools were also developed to detect and recover from replication failures. The directory monitoring system has been augmented with tests to alert administrators if replication appears stuck (for example, if the replication queue gets too big). Tools were also developed to make the process of recovering from a replication failure easier. These include scripts that automate the process of creating one directory replica from another. The process of clearing out "bad" changes in a replication log remains manual, although more recently directory administrators have created surgical techniques for repairing entries damaged by replication errors without causing service interruptions.

Leveraging the Directory Service

After the directory service infrastructure was laid down, Big State deployed more applications to leverage the directory. The directory world was filled with possibilities.

Applications

The Big State directory service was driven by the white pages and email applications described earlier in this chapter. Many new applications from all parts of the campus began to be developed as soon as the directory infrastructure was available and robust. Following are a few of the more interesting applications:

- *Card key access.* The university operates several unstaffed computing sites for the exclusive use of current faculty, staff, and students. The departments have deployed card reader door locks at these sites and developed software for the readers that consult the directory to determine the status of individuals requesting access.

- *Software license tracking.* For funding purposes, the university wanted to track application usage on a school and college basis, so it developed its own license-tracking software. The campus software license server was modified to consult the directory to determine the school or college affiliation of users accessing licensed software.

- *Bulk email communications.* Occasionally, offices on campus need to communicate with all users in a certain department, school, or college, or with users who have a certain title or job description. For examples, sometimes the Registrar's office needs to communicate financial aid information to students, or the Personnel office needs to communicate benefit information to staff members. The directory team developed software that consults the directory and contacts the appropriate users. Because of the potential for abuse of this service to send "spam" (unwanted junk email), use of the service is carefully controlled.

- *Course registration.* The university developed an automated telephone registration system that allows students to register for classes over the phone. The directory is used to email students the schedule of the classes they register for.

- *Legacy email address book population.* As mentioned earlier, departments throughout the university have deployed various LAN email products. These systems generally do not have the ability to query the LDAP directory directly, so the campus directory is used as a data source to populate these directories with name and email address information.

- *Documentation finder*. The university's IT division uses the directory to store an index of campus computing documentation. This index is accessed by a Web application that can be used to locate and access documentation. In this case, the directory contains only documentation index information—not the documentation itself.

- *Personal Web page finder*. A simple application allows users to locate the personal Web pages of other users. The directory is mined periodically as the source of this information.

The easy availability of the directory, coupled with some good, basic development tools, makes it easy for people to develop directory-enabled applications. As the scope of people developing directory-enabled applications increases, Big State is finding the need to develop more formal documentation and courses explaining how to program directory-enabled applications, how to design new schemas, how to avoid abusing the directory, and other topics.

Directory Deployment Impact

The directory world at Big State University is generally an improvement over the old one. On- and off-campus users have easy access to accurate white pages information about university faculty, staff, and students via a variety of clients. All users have access to the popular bigstate.edu email service, whose group feature is especially liked. Many new directory-enabled applications have been deployed across the campus to serve a variety of needs.

The administration aspect of the directory is both good and bad. The good news is that the directory provides a valuable service to the Big State community; the number of people accessing the service every day is a testament to its success. The bad news is that maintaining the directory is more expensive than the university's directory team would like. Decisions made in haste or using bad information at the beginning of the project (for example, its namespace design) have come back to haunt the directory maintenance team. The success of the service makes it difficult to go back and make fundamental changes; this would be too disruptive.

Summary and Lessons Learned

We want to stress again that this case study does not describe the University of Michigan's directory service, although many of our experiences designing and deploying that system are reflected.

Many of the decisions Big State made were a result of leading the charge into an immature and developing market. There were no books like this one available when Big State set about designing its service. Indeed, no one was quite sure what a directory was and all the things it would be used for. So the design and deployment was definitely a learning experience.

One important lesson learned was that it is easy to become a victim of your own success. This happened to Big State, whose initial directory deployment should have been redesigned to address problems with the namespace and data handling procedures and to introduce vendor-supplied software. Unfortunately, the service was popular enough that making these kinds of sweeping changes proved problematic.

Another important lesson learned was that the quality of data contained in various university data sources is relatively poor. These sources were thought to be the source of truth for information, but in fact they contained many errors. The increased visibility of these errors through the directory was partly responsible for raising general awareness of these data quality issues.

Looking Ahead

This concludes the second of our four case studies. The following two case studies will examine more-typical commercial deployments of directories and how those directories can be used to help deploy extranet applications.

## CHAPTER 25

Case Study: A Large Multinational Enterprise

In this chapter we look at how a large multinational enterprise might design and deploy an LDAP directory service. Large organizations typically spend much more time and money up front to design a good directory service than small organizations do. There are several reasons why the extra investment is necessary:

- Large organizations tend to be more decentralized in terms of geography, political control, and information systems management. It is difficult to bring an organizationwide service such as a directory online because of all the physical and political boundaries that separate the different parts of the organization.

- Data about important organizational assets (including people) is typically controlled by a group different from the one charged with deploying the directory service. This increases the amount of coordination and political cooperation needed to obtain the data and deploy the directory.

- The complexity and cost of managing a directory service consisting of a large number of servers is significant enough that a lot of time and money is typically spent designing and piloting to ensure that the process of putting the service into production goes smoothly.

- The cost of a design error is greater than in smaller deployments. Because of the large number of servers rolled out and the complexity of data maintenance and other issues, a redesign of a large-scale directory late in the design process causes more pain and expense than it would in smaller deployments.

The large multinational enterprise case study discussed in this chapter is fictional—it is not based directly on any real-world directory deployments. However, this case study draws from knowledge of several actual deployments we are familiar with. The enterprise we describe is patterned after a manufacturing company such as Ford Motor Company, Boeing, or Intel. The name of our fictitious company is HugeCo. This case study is written as if HugeCo's directory service has been deployed as a production service for approximately six months.

An Overview of the Organization

HugeCo is a very widely dispersed organization with 225,000 employees and contractors located in 34 countries around the world. Most employees live and work in countries where HugeCo's manufacturing facilities are located: the United States, Canada, Mexico, the United Kingdom, Germany, Japan, and Australia. HugeCo has relationships with hundreds of other companies that serve as suppliers, dealers, and customers for the products it produces.

HugeCo has a strong, well-funded central information services (IS) organization that operates out of the corporate headquarters site in Chicago, Illinois. There are four regional IS departments to serve the needs of HugeCo sites in North America, Latin America, Europe, and the Asia Pacific region. The primary role of the central IS organization is to design the network and applications architecture, run several central services (such as a corporate electronic mail hub), and coordinate the activities of HugeCo's regional IS departments. The regional IS departments are responsible for the installation and maintenance of all hardware and software within their regions.

The information technology infrastructure at HugeCo includes a modern, high-speed TCP/IP network. Within each site, a combination of 10Base-T and 100Base-T twisted-pair Ethernets is used to connect desktop machines and servers. Larger sites also have an internal fiber optic backbone network that operates at 100Mbps. Most sites are connected with leased T1 (1.54Mbps) or T3 (45Mbps) lines to regional data centers that are connected to each other with leased T3 lines. Some of HugeCo's smallest sites are connected via the public

Internet using virtual private network (VPN) technology and local Internet service providers (ISPs). An overview of the HugeCo network is shown in Figure 25.1.

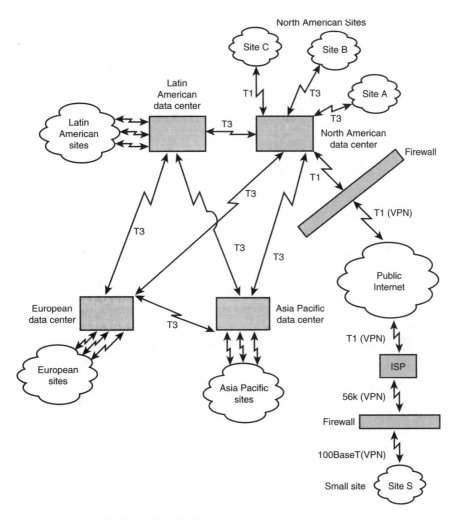

FIGURE 25.1 *The HugeCo TCP/IP network.*

The central IS organization, along with the regional IS departments, provides a rich, robust set of electronic mail, discussion forum, group scheduling, and document publishing services to HugeCo's professional employees. Following is a list of the most important applications in use at HugeCo:

- Netscape Messaging Server is used to provide electronic mail routing, delivery, and reading services for most of HugeCo's sites. Sendmail.org's `sendmail` mail transfer agent (MTA) and the University of Washington's `imapd` mail store software are used in some sites, but both packages are being phased out. A variety of desktop email clients are used, including QUALCOMM's Eudora, Netscape Messenger, and Microsoft's Outlook and Outlook Express clients.

- Lotus Notes servers and clients are used to support group discussion forums and certain collaborative applications developed in house. Notes is used only by HugeCo's executive staff and their assistants.

- Netscape Enterprise Server is used to provide document publishing services and to support a variety of custom Web-based applications. Microsoft's Internet Explorer browser and Netscape's Navigator browser are both widely used within HugeCo.

Most of the applications are hosted on Sun Enterprise servers that run the Solaris UNIX operating system. The notable exceptions are the servers for Lotus Notes, which are deployed on Dell PowerEdge servers that run Microsoft Windows NT Server.

The central IS organization also employs several dozen software engineers who develop and maintain a variety of custom Web-based applications. These software engineers also assist employees in the regional IS departments and within HugeCo departments that are developing their own applications.

HugeCo benefits from strong centralized leadership that makes it possible for the central IS organization to dictate which software and hardware are used throughout much of the company. Still, there is a high degree of independence within regions, especially with respect to how services and data are administered.

Directory Drivers

To better serve its internal customers, HugeCo's central IS organization decided to design and deploy an organizationwide LDAP directory service. The motivation to create a comprehensive corporate directory was driven by the following goals, some of which addressed immediate needs and others long-term needs:

- *Improve internal communication*—HugeCo's executive staff handed down a mandate that internal communication should be improved. The IS organization decided that a good way to streamline internal communication would be to make it easier to locate and share information about people and resources such as conference rooms. Before the arrival of an organizationwide LDAP directory, most applications had their own database of users, groups, and resources, which added to end user confusion and created a high administrative burden. IS managers believed that by deploying a shared, organizationwide directory, the quality and the timeliness of information accessed by users and applications could be improved and that data management costs could be lowered through the elimination of redundant information.

- *Make it easier to develop and deploy Web applications*—As more and more Web-based applications were being developed and deployed, it became clear that a shared authentication and group database was needed. A common directory service used by all of the custom applications would allow HugeCo to provide a form of single sign-on and decrease the costs of developing, deploying, and maintaining the custom applications. It also would lower the cost of entry so that smaller departments without the resources to develop and maintain their own infrastructure could develop their own applications.

- *Increase security and privacy*—Within the next two years, HugeCo plans to issue public key certificates that employees can use to authenticate to email and workflow applications. Deployment of the necessary public key infrastructure (PKI) would be a time-consuming task, but it would be made easier by the presence of a directory service. In the short run, the HugeCo directory could provide a single point of management for passwords and distribution of role-based access rights used by Web-based applications.

  The security and privacy of the directory data itself were important issues because of the wide geographical dispersion of HugeCo's employees and because some of the corporate traffic is tunneled through the public Internet using VPN technology.

- *Improve communication with dealers and suppliers*—HugeCo's upper management knows that the company needs to maintain close ties to its dealers (sales offices) and suppliers to stay competitive. Because these entities operate independently of HugeCo, they do not share any information technology infrastructure. Without exception, HugeCo has a more highly developed infrastructure and more expertise than its dealers and suppliers. At the present time, most communication outside the company is done using simple file transfers and fax machines. Although we do not discuss it in this chapter, HugeCo hopes to leverage the knowledge gained from deployment of its corporate directory service to create a directory to link it closely and securely with its suppliers and dealers. A directory deployment motivated by similar needs is discussed in Chapter 26, "Case Study: An Enterprise with an Extranet."

Directory Service Design

The first phase in HugeCo's directory service adventure was to analyze its needs and design the service itself. This task was accomplished over the course of four months by a team of five people from the central IS organization. An IS employee from each of the four regional IS departments was asked to participate in a weekly conference call and occasional face-to-face meetings to review the detailed directory design as it was drafted.

HugeCo's chief information officer (CIO), who oversees all IS activities within the company, was involved early in the decision to develop an LDAP directory service. To bring the CIO up to speed and expose her to the short- and long-term benefits a directory would provide, the IS group arranged a private presentation and demonstration for her. An entire week was spent preparing for the meeting with the CIO, but the good will and support it generated in her helped the directory deployment process immensely. Having the CIO on board lowered the political barriers that occasionally threatened to block the progress of the design and deployment of HugeCo's directory service.

Needs

When the directory design team was formed by HugeCo's senior IS managers, the reasons for the directory were clearly spelled out to the team. This and the fact that the overall computing environment was already well-known and documented by the central IS organization made the directory needs analysis a relatively easy step.

The following applications were identified as good candidates to take advantage of a directory service immediately:

- Netscape Messaging Server (electronic mail transfer and delivery)

- A variety of electronic mail clients (used by end users to manage their email)

- Netscape Enterprise Server (used to publish Web documents and support custom applications)

- Lotus Notes (used for group discussions)

This list is in order of priority, although the explosion of Web-based applications that was underway made Netscape Enterprise Server increasingly important. Integration of the new LDAP directory service with Lotus Notes was a relatively low priority because of Notes' small user base (limited to HugeCo's executive staff). In contrast, almost all of HugeCo's professional employees use email daily.

The directory design team also thought it would be cost-effective and useful to replace printed departmental employee phone lists with a Web-based phonebook application. This application could even be used by directory administrators and help desk staff to perform simple directory maintenance tasks, such as correcting an employee's information or resetting a password.

Because of the wide geographic distribution of HugeCo's facilities, it was clear from the start that the directory service would need to be available to end users and applications 24 hours a day, seven days a week. The IS staff already was already required to provide similar levels of service for most of the shared network infrastructure and important applications such as email.

The design team also took time to develop a directory project plan. This plan included several goals, each with an associated target date. The goals were as follows:

- Publish a directory service requirements document (within 1 month).

- Complete and publish the initial directory design (within 3 months).

- Complete a directory pilot involving at least two regions of HugeCo (within 8 months).

- Deploy a production-quality directory service used for phonebook lookups, email routing, and at least one important Web-based application (within 18 months).

Everyone agreed that this was an aggressive set of goals, but the team thought all of them could be achieved. The initial draft of the requirements document was created and published soon after the needs analysis stage was complete. The leader of the design team shared the goals with IS upper managers and other IS employees—but not before padding the target dates by a few months to give the team more room to meet them.

Data

As soon as the list of applications was in hand, the HugeCo design team worked with an existing data architecture team within the IS organization to craft a directory data policy statement. The core tenants of the statement included the following points:

- Data that is shared by more than one application should be stored in the directory service.

- The authoritative source for each data element stored in the directory must be defined.

- Data that is extremely sensitive or private should not be stored in the directory service unless there is an operational reason to do so. This kind of data includes payroll and employee benefit information.

- All legal requirements, including country and regional privacy laws in effect where HugeCo operates, must be followed.

IS quickly produced a list of data elements needed by each application. This was a relatively easy task; many of the applications supported LDAP already and therefore came with a set of well-documented data elements and schemas. For HugeCo's custom Web-based applications, a role-based access control system used by some of the newest applications was adopted and modeled in the directory.

Roles at HugeCo include `helpDesk`, `emailAdmin`, `systemAdmin`, `payrollClerk`, `seniorManager`, `lineManager`, and dozens of others. The Web-based applications use a combination of the roles that a person is allowed to adopt, along with information about the department they are in, to grant or deny access to application functions. Many of the newest applications manage workflow tasks in which the appropriate flow of information is especially critical. The directory design team decided that in addition to a standard department number data element, a list of roles should be stored with each person entry in the directory service to facilitate the use of role-based access control by applications.

Next, the team created a table of all the data elements that would initially need to be stored in the directory service. As recommended in Chapter 6, "Data Design," the table included a comprehensive set of characteristics for each data element. The team discovered that most of the data elements were shared by several applications and would not contain any sensitive information, which fit well within the directory data policy statement. The team also noted that many of the data elements had to accommodate data values of several different character sets and languages because of the multinationality of HugeCo. Although most official communication takes place in English, most of the sites located in non–English-speaking countries communicate internally using the native language.

The final data design task was to examine an existing inventory of HugeCo's data sources. The team's goal was to determine which data elements that were to be stored in the directory were already available in existing stores. The team discovered that many of the employee-related data elements were already present in HugeCo's PeopleSoft human resources (HR) system. A series of meetings was planned with the PeopleSoft experts within the IS organization to determine how to best manage the relationship between the HR database and the directory service.

Schema

To accommodate the data elements, the HugeCo team chose to use standard schemas and schemas provided by the application vendors when available. In some cases the team members found that they needed to subclass standard schema elements to meet their needs. Some of the LDAP object classes selected for use in the HugeCo directory are shown in Figure 25.2.

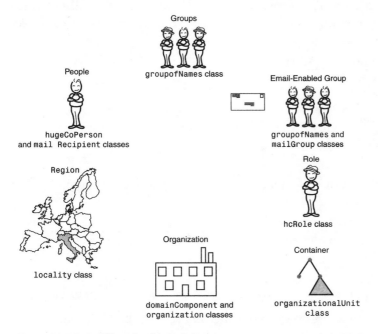

FIGURE 25.2 *HugeCo object classes.*

To allow the storage of values for a few custom attributes in each employee entry, the standard inetOrgPerson object class was subclassed to create a hugeCoPerson object class. The first three custom attributes defined as part of the hugeCoPerson class were

- hcEmployeeRole, to store the list of roles described earlier.

- hcBuildingNumber, to store a number that uniquely identifies the building where an employee works.

- hcBuildingFloor, to store the floor or building level where an employee works.

By subclassing a standard LDAP object class, maximum compatibility with existing directory-enabled applications was maintained, and company-specific extensions could be made cleanly and easily in the future.

For the routing of electronic mail, the mailRecipient object class defined by Netscape for use with its Messaging Server was the natural choice. For email and access control groups, the standard groupOfNames object class was used with Netscape's mailGroup auxiliary class to email-enable entries as needed.

A new object class called hcRole was created to allow the entire list of available roles to be stored as a set of directory entries. The design of the hcRole object class is shown in Listing 25.1.

LISTING 25.1 THE hcRole OBJECT CLASS

```
objectclass hcRole
    superior top
    oid 1.2.3.4.5.6.7
    required
        cn
    allowed
        description
```

The cn attribute is used to hold the name of the role itself. A sample role entry is shown in Listing 25.2.

LISTING 25.2 A SAMPLE hcRole ENTRY.

```
dn: cn=helpDesk, ou=Roles, ou=Global, dc=hugeco, dc=com
objectclass: top
objectclass: hcRole
cn: helpDesk
description: people who handle questions sent to the IS help desk
```

Storing all the available roles in the directory service allows directory-enabled administration tools and Web-based applications to easily obtain and present the complete list of roles to their users if needed.

To accommodate international data, the language attribute subtypes and Unicode (UTF-8) character set specified by LDAPv3 were adopted. By convention, an ASCII-only value that is not tagged with any language is always stored for all attribute types. This provides maximum compatibility with directory-enabled applications that are not able to handle Unicode data.

Namespace

The HugeCo team made an early decision to follow a domain component (dc) naming scheme. This allowed them to leverage their existing Domain Name System (DNS) names for the top part of their namespace. Their top-level suffix of dc=hugeco, dc=com was simply derived from the company's existing Internet domain name (hugeco.com).

The HugeCo design team wanted to keep the directory namespace fairly flat to reduce the overhead of managing distinguished name (DN) changes. A hierarchy was incorporated into the namespace to allow for delegation of responsibility and provide subtree roots to facilitate replication. HugeCo's initial directory namespace design is shown in Figure 25.3.

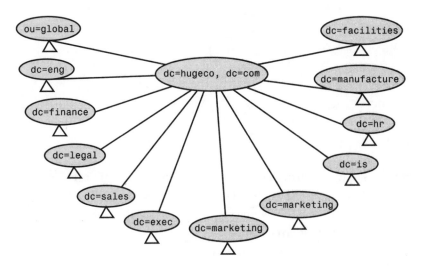

FIGURE 25.3 *The initial design of HugeCo's directory namespace.*

By splitting the directory tree along DNS subdomain lines, a useful hierarchy of directory entries was produced. This scheme fit well with the way electronic mail accounts are managed within HugeCo. It allowed different access control to be placed at the top of each dc container to allow for a rough mapping of authority based on departments.

However, this namespace design did not mesh well with HugeCo's need to replicate its directory information in all locations. The main reason for this was the complexity of managing and setting up replication between 11 directory partitions. When revising the namespace design, the HugeCo team decided instead to separate the tree along regional lines. The final, revised namespace design is shown in Figure 25.4.

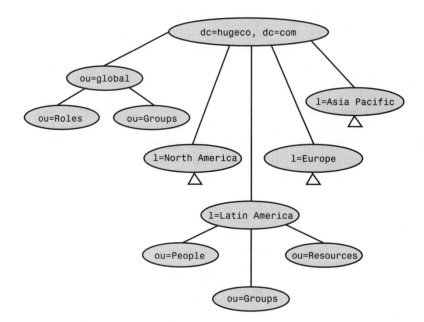

FIGURE 25.4 *The final design of HugeCo's directory namespace.*

In Figure 25.4, *locality* entries are used to represent each region. The relative distinguished name (RDN) of these entries is formed using the l (locality) attribute. The entry for the Asia Pacific region is shown in Listing 25.3.

LISTING 25.3 A SAMPLE hcPersonEntry ENTRY

```
dn: l=Asia Pacific, dc=hugeco, dc=com
objectclass: top
objectclass: locality
l: Asia Pacific
description: includes all sites in Japan and Australia
```

There are three subtrees under each of the four locality entries: ou=People, ou=Groups, and ou=Resources. The namespace is flat under each of these containers.

The ou=Global subtree rooted at the same level as the regional entries is used to store groups that are global to the entire company, along with the master list of HugeCo roles.

Limiting the number of major directory partitions to only five makes replication easier to manage. In the new namespace design, delegation of authority over directory entries is accomplished by basing access control on attribute values stored in specific entries rather than on the structure of the tree. For example, a departmental directory administrator group can be granted authority over its own employees' directory information by creating an access control rule that refers to the departmentNumber attribute within each employee's entry.

Every HugeCo employee and contractor is assigned a unique, nonrecycled identification (ID) number by the HR department. The directory team decided to use these ID numbers to form the RDN of all people entries. A typical employee entry is shown in Listing 25.4

LISTING 25.4. A SAMPLE hcPersonEntry ENTRY

```
dn: employeeNumber=12397, ou=People, l=North America, dc=hugeco, dc=com
objectclass: top
objectclass: person
objectclass: organizationalPerson
objectclass: inetOrgPerson
objectclass: hugeCoPerson
cn: Babs Jensen
cn: B Jensen
sn: Jensen
employeeNumber: 12397
uid: babs
telephoneNumber: +1 555 1234
roomNumber: 42
manager: employeeNumber=9837, ou=People, l=North America,
  dc=hugeco, dc=com
hcBuildingNumber: 747
hcBuildingFloor: 3
hcRole: lineManager
...
```

As we already saw, the four location entries are named using the l (locality) attribute. The cn attribute is used to form the RDN of all other entries.

Topology

The HugeCo IS organization's general strategy for managing important, widely used services such as electronic mail is to deploy a small number of relatively large server machines within each site. The company followed this same philosophy when designing its directory topology. For directory-enabled applications that have high search and read performance requirements, the design allows a directory replica to be located on the same machine or on the same network segment as the application. Because HugeCo was already leaning toward choosing directory server software that can support more than a million entries in one server partition, there was no need to partition the data across servers for scaling reasons. Partitioning along regional lines to accommodate HugeCo's replication strategy is discussed in the next section.

Special thought was given to the configuration of the read-write master directory servers on which updates are applied. Because the master servers are single points of failure, the HugeCo designers wanted to use high availability (HA) hardware to reduce the risk of total failure. Each master server (there is one in each region) is paired with a hot standby master. The hot standby machines contain identical server software and are configured the same as the master server they are paired with. Each master server and its hot standby share a dual-ported RAID level 5 disk array, but they do not share any other components or network connections. The logical arrangement is shown in Figure 25.5.

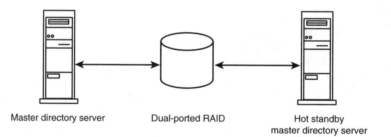

Master directory server   Dual-ported RAID   Hot standby
                                                            master directory server

FIGURE 25.5 *A master directory server with hot standby.*

If the master server fails for any reason, the directory server application on the hot standby machine can be quickly started to take the master's place, thereby minimizing downtime for end users and applications.

Replication

The main goal of replication in the HugeCo design is to allow increased directory search and read capacity to be provided in an incremental way. This is accomplished by copying all of HugeCo's directory data to as many replicas as needed to provide adequate capacity. HugeCo uses a single-master configuration, in which each directory entry can be updated on only one server. Typically, a read-only replica is located near each important directory-enabled application such as a large mail server, a busy phonebook service, or a Web-enabled workflow application.

20-20 Hindsight: The Need for Better HA Support

HugeCo's solution for HA is not ideal. Switching from the master server to the hot standby master is a manual process that must be done by a systems administrator. HA software and hardware solutions available from leading vendors such as Sun Microsystems automate the switch to a hot standby server. Unfortunately, most directory server vendors do not yet support these HA solutions.

In addition, the hot standby machine is a relatively expensive piece of hardware that sits idle nearly all the time. It would be more cost-effective if the hot standby server could handle some of the directory service load even while the master server functions normally. As soon as multimaster replication features are available in the directory service software itself, HugeCo plans to turn the hot standby servers into read-write replicas that are operational all the time.

Directory data is mastered in five servers. The master servers and the data they hold are shown in Figure 25.6.

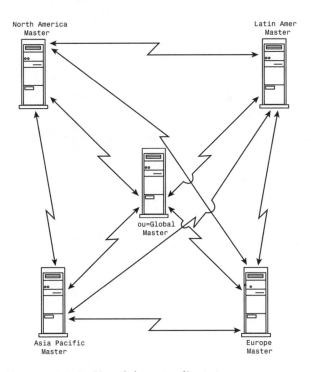

FIGURE 25.6 *HugeCo's master directory servers.*

One master directory server is located in each region, and one additional master server located in North America manages the directory entries that are not region-specific (the `ou=Global, dc=hugeco, dc=com` subtree). HugeCo chose a two-tiered replication scheme in which each master server supplies exactly one replica, which is in turn responsible for supplying all the other replicas (see Figure 25.7).

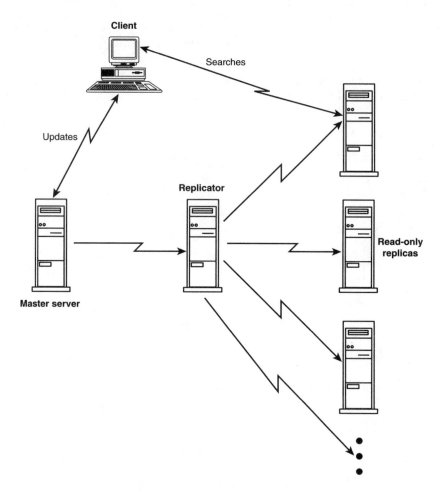

FIGURE 25.7   *A two-tiered replication scheme.*

The two-tiered scheme was selected to reduce the load on the master servers in an effort to maximize update performance. Aside from handling the update traffic for the entries it masters, each master server needs to supply only a single replication server.

The HugeCo team plans to switch to a multimaster replication topology as soon as the feature is available from the directory server vendor. This will allow the team to increase the availability of the directory service for updates and eliminate the hot standby servers paired with each master server.

Because the Netscape Directory Server product's unit of replication must be defined as an entire subtree, the top-most entry in the HugeCo directory namespace (the dc=hugeco, dc=com entry) can not be automatically replicated. Instead, each server has its own copy of that entry, and access control rules are used to ensure that no changes are made to it.

20-20 Hindsight: Awash in Replication Agreements

As HugeCo moved beyond the directory pilot and rolled out its production service worldwide, it found that setting up the large number of server-to-server replication agreements was a large chore. Now that the servers are set up, maintenance of the replicated servers is fairly easy, but there are still a lot of replication connections to monitor. For example, each of the five replication servers paired with a master server must supply its four peers, resulting in a total of 20 replication agreements. To reduce the number of replication agreements needed, a new design that includes one or more replication hubs is being considered. As shown in Figure 25.8, a simple star topology can be used to replicate data across five servers—requiring only 10 agreements.

Privacy and Security

HugeCo generally trusts its own employees, but it is wary of outside security threats. Because no directory data is currently published outside HugeCo's corporate firewall, the threat from outsiders is minimized. However, some small sites are connected via VPNs, which originate at a local ISP, tunnel TCP/IP traffic across the Internet through an encrypted pipe, and enter HugeCo's corporate network through its Internet firewall (see Figure 25.9).

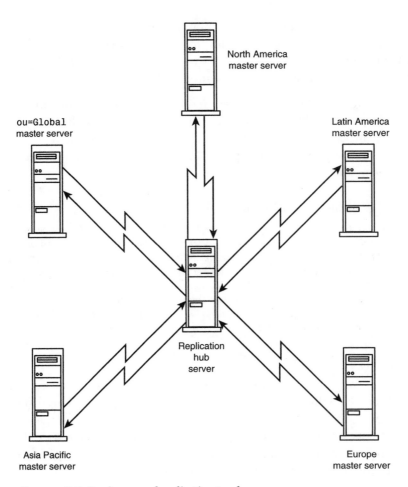

FIGURE 25.8   *A proposed replication topology.*

Although the VPN encryption technology is thought to be nearly uncrackable, to be on the safe side directory access control was set up to disallow any changes to directory data from connections that come in through a VPN. A manual process (usually handled through email) is used by employees at VPN-connected sites to request updates of information in the directory service. Change requests are monitored and handled by directory services data administrators located in the IS department.

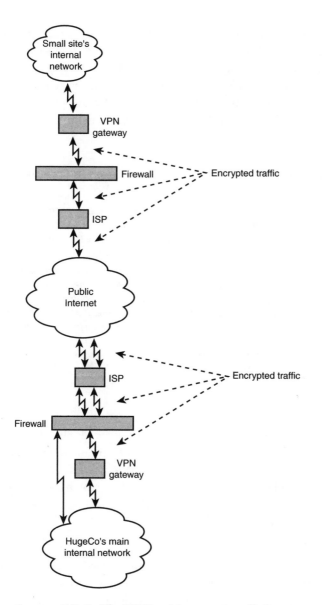

FIGURE 25.9 *The VPN used to connect small sites.*

To protect data against naive or misguided employees who might try to download large lists of employees from the directory service, two precautions were taken. First, all server-to-server replication transfers are done over 128-bit encrypted secure sockets layer (SSL) channels. Second, conservative size and time limits were specified for all directory servers to make it very difficult to collect large numbers of entries (a process called *trawling*).

There is also a lot of concern at HugeCo about keeping employee data private, and the CIO believes strongly in the right to personal privacy. To meet employees' privacy needs, the directory design team developed a conservative access control scheme that allows only an employee's manager to see the employee's home address and phone number. In addition, access control for groups was designed so that only the owners (maintainers) of a group can see the complete list of members.

20-20 Hindsight: Giving Individuals Greater Control over Access to Their Personal Information

After the HugeCo team rolled out its production directory service, it discovered that employees wanted finer control over the access granted to their personal information. The most common request was for home addresses and phone numbers to be accessible to more than just a person's manager.

To meet legal requirements, and because not all employees want to share their home information, a small redesign is under way to allow each employee to choose whether his or her home information is readable by everyone. This option will be provided by defining access control rules that allow anonymous access to the homePhone *and* homePostalAddress *attributes if a Boolean attribute within a person's* hcHomeInfoIsPublic *entry is set to* TRUE. *The phonebook front end is being altered to provide a "Home Information Is Public"*
check box that employees can toggle to change the value of the hcHomeInfoIsPublic *attribute, granting or denying anonymous access if they so desire.*

Deployment

While the directory design was being completed and reviewed, HugeCo formed a directory deployment team. The deployment team included all the people who participated in the design process, plus system administrators responsible for the actual rollout and for running the service on a day-to-day basis. An IS employee who had expertise in network monitoring and escalation procedures was also added to the team.

Product Choice

Before making a final choice of LDAP server software, HugeCo performed an extensive in-house evaluation. After talking to a large number of directory server vendors, HugeCo narrowed its choice to three products: Netscape Directory Server, ISOCOR's Global Directory Server, and OpenDirectory's Dxserver. Evaluation copies of each of the three products were obtained, and each was subjected to a thorough evaluation that involved installing the products, configuring them with HugeCo's custom schema, setting up replication, and conducting performance and scalability testing using custom tools.

In the end, the team selected the Netscape Directory Server product for the following reasons:

- Best performance and scalability, as observed during performance tests

- Support for SSL security, as required by HugeCo's replication and security design

- Flexible, powerful access controls

- Good support for international data

- Comprehensive management tools that provide a Java GUI and a command-line interface

- Customizable HTML-to-LDAP gateway for building phonebook interfaces and directory management applications

HugeCo also evaluated several LDAP software development kits (SDKs), including Netscape's C and Java SDKs, a few LDAP Perl modules they found on the Internet, Microsoft's ADSI, and JavaSoft's JNDI. The team found that all these SDKs were functional but decided to focus on Netscape's SDKs and the PerLDAP Perl module for most of its own development projects. Availability of source code for the SDKs was considered a nice bonus, but the main reason the team recommended the Netscape SDKs was because it felt confident that they would work well with the Netscape server products already selected.

Piloting

A fairly extensive directory service pilot was conducted to prove the directory design, become familiar with the directory software, and determine the level of effort required to roll out and maintain the production service. HugeCo's North America and Asia Pacific regions participated in the pilot, which was conducted over four months. During the pilot, the directory service was deployed in a limited number of physical sites within each region. Figure 25.10 shows the pilot topology.

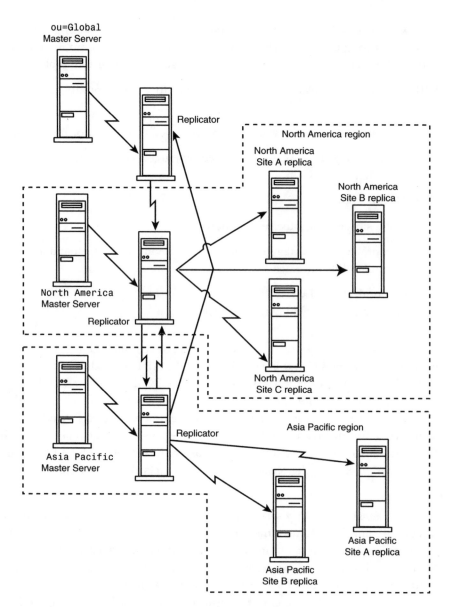

ou=Global
Master Server

Replicator

North America region

North America
Site A replica

North America
Site B replica

North America
Master Server

Replicator

North America
Site C replica

Asia Pacific region

Asia Pacific
Master Server

Replicator

Asia Pacific
Site A replica

Asia Pacific
Site B replica

FIGURE 25.10   *HugeCo's directory pilot topology.*

The directory-enabled applications used in the pilot included the following:

- Netscape Messaging Server to provide electronic mail routing and delivery for end users.

- A simple workflow application to allow employees to request vacations and other time off. This was hosted by a Netscape Enterprise (Web) Server and included an interface for employees (used to request time off) and an interface for managers (used to approve time off requests). The application uses the `hcEmployeeRole` and `manager` attributes within employee entries to route time off requests appropriately and verify that a specific manager is allowed to approve or deny an employee's request.

- An employee phonebook to support anonymous directory lookups and employee self-service activities such as setting passwords or changing home telephone numbers. This was built using a customized version of Netscape's HTML-to-LDAP directory gateway.

Apart from testing the directory-enabled applications, an important goal of the pilot project was to obtain feedback on the directory service from end users and system administrators. To collect feedback from end users, the directory phonebook was modified halfway through the pilot to occasionally display a simple survey form before providing access to the phonebook itself. Face-to-face and telephone interviews were conducted to collect feedback from system administrators of directory-enabled applications and the directory service.

The pilot showed that most of HugeCo's directory design choices were sound. One major redesign was done halfway through the pilot after the team experienced the pain of managing a replication topology that included a large number of partitions. (As discussed earlier in this case study, the directory namespace was redesigned to use a simpler structure based on regions instead of DNS subdomains.)

After the pilot project was complete, most of the hardware used was incorporated into the production directory service. A few servers were reserved to form a testbed for future experiments with new applications, new directory server software, and directory design changes. Figure 25.11 shows the testbed topology.

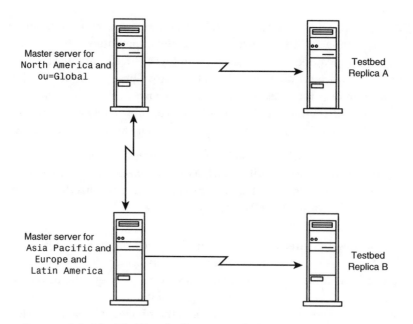

FIGURE 25.11 *The HugeCo directory testbed.*

Normally, none of the servers in the testbed are connected to the production directory service, although sometimes they are temporarily incorporated into the production topology to prepare for software upgrades or obtain data for testing purposes.

Analyzing and Reducing Costs

HugeCo tried to minimize the ongoing cost for its directory service by saving money in the following ways:

- All routine directory administrative tasks were automated, including nightly backups, service monitoring, creation of entries for new employees, and deletion of entries for terminated employees.

- Pilot hardware was reused to deploy the production service and form a directory service testbed.

- A relatively small number of larger, more expensive server machines was used instead of many smaller ones. This followed the principle that personnel costs are more significant than hardware costs, and it fit well with HugeCo IS's general approach toward service deployment.

HugeCo has not conducted a thorough analysis of directory costs and has no immediate plans to do so.

Going Production

Because HugeCo's directory deployment involved a large number of sites, servers, and applications, the production rollout was a complex undertaking. The key to success was to roll out the service in four phases:

1. Roll out directory servers and the phonebook application in one region (North America).

2. Roll out directory servers and the phonebook application in the remaining three regions using the same server configuration and enlisting the assistance of IS staff members who deployed the North American service.

3. Deploy directory-enabled email services in each region. This was handled by the regional IS staff, with help from some directory experts in the central IS organization.

4. Deploy other directory-enabled applications, including Web-based workflow applications.

In conjunction with the production rollout, training sessions were conducted within each region for IS system administrators and help desk staff. The IS communication group spread the word about the directory service by publishing a series of how-to articles in the employee newsletter and through a "Do you know where your directory entry is?" poster campaign. Posters were placed in every HugeCo building to encourage employees to try the phonebook application and update their own directory entry. The poster campaign raised awareness of the new service and improved the accuracy and completeness of employee information in the directory.

Maintenance

Ongoing maintenance of HugeCo's large directory service requires a lot of attention from IS system administrators. This is especially true at the present time because the service is still evolving as new directory-enabled applications are being integrated. All basic maintenance is handled using automated procedures that are similar to those used for other systems the IS organization manages. The sections that follow provide specific information on each aspect of directory maintenance within HugeCo's deployment.

Data Backups and Disaster Recovery

As discussed earlier in this chapter, each master server is paired with a hot standby master server to protect against machine failures. Written procedures were created that system administrators can follow to bring a standby master online. Once a month the standby servers are tested to ensure that they are functional.

The master servers are backed up to disk nightly and archived to tape using 4mm DAT drives. Twice a week each region sends a set of backup tapes to another region for offsite storage. The backup procedures are largely automated and similar to those used for all the services HugeCo's IS organization supports.

HugeCo outsources all its disaster recovery planning and services to IBM Business Recovery Systems, which maintains cold sites in each of HugeCo's four regions.

Maintaining Data

The IS organization spends a lot of time and money on data maintenance across all of HugeCo's systems. Corporate data is held in a variety of databases, and keeping the data up-to-date is largely a manual process. One of the goals of the directory service team was to increase the overall data maintenance burden as little as possible. This was accomplished though a combination of automated processes and the distribution of data maintenance responsibilities.

To integrate with its PeopleSoft HR database, HugeCo contracted with Netscape Professional Services to create a custom directory synchronization tool. The synchronization tool runs once per hour to transfer changes made in the HR database to the directory service. Basic information about employees is synchronized, including name, contact information, ID number, and location. The synchronization tool takes care of creating new hugeCoPerson entries in the directory service when employees join HugeCo, and it disables user accounts by altering passwords after an employee leaves the company. The synchronization tool, written in Perl, operates on text extracts generated from the PeopleSoft database, and it uses the PerLDAP module to access the LDAP directory.

To distribute directory data maintenance responsibilities, the HugeCo team defined the following categories of directory data managers:

- Directory administrators, who are granted full access rights to all the data in the directory service.

- Departmental administrators, who are granted nearly full access rights to the people and group entries for their department. Departmental administrators are not, however, allowed to change any attributes managed by the HR database synchronization process.

- Help desk staff, who are permitted to set passwords for all people entries.

- End users, who are allowed to change home contact information, URLs, descriptions, and a few other fields within their own entries.

For access control purposes, groups are maintained in the directory for each category of data administrators. The one exception is the end user category: End users are identified by the absence of group membership. Access control rules were placed in the directory to give people in each category an appropriate level of access. By allowing departmental administrators and end users to manage some of their own information, the data management burden carried by the IS employees (the directory administrators and help desk staff) is minimized.

20-20 Hindsight: Improving Data Quality

As an increasing number of HugeCo employees found out about the new directory service and began to examine their own data, the IS help desk started to receive quite a few reports of erroneous information. To get a better handle on the problem and determine the cause, the central IS organization is developing an email survey tool that will extract information from both the PeopleSoft HR database and the directory service. Surveys will be sent to a random sample of 5,000 employees in an effort to determine how widespread the data quality problems are. The results will be checked against directory audit logs to determine the source of the incorrect information, and the data gathered by the survey will be used to decide where to focus future data quality improvement efforts.

Monitoring

The overall HugeCo strategy for network monitoring revolves around HP OpenView, a commercial network monitoring system (NMS). Each regional IS department runs an HP OpenView system that monitors the network and the applications located in that region. In addition, the central IS organization runs an HP OpenView system that monitors the global network and centrally managed applications such as the PeopleSoft system.

A combination of techniques was used to integrate the Netscape Directory Server software and important directory-enabled applications into the NMSs. First, the built-in SNMP support provided by the server software was used to provide basic service and performance monitoring. Then a set of Perl scripts was developed using the PerLDAP module to probe all the critical directory servers from several locations on HugeCo's network. Finally, indirect monitoring of the directory service was started through extensive observing of critical directory-enabled applications, including the email servers, the PeopleSoft synchronization process, the phonebook servers, and the Web servers that support critical applications. As much as possible, probes mimic the operations that end users and applications frequently perform.

20-20 Hindsight: The Value of Indirect Probes

About a month after the HugeCo directory service was first rolled out worldwide, the IS email team received a complaint from one of the executive vice presidents in the Latin America region: Electronic mail was being delayed for up to 30 minutes before reaching all the intended recipients. This was puzzling because most messages were routinely delivered by the Netscape Mail Transfer Agent (MTA) network within five minutes.

After an afternoon of investigation, the email administrators discovered that all the delayed messages had been sent to a dynamic group (one in which membership is determined by a search of the directory). They quickly brought some directory experts over to look at the problem. In the end, the root cause of the problem was traced to a missing index in the configuration of the directory servers used by the MTAs. Although easily corrected, the problem had gone unnoticed for almost a month (much to the chagrin of the IS staff).

This incident prompted the IS employees to design and implement a series of indirect directory probes that closely emulate the behavior of important applications such as the messaging servers. By proactively monitoring the performance of the system as experienced by end users, the HugeCo IS staff hopes to detect problems earlier in the future.

When a problem is detected by HugeCo's OpenView monitoring system, the following automated notification methods are used to bring the problem to the attention of the appropriate system administrator:

- Text pager messages are sent when an urgent system outage is detected.

- Electronic mail messages are used to send weekly directory activity summaries and notify administrators immediately about problems such as reduced performance of a directory application.

- IS staff and end users can access a continuously updated Web page that lists information about all known outages.

Overall, the directory service and associated applications have proved to be very reliable. So far there has been no need to automate such actions as restarting failed directory server processes or machines.

Troubleshooting

HugeCo's IS organization maintains a well-documented set of escalation procedures stating that senior members of the IS staff will be called in over time to address critical problems. Directory-specific procedures were developed during the directory pilot deployment and refined over time to ensure that problems are addressed quickly by the right people.

Leveraging the Directory Service

Now that the LDAP directory service has been successfully deployed worldwide, HugeCo is finding a number of new and interesting ways to leverage the directory. In this section we describe applications that are in the process of being developed and integrated with HugeCo's directory, and we take a look at how things have changed at HugeCo since the directory was deployed.

Applications

The central IS organization, the regional IS departments, and several independent departments within HugeCo are all leveraging the directory service to enhance existing applications and develop new ones. Efforts underway include the following:

- Savvy end users quickly discovered that many of their favorite email clients have LDAP search features built in. The IS departments picked up on the movement, and a series of articles was published in the employee newsletter that explained how to configure the Eudora, Outlook Express, and Netscape Messenger email clients to access the corporate LDAP directory service. Before the introduction of LDAP, it was impossible for clients from different vendors to share one directory.

- Pleased with the success of the employee time off request application, the HR department is working with IS programmers to create a variety of Web-based, directory-enabled workflow applications to automate common employee processes required when an employee joins or leaves the company, enrolls in employee health benefit plans, and more. These applications are being developed using HTML, JavaScript, and Java.

- The North American engineering group has embarked on an ambitious project to tie its existing database of engineering drawings into the directory. The integrated system will make it easier to locate the persons responsible for an existing design and will eventually be used to build a workflow system to automate the design approval process.

- The central IS department is developing an enhanced employee phonebook application that will provide access to information about people, conference rooms, office equipment (such as computers and fax machines), and building locations. The new phonebook is an extension of an existing one based on Netscape's HTML- and JavaScript-based Directory Server Gateway. Custom CGIs are being written in Perl to integrate location information with building maps and create organizational charts from the employee data. A variant of the same application will be used by IS, HR, and departmental administrators to manage directory information.

- A pilot project underway within the IS and HR departments will require public key certificates for authentication to email servers and the time off request workflow application. The directory service is being used to manage personal certificates, perform revocation checking, and streamline the process of issuing and renewing certificates.

Without exception, it is now easier and much more practical to create these applications than it was before the HugeCo directory service existed.

Directory Deployment Impact

After the directory was deployed and people started to use it, the HugeCo directory team observed that the service rapidly became indispensable to people. Some of their observations are captured in this section.

Richer services are now available to end users. It is much easier to find timely information about other employees, which has increased communication among employees. Paper lists of phone numbers are a thing of the past for the many employees who have come to rely on the directory-enabled phone book application. Employees can more easily update information about themselves, and new automated services such as time off and benefit request systems are coming online.

A richer set of functionality is available to application developers. Application writers can easily access and update information about a variety of important HugeCo resources without incurring the burden of managing their own directory or database. Simple authentication and attribute-based role information can be used to make applications more secure.

The HR and IS organizations have used the directory service to get closer to their customers and place more control (and more of the work) in employees' hands. Timeliness and manageability of important information has improved dramatically.

Finally, the HugeCo directory design and deployment team has greatly increased its knowledge of directory service design and is now well-positioned to tackle additional directory projects. First up: design and deployment of an extranet directory that will store information about HugeCo's dealer network. This new directory service will allow the deployment of a new class of secure, Web-based information delivery applications. The extranet directory design team will draw on lessons learned during the internal HugeCo directory deployment.

Summary and Lessons Learned

Now let's step back and take a critical look at the HugeCo directory design and deployment process. A large investment was made by HugeCo to ensure that its directory service would be a success—and it is. As always, we can learn from the company's experience, successes, and failures.

Although HugeCo's directory design team clearly did its homework, there were still a number of times it found problems with the design. In some cases a redesign was required before the deployment of the production service. Some problems are yet to be resolved, and more redesign and redeployment activities are on the horizon. Interesting design problems HugeCo's team encountered include the following:

- The original namespace design proved too cumbersome and had to be redesigned during the directory pilot.

- Support for HA hardware and software was lacking in the available directory server products.

- Setting up and managing a large number of replication agreements was burdensome, and alternative designs are being examined to reduce the number of agreements required.

- Individual employees made their voices heard in asking for more control over who can access their personal information.

- Several data quality problems must be investigated and remedied.

- The initial plan for monitoring the directory service did not include any indirect probing. This was added only after an embarrassing directory configuration error was unearthed following a vice president's complaint.

As more applications are integrated with the directory service, new challenges will no doubt surface.

Overall, HugeCo's directory design and deployment process was well-conceived and well-executed. By conducting a serious pilot, the team members discovered some critical problems before they deployed the entire service. They were not afraid to revisit design decisions to improve the service. And although deploying a directory service for their large organization was a big task, the service is now being leveraged in some interesting and unexpected ways.

Further Reading

IBM Business Recovery Systems. Information is available on the Web at `http://www.ibm.com`.

Netscape Professional Services. Information is available on the Web at `http://home.netscape.com/proservices/`.

PerLDAP, an Object-Oriented LDAP Perl Module for Perl5. Available on Netscape's Directory Developer Central Web site at `http://developer.netscape.com/tech/directory/`.

Looking Ahead

In Chapter 26, we will continue our parade of LDAP directory deployment case studies with an example of an extranet directory service.

CHAPTER 26

Case Study:

An Enterprise with an Extranet

In this chapter we examine how a hypothetical company might extend its intranet-based services to its external trading partners. Such an arrangement, called an extranet, is an effective way to leverage existing systems and expertise.

In such a deployment, a directory service is usually already designed and deployed. However, to expand its service, the directory must be extended beyond the organization's internal network (and outside any firewalls). This creates additional requirements, especially in the area of security and access control, that might necessitate a reassessment of the basic directory design.

In this chapter we build on the fictional company HugeCo that was introduced in Chapter 25, "Case Study: A Large Multinational Enterprise." We discuss changes and improvements to HugeCo's existing directory service that extend the intranet application suite to the extranet.

An Overview of the Organization

HugeCo is a supplier of a wide range of custom-built home renovation products, from cabinetry and replacement windows to completely prefabricated homes. Its Home Renovation Products (HRP) division produces cabinets, counters, windows, and other products built to customer specifications and shipped to local home improvement retailers and contractors in the United States and Canada.

Instead of maintaining a direct sales force, HugeCo partners with home improvement retailers and contractors who become certified retailers of HugeCo products. Certified retailers place orders for custom-built items, which are manufactured at HugeCo's main factory and shipped to the retailer or directly to the customer site. Retailers can become certified on any of a number of different product lines—and may sell only those products for which they are authorized.

HugeCo currently has about 800 authorized retailers in the United States and Canada. To support each of these retailers, updated product literature and price lists are shipped to each retailer monthly. Because the ordering process is quite complex and varies from product to product, the literature includes worksheets that describe the options available for each product and any measurements, which must be supplied before the manufacturing process can begin.

HugeCo, an early adopter of database technology, uses a large Oracle installation to track the progress of orders through the system, from initial order to final shipment. Although the order tracking system had provided large gains in productivity at lower cost compared to the older system, its user interface was somewhat lacking. With the advent of World Wide Web technology, HugeCo's IS staff developed a Web-based interface for the system, making it easier to use, and therefore, lowering training costs.

Spurred on by the initial success of the order management system, HugeCo staff established an email link between the manufacturing staff and the sales staff. The craftsperson responsible for building a custom set of cabinets, for example, can send electronic mail to the sales representative who originally took the order to request clarification on some aspect of the work order.

Recently, HugeCo management started a new project—a corporate extranet that aimed to extend the benefits of HugeCo's intranet to its authorized retailers. The primary motivators behind this extranet deployment were to improve service to retailers and customers and to lower costs. This case study describes the planning and execution of the directory component of this project.

The way that authorized retailers used to place orders and learn about status was inefficient and error-prone: All interactions were performed via telephone. The original order was called into a data entry operator, who keyed the information into the order entry application. This transcription step was a source of errors. And if a retailer needed to check on the status of an existing order, a call had to be placed to the central office during business hours. This order management system architecture is shown in Figure 26.1.

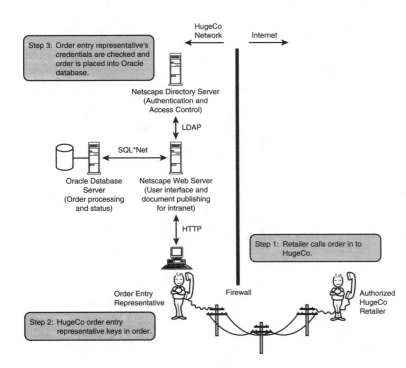

FIGURE 26.1 *The old order entry system architecture.*

As shown in Figure 26.1, the Web server provides an easy-to-use front end to the order entry and tracking database, which is hosted by an Oracle database server. The directory stores the Oracle login passwords so that they can be made available to the Web server CGI programs that comprise the order entry system.

A much more attractive alternative would be to allow employees at authorized retailers to place their own orders directly into the Web-based order system, bypassing the data entry operators and improving accuracy. Such a system would also allow retailers to directly check order status 24 hours per day, seven days per week, resulting in better customer service. Such a system is depicted in Figure 26.2.

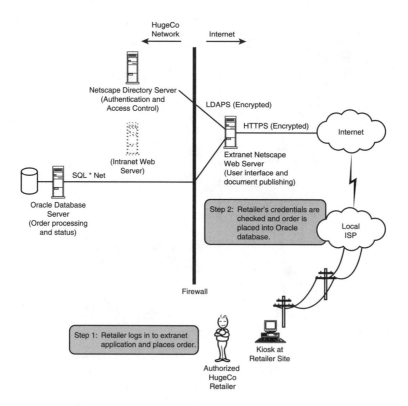

FIGURE 26.2 *The new order entry system architecture.*

Note that there is a much closer coupling between the retailer and the craftsperson in this system. Such a system should significantly improve responsiveness to retailer needs and higher customer satisfaction.

New product information and ordering procedures were distributed along with regular product literature updates shipped to retailers every eight weeks. Because new product notices were distributed so infrequently, a long time could pass between the time a new product was available and the time that orders for it could be placed. An alternative approach was to publish notices about new products and procedures to the extranet. When a new product is available or a new procedure is released, each retail employee can be informed about this via items on a personalized start page. Information about products that the retailer is authorized to sell can be highlighted, whereas information about products not authorized can be hidden. New product literature and price sheets can be published to the extranet Web server, making the new product immediately available for ordering.

Directory Drivers

In planning for these extranet applications, having several drivers led the designers to conclude that a directory service was essential to the deployment. The following requirements led them to this conclusion:

- *Extranet applications must be manageable though delegation*—Because there are over 800 retailers, each of which has several employees authorized to sell HugeCo products, it is expected that there will be at least several thousand user entries in the database at any time. To further complicate the management of this user information, each retailer is an independent business with its own employees. Clearly, to make it possible to manage user information, the creation, deletion, and maintenance of user account information must be delegated to the individual retailers.

- *User information must be shared among multiple applications*—There are several different extranet applications (order entry, personalized product notice generation, and so on) that would comprise the extranet suite, each of which needs to authenticate users and store customization information. Because a directory provides a standard method for storing and accessing this information over the network, it would make sense to place shared user information in a directory.

Directory Service Design

To support its new extranet applications, the HugeCo corporate directory design had to be revisited and altered. To start the redesign process, HugeCo's IS staff began by analyzing the needs of the new extranet applications.

Needs

A number of needs drove the direction of the directory design for the HugeCo HRP extranet:

- The applications demand a flexible access control model that supports delegation of user account maintenance. Conceptually, two roles would be defined for the applications: manager and employee. One manager would be defined per authorized retailer, and that person would be responsible for creating, maintaining, and deleting entries in the directory for all the employees allowed to use the HugeCo extranet applications. The directory must support this capability.

- It was anticipated that the extranet applications would have roughly the same performance requirements as the equivalent intranet applications. For example, the extranet Web servers that support the order tracking system should place the same load on the directory as the existing intranet servers. The other applications place a much lighter load on the directory.

- The directory must be highly available and deliver a high level of service. This means that the directory needs to be replicated for fault tolerance.

- The directory must support configuration of customized schema to support the specialized schema requirements of these extranet applications.

All these needs taken together are not too different from the needs of HugeCo's intranet. The main difference is the need for delegation capabilities.

Data

Because the extranet would be a set of new applications that leveraged an existing directory installation, HugeCo needed to review its existing data policy statement to see if it was valid for the new extranet applications. Recall the policy statement presented in Chapter 25:

- Data that is shared by more than one application should be stored in the directory service.

- The authoritative source for each data element stored in the directory must be defined.

- Data that is extremely sensitive or private should not be stored in the directory service unless there is an operational reason to do so. This kind of data includes payroll and employee benefit information.

- All legal requirements, including country and regional privacy laws in effect where HugeCo operates, must be followed.

After review, it was apparent that this data policy statement was suitable for the new extranet, and HugeCo staff began to define the new data elements needed to support these applications, determine if the data was already available in the directory or other HugeCo databases, and identify the authoritative data sources for each item.

Building on the concept of roles, two new roles were defined: hcHrpRetailEmployee and hcHrpRetailManager. The hcHrpRetailEmployee role represents an employee at a retailer authorized to sell HugeCo's home renovation products, and the hcHrpRetailManager represents a manager at an authorized retailer.

Newly identified data elements necessary to support the extranet applications are discussed in the following section.

Schema

As with the existing schema described in Chapter 25, HugeCo chose to subclass standard object classes to represent the new objects that would be stored in the directory. Two new object classes were defined—hcHrpRetailer, which represents an authorized retail outlet; and hpHrpRetailEmployee, which describes an employee of a HugeCo home products retail outlet. The definition of the hcHrpRetailer object class is shown in Listing 26.1.

LISTING 26.1. THE hcHrpRetailer OBJECT CLASS

```
objectclass hcHrpRetailer
    superior top
    oid 1.2.3.4.5.6.8
    required
        hcHrpRetailerID
    allowed
        hcHrpProductAuthorized
```

The hcHrpRetailerID attribute, used to name the entry, contains the unique authorized retailer ID assigned to that retailer. The hcHrpProductAuthorized attribute contains a value for each HugeCo home renovation product line the retailer is authorized to sell.

A sample hcHrpRetailer entry might look like the one shown in Listing 26.2.

LISTING 26.2. A SAMPLE hcHrpRetailer ENTRY

```
dn: hcHrpRetailerID=882-501, ou=hcHrpRetailers, ou=Extranet,
 dc=HugeCo, dc=com
objectclass: top
objectclass: organization
objectclass: hcHrpRetailer
hcHrpRetailerID: 882-501
o: Jensen Home Improvement Products, Inc.
postalAddress: 123 Anystreet $ Tucson, AZ $ USA 94432
st: AZ
postalCode: 94432
telephoneNumber: +1 520 555 0499
facsimileTelephoneNumber: +1 520 555 3882
hcHrpProductAuthorized: A733
hcHrpProductAuthorized: J812
hcHrpProductAuthorized: J813
hcHrpProductAuthorized: J814
```

The entry shown in Listing 26.2 describes an authorized retailer of HugeCo products. The retailer, located in Tucson, Arizona, is authorized to sell four different HugeCo product lines.

The definition of the hcHrpRetailEmployee objectclass is shown in Listing 26.3.

LISTING 26.3 THE hcHrpRetailEmployee OBJECT CLASS

```
objectclass hcHrpRetailEmployee
    superior inetOrgPerson
    oid 1.2.3.4.5.6.9
    allowed
        hcHrpRetailerID
        hcHrpLastLogin
        hcHrpEmployeeExpireDate
        hcEmployeeRole
```

The hcHrpRetailerID attribute contains the retailer ID of the authorized HugeCo dealer that employs this person. The hcHrpLastLogin attribute contains the date and time that the employee last logged in to the system. The initial page shown to each employee contains a list of new product notices, promotions, and alerts, and the hcHrpLastLogin attribute allows the Web server that generates the start page to show only those notices posted since the last time the employee logged in. The hcHrpEmployeeExpireDate attribute contains the expiration date for this entry (which is removed on or after that date). The hcEmployeeRole attribute contains the value hcHrpRetailEmployee if the entry describes an employee at a retailer, or the value hcHrpRetailManager if the entry describes a manager at a retailer.

A sample hcHrpRetailEmployee entry might look like the one shown in Listing 26.4.

LISTING 26.4 A SAMPLE hcHrpRetailEmployee ENTRY

```
dn: uid=hreming, hcHrpRetailerID=882-501, ou=hcHrpRetailers,
 ou=Extranet, dc=HugeCo, dc=com
objectclass: top
objectclass: person
objectclass: organizationalPerson
objectclass: inetOrgPerson
objectclass: hcOracleUser
objectclass: hcHrpRetailEmployee
cn: Harold Remington
sn: Remington
uid: hreming
...
(other inetOrgPerson attributes)
...
hcHrpRetailerID: 882-501
hcHrpLastLogin: 199808300061302Z
hcHrpEmployeeExpireDate: 19990127
```

```
hcEmployeeRole: hcHrpRetailManager
hcOracleLogin: hreming
hcOraclePassword: FooD%golf!!
```

As you can see, the entry contains the attributes you would expect to see in a typical inetOrgPerson object, such as cn (common name), sn (surname), and uid (user identifier). However, this entry can also contain two additional attributes because it is of the hcHrpRetailEmployee object class. The hcHrpRetailerID attribute shows that this person works for retailer number 882-501, the hcHrpLastLogin attribute shows the time that the employee last accessed the system, and the hcHrpEmployeeExpireDate attribute gives the date on which the employee record will expire if it is not renewed by the manager. More information on the employee expiration policy is given later in this chapter in the "Maintenance" section.

Several other attributes allow a person to access the HugeCo Oracle database servers. The auxiliary objectclass hcOracleUser has two optional attributes, hcOracleLogin and hcOraclePassword, which respectively specify the Oracle login ID and password that should be used by Web server CGIs that need to connect to the Oracle database on behalf of the user.

Namespace

To satisfy the delegation requirements of the extranet application framework, HugeCo decided to place the information about authorized retailers and their employees into a separate subtree. The complete HugeCo directory namespace design is shown in Figure 26.3.

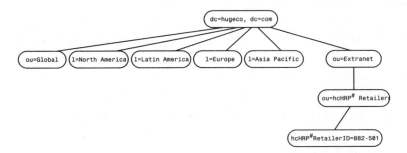

FIGURE 26.3   *HugeCo directory namespace design, including extranet data.*

Placing all the information about authorized retailers into the ou=hcHrpRetailers, ou=Extranet, dc=HugeCo, dc=com subtree allows this information to be selectively replicated across the firewall without requiring that all other corporate data in the directory also be made available outside the firewall.

The initial design for HugeCo's Home Renovation Products extranet directory namespace called for a single container named ou=Retailers, dc=HugeCo, dc=com that would contain all the HRP division retailers. Soon after completing the initial design, the extranet application developers realized that, if successful, their extranet application would encourage the development of other extranet applications within other HugeCo divisions. The original namespace design was clearly inadequate; placing all retailers underneath a single subtree would present problems as soon as the thousands of retailers of other HugeCo products were placed there.

To address this issue, the HRP extranet developers opted to create a container named ou=Extranet that could be subdivided as more extranet applications were developed. Within the ou=Extranet container, additional containers could be created to accommodate each new extranet application.

Underneath the retailers subtree, there is one tree for each retailer. The entries at the top of each tree are of the hcHrpRetailer object class and contain information about the actual retailer (see the "Schema" section earlier in this chapter for more information about the hcHrpRetailer objectclass). Within each retailer subtree, there is an entry for the primary contact person (usually the department manager) and a container named ou=employees. This container holds information about additional employees, if any, who are authorized to place and track orders.

The intent of placing data about each retailer into its own subtree is to allow easy delegation of the administration of that information. For example, the manager at any particular retailer could be delegated the ability to update information about the retailer and create new employee entries, but only within his or her particular retailer subtree. Early in the design process it was unclear whether it was a good idea to allow such delegation, but the designers decided to construct a directory namespace that could support delegation if needed. Delegation can be enabled by placing the appropriate access control directives in the hcHrpRetailer entries.

You may be wondering why HugeCo decided to add the hcHrpRetailerID attribute to entries representing employees. On the surface, it seems unnecessary because all the employees of a given retailer are held underneath the entry describing the retailer (see Figure 26.4). However, if you want to find all the employees of a given retailer, this construction allows you to perform a subtree search rooted at the retailer entry with a filter of (objectclass=hcHrpEmployee).

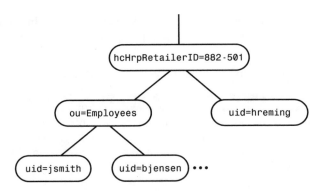

FIGURE 26.4 *A portion of HugeCo's directory representing a single retailer and its employees.*

So why is it desirable to include the retailer ID in each person entry? Sometimes it is necessary to map from an employee's entry back to his or her retailer. Although it would be possible to walk up the directory tree until an hcHrpRetailer entry is located, storing the retailer number in the entry allows the corresponding retailer record to be located with a single search operation. (For an example of an application that performs exactly this operation, see the discussion of how personal start pages are generated in the "Deployment" section of this chapter.)

Topology

As discussed in Chapter 25, HugeCo's directory is partitioned along regional lines, with each major locality mastered in a different server and replicated to all the other servers via a central replication hub (refer to Figure 25.8).

When adding the extranet subtree to the directory tree, HugeCo's directory designers opted to create an additional directory partition holding all the data at or below the ou=Extranet entry. This approach, which is consistent with the existing partitioning scheme, is depicted in Figure 26.5.

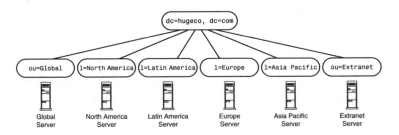

FIGURE 26.5 *HugeCo directory partitions, including extranet data.*

The designers initially used referrals in each of the regional servers to link the extranet data into the directory information tree (DIT). Whenever any of the regional servers receive an LDAP operation that needs data from the `ou=Extranet` subtree, a referral to the extranet server is generated.

20-20 Hindsight: Search Performance Across All Corporate Directory Data

One negative consequence of linking the extranet directory data into the HugeCo main directory tree is that searches across the whole organization (e.g., searches rooted at `dc=HugeCo, dc=com`) require the LDAP client to chase a referral and then combine results from the two servers before presenting them to the client or directory-enabled application. Performance is slower than it would be if all entries were held within a single server.

Also, some server capabilities become less useful in a distributed environment. For example, server-side sorting and paging through result sets works only within a single server. If a client application needs to contact two servers to satisfy a user's search request, and the user has specified that the results should be sorted, the client application needs to merge the entries returned from each server into a single list before presenting it to the user.

After some more thought, HugeCo staff realized that the HRP extranet applications didn't really need to be aware of the intranet directory data, and the intranet applications had no real need to be aware of the extranet data. In light of this, the designers decided to remove the referrals from the regional servers, essentially making the extranet data a separate, unconnected directory—which is acceptable for the time being. In the future, if the extranet and intranet directory data need to be combined, the replication architecture can be altered so that extranet data is replicated to each of the regional servers.

Replication

As stated in Chapter 25, the primary goal of replication in HugeCo's directory deployment is to increase the read and search capacity of the directory in an incremental fashion. HugeCo decided to stick with this approach as it extended its applications to the extranet.

Extranet data can be replicated as needed to increase capacity for the extranet applications. HugeCo planned to initially deploy two read-only replicas, which increased the reliability and scalability of the extranet directory data. Both read-only replicas are known by a single domain name, `hrpdirectory.extranet.hugeco.com`. This domain name is associated with the IP addresses of both replicas, and the addresses are returned in round-robin fashion. If additional replicas need to be added, they can be deployed and their IP addresses added to the domain name system.

Privacy and Security

Security design for HugeCo's internal directory server deployment focused on two major issues: access control on directory data to support delegated administration, and protection against attack.

Security Design: Access Control

Before we discuss the access control policies in effect for the directory, we should clarify that the order entry and tracking application has its own set of access control policies that are separate from the directory access control policy. The directory is used to authenticate users, produce the personalized start page for retail employees, and determine whether a given user may access a given URL within the order entry application. The directory is merely used as a repository for the information that the Web application uses to make its access control decisions.

The access control policy in effect for the directory itself controls who may access the actual directory content. HugeCo has a restrictive access control policy in effect for its directory data. Employees may update only a few fields in their own entries, as described in Chapter 25.

Within the subtree used to hold information about employees of authorized retailers, a different set of access control policies is in force. The goal of these policies is to delegate administration of the individual retailer information to a responsible person at each retailer. This not only reduces costs for HugeCo, but it's absolutely necessary: Employees of the retailers are not HugeCo employees, so HugeCo has no knowledge of when these employees are hired or terminated.

To meet this requirement, the following access control policies were developed:

- Each retailer must designate a single point of administrative contact. This person is responsible for adding and deleting local users and updating certain information about the retailer.

- The administrative contacts may create and delete users as they see fit.

- Users created by an administrative contact may not update their own entries.

- Only HugeCo personnel may add or delete the entry representing the retailer.

- Only HugeCo personnel may add or delete the entry representing the administrative contact.

See Figure 26.6 for an illustration of this delegated access control policy.

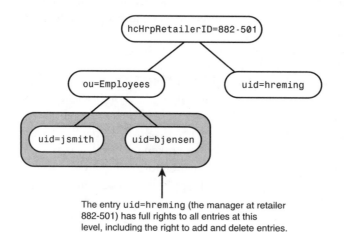

The entry uid=hreming (the manager at retailer
882-501) has full rights to all entries at this
level, including the right to add and delete entries.

FIGURE 26.6 *The delegated access control policy.*

Dangers of Delegation

When delegating privileges, it's also important to consider the capabilities that those privileges grant, especially with respect to directory-enabled applications. For example, what would happen if administrative contacts at retailers were able to create entries with the same user identifier (UID) as an existing entry somewhere else in the directory? If the new entry were within a separate directory tree, its name wouldn't collide with the other entry; however, applications that expect UIDs to be unique across the directory (authentication applications behave this way) may malfunction when they discover multiple matching entries.

To prevent this, applications should check before adding new entries to make sure that no undesirable attribute collisions occur. If, for example, someone attempts to add a new entry with the UID jsmith to a directory, but there is an existing jsmith somewhere else in the directory, the application could reject the addition with a helpful error message. Similarly, the application could check whether modifying or renaming an entry is legal and does not cause a collision.

However, this approach requires that you force all updates to the directory through a single application such as a Web front end. This way you lose the ability to deploy general-purpose clients. And there may be no practical way to prevent someone from using one of these general-purpose clients.

continues

continued

A much more bulletproof solution is to enforce the attribute uniqueness constraints on the server itself. Netscape Directory Server (version 4.0 and later) includes a general attribute-uniqueness plug-in that allows the server to reject any update to the directory that causes an undesired attribute value collision. For example, the plug-in can be configured to reject any modifications to directory data that would cause two entries to have the same UID. Using this plug-in means that no matter how clever or determined a person is, he or she cannot bypass the uniqueness constraints you have configured.

Security Design: Protection Against Attack

Connections from HugeCo's authorized retailers to the Web-based application and to the directory traverse the public Internet. To protect against eavesdropping and man-in-the-middle attacks, it was decided to use secure sockets layer (SSL) session-layer encryption to protect sensitive data during transit. All protocols used to communicate with authorized retailer sites (HTTP, LDAP, IMAP) are performed over SSL-secured connections. SSL-capable web browsers and electronic mail user agents were deployed at each retailer site. Using this approach, even if data were intercepted in transit, the eavesdropper would not be able to make use of the encrypted data without a great deal of effort.

Deployment

After HugeCo completed the design of the extranet applications and directory, it embarked on the deployment phase of the project. HugeCo used a phased approach, similar to the intranet directory deployment: Products were chosen, an extranet pilot project was deployed, and then the production service was rolled out to all retailers.

Product Choice

Because HugeCo had already deployed the Netscape Directory Server for its corporate intranet, it made sense to continue to use it for the extranet applications. Nevertheless, HugeCo analyzed the requirements of the extranet directory to verify that the Netscape product was, in fact, suitable. This was accomplished by detailing the types of operations the extranet applications would perform against the directory. These included the following operations:

- *User authentication*—Whenever a user requests a Web page or CGI from the order entry and tracking system, his or her user ID and password are sent to the Web server, which verifies it and looks up the corresponding entry in the directory. Although the Web servers cache the lookup results for five minutes, the directory server sees quite a bit of this type of lookup traffic—typically one lookup every five minutes per user.

- *User start page generation*—When a user displays his or her personalized start page, it includes a list of relevant product bulletins or announcements that the user has not yet viewed. To generate this list, two directory entries are retrieved. First, the user's entry is retrieved and its hcHrpRetailerID attribute examined. Then the corresponding retailer entry is retrieved from the directory and the hcHrpProductAuthorized attribute is extracted. When these pieces of information have been retrieved, the application has enough information to display the new product notices for only those products the retailer is authorized to sell.

  When a new order is placed, the order entry and tracking system consults the retailer's directory entry to verify that the retailer is authorized to sell the ordered product.

Because the extranet Web server resides outside HugeCo's corporate firewall, all traffic between the Web server and the directory should be encrypted. Because Netscape Directory Server supports LDAPS (LDAP over SSL) connections, this requirement is met.

The types of queries required by these applications are well within the capabilities of the Netscape Directory Server. Hence, HugeCo decided to simply install additional instances of the Netscape Server to support the extranet application.

Piloting

As with the original directory deployment, HugeCo rolled out the extranet applications and directory in an incremental fashion. The process began with a small-scale pilot that provided valuable feedback and validation of the directory design. The pilot involved three different types of retailers—a home improvement superstore, a small-town hardware store, and a home builder—in different parts of the United States. Selecting these three types of retailers provided a set of users with a wide range of computer experience. The large home improvement center, for example, has its own computer consultant (shared with the other stores in the region), whereas the home builder serves as his own computer consultant.

HugeCo staff visited each pilot site. They assisted the retailer at each site with hardware and software installation, created entries and issued passwords for the users, and then stayed for three days as the pilot users began to use the extranet system. During this time, any difficulties the users encountered while using the system were noted and fed back to the system developers at HugeCo. Of particular interest to the developers were the experiences of the local administrators as they created and removed accounts for their staff using the administration utility hosted on the extranet Web server.

Also of interest to the extranet developers was the quantity of directory load placed on the extranet directory servers. During the pilot, the developers kept logs for the extranet directory servers and observed how each individual retailer generated load on the directory. Extrapolating from the pilot usage data allowed the developers to validate their assumption that two directory servers (a writable master and a read-only slave) would be sufficient for the needs of the extranet applications. Of course, if any new applications are deployed in the future, the load on the directory might change significantly, so this assumption must be revisited periodically throughout the lifetime of the extranet.

After a pilot site was installed, the HugeCo staff moved on to the next pilot site but remained available by telephone for assistance. After all the pilot sites were installed and operational, the pilot staff returned to each pilot site in order and interviewed the pilot users. The collected feedback from all the pilot sites and the usage data from the extranet directory servers were reviewed by the developers, and changes were incorporated into the system. Most of these changes involved alterations to the user interface of the order entry system.

Based on the experiences with hardware and software installation, HugeCo staff decided to pre-install all the software on the kiosk hardware and produce a quick-start setup guide. All that a retailer needed to do was unpack the kiosk, connect the cables as pictured in the setup guide, and plug the modem into a phone line.

Going Production

After the pilot was completed and applications were updated to incorporate feedback, HugeCo planned its production rollout of the service. Although HugeCo believed that the kiosk kits would be easy to install and configure, it decided to be conservative in the number of sites to be brought online, just in case the retailers needed a lot of telephone support. To avoid swamping the help desk with calls, only 25 kiosk kits were shipped initially. One week after the kiosks were shipped, a follow-up call was placed to each retailer to make sure that they were installed successfully.

After several weeks of shipping 25 kits per week, HugeCo was confident that it could handle a larger volume. This conclusion was based on the frequency of support calls and the usage patterns on the extranet directory servers, which were increasing as expected but well within the capacity limits of the servers. Volume was increased to 100 kiosks per week, and all kits were shipped within 10 weeks.

To encourage usage of the new kiosks, HugeCo tracked the usage of the extranet applications and the telephone order center. Initial results were disappointing, as the call center volume actually increased for a period of time; but this eventually began to decline as retailers became more comfortable using the system.

Data was collected and analyzed during the entire process to determine if the directory was in danger of becoming overloaded. Based on the experience gained while deploying HugeCo's corporate intranet directory, staff members felt confident about the abilities to perform capacity planning for the new extranet applications. Basic performance metrics, such as average search response time, were developed and measured throughout the directory deployment phase; directory load remained well within expected levels.

Maintenance

In this section we describe the various procedures used to maintain HugeCo's extranet directory.

Data Backup and Disaster Recovery

Backups of the extranet directory servers are handled in the same manner as backup of the other directory servers. A 4mm DAT drive is attached to the master extranet directory server, and backups are performed nightly. The backups are transferred off-site as part of the twice-weekly schedule described in Chapter 25. Disaster recovery services for extranet applications were added to the contract that HugeCo maintains with a disaster recovery vendor.

Maintaining Data

Maintenance of extranet directory data involves two data sources—the Oracle database that tracks information about the authorized HugeCo retailers, and the managers at the individual retailers. Each of these data sources is considered authoritative for certain directory information.

The Oracle database is considered the authoritative source for information about the individual retail outlets. The retailer name, telephone and fax numbers, mailing address, retailer number, and list of authorized products are all synchronized from the Oracle database into the directory on a regular basis using a set of Perl scripts developed by HugeCo's IS staff. An established procedure is used to add or remove retailers from the Oracle database, and these changes propagate to the directory via the synchronization scripts.

The entries corresponding to individual employees at the retailers, on the other hand, are owned by the manager at each particular retailer. When a new employee is to be granted access to the extranet applications, the manager uses a special Web-based application to create a new entry in the directory; this creates the directory entry for the employee and sets an initial password. Similarly, when an employee leaves a retailer, access must be revoked. The manager can accomplish this by using the same Web-based application.

20-20 Hindsight: Preventing Stale Directory Data from Accumulating

Delegating the creation of new employee entries to the individual retail managers is an effective way to cut down on costs. In fact, it's absolutely necessary because HugeCo's human resources division has no record of these employees at all.

However, it's also necessary to take steps to ensure that stale directory entries do not accumulate. When employees are terminated, it's the responsibility of the retailer's manager to remove their records. But what happens if the manager forgets to do this? The initial directory design depended on managers to perform this task, and it did not include any method for alerting the manager to the presence of stale data.

To prevent stale directory entries from accumulating, an automatic expiration system was put in place. Each employee entry in the database (except for the manager's entry) is created with an expiration date six months in the future. One month before expiration, the manager is alerted to the fact that the entry is about to expire. The manager can easily reinstate the employee for an additional six-month period by clicking on a button in the user management application; if not reinstated, the employee's entry is removed from the directory. Behind the scenes, a Perl script (which uses the PerLDAP module) runs nightly and searches for employee directory entries that are about to expire. For each such entry found, the script arranges for the manager for that entry to be notified. The same script removes entries that have expired.

When a manager leaves his or her position with a retailer, HugeCo administrative staff remove his or her entry and add a new record when a new manager is hired. HugeCo representatives periodically contact the HRP retailers via telephone as part of a regular administrative procedure, and this is frequently the point when they discover that a manager has left a retailer. If a new manager has been appointed, a new entry is created, and ACLs in the directory are altered to grant appropriate privileges to the new manager.

These steps keep directory data from becoming stale, thereby improving its quality and usefulness.

Monitoring

Monitoring of the extranet application and directory servers is handled by the existing monitoring system described in Chapter 25.

Troubleshooting

Procedures were added to the existing HugeCo directory escalation process to accommodate the Web and directory servers that support the new extranet applications.

Leveraging the Directory Service

With the successful deployment of the HRP extranet, HugeCo directory designers have begun to make plans for additional directory-enabled extranet applications. These applications will continue to leverage the directory to improve service to HugeCo retailers and customers.

Applications

HugeCo plans to extend its extranet to support a new application through which authorized retailers can become certified to sell new HugeCo product lines. This application would be a combination of an online education application and a database of certified employees. The directory could be leveraged to store information about the online courses the employee has taken, and it could even be used to store information about the current course the employee is taking. After the employee completes the appropriate course and passes an online examination, the store would be marked as authorized to sell the new product.

Other extranet applications being considered might extend HugeCo resources directly to consumers. In particular, an application being prototyped allows consumers to take a virtual tour of a home finished with various HugeCo products. Consumers can select from a number of different model homes one that closely matches theirs, and they can experiment with "virtual installation" of various products. If the customers find a combination they like, they can travel to an authorized retailer who can retrieve the virtual plans and begin the ordering process for the customer. Customer information and virtual plan choices are stored in the directory.

Directory Deployment Impact

The HRP retailer extranet has enhanced HugeCo's business in the following ways:

- Product literature and prices are disseminated more quickly and at a lower cost to HugeCo.

- Retailers receive more proactive notification of product announcements, special promotions, and so on via the personalized start page.

- Retailers can communicate more effectively with HugeCo concerning outstanding orders. Orders can be placed and tracked 24 hours per day, 365 days per year, and any clarifications required by craftspersons on the assembly line can be handed electronically.

Summary and Lessons Learned

As with any complex process such as deploying a directory, there is always room for improvement. Here are a few words of advice based on lessons learned during the extranet directory deployment at HugeCo.

During the design, pilot, and deployment phase, HugeCo developers chose to revisit several decisions they had made, including the following:

- The original namespace design, in which all extranet application data was held within a single ou=Retailers subtree, would not have scaled well as additional types of extranet applications were added. Many additional container entries would have needed to be created at the dc=HugeCo, dc=com level of the DIT to accommodate the applications. By placing an additional ou=Extranet container at this level, HugeCo's developers gained additional flexibility to arrange the extranet namespace in a more scalable fashion.

- The original server topology, which tied the extranet and intranet directory data together via referrals, had negative performance implications. The developers chose to keep the intranet and extranet directories separate for the time being because no applications needed to use both sets of directory data. This decision might be revisited in the future if intranet and extranet data needs to be shared between applications.

- Maintaining the quality of the retailer employee information was delegated to the managers at each authorized retailer, but there was initially no way for the manager to find out about stale directory data. A system was developed in which entries automatically expire unless reinstated by the manager, who is notified of the impending expiration.

- Associating entries with one another based on location in the DIT proved to be troublesome. It is possible to locate the retailer entry for any given employee by moving up exactly two levels in the DIT. However, what happens if the layout of directory entries changes at some point? What if all the employee entries are moved beneath another container within the retailer subtree? Retailer entries would then be three levels above, instead of two. A better choice, implemented in the HugeCo HRP extranet, is to place an attribute in an employee's entry that associates it with a particular retailer. The hcHrpRetailerID attribute serves this purpose and decouples the method of locating a retailer's entry from the DIT structure.

As new extranet applications are designed and deployed, some of the design decisions will no doubt need to be revisited. The process of incrementally adding new directory-enabled extranet applications is a process of constant evolution and refinement.

The Big Picture

Overall, the HugeCo HRP extranet was an excellent first step into the world of extranet applications, and it expanded on the expertise developed when HugeCo designed and deployed its intranet directory service. The expertise developed should serve HugeCo well as it moves forward and leverages its directory to enable even more interesting extranet applications.

Further Reading

Netscape Professional Services. Information is available on the Web at
http://home.netscape.com/proservices/.

Index

B

Q